Texts in Computer Science

Editors
David Gries
Fred B. Schneider

For other titles published in this series, go to
www.springer.com/series/3191

A.W. Roscoe

Understanding Concurrent Systems

 Springer

Prof. A.W. Roscoe
Oxford University Computing Laboratory
Wolfson Bldg., Parks Road
Oxford OX1 3QD
UK
Bill.Roscoe@comlab.ox.ac.uk

Series Editors
David Gries
Department of Computer Science
Upson Hall
Cornell University
Ithaca, NY 14853-7501, USA

Fred B. Schneider
Department of Computer Science
Upson Hall
Cornell University
Ithaca, NY 14853-7501, USA

ISSN 1868-0941   e-ISSN 1868-095X
ISBN 978-1-4471-2600-3   ISBN 978-1-84882-258-0 (eBook)
DOI 10.1007/978-1-84882-258-0
Springer London Dordrecht Heidelberg New York

British Library Cataloguing in Publication Data
A catalogue record for this book is available from the British Library

Cover design: VTEX, Vilnius

Printed on acid-free paper

Springer is part of Springer Science+Business Media (www.springer.com)

Preface

Since C.A.R. Hoare's text *Communicating Sequential Processes* [60] was published in 1985, his CSP notation has been extensively used for teaching and applying concurrency theory. I published a book [123] on this topic in 1997 entitled "The Theory and Practice of Concurrency". We will be referring to the latter many times in the present book, and will abbreviate it *TPC*. Hoare's book and TPC are now freely available via the web. The present book draws heavily on material from TPC: parts of the text are updated versions of sections of TPC, mainly in Part I, and we will frequently refer to material in it. However, we omit most advanced material from TPC that does not require updating. Chapter 4 and each of Chaps. 8–20 are either mainly or entirely new.

When I started writing this book, I thought of it as a much revised second edition of TPC. That remains true for the first (introductory) part, but for the rest the completed book is perhaps better described as a "sequel".

Overview and Goals

The aim of this book is to be a comprehensive introduction and reference volume for CSP, providing the material for a number of different courses. It should also be the first point of reference for anyone wanting to use CSP or find out about its theory. It introduces other views of concurrency, using CSP to model and explain these. This book is integrated with, and uses, CSP-based tools and especially FDR to a much greater extent than TPC, and in addition describes how to create new tools based on FDR.

FDR is freely downloadable for all but commercial use. Almost all chapters either explain or illustrate the use of FDR, and there are two chapters (8 and 16) specifically about it.

This book is divided into parts on similar lines to TPC: the first three are, respectively, an introductory course on CSP, a review of the theory of CSP, and some topics on the application of CSP and its tools. Whereas TPC has extensive appendices on the mathematical background, the CSP$_M$ language and FDR, the present book has a fourth proper part.

I have become convinced that CSP and FDR are ideal vehicles for understanding and reasoning about a wide variety of concurrent systems, not just those initially described in this language. I and others have written a number of compilers that take programs written in other notations and translate them to CSP for analysis on FDR—and most also take the output of FDR and translate it back to give feedback appropriate to the non-CSP input notation. The fourth part is devoted to this topic, while simultaneously providing an introduction to the other sorts of concurrent systems that we explain in CSP.

Organisation and Features

Part I: An Introduction to CSP

This part is designed to be used for an introductory course on CSP.

It owes much to TPC, though some of the more difficult topics in Part I of TPC have been delayed to later parts, or removed. In their place we have included some hopefully more interesting case studies.

Part II: Theory

The theory of CSP has made considerable advances since 1997 in a number of directions, notably the following:

- Models have been developed [126] that do not need the sometimes controversial *divergence strictness* previously needed in all models that handle infinite behaviours.
- Our understanding of the overall hierarchy of CSP's semantic models [129, 130] has advanced: new models have been discovered, and we also know that there is no alternative to the weakest few models.
- We now have compositional models [99] for *Discrete Timed CSP*, lying between the informal *tock*-CSP language from Chap. 14 of TPC and the (continuous) *Timed CSP* of [111, 146]. Importantly, advances [98, 99] have been made in linking all these together.
- Links have been made between operational semantics in a general setting and CSP models [132]: it has thus been *proved* that one can give a semantics *in CSP* to a wide variety of languages.
- We now understand [89, 128] what properties can be specified using the (FDR-like) refinement check $F(P) \sqsubseteq G(P)$ for CSP contexts F and G.
- Impressive theories, for example [116], have been built on mechanical theorem provers to check the properties of CSP models and semantics.

- It is necessary to change much of the structure of the algebraic semantics for CSP presented in TPC if they are to encompass some of the new models now available.
- The theory of model checking CSP (which is what FDR does) has developed substantially in a number of ways.

In this book we will discuss most of these topics, some in Part II and some in Part III.

It would be impossible to give an in-depth presentation of the theory of CSP as it now is, as TPC largely did (with the exception of Timed CSP) in 1997. In the present book we explain some basic concepts in detail and introduce the main ideas behind the advanced theory, referring the reader to the resources provided by TPC and many academic papers. Thus Part II provides the core of a textbook, building on itself by referencing these on-line resources. There are chapters on:

- Operational semantics
- The usual denotational models
- The hierarchy of models where everything is finitely observable
- The hierarchy of models that include infinite observations
- Algebraic semantics

Part III: Using CSP

This part covers a number of topics in the application of CSP, and has chapters on:

- Timed modelling and analysis using the "*tock*-time" model introduced in TCP.
- The discrete modelling and verification of Timed CSP.
- More about FDR: advanced topics in the use of FDR and advanced specification techniques.
- Parameterised verifications and the state explosion problem: we introduce some techniques for coping with the exponential growth in the number of states to explore as we look at instances of networks with more processes, and techniques for proving properties of large classes of network. These include data independence, induction, and buffer tolerance.

Part IV: Exploring Concurrency

Here we emphasise the ability of CSP to describe and enable reasoning about parallel systems modelled in other paradigms. There are chapters on:

- Compiling shared variable programs into CSP
- Shared variable concurrency
- Priority and mobile processes

The two chapters on shared variable concurrency introduce a new tool called SVA, created by myself and David Hopkins, as a front end for FDR. We will see that it is highly effective in revealing how shared variable programs behave.

As in TPC I have attempted, in writing Parts III and IV, to rely as little as possible on the theory presented in Part II. Therefore either of these, or various combinations of chapters and sections chosen from them, can be used as the basis of a course on concurrency to follow up Part I.

Target Audience

This book is aimed at everyone who wants to get an in-depth understanding of concurrent systems, and will be essential reading for anyone interested in Hoare's CSP.

Part I is designed for an audience of undergraduate and Masters'-level graduate computer science students. At Oxford it is used for a second-year undergraduate course, and for both full-time and part-time M.Sc. students.

Part II is designed for people who are familiar with Part I and have fairly theoretical interests. These could be students taking an advanced course based on this material, or researchers interested in the state of the art.

Part III is intended for people who already have some experience in using CSP and FDR in practice, and want to be able to use them better or who are specifically interested in timed systems.

Part IV is designed for people who already understand CSP. They might want to understand other models of concurrent systems in terms of CSP. They might want model shared-variable, mobile or prioritised systems in CSP. Or they might want to write a translator from another language into CSP.

Most of the present book relies on no theoretical background other than a basic knowledge of sets and sequences. Some of Part II relies on a knowledge of basic partial order and metric space theory such as can be obtained by studying Appendix A of TPC. Except in Part II, I have tried to avoid making the reader follow sophisticated mathematical arguments, though this proved unavoidable in parts of Chap. 17.

Whilst I was writing this book, many people asked me to provide many examples of how to program in CSP: *design patterns*. While this is not the book of case studies that some wanted, I have tried to include enough to keep them happy. The main case studies can be found in Chaps. 4, 8, 9, 14, 15, 17, 18, 19 and 20.

Notes to the Instructor

Chapters 1–6 (with Chap. 7 being optional) provide a comprehensive introductory course on CSP, dipping into Chap. 8 on FDR as required during the course. When deciding whether or not to include Chap. 7, the instructor should bear in mind that Chaps. 18 and 19 (on shared variables) depend heavily on sequential composition.

For an audience already familiar with CSP one could give a theory course based on Part II. Many different courses on the practical uses of CSP and FDR could be based on Chaps. 4, 8 and 14–19 of the present book and Chaps. 12–15 of TPC, and indeed there is probably enough material in Chaps. 18 and 19 on which to base a course on shared variable concurrency.

Teaching Resources

This book has a web-site www.comlab.ox.ac.uk/ucs where you can find links to complete texts of Hoare's book [60] and TPC and links from which FDR, the ProBE CSP animator, SVA and other CSP-based tools can be down-loaded.

You can also find machine-readable CSP_M versions of almost all the CSP programs in this book and in TPC, as well as overheads covering most of the material in the two books. Additionally there are practical exercises in the use of FDR that those learning this material can use, whether personally or in a course.

Further practicals and solutions to all the exercises in this book can be obtained from the author by academics using this book for teaching.

And Finally...

When I started to write this book I assumed that it would include a chapter or two on security. In fact there is very little here on this subject, and that is mainly a summary of material in TCP. This is not because there is no new material on the mixture of CSP and security, but rather the reverse. There is now a book on security protocols via CSP [142] and a lot of additional material that goes well beyond that. It has become too large a subject to be included in a general book about CSP, at least if we want to discuss the state of the art.

While this book is focused on CSP, it covers a very wide variety of concurrent systems including combinatorial, timed, priority-based, mobile, shared variable, statecharts, buffered and asynchronous systems. Furthermore, we see how to translate several other notations into CSP. I hope, therefore, that it justifies its title *Understanding Concurrent Systems*.

Oxford, UK   Bill Roscoe
June 2010

Acknowledgements

I had the good fortune to become Tony Hoare's research student in 1978, which gave me the opportunity to work with him on the development of the 'process algebra' version of CSP and its semantics from the first.[1] I have constantly been impressed that the decisions he took in structuring the language have stood so well the twin tests of time and practical use in circumstances he could not have foreseen. The work in the present book all results, either directly or indirectly, from his vision. Those familiar with his book will recognise that much of my presentation, and many of my examples, have been influenced by it.

The core theory of CSP was developed in the late 1970s and 1980s. The two people most responsible, together with Tony and myself, for the development of the basic theoretical framework for CSP were Steve Brookes and Ernst-Rüdiger Olderog, and I am delighted to acknowledge their contributions. We were, naturally, much influenced by the work of those such as Robin Milner, Matthew Hennessy and Rocco de Nicola who were working at the same time on other process algebras.

The last few months have seen the deaths of Robin Milner and Amir Pnueli, both giants of computer science and concurrency theory in particular. A small aspect of Amir's influence can be seen in Sect. 16.4 of this book. Both were wonderful and generous men who influenced generations of researchers. They will be sadly missed.

Over the years, both CSP and my understanding of it have benefited from the work of too many people for me to list their individual contributions. I would like to thank the following present and former students, colleagues, collaborators and correspondents for their help and inspiration: Samson Abramsky, *Phil Armstrong*, Geoff Barrett, Stephen Blamey, Tilo Buschmann, *Sadie Creese*, Naiem Dathi, Jim Davies, *John Fitzgerald*, Richard Forster, Paul Gardiner, *Michael Goldsmith*, Anthony Hall, He Jifeng, *Philippa Hopcroft (née Broadfoot)*, *David Hopkins*, *Huang Jian*, Jason Hulance, David Jackson, Lalita Jategaonkar Jagadeesan, Alan Jeffrey, Mark Josephs, Maneesh Khattri, Jonathan Lawrence, *Ranko Lazić*, *Eldar Kleiner*,

---

[1]An account of the development of CSP, and in particular the transition to the process algebra version of [60] from the "imperative" version of [58], can be found in [71].

Gavin Lowe, Helen McCarthy, Christie Marr (née Bolton), Jeremy Martin, Albert Meyer, Michael Mislove, *Nick Moffat*, Lee Momtahan, *Tom Newcomb*, *Long Nguyen*, David Nowak, *Joël Ouaknine*, *Hristina Palikareva*, Ata Parashkevov, David Park, *Sriram Rajamani*, *Joy Reed*, Mike Reed, *Jakob Rehof*, *Markus Roggenbach*, Bill Rounds, Peter Ryan, Jeff Sanders, Bryan Scattergood, Steve Schneider, Brian Scott, Karen Seidel, *Jane Sinclair*, *Antti Valmari*, *Rob van Glabbeek*, *David Walker*, *Wang Xu*, *Peter Welch*, Paul Whittaker, Jim Woodcock, James (Ben) Worrell, Zhenzhong Wu, Lars Wulf, Jay Yantchev, Irfan Zakiuddin and Zhou Chao Chen.

Many of them will recognise specific influences their work has had on my two books. Those *italicised* have had a direct influence on the new work reported in the present book.

Special thanks are due to the present and former staff of Formal Systems (some of whom are listed above) for their work in developing FDR and ProBE. The remarkable capabilities of FDR transformed my view of CSP. One of my main motivations for writing this book is to show how to use FDR effectively. Bryan Scattergood was chiefly responsible for both the design and the implementation of the ASCII version of CSP used on these and other tools. The passage of time since FDR 2 was released has only emphasised the amazing job he did in designing CSP_M, and the huge expressive power of the embedded functional language.

In the last few years the development and maintenance of FDR have become the responsibility of my team at Oxford University Computing Laboratory, led by Phil Armstrong. I am pleased to say that this has led to many exciting developments with the tool and should soon lead to a third major release: FDR 3.

The presentation of this book has been greatly assisted by all those who have commented on and pointed out errors in drafts. In particular I would like to thank Irfan Zakiuddin, who read through the entire final draft and gave many useful comments. Wayne Wheeler and Simon Rees from Springer have given me just the right mixture of help, encouragement and cajoling.

My work on CSP, including the writing of both this book and TPC, has benefited from funding from several bodies over the years, including EPSRC, DRA, QinetiQ, ESPRIT, industry and the US Office of Naval Research. I am particularly grateful to Ralph Wachter from the last of these, without whom most of the research on CSP tools would not have happened.

This book could never have been written without the support of my wife Coby. For the third time (the previous ones being my doctoral thesis and TPC) she has read through hundreds of pages of text on a topic entirely foreign to her, expertly pointing out errors in spelling and style. And, yet again, she put up with me writing it.

Contents

Part I
A Foundation Course in CSP

The following 8 chapters are intended to give the reader a good basic knowledge of CSP, and are similar in content to the *Concurrency* course that has been given to undergraduate and Masters' students at Oxford for many years.

CSP is a programming language, a specification language and a theory to help you understand concurrent systems and decide whether a program meets its specification. It belongs to a class of notations known as *process algebras*, where concepts of communication and interaction are presented in an algebraic style. The odd-numbered chapters successively introduce more of the language, with the even-numbered ones being used to explain reasoning techniques and provide larger examples. Each of Chaps. 1–7 shows how to use the FDR tool in connection with its material; Chap. 8 gives much more information about FDR and is intended to be studied in parallel with a course based on Chaps. 1–7, with its later Sects. 8.5–8.8 being optional.

It is strongly recommended that courses based on this Part are accompanied by practical work using FDR. As described in the Preface, teaching and practical materials are available from this book's web-site and the author.

Chapter 1
Building a Simple Sequential Process

A CSP process is completely described by the way it can communicate with its external environment. In constructing a process we first have to decide on an *alphabet* of communication events—the set of all events that the process (and any other related processes) might use. The choice of this alphabet is perhaps the most important modelling decision that is made when we are trying to represent a real system in CSP. The actions we use determine the level of detail or abstraction in the final specification, and also whether it is possible to get a reasonable result at all. But this will only really become clear once we have a grasp of the basic notation and start to look at some examples, though some guidance is given in Sect. 1.5. So let us assume for now that the alphabet Σ of all events has been established.

The fundamental assumptions about communications in CSP are these:

- They are instantaneous: we abstract the real time intervals during which individual events are performed into single moments—conceptually the moments when an event becomes inevitable.
- They only occur when both the process and its environment allow them; but at any moment when the process and its environment *do* agree on an event then it or some other event must happen.

CSP is about setting up and reasoning about processes that interact with their environments using this model of communication. Ultimately, of course, we will want to set up parallel systems of processes which communicate with each other, but in this chapter we will meet a basic collection of operators that allow us to create processes that simply describe (internally sequential) patterns of communication.

1.1 Basic Operators

1.1.1 Prefixing

The simplest of all CSP processes is the one which never does anything. It is written *STOP* and never communicates.

A.W. Roscoe, *Understanding Concurrent Systems*, Texts in Computer Science, DOI 10.1007/978-1-84882-258-0_1, © Springer-Verlag London Limited 2010

Given an event a in Σ and a process P, $a \to P$ is the process which is initially willing to communicate a and will wait indefinitely for this a to happen. After a it behaves like P. Thus

$$up \to down \to up \to down \to STOP$$

will communicate the cycle up, $down$ twice before stopping. This operation on processes (turning P into $a \to P$) is known as *prefixing*.

Clearly $STOP$ and prefixing, together, allow us to describe just the processes that make a fixed, finite sequence of communications before stopping. For example,

$$Day = getup \to breakfast \to work \to lunch \to play$$
$$\to dinner \to tv \to gotobed \to STOP$$

is a process describing someone's day.

1.1.2 Recursion

If we want to use versions of the processes above which, instead of quickly stopping, can go on performing events indefinitely, we can use *recursion*. Two different processes which achieve this effect for up and $down$ are defined by the equations

$$P_1 = up \to down \to P_1$$
$$P_2 = up \to down \to up \to down \to P_2$$

The idea is that any use of the recursively defined process's name (P_1 or P_2) on the right-hand side of the equations means exactly the same as the whole. It should be intuitively clear that any process satisfying either of these equations has the desired behaviour. The form of a recursive definition by a single equation is that an identifier representing the process being defined is at the left-hand side, and a process term, probably involving the identifier, is on the right. (If the identifier does not appear then the recursion is not really a recursion and simply defines the identifier on the left to be the process on the right.) We can draw a picture illustrating the behaviour of P_1 and P_2: see Fig. 1.1. Clearly we could do the same for Day, turning it into a process representing an eternal but repetitive existence:

$$Groundhog\_Day = getup \to breakfast \to work \to lunch \to play$$
$$\to dinner \to tv \to gotobed \to Groundhog\_Day$$

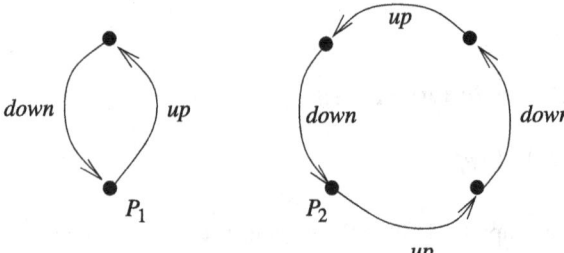

Fig. 1.1 Examples of repetitive behaviour: P_1 and P_2

Instead of defining one process by a single equation we can define a number simultaneously by a *mutual* recursion. For example, if we set

$$P_u = up \to P_d$$
$$P_d = down \to P_u$$

then P_u should behave in just the same way as P_1 and P_2 defined earlier. We could produce separate definitions of processes *Monday, Tuesday, . . . , Sunday*, each describing a particular day's activities leading to the next.

Most of the recursions in this book will be written in this equational style, but sometimes it is useful to have a way of writing down a recursive term without having to give it a name and a separate line. The single recursion $P = F(P)$ (where $F(P)$ is any CSP term involving P) defines exactly the same process as the 'nameless' term $\mu P.F(P)$. (μ is the Greek letter 'mu'.) Thus

$$up \to (\mu p.down \to up \to p)$$

defines yet another process alternating *up*s and *down*s.

We have seen quite a few ways of defining recursive processes with many of our examples (e.g. P_1, P_2 and P_u) having very similar behaviour. They were invariably rather dull since we still can only create processes whose sequence of communications is completely fixed. In fact the theories we explain in this book will allow us to prove that the three processes P_1, P_2 and P_u are equal. But that is a subject for later.

1.1.3 Guarded Alternative

It is still only possible to define processes with a single thread of behaviour: all we can do so far is to define processes which execute a fixed finite or infinite sequence of actions. CSP provides a few ways of describing processes which offer a choice of actions to their environments. They are largely interchangeable from the point of view of what they can express, each being included because it has its distinct uses in programming.

The simplest choice construct takes a list of distinct initial actions paired with processes and extends the prefix operator by letting the environment choose any one of the events, with the subsequent behaviour being the corresponding process.

$$(a_1 \to P_1 \mid \ldots \mid a_n \to P_n)$$

can do any of the events $a_1, \ldots, a_n$ on its first step and, if the event chosen is a_r, subsequently behaves like P_r. This construct is called *guarded alternative*. The process

$$UandD = (up \to down \to STOP \mid down \to up \to STOP)$$

can do the two events *up* and *down* in either order.

Fig. 1.2 The behaviours of
two processes with choice

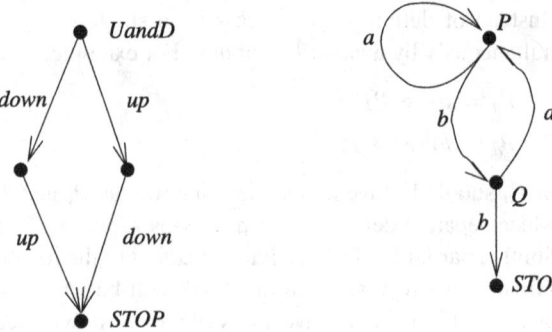

Combining this operator with recursion, it is possible to define some complex behaviours. As a relatively simple example, consider the processes

$$P = (a \to P \mid b \to Q)$$
$$Q = (a \to P \mid b \to STOP)$$

where P will accept any sequence of as and bs except that it stops if given two consecutive bs. Indeed, it should not be hard to see that any *deterministic finite-state machine*—a finite collection of states, each of which has a finite set of actions available, and where the next state depends deterministically on which of this set occurs (i.e., only one possible state per action)—can be encoded using this operator and mutual recursion with finitely many equations. The behaviours of this P and of *UandD* are illustrated in Fig. 1.2

We can now put some choice into the person whose life we have been describing. We might, for example, define:

$$Asleep = (sleep \to Asleep \mid wake \to InBed)$$
$$InBed = (sleep \to Asleep \mid read \to InBed \mid tv \to InBed \mid getup \to Up)$$
$$Up = (gotobed \to InBed \mid read \to Up \mid eat \to Up \mid tv \to Up$$
$$\mid work \to Up \mid play \to Up)$$

By combining guarded choice with an *infinite* mutual recursion which defines one process $COUNT_n$ for every natural number $n \in \mathbb{N}$, we can define a system of counter processes as follows:

$$COUNT_0 = up \to COUNT_1$$
$$COUNT_n = (up \to COUNT_{n+1}$$
$$\mid down \to COUNT_{n-1}) \quad (n > 0)$$

$COUNT_n$ is the process which will communicate any sequence of *up*s and *down*s, as long as there have never been $n+1$ more *down*s than *up*s. These are not, of course, finite-state machines: there are infinitely many fundamentally different states that any one of the $COUNT_n$ processes can pass through. The distinction between finite-state and non-finite-state CSP processes is extremely important for model checking, the term usually used for state exploration tools such as FDR, since that method

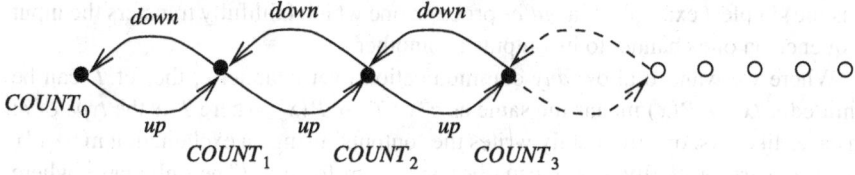

Fig. 1.3 The behaviour of $COUNT_n$

relies on being able to visit every state. Of course the pictures of these processes are also infinite—see Fig. 1.3.

If $A \subseteq \Sigma$ is any set of events and, for each $x \in A$, we have defined a process $P(x)$, then

$$?x : A \rightarrow P(x)$$

is the process which accepts any element a of A and then behaves like the appropriate $P(a)$. This construct is known as *prefix-choice* for obvious reasons. Clearly it generalises the guarded alternative construction, since any guarded alternative can be recast in this form, but if A is infinite the reverse is not true. $?x : \emptyset \rightarrow P(x)$ means the same as $STOP$ and $?x : \{a\} \rightarrow P(x)$ means the same as $a \rightarrow P(a)$.

This operator *tends* to be used in cases where the dependency of $P(x)$ upon x is mainly through its use of the identifier x in constructing subsequent communications, in constructing the index of a mutual recursion, or similar. Thus we can write a process which simply repeats every communication which is sent to it:

$$REPEAT = ?x : \Sigma \rightarrow x \rightarrow REPEAT$$

or one which behaves like one of the counters defined above, but depending on what its first communication is:

$$Initialise = ?n : \mathbb{N} \rightarrow COUNT_n$$

In many situations it is useful to have an alphabet Σ which contains compound objects put together by an infix dot. So if c is the name of a 'channel' and T is the type of object communicated down it, we would have $c.T = \{c.x \mid x \in T\} \subseteq \Sigma$. It is natural to think of processes inputting and outputting values of type T over c: an inputting process would typically be able to communicate any element of $c.T$ and an outputting process would only be able to communicate one. Rather than write the input in the form $?y : c.T \rightarrow P(y)$, where the uses of y in $P(y)$ have to extract x from $c.x$, it is more elegant to use the 'pattern matching' form

$$c?x : T \rightarrow P'(x)$$

where the definition of P' is probably slightly simpler than that of P because it can refer to the value x input along c directly, rather than having to recover it from a compound object. For example, the process $COPY$, which inputs elements of T on channel *left* and outputs them on channel *right* is defined

$$COPY = left?x : T \rightarrow right.x \rightarrow COPY$$

It is the simplest example of a *buffer* process: one which faithfully transfers the input sequence on one channel to its outputs on another.

Where we want to allow *any* communication over channel c, the set T can be omitted: $c?x \to P(x)$ means the same as $c?x : T \to P(x)$, where T is the *type* of c: In cases like this, one frequently writes the 'outputs' using an exclamation mark $c!x$ for symmetry or clarity. $c!x$ is usually a synonym for $c.x$. (The only cases where this does not apply arise where a communication is more highly structured than we have seen here and has both 'input' and 'output' components—see p. 15, where this subject is discussed further.) So, where T is understood, we might write

$$COPY = left?x \to right!x \to COPY$$

It is important to remember that, even though this syntax allows us to model input and output over channels, the fundamental CSP model of communication still applies: neither an input nor an output can occur until the environment allows it.

We broaden the guarded alternative operator to encompass arguments of the form $c?x : T \to P(x)$ as well as ones guarded by single events. For now we will assume, as an extension of the earlier assumption of disjointness, that all of the events and input channels used in the guards are distinct and that none of the single events belongs to more than one of the input channels.

For example, we could extend our human subject's alphabet so that *eats* becomes a channel of type {*breakfast, lunch, dinner, snack*} and *tv* offers a range of television channels.

We can define a buffer process which, unlike *COPY*, does not insist upon outputting one thing before inputting the next. If T is the type of objects being input and output, and $left.T \cup right.T \subseteq \Sigma$, we can define a process B_s^∞ for every $s \in T^*$ (the set of finite sequences of elements of T) as follows:

$$B_{\langle\rangle}^\infty = left?x : T \to B_{\langle x \rangle}^\infty$$
$$B_{s^\smallfrown\langle y \rangle}^\infty = (left?x : T \to B_{\langle x \rangle^\smallfrown s^\smallfrown \langle y \rangle}^\infty$$
$$| \; right!y \to B_s^\infty)$$

So B_s^∞ is the buffer presently containing the sequence s, and $B_{\langle\rangle}^\infty$ is the initially empty one. Notice the basic similarity between this recursive definition and the ones (particularly *COUNT*) seen earlier. This *tail recursive* style, particularly when each recursive call is guarded by exactly one communication (*one-step* tail recursion) shows the state space of a process extremely clearly. This style of definition is important both in presenting CSP specifications and in verification techniques.

The use of sequence notation should be self-explanatory here. We will, however, discuss the language of sequences in more detail in Sect. 2.2.

The example B^∞ above illustrates two important and related aspects of CSP style that have also been seen in earlier examples: the uses of parameterised mutual recursions and of identifiers representing 'data' values. The value of a parameterised recursion such as this one or *COUNT* is that it allows the succinct presentation of a large (and even, as in both these cases, infinite) set of processes. We will think of the parameters as representing, in some sense, the *state* of such a process at the points of recursive call. A parameterised process can have any fixed number of parameters, which can be numbers, events, tuples, sets, sequences etc., though they must not be processes (or tuples etc. that contain processes).

The parameters can be written as subscripts (as in B_s^∞ above), superscripts (e.g., $R^{(a,b)}$) or as 'functional arguments' (e.g., $R(n, x)$). The first two of these were the traditional style before the advent of machine readable CSP, which is usually denoted CSP_M, which only accepts the third. There is no formal difference between the various positions, the choice being up to the aesthetic taste of the programmer. Often, in more complex examples, they are combined.

The identifiers used for input (i.e., those following '?') are the second main contributor to process state. Each time an input is made it has the effect of creating a new binding to the identifier, whose scope is the process it enables (i.e., in $c?x \to P$ and $(c?x \to P \mid d \to Q)$ it is P). Both these identifiers and the ones introduced as parameters can be used freely in creating events and parameters, and in deciding conditionals (see later). There is, however, no assignment statement in CSP, meaning that an identifier is bound to the same value throughout its *scope*. In this sense CSP is like a functional language such as Haskell: it is *declarative*.

We will see later that CSP can model languages that do have assignment statements: assignable variables can be implemented as separate parallel processes.

Exercise 1.1 Summarise your life using a CSP process of the type used in examples above. You might like to distinguish between weekdays and weekends, term and vacation etc.

Exercise 1.2 A *bank account* is a process into which money can be deposited and from which it can be withdrawn. Define first a simple account $ACCT_0$ which has events *deposit* and *withdraw*, and which is always prepared to communicate either.

Exercise 1.3 Now extend the alphabet to include *open* and *close*. $ACCT_1$ behaves like $ACCT_0$ except that it allows no event before it has been opened, and allows no further event after it has been closed (and is always prepared to accept *close* while open). You might find it helpful to define a process *OPEN* representing an open account.

Exercise 1.4 $ACCT_0$ and $ACCT_1$ have no concept of a balance. Introduce a parameter representing the balance of an *OPEN* account. The alphabet is *open* and *close* as before, *deposit*.$\mathbb{N}$ and *withdraw*.$\mathbb{N}$ (which have now become channels indicating the amount of the deposit or withdrawal) plus *balance*.$\mathbb{Z}$ ($\mathbb{Z}$ is the set of positive and negative integers), a channel that can be used to find out the current balance. An account has a zero balance when opened, and may only be closed when it has a zero balance. Define processes $ACCT_2$ and $ACCT_3$ which (respectively) allow *any* withdrawal and only allow those which would not overdraw the account (make the balance negative).

1.2 Choice Operators

1.2.1 External Choice

The various ways of defining a choice of events described in the last section all set out *as part of the operator* what the choice of initial events will be. In particular, in guarded alternatives such as $(a \rightarrow P \mid b \rightarrow Q)$, the a and b are an integral part of the operator even though it is tempting to think that this process is a choice between the processes $a \rightarrow P$ and $b \rightarrow Q$. From the point of view of possible implementations, the explicitness of the guarded alternative has many advantages, but from an algebraic standpoint and also for generality it is advantageous to have a choice operator which provides a simple choice between processes; this is what we will now meet.

$P \square Q$ is a process which offers the environment the choice of the first events of P and of Q, and then behaves accordingly. This means that if the first event chosen is one from P only, then $P \square Q$ behaves like P, while if one is chosen from Q it behaves like Q. Thus $(a \rightarrow P) \square (b \rightarrow Q)$ means exactly the same as $(a \rightarrow P \mid b \rightarrow Q)$. This generalises totally: any guarded alternative of the sorts described in the last section is equivalent to the process that is obtained by replacing all of the |s of the alternative operator by $\square$s.[1] Therefore we can regard $\square$ as strictly generalising guarded alternative: for that reason we will henceforth tend to use only $\square$ even in cases where the other would have been sufficient. (In fact, in ordinary use it is rare to find a use of $\square$ which could not have been presented as a guarded alternative, at least if, in a way similar to that described on p. 14, we extend the idea of a guarded alternative to allow conditional clauses on the guards.)

One important property of $\square$ is the law $P = P \square STOP$: to offer the environment the actions of $STOP$ in addition to those of P has no effect on P. So, in particular, $P \square STOP$ cannot deadlock unless P can.

The discussion above leaves out one important case that does not arise with guarded alternatives: the possibility that P and Q might have initial events in common so that there is no clear prescription as to which route is followed when one of these is chosen. We define it to be ambiguous: if we have written a program with an overlapping choice we should not mind which route is taken and the implementation may choose either. Thus, after the initial a, the process $(a \rightarrow a \rightarrow STOP) \square (a \rightarrow b \rightarrow STOP)$ is free to offer a or b *at its choice* but is not obliged to offer both. It is thus a rather different process to $a \rightarrow ((a \rightarrow STOP) \square (b \rightarrow STOP))$, which *is* obliged to offer the choice of a and b. This is the first example we have met of a *nondeterministic* process: one which is allowed to make internal decisions which affect the way it looks to its environment.

---

[1]This transformation is trivial textually, but less so syntactically since the prefixes move from being part of the operator to become part of the processes being combined, and also we are moving from a single operator of arbitrary 'arity' to the repeated use of the binary operator $\square$. The fact that $\square$ is associative (see later) means that the order of this composition is irrelevant.

We will later find other examples of how nondeterminism can arise from natural constructions, more fundamentally—and inevitably—than this one when studying concurrent systems.

A *deterministic* process is one where the range of events offered to the environment depends only on things it has seen (i.e., the sequence of communications so far). In other words, it is formally *nondeterministic* when some internal decision can lead to uncertainty about what will be offered. The distinction between deterministic and nondeterministic behaviour is an important one, and we will later (Sect. 6.1) be able to specify it exactly.

If $S = \{a, b, \ldots, q\}$ is a set that indexes any finite collection of processes, one can write $\Box\{P_a \mid a \in S\}$ or $\Box_{x \in S} P_x$ as synonyms for $P_a \Box P_b \Box \cdots \Box P_q$. This simply offers all the choices of the processes in the collection, and if S is empty gives the same behaviour as *STOP*.

1.2.2 Nondeterministic Choice

Since nondeterminism does appear in CSP whether we like it or not, it is necessary for us to be able to reason about it cleanly. Therefore, even though they are not constructs one would be likely to use in any program written for execution in the usual sense, CSP contains two closely related ways of presenting the nondeterministic choice of processes. These are

$$P \sqcap Q \quad \text{and} \quad \sqcap S$$

where P and Q are processes, and S is a *non-empty* set of processes. The first of these is a process which can behave like either P or Q, the second is one that can behave like any member of S. Applying $\sqcap$ to the empty set simply does not make sense: $\sqcap S$ is a process in which the process *must* behave like some member of S, which is impossible when $S = \emptyset$.

Clearly we can represent $\sqcap S$ for finite S using $\sqcap$. The case where S is infinite leads to a number of difficulties in modelling since (obviously) it introduces infinite, or *unbounded*, nondeterminism. It turns out that this is somewhat harder to cope with than finite nondeterminism, so we will sometimes have to exclude it from consideration. Apart from the explicit operator $\sqcap S$ there are several other operators we will meet later which can introduce unbounded nondeterminism. We will mention this in each case where it can arise, and the precautions necessary to avoid it.

It is important to appreciate the difference between $P \Box Q$ and $P \sqcap Q$. The process $(a \to STOP) \Box (b \to STOP)$ is obliged to communicate a or b if offered only one of them, whereas $(a \to STOP) \sqcap (b \to STOP)$ may reject either. The latter is only obliged to communicate if the environment offers *both* a and b. In the first case, the choice of what happens is in the hands of the environment, in the second it is in the hands of the process. Some authors call these two forms of choice *external* and *internal* nondeterminism respectively, but we prefer to think of 'external nondeterminism' as 'environmental choice' and not to confuse it with a form of nondeterminism.

Recall the processes such as *Asleep*, *InBed* and *Up* that describe people's lives. We can look at these as describing the behaviour of an actual person or as a "diary"-like process that a person (as the environment) interacts with when deciding what to do next. If the process is a diary, then probably the right thing to do is to leave all the choices external: the person then always gets to pick what to do next from the available options. If, on the other hand, the process represents a person, then we would want to represent any choice made by this individual as *free will* by $\sqcap$, leaving ones where he or she is willing to take instructions as $\square$.

Functionally, the process P can be used in any place where $P \sqcap Q$ would work, since there is nothing we can do to stop $P \sqcap Q$ behaving like P every time anyway. If R is such that $R = R \sqcap P$ we say that P is more deterministic than R, or that it *refines* R. Since $(P \sqcap Q) \sqcap P = P \sqcap Q$ for any P and Q, it follows that P is, as one would expect, always more deterministic than $P \sqcap Q$. This gives the basic notion of when one CSP process is 'better' than another, and forms the basis of the most important partial orders over CSP models. When $P \sqcap R = R$ we will write

$$R \sqsubseteq P$$

The concept of refinement will turn out to be exceptionally important. Any definition of what it means for two processes to be equivalent gives rise to its own definition of refinement through the equation $P = P \sqcap Q$. We will meet the first of these shortly.

Remember the process $B_{\langle\rangle}^{\infty}$ defined above. It is always prepared to input. We can make it more nondeterministic by making it optional as to whether or not it inputs when it is non-empty, but insist that it can accept any input when empty.

$$Buff_{\langle\rangle} = left?x : T \rightarrow Buff_{\langle x\rangle}$$
$$Buff_{s^\smallfrown\langle y\rangle} = (STOP \sqcap left?x : T \rightarrow Buff_{\langle x\rangle^\smallfrown s^\smallfrown \langle y\rangle})$$
$$\square \, right!y \rightarrow Buff_s$$

This—we assert—is the most nondeterministic process that can unequivocally be called a buffer, and in general $Buff_{\langle\rangle} \sqsubseteq P$ if and only if P is a buffer. We will amplify this point in later chapters.

1.2.3 Conditional Choice

Since we allow identifiers into CSP processes that hold non-process values, through input and process parameters, a further form of choice is needed: conditional choice based on the value of a boolean expression. In the informal style of presenting CSP there is no need to be very prescriptive about the way these choices are written down,[2] though obviously a tighter syntax will be required when we consider CSP_M. However a choice is written down, it must give a clear decision about which process

---

[2]Indeed, in many presentations of CSP they seem to be considered so informal that they are not described as part of the language.

Fig. 1.4 The nine cases: different sets of initial events in *Counter*(*i*, *j*)

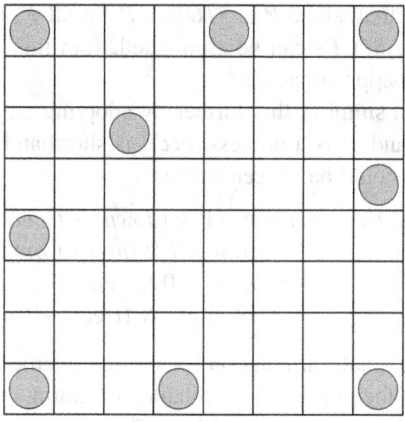

the construct represents for any legitimate value of the state identifiers in scope, and only depend on these.

Conditionals can thus be presented as *if … then … else …* constructs (as they are in CSP$_M$), as case statements (implemented in CSP$_M$ via pattern matching: see p. 151), or in the following syntax due to Hoare, which elegantly reduces the conditional to an algebraic operator: $P \triangleleft b \triangleright Q$ means exactly the same as *if b then P else Q*. Because it fits in well with the rest of CSP notation, we will tend to quote this last version when discussing or using conditionals in "blackboard" CSP as opposed to CSP$_M$. It is also legitimate to use conditionals in computing sub-process objects such as events. Thus the two processes

$$ABS_1 = left?x \rightarrow right!((-x) \triangleleft x < 0 \triangleright x) \rightarrow ABS_1$$

$$ABS_2 = left?x \rightarrow ((right!(-x) \rightarrow ABS_2) \triangleleft x < 0 \triangleright (right!x \rightarrow ABS_2))$$

are equivalent: both input numbers and output the absolute values.

The use of conditionals can obviously reduce the number of cases of a parameterised mutual recursion that have to be treated separately to one (simply replacing each case by one clause in a conditional), but they can, used judiciously, frequently give a substantial simplification as well. Consider, for example, a two-dimensional version of our *COUNT* process which now represents a counter on a chess board. It will have two parameters, both restricted to the range $0 \leq i \leq 7$. One is changed by the events {*up*, *down*}, the other by {*left*, *right*}. There are no less than nine separate cases to be considered if we were to follow the style (used for *COUNT* earlier) of dealing with the different possible initial events one by one: see Fig. 1.4. Fortunately these all reduce to a single one with the simple use of conditionals:

$$Counter(n, m) = (down \rightarrow Counter(n - 1, m)) \triangleleft n > 0 \triangleright STOP$$
$$\square (up \rightarrow Counter(n + 1, m)) \triangleleft n < 7 \triangleright STOP$$
$$\square (left \rightarrow Counter(n, m - 1)) \triangleleft m > 0 \triangleright STOP$$
$$\square (right \rightarrow Counter(n, m + 1)) \triangleleft m < 7 \triangleright STOP$$

Notice that, since $P \square STOP = P$ for all P, for any of the values of parameters (n, m) the $STOP$s can be eliminated from this to leave 2, 3 or all 4 of the above clauses as appropriate.

We can simplify this further by adopting an abbreviation: if b is a boolean expression and P is a process, $b \& P$ is shorthand for $P \mathbin{\triangleleft} b \mathbin{\triangleright} STOP$. Thus the above definition could have been written:

$$
\begin{aligned}
Counter(n, m) = \; & n > 0 \; \& \; (down \rightarrow Counter(n - 1, m)) \\
& \square \; n < 7 \; \& \; (up \rightarrow Counter(n + 1, m)) \\
& \square \; m > 0 \; \& \; (left \rightarrow Counter(n, m - 1)) \\
& \square \; m < 7 \; \& \; (right \rightarrow Counter(n, m + 1))
\end{aligned}
$$

This is a natural notation for writing guarded alternatives where a variable collection of the clauses are available depending on the parameters. You can think of these booleans as *conditional guards*.

The most nondeterministic buffer process $Buff_{\langle\rangle}$ is infinite state, even if the type the buffer contains is finite. We can use conditional choice to construct the most nondeterministic buffer that never contains more than N items ($N \geq 1$):

$$
\begin{aligned}
Buff^N_{\langle\rangle} &= left?x : T \rightarrow Buff^N_{\langle x \rangle} \\
Buff^N_{s \hat{} \langle y \rangle} &= \#s < N - 1 \; \& \; (STOP \sqcap left?x : T \rightarrow Buff^N_{\langle x \rangle \hat{} s \hat{} \langle y \rangle}) \\
& \quad \square \; right!y \rightarrow Buff^N_s
\end{aligned}
$$

1.2.4 Multi-Part Events: Extending the Notation of Channels

Thus far all events we have used have been atomic (such as *up* and *down*) or have comprised a channel name plus one 'data' component (such as *left*.3). In general we allow events that have been constructed out of any finite number of parts using the infix dot '.' (which is assumed to be associative). In written CSP it is a convention, which is enforced as a rule in CSP_M, that a *channel* consists of an identifier (its name or tag) plus a finite (perhaps empty) sequence of data-types, and that Σ then consists of all events of the form

$$c.x_1. \ldots .x_n$$

where c is such a name, $T_1, \ldots, T_n$ is its sequence of types, and $x_i \in T_i$ for each i.

The most common use for communications with more than two parts is when we want to set up what is effectively an array of channels for communication in a parallel array where the processes are probably similarly indexed. Thus if we had processes indexed $P(i)$ for $i \in A \subseteq \mathbb{N}$, we might well have a channel of type $\mathbb{N}.\mathbb{N}.T$ where T is a data-type that these processes want to send to each other. If c were such a channel, then $c.i.j.x$ might represent the transmission of value x from $P(i)$ to $P(j)$. We will see many examples like this once we have introduced parallel operators.

Channels can also, however, be used to achieve multiple data transfers in a single action. This can even be in several directions at once, since the input (?) and output (!) modes of communication can be mixed in a multi-part communication. Thus

$$c?x : A!e \rightarrow P$$

represents a process whose first step allows all communications of the form $\{c.a.b \mid a \in A\}$ where b is the value of the expression e. The identifier x is then, of course, bound to the relevant member of a in the body of P. The advent of CSP_M and FDR has proved the usefulness of this type of construct, and has led to the adoption of conventions to deal with various cases that can arise. One of these shows the subtle distinction between the use of the infix dot '.' and the output symbol ! in communications. For example, if d is a channel of type $A.B.C.D$ then, if the communication $d?x.y!z.t$ appears in a process definition, it is equivalent to $d?x?y!z!t$ because an infix dot following a ? is taken to be part of a pattern that is matched by the input. Thus one ? can bind multiple identifiers until overridden by a following !. None of the examples in this book uses this or any other related convention—in the examples where more than one data component follows a ? we will follow the good practice of using only ? or ! as appropriate for each successive one.

One very useful notation first introduced in CSP_M, which we will use freely, allows us to turn any set of channels and partially defined events into the corresponding events. This is the $\{|c_1, c_2|\}$ notation, which forms the appropriate set of events from one or more channels: it is formally defined as follows. If c has type $T_1.T_2 \ldots T_n$ as above, $0 \le k \le n$ and $a_i \in T_i$ for $1 \le i \le k$, then

$$events(c.a_1 \ldots a_k) = \{c.a_1 \ldots a_k.b_{k+1} \ldots b_n \mid b_{k+1} \in T_{k+1}, \ldots, b_n \in T_n\}$$

is the set of events which can be formed as extensions of $c.a_1 \ldots a_k$. We can then define

$$\{|e_1, \ldots, e_r|\} = events(e_1) \cup \cdots \cup events(e_r)$$

Exercise 1.5 Extend the definition of $COUNT_n$ so that it also has the events $up5$, $up10$, $down5$ and $down10$ which change the value in the register by the obvious amounts, and are only possible when they do not take this value below zero.

Exercise 1.6 A *change-giving* machine takes in £1 coins and gives change in 5, 10 and 20 pence coins. It should have the following events: $in£1$, $out5p$, $out10p$, $out20p$. Define versions with the following behaviours:

(a) *CMA* gives the environment the choice of how it wants the change, and if an extra £1 is inserted while it still has a non-zero balance it increases the amount of change available accordingly.
(b) *CMB* behaves like *CMA* except that it will only accept a further £1 if its balance is less than 20p.
(c) *CMC* is allowed to choose any correct combination of change nondeterministically, only allowing the insertion of £1 when it has zero balance.

Exercise 1.7 *COPY* represents a one-place buffer and $B_{\langle\rangle}^{\infty}$ represents an unbounded one. These are just two examples of processes representing communication media for transmitting information from channel *left* to channel *right*. Describe ones with the following behaviours (except for the last one, their output streams must always copy the input ones without loss, preserving order):

(a) *FCOPY* behaves like *COPY* except that it is allowed to input a second item when it already contains one, but if it does it breaks (*STOP*).
(b) *DELAY* can hold up to two items, but cannot output the first one unless it is full. Thus its outputs are (after the initial input) always one or two behind its inputs, unlike the case with *COPY* where they are always zero or one behind.
(c) *LEAKY* behaves like *COPY* except that it loses every third item.

Exercise 1.8 Create a model of *Duncan*, who has three states modelled on *Asleep*, *InBed* and *Up*. He chooses nondeterministically between *read* and *sleep* when *InBed*, always offers to *eat* and *play* when *Up*, but may or may not offer to *work*.

1.3 A Few Important Processes

There are a few processes with very basic behaviour for which it is useful to have standard names. We have already met *STOP*, the process that does nothing at all. Two more are

$$RUN_A = ?x : A \rightarrow RUN_A$$

the process which, for a set of events $A \subseteq \Sigma$, can always communicate any member of *A* desired by the environment, and

$$Chaos_A = STOP \sqcap (?x : A \rightarrow Chaos_A)$$

which can always choose to communicate or reject any member of *A*. Evidently $Chaos_\emptyset$ and $RUN_\emptyset$ are both equivalent to *STOP*. If no alphabet is specified for one of these processes (*RUN* or *Chaos*) then we understand it (the alphabet) to be the whole of Σ. Clearly $Chaos_A$ is refined by both *STOP* and RUN_A.

Two other important constants (**div** and *SKIP*) will be introduced later (respectively Sects. 5.1.1 and 7.1.1) once the concepts they involve have been established.

1.4 Traces Refinement

Imagine you are interacting with a CSP process. The most basic record you might make of what happens is to write down the *trace* of events that occur: the sequence of communications between you (the environment) and the process. In general, a trace might be finite or infinite: finite either because the observation was terminated or because the process and environment reach a point where they cannot agree on any event; infinite when the observation goes on for ever and infinitely many events are transacted.

Traces are typical of the sort of behaviours we use to build models of CSP processes: they are clearly observable by the environment interacting with the process, and each of them is the record of a single interaction with the process. We will see more details of the *traces model* in the next chapter, but we now introduce a fundamental way in which we can specify the correctness of a CSP process. Using *traces(P)* to denote P's finite traces we can write

$$P \sqsubseteq_T Q \quad \text{if and only if} \quad traces(P) \supseteq traces(Q)$$

and read this as Q *trace-refines* P. In other words, every trace of Q is a trace of P. This is the simplest of a number of versions of refinement that we will meet in this book.

FDR allows you to decide $P \sqsubseteq_T Q$ for any *finite-state* processes P and Q: we will discuss this restriction further in Sect. 1.6.1.

The most common use of this function in FDR is when P represents the set of all the traces that are allowable for processes satisfying some specification, and Q is a process we want to test against it.

RUN_A can be regarded as the specification that no event outside A ever happens, and

$$ALT(a, b) = (a \rightarrow ALT(b, a)) \,\square\, (?x : (\Sigma \backslash \{a, b\}) \rightarrow ALT(a, b))$$

specifies that the events a and b alternate, whatever other events happen. *Note that the parameters swap in this definition after recursion.*

Either $B_{\langle\rangle}^{\infty}$ or *Buff*$_{\langle\rangle}$ (two processes with the same set of traces) might be regarded as the trace-refinement specification for a buffer as well as being a buffer itself, since they have every trace (for the given input and output channels) where the sequence of values output is always an initial subsequence of the inputs. This specification, however, is not finite state in either (or indeed any) form.

Almost all the properties we will want to prove of processes in this book can be expressed in terms of refinement, though sometimes in richer models than traces. Most of these properties of a process P will take the form $Spec \sqsubseteq P$ over some model—we call these *behavioural specifications* since they say that every behaviour of P is one of *Spec*—but refinement allows us to formulate more general properties of P: $F(P) \sqsubseteq G(P)$ for CSP-defined functions or *contexts* F and G. We will occasionally use this generality in later chapters.

Readers should notice a very important fact about CSP: it is not only a language for writing descriptions of proposed implementations, but also one for writing specifications. So, when using CSP to describe systems, there is usually no need to appeal to a second language for specification.

1.5 What is a Communication?

CSP is a calculus for studying processes which interact with each other and their environment by means of communication. The most fundamental object in CSP is therefore a communication event. These events are assumed to be drawn from a set Σ (the Greek capital letter 'Sigma') which contains all possible communications for processes in the universe under consideration. Think of a communication as a transaction or synchronisation between two or more processes, rather than as necessarily being the transmission of data one way. A few possible events in very different examples of CSP descriptions are given below.

- In a railway system where the trains and signal boxes are communicating, a typical event might be a request to move onto a segment of track, the granting or refusing of permission for this, or the actual movement.
- If trying to model the interaction between a customer and a shop, we could either model a transaction as a single event, so that $buys.A.X.Y$ might mean A *buys* X *for £Y*, or break it up into several events (offer, acceptance, money, change, etc.). The choice of which of these two approaches to follow would depend on taste as well as the reason for writing the CSP description.
- The insertion of an electronic mail message into a system, the various internal transmissions of the message as it makes its way to its destination, and its final receipt would all be events in a description of a distributed network. Note that the user is probably not interested in the internal events, and so would probably like to be able to ignore, or *abstract away* their presence.
- If we were using CSP to describe the behaviour of VLSI circuits, an event might be a clock tick, seen by a large number of parallel communications, or the transmission of a word of data, or (at a lower level) the switching of some gate or transistor.

More than one component in a system may have to cooperate in the performance of an event, and the 'real' phenomenon modelled by the event might take some time. In CSP we assume firstly that an event only happens when all its participants are prepared to execute it (this is what is called *handshaken* communication), and secondly that the abstract event is instantaneous. The instantaneous event can be thought of as happening at the moment when it becomes inevitable because all its participants have agreed to execute it. These two related abstractions constitute perhaps the most fundamental steps in describing a system using CSP.

The only things that the environment can observe about a process are the events which the process communicates with it. The interaction between the environment and a process takes the same form as that between two processes: events only happen when both sides agree.

One of the fundamental features of CSP is that it can serve as a notation for writing programs which are close to implementation, as a way of constructing specifications which may be remote from implementation, and as a calculus for reasoning about both of these things—and often comparing the two. For this reason it contains a number of operators which would either be hard to implement in a truly parallel system, or which represent some 'bad' forms of behaviour, thus making them unlikely candidates for use in programs as such. Examples are *STOP*, *Chaos* and ⊓. The reason for having the bad forms of behaviour such as deadlock and nondeterminism represented explicitly and cleanly is to enable us to reason about them, hopefully proving them absent in practical examples.

1.6 Tools

The automated tools available to help us understand a CSP process fall into two categories: ones that let us see how it behaves directly, and ones that attempt to prove properties such as trace refinement of them.

Examples of the former are the CSP animator ProBE and FDR's ability to draw a graphical representation of a process's actions, and the main example of the latter (at least for us) will be the verification functions of FDR.

With ProBE you can write an arbitrary process description and interact with it much as described in the text. In other words, you can play at being 'the environment'. In fact, an animator may give you various options about how much control you want over the process (i.e., how much of its behaviours you want to be automatic) and, in particular, it will give you the option of controlling the process more precisely than the real environment could. For example, if you like, it will let you make all its internal decisions: an internal choice $P \sqcap Q$ will be implemented as a process which can take an invisible τ (tau) action to each of P and Q. If you take control over the τ actions, then you have the power to resolve the nondeterministic choices and can thus explore whichever avenue you desire. τ actions will be discussed properly in Chap. 5: but they are assumed to be neither observable nor controllable by the "real" environment.

Chapter 8 is designed to introduce the reader to the use of FDR. Section 8.1 provides a basic introduction for readers whose knowledge of CSP is limited to the contents of the present chapter. In particular, it introduces the ASCII version of CSP, namely CSP_M, that is used as the input format for FDR, ProBE, and a number of other CSP tools, as well as the distinction between finite-state and infinite-state processes that is so important to FDR (though not ProBE).

We restrict ourselves here to describing the ways of representing the constructs introduced in this chapter in CSP_M.

All events used explicitly in a CSP_M script have to be declared explicitly using lines such as

```
channel sleep, getup, gotobed
channel eat:Meals
channel tv:Channels
channel walk:Place.Place
```

The first of these lines defines a number of data-less channels, namely individual events, and the rest define channels that have one or more components of data. All

events in CSP$_M$ consist of a channel name and zero or more data components in this
way. A `channel` declaration creates a name for use in the script: you should not
use the same name for anything else or you are likely to get some strange behaviour
and error messages.

In the rest of this book we will, in "blackboard" as well as ASCII CSP, follow
the convention that an event is a channel name followed by zero or more "data"
fields.

The prefix-construction $a \to P$ is written `a -> P`, and external and internal
choice are written `P [] Q` and `P |~| Q` respectively. Both of these operators
have indexed forms that allow you to apply them to indexed finite collections of
processes. So if `P(i)` is a process for each `i` in the set `S`, `[] i:S @ P(i)` and
`|~| i:S @ P(i)` respectively represent $\square\{P(i) \mid i \in S\}$ and $\sqcap\{P(i) \mid i \in S\}$.
`S` is allowed to be empty in the case of `[]` (giving the result `STOP`) but not
for `|~|`.

Of the constructs defined in this chapter, two are not supported in the machine-
readable version CSP$_M$ because their effects can easily be achieved in other ways.
These are guarded alternative $(a \to P \mid \ldots \mid z \to Q)$ and the form of prefix-choice
without a channel name preceding the '?': one can write `c?x`, `c.n?x:T`, etc., but
there is no direct equivalent of $?a : A \to P$. Both of these can be written in terms of
the external choice operator: the case of guarded choice has already been discussed
in the text, and the prefix-choice above can be written `[] a:A @ a -> P` which
is the literal translation of $\square_{a \in A} a \to P$. Several other operators we will meet later
also have indexed forms like this.

If, when inputting on a channel, you have no further need of the value
that is communicated, you may replace the usual identifier with an underscore.
Thus `c?_ -> STOP` and `d?x?_:A -> c!x -> STOP` mean the same as
`c?x -> STOP` and `d?x?y -> c!x -> STOP`.

The CSP$_M$ version of conditional is `if..then..else..` rather than
$P \lhd b \rhd Q$. Process parameters are written in 'argument' style `P(a,b,...,z)`.
Look at the demonstration files for examples of all these things and more. An alter-
native to conditional choice is pattern matching (see Sect. 8.1.3).

The processes `STOP` and `CHAOS(X)` are implemented in CSP$_M$, but for
some reason[3] `RUN(X)` is not. It may be defined `RUN(X) = [] x:X @ x ->`
`RUN(X)`.

The alphabet Σ of all events is written `Events` in machine-readable CSP.

Most recursive definitions in CSP$_M$ scripts are defined by equations as they are
in the text. In definitions, analogous to B^∞, where processes have parameters it
is frequently useful to use *pattern matching*, giving different clauses for different
sorts of parameter values (see example scripts and Sect. 8.1.3 for details). CSP$_M$
allows local definitions using `let` *definitions* `within` *value* clauses, and these can
be used to emulate in-line recursions $\mu p.P$: `let p=P within p`, where P is a
term involving p.

---

[3]RUN could, of course, easily be inserted into the language, but this would create a problem for the
many existing scripts that give their own local definitions of it.

The checks for FDR to perform can be pre-loaded into FDR by including lines such as

```
assert Spec [T= Imp
```

in the scripts you write for it. (This represents the check of process Imp trace-refining process Spec.) Note that it gives you a choice of modes and models for checks; the only thing we are in a position to understand yet is *trace* checks in the *refinement* mode.

1.6.1 Finite-State Machines

Thanks to the existence of infinite types it is all too easy to write process descriptions, such as $COUNT_0$ and $B_{\langle\rangle}^{\infty}$, that have infinitely many states. Since FDR works by expanding the state spaces of processes it will not terminate if asked to do much with one of these. There is nothing to stop you applying an animator to an infinite-state process, though obviously you will never be able to explore one completely!

One can usually get round this problem by restricting the range of the offending parameter(s) to that which will be encountered in the example being considered. Examples of this can be found in this chapter's demonstration file, and we have already seen one: the process $Counter(n, m)$ restricts both its parameters to the range $\{0, 1, \ldots, 7\}$ and thus has 64 states. Like many finite-state processes, this has an infinite set of traces.

This restriction is most often annoying at the specification end of refinement, since it is sometimes the case that we would (as with buffers) like to have an infinite-state specification, since this is what best represents our requirements. The only elementary thing one can do at the time of writing is to choose a finite-state specification which we know refines the 'real' one (for example, the specification that a process is a buffer with capacity no greater than 5) and prove it. It is possible that future releases of the tool will be able to handle some infinite-state specifications (though not implementations), but you should always expect this to be less efficient.

You will, with experience, get to know the sizes of process that your version of FDR can handle. With the restricted syntax in this chapter it will comfortably deal with processes that have tens of thousands of states at the time of writing: the extra constructs in Chap. 3 and beyond will lift this limit greatly.

Chapter 2
Understanding CSP

In the previous chapter we learned how to build simple CSP descriptions of sequential systems. We also saw that the specifications of CSP processes are frequently other CSP processes. In this chapter we see some of the methods we can use to prove processes equal to each other and understand how they behave.

Since the early 1980s there have been three complementary approaches to understanding the semantics of CSP programs. These are *algebra*, where we set out laws that the syntax is assumed to satisfy, *behavioural models* such as traces that form the basis of refinement relations and other things, and *operational models*, which try to understand all the actions and decisions that process implementations can make as they proceed. This chapter introduces the reader to the basics of each of these.

2.1 Algebra

An algebraic law is the statement that two expressions, involving some operators and identifiers representing arbitrary processes (and perhaps other things such as events) are equal. By 'equal', we mean that the two sides are essentially the same: for CSP this means that their communicating behaviours are indistinguishable by the environment.

Everyone with the most basic knowledge of arithmetic or set theory is familiar with the sort of algebra we are now talking about. There are a number of basic patterns that many laws conform to; the following are a few familiar examples illustrating these:

$$x + y = y + x$$ a *commutative*, or *symmetry* law
$$x \times y = y \times x$$ ditto
$$x \cup y = y \cup x$$ ditto
$$(x + y) + z = x + (y + z)$$ *associativity*
$$(x + y) \times z = (x \times z) + (y \times z)$$ (right) *distributive* law
$$0 + x = x$$ *unit* law (0 is a left unit of $+$)

A.W. Roscoe, *Understanding Concurrent Systems*, Texts in Computer Science, DOI 10.1007/978-1-84882-258-0_2, © Springer-Verlag London Limited 2010

$$\emptyset \cap x = \emptyset \qquad \textit{zero} \text{ law } (\emptyset \text{ is a left zero of } \cap)$$
$$x \cup x = x \qquad \textit{idempotence}$$

We will find all of these patterns and more amongst the laws of CSP. Let us now consider what laws ought to relate the CSP operators we have met so far: prefixing, external choice, nondeterministic choice, and conditionals.

We would expect the choice between P and itself to be the same as P, the choice between P and Q the same as that between Q and P, and the choice between three processes P, Q and R to be the same however bracketed. And this will all apply whether we are talking about internal (nondeterministic) choice or external choice. In other words, these properties all hold whether the environment or the process gets to decide which path is chosen. Thus there are idempotence,[1] symmetry and associative laws for both $\square$ and $\sqcap$:

$$P \square P = P \qquad\qquad \langle\square\text{-idem*}\rangle \ (2.1)$$
$$P \sqcap P = P \qquad\qquad \langle\sqcap\text{-idem}\rangle \ (2.2)$$
$$P \square Q = Q \square P \qquad\qquad \langle\square\text{-sym}\rangle \ (2.3)$$
$$P \sqcap Q = Q \sqcap P \qquad\qquad \langle\sqcap\text{-sym}\rangle \ (2.4)$$
$$P \square (Q \square R) = (P \square Q) \square R \qquad\qquad \langle\square\text{-assoc}\rangle \ (2.5)$$
$$P \sqcap (Q \sqcap R) = (P \sqcap Q) \sqcap R \qquad\qquad \langle\sqcap\text{-assoc}\rangle \ (2.6)$$

These three laws[2] (idempotence, symmetry and associativity) are just what is needed to ensure that the nondeterministic choice operator over sets, $\sqcap S$, makes sense (see Exercise 2.5). For what we mean by this (for finite $S = \{P_1, \ldots, P_n\}$) must be the same as $P_1 \sqcap \cdots \sqcap P_n$, and since sets are oblivious to the repetition and order of their elements, we need $\sqcap$ to be idempotent (ignoring repetitions), symmetric (ignoring order) and associative (so that bracketing is not required). Clearly the operator $\sqcap S$ has laws that we could write down too, but these would not follow such conventional forms as it is not an ordinary binary operator. We will always feel at liberty to rewrite $\sqcap\{P_1, \ldots, P_n\}$ as

$$P_1 \sqcap \cdots \sqcap P_n$$

and similar, without formal recourse to laws.

----

[1] The reader will notice that $\langle\square\text{-idem*}\rangle$ has a * in its name. This is because, while this law is true in the most standard models of CSP, there are models in the hierarchy discussed in Chaps. 11 and 12 where it is not true. This point is examined in Chap. 13. We will follow the *-ing convention throughout the book: any law without one is true throughout the hierarchy of behavioural equivalences for CSP; sometimes * will be replaced by an indication of the class of models in which the law is true.

[2] We have given each law a descriptive name and a number. The many laws that are common to this book and TPC are given the same name in each, but not usually the same number. In each book the number refers to the chapter in which the law was first asserted, and the number within that chapter.

Notice that each law has been given a name and a number to help us refer to it later. Laws will be quoted throughout this section and Chap. 13. A consolidated list can be obtained from this book's web-site.

If we have any operator or construct $F(\cdot)$ which, in any 'run', takes at most one copy of its argument, then it is natural to expect that $F(\cdot)$ will be *distributive*, in that

$$F(P \sqcap Q) = F(P) \sqcap F(Q)$$

$$F(\sqcap S) = \sqcap\{F(P) \mid P \in S\}$$

(i.e., the operator distributes over $\sqcap$ and distributes through $\sqcap$). In the first of these, this is because the argument on the left-hand side can act like P or like Q, so the effect of running $F(P \sqcap Q)$ must be either like running $F(P)$ or like running $F(Q)$. Since that is precisely the set of options open to $F(P) \sqcap F(Q)$, the two sides are equal. The second is just the same argument applied to an arbitrary, rather than two-way, choice. All of the operators, other than recursion, which we have described so far fall into this category. The distributive laws for some of the constructs seen to date are:

$$P \,\square\, (Q \sqcap R) = (P \,\square\, Q) \sqcap (P \,\square\, R) \qquad\qquad \langle\square\text{-dist}\rangle \quad (2.7)$$

$$P \,\square\, \sqcap S = \sqcap\{P \,\square\, Q \mid Q \in S\} \qquad\qquad \langle\square\text{-Dist}\rangle \quad (2.8)$$

$$a \rightarrow (P \sqcap Q) = (a \rightarrow P) \sqcap (a \rightarrow Q) \qquad\qquad \langle\text{prefix-dist}\rangle \quad (2.9)$$

$$a \rightarrow \sqcap S = \sqcap\{a \rightarrow Q \mid Q \in S\} \qquad\qquad \langle\text{prefix-Dist}\rangle \quad (2.10)$$

$$?x : A \rightarrow (P \sqcap Q) = (?x : A \rightarrow P) \sqcap (?x : A \rightarrow Q) \qquad\qquad \langle\text{input-dist}\rangle \quad (2.11)$$

$$?x : A \rightarrow \sqcap S = \sqcap\{?x : A \rightarrow Q \mid Q \in S\} \qquad\qquad \langle\text{input-Dist}\rangle \quad (2.12)$$

Note that there is a pair for each. In fact, of course, the second of each pair implies the first. An operator that distributes over $\sqcap S$ might be called *fully* distributive, whereas one that distributes over $\sqcap$ might be called *finitely* distributive. In future, we will generally only quote one of each pair of distributive laws explicitly, to save space. It may be assumed in CSP that they both hold if either does, noting that they are always equivalent when infinite (unbounded) nondeterminism is banned.

In general, an operator $F(P)$ should be distributive unless it has the chance, in a single run, to compare two different copies of P. If it can make such a comparison then $F(P \sqcap Q)$ may be different from $F(P) \sqcap F(Q)$. In the first case the two copies it compares may be different (one P and one Q) whereas, in the second, they must be the same (whichever they are). This is why recursion is not distributive. We only have to consider a simple example like

$$\mu p.((a \rightarrow p) \sqcap (b \rightarrow p)) \quad \text{and} \quad (\mu p.a \rightarrow p) \sqcap (\mu p.b \rightarrow p)$$

where the left-hand side can perform any sequence of as and bs (at its own choice) while the right-hand side has to be consistent: once it has communicated one a it must keep on doing as.

⟨□-dist⟩ is actually only one of the two distributive laws for □ over ⊓. The other one (the right distributive law) follows from this one and ⟨□-sym⟩. There are also (left and right) distributive laws for ⊓ over itself—provable from the existing set of laws for ⊓ (see Exercise 2.1 below).

Distributivity of most operators, and in particular $a \rightarrow \cdot$, over ⊓ is something that is true in CSP but frequently not in other process algebras. The main reason for this is the type of models—traces etc.—that we use for CSP. Each observation these make of a process records only a single evolution through time, with no branching. It should not be too hard to see that if we could *freeze* a process after a non-empty trace and run several copies of the result, then we could distinguish between $(a \rightarrow b \rightarrow STOP) \sqcap (a \rightarrow c \rightarrow STOP)$ and $a \rightarrow (b \rightarrow STOP \sqcap c \rightarrow STOP)$. If we froze the second version after a and ran it twice then one copy might perform b and the other c, but since the nondeterministic choice in the first version gets committed before a, the two frozen copies made after a are bound to behave the same. We will learn more about this in Chaps. 9 and 10. Observations of a single evolution through time are sometimes called a *linear* or *linear time* observation, in contrast to *branching time* where we can freeze or backtrack.

There is a close relationship between this last argument and the earlier one that an operator which uses several copies of an argument need not be distributive. We can conclude that copying arguments is incompatible with distributivity whether it is done by an operator or by the underlying model.

There is a further law relating the two forms of choice whose motivation is much more subtle. Consider the process $P \sqcap (Q \ \square \ R)$. It may *either* behave like P or offer the choice between Q and R. Now consider

$$(P \sqcap Q) \square (P \sqcap R)$$

a process which the distributive laws of □ can expand to

$$(P \square P) \sqcap (P \square R) \sqcap (Q \square P) \sqcap (Q \square R)$$

The first of these four equals P by ⟨□-idem*⟩. It follows that the first and last alternatives provide all the options of the first process. Every behaviour of the second and third is possible for one of the other two: every set of events they reject initially is also rejected by P (for they offer the choice of the first actions of P and another process), and every subsequent behaviour belongs to one of P, Q and R. It is therefore reasonable[3] to assert that the processes on the left- and right-hand sides below are equal. In other words, ⊓ distributes over □, at least in the most used models of CSP.

$$P \sqcap (Q \square R) = (P \sqcap Q) \square (P \sqcap R) \qquad \langle\sqcap\text{-}\square\text{-dist*}\rangle \ \ (2.13)$$

---

[3]In some sense this is the most important law that characterises the most standard equivalences for CSP. As we can see from the *, there are models where it is not true.

The following is the chief law relating prefixing and external choice. It says that if we give the environment the choice between processes offering A and B, then we get a process offering $A \cup B$ whose subsequent behaviour depends on which of A and B the first event belongs to:

$$(?x : A \rightarrow P) \,\square\, (?x : B \rightarrow Q)$$
$$= ?x : A \cup B \rightarrow ((P \sqcap Q) \lhd x \in A \cap B \rhd (P \lhd x \in A \rhd Q))$$

$$\langle \square\text{-step}\rangle \quad (2.14)$$

We have called this a *step* law because it allows us to compute the first step of the combination's behaviour (i.e., the selection of initial actions plus the process that succeeds each action) from the first-step behaviour of the processes we are combining.[4]

STOP is the process that offers no choice of initial actions. This can of course be written as the prefix-choice over an empty set:

$$STOP = ?x : \emptyset \rightarrow P \qquad\qquad \langle STOP\text{-step}\rangle \quad (2.15)$$

It is an immediate consequence of the last two laws that

$$STOP \,\square\, (?x : A \rightarrow P) = ?x : A \rightarrow P$$

Of course we would expect that the external choice of *any* process with *STOP* would have no effect. This gives us our first unit law:

$$STOP \,\square\, P = P \qquad\qquad \langle \square\text{-unit}\rangle \quad (2.16)$$

(There is no need for a right unit law as well as this one, since it is easily inferred from this one and the symmetry law $\langle \square\text{-sym}\rangle$.)

Conditional choice is idempotent and distributive:

$$P \lhd b \rhd P = P \qquad\qquad\qquad \langle \lhd \cdot \rhd\text{-idem}\rangle \quad (2.17)$$

$$(P \sqcap Q) \lhd b \rhd R = (P \lhd b \rhd R) \sqcap (Q \lhd b \rhd R) \qquad \langle \lhd \cdot \rhd\text{-dist-l}\rangle \quad (2.18)$$

$$R \lhd b \rhd (P \sqcap Q) = (R \lhd b \rhd P) \sqcap (R \lhd b \rhd Q) \qquad \langle \lhd \cdot \rhd\text{-dist-r}\rangle \quad (2.19)$$

Left and right distributive laws are required here because conditional choice is not symmetric.

---

[4]From here on, in quoting laws about prefixed processes, we will usually refer only to the form $?x : A \rightarrow P$. The others, namely $a \rightarrow P$ and $c?x : A \rightarrow P$ (and the more complex forms for multi-part events discussed above) can be transformed into this form easily, and so quoting a lot of extra laws to deal with them would serve no particular purpose.

The conditional behaviour is brought out by the following pair of laws:

$$P \lessdot true \gtrdot Q = P \qquad\qquad\qquad\qquad \langle \lessdot true \gtrdot \text{-id} \rangle \ (2.20)$$

$$P \lessdot false \gtrdot Q = Q \qquad\qquad\qquad\qquad \langle \lessdot false \gtrdot \text{-id} \rangle \ (2.21)$$

There are other laws in which conditional choice interacts with boolean operators on the condition(s), but we do not attempt to enumerate them here (though see the exercises below). One interesting class of laws is that almost all operators distribute over this form of choice as well as over $\sqcap$. The only ones that do not are ones (in particular prefix-choice) that may modify the bindings of identifiers used in the boolean condition. An example of a law that does hold is

$$P \,\square\, (Q \lessdot b \gtrdot R) = (P \,\square\, Q) \lessdot b \gtrdot (P \,\square\, R) \qquad\qquad \langle \lessdot \cdot \gtrdot \text{-}\square\text{-dist} \rangle \ (2.22)$$

while the failure of this distribution in the presence of binding constructs is illustrated by

$$?x : \mathbb{N} \rightarrow ?x : \mathbb{N} \rightarrow (P \lessdot x \text{ is even} \gtrdot Q) \neq$$

$$?x : \mathbb{N} \rightarrow ((?x : \mathbb{N} \rightarrow P) \lessdot x \text{ is even} \gtrdot (?x : \mathbb{N} \rightarrow Q))$$

since the distribution of $\lessdot x$ is even$\gtrdot$ through the inner prefix-choice results in x being bound to the first input rather than the second.

The fundamental law of *recursion* is that a recursively defined process satisfies the equation defining it. Thus the law is (in the case of equational definitions) just a part of the program. For the μ form of recursion this law is

$$\mu p.P = P[\mu p.P/p] \qquad\qquad\qquad\qquad \langle \mu\text{-unwind} \rangle \ (2.23)$$

where the notation $Q[R/p]$ means the substitution of the process R for all free (i.e., not bound by some lower-level recursion) occurrences of the process identifier p. (We will sometimes denote the set of *all* a term's free identifiers, both process and non-process, as $fv(P)$.)

We have already noted that recursion fails to be distributive.

Laws of the sort seen in this section serve several functions: they provide a useful way of gaining understanding and intuition about the intended meaning of constructs, they can (as we will see later) be useful in proofs about CSP processes, and finally, if presented and analysed highly systematically, they can be shown to completely define the meaning, or *semantics* of language constructs (in a sense we are not yet in a position to appreciate but which is fully explained in Chap. 13). Whenever we introduce a new operator in later chapters, we will use some of its laws to help explain how it behaves.

Exercise 2.1 Using the laws quoted in the text for $\sqcap$, prove that it distributes over itself (i.e., that $P \sqcap (Q \sqcap R) = (P \sqcap Q) \sqcap (P \sqcap R)$).

Exercise 2.2 Suggest some laws for $\sqcap S$ and how it relates to $\sqcap$.

Exercise 2.3 Write down the left and right distributive laws of $\cdot \triangleleft b \triangleright \cdot$ through $\sqcap$.

Exercise 2.4 Use $\langle\Box\text{-step}\rangle$ and other laws given above to prove that

$$(?x : A \rightarrow P) \,\Box\, (?x : A \rightarrow Q) = (?x : A \rightarrow P) \sqcap (?x : A \rightarrow Q)$$

Exercise 2.5 Suppose we try to extend the binary operator $\oplus$ (e.g. $\sqcap$) to finite non-empty sets by defining

$$\bigoplus\{P_1, \ldots, P_n\} = P_1 \oplus (P_2 \oplus \cdots (P_{n-1} \oplus P_n) \cdots)$$

Show that this makes sense (i.e., the value of $\bigoplus S$ is independent of the way S is written down) only if $\oplus$ is idempotent, symmetric and associative. For example, it must be idempotent because $\{P, P\} = \{P\}$, and hence $P \oplus P = \bigoplus\{P, P\} = \bigoplus\{P\} = P$.

In this case prove that $\bigoplus(A \cup B) = (\bigoplus A) \oplus (\bigoplus B)$ for any non-empty A and B.

What additional algebraic property must $\oplus$ have to make $\bigoplus \emptyset$ well defined in such a way that this union law remains true? [*Hint*: $\Box$ *has this property but* $\sqcap$ *does not*.] What is then the value of $\bigoplus \emptyset$?

Exercise 2.6 Complete the following laws of the conditional construct by filling in the blank(s) ($\ldots$) in each

(a) $P \triangleleft \neg b \triangleright Q = \cdots \triangleleft b \triangleright \cdots$
(b) $P \triangleleft b \triangleright (Q \triangleleft b \wedge c \triangleright R) = \cdots \triangleleft b \triangleright R$
(c) $(P \triangleleft c \triangleright Q) \triangleleft b \triangleright R = \cdots \triangleleft c \triangleright \cdots$

2.2 The Traces Model and Traces Refinement

Recall that we defined that P *trace-refines* Q, written $Q \sqsubseteq_T P$, to mean that every finite trace of P is one of Q. Note that a trace is a sequence of visible actions in the order they are observed, but that the actual time these actions happen are not recorded.

It is natural to model an untimed CSP process by the set of all traces it can perform. It turns out that recording only *finite* traces is sufficient in the majority of cases—after all, if u is an infinite trace then all its finite *prefixes* (initial subsequences) are finite traces—and for the time being we will only record finite ones. In Sect. 9.5.2 and Chap. 12 we will see the subtle distinctions infinite traces can make in some cases—though at some cost in terms of theoretical difficulty. As we will see later in this book, for example Chaps. 6, 11 and 12, there are many other choices of behaviours we can use to model processes.

2.2.1 Working out traces(P)

Recall that, any process P, $traces(P)$ is the set of all its finite traces—members of Σ^*, the set of finite sequences of events. For example:

- $traces(STOP) = \{\langle\rangle\}$—the only trace of the process that can perform no event is the empty trace;
- $traces(a \rightarrow b \rightarrow STOP) = \{\langle\rangle, \langle a\rangle, \langle a, b\rangle\}$—this process may have communicated nothing yet, performed an a only, or an a and a b;
- $traces((a \rightarrow STOP) \,\square\, (b \rightarrow STOP)) = \{\langle\rangle, \langle a\rangle, \langle b\rangle\}$—here there is a choice of first event, so there is more than one trace of length 1;
- $traces(\mu p.((a \rightarrow p) \,\square\, (b \rightarrow STOP))) = \{\langle a\rangle^n, (\langle a\rangle^n)^\frown\langle b\rangle \mid n \in \mathbb{N}\}$—this process can perform as many as as its environment likes, followed by a b, after which there can be no further communication.

Note the use of finite sequence notation here: $\langle a_1, a_2, \ldots, a_n\rangle$ is the sequence containing a_1, a_2 to a_n in that order. Unlike sets, the order of members of a sequence *does* matter, as does the number of times an element is repeated. Thus $\langle a, a, b\rangle$, $\langle a, b\rangle$ and $\langle b, a\rangle$ are all different. $\langle\rangle$ denotes the empty sequence. If s and t are two finite sequences, then $s^\frown t$ is their *concatenation*: the members of s followed by those of t: for example $\langle a, b\rangle^\frown\langle b, a\rangle = \langle a, b, b, a\rangle$. If s is a finite sequence and $n \in \mathbb{N}$, then s^n means the n-fold concatenation of s: $s^0 = \langle\rangle$ and $s^{n+1} = (s^n)^\frown s$. If s is an initial subsequence, or *prefix* of t, in that there is a (possibly empty) sequence w with $t = s^\frown w$, then we write $s \leq t$. We will meet more sequence notation later when it is required.

For any process P, $traces(P)$ will always have the following properties:

- $traces(P)$ is non-empty: it always contains the empty trace $\langle\rangle$;
- $traces(P)$ is prefix-closed: if $s^\frown t$ is a trace then at some earlier time during the recording of this, the trace was s.

There are two important things we can do with $traces(P)$: give a meaning, or semantics, to the CSP notation, and specify the behaviour required of processes. The set of all non-empty, prefix-closed subsets of Σ^* is called the *traces model*— the set of all possible representations of processes using traces. It is written $\mathcal{T}$ and is the first—and simplest—of a number of models for CSP processes we will be meeting in this book: the rest are introduced in Chap. 6, Part II and (in a timed context) Chap. 15

Hopefully, given the earlier explanations of what the various constructs of CSP 'meant', the example sets of traces are all obviously correct in the sense that they are the only possible sets of traces that the various processes might have. We can, in fact, *calculate* the trace-set of any CSP process by means of a set of simple rules— for in every case we can work out what the traces of a compound process (such as $a \rightarrow P$ or $P \,\square\, Q$) are in terms of those of its components (P and Q). Thus the traces of any process can be calculated by following its syntactic construction.

The rules for the prefixing and choice constructs are all very easy:

1. $traces(STOP) = \{\langle\rangle\}$

2. $traces(a \rightarrow P) = \{\langle\rangle\} \cup \{\langle a\rangle\hat{\ }s \mid s \in traces(P)\}$—this process has either done nothing, or its first event was a followed by a trace of P.

3. $traces(?x : A \rightarrow P) = \{\langle\rangle\} \cup \{\langle a\rangle\hat{\ }s \mid a \in A \wedge s \in traces(P[a/x])\}$—this is similar except that the initial event is now chosen from the set A and the subsequent behaviour depends on which is picked: $P[a/x]$ means the substitution of the value a for all free occurrences of the identifier x.

4. $traces(c?x : A \rightarrow P) = \{\langle\rangle\} \cup \{\langle c.a\rangle\hat{\ }s \mid a \in A \wedge s \in traces(P[a/x])\}$—the same except for the use of the channel name.

5. $traces(P \ \square \ Q) = traces(P) \cup traces(Q)$—this process offers the traces of P and those of Q.

6. $traces(P \ \sqcap \ Q) = traces(P) \cup traces(Q)$—since this process can behave like either P or Q, its traces are those of P and those of Q.

7. $traces(\sqcap S) = \bigcup\{traces(P) \mid P \in S\}$ for any non-empty set S of processes.

8. $traces(P \ {\triangleleft}b{\triangleright} \ Q) = traces(P)$ if b evaluates to $true$; and $traces(Q)$ if b evaluates to $false$.[5]

The traces of a guarded alternative can be computed by simply re-writing it as an external choice (i.e., replacing all |s by $\square$s).

Notice that the traces semantics of internal and external choice are indistinguishable. What this should suggest to you is that $traces(P)$ does not give a complete description of P, since we certainly want to be able to tell $P \ \square \ Q$ and $P \ \sqcap \ Q$ apart. We will see the solution to this problem later, but its existence should not prevent you from realising that knowledge of its traces provides a great deal of information about a process.

This style of calculating the semantics of a process is known as *denotational*. We will see other denotational semantics for CSP in Chap. 6 and study this style in detail in Chaps. 10–12. The final construct we need to deal with is recursion. Think first about a single, non-parameterised, recursion $p = Q$ (or equivalently $\mu p.Q$), where Q is any process expression possibly involving the identifier p. This means the process which behaves like Q when the whole recursively defined object is substituted for the process identifier p in its body: $Q[\mu p.Q/p]$ as in the law $\langle\mu\text{-unwind}\rangle$. The way traces have been calculated through the other constructs means that a term, like Q, with a free process identifier p, represents a function F from sets of traces to sets of traces: if p has set of traces X, then Q has traces $F(X)$. For example, if Q is $a \rightarrow p$, $F(X) = \{\langle\rangle\} \cup \{\langle a\rangle\hat{\ }s \mid s \in X\}$. $traces(\mu p.Q)$ should be a set X that solves the equation $X = F(X)$.

Now it turns out that the functions F over $\mathcal{T}$ that can arise from CSP process descriptions always have a least *fixed point* in the sense that $X = F(X)$ and $X \subseteq Y$

---

[5]*Technical note*: The treatment of identifiers representing input values and process parameters, and appearing in boolean expressions, is very lightweight here. This treatment implicitly assumes that the only terms for which we want to compute $traces(P)$ are those with no free identifiers—so that for example any boolean expression must evaluate to $true$ or $false$. The advantage of this approach is that it frees us from the extra notation that would be needed to deal with the more general case, but there is certainly no reason why we could not deal with processes with free identifiers as 'first class objects' if desired.

whenever $Y = F(Y)$—this least fixed point always being the appropriate value to pick for the recursion (see Chap. 10). Two separate mathematical theories can be used to demonstrate the existence of these fixed points, namely metric spaces and partial orders. There are introductions to each of these and their most important fixed point methods in Appendix A of TPC. Readers interested in getting full background in this area should study that.

The case of parameterised and other mutual recursions is little different, though the greater generality makes it somewhat harder to formulate. In this case we have a definition for a collection of processes, where the definition of each may invoke any or all of the others. This defines what we might term a *vector* of process names (where, in the case of a parameterised family, the parameter value is part of the name, meaning that there are as many names as there are parameter values) to be equal to a vector of process expressions. The problem of determining the trace-set of one of these mutually defined processes then comes down to solving an equation $\underline{X} = F(\underline{X})$ where $\underline{X}$ is a vector of trace-sets—one for each process name as above—and $F(\cdot)$ is now a function which both takes and delivers a vector of trace-sets. For example, in the mutual recursion

$$P = (a \rightarrow P) \,\Box\, (b \rightarrow Q)$$
$$Q = (c \rightarrow Q) \,\Box\, (b \rightarrow P)$$

all the vectors have length 2—one component corresponding to each of P and Q. Given a vector $\underline{X} = \langle X_P, X_Q \rangle$, the function F produces a vector, $\langle Y_P, Y_Q \rangle$ say, where

- $Y_P = \{\langle\rangle\} \cup \{\langle a \rangle\hat{\ }s \mid s \in X_P\} \cup \{\langle b \rangle\hat{\ }s \mid s \in X_Q\}$ i.e., the result of substituting $\underline{X}$ into the recursive definition of P, and
- $Y_Q = \{\langle\rangle\} \cup \{\langle c \rangle\hat{\ }s \mid s \in X_Q\} \cup \{\langle b \rangle\hat{\ }s \mid s \in X_P\}$ i.e., the result of substituting $\underline{X}$ into the recursive definition of Q.

In the case of *COUNT*, the vectors would be infinite—with one component for each natural number. B^∞ will also produce infinite vectors, but this time there is one component for each finite sequence of the type being transmitted.

The extraction of fixed points is mathematically the same whether the functions are on single trace-sets or on vectors. The only difference is that the intended process value in the case of a mutual recursion will be one of the components of the fixed point vector, rather than the fixed point itself.

All of the recursions we have seen to date (and almost all recursions one meets in practice) have a property that makes them easier to understand—and reason about. They are *guarded*, meaning that each recursive call comes after (i.e., is prefixed by) a communication that is introduced by the recursive definition[6] rather than being exposed immediately. Examples of *non*-guarded recursions are $\mu p.p$ (perhaps the archetypal one), $\mu p.p \,\Box\, (a \rightarrow p)$, and the parameterised mutual recursion (over the

---

[6]This definition will be modified later to take account of language constructs we have not met yet.

natural numbers)[7]

$$P(n) = (a \rightarrow P(1)) \triangleleft n = 1 \triangleright P((3n+1) \text{ div } 2 \triangleleft n \text{ odd} \triangleright n \text{ div } 2)$$

The point about a guarded recursion is that the first-step behaviour does not depend at all on a recursive call, and when a recursive call is reached, the first step of its behaviour, in turn, can be computed without any deeper calls, and so on. In other words, we are guaranteed to have communicated at least n events before a recursive call is made at depth n.

2.2.2 Traces and Laws

In Sect. 2.1 we introduced the notion of equality between processes provable by a series of laws. One can have two quite different processes, textually, which are provably equal by a series of these laws. Whatever the text of a process, the previous section gives us a recipe for computing its set of traces. We should realise that these two theories have to be squared with each other, since it would be a ridiculous situation if there were two processes, provably equal in the algebra, that turned out to have different trace-sets.

Of course this is not so, since all the laws quoted are easily shown to be valid in the sense that the traces of the processes on the left- and right-hand sides are always the same. For example, since the traces of $P \square Q$ and $P \sqcap Q$ are both given by union, the trace-validity of their idempotence, symmetry and associative laws follow directly from the same properties of set-theoretic union ($\cup$). Since $\sqcap$ and $\square$ are indistinguishable from each other in traces, their distributive laws over each other are equally simple, for example

$$traces(P \sqcap (Q \square R)) = traces(P) \cup (traces(Q) \cup traces(R))$$
$$= (traces(P) \cup traces(Q))$$
$$\cup (traces(P) \cup traces(R))$$
$$= traces((P \sqcap Q) \square (P \sqcap R))$$

On the other hand, since there are distinctions we wish to make between processes that we know are not made by traces, we would expect that there are processes P and Q such that $traces(P) = traces(Q)$ (which we can abbreviate $P =_T Q$) but such that $P = Q$ is *not* provable using the laws. This is indeed so, as our investigations of more refined models in later chapters will show.

Clearly the validity of the various laws with respect to traces means we can prove the equality of $traces(P)$ and $traces(Q)$ by transforming P to Q by a series of

---

[7]The interesting thing about this particular example is that it is not known whether or not the series (of parameters) generated by an arbitrary starting value will always reach 1, so in fact we *do not know* whether all the components of this recursion will always be able to communicate an a. Of course not nearly this amount of subtlety is required to give unguarded mutual recursions!

laws. The rather limited set of operators we have seen to date means that the range of interesting examples of this phenomenon we can discuss yet is rather limited. However, there is one further proof rule which greatly extends what is possible: the principle of unique fixed points for guarded recursions.

2.2.3 Unique Fixed Points

If $Z = F(Z)$ is the fixed-point equation generated by any guarded recursion (single, parameterised or mutual) for trace-sets and Y is a process (or vector of processes) whose trace-sets satisfy this equation, then $X =_T Y$ where X is the process (or vector) defined by the recursion. In other words, the equation has precisely one solution over[8] T or the appropriate space of vectors over T. This rule is often abbreviated UFP; its theoretical justification can be found in Sect. 10.2, but in essence it is true because guardedness means that we can completely determine the traces of the fixed point P of a guarded function F, with length n or less, from the equation $P = F^n(P)$.

Recall for example, the first two recursive processes we defined:

$$P_1 = up \rightarrow down \rightarrow P_1$$
$$P_2 = up \rightarrow down \rightarrow up \rightarrow down \rightarrow P_2$$

We know, by unwinding the first of these definitions twice, that

$$P_1 = up \rightarrow down \rightarrow up \rightarrow down \rightarrow P_1 \qquad\qquad (\dagger)$$

Thus P_1 satisfies the equation defining P_2. Since P_2 is guarded we can deduce that $P_1 =_T P_2$—in other words, $traces(P_1)$ solves an equation with only one solution, namely $traces(P_2)$. Of course it was obvious that these two processes are equivalent, but it is nice to be able to prove this!

In applying this rule in future we will not usually explicitly extract the trace-sets of the process we are claiming is a fixed point. Instead, we will just apply laws to demonstrate, as in ($\dagger$) above, that the syntactic process solves the recursive definition.

Most interesting examples of the UFP rule seem to derive from mutual recursions, where we set up a vector $\underline{Y}$ that satisfies some mutual recursion $\underline{X} = F(\underline{X})$. Indeed, the mutual recursion is usually in the form of a one-step tail recursion (precisely one event before each recursive call). The thing to concentrate on is how these vectors $\underline{Y}$ are constructed to model the state spaces that these tail recursions so clearly describe.

---

[8]IMPORTANT: though the UFP rule is stated here in terms of the traces model T, because this is the only model we have seen so far, it applies equally to all models of CSP to be found in this book except for some introduced in Chap. 12.

As an easy but otherwise typical example, suppose our *COUNT* processes were extended so that the parameter now ranges over *all* the integers $\mathbb{Z}$ rather than just the non-negative ones $\mathbb{N}$:

$$ZCOUNT_n = up \rightarrow ZCOUNT_{n+1} \ \square \ down \rightarrow ZCOUNT_{n-1}$$

The striking thing about this example, when you think about it, is that the value of the parameter n actually has no effect at all on the behaviour of $ZCOUNT_n$: whatever its value, this process can communicate any sequence of *ups* and *downs*. This might lead us to believe it was equal to the process

$$AROUND = up \rightarrow AROUND \ \square \ down \rightarrow AROUND$$

and indeed we can use the UFP rule to prove $AROUND =_T ZCOUNT_n$ for all n. Let $\underline{A}$ be the vector of processes with structure matching the *ZCOUNT* recursion (i.e., it has one component for each $n \in \mathbb{Z}$) where every component equals *AROUND*. This is a natural choice since we conjecture that every $ZCOUNT_n$ equals *AROUND*. Applying the function F_{ZC} of the *ZCOUNT* recursion to this vector we get another, whose nth component is

$$F_{ZC}(\underline{A})_n = up \rightarrow A_{n+1} \ \square \ down \rightarrow A_{n-1}$$
$$= up \rightarrow AROUND \ \square \ down \rightarrow AROUND$$
$$= AROUND$$
$$= A_n$$

(where the second line follows by definition of $\underline{A}$ and the third by definition of *AROUND*). Thus $\underline{A}$ is indeed a fixed point of F_{ZC}, proving our little result.

The basic principle at work here is that, in order to prove that some process P (in this case *AROUND*) is equivalent to a component of the tail recursion $\underline{X} = F(\underline{X})$ (in this case *ZCOUNT*), you should work out what states P goes through as it evolves. Assuming it is possible to do so, you should then form a hypothesis about which of these states each component of $\underline{X}$ matches up with. In our case there is only one state of P, and *all* the components of *ZCOUNT* match up with it. You then form the vector $\underline{Y}$ by replacing each component of $\underline{X}$ by the state of P conjectured to be equivalent, and then try to prove that this creates a solution to the tail recursion: if you can do this, you have completed the proof.

Both in the text and the exercises, there will be a number of examples following basically this argument through the rest of Part I (see, for example, pp. 52, 101 and 133, and Exercises 3.9 and 7.3).

Exercise 2.7 Prove the validity in traces of the laws ⟨prefix-dist⟩ (2.9) and ⟨□-step⟩ (2.14).

Exercise 2.8 Recall the processes P_1, and P_u and P_d from Sect. 1.1.2. Prove that $P_u =_T P_1$ by the method above. [*Hint: show that a vector consisting of P_1 and one other process is a fixed point of the $\langle P_u, P_d \rangle$ recursion.*]

Exercise 2.9 Use laws and the UFP rule to prove that

$$Chaos_A \sqcap RUN_A =_T Chaos_A$$

for any alphabet A.

2.2.4 Specification and Refinement

Traces are not just a dry and abstract model of processes to help us decide equality, but give a very usable language in *specification*. A specification is some condition that we wish a given process to satisfy. Since a CSP process is, by assumption, characterised completely by its communicating behaviour, it is obviously the case that we will be able to formulate many specifications in terms of *traces(P)*. In fact, most trace specifications one meets in practice are what we term *behavioural* specifications: the stipulation that each $s \in traces(P)$ meets some condition $R(s)$. This is termed a behavioural specification because what we are doing is 'lifting' the specification R on the individual recorded behaviours (i.e., traces) to the whole process.

There are two different approaches to behavioural specifications and their verification. The first (which is that adopted in Hoare's book, where you can find many more details than here) is to leave R explicitly as a specification of traces (generally using the special identifier *tr* to range over arbitrary traces of P). The second, and essentially equivalent, method, and the one required for FDR, is to define a process *Spec* that has just those traces that can occur in a process satisfying the specification, and test $Spec \sqsubseteq_T P$. There are merits in both of these ways of expressing specifications, as well as others such as *temporal logics*. The functionality of FDR means, however, that the main emphasis of this book will be on processes-as-specifications.

In Hoare's notation

$$P \text{ sat } R(tr) \quad \text{means} \quad \forall tr \in traces(P).R(tr)$$

This is meaningful however R is constructed, though usually it is expressed in predicate logic using trace notation.

In order to be able to express this sort of property it is useful to extend our range of trace notation:

- If s is a finite sequence, $\#s$ denotes the *length* of s (i.e., the number of members).
- If $s \in \Sigma^*$ and $A \subseteq \Sigma$ then $s \upharpoonright A$ means the sequence s *restricted* to A: the sequence whose members are those of s which are in A. $\langle\rangle \upharpoonright A = \langle\rangle$ and $(s^\frown\langle a\rangle) \upharpoonright A = (s \upharpoonright A)^\frown\langle a\rangle$ if $a \in A$, $s \upharpoonright A$ otherwise.
- If $s \in \Sigma^*$ then $s \downarrow c$ can mean two things depending on what c is. If c is an *event* in Σ then it means the number of times c appears in s (i.e., $\#(s \upharpoonright \{c\})$), while if c is a *channel name* (associated with a non-trivial data-type) it means the sequence of values (without the label c) that have been communicated along c in s. For example,

$$\langle c.1, d.1, c.2, c.3, e.4\rangle \downarrow c = \langle 1, 2, 3\rangle$$

The following are some examples of specifications describing features of some of the processes we have already met.

- Various processes in Sect. 1.1.2 all satisfy the condition:

$$tr \downarrow down \leq tr \downarrow up \leq tr \downarrow down + 1 \qquad (\ddagger)$$

which states that they have never communicated more *down*s than *up*s, and neither do they fall more than one behind.
- The specification of $COUNT_n$ is similar but less restrictive:

$$tr \downarrow down \leq tr \downarrow up + n$$

- $B_{\langle\rangle}^{\infty}$ and *COPY* both satisfy the basic *buffer* specification:

$$tr \downarrow right \leq tr \downarrow left$$

(noting that here $\leq$ means prefix and the things to its left and right are sequences of values). This is in fact the strongest trace specification that $B_{\langle\rangle}^{\infty}$ meets, but *COPY* meets further ones.

Hoare gives a set of proof rules for establishing facts of the form P sat $R(tr)$— essentially a re-coding into logic of the rules we have already seen for computing $traces(P)$. The following rules cover the operators we have seen to date (bearing in mind the known equivalences between forms of prefixing).

$$STOP \, \mathbf{sat}(tr = \langle\rangle)$$

$$\frac{\forall a \in A.P(a) \, \mathbf{sat} \, R_a(tr)}{?a : A \rightarrow P \, \mathbf{sat}(tr = \langle\rangle \vee \exists a \in A.\exists tr'. \, tr = \langle a\rangle^\frown tr' \wedge R_a(tr'))}$$

$$\frac{P \, \mathbf{sat} \, R(tr) \wedge Q \, \mathbf{sat} \, R(tr)}{P \, \Box \, Q \, \mathbf{sat} \, R(tr)}$$

$$\frac{P \, \mathbf{sat} \, R(tr) \wedge Q \, \mathbf{sat} \, R(tr)}{P \, \sqcap \, Q \, \mathbf{sat} \, R(tr)}$$

$$\frac{P \, \mathbf{sat} \, R(tr) \wedge \forall tr.R(tr) \Rightarrow R'(tr)}{P \, \mathbf{sat} \, R'(tr)}$$

$$\frac{P \, \mathbf{sat} \, R(tr) \wedge P \, \mathbf{sat} \, R'(tr)}{P \, \mathbf{sat} \, R(tr) \wedge R'(tr)}$$

The most interesting is that relating to recursion, and in fact Hoare's rule can usefully (and validly) be generalised in two ways: his assumption that the recursion is guarded is not necessary for this style of proof (though it is in many similar proof rules, some of which can be found later in this book or in TPC), and we can give a version for mutual recursion by attaching one proposed specification to each component of the vector of processes being defined.

PROOF RULE FOR RECURSION   *Suppose $\underline{X} = F(\underline{X})$ is the fixed point equation for (vectors of) trace-sets resulting from some recursive definition, and that $\underline{X}$ is the (least) fixed point which it defines. Let Λ be the indexing set of the vectors, so that $\underline{X} = \langle X_\lambda \mid \lambda \in \Lambda \rangle$. Suppose that for each λ there is a specification R_λ such that*

- *$STOP$ sat $R_\lambda(tr)$ for all $\lambda \in \Lambda$, and*
- *$\forall \lambda \in \Lambda.Y_\lambda$ sat $R_\lambda(tr) \Rightarrow \forall \lambda \in \Lambda.F(\underline{Y})_\lambda$ sat $R_\lambda(tr)$*

then X_λ sat $R_\lambda(tr)$ for all $\lambda \in \Lambda$.

Paraphrasing this: we attach a specification R_λ to each component of the mutual recursion, and provided all of these are satisfied by *STOP* and, on the assumption that they all hold of recursive calls, they hold of the body of the recursion, then we can infer they hold of the actual process(es) defined by the recursion. This rule is formally justified in Sect. 9.2 of TPC, which discusses a number of related proof rules collectively known as *recursion induction*.

The above can be used to prove that the *COUNT* processes meet the vector of specifications quoted for them above and, provided one can come up with appropriate specifications for the B_s^∞ processes for $s \neq \langle \rangle$, one can prove that $B_{\langle \rangle}^\infty$ meets its specification.

The most curious feature of this is the role played by *STOP*. It does not seem a very useful process and yet its satisfying R is a precondition to the above rule (and Hoare's). At first sight it seems unlikely that many useful specifications will be met by *STOP*, but in fact *any* behavioural trace specification which is satisfied by any process at all is satisfied by *STOP*. For $traces(STOP) = \{\langle \rangle\} \subseteq traces(P)$ for any P, and so if all the traces of P satisfy R, so do all those of *STOP*.

This shows precisely the limitation of trace specifications: while they can say that a process P cannot do anything stupid, they cannot force it to do anything at all. For this reason they are often termed *safety* or *partial correctness* conditions, while *liveness* or *total correctness* conditions are ones that additionally force a process to be able to do things. In later chapters we will develop models that allow us to build liveness specifications.

In order to satisfy 'sat $R(tr)$' a process's traces must be a *subset* of the traces which R allows. In fact, most of the example specifications given above have the property that the target process has the *largest possible* set of traces of any process satisfying it. This can be expressed in several different, but equivalent, ways (where P is the process and R the trace condition):

- $P =_T \sqcap \{Q \mid Q$ sat $R(tr)\}$ or, in other words, P is trace equivalent to the nondeterministic choice over all processes meeting the specification.
- Q sat $R(tr) \Rightarrow traces(Q) \subseteq traces(P)$
- $traces(P) \subseteq \{s \mid \forall t \leq s.R(t)\}$, the largest prefix-closed set of traces satisfying R. (It is worth noting that the set of traces satisfying each of the trace specifications on p. 37 is *not* prefix-closed. For example, the trace $\langle down, up \rangle$ satisfies the specification ($\ddagger$) there, but since the prefix $\langle down \rangle$ does not, the longer trace is not possible for a process *all* of whose traces satisfy ($\ddagger$).)

Remember we defined that Q *refines* P, written $P \sqsubseteq Q$ if $P = Q \sqcap P$. Interpreted over the traces model, this leads to the concept of *traces refinement*

$$P \sqsubseteq_T Q \equiv P =_T Q \sqcap P \equiv traces(Q) \subseteq traces(P)$$

The above properties demonstrate that, for any satisfiable behavioural trace specification R there is always a process P_R (given by the formula in the first bullet point, and whose traces are the expression in the third) that is the most nondeterministic satisfying R and such that

$$Q \text{ sat } R(tr) \Leftrightarrow P_R \sqsubseteq_T Q$$

Let us say that P_R is the *characteristic* process of R. In other words, satisfaction (**sat**) can always be determined by deciding refinement against a suitably chosen process.

For example, $B_{\langle\rangle}^{\infty}$ is the (characteristic process of the) trace specification of a buffer, and a process will trace-refine it if, and only if, it meets the trace-based buffer specification. Thus $COPY \sqsupseteq_T B_{\langle\rangle}^{\infty}$, and all but the last of your answers to Exercise 1.7 should have the same property. (Here, we are taking the liberty of writing $P \sqsupseteq_T Q$ as the equivalent of $Q \sqsubseteq_T P$. We will do this for all order relations in future without comment, as the need arises.)

There are some major advantages in identifying each specification with the most nondeterministic process satisfying it.

- This is the form in which FDR codes specifications and allows them to be mechanically verified or refuted.
- Refinement has many properties that can be exploited, for example it is *transitive*:

$$P \sqsubseteq Q \wedge Q \sqsubseteq T \Rightarrow P \sqsubseteq T$$

and *monotone*: if $C[\cdot]$ is any process context, namely a process definition with a slot to put a process in, then

$$P \sqsubseteq Q \Rightarrow C[P] \sqsubseteq C[Q]$$

If $C[Q]$ is a process definition with component Q, with an overall target specification S, we might be able to factor the proof of $S \sqsubseteq C[Q]$ into two parts. First, find a specification P such that $S \sqsubseteq C[P]$. Second, prove $P \sqsubseteq Q$, which implies thanks to monotonicity that $C[P] \sqsubseteq C[Q]$. Transitivity then gives $S \sqsubseteq C[Q]$. This software engineering technique is known as *compositional development*.

Note how the identification of processes and specifications allowed us to consider the object $C[P]$, which we might read as '$C[Q]$, on the assumption that the process Q satisfies the specification P'.

- It allows one to move gradually from specification to implementation, using the transitivity property quoted above, creating a series of processes

$$Spec \sqsubseteq P_1 \sqsubseteq \cdots \sqsubseteq P_n \sqsubseteq Impl$$

where the first is the specification, and each is created by refining the previous one till an acceptable implementation is reached. This is known as *stepwise refinement*.

It is worth noting that, since the refinement $P \sqsubseteq Q$ is expressible as the equality $P \sqcap Q = P$, it makes sense to try to prove it algebraically. Recall Exercise 2.9.

Of course, the limitations of trace specification discussed earlier still apply here. It is worth noting that $STOP \sqsupseteq_T P$ and $RUN \sqsubseteq_T P$ for all processes P.

Our emphasis on refinement-based proof means that we will not give any of the **sat** rules for the further operators and models we introduce later in this book; the interested reader can, of course, find many of them in Hoare's text.

2.2.5 Afters and Initials

If P is any process, *initials*(P) (abbreviated P^0 in some publications on CSP) is the set of all its initial events

$$initials(P) = \{a \mid \langle a \rangle \in traces(P)\}$$

This set is often used in specifications and other definitions.

For example, *initials*$(STOP) = \emptyset$ and *initials*$(?x : A \rightarrow P(x)) = A$.

If $s \in traces(P)$ then P/s (pronounced 'P *after* s') represents the behaviour of P after the trace s is complete. Over the traces model, P/s can be computed

$$traces(P/s) = \{t \mid s\hat{\ }t \in traces(P)\}$$

This operator should not be thought of as an ordinary part of the CSP language, rather as a notation for discussing behaviour of processes in fairly abstract contexts, to represent the behaviour of P on the *assumption* that s has occurred. The best reason for not including it as an operator you could use in programs is that it is not implementable in a conventional sense: the process

$$(STOP \sqcap a \rightarrow a \rightarrow STOP)/\langle a \rangle$$

is equivalent to $a \rightarrow STOP$, but no reasonable implementation acting on the nondeterministic choice here can force it to do anything.

Over the traces model it is true that

$$P =_T ?x : initials(P) \rightarrow P/\langle x \rangle$$

but we will find that this is not true over more discriminating models.

Exercise 2.10

(a) Let $N \geq 0$. Give a trace specification for a process with events a, b and c which states that the absolute value of the difference between the number of as and the total number of bs and cs is at most N.

(b) Now find a CSP definition of a process D_N for which this is the strongest spec-ification. [*Hint: give a parameterised recursion whose parameter is the present difference.*] D_0 is equivalent to a well-known simple process: what is it and why?

(c) What traces refinements hold between the D_N?

Exercise 2.11 Give the strongest trace specification satisfied by $COPY = left?x \rightarrow right!x \rightarrow COPY$. Use the proof rules for **sat** given above to prove that $COPY$ meets it.

Exercise 2.12 See Exercise 1.6. Give a trace specification that a machine with events $\{in£1, out5p, out10p, out20p\}$ has never given out more money than it has received.

2.3 Operational Semantics and Labelled Transition Systems

Unlike algebraic laws and behavioural models, an *operational* semantics does not attempt to capture some sort of extensional[9] equivalence between processes. Rather it gives a formalisation of how a process can be implemented. We will see several styles of operational semantics for CSP in this book. The most practically important of these are based on the idea of *labelled transition systems*, usually abbreviated LTS.

A labelled transition system consists of a non-empty set of states S, with a desig-nated initial state P_0, a set of labels L (which for us will always be the set of visible actions processes can perform plus a special, invisible action τ, the Greek letter tau), and a ternary relation $P \xrightarrow{x} Q$ meaning that the state P can perform an action labelled x and move to state Q. All the transition pictures we showed in Chap. 1 are examples of LTSs, for example Figs. 1.1 and 1.2. A further one, the behaviour of the process *Asleep* (p. 6) is shown in Fig. 2.1.

Many operational semantics consist of rules for extracting an LTS from the syn-tax of a program: from any program state P they provide rules for calculating what

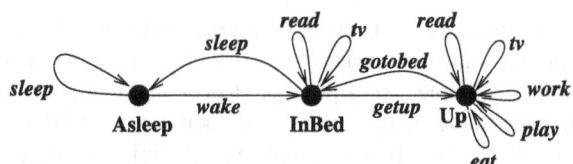

Fig. 2.1 Example LTS: the process *Asleep*

---

[9]Here, *extensional* means equality between objects based on the properties that can be observed of them. Thus the *axiom of extension* in set theory says that two sets are equal if and only if they have the same members. The opposite of extensional is *intensionality*, and intensional semantics capture not only what a program does but some element of how it does it. Thus operational semantics have at least an element of intensionality about them.

the initial labels are of actions that P can perform, together with the state the process moves to resulting from each action. In CSP these program states are usually just pieces of CSP syntax. A given state may have more than one result for a given label: for example the operational semantics of $P \sqcap Q$ has two different results of τ (namely P and Q) and $(a \to P) \,\square\, (a \to Q)$ has the same two results for a. We will see in Chap. 9 that the rules for reducing a process description to an LTS can take a number of different forms.

FDR operates on the LTS representation of a process, which it calculates from the syntax. When we refer to a *state* or number of states in the context of an FDR check, we are always referring to states in the resulting LTS. While the nodes of an LTS are often marked with a representation of the processes they represent, these node markings are irrelevant: the behaviour comes only from the actions.

It is clear that we can calculate[10] the traces of a process from its LTS semantics: just start from the initial state and see what sequences of actions are possible from there, deleting the τs. Everything that FDR does with traces is based on this correspondence: the tool *never* calculates an explicit trace-set for any process.

We will not give the explicit rules of an operational semantics here: by and large you can rely on FDR calculating a process's transitions either to use itself or to display the transitions in graph mode. For most simple sequential processes (such as those whose transition systems we have already seen), the shape of the LTS is fortunately obvious: indeed it would make a lot of sense to have a graphical input mode for FDR and other tools that would allow the user to draw an LTS and automatically generate the corresponding CSP (we will later have an exercise (5.12) to show that every LTS can be implemented as a CSP process.

It is important for using FDR that you know what an LTS is and what our assumptions are about how they behave:

- Starting from the initial state, a process is always in one of the states of its LTS.
- When a process is in a state that has visible (outward-pointing) actions, it may allow the environment to synchronise with one of these.
- If it has no τ actions, it must agree to one of its visible actions if offered by the environment.
- If it does have one or more τ actions, then either it synchronises quickly on a visible action with the environment, or follows one of its τ options. Following a τ option is both unobservable and uncontrollable by the environment.

Two processes can easily be equivalent in every behavioural model and yet have different transition systems. This is clear from the two examples in Fig. 1.1. As another example, every process P is behaviourally equivalent to the one in which the initial node leads directly, by a τ action to the initial node of P. (Following some other process algebras it is convenient to write this process as τP.)

We will find in later chapters (particularly Chap. 9) that there are theories that allow us (and FDR) to compare and manipulate LTSs. It is not necessary to understand these now.

---

[10]It should also be clear to those familiar with automata theory that the trace set of any finite-state process is a *regular language*.

Fig. 2.2 See Exercise 2.13

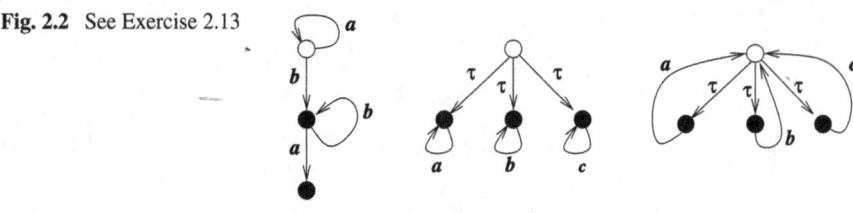

(i)   (ii)   (iii)

Exercise 2.13 Give CSP definitions of processes whose natural LTS implementations are the diagrams shown in Fig. 2.2. In each case the initial node is indicated by the white circle.

2.4 Tools

As stated above, FDR works by calculating the LTS semantics of the specification and implementation processes of each refinement check Spec T=[Imp and then running an algorithm on these that produces the same answer we would have got by working out the traces of both sides and comparing them directly. You can find some details of this algorithm in Chap. 8. One obvious advantage of this approach is that it works for any finite-state system, even when they have infinite trace sets.

There is, unfortunately, no way of checking the various laws of CSP on FDR in their full generality. All we can do is check particular cases of the laws when all the processes and other parameters have been substituted by concrete values. This demonstrates the main weakness of the style of reasoning that FDR represents: excellent at concrete examples, but much more difficult to use for proving general results.

A number of techniques where, by doing a few carefully chosen FDR checks, one can establish general results, can be found in Chap. 17. None of these applies to the laws. Until recently the only option was to prove them by hand. Several groups, in particular that of Markus Roggenbach at Swansea [115, 116], and [156], have shown how to embed the theories of several CSP models in theorem proving tools such as Isabelle [103], and then prove both the laws in general and other coherency properties of the definitions of CSP operators over the models. This type of tool is not recommended for CSP beginners unless they happen to be experts in theorem proving technology.

Chapter 3
Parallel Operators

All the processes defined so far have, at least in their obvious executions, only one thread of action. The whole idea of concurrency is to be able to reason about systems where there are a number of processes with independent control, interacting where necessary. In this chapter we see how to add operators which model this within our framework.

3.1 Synchronous Parallel

We have already set down the principle that processes interact by agreeing, or hand-shaking, on communications. The simplest form of the CSP parallel operator insists that processes agree on *all* actions that occur. It is written $P \parallel Q$. For example, if $a \in \Sigma$, then

$$(a \to REPEAT) \parallel REPEAT$$

will have the same behaviour (except, perhaps, for precise timing details that we choose to ignore) as $\mu p.a \to p$. We can see this by following through how this combination works. Recall that

$$REPEAT = ?x : \Sigma \to x \to REPEAT$$

Since both sides have to agree on all events, it is clear that the only possible first event is a, and this indeed is a possible event for the right-hand process. The copy of *REPEAT* on the right-hand side then forces the second event to be an a, which is accepted by *REPEAT* on the left-hand side, forcing the third event to be a also, and so on for ever like a game of ping pong.

Perhaps the clearest description of this parallel operator is the following law:

$$?x : A \to P \parallel ?x : B \to Q = ?x : A \cap B \to (P \parallel Q) \qquad \langle \parallel\text{-step} \rangle \ (3.1)$$

$\parallel$ is also symmetric, associative and distributive. We do not quote these laws explicitly here since they will be subsumed later into laws for generalisations of $\parallel$.

A.W. Roscoe, *Understanding Concurrent Systems*, Texts in Computer Science,
DOI 10.1007/978-1-84882-258-0_3, © Springer-Verlag London Limited 2010

Think back to our example of describing the events of someone's life as a CSP process as on p. 6. If a couple decide to synchronise their lives and do *everything* together, this is the equivalent of putting them in parallel using $\|$. They can only do things that they both agree on. So, for example the pair

$$Peter = getup \rightarrow (breakfast \rightarrow jog \rightarrow work \rightarrow Peter'$$
$$\square\, jog \rightarrow breakfast \rightarrow work \rightarrow Peter'$$

$$Maggie = getup \rightarrow (breakfast \rightarrow swim \rightarrow work \rightarrow Maggie'$$
$$\square\, swim \rightarrow breakfast \rightarrow work \rightarrow Maggie'$$

will, in *Peter* $\|$ *Maggie*, agree on getting up and breakfast, but then *deadlock*, even though they would later agree on *work*.

3.1.1 Turning Parallel Processes into Sequential Ones

It is important to realise that CSP makes no fundamental distinction between 'parallel' and 'sequential' processes. There are just processes, and you can use any operator on any process. Indeed, any parallel CSP process is equivalent to sequential processes with the same pattern of communications.

The law $\langle\|\text{-step}\rangle$ (together with the other properties listed above, and the laws quoted in the previous chapter) can be used to transform a parallel process into a sequential one. For example, if

$$P = (a \rightarrow a \rightarrow STOP) \,\square\, (b \rightarrow STOP)$$
$$Q = (a \rightarrow STOP) \,\square\, (c \rightarrow a \rightarrow STOP)$$

these laws prove $P \| Q = a \rightarrow STOP$.

When the component processes are recursively defined, the algebraic laws alone will probably not be enough. In this case we use a combination of laws and the UFP rule: the parallel combination is expanded until we have a guarded expression for it and every other parallel combination discovered during the exploration. Consider, for example, the combination

$$(a \rightarrow REPEAT) \| REPEAT$$

discussed earlier:

$$= (a \rightarrow REPEAT) \| (?x : \Sigma \rightarrow x \rightarrow REPEAT)$$
$$= a \rightarrow \underline{(REPEAT \| (a \rightarrow REPEAT))}$$

The underlining here indicates the parallel expression we have uncovered behind the guard a. Now we could use the symmetry of $\|$ to observe that this second combination equals the original one, so that

$$(a \rightarrow REPEAT) \| REPEAT = a \rightarrow (a \rightarrow REPEAT) \| REPEAT$$

showing that the process satisfies the guarded recursion $P = a \to P$. Alternatively (as would have been the only option if this example were not so symmetric) we could expand this second parallel combination in the same way that we did the first, and would find

$$REPEAT \parallel (a \to REPEAT) = a \to \underline{(a \to REPEAT) \parallel REPEAT}$$

At this point we notice that the parallel combination reached here is one we have seen before, so there is no need to expand it again (in general you should proceed by expanding each combination you find until there is none you have not seen before). We have thus expanded two processes and shown that they satisfy the guarded mutual recursion

$$R = a \to Q$$
$$Q = a \to R$$

Depending on which route we have followed, this has proved via the UFP rule that the parallel combination is trace equivalent to one of the processes P and R above. Of course, the fact that P, Q and R are equivalent is itself an easy consequence of the UFP rule.

This idea and variations on it work for every system built as the parallel combination of sequential processes under $\parallel$ and the other parallel operations we will introduce in this chapter. When the sequential processes contain nondeterminism ($\sqcap$), the distributive law of parallel is also used in this transformation. For example if $P = a \to P \sqcap b \to P$ and $Q = a \to Q$, we can see that

$$P \parallel Q = ((a \to P) \parallel (a \to Q)) \sqcap ((b \to P) \parallel (a \to Q))$$
$$= (a \to (P \parallel Q)) \sqcap STOP$$

by distributivity and $\langle \parallel\text{-step}\rangle$, demonstrating that this process is equivalent (by UFP) to $\mu p.((a \to p) \sqcap STOP)$.

This illustrates that when a pair of processes can deadlock, one of the states in their equivalent sequential form will be $STOP$, which is equivalent to $?x : \emptyset \to P$ by $\langle STOP\text{-step}\rangle$. When, as in $Peter \parallel Maggie$ from p. 46, all traces lead to certain deadlock, the parallel process expands finitely (here to $getsup \to breakfast \to STOP$) and there is no need to use UFP.

When the processes in parallel depend on a parameter introduced by recursion or input, it is likely that the family of processes uncovered by the exploration will be another parameterised one. Some examples can be found in the exercises below and in later sections, and an interesting application of this idea can be found in Sect. 4.2.3.

Example 3.1 (Bargaining) The two processes put in parallel by $\parallel$ can influence each other. Typically one offers a range of actions and the other picks one of them, but more generally they can both narrow down the choice. For example, imagine a buyer coming up to a market stall whose stock is a subset of some set *Item*. A transaction might be represented by the event $buy.x.y$ where x is an item and y is an amount of money. In a simple model, our buyer might have a fixed amount of money Y and have a maximum amount $pval(x)$ she is prepared to pay for any item x. Similarly the merchant will have a minimum amount $mval(x)$ he is prepared to accept for any item. We might describe a merchant with stock X by

$$Merchant(X) = \Box\{buy.x.y \to Merchant(X \setminus \{x\}) \mid x \in X, y \geq mval(x)\}$$
$$\Box\ outofstock?x : Item \setminus X \to Merchant(X)$$

This is a deterministic process because the merchant is always prepared to sell for the right amount of money. The customer, on the other hand, selects an item to try and buy nondeterministically. She is parameterised by her remaining amount of money:

$$Customer(Y) = \sqcap\{buy.x?y : \{y' \mid y' \leq \min(pval(x), Y)\} \to Customer(Y - y)$$
$$\Box\ outofstock.x \to Customer(Y)$$
$$\mid x \in Item\}$$

The parallel process $Customer(Y) \parallel Merchant(X)$ lets the customer choose a succession of items she wants to buy. For each of these, either the merchant signals he is out of stock, or they are prepared to agree on any amount of money between (at the low end) the merchant's valuation and the minimum of the customer's valuation and the amount of money she has left. They deadlock if, for any such item, they cannot agree on a price.

The traces of $P \parallel Q$ are easy to compute: since this process can perform an action just when its two arguments can, it follows that

$$traces(P \parallel Q) = (traces(P)) \cap (traces(Q))$$

It is worth noting that, even though this implies $traces(P \parallel P) = traces(P)$, the existence of nondeterminism (which we know is not described fully by traces) makes it possible that $P \parallel P$ will not behave like P: both sides may make different nondeterministic choices and so fail to agree on any communication. This means $\parallel$ is not idempotent. For example, if $P = (a \to STOP) \sqcap (b \to STOP)$, which cannot deadlock on its first step, then $P \parallel P = P \sqcap STOP$, which can. The reasons for this are closely connected with our discussion of distributivity in Sect. 2.1: $P \parallel P$ clearly requires two copies of P and so can compare them.

Exercise 3.1 How do $COUNT_0 \parallel COUNT_3$, $COUNT_0 \parallel Counter(0, 0)$ and $COUNT_0 \parallel REPEAT$ behave, where they are all as described in the previous chapter? For each either find an existing process that behaves like the appropriate combination, or define a new (sequential) process that does.

Prove trace equivalence in at least one case using the UFP rule.

Exercise 3.2 Suggest a modification to the *Customer* process in the example above so that even if she cannot agree the price of one article she can agree to purchase another. *There are a number of different approaches to achieving this.*

3.2 Alphabetised Parallel

The more processes we combine using ∥, the more have to agree on every event. This is not what we will usually want (though it is a theme we will expand on in Sect. 3.5), and so we require a more general version of the parallel operator. What we need to reflect is the likelihood that, when two processes P and Q are placed in parallel, some of the communications of P are with Q, and some are not.

If X and Y are subsets of Σ, $P\ _X\|_Y\ Q$ is the combination where P is allowed to communicate in the set X, which we will call its *alphabet*, Q is allowed to communicate in its alphabet Y, and they must agree on events in the intersection $X \cap Y$. Thus $P\ _\Sigma\|_\Sigma\ Q = P \parallel Q$. So, for example,

$$(a \rightarrow b \rightarrow b \rightarrow STOP)\ _{\{a,b\}}\|_{\{b,c\}}\ (b \rightarrow c \rightarrow b \rightarrow STOP)$$

behaves like

$$a \rightarrow b \rightarrow c \rightarrow b \rightarrow STOP$$

since initially the only possible event is a (as the left-hand side blocks b); then both sides agree on b; then the right-hand side blocks b so only c is possible, and finally they agree on b again. In most cases, as in this one, the alphabets of individual processes composed in parallel will be the sets of events which they can communicate. But they have to be given explicitly for a number of subtle reasons—for example, we often give processes strictly larger alphabets than the sets of events they actually use (frequently the process is then *STOP*). You should note that the same process can be used in different parallel compositions with different alphabets.[1]

The nature of the synchronous parallel operator meant that the unlikely couple we discussed had to agree on everything they did, or they deadlocked. If we were to place *jog* in only Peter's alphabet and *swim* in Maggie's, there is no evidence from the partial definitions on p. 46 that they would deadlock. The greater flexibility of our new operator is also shown by the following example of the two actors inside a pantomime horse: one playing the front and one the back: see Fig. 3.1. Because they exist inside the same costume the two halves have to agree on which way their character moves, but each can have individual control of other activities:

Front $_F\|_B$ *Back*

where $F = \{forward, backward, nod, neigh\}$
$\qquad\ B = \{forward, backward, wag, kick\}$

---

[1] In allowing this we are giving a different presentation to that in Hoare's book, where a process has an intrinsic alphabet αP. These alphabets make the presentation of this particular parallel operator easier, while adding complications elsewhere. See Sect. 3.7 for more details of this difference.

Fig. 3.1 A parallel process

If, in fact, *Front* will only nod the horse's head until it has moved forwards, and *Back* will only wag its tail until it has moved backwards:

$$Front = forward \rightarrow Front'$$
$$\square\, nod \rightarrow Front$$
$$Back = backward \rightarrow Back'$$
$$\square\, wag \rightarrow Back$$

then the composition will never move whatever the processes *Front'* and *Back'* are (since they are never reached), but it will simply nod and wag for ever. It will be equivalent to $RUN_{\{nod,wag\}}$.

When P can perform any of the events A (being equivalent to a process of the form $?x : A \rightarrow P'$) and Q can perform the events B (respectively $?x : B \rightarrow Q'$), then P $_X\|_Y$ Q can perform any of

$$C = (A \cap (X \setminus Y)) \cup (B \cap (Y \setminus X)) \cup (A \cap B \cap X \cap Y)$$

The first component of this union are the events P can perform on its own (because they are in X and not Y); similarly, the second are the events Q can do by itself. The final component are the events which they can synchronise on: the ones that both processes can perform, and are in both their alphabets. The law expressing this is the following

$$P \;_X\|_Y\; Q =?x : C \rightarrow (P' \;\mbox{$<\!\!\!<$}\, x \in X \,\mbox{$>\!\!\!>$}\; P$$
$$ {}_X\|_Y$$
$$ Q' \;\mbox{$<\!\!\!<$}\, x \in Y \,\mbox{$>\!\!\!>$}\; Q) \qquad\qquad \langle {}_X\|_Y\text{-step}\rangle \;\; (3.2)$$

where C is as above. $_X\|_Y$ is distributive, like most operators, over $\sqcap$ and $\mbox{$<\!\!\!< b >\!\!\!>$}$.

The rest of its basic laws are given below. It has symmetry and associativity laws that are slightly more complex than usual because of the alphabets.

$$P \;_X\|_Y\; (Q \sqcap R) = (P \;_X\|_Y\; Q) \sqcap (P \;_X\|_Y\; R) \qquad\qquad \langle {}_X\|_Y\text{-dist}\rangle \;\; (3.3)$$

Fig. 3.2 A simple chain connected in parallel

$$P _X\|_Y Q = Q _Y\|_X P \qquad\qquad \langle _X\|_Y\text{-sym}\rangle \ (3.4)$$

$$(P _X\|_Y Q) _{X\cup Y}\|_Z R = P _X\|_{Y\cup Z} (Q _Y\|_Z R) \qquad\qquad \langle _X\|_Y\text{-assoc}\rangle \ (3.5)$$

As the associative law above begins to show, composing a large network using this binary operator gets rather clumsy because of the bookkeeping required on the alphabets. We therefore include a better, indexed notation for n-way parallel composition:

$$\|_{i=1}^{n}(P_i, X_i) = P_1 \ _{X_1}\|_{X_2\cup\cdots\cup X_n} (\ldots(P_{n-1} \ _{X_{n-1}}\|_{X_n} P_n)\ldots)$$

So, for example, if

$$COPY'(c, d) = c?x : T \to d.x \to COPY'(c, d)$$

and $X_r = c_r.T \cup c_{r+1}.T = \{|c_r, c_{r+1}|\}$ (with $c_0, c_1, \ldots, c_n$ all being distinct) then

$$\|_{r=0}^{n-1}(COPY'(c_r, c_{r+1}), X_r)$$

represents a chain of n one-place buffer processes. $COPY'(c_0, c_1)$ can input a value on channel c_0 without requiring the cooperation of any other process in the network. This value is then communicated across the channels $c_1, \ldots, c_{n-1}$ in turn (each transfer requiring the agreement of the two processes involved) until it appears at the far end and $COPY'(c_{n-1}, c_n)$ is able to output it without needing any other process to agree. The network is shown in Fig. 3.2. It is natural to think of the channels c_0 and c_n as external, because they are only in the alphabet of one process each, and the rest are internal.

The reason it is natural to think of the above network as a chain is because the alphabets X_r of the processes only have non-empty intersection—corresponding to the possibility of communication between them—for consecutively numbered cells. By appropriate choices of alphabets it is possible to construct networks using $\|$ which have any chosen finite graph structure. The graph with one node per process and an edge between processes with non-empty intersection of alphabets is termed the *communication graph*. One might be tempted to put arrows on this graph to correspond to the direction of the channels, but this would be a mistake: you should remember that communication in CSP is symmetric and that channels are just a gloss on this.

Just as with the synchronous parallel operator, any system of sequential processes put in parallel with $_X\|_Y$ can be expanded into a (usually recursive) sequential one using the laws (predominantly $\langle _X\|_Y\text{-step}\rangle$) and the UFP rule. Consider, for example, the combination

$$COPY'(a, b) \ _{\{|a,b|\}}\|_{\{|b,c|\}} COPY'(b, c)$$

The initial events of the two processes are respectively $\{|a|\}$ and $\{|b|\}$ (since they are both ready to input). The initial events of the combination are therefore (showing the full calculation!)

$$(\{|a|\} \cap \{|b|\} \cap \{|a,b|\} \cap \{|b,c|\})$$
$$\cup (\{|a|\} \cap (\{|a,b|\} \setminus \{|b,c|\}))$$
$$\cup (\{|b|\} \cap (\{|b,c|\} \setminus \{|a,b|\}))$$

which reduces to $\emptyset \cup \{|a|\} \cup \emptyset = \{|a|\}$ (i.e., there is no shared event possible initially, no event possible for the right-hand process, but the left-hand one can input). This is, of course, exactly what one would have expected.

Thus the original process (which we will name CC_0) equals (by $\langle_X\|_Y\text{-step}\rangle$)

$$a?x \to ((b!x \to COPY'(a,b)) \,_{\{|a,b|\}}\|_{\{|b,c|\}}\, COPY'(b,c))$$

Call the parallel combination here $CC_1(x)$ (the x is needed because it depends on the input value). Now both processes can only perform shared (b) events, and agree on one, so another use of $\langle_X\|_Y\text{-step}\rangle$ turns $CC_1(x)$ into

$$b!x \to (COPY'(a,b) \,_{\{|a,b|\}}\|_{\{|b,c|\}}\, c!x \to COPY'(b,c))$$

If we similarly call the parallel combination here $CC_2(x)$, we find that neither of its parallel components can perform any b action, but each can perform some of its own actions independently. It equals

$$a?y \to (b!y \to COPY'(a,b) \,_{\{|a,b|\}}\|_{\{|b,c|\}}\, c!x \to COPY'(b,c))$$
$$\Box\, c!x \to (COPY'(a,b) \,_{\{|a,b|\}}\|_{\{|b,c|\}}\, COPY'(b,c))$$

which, naming the first parallel combination $CC_3(y,x)$, equals

$$a?y \to CC_3(y,x) \,\Box\, c!x \to CC_0$$

In $CC_3(y,x)$, the left-hand process can only perform the shared event $b!y$, while the right-hand one can only perform its own action $c!x$. It follows that this process equals

$$c!x \to ((b!y \to COPY'(a,b)) \,_{\{|a,b|\}}\|_{\{|b,c|\}}\, COPY'(b,c))$$

which is $c!x \to CC_1(y)$. Since there are no more parallel combinations to expand, the state exploration is complete and we have shown that the processes CC_0, $CC_1(x)$, $CC_2(x)$ and $CC_3(y,x)$ satisfy a guarded mutual recursion:

$$CC_0' = a?x \to CC_1'(x)$$
$$CC_1'(x) = b!x \to CC_2'(x)$$
$$CC_2'(x) = (c!x \to CC_0') \,\Box\, (a?y \to CC_3'(y,x))$$
$$CC_3'(y,x) = c!x \to CC_1'(y)$$

Thus the CC and CC' systems are trace equivalent by the UFP rule. A picture of their joint system of states is in Fig. 3.3 (the picture over-simplifies the values input

Fig. 3.3 The states of two
one-place buffers in parallel

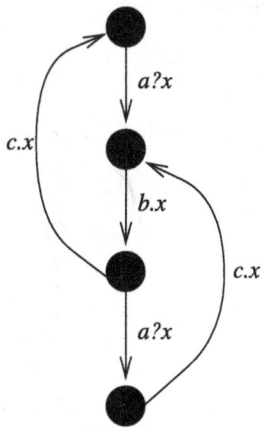

and output in that it does not allow you to reconstruct the relationship between
the values going in and those going out). Clearly this simple example is already
getting a bit tedious to expand. Much larger examples are impractical by hand—
fortunately, however, tools like FDR are much better able to deal with the expansion
and bookkeeping than we are, and in fact a large part of what they do is precisely
this.

The traces of $P_X \|_Y Q$ are just those which combine a trace of P and a trace of
Q so that all communications in $X \cap Y$ are shared.

$$traces(P_X \|_Y Q) = \{s \in (X \cup Y)^* \mid s \restriction X \in traces(P) \wedge s \restriction Y \in traces(Q)\}$$

Example 3.2 (The five dining philosophers) This is perhaps the best known of all
examples in this field. As shown in Fig. 3.4, five philosophers share a dining table
at which they have allotted seats. In order to eat (in the figure, from a tangled bowl
of spaghetti in the middle of the table!), a philosopher must pick up the forks on
either side of him or her (i.e., both of them) but, as you see, there are only five forks.
A philosopher who cannot pick up one or other fork has to wait. We can model this
story in various ways in CSP by choosing different episodes of philosophers' lives
as events, but the essential events from the point of view of interaction are when
they pick up or put down their forks. In order to make sure no fork can be held by
two philosophers at once, we also require a process to represent each fork.

We will therefore describe two classes of process: $PHIL_i$ and $FORK_i$, in each
case for $i \in \{0, 1, 2, 3, 4\}$. The events of $FORK_i$ are

- *picksup.i.i* and *picksup.i⊖1.i* where ⊖ represents subtraction *modulo* 5 (with ⊕
  being the corresponding addition operator). These respectively represent $FORK_i$
  being picked up by $PHIL_i$ and $PHIL_{i⊖1}$.
- *putsdown.i.i* and *putsdown.i⊖1.i*, representing the fork being put down again.

$$FORK_i = (picksup.i.i \rightarrow putsdown.i.i \rightarrow FORK_i)$$
$$\square \ (picksup.i⊖1.i \rightarrow putsdown.i⊖1.i \rightarrow FORK_i)$$

Fig. 3.4 The five dining
philosophers

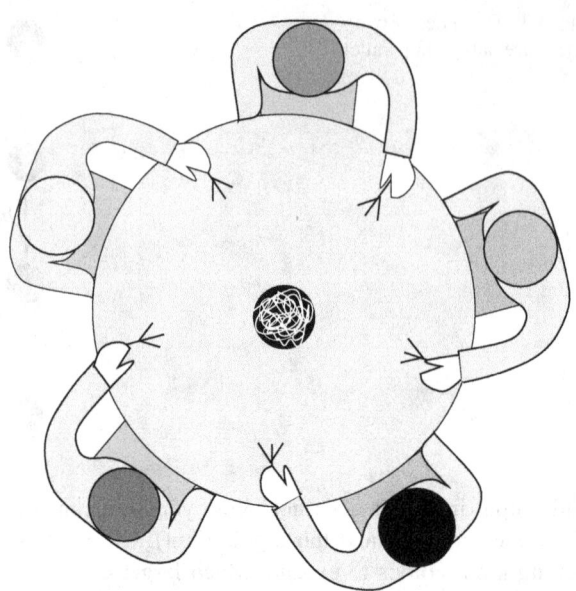

The philosophers have these same events, plus some individual ones. What turns
out to be crucial in describing the philosophers is the order in which they pick up
their forks. There are various options: either left-hand one first, right-hand one first,
or some form of choice between the two. And of course different philosophers might
have different preferences. For simplicity, the following definition asserts that each
philosopher picks up the left fork first and puts it down last.

$$PHIL_i = thinks.i \rightarrow sits.i \rightarrow picksup.i.i \rightarrow$$
$$picksup.i.i \oplus 1 \rightarrow eats.i \rightarrow putsdown.i.i \oplus 1 \rightarrow$$
$$putsdown.i.i \rightarrow getsup.i \rightarrow PHIL_i$$

The complete system is then formed by putting all of these processes in parallel,
each having as its alphabet the set of events it can use. If AF_i and AP_i are these sets
for $FORK_i$ and $PHIL_i$ respectively, the network is formed by composing together
the ten pairs

$$\{(FORK_i, AF_i), (PHIL_i, AP_i) \mid i \in \{0, 1, 2, 3, 4\}\}$$

in parallel. The communication graph of the resultant network, with an edge between two processes if their alphabets have non-empty intersection, is shown in
Fig. 3.5.

So how does this system behave? We have already noted that one philosopher
might have to wait for a neighbour to put down a fork. The greatest danger, however,
is that they might all get hungry at once and all manage to pick up their left-hand
fork (as is about to happen in Fig. 3.4). For then none can make any progress and
the system is deadlocked. The philosophers starve to death.

Fig. 3.5 The communication network of the dining philosophers

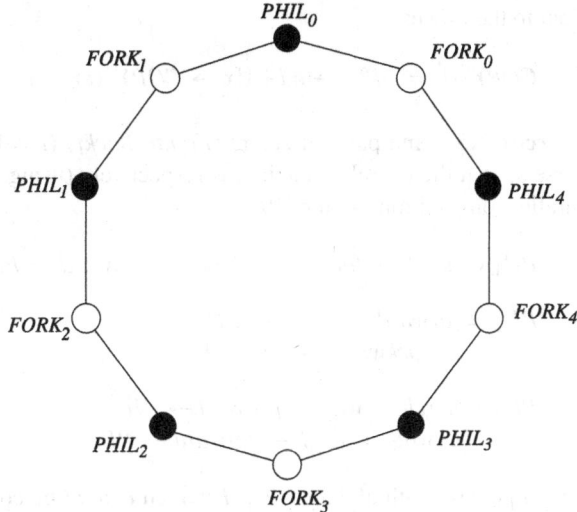

There are two standard ways of avoiding this deadlock. The first is to introduce a *butler* or *footman* process with alphabet $\{|sits.i, getsup.i|\}$ whose job is to prevent the philosophers from all sitting down at once:

$$BUTLER(n) = n < 4 \& sits?i \rightarrow BUTLER(n+1)$$
$$\square \; n > 0 \& getsup?i \rightarrow BUTLER(n-1)$$

The second is to ensure that the ring is *asymmetric* and contains at least one left-handed philosopher and one right-handed. Notice that if the deadlock occurs with each holding one fork, then *either* it is everyone's right-hand fork *or* everyone's left-hand one. The first of these is impossible if there is at least one left-hander, and the second if there is at least one right-hander. We will see the dining philosophers on a number of further occasions in this book: consult the index.

As well as demonstrating the use of the parallel operator, this example also illustrates uses of events we have not seen before. Like many networks we will see, this one has numbers of processes which behave similarly except for the precise events they use. Of course the easy way to define these is to use parameterisation: $PHIL_i$ rather than $PHIL_0, \ldots, PHIL_4$ separately. Notice, however, that unlike previous parameterised recursions, these processes do not depend on each other: $PHIL_2$ only makes recursive calls to $PHIL_2$, for example. To create the arrays of events that are needed to tie in with these arrays of processes, we use the channel notation to create arrays of events as anticipated on p. 14. Sometimes, as with the *picksup* and *putsdown* events, we need a two-dimensional array (or even more).

One can mix the array and data-passing uses of channels. The best way of implementing the chain of $COPY'$ processes is to create an array of channels c whose communications look like $c.i!x$ or $c.i?x$. $COPY'(c.i, c.i + 1)$ would then be equivalent to the process

$$COPY''(i) = c.i?x \rightarrow c.i+1!x \rightarrow COPY''(i)$$

Exercise 3.3 Find pairs of actors $(Front_i, Back_i)$ $(i = 1, 2, 3)$ for the pantomime horse so that the overall behaviour is respectively (using the same alphabets for the parallel composition as on p. 49)

$$PH_1 = neigh \rightarrow forward \rightarrow kick \rightarrow backward \rightarrow PH_1$$

$$PH_2 = forward \rightarrow neigh \rightarrow PH_2$$
$$\square\, backward \rightarrow kick \rightarrow PH_2$$

$$PH_3 = neigh \rightarrow wag \rightarrow forward \rightarrow PH_3$$
$$\square\, wag \rightarrow neigh \rightarrow forward \rightarrow PH_3$$

Find a process with alphabet $F \cup B$ which *cannot* be constructed in this way, and explain why it is impossible.

Exercise 3.4 Let $X = \{a, b, c, d\}$ and $Y = \{c, d\}$, and let

$$P = (a \rightarrow c \rightarrow P) \,\square\, (b \rightarrow d \rightarrow P)$$
$$Q = c \rightarrow d \rightarrow Q$$

What are the traces of $P \;_X\|_Y\; Q$? Which of these traces are terminal, in the sense that they are not prefixes of any other trace? What can you say about the behaviour of a process after it has performed such a trace?

Exercise 3.5 Use the methods illustrated in this section to expand $P \;_X\|_Y\; Q$ to a sequential process (where P and Q are as in the previous question). You should find some states in this expansion equivalent to *STOP*—corresponding to deadlock. Compare these states to the terminal traces.

  Find a process R with alphabet $Z = \{a, b\}$ such that $R \;_Z\|_X\; (P \;_X\|_Y\; Q)$ is deadlock-free.

Exercise 3.6 Formulate trace specifications of the following properties in the alphabets of the examples to which they refer.

(a) The numbers of times the pantomime horse has wagged its tail and neighed always differ (in absolute value) by at most one.
(b) It has always wagged its tail at least twice as often as it has kicked.
(c) Whenever $PHIL_i$ eats, $PHIL_{i\oplus 1}$ is not holding any fork.

Find the characteristic process (over the respective alphabet) for each. How do you deal with the events each system can do which are irrelevant to the specification? Which of these is finite state? If any is infinite state can you suggest a stronger, finite-state one which the appropriate network will still satisfy and which is as close in meaning to the original as possible? Prove (either manually or using FDR or a similar tool) that each holds of one or more of the systems we have already seen (in the first case in Exercise 3.3 (c)).

3.3 Interleaving

The parallel operators seen so far ($\|$ and $_X\|_Y$) have the property that all partners allowed to make a particular communication must synchronise on it for the event to occur. The opposite is true of parallel composition by *interleaving*, written $P \mathbin{|\!|\!|} Q$. Here, the processes run completely independently of each other. Any event which the combination communicates arose in precisely one of P and Q. If they could both have communicated the same event then the choice of which one executed it is nondeterministic, but only one did. The law governing this is the following: if $P = ?x : A \to P'$ and $Q = ?x : B \to Q'$ then

$$P \mathbin{|\!|\!|} Q = ?x : A \cup B \to (P' \mathbin{|\!|\!|} Q) \sqcap (P \mathbin{|\!|\!|} Q')$$
$$\mathbf{\{} x \in A \cap B \mathbf{\}}$$
$$(P' \mathbin{|\!|\!|} Q) \mathbf{\{} x \in A \mathbf{\}} (P \mathbin{|\!|\!|} Q') \qquad \langle \mathbin{|\!|\!|}\text{-step} \rangle \ (3.6)$$

As one would expect, $\mathbin{|\!|\!|}$ is symmetric, associative and distributive.

$$P \mathbin{|\!|\!|} Q = Q \mathbin{|\!|\!|} P \qquad\qquad \langle \mathbin{|\!|\!|}\text{-sym} \rangle \ (3.7)$$

$$(P \mathbin{|\!|\!|} Q) \mathbin{|\!|\!|} R = P \mathbin{|\!|\!|} (Q \mathbin{|\!|\!|} R) \qquad\qquad \langle \mathbin{|\!|\!|}\text{-assoc} \rangle \ (3.8)$$

$$P \mathbin{|\!|\!|} (Q \sqcap R) = (P \mathbin{|\!|\!|} Q) \sqcap (P \mathbin{|\!|\!|} R) \qquad\qquad \langle \mathbin{|\!|\!|}\text{-dist} \rangle \ (3.9)$$

The process $L_1 = up \to down \to L_1$ keeps $tr \downarrow down$ (the number of *down*s it has communicated to date) between $tr \downarrow up - 1$ and $tr \downarrow up$. By interleaving a number of these we can increase this margin:

$$L_n = L_1 \mathbin{|\!|\!|} L_1 \mathbin{|\!|\!|} \ldots \mathbin{|\!|\!|} L_1 \quad n \text{ copies of } L_1$$

keeps $tr \downarrow down$ between $tr \downarrow up - n$ and $tr \downarrow up$. Even though which of a number of processes performs a given event is usually nondeterministic, the overall effect here is actually deterministic.

Clearly $L_n \mathbin{|\!|\!|} L_m = L_{n+m}$, whereas $L_n \| L_m = L_{\min\{n,m\}}$.

The combination of interleaving and recursion can allow us to describe complex behaviours which would otherwise need infinite mutual recursions. For example, we can simulate the infinite-state recursion *COUNT* by a single line

$$Ctr = up \to (Ctr \mathbin{|\!|\!|} down \to STOP)$$

or, more subtly

$$Ctr' = up \to (Ctr' \mathbin{|\!|\!|} \mu P.down \to up \to P) \quad \text{or even}$$
$$Ctr'' = up \to (Ctr'' \mathbin{|\!|\!|} down \to Ctr'')$$

All of these behave the same as $COUNT_0$. In each case see if you can understand why.

The above uses of ||| have all involved combinations of processes that use the same events, creating nondeterminism about which side carries out an event. In practice such uses, though clever when they work, are rather rare. In creating practical networks, it is usual to find processes which use disjoint sets of events or perhaps soon come into a state where they do this. Think back to the five dining philosophers: the five philosophers do not (in our model!) talk to each other, and neither do the five forks. Therefore we can achieve exactly the same effect as previously by first composing these two groups by interleaving:

$$FORKS = FORK_0 \;|||\; FORK_1 \;|||\; \ldots \;|||\; FORK_4$$
$$PHILS = PHIL_0 \;|||\; PHIL_1 \;|||\; \ldots \;|||\; PHIL_4$$

and then, if $AFS = AF_0 \cup AF_1 \cup AF_2 \cup AF_3 \cup AF_4$, we can form the complete system

$$FORKS \;_{AFS}\|_{\Sigma}\; PHILS$$

See p. 179 to see why, though this formulation is elegant, it also has a disadvantage.

The traces of $P \;|||\; Q$ are just the interleavings of traces of P and Q. We need to define an operator for producing the interleavings of a given pair of traces: this is defined recursively below

$$\langle \rangle \;|||\; s = \{s\}$$
$$s \;|||\; \langle \rangle = \{s\}$$
$$\langle a \rangle\hat{\;}s \;|||\; \langle b \rangle\hat{\;}t = \{\langle a \rangle\hat{\;}u \mid u \in s \;|||\; \langle b \rangle\hat{\;}t\}$$
$$\cup \{\langle b \rangle\hat{\;}u \mid u \in \langle a \rangle\hat{\;}s \;|||\; t\}$$

Given this

$$traces(P \;|||\; Q) = \bigcup \{s \;|||\; t \mid s \in traces(P) \wedge t \in traces(Q)\}$$

Exercise 3.7 A *bag* is a process with channels *left* and *right* which behaves like a buffer except that the order in which things come out is not necessarily that in which they are put in. Use ||| and *COPY* to define a bag with capacity N. Explain your definition. Now define an infinite capacity bag by following the style of recursion in the process *Ctr* above.

Exercise 3.8 Prove that $COUNT_0 \;|||\; COUNT_0$ is trace equivalent to $COUNT_0$. You should do this by calculating the sets of traces directly (bearing in mind what has already been established about $traces(COUNT_0)$).

Exercise 3.9 Consider the following mutual recursion indexed by pairs of natural numbers $\mathbb{N} \times \mathbb{N}$:

$$CT2(n, m) = up \rightarrow (CT2(n + 1, m) \sqcap CT2(n, m + 1))$$
$$\square ((down \rightarrow CT2(n - 1, m)) \triangleleft n > 0 \triangleright STOP)$$
$$\square ((down \rightarrow CT2(n, m - 1)) \triangleleft m > 0 \triangleright STOP)$$

Show that it is satisfied by the vectors $\langle COUNT_{n+m} \mid (n, m) \in \mathbb{N} \times \mathbb{N} \rangle$ and

$$\langle COUNT_n \parallel\!\!\parallel COUNT_m \mid (n, m) \in \mathbb{N} \times \mathbb{N} \rangle$$

and deduce that $COUNT_n \parallel\!\!\parallel COUNT_m$ and $COUNT_{n+m}$ are trace equivalent for all $(n, m) \in \mathbb{N} \times \mathbb{N}$.

If you look at this question carefully, you will see that it shows a way of using the UFP rule to prove the equivalence to two systems where there is a many–one relation of equivalence between the underlying state spaces.

3.4 Generalised Parallel

The effects of all the parallel operators we have seen so far, and more, can be achieved with a single operator which, for whatever reason, has become the most commonly used with FDR even though it does not appear in Hoare's book. In $P_X\|_Y Q$, we decide which events are synchronised and which are not by looking at X and Y. In the new operator, we simply give the interface: $P \underset{X}{\parallel} Q$ is the process where all events in X must be synchronised, and events outside X can proceed independently. It is called *generalised* or *interface* parallel. We will always have

$$P \parallel\!\!\parallel Q = P \underset{\emptyset}{\parallel} Q$$

and, provided P and Q never communicate outside X and Y,

$$P_X\|_Y Q = P \underset{X \cap Y}{\parallel} Q$$

(The case when P or Q do not satisfy this condition is left as an exercise.)

In almost all cases one meets, this new operator just gives a different presentation of something we could have written with $_X\|_Y$. However, you should realise there are new effects that could not have been achieved without it: if X is non-empty but does not cover all events that can be used by P and by Q then $P \underset{X}{\parallel} Q$ acts a little bit like the alphabetised parallel and a little bit like $P \parallel\!\!\parallel Q$. There are some events that are synchronised and some which can ambiguously come from either side. For example, $COUNT_0 \underset{\{up\}}{\parallel} COUNT_0$ is a process that will allow *twice* as many *down*s as *up*s, since the *down* events proceed independently.

If $P = ?x : A \to P'$ and $Q = ?x : B \to Q'$ then the initial events of $P \parallel_X Q$ are $C = (X \cap A \cap B) \cup (A \setminus X) \cup (B \setminus X)$. The behaviour is shown by the following step law, whose complexity reflects the operator's generality: an event may now be synchronised, unsynchronised but ambiguous, or from one side only

$$P \parallel_X Q = ?x : C \to (P' \parallel_X Q') \lessdot x \in X \gtrdot$$
$$(((P' \parallel_X Q) \sqcap (P \parallel_X Q')) \lessdot x \in A \cap B \gtrdot$$
$$((P' \parallel_X Q) \lessdot x \in A \gtrdot (P \parallel_X Q'))) \qquad\qquad \langle \parallel\text{-step} \rangle \; (3.10)$$

It is symmetric and distributive:

$$P \parallel_X Q = Q \parallel_X P \qquad\qquad\qquad\qquad \langle \parallel\text{-sym} \rangle \; (3.11)$$

$$P \parallel_X (Q \sqcap R) = (P \parallel_X Q) \sqcap (P \parallel_X R) \qquad\qquad \langle \parallel\text{-dist} \rangle \; (3.12)$$

It has the following weak (in that both interfaces are the same) associativity property

$$P \parallel_X (Q \parallel_X R) = (P \parallel_X Q) \parallel_X R \qquad\qquad \langle \parallel\text{-assoc} \rangle \; (3.13)$$

but the possibility, in $P \parallel_X (Q \parallel_Y R)$, of X containing an event not in Y that Q and R can both perform, makes it hard to construct a universally applicable and elegant associative law.

The traces of $P \parallel_X Q$ are simply combinations of traces of P and Q where actions in X are shared and all others occur independently. As with the interleaving operator, the best way to calculate the trace-set is in terms of an operator that maps each pair of traces to the set of possible results (which is always empty when they do not agree on X). The following clauses allow one to calculate $s \parallel_X t$ (a set of traces, like $s \parallel\!\parallel\!\parallel t$) for all $s, t \in \Sigma^*$; below x denotes a typical member of X and y a typical member of $\Sigma \setminus X$.

$$s \parallel_X t = t \parallel_X s$$

$$\langle\rangle \parallel_X \langle\rangle = \{\langle\rangle\}$$

$$\langle\rangle \parallel_X \langle x \rangle = \emptyset$$

$$\langle\rangle \parallel_X \langle y \rangle = \{\langle y \rangle\}$$

$$\langle x \rangle \hat{\,} s \parallel_X \langle y \rangle \hat{\,} t = \{\langle y \rangle \hat{\,} u \mid u \in \langle x \rangle \hat{\,} s \parallel_X t\}$$

$$\langle x \rangle \hat{\,} s \parallel_X \langle x \rangle \hat{\,} t = \{\langle x \rangle \hat{\,} u \mid u \in s \parallel_X t\}$$

$$\langle x\rangle\hat{\ }s \parallel_{X} \langle x'\rangle\hat{\ }t = \emptyset \qquad \text{if } x \neq x'$$

$$\langle y\rangle\hat{\ }s \parallel_{X} \langle y'\rangle\hat{\ }t = \{\langle y\rangle\hat{\ }u \mid u \in s \parallel_{X} \langle y'\rangle\hat{\ }t\}$$

$$\cup \{\langle y'\rangle\hat{\ }u \mid u \in \langle y\rangle\hat{\ }s \parallel_{X} \hat{\ }t\}$$

Given this, it is possible to define

$$traces(P \parallel_{X} Q) = \bigcup\{s \parallel_{X} t \mid s \in traces(P) \wedge t \in traces(Q)\}$$

Exercise 3.10 If we do not assume that P and Q never communicate outside X and Y, how can we express $P_{X}\parallel_{Y} Q$ in terms of $\parallel_{Z}$? [*Hint: use STOP.*]

Exercise 3.11 Describe the behaviours of the following processes; in each case find a tail-recursive process equivalent to it.

(a) $COPY \parallel_{\{\mid left\mid\}} COPY$

(b) $COPY \parallel_{\{\mid right\mid\}} COPY$

Exercise 3.12 Show that $(P \parallel\parallel\parallel Q) \parallel R$ and $P \parallel\parallel\parallel (Q \parallel R)$ need not be equivalent. What does this tell you about the 'law'

$$P \parallel_{X} (Q \parallel_{Y} R) =? (P \parallel_{X} Q) \parallel_{Y} R$$

3.5 Parallel Composition as Conjunction

The uses seen so far of the synchronised parallel operator $\parallel$ and the alphabetised one $_{X}\parallel_{Y}$ have all had broadly the intuition one would have expected of a parallel operator, namely describing interactions between processes which might reasonably be expected to run concurrently and communicate with each other. But they can be used in a rather different way in situations where we are using CSP more in the manner of a *specification* language than as a method of describing systems as implemented.

It turns out to be very difficult, even impractical, to implement handshaken communication in anything like the generality implied by the CSP parallel operators, at least if a genuinely parallel implementation is required. In particular, handshakes involving more than two parties often come into this 'impractical' category. Except in special circumstances, CSP descriptions which are intended to model the construction of parallel systems tend to respect this restriction.

Multi-way handshaking is nevertheless an extremely useful construct in CSP: it can be used to build up specifications of intended behaviour (i.e., processes that are probably going to be used on the left-hand side of a refinement check). In fact, parallel composition turns out to be equivalent to the conjunction (i.e. logical 'and') of trace specifications. In this style of use, you should view parallel as belonging to the category of CSP operators (for example $\sqcap$) whose main role is in constructing specifications rather than implementations. Look up "many-way synchronisation" in the index for more applications of this construct.

Suppose Q is a process using only events from Y. In $P \sideset{_\Sigma}{_Y}{\mathop{\|}} Q = P \underset{Y}{\|} Q$, it can be thought of as adding to P, since every communication of P in Y must be possible for Q. As P participates in all of the combination's events, we can think of Q's role as simply being to restrict P's behaviour. If P represents a trace specification, then $P \sideset{_\Sigma}{_Y}{\mathop{\|}} Q$ is a stronger one.

As a simple example, consider a robot which roams around the plane by making movements in the four directions $\{N, S, E, W\}$. It can also report its position. If its initial coordinates are $(0, 0)$, it becomes the process $ROBOT_{0,0}$ where

$$ROBOT_{n,m} = position.(n, m) \rightarrow ROBOT_{n,m}$$
$$\square\, N \rightarrow ROBOT_{n+1,m}$$
$$\square\, S \rightarrow ROBOT_{n-1,m}$$
$$\square\, E \rightarrow ROBOT_{n,m+1}$$
$$\square\, W \rightarrow ROBOT_{n,m-1}$$

We can restrict the area it can roam over by placing it parallel with processes stopping it entering forbidden areas. For example, if it is actually sitting on a rectangular table whose corners are $\{(0, 0), (n, 0), (n, m), (0, m)\}$ then we can enforce this either by putting it in parallel with four $COUNT$-like processes:

$CT(E, W)_0$	alphabet $\{E, W\}$
$CT(W, E)_m$	alphabet $\{E, W\}$
$CT(N, S)_0$	alphabet $\{N, S\}$
$CT(S, N)_n$	alphabet $\{N, S\}$

where

$$CT(a, b)_r = a \rightarrow CT(a, b)_{r+1}$$
$$\square\, r > 0 \,\&\, b \rightarrow CT(a, b)_{r-1}$$

or by using two processes (each imposing both limits in one dimension) or just one (imposing all four limits). We could prevent it entering a specific square, (r, s), say, by placing it in parallel with the following process with alphabet $\{N, S, E, W\}$:

$$BLOCK(r, s)_{n,m} = (n \neq r-1 \vee m \neq s \,\&\, N \rightarrow BLOCK(r, s)_{n+1,m})$$
$$\square\, (n \neq r+1 \vee m \neq s \,\&\, S \rightarrow BLOCK(r, s)_{n-1,m})$$
$$\square\, (n \neq r \vee m \neq s+1 \,\&\, E \rightarrow BLOCK(r, s)_{n,m-1})$$
$$\square\, (n \neq r \vee m \neq s-1 \,\&\, W \rightarrow BLOCK(r, s)_{n,m+1})$$

Note the use we have again made here of the conditional construct to reduce the number of clauses. Clearly we can use as many of these as we like to ban any finite region of space. Notice that $BLOCK(0,0)$ stops the robot from re-entering the origin once it has left it—it cannot be prevented from being there initially!

Other things we could do would be to stop it doing more than K actions in total say, representing its fuel capacity, or from communicating its position when in specified areas.

One of the simplest and most useful examples of this style is the banning of events: $P \,_{\Sigma}\|_X STOP = P \parallel_X STOP$ is the process which behaves like P except that events in X are banned.

This style of use of the parallel operator amounts to building up a complex behaviour by adding together a number of simple constraints. Clearly the number of participants in a given action in this example might get very large. But this need not worry us since, as we already know, it is quite possible to have a parallel process equivalent to a sequential one, and the eventual implementation of our specification will almost certainly be very different from the combination of the parallel constraints.

The exercises below illustrate this style well, and we will see further examples at various points in this book.

Exercise 3.13 We can describe a bank as a process that simply opens and closes:

$$BANK = bank\_open \rightarrow bank\_close \rightarrow BANK$$

Interleave this with the process that records what day of the week it is:

$$DAYS = Monday \rightarrow Tuesday \rightarrow \cdots \rightarrow Sunday \rightarrow DAYS$$

Express the following as parallel constraints to this system:

(a) It opens no more than once per day.
(b) It is always closed at midnight (the time when the *day* events occur).
(c) It is never open on a Sunday.
(d) It is always open at least two times per week.

Exercise 3.14 Put your solutions to the previous exercise and Exercise 1.4 in parallel via interleaving. Impose the following constraints:

(a) An account can only be opened or closed when the bank is open.
(b) Balance enquiries may not be made on Sundays.

Exercise 3.15 Figure 3.6 shows a section of a railway network. There are signals at A, B, C governing entry to the section, and points at P which connect the line from A to either B or C. The alphabet is as follows:

signal.X.Y for $X \in \{A, B, C\}$ and $Y \in \{red, green\}$ indicates the change of the signal at X to colour Y

Fig. 3.6 Some railway track
(see Exercise 3.15)

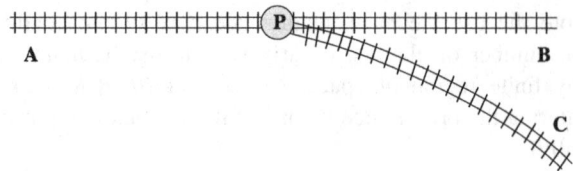

point.X   for $X \in \{B, C\}$ represents the points being switched to connect A to X

enter.X.t   for $X \in \{A, B, C\}$ and $t \in$ *Trains* represents train t entering the section
at X

leave.X.t   (X and t as above) represents t leaving at X.

Assume that initially all signals are red, the points connect A to B, and the track
is empty.

Give trace specifications for each of the following properties:

(a) Each signal alternates between turning green and red.
(b) Only one signal can be green at any time.
(c) The points alternate between the two directions.
(d) The points only switch when all signals are red and there is no train on the track.
(e) A signal can only turn green when there is no train on the track.
(f) The signals at B and C only turn green when the points are appropriately set.

Build a process that meets all of these specifications and which has, within reason, all of the traces which they allow. Do this by building one or more processes
for each constraint and combining them appropriately in parallel.

The above specifications allow a train to enter against a red signal. Introduce an
extra event *alarm* which occurs (before anything else) if this happens, and modify
your process definition appropriately.

3.6 Tools

The last three binary parallel operators we have seen are supported in machine-
readable CSP. They are written as follows:

$P \,_X\|_Y\, Q$ becomes P [X||Y] Q

$P \,\|\|\, Q$ becomes P ||| Q

$P \,\|_X\, Q$ becomes P [|X|] Q

($P \,\|\, Q$ can easily be represented as P [|Events|] Q.)

Indexed versions are written as follows:

$\|_{i=1}^{N}(P_i, A_i)$ becomes `|| i:1..N @ [A(i)] P(i)`

$\||_{i=1}^{N} P_i$ becomes `||| i:1..N @ P(i)`

$\|_{X_{i=1}}^{N} P_i$ becomes `[|X|] i:1..N @ P(i)`

Note that the last of these assumes that all the P_i synchronise on the set X, and that no other event is synchronised at all.

The addition of parallel operators has an enormous effect on the expressive power of the language, in the sense that it becomes possible to describe many complex and interesting systems concisely and naturally. One effect that is very noticeable is the exponential *state explosion* that can, and frequently does, occur when we put a lot of processes in parallel. If each P_i has just two states, then $\||_{i=1}^{N} P_i$ has 2^N. Synchronising events, as in $\|_{i=1}^{N}(P_i, A_i)$, usually prevents the combination reaching *some* arrangements of component states; however it often (it is safe to say *usually*) leaves enough arrangements to cause an exponential state explosion.

We will see evidence of both this expressive power and this *state explosion problem* in the next chapter. The ways in which FDR attempts to tackle this problem are addressed in Chap. 8 and several later ones including Chap. 17.

3.7 Postscript: On Alphabets

The most significant difference between the version of CSP used in this book (and TPC) and that in Hoare's text is the treatment of *alphabets*. Hoare stipulates that every process P has its own associated alphabet αP. One can think of the alphabet of a process as representing its type. A process may only communicate events from its alphabet, but there may be events in its alphabet which it can never communicate and which do not even appear in its description. The presence of alphabets makes the parallel operator more elegant, since by writing $P \parallel Q$ we know immediately that P has control over αP and Q has control over αQ, and so they interact in, and must cooperate on, $\alpha P \cap \alpha Q$. This is in contrast with our version where alphabets are given explicitly: $P _X\parallel_Y Q$. Hoare makes a number of stipulations about the alphabets of the processes that are composed together; most of the operators require that all processes combined have the same alphabet and that the resulting alphabet is the same again. Others, such as $\parallel$ and hiding (see Chap. 5), have special rules. The CSP operators in the alphabetised theory are thus *polymorphic* in a sense very close to the usual one.

The disadvantages of the alphabetised version of CSP are firstly the need to give *all* processes alphabets (which can clutter definitions, especially recursions), the occasional need for special language constructs to get the 'typing' right, and additional theoretical complexity. The main manifestation of the last is the need to construct separate mathematical models for every different alphabet, where we can get away with just one.

The choice of one version or the other is largely a matter of taste, though it is certainly the case that the balance changes from application to application. We do not regard this as an important issue, since everything done in one version of CSP can be done in the other with trivial changes.

In this book we sometimes refer to the 'alphabet' of a process. This, in an informal sense, means the same as Hoare's alphabets, namely the set of communications it might use. However, whenever *we* need such an alphabet to have semantic significance (as in the set of events a P controls in a parallel combination), it has to be defined and used explicitly.

The author is often asked why one cannot define alphabets formally in the way described in the last paragraph. One answer is that it would invalidate many of the laws of CSP, as in many cases the processes on the two sides of laws (examples being $\langle STOP\text{-step}\rangle$ (2.15) and $\langle \underset{X}{\parallel}\text{-step}\rangle$ (3.10) can include different events in their definitions. Another is that when alphabets of processes include some but not all members of an array of channels such as $a.\mathbb{N}$, where the components used are calculated, there may be no way of pre-computing which components will actually be used by a given process.

The idea of a process alphabet will re-emerge later in this book when we discuss hierarchical compression in FDR (for example Sect. 8.8) and mobile systems (Sect. 20.3).

Chapter 4
CSP Case Studies

In this chapter we work on a few larger examples of CSP descriptions. The first is one of many types of combinatorial puzzle that can be modelled in CSP and solved on FDR. The second shows how we can develop deadlock-free routing networks as well as providing an introduction to deadlock analysis, and the third develops a communications protocol.

All of these examples are formulated in terms of the language of sequential processes and parallel operators that we have studied up to this point in the book, but in every case, as we will discover in the next chapter, the hiding and/or renaming operators can also be used to good effect. We will re-visit these case studies frequently in the rest of this book.

4.1 Sudoku in CSP

In the usual version of this game the solver is presented with a 9×9 grid in which numbers from the set $\{1, \ldots, 9\}$ have been inserted into some of the 81 squares. The objective is to complete the grid so that each row, each column and each of the 9 3×3 squares that are ruled off contains each of the digits $1, \ldots, 9$ (and therefore no repetitions). We will call these 27 sets of 9 squares the *domains* of the puzzle. An example[1] is shown in Fig. 4.1. So popular has Sudoku become that most newspapers print several per day and many variants on the rules have been devised. An easy generalisation is that, for any integers a and b, one can arrange ab $a \times b$ blocks, as shown in Fig. 4.2, for $a = 2$ and $b = 3$ into a puzzle with $(ab)^2$ squares into which to arrange the numbers $1 \ldots ab$. We will describe this version in CSP in such a way that we can search for a solution on FDR.

The author has enjoyed rendering puzzles into CSP for many years, with one example (peg solitaire) used as a case study in TPC (Sect. 15.1). Such models are

---

[1]This puzzle, created using FDR, has a unique solution like those in newspapers. It also has the property that removing any one of the hints would mean it had multiple solutions.

A.W. Roscoe, *Understanding Concurrent Systems*, Texts in Computer Science, DOI 10.1007/978-1-84882-258-0_4, © Springer-Verlag London Limited 2010

Fig. 4.1 Example Sudoku puzzle

		9		2	3			7
		5		6	7	8		
			8					
	1					9		3
				5				
7		2					1	
					5			
			9	4		2		
6		4	2	7		5		

Fig. 4.2 Small Sudoku puzzle

		5			6
	2	4			
		1		3	
3				2	
			5		4

almost always parallel systems (though see Exercise 4.3) designed to avoid creating unnecessary transitions or states. Typically each move should be a decisive step that makes a definite decision about a possible solution. It should therefore not surprise the reader that the first time the author saw a Sudoku puzzle (in 2005), his immediate reaction was to sit down and write a CSP program to solve it.

There is an obvious alphabet for our coding of Sudoku: events of the form *select.*$(i, j).k$ where (i, j) are the coordinates of a place on the board (we will have both i and j ranging over $\{0, \ldots, ab - 1\}$) and k is one of the ab symbols that have to be placed in each row, column and $a \times b$ block. We will let these symbols range over $\{1, \ldots, ab\}$ with the additional value 0 representing a blank square. *select.p.k* means "place k at square p". It is helpful to have an event *done* that signifies that the puzzle has been solved. This greatly simplifies the FDR check we use to find a solution since all we then have to do is assert that *done* can never happen: if there is a solution then *done* will occur and the debugger will find us the trace telling us which number to put where.

Our approach will be to combine a number of processes in parallel that enforce the rules of the game, such as not allowing a given digit to be placed where it clashes with an equal digit in the same row, column or $a \times b$ rectangle. Once we realise the power of many-way synchronisation, this is not at all hard: we make each square notice the placing of symbols not only into it, but also into the other squares with which it shares a row, column or block (there are $3ab - a - b - 1$ of these: 20 in

the case of a 9 × 9 puzzle). The set of these "neighbours" can be defined as follows
in CSP$_M$:

```
ab = a*b      -- for convenience and efficiency
Coord = {0..ab-1}
Coords = {(i,j) | i <- Coord, j <- Coord}
Row(i) = {(i,j) | j <- Coord}
Col(j) = {(i,j) | i <- Coord}
Box(i,j) = {(i*a+k,j*b+l) | k <- {0..a}, l <- {0..b}}

nhd((i,j)) = Union({Row(i),Col(j),Box((i-1)/a,(j-1)/b)})
adj((i,j)) = diff(nhd(p),{p})
```

We can represent the initial configuration of a puzzle as a square list-of-lists, such
as (with $(a,b) = (3,2)$):

```
puzzle = <<0,0,5,  0,0,6>,
          <0,2,4,  0,0,0>,

          <0,1,0,  0,3,0>,
          <3,0,0,  0,2,0>,

          <0,0,0,  5,0,4>,
          <0,0,0,  0,0,0>>
```

The initial value of point p=(i,j) is thus

```
init((i,j)) = nth(j,nth(i,puzzle))
```

Here, nth(k,xs) is the function that gives the kth member of list xs, counting
from 0 (see p. 150). Notice how we have arranged the lists and spacing to suggest
the puzzle structure, and used 0 for squares without a predefined "hint".

There are at least two different ways in which we can avoid placing clashing
symbols in squares in the same row, column or block:

- Make each empty square keep a record of the values that can legally be put into
  it, removing each value that is placed in a member of adj(p).
- Make each member q of adj(p) refuse to synchronise on select.p.k when
  q already contains k.

The following is a coding of a single square implementing the first of these:
p tells us which square it is, and X tells us which symbols can still be put here.

```
EmptyM(p,X) = select.p?v:X -> FullM(p)
           [] select?q:adj(p)?v -> EmptyM(diff(X,{v}))
```

```
FullM(p) = select?q:adj(p)?v -> FullM(p)
             [] done -> FullM(p)
```

The M in these names stands for "memo", as the B in the following processes implementing the second method stands for "block":

```
EmptyB(p) = select.p?v -> FullB(p,v)
             [] select?q:adj(p)?v -> EmptyB{p}

FullB(p,v) = select?q:adj(p)?v:diff(Symbol,{v})
                                    -> FullB(p,v)
             [] done -> FullB(p,v)
```

We can respectively initialise a process representing square p as follows:

```
CellM(p) =
if init(p)==0 then
    EmptyM(p,diff(Symbol,{init(q) | q <- adj(p)}))
    else FullM(p)

CellB(p) = if init(p)==0 then EmptyB(p)
                           else FullB(p,init(p))

Alpha(p) = {|select.p, done | p <- adj(p)|}
```

These processes are combined in parallel with the above alphabets to form either PuzzleM or PuzzleB. Note that the event done can only happen when all the cells are in their Full state. Since one way or another the environment is prevented from adding any symbols that create duplicates in a row, column or box, if done occurs then the puzzle has been solved.

In fact, it should not be to hard to see that PuzzleM and PuzzleB have exactly the same traces, and that the puzzle represented by the array puzzle is soluble if and only if the equivalent refinement checks

```
CHAOS({|select|}) [T= SystemM/B
```

fail. The trace reported by FDR's debugger will then tell you which symbols go in each empty square.

These checks are very inefficient for running in FDR's standard mode.[2] We can see this from the fact that if there are m empty squares in the initial puzzle then there are 2^m subsets of these that can be filled in with the symbols they get in the complete answer. Each of the subsets gives a different state for FDR to find, besides the ones that have at least one symbol that is not in the right place. So, for example,

---

[2]They can be expected to work much better using SAT checking, for example: see p. 186.

a 9×9 puzzle with 50 empty squares would have more than 10^{15} states, not counting those that lead to dead ends!

By putting the `Puzzle` process in parallel with what we might call a *regulator* process, we can control the order in which moves are made. We want to specify how the moves are made so that there will still be a way of filling in the symbols for the correct solution, but not too much choice. The most obvious way of doing this is to specify the order in which the squares are filled in, as in

```
scan = <(i,j) | i <- <0..ab-1>,
                 j <- <0..ab-1>, init((i,j))==0>

Reg(<>) = STOP
Reg(<p>^ps>) = select.p?v -> Reg(ps)


RegPuzzleM = Reg(scan) [|{|select|}|] PuzzleM
RegPuzzleB = Reg(scan) [|{|select|}|] PuzzleB
```

The reader will find that trying out the check against `Chaos({|select|})` for either of these solves the typical 9×9 puzzle quite easily. The trace FDR gives for the 6×6 puzzle above is

```
<select.(0,0).1,select.(0,1).3,select.(0,3).2,select.(0,4).4,
  select.(1,0).6,select.(1,3).1,select.(1,4).5,select.(1,5).3,
  select.(2,0).4,select.(2,2).2,select.(2,3).6,select.(2,5).5,
  select.(3,1).5,select.(3,2).6,select.(3,3).4,select.(3,5).1,
  select.(4,0).2,select.(4,1).6,select.(4,2).3,select.(4,4).1,
  select.(5,0).5,select.(5,1).4,select.(5,2).1,select.(5,3).3,
  select.(5,4).6,select.(5,5).2,done>
```

Notice that the squares are addressed in exactly the order implied by the regulator process. This trace easily implies the following solution:

```
<<1,3,5, 2,4,6>,
 <6,2,4, 1,5,3>,

 <4,1,2, 6,3,5>,
 <3,5,6, 4,2,1>,

 <2,6,3, 5,1,4>,
 <5,4,1, 3,6,2>>
```

There is an interesting way in which we can improve the coding of `PuzzleM` and hence `RegPuzzleM`. The process `EmptyM(p,X)` can never be filled if `X` is empty, so there is no point in adding symbols to any other squares. It would therefore make sense if no square could be filled in as soon as *any* `X` becomes empty. The easiest way to achieve this is to make each `select.p.v` require the permission of every `CellM(q)`, with an empty square with X empty refusing this permission.

```
EmptyM2(p,X) =
card(X)>0 &
   (    select.p?v:X -> FullM2(p)
     [] select?q:adj(p)?v -> EmptyM2(p,diff(X,{v})))
     [] select?q:diff(Coords,nhd(p))?v -> EmptyM2(p,X))

FullM2(p) = select?q:diff(Coords,{p})?v -> FullM2(p)
            [] done -> FullM2(p)
```

The resulting `RegPuzzleM2` has fewer states than `RegPuzzleM` but takes longer for FDR to compile. We already know why there are fewer states; and compilation takes longer simply because all the `CellM2` processes have a lot more transitions to calculate.

We will see a way of avoiding most of this extra effort in the next chapter (see p. 113), and will return to the Sudoku case study at several later points in the book.

General things to note from this example are:

- It is possible to use the CSP parallel operator to build up a model of a system that one would not naturally think of as a parallel process, with the various processes adding in constraints one after another. In this sense this is rather similar to the idea developed in Sect. 3.5 of building up a specification using parallel composition between sub-specifications.
- We can use a "flag" event such as `done` to discover whether a system can reach a state with a particular property. Where more than one of the component processes need to agree on the property (in our case that all the squares are full), they can synchronise on the flag event.
- We can use multi-way parallel composition both to communicate information around a system—in `PuzzleM` it tells squares the values in their neighbours— and to impose constraints on what can be communicated, as in `PuzzleB`.
- In cases where events can happen in many different orders, it can help FDR to break symmetries using a regulator process.
- FDR can be programmed in CSP_M to solve problems that humans find difficult. The main message in this is that we can therefore expect it to find things out about "real" parallel programs and system designs that are also beyond what humans can normally discover.

  With typical 9×9 puzzles, while it can take longer than one might wish to fill in the hints in the array for our files to process, FDR usually solves them insultingly quickly. For larger ones such as 16×16 the codings seen above sometimes work very quickly and sometimes more slowly: ideas in Exercise 4.2 below and later chapters will help to improve the CSP coding.

Exercise 4.1 Create a third version of `Puzzle` which, instead of having one process per square of the original puzzle, has one for each row, column and $a \times b$

box, each of whose alphabets is done together with all select.p.b for p in the respective area.

Exercise 4.2 After becoming familiar with CSP_M's sub-process language as described in Sect. 8.1.3, create some more intelligent orders from which to build Reg(order). For example, you might address the empty squares in increasing order of the number of legal symbols that remain available for them in the initial state. (A symbol v is legal if the row, column and box of the point contain no v.)

Exercise 4.3 A man has to take all the following cargo across a river:

datatype cargo = Wolf | Goat | Cabbage

He has a boat that is only large enough one of the three items plus him. He is not willing to leave the goat alone with either the wolf or the cabbage, for fear that one of his items might get eaten! Create a CSP script that describes this problem and can show the man how to get the items across safely.

It is possible to solve this with a sequential script, or to factor it in different ways into a parallel one.

4.2 Deadlock-Free Routing

One of the most common tasks in distributed systems is that of routing information from a sender to a receiver across a network composed of many nodes. The Internet is one of the best-known examples of this. There are two separate issues in creating such a network: firstly we should ensure that the route chosen for a message is one that will actually get it to the intended recipient, and secondly we should avoid mis-behaviours that might prevent a message ever getting through. We need to decide whether we want the network to be absolutely reliable in that every message sent gets through, or are prepared (as happens on the Internet) for some failure rate. We also need to decide whether our network has to tolerate some of its nodes "going down", in which case the routing needs to adapt to avoid such places.

One can, of course, address all these possibilities in CSP, but in this section we will consider only networks that are fixed and where we are *not* prepared to throw away messages to avoid deadlock and similar pathologies.

In each of the networks we consider, a typical message packet takes the form (a, b, m) where a is the sender, b is the addressee, and m is the contents of the message. Each node n will also have communications which respectively accept messages from the local user and give messages from the network to the local user:

- *send.n.*(n', m) represents the user at n sending m to n' and
- *receive.n.*(n', m) represents n receiving m from n'.

Naïve attempts to create a routing system in a non-tree network almost inevitably introduce the possibility of deadlock. The classic example of this is provided by a simple ring composed of N nodes:

$$D_i = send.i?(b, m) \rightarrow D'_i(i, b, m)$$
$$\square \, ring.i?(a, b, m) \rightarrow D'_i(a, b, m)$$

$$D'_i(a, b, m) = receive.i!(a, m) \rightarrow D_i$$
$$\triangleleft b = i \triangleright$$
$$ring.(i \oplus 1)!(a, b, m) \rightarrow D_i$$

Here every node has one 'slot' for a message: this can be occupied either by a message input from the local user over $send.i$ or by one from the ring. One way to deadlock the resulting ring is for all the users simultaneously to transmit a message addressed to some different user. All the processes are then stuck waiting to output to the next member of the ring. Throughout this section we will use similar alphabets and message structures to the above, labelling each message with its sender and receiver as it passes through the network.

One's first reaction to this deadlock might be to add more buffering capacity to the nodes. But this in itself does not help, since however large a finite capacity we give each node we cannot stop them becoming full if the external users are very keen to send messages.

It is all too easy to imagine that in a more complex topology, if many messages converge on a particular region at once, it may get so full that no progress is possible. So even if an overall network is much bigger than the number of messages that could conceivably be present, local congestion can still cause deadlock. See Exercise 4.4 below for one example of this, together with a strategy for avoiding it.

There are basically three strategies for avoiding deadlock in general message passing systems of the type we are discussing:

A. Ensure that any contention ends up in parts of the network with no cycles in them, so that deadlock is much easier to avoid.
B. Control the way in which messages enter potentially contentious parts of the network, to the extent that deadlock is impossible.
C. Ensure that messages leaving part of the network never get blocked by those entering it. (The solution implied in Exercise 4.4 falls into this class.)

Exercise 4.4 Figure 4.3 shows a road layout allowing visitors to drive round a monument. Cars all enter the road at A and pass round the loop until they exit at B. As you can see, a pair of rocks have meant that one stretch of road is too narrow for cars to pass each other: it is single-lane there and two-lane elsewhere.

Code CSP processes which implement this layout, with one process per lane segment under the assumption that no more than one car can occupy each with, for the moment, no other restriction on who can move forward onto the next segment on their route. (Except for segment C, each should have two states, *Empty* and *Full*; C should have three states, *Empty*, *Leftwards* and *Rightwards*.) Show that this can lead to deadlock.

Fig. 4.3 Road with a narrow
section: see Exercise 4.4

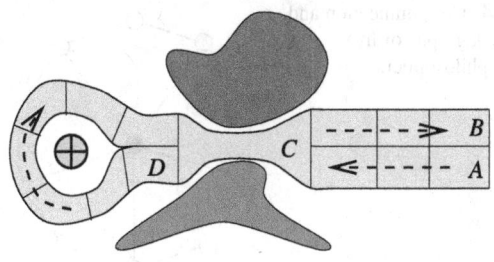

It is later decided to give outgoing (i.e., rightward in our picture) cars priority over incoming ones, in the sense that an incoming car is not allowed to enter the single-lane segment (C) until segment D is empty. Modify your coding
to achieve this, it will require extra communication between C and D. Your aim
should be to produce a system that is now deadlock free. Either create an argument that demonstrates why the revised version is deadlock free, or verify this
on FDR.

Would it work to give incoming traffic priority rather than outgoing?

4.2.1 Head for the Trees!

Deadlock is much easier to avoid when one is designing a network with no proper
cycles in it. Here, a *proper cycle* means a sequence of component processes
$\langle P_0, P_1, \ldots, P_{r-1}\rangle$ with $r \geq 3$ and such that $A_i \cap A_{i \oplus 1} \neq \emptyset$ for $i \in \{0, \ldots, r-1\}$
for the corresponding alphabets A_i. Informally, this is because each process round
a cycle might want communication with the next, which refuses because it is waiting for the one after, and so on. We call this is a *proper cycle of ungranted requests*.

There is a detailed study of deadlock and how to avoid it in Chap. 13 of TPC.
Here and in the next two subsections we summarise and apply some of the most
important principles from that chapter.

Suppose we have a parallel network $N = \|_{i=1}^{n}(P_i, A_i)$ in which each P_i is itself
deadlock free and where all communication is point-to-point (i.e. there is no 3-way
synchronisation or more: $A_i \cap A_j \cap A_k = \emptyset$ whenever i, j, k are all different), then in
any deadlocked state it is clear that every P_i must have one or more communications
it can perform with other P_js, which in turn reject them. If neither P_i nor the P_js
have any internal nondeterminism,[3] this is just saying that P_i $_{A_i}\|_{A_j}$ P_j has a trace
s such that $(s \upharpoonright A_i)^\frown\langle a\rangle \in traces(P_i)$ for some $a \in A_i \cap A_j$, but there is no $b \in$
$A_i \cap A_j$ such that $(s \upharpoonright A_i)^\frown\langle b\rangle \in traces(P_i)$ and $(s \upharpoonright A_j)^\frown\langle b\rangle \in traces(P_j)$. This is
just a formalisation of the idea of an ungranted request.

---

[3]For general formulations of this idea, see Sects. 6.3 and 11.2.3.

Fig. 4.4 Communication and
deadlock graphs of five
dining philosophers

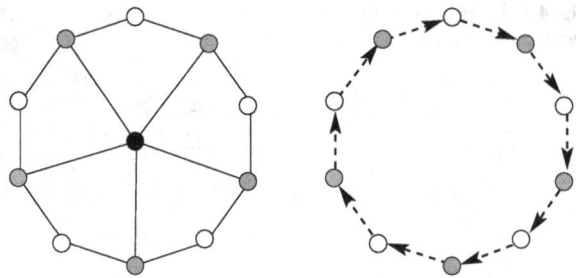

For any network N we can draw two pictures. One shows the processes and draws an edge between two of them if their alphabets intersect: the *communication graph* introduced in the previous chapter. This is an *undirected* graph because there is no sense in which an edge points from one of the two nodes it connects to the other. In any deadlocked state we can also draw a *directed* graph, in which there is an edge from P_i to P_j when P_i has an ungranted request to P_j. We can call the latter the *deadlock* graph. It is clear that the deadlock graph is in some sense a subgraph of the communication graph, since there cannot be an ungranted request from P_i to P_j when they have no common alphabet. The left-hand side of Fig. 4.4 shows the communication graph of the five dining philosophers with a butler (the process in the middle connected to the five philosophers), and the right-hand side shows the deadlock graph of the deadlock that sometimes occurs without him.

It is clear that under the conditions laid out above a network that is deadlocked has one or more cycles (paths $Q_0, Q_1, \ldots, Q_{r-1}, Q_0, r \geq 2$) in its deadlock graph. This is because any unending path in a finite graph must visit some node twice.

Note that we have allowed the degenerate cycle of length 2 here, but there is a straightforward and useful way of eliminating these from consideration. Say a pair of nodes P_i and P_j are in *strong conflict* if each has an ungranted request to the other (at the same time) and furthermore one of these can perform no other communication at all. Thus P_i (say) is both asking to communicate with P_j while at the same time preventing P_j from performing any action. In the author's experience, well-designed networks representing communicating systems always satisfy the principle of *freedom from strong conflict*: no neighbouring pair of processes in such a network ever reach a strong conflict.

It is, of course, possible to check both for the existence of ungranted requests and strong conflict in a pair of neighbouring processes by looking at just their parallel composition, not the entire system. We will see ways of checking for these properties in Sect. 11.2.3.

The crucial property of networks that are free of strong conflict is that whenever P_i has an ungranted request to P_j in a deadlock state, then P_j has one to a P_k with $k \neq i$. Thus, starting from an arbitrary $P_i = Q_0$, we can find an unending sequence of nodes where each has an ungranted request to the next, and every three consecutive nodes are distinct from each other. Thus each such network, when deadlocked, contains a *proper* cycle of ungranted requests. Therefore, if its communication graph is a tree, it is deadlock free.

This last principle (referred to as *Deadlock Rule 1* in TPC) can be generalised to non-tree networks provided that there is a subset S of the edges of the communication graph such that (i) S is a tree and (ii) it can be proved that, in a deadlock state, no ungranted request occurs on any edge not in S.

We can develop both Rule 1 and this extension into deadlock-free routing networks. So let us suppose first that we have a tree in which the neighbours of each node n are $tnbrs(n)$, and that each node n has channels to and from each of its neighbours: for n to send message m, originally from a, to n', for eventual transmission to b, will be the communication: $pass.(n, n').(a, b, m)$.

The most obvious network with this alphabet is perhaps the one where node n is programmed:

$$NodeE1(n) = \square\{pass.(n', n)?(a, b, m) \rightarrow NodeF1(n, a, b, m)$$
$$| \, n' \in tnbrs(n)\}$$
$$\square \, send.n?(b, m) \rightarrow NodeF1(n, n, b, m)$$

$$NodeF1(n, a, b, m) = receive.n.(a, m) \rightarrow NodeE1(n)$$
$$\not< n = b \not>$$
$$pass.(n, tnext(n, b)).(a, b, m) \rightarrow NodeE1(n)$$

where $tnext(n, b)$ is the first node on the unique direct path from n to b through the tree.

Unfortunately these nodes can easily get into strong conflicts whenever two neighbouring nodes n and n' are each trying to send the other a message: one on $pass.(n, n')$ and the other on $pass.(n', n)$. Simply adding extra storage capacity to nodes will not do any good, because whatever finite capacity they have, two nodes may still be full and waiting to send each other messages. What we need to do is arrange that, whenever node n wants to send a message to n' over $pass$, it will accept one from there. This creates the danger that n' might then send it infinitely many messages while n is still waiting, which might well end up requiring that n has infinite capacity.

This can, however, be avoided since we can have n accept this exceptional message over a second channel *swap*, thereby notifying n' that a swap is in progress:

$$NodeE2(n) = \square\{pass.(n', n)?(a, b, m) \rightarrow NodeF2(n, a, b, m)$$
$$| \, n' \in tnbrs(n)\}$$
$$\square \, send.n?(b, m) \rightarrow NodeF2(n, n, b, m)$$

$$NodeF2(n, a, b, m) = receive.n.(a, m) \rightarrow NodeE2(n)$$
$$\not< n = b \not>$$
$$(pass.(n, tnext(n, b)).(a, b, m) \rightarrow NodeE2(n)$$
$$\square \, swap.(n, tnext(n, b))!(a, b, m) \rightarrow$$
$$swap.(tnext(n, b), n)?(a', b', m') \rightarrow$$

$$NodeF2(n, a', b', m')$$
$$\square \; swap.(tnext(n, b), n)?(a', b', m') \rightarrow$$
$$swap.(n, tnext(n, b))!(a, b, m) \rightarrow$$
$$NodeF2(n, a', b', m')$$

Notice that a communication over $swap.(n, n')$ can only happen when each of n and n' wants to output to the other, and then they always happen as a pair. It should be easy to see that this eliminates the strong conflict, meaning that a network composed of $NodeE2$s does indeed deliver a deadlock-free routing service.

Having achieved this, we can take advantage of our extension to Rule 1 and let nodes exploit links that lie outside the tree, *provided* that ungranted requests still only happen within the tree. The strategy we use is to allow the network to use all links, whilst always reverting to the behaviour above when there is a danger of deadlock.

We could make any routing strategy deadlock free by having each node n ask before it sends any n' a message, ensuring that such requests are answered with a "yes" or "no", with no node that says "yes" ever refusing the message that follows. We can apply this idea to our first (deadlocking) network, without even needing the assumption that the network is a tree:

$$NodeE3(n) = \square \{yes.(n', n) \rightarrow pass.(n', n)?(a, b, m) \rightarrow$$
$$NodeF3(n, a, b, m) \mid n' \in nbrs(n)\}$$
$$\square \; send.n?(b, m) \rightarrow NodeF3(n, n, b, m)$$

$$NodeF3(n, a, b, m) = (receive.n.(a, m) \rightarrow NodeE3(n)$$
$$\text{\large\guillemotleft} b = n \text{\large\guillemotright}$$
$$(yes.(n, next(n, b)) \rightarrow pass.(n, next(n, b)).(a, b, m) \rightarrow$$
$$NodeE3(n)$$
$$\square \; no.(n, next(n, b)) \rightarrow NodeF3(n, a, b, m))$$
$$\square \square \{no.(n', n) \rightarrow NodeF3(n, a, b, m) \mid n' \in nbrs(n)\}$$

Here, $nbrs(n)$ is the set of *all* neighbours of n, and $next(n, b)$ selects the member of $nbrs(n)$ that a message to b is passed to. Notice that the only time that a node is *not* in a position to say *yes* or *no* to a request is when it is either sending or receiving an earlier message where the answer has been *yes*—and it is not possible for such communications to be blocked. It easily follows that a network consisting of these nodes is deadlock free.

It should not take the reader long to spot the fatal flaw in this version, however, since in any configuration where the first network would have been deadlocked, this one will be in a state where requests are constantly being made and refused. We have replaced deadlock by an equally useless "busy wait" state.

We can, however, combine this idea with Network 2 to produce a useful implementation. When passing on a message, we can allow a node some finite number of attempts to send it over a non-tree link using the protocol of Network 3, with it reverting to Network 2 behaviour if these attempts all fail. In the following, a node is allowed only one such attempt.

$$NodeE4(n) = \square\{pass.(n', n)?(a, b, m) \rightarrow NodeF4(n, a, b, m)$$
$$| n' \in tnbrs(n)\}$$
$$\square \square\{yes.(n', n) \rightarrow pass.(n', n)?(a, b, m) \rightarrow$$
$$NodeF4(n, a, b, m) \mid n' \in ntnbrs(n)\}$$
$$\square send.n?(b, m) \rightarrow NodeF4(n, n, b, m)$$
$$NodeF4(n, a, b, m) = NodeF4_L(n, a, m) \blacktriangleleft n = b \blacktriangleright$$
$$(NodeF4_T(n, a, b, m) \blacktriangleleft next(n, a) \in tnbrs(n) \blacktriangleright$$
$$NodeF4_O(n, a, b, m))$$
$$NodeF4_L(n, a, m) = \square\{no.(n', n) \rightarrow NodeF4_L(n, a, m) \mid n' \in ntnbrs(n)\}$$
$$\square receive.n.(a, m) \rightarrow NodeE4(n)$$
$$NodeF4_T(n, a, b, m) = \square\{no.(n', n) \rightarrow NodeF4_T(n, a, m) \mid n' \in ntnbrs(n)\}$$
$$\square (pass.(n, tnext(n, b)).(a, b, m) \rightarrow NodeE4(n)$$
$$\square swap.(n, tnext(n, b))!(a, b, m) \rightarrow$$
$$swap.(tnext(n, b), n)?(a', b', m') \rightarrow$$
$$NodeF4(n, a', b', m')$$
$$\square swap.(tnext(n, b), n)?(a', b', m') \rightarrow$$
$$swap.(n, tnext(n, b))!(a, b, m) \rightarrow$$
$$NodeF4(n, a', b', m')))$$
$$NodeF4_O(n, a, b, m) = \square\{no.(n', n) \rightarrow NodeF4_O(n, a, b, m)$$
$$| n' \in ntnbrs(n)\}$$
$$\square yes.(n, next(n, b)) \rightarrow$$
$$pass.(n, next(n, b)).(a, b, m) \rightarrow NodeE4(n)$$
$$\square no.(n, next(n, b)) \rightarrow NodeF4_T(n, a, b, m)$$

Note that a node holding a message behaves differently depending on whether that message is for the local user $NodeF4_L$, is routed by *next* to a tree neighbour $NodeF4_T$, or routed to a non-tree neighbour $NodeF4_O$. In the middle case no *yes/no* negotiation is necessary, and the last case reverts to tree mode as soon as it has had one rejection. This reversion means it can never perform an infinite number of actions without at least moving a message, as Network 3 can. It is also, by design, deadlock free.

Fig. 4.5 Two routing
strategies resulting in a cycle

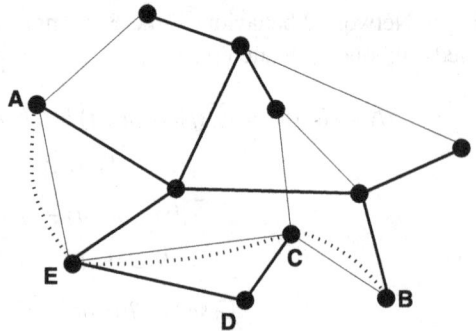

There is, however, one danger that remains. As shown in Fig. 4.5, it is possible that a message can go round a cycle and end up back where it started, even though all the *next*(n, b) and *tnext*(n, b) calculations make sense. This is because the only route through the tree might not be the one chosen in the complete network, and each time our message from A to B reaches node C it might get blocked and so move back to through D to E, completing a cycle that might go on for ever. The thick edges represent tree edges, and the thinner ones the additional ones. The dotted line is the path from A to B that we assume *next* picks.

This could in turn be cured by ensuring that the number of steps through the tree from *next*(n, b) to b is never greater than the corresponding number for the one from n to b, giving each message a finite limit on the number of non-tree hops it can make, or a combination of the two.

Exercise 4.5 Re-program Network 2 so that a swap is executed in a single communication rather than two.

Exercise 4.6 Do you think that it would be more efficient to use a richly branching tree to implement Network 2 or to connect the nodes in a straight line? Which part of the network, if any, would you expect to get most congested?

4.2.2 Uncloggable Rings

Imagine a roundabout or traffic circle, which cars enter, travel round in a predetermined direction (clockwise in countries that drive on the left-hand side of the road, and anti-clockwise in the rest of the world) and leave upon reaching the exit their drivers want. There are two protocols that have been implemented for these in different countries:

A. Cars already on the roundabout have priority over those trying to get on.
B. Cars already on the roundabout have to give way to those trying to get on: a version of the *priorité à droit* rule for countries where one drives on the right.

Fig. 4.6 Roundabout

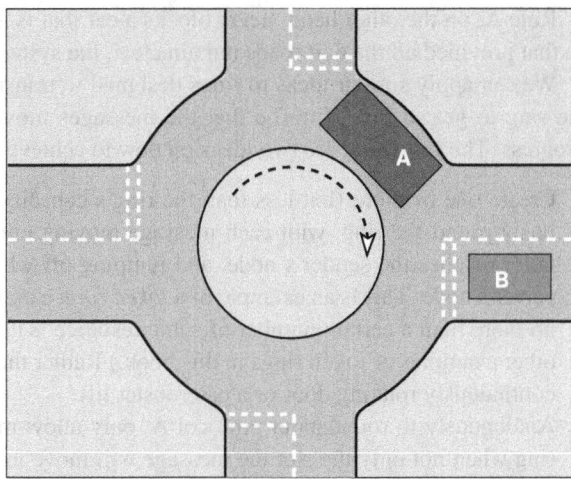

Fig. 4.7 Deadlocked
roundabout

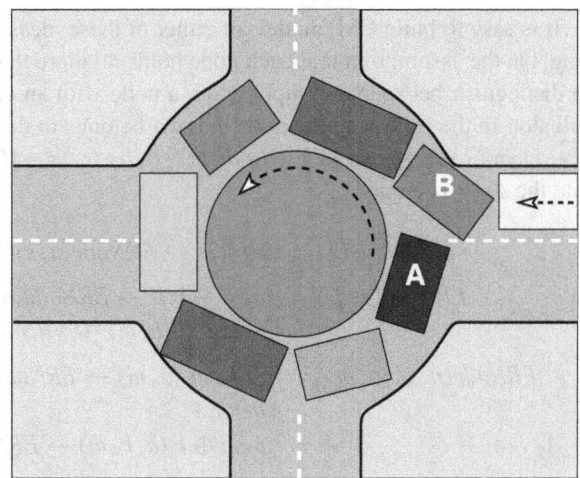

In Fig. 4.6 the question is whether B, attempting to get onto the roundabout, has to
give way to A (who is making for the bottom road) as implied by these road markings, or vice-versa. Of course in some countries the observed protocol seems to be
that everyone thinks they have priority; and increasingly often in the UK roundabouts seem to be equipped with traffic lights—but we will not dwell on such variations.

It is easy to see that Rule B, in the situation illustrated in Fig. 4.7, leads immediately to deadlock. Here all the vehicles want to get to an exit beyond the one they
are at or coming up to. The *priorité à droit* rule forces car A to give way to car B
and no-one on the roundabout can move.[4]

---

[4]The two roundabouts in Figs. 4.6 and 4.7 have opposite orientation in the pictures so that driving
readers in all countries have something to relate to! The orientation naturally makes no difference

Rule A, on the other hand, never blocks a car that is already on the roundabout, so that provided all the exit roads remain clear, the system never deadlocks.

We can apply similar ideas to rings designed to transmit messages: never allow the ring to get so full of traffic that the messages moving round it can make no progress. The following are two ideas on how to achieve this:

1. Create one or more (but less than the ring's capacity) slots that move continuously round the ring, with each message moving onto an empty slot when the latter reaches the sender's node, and jumping off when the slot reaches the receiver's node. This is an example of a *token ring*: a common way of ensuring that no more than a certain number of some resource is allocated. (See the index for other examples of token rings in this book.) Rather than a roundabout, think of a continuously rotating door or a paternoster lift.
2. Analogously to roundabout protocol A, only allow messages to be put into the ring when not only the slot the message will move into, but also the slot behind the message, is free.

It is easy to build CSP models of either of these ideas. We first look at the token ring. On the assumption that each node holds no more than one slot/token, we need to distinguish between an empty node, a node with an empty slot, and one with a full slot. In the following the node index n belongs to the node indices $I = \{0, \ldots, N-1\}$ and s varies over $\{E\} \cup \{(a, b, m) \mid a, b \in I, m \in Messages\}$, with E meaning that the slot s is empty.

$$ERNode(n) = ring.n?s \rightarrow FRNode(n, s)$$

$$FRNode(n, E) = ring.n \oplus 1.E \rightarrow ERNode(n)$$
$$\square\, send.n?(b, m) \rightarrow FRNode(n, (n, b, m))$$

$$FRNode(n, (a, b, m)) = receive.n.(a, m) \rightarrow FRNode(n, E)$$
$$\nleftarrow b = n \nrightarrow$$
$$ring.n \oplus 1.(a, b, m) \rightarrow ERNode(n)$$

This works provided some, but not all, of the nodes are initially empty ($ERNode(n)$) and the rest have an empty slot ($FRNode(n, E)$). If we want to give the node users the ability to send messages at any time rather than just the short periods when an empty slot happens to be present, we could add a buffer at each node to hold queued messages waiting to get onto the ring.

Two ways in which we might want to change the ring's behaviour are examined in exercises below.

We now turn to the second approach: ensuring that no slot accepts an input from outside unless it and the previous slot are empty. We could of course do this when every slot was potentially able to accept external messages, but we make life easier

---

to how the examples behave; however with driving on the left the rule in the second would be *priorité à gauche*, not *droit*.

for ourselves by providing two slots for each user, and preventing them *send*ing a message when either of the slots is full.

$$NB0(n) = ring.n?(a, b, m) \to NB1(n, (a, b, m))$$
$$\square\, send.n?(b, m) \to NB1(n, (n, b, m))$$

$$NB1(n, (a, b, m)) = ring.n?(a', b', m') \to$$
$$NB2(n, (a, b, n), (a', b', m'))$$
$$\square\, (receive.n.(a, m) \to NB0(n)$$
$$\nmid b = n \nmid$$
$$ring.n \oplus 1.(a, b, m) \to NB0(n))$$

$$NB2(n, (a, b, m), (a', b', m')) = receive.n.(a, m) \to NB1(n, (a', b', m'))$$
$$\nmid b = n \nmid$$
$$ring.n \oplus 1.(a, b, m) \to$$
$$NB1(n, (a', b', m'))$$

It is clear that the only possible cycles of ungranted requests in this network are where all nodes are empty and asking their predecessor for an output, and where all are completely full and asking their successor to accept an input. The first of these is not a deadlock since all the external users can *send*, and the second is impossible since this ring can never become full.

It is easy (as described in TPC) to generalise this to the case where nodes have larger capacities, provided that no *send* action ever fills up the node that accepts it.

A substantial case study (most of which is cast in OCCAM rather than CSP) of how this ring mechanism can be extended to a deadlock-free routing protocol for use on an arbitrarily connected network can be found in [119]. This essentially follows the same methods as we did in Sect. 4.2.1 where we extended the deadlock-free tree.

Exercise 4.7 Re-program the token-ring node as the combination of a cell performing the ring protocol and a process which can hold one message that the local user has sent. The two should ensure that when there is such a queued message and an empty slot comes along, then the message is placed in this slot.

Exercise 4.8 An interesting feature of the token ring is that when there are no messages being sent, the slots still circulate. There is usually no practical disadvantage to this, but in some circumstances it might be better if an empty ring eventually became quiescent, only resuming communications when a new message was sent. Of course, this can only work if some signal can tell the slot(s) to begin circulating again. How would you implement a ring based on these ideas? If it is helpful, you can assume that there is just one token.

4.2.3 The Mad Postman

It should not be too hard to see that any routing algorithm in a network where the following hold is deadlock free:

- The directed graph formed by drawing an edge from node n to n' if a message is ever passed from n to n' has no cycles in it. Thus, for any node, some of the nodes may be "upstream", some "downstream", some neither, but none both.
- Whenever a node is empty it will accept a message from *any* of its upstream neighbours and, when the message is not for itself, route it to one of its downstream neighbours. Furthermore, nodes never input selectively: if they accept one input, they accept any.
- Whenever a node is empty it will accept a message from its user to any downstream node and route it appropriately.

This is because any cycle of ungranted requests must have a *maximally downstream* point in it (i.e. a node that inputs from both its neighbours in the cycle). But this node cannot request an input from one of them without also requesting one from the other, meaning that it actually cannot refuse the request from the neighbour that is trying to output to it.

This seems straightforward but very limiting, since it seems to imply that one cannot route from any n to any n'. The solution to this was discovered by Jay Yantchev [158], which he called 'virtual networks'.[5] Suppose we have a rectangular[6] grid of nodes $\{N_{i,j} \mid 1 \leq i \leq A, 1 \leq j \leq B\}$ and might want to send a message packet from any one of these nodes to any other. On the face of it, this system is too symmetric to apply the above rule: messages can be sent in any direction so there cannot be some downstream nodes which cannot send to others upstream. The trick is to divide each node $N_{i,j}$ into the parallel composition of two processes $I_{i,j}$ and $O_{i,j}$. If every message enters the pair via $I_{i,j}$ with destination (k, l) it is then

- routed to $I_{m,n}$ through the Is, where $m = \max(i, k)$ and $n = \max(j, l)$;
- passed to $O_{m,n}$;
- routed to $O_{k,l}$ through the Os

and then output. The amazing thing about this is that there are no cycles the graph formed from the Is and Os with an edge from one to another, if there is ever an output from the first to the second. The most upstream node of all is $I_{1,1}$, and the most downstream is $O_{1,1}$. A picture of the 4×3 version of this network is shown in Fig. 4.8, with the routing technique illustrated by the path a message takes from $N_{1,3}$ to $N_{2,1}$.

---

[5]He also invented a clever hardware-level packet propagation mechanism which minimises propagation latency in this network. He called this the *mad postman* algorithm, but the details are not relevant to the present discussion.

[6]In fact the algorithm works equally well in any number of dimensions.

Fig. 4.8 Virtual network routing and detail of $N_{i,j}$

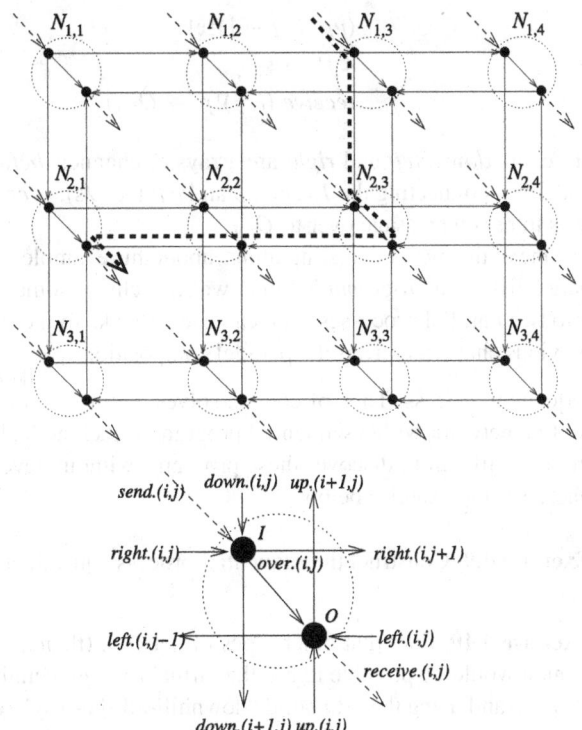

The simplest implementation of this that follows the rules above is given by the following process descriptions:

$$I_{i,j} = send.(i,j)?((x,y),m) \rightarrow I'_{i,j}((i,j),m)$$
$$\Box\, down.(i,j)?(x,y)?p \rightarrow I'_{i,j}((x,y),p)$$
$$\Box\, right.(i,j)?(x,y)?p \rightarrow I'_{i,j}((x,y),p)$$
$$I'_{i,j}((x,y),p) = right.(i+1,j)!(x,y)!p \rightarrow I_{i,j}$$
$$\langle\!\langle i < x \rangle\!\rangle$$
$$(down.(i,j+1)!(x,y)!p \rightarrow I_{i,j}$$
$$\langle\!\langle j < y \rangle\!\rangle$$
$$over.(i,j)!(x,y)!p \rightarrow I_{i,j})$$
$$O_{i,j} = over.(i,j)?(x,y)?p \rightarrow O'_{i,j}((x,y),p)$$
$$\Box\, up.(i,j)?(x,y)?p \rightarrow O'_{i,j}((x,y),p)$$
$$\Box\, left.(i,j)?(x,y)?p \rightarrow O'_{i,j}((x,y),p)$$
$$O'_{i,j}((x,y),p) = left.(i-1,j)!(x,y)!p \rightarrow O_{i,j}$$
$$\langle\!\langle i > x \rangle\!\rangle$$

$$(up.(i, j - 1)!x!y!p \to O_{i,j}$$
$$\Box j > y \Box$$
$$receive.(i, j)!p \to O_{i,j})$$

Here, *up*, *down*, *left* and *right* are arrays of channels *between* the nodes (with *right* and *down* connecting the *I*s and *up* and *left* the *O*s), *over*.(i, j) is a channel that $I_{i,j}$ uses to pass a message over to $O_{i,j}$.

One of the most interesting things about this example is that it shows the power of parallelism as a *programming tool*: we can achieve something by splitting up a node into two parallel processes. You can even, thanks to the techniques discussed in the previous chapter, convert the parallel composition $I_{i,j} \underset{\{|over|\}}{\|} O_{i,j}$ into an equivalent sequential process. This, of course, solves the problem of creating a deadlock-free routing network with a sequential program at each node, but it would have been extremely difficult to discover these programs without developing them from parallel ones. See the exercise below.

Exercise 4.9 Construct the sequential process equivalent to $I_{i,j} \underset{\{|over|\}}{\|} O_{i,j}$.

Exercise 4.10 For what other types of network (than n-dimensional grids) do you think it would be possible to use the virtual routing technique of splitting each node into two and using these to build "downhill-all-the-way" routing? Would it ever help to use more than two processes per node?

4.3 Communications Protocols

A communications protocol is a method that two or more processes use to pass information to each other. It provides rules on the format in which data is sent, and what messages each process is required to send and receive. It might be designed to achieve some particular goal such as efficiency, fault tolerance, or security. Equally, it might implement an agreed Standard used either by one set of designers or multiple manufacturers so that the components they design can interface successfully and "understand" each other.

Rather than design a single protocol that meets multiple goals at once (e.g. assembling packets, overcoming data corruption, avoiding message re-ordering, tolerating message loss/duplication, security and formatting) protocols are frequently designed in layers. So we first design a protocol that solves only the lowest-lever problem posed by the real communications medium, recasting the result as a slightly better medium before solving the second lowest-level problem, and so on.

For example, we might solve the problem of data corruption using a combination of error-correcting codes [105] and check-sums, and avoid message re-ordering through adding counters onto messages. You can see protocols designed to achieve security in Chap. 15 of TPC and [142]. In the rest of this section we will concentrate on a well-known protocol that overcomes bounded message loss and duplication. (Message duplication might well have been eliminated at lower levels, but message loss can easily be introduced by check-sums, when erroneous ones are discarded, as well as the bottom level medium.)

If one can put a fixed bound on the amount of message loss, such as "E loses no more than 3 messages from any consecutive 5", then it is possible to construct processes S and R such that $(S \underset{\{|a|\}}{\|} E) \underset{\{|b|\}}{\|} R$ behaves like a buffer between the input channel of S and the output channel of R, where a is a channel from S to E and b one from E to R. In this case, one could tag alternate messages with 0 and 1 and replicate them 4 times each so that at least one gets through. If M only handles bits, we can still solve this problem by having S send different length sequences of alternating bits depending on which of 0 or 1 it wants to send. It might send a run of 4 (the shortest sequence of which one is guaranteed to get through) to transmit a 0, and a run of 14 (the shortest sequence of which at least 5 will get through) to transmit a 1. R can then easily interpret this: a run of 1–4 identical bits represents a 0, and a run of 5–14 a 1. See Exercise 4.11 below.

However, as this example shows, even if the maximum error happens extremely infrequently, this style of solution needs to allow for it all the time because the sender never knows what errors the medium has committed. This leads to considerable inefficiency.

There are more advanced techniques that can be used in cases where we can send more than a single bit and where it is possible to implement an acknowledgement channel (albeit faulty in the same sense as the forward channel) back from R to S.

When we can implement the acknowledgement channel there are a number of protocols that can be used to exploit it. We might want to implement a buffer between two distant points but only have unreliable channels available. By this, we mean error-prone channels that can lose or duplicate as many messages as they wish—though not an infinite consecutive sequence—but preserve the value and order of those they do transmit. There are a number of protocols available to overcome this sort of error, the simplest of which is known as the *alternating bit protocol* (ABP). In fact, there are (as we will see in this and later chapters, where we will sometimes use it as an example to illustrate new ideas) a number of variants of this protocol, but the basic idea is the same in all of them. The structure of the network used is shown in Fig. 4.9, where the two error-prone channels are $C1$ and $C2$.

The basic idea is to add an extra bit to each message sent along the leaky channels which alternates between 0 and 1. The sending process sends multiple copies of each message until it is acknowledged. As soon as the receiving process gets a new message it sends repeated acknowledgements of it until the next message arrives. The two ends can always spot a new message or acknowledgement because of the alternating bit.

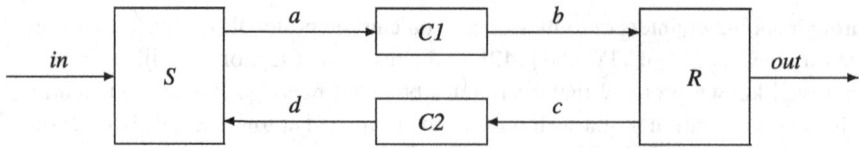

Fig. 4.9 The process structure of the alternating bit protocol

This is usually described using real-time features such as time-outs (for deciding when to re-send messages and acknowledgements; we will return to this in Example 15.2), but in fact with a little care it is possible to construct a version whose correctness is independent of timing details. Below we present sender (S) and receiver (R) processes which can readily be proved to work, in the sense that if $C1$ and $C2$ behave as described above, then the complete system behaves like a reliable buffer.

Very general error-prone channel processes are described by the following, where no limit is placed on the number of losses or duplications:

$$C(in, out) = in?x \rightarrow C'(in, out, x)$$

$$
\begin{aligned}
C'(in, out, x) = {}& out!x \rightarrow C(in, out) && \text{(correct transmission)} \\
& \sqcap out!x \rightarrow C'(in, out, x) && \text{(potential duplication)} \\
& \sqcap C(in, out) && \text{(loss of message)}
\end{aligned}
$$

With the channel names implied by Fig. 4.9, we get $C1 = C(a, b)$ and $C2 = C(c, d)$.

This sort of erroneous medium may lose as many messages as it likes, and repeat any message as often as it wishes. We can reasonably hope to create a system using such media which works as long as they do not commit an infinite unbroken series of errors.

The model above decides to commit an error or not by nondeterministic choice $\sqcap$. This is a rather realistic model of how such a medium looks to the users, but it gives us no direct way of seeing from a system's behaviour that *provided* that the errors are sufficiently limited, the system satisfies some specification.

It can therefore be useful to construct alternative models of erroneous processes in which, instead of error behaviours being chosen by $\sqcap$, we introduce visible events that some demon or gremlin can use to trigger them. The above definition then becomes

$$CE(in, out) = in?x \rightarrow CE'(in, out, x)$$

$$
\begin{aligned}
CE'(in, out, x) = {}& out!x \rightarrow CE(in, out) && \text{(correct transmission)} \\
& \square\, dup \rightarrow out!x \rightarrow CE'(in, out, x) && \text{(potential duplication)} \\
& \square\, loss \rightarrow CE(in, out) && \text{(loss of message)}
\end{aligned}
$$

where the gremlin gets the alphabet $\{dup, loss\}$. Notice that if our gremlin does nothing then this process behaves perfectly: this is something we will always expect of faulty processes described in this *controlled error* style: in other words for any component C with error events in E, we expect that $C \parallel_{E} STOP$ (for $E = \{loss, dup\}$) is equivalent to how C should behave if none of its errors occur—in the case above a one-place buffer.

In Sect. 6.5 we will give further insight into the controlled error model, including a second basic criterion for how the erroneous components must behave.

The sender and receiver processes are now $S(0)$ and $R(0)$, where for $s \in \{0, 1\}$:

$$S(s) = in?x \to S'(s, x)$$

$$\begin{aligned} S'(s, x) = \ &a.s.x \to S'(s, x) \\ &\Box d.s \to S(1-s) \\ &\Box d.(1-s) \to S'(s, x) \end{aligned}$$

$$\begin{aligned} R(s) = \ &b.s?x \to out!x \to R(1-s) \\ &\Box b.(1-s)?x \to R(s) \\ &\Box c!(1-s) \to R(s) \end{aligned}$$

In order to study the transmission of messages it is easiest to consider the sequences of messages on a, b, c and d in which any message following another with the same tag bit is removed, as are any initial messages on c and d with tag bit 1. Call these stripped sequences $\overline{a}, \overline{b}, \overline{c}$ and $\overline{d}$. The structures of the processes involved then imply the following facts:

- $C1$ implies that $\#\overline{a} \geq \#\overline{b}$: the stripping process clearly removes any duplication.
- R implies that $\#\overline{b} \geq \#\overline{c}$: R can only change the bit it outputs along c in response to a change in the input bit on b. It only initiates the first member of $\overline{c}$ in response to the first 0 in $\overline{b}$.
- $C2$ implies that $\#\overline{c} \geq \#\overline{d}$.
- S implies that $\#\overline{d} \geq \#\overline{a} - 1$: S can only change the bit it outputs along a in response to a change in the input bit on d.

We can piece all of these together to get

$$\#\overline{a} \geq \#\overline{b} \geq \#\overline{c} \geq \#\overline{d} \geq \#\overline{a} - 1$$

or, in other words, these four sequences are, in length, all within one of each other. From this it is implied that $C1$ must, at each moment, have transmitted at least one of each equal-bit block of outputs sent by S except perhaps the current one (for it to have completely lost one would imply that $\#\overline{b}$ is at least two less than $\#\overline{a}$). This, the structure of S, and the fact that R outputs a member of each block it receives on *right*, imply that each trace s of the protocol satisfies

$$s \downarrow right \leq s \downarrow left \quad \text{and} \quad \#(s \downarrow left) \leq \#(s \downarrow right) + 1$$

or, in other words,

$$COPY \sqsubseteq_{T} ABP$$

Having gained this understanding of its traces, it is easy to show that our network is deadlock free. If $\bar{a} \ldots \bar{d}$ are all equal in length then S can accept any input on *in*. Otherwise S wants to re-send a message, and the only way a cycle of ungranted requests (see p. 75) can occur is if S is rejecting a communication on d. But whenever S offers an output on a it also accepts any input on d.

S and R can equally be combined with the nondeterministic or controlled error versions of the medium processes. The difference, of course, is that in the first version there is no easy way to see what errors have occurred, while in the second we can ask questions such as "If k or less errors occur, is there a bound on the length of trace required to transmit s messages?"

We will return to this example at several points later in this book, including Sects. 5.1, 15.2 and 17.4.1.

The alternating bit protocol is too simple and inefficient to be used much in practice. However, a reasonably straightforward development of it called the *sliding window* protocol, where the transmission of sequences of consecutive messages overlap, is much more practical and is the core of a number of practical systems. There is an implementation of the sliding window protocol in CSP_M on this book's web-site.

Exercise 4.11 Design processes S and R such that $(S \parallel_{\{a\}} E) \parallel_{\{b\}} R$ behaves like a buffer of bits, where E is the process that can lose up to 3 bits from any 5. How would your processes have to change if E can also duplicate or triplicate any bit and send it up to 3 times?

Exercise 4.12 The answer to the question above about whether a bound on the number of errors that occur in our model of the ABP bounds the length of trace to transmit s messages is actually "no"! This is because there is nothing to stop the infinite trace in which S sends and re-sends the first message over and over again, and R never bothers to acknowledge it.

(a) Revise the definition of R so that it acknowledges each message it receives on b exactly once.
(b) The arguments made above about trace correctness and deadlock freedom still apply to this revised system. Why?
(c) Give an estimate for the maximum length of trace that transmits k messages when there are no errors.
(d) There is an elegant way to verify this estimate for any fixed k using the controlled error model of the protocol. Try to discover it.

Exercise 4.13 What would happen if the two channels $C1$ and $C2$ of the alternating bit protocol were replaced by the following single medium process that only handles messages in one direction at a time?

$$M = a?x \rightarrow M'(b, x)$$
$$\square \, c?x \rightarrow M'(d, x)$$

$$M'(out, x) = out!x \rightarrow M'(in, out)$$
$$\sqcap \, out!x \rightarrow M'(in, out, x)$$
$$\sqcap \, M$$

Modify the sender and receiver processes by adding extra messages between them, so that this medium can be used successfully. *This is a difficult question!*

Chapter 5
Hiding and Renaming

It is often useful either to remove certain actions from the view of the environment or to apply mappings to a process's events. In this chapter we introduce the operators that allow us to do these things.

5.1 Hiding

Consider the parallel combination of $COPY'(c_r, c_{r+1})$ processes we saw on p. 51. We said there that it would be natural to think of c_0 and c_n as being external channels, and the others as internal ones. If they really are internal then the fact that we can still see the communications passing along them is unfortunate from several points of view.

- Seeing these communications clutters up our picture of the process and makes it impossible to show that this system behaves like an n-place buffer implemented some other way such as a sequential process. We should not have to see unnecessary internal details of a system.
- By leaving the internal communications visible we are leaving open the possibility that another process might be put in parallel with the currently defined network, with some of the internal events in its alphabet. The second process would be able to stop these events from happening. In this case, and in many like it, we would expect 'internal' communications to proceed without requiring further control from outside.

Both of these difficulties can be avoided by *hiding* the internal events, making them invisible to and uncontrollable by the environment.

Exactly the same arguments apply to the internal messages of the routingnetworks discussed in Sect. 4.2, and to both the alternating bit protocol and the 2-from-5 example in Sect. 4.3.

Given any process P and any set of events X, the process $P \setminus X$ behaves like P except that the events from X have been internalised: turned into τs. If we want

A.W. Roscoe, *Understanding Concurrent Systems*, Texts in Computer Science,
DOI 10.1007/978-1-84882-258-0_5, © Springer-Verlag London Limited 2010

Fig. 5.1 The effects of hiding on a transition system

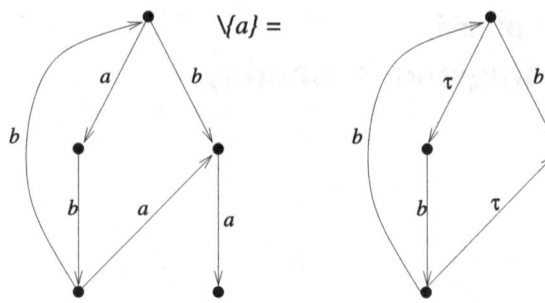

to hide a single event or channel a then we will sometimes write $P \setminus a$ rather than $P \setminus \{a\}$ or $P \setminus \{|a|\}$.

Thus, if we want to hide all the communication between a pair of parallel processes, we would write $(P \mathbin{_X\|_Y} Q) \setminus (X \cap Y)$ or $(P \mathbin{\underset{Z}{\|}} Q) \setminus Z$. This creates point-to-point, invisible communication, which is arguably closest to the 'natural' parallel operator of implementations. In specifying a real parallel communicating system, rather than one devised as a specification where the parallel operator takes the role of conjunction as described in Sect. 3.5, one almost always uses a combination of the parallel and hiding operators.[1] The natural view of the chain of buffers would be

$$\left(\|_{r=0}^{n-1} (COPY'(c_r, c_{r+1}), \{|c_r, c_{r+1}|\}) \right) \setminus (\{|c_1, \ldots, c_{n-1}|\})$$

while in the alternating bit protocol example we would hide $\{|a, b, c, d|\}$.

The only communications visible in the system displayed above are its inputs and outputs, namely $\{|c_0, c_n|\}$. Since we are no longer seeing the internal workings, we can potentially prove this system equivalent to a totally different one which might have different internal channels or none at all, or to another CSP description intended as a specification.

Perhaps the easiest way of understanding the effect of the hiding operator is to see how it transforms the picture of a process's transitions. We saw a few of pictures in previous chapters (Figs. 1.1, 1.2, etc.). As previously discussed in Sect. 2.3, any process can be given such a *labelled transition system* or LTS, which provides a much less abstract view of the way it behaves than its set of traces. The shape of the transition system remains exactly the same after hiding, but hidden actions are transformed into invisible τ actions of the same sort used to implement nondeterministic choice. An example is shown in Fig. 5.1. Invisible (or internal) actions are to be thought of as ones which (a) do not contribute to the trace, because the environment cannot see them and (b) the process can perform by itself. τ is a special event that is never in Σ.

Since hiding is a unary (one-place) rather than binary operator (on processes), the only one of the 'usual' sorts of algebraic laws that applies to it is the distributive

---

[1] Some other process algebras, notably CCS, combine parallel and hiding into a single operator: they do not factor the 'natural' operator into two parts like CSP.

law. There is a rich collection of laws, nevertheless, of which the following are a few:

$$(P \sqcap Q) \setminus X = (P \setminus X) \sqcap (Q \setminus X) \qquad \langle \text{hide-dist} \rangle \ (5.1)$$

$$(P \setminus Y) \setminus X = (P \setminus X) \setminus Y \qquad \langle \text{hide-sym} \rangle \ (5.2)$$

$$(P \setminus Y) \setminus X = P \setminus (X \cup Y) \qquad \langle \text{hide-combine} \rangle \ (5.3)$$

$$P \setminus \emptyset = P \qquad \langle \text{null hiding} \rangle \ (5.4)$$

$$(a \rightarrow P) \setminus X = \begin{cases} P \setminus X & \text{if } a \in X \\ a \rightarrow (P \setminus X) & \text{if } a \notin X \end{cases} \qquad \langle \text{hide-step 1} \rangle \ (5.5)$$

The second of these is an easy consequence of the third. The final law above shows the hiding actually happening: the a disappears when it is an element of X. Note that this shows that a process whose only initial action is a single τ is equivalent to whatever state follows the τ.

This is not a full 'step' law, in the sense we have already used to describe other operators, since that requires the process to have an arbitrary subset of Σ as its initial actions. The full version is more complex because it has to deal with what happens when (i) there is a choice of hidden actions and (ii) there is a choice between hidden and visible actions. Rather than writing down the whole law immediately, let us look at each of these two situations separately.

$$(a \rightarrow P \square b \rightarrow Q) \setminus \{a, b\}$$

has two hidden actions possible. Now only one happens, and we cannot be sure which, so in fact this equates to $(P \setminus \{a, b\}) \sqcap (Q \setminus \{a, b\})$. This creates the first principle we are looking for here: when there is more than one hidden action possible, it is nondeterministic which occurs. And in fact the usual[2] way of creating a transition picture of the process $P \sqcap Q$ is by creating one whose initial state has two τ actions: one to P and one to Q.

It is tempting to think that we should either give hidden actions the ability to exclude visible ones from the same choice—because the hidden action occurs as soon as it is possible—or perhaps the reverse. In fact, neither is consistent with what we already know. Consider the process

$$(a \rightarrow P \square b \rightarrow Q) \setminus b$$

(the same as above except that only one of the two events is hidden). If either the unhidden or the hidden event (τ) were preferred, this would equal

$$a \rightarrow P \setminus b \quad \text{or} \quad Q \setminus b$$

---

[2]This is exactly how FDR and ProBE represent nondeterministic choice, as previously described in Sect. 1.6.

Fig. 5.2 Hiding creating '▷'

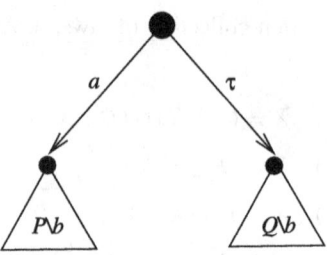

which, if we then hid a, would in either case give a different answer from hiding $\{a, b\}$ together, in contradiction to the law ⟨hide-combine⟩. Thus both the hidden and unhidden actions must remain possible. The right way to think about the way this type of process behaves is that as soon as an internal action becomes available then *something* must happen, but it might be a visible action rather than a hidden one. Unless we do manage to get a visible communication, a hidden one must occur. This is actually a new form of choice between two processes that is different from $\square$ and $\sqcap$.[3] $P \triangleright Q$ *may* offer initial events of P, and if one is chosen it resolves the choice in P's favour. If no event is picked from P, an internal τ action will happen that resolves the choice in Q's favour. It is perhaps easiest to understand this by considering transition pictures like Fig. 5.2.

$P \triangleright Q$ can be thought of as analogous to a *time-out*: the choices of P are offered, but if one is not picked soon enough these options disappear and the combination times out to Q. This analogy is not *that* close, simply because there is no concept of the passage of time in the usual view of CSP. We will call this operator *sliding*, or *asymmetric*, choice.

In fact, of course, since $P \triangleright Q = (P \square a \to Q) \setminus a$ for any event a not appearing in P or Q, it is possible to derive the traces of $P \triangleright Q$ and its algebraic laws from those of the operators used in this expression. It is, of course, distributive, associative and idempotent, but obviously not symmetric. *STOP* is a left unit for it (i.e. *STOP* $\triangleright$ $P = P$).

We will find in Chap. 13 that $\triangleright$ is one of the most important operators when trying to understand CSP using its laws. Many laws of this operator can be found there.

The complete step law for hiding is given below:

$$(?x : A \to P) \setminus X$$

$$= \begin{cases} ?x : A \to (P \setminus X) & \text{if } A \cap X = \emptyset \\ (?x : (A \setminus X) \to (P \setminus X)) & \\ \quad \triangleright \sqcap\{(P[a/x]) \setminus X \mid a \in A \cap X\} & \text{if } A \cap X \neq \emptyset \end{cases} \qquad \text{⟨hide-step⟩ (5.6)}$$

---

[3]TPC identifies the process $P \triangleright Q$ with $(P \sqcap STOP) \square Q$. This identification is correct, if a little hard to understand, in the theories of CSP that TPC considers. Since we will consider a number of theories in later chapters where it is not correct to identify these two terms, we prefer to think of $\triangleright$ as a primitive operator rather than one derived from others.

It should be noticed that this step law is unlike all of the ones we have seen before, in that, while it obviously uses one step of the process it is applied *to*, it does not necessarily give us the first visible action of the *result*. Of course this is perfectly natural with a hiding operator, but it does mean that one might never come to a conclusion from it about what the initial actions of $P \setminus X$ are: just think what would happen if you were to apply it to $(\mu p.a \to p) \setminus a$.

Notice that in the buffer example above we hid all the internal communications at once, at the outermost level, where we could have combined the cells in steps hiding the internal channels as we went. This is represented by the complex expression

$$((\ldots(COPY'(c_0, c_1) \; {}_{\{|c_0,c_1|\}}\|{}_{\{|c_1,c_2|\}} \; COPY'(c_1, c_2)) \setminus \{|c_1|\} \ldots)$$

$$ {}_{\{|c_0,c_{n-1}|\}}\|{}_{\{|c_{n-1},c_n|\}} \; COPY'(c_{n-1}, c_n)) \setminus \{|c_{n-1}|\}$$

(We will see much more convenient ways of writing this down in Sect. 5.3.) Provided that moving the hiding does not influence the number of processes that have to agree on an action, it should not matter whether we hide that action at an inner or an outer level of a parallel combination. Thus, we can expect

$$(P \; {}_X\|_Y \; Q) \setminus Z = (P \setminus Z \cap X) \; {}_X\|_Y \; (Q \setminus Z \cap Y)$$

$$\text{provided } X \cap Y \cap Z = \emptyset \qquad \langle \text{hide-}{}_X\|_Y\text{-dist} \rangle \;\; (5.7)$$

$$\left(P \; \underset{X}{\|} \; Q \right) \setminus Z = (P \setminus Z) \; \underset{X}{\|} \; (Q \setminus Z)$$

$$\text{provided } X \cap Z = \emptyset \qquad \langle \text{hide-}\underset{X}{\|}\text{-dist} \rangle \;\; (5.8)$$

These laws are helpful in understanding how a network put together with parallel and hiding operators behaves: we can move all the hiding to the outermost level so we can 'see' all of the communications in the network at once before applying a single hiding operator to get rid of the ones we don't want to see. We will see in later chapters that these laws are vital to the effective use of FDR's *compression* functions, and Chap. 13 of TPC demonstrates that they are also extremely helpful in reasoning about deadlock.

The traces of $P \setminus X$ are very easy to compute: if we define $s \setminus X$, for any trace s, to be $s \upharpoonright (\Sigma \setminus X)$, then

$$traces(P \setminus X) = \{s \setminus X \mid s \in traces(P)\}$$

5.1.1 The Consequences of Hiding

Hiding is the most common source of nondeterminism in CSP descriptions. It often shows up in real systems where one parallel partner has to arbitrate between two others. For example, we know that the process

$$P = a \to c \to STOP \; \square \; b \to d \to STOP$$

offers the environment the choice between a and b, with subsequent behaviour depending on which option is chosen. If we give it the alphabet $X = \{a, b, c, d\}$ of all events it can perform, then simply putting it in parallel with processes which choose a and b respectively does not change the way it looks to the outside world:

$$N \ = \ P \ _X\|_{\{a,b\}} \ (a \rightarrow STOP \ _{\{a\}}\|_{\{b\}} \ b \rightarrow STOP)$$

N can be expected to behave in the same way as P. If, however, we 'complete' the parallel composition by hiding the internal events $N \setminus \{a, b\}$ then we introduce nondeterminism. The result will behave like

$$(c \rightarrow STOP) \sqcap (d \rightarrow STOP)$$

This type of behaviour is what makes nondeterminism an inevitable constituent of any theory describing concurrency where arbitration is present in some form.

In Sect. 4.2 we saw a number of approaches to designing routing networks, including several that are deadlock free. The user's view of such a network would be far clearer if all the internal messages were hidden, leaving only $\{|send, receive|\}$ visible.

Even in the simplest of these networks, namely the deadlockable ring consisting of D_i on p. 74, the hiding leads to nondeterminism, by which we mean that the users cannot be certain what the response of the system will be based solely on its trace. Here are some examples:

- Suppose nodes D_i, D_j and D_k are in that order on the ring, with several other nodes in both the gaps. After the trace $\langle send.i.(k, m1), send.j.(k, m2)\rangle$ there are two messages, both heading for k. We do not know which order they will arrive in, since without seeing the hidden actions it is uncertain whether or not D_i's message was already past D_j at the time that node's message was sent.
- Suppose that in the same situation D_i has sent more messages to D_k than there are nodes from D_j to D_k, but that the user of D_k has not accepted any of them. So each of the messages is sitting somewhere on the ring between D_i and D_k. Ultimately these messages will sit in the nodes leading up to D_k with no gaps, since systems never sit still for ever while a hidden (τ) action is available. This means that eventually the user of D_j will be unable to *send* a message until the ones for D_k are *receive*d. However, a $send.j$ event is possible between all the $send.i.(k, \_)$ events and the time when all the nodes from D_j to D_k are full. So, after a trace consisting of all these $send.i(k, \_)$s, the system looks like $(send.j?p \rightarrow R) \rhd STOP$ to the user of D_j. This, of course, is a sort of nondeterminism.

In other words, we can know a lot more about how our system will respond in a given situation when we can see what internal actions have taken place; but since we do not want our external user(s) to be cluttered with this knowledge, the system behaves nondeterministically to them.

Very similar issues occur with all the routing networks in Sect. 4.2. Two of them suffer from an additional problem. In Network 4 of Sect. 4.2.1 (p. 75) we showed how to supplement a deadlock-free tree-based routing network by polling links that lay outside the tree. We identified (Fig. 4.5) a problem that might then arise: a message moving round and round the ring for ever without ever reaching its destination. Provided (as in the D_i example considered above) enough users do not accept available *receive* events, it is not too hard to see that a message could circulate for ever without any external communication happening at all. In the hidden system this becomes an infinite, unbroken, sequence of τ actions. In other words, the network becomes *livelocked* as opposed to *deadlocked*.

In fact a similar situation can arise whenever the process P, in $P \setminus X$, can perform an infinite unbroken sequence of τ actions. We call such behaviour *divergence*. It can, in fact, happen without the use of hiding in recursions like $P = P \sqcap a \to P$ and $P = P \,\square\, a \to P$: in the first of these there is the possibility of an infinite sequence of τs, always resolving the nondeterministic choice to the left. In the second the recursion unfolds infinitely in the vain hope of calculating what the initial actions of the left-hand process are.[4]

In CSP, divergence, when it is considered at all, is usually treated as a serious sort of misbehaviour: we will see just how serious on p. 118. This is clearly a reasonable view in the Network 4 case. The token ring (see p. 82), however, is clearly *intended* to diverge when there are no full slots circulating. In other words, there are some sorts of systems where we allow one or more processes to engage in a *busy wait*: typically they poll parts of the system from where stimuli might come, as the tokens do here looking for messages to hold. For such a system to be successful, we need to ensure that the series of actions that constitute this polling do not run to the exclusion of the ones that they are waiting for. In other words, we would need to be sure that a node holding an empty token is not so intent on passing it to the next process in the ring that it does not allow its user to *send*.

Reasoning about this idea of *fairness* [42] can get complicated, and we will not treat it in detail in this book. We will, however, introduce a new model in Sect. 12.4 that allows sensible consideration of examples like this token ring: divergence is modelled but not considered disastrous. We will see a timed model of this ring in Chap. 14.

It is useful to have a constant **div** in our language to represent a process that does nothing but diverge, just as *STOP* is one that does nothing but deadlock. As in TPC, the constant $Chaos_\Sigma$ represents the most nondeterministic process that cannot diverge.

Particular care has to be exercised in dealing with *infinite* hiding, i.e., $P \setminus X$ for infinite sets of events X. For it can introduce unbounded nondeterminism in just the same way as the unconstrained use of $\sqcap$. That this is so is readily demonstrated: if $S = \{P_\lambda \mid \lambda \in \Lambda\}$ for a set of events Λ chosen to be disjoint from those which the P_λ themselves can communicate, then clearly

$$\sqcap S = (?\lambda : \Lambda \to P_\lambda) \setminus \Lambda$$

It is interesting to study the consequences of hiding on the alternating bit protocol (Sect. 4.3). Divergence can occur for two reasons in ABP:

---

[4]See p. 203 for further discussion of this point.

- In the version where message loss and duplication are controlled by nondeterministic choice rather than demonic events, it is clear that when these choices are resolved in the direction of error sufficiently then the system can diverge. This can happen in several ways such as the first medium process losing an infinite consecutive sequence of the messages it is sent, or the second one duplicating one acknowledgement infinitely.

  To avoid this sort of divergence we either need to build an assumption into our model of a medium so that it never commits an infinite sequence of errors, or to use the controlled error version in which divergence is replaced by an infinite sequence of demon events. There is a clear sense in which we must expect these types of misbehaviour when dealing with an error-prone medium.

- More worryingly, in the absence of any errors, the receiver process R might send an infinite sequence of acknowledgement messages without accepting a message from S. Thus it will forever be an old message that R is acknowledging, so these messages will be received but ignored by S. This issue is closely related to Exercise 4.12.

This divergence in our model appears because of the way in which the model on p. 87 abstracts away from time. The usual implementation of this protocol would have S and R repeat messages only after waiting some non-zero time for an acknowledgement or new message respectively. In this set-up the divergence we described cannot occur. We will see how to model the alternating bit protocol in a timed setting in Chap. 15.

5.1.2 Hiding versus Constructiveness

It must be pointed out that the very useful notion of a guarded recursion fits uneasily with hiding. For the meaning of 'guarded' is that information—in the sense of communications—is added by a recursion. Another (and, in general, more accurate) term we can use is 'constructive'. Hiding deletes events: consider the recursion

$$P = a \to (P \setminus a)$$

which, according to our earlier definition, is guarded because the recursive call is prefixed by an event. The problem is that communications are deleted by the hiding, so that what the recursion gives with one hand it takes away with the other. In fact this recursion does not have a unique fixed point over the traces model $\mathcal{T}$: if S is any member of $\mathcal{T}$ at all (possibly able to communicate events other than a), then

$$\{\langle\rangle\} \cup \{\langle a\rangle^\frown(s \setminus a) \mid s \in S\}$$

is a solution to the fixed point equation we get from the recursion. The least and natural solution is, of course, $\{\langle\rangle, \langle a\rangle\}$. After the trace $\langle a\rangle$ we would expect that this process would diverge, since it would perform a sequence of increasingly deeply hidden as. Our intuition, therefore, is that this $P = a \to \mathbf{div}$.

This behaviour forces us to add a caveat to the definition of guardedness: no recursion in which the hiding operator is applied (directly or indirectly) to a recursive call should be considered guarded (at least, without a careful analysis based on mathematical models).

Of course, this restriction applies equally to the *derived* operators we will meet later that use hiding in their definition. In a few cases it is possible to assert that recursions involving hiding are constructive, but to do this you need to understand the mathematics of constructiveness a great deal better: this is discussed in Chap. 4 of TPC.

It is easy to think that the above restriction prevents us from applying the UFP rule to any process involving hiding: this is not so, it is only the recursion to which the rule is applied that has to be constructive. A good example is the process we get when we hide the internal channel of the combination we studied in the last chapter:

$$(COPY'(a, b) \ {}_{\{|a,b|\}}\|_{\{|b,c|\}} COPY'(b, c)) \setminus \{|b|\}$$

Now of course we already know that the process inside the hiding is equivalent to CC_0', where

$$CC_0' = a?x \rightarrow CC_1'(x)$$
$$CC_1'(x) = b!x \rightarrow CC_2'(x)$$
$$CC_2'(x) = (c!x \rightarrow CC_0') \ \square \ (a?y \rightarrow CC_3'(y, x))$$
$$CC_3'(y, x) = c!x \rightarrow CC_1'(y)$$

When we hide $\{|b|\}$ in this we find (applying $\langle$hide-step$\rangle$) that

$$CC_0' \setminus b = a?x \rightarrow CC_1'(x) \setminus b$$
$$CC_1'(x) \setminus b = CC_2'(x) \setminus b$$
$$CC_2'(x) \setminus b = (c!x \rightarrow CC_0' \setminus b) \ \square \ (a?y \rightarrow CC_3'(y, x) \setminus b)$$
$$CC_3'(y, x) \setminus b = c!x \rightarrow CC_1'(y) \setminus b$$

which is not (applying the usual trick of replacing each term on the left-hand side by a new recursive identifier) guarded. However, the above equations imply trivially that $CC_0' \setminus b$, $CC_1'(x) \setminus b$ and $CC_3'(y, x) \setminus b$ satisfy the recursive definition

$$B_0^2 = a?x \rightarrow B_1^2(x)$$
$$B_1^2(x) = (a?y \rightarrow B_2^2(y, x)) \ \square \ (c!x \rightarrow B_0^2)$$
$$B_2^2(y, x) = c!x \rightarrow B_1^2(y)$$

which *is* guarded. (Note that B_0^2, $B_1^2(x)$ and $B_2^2(x, y)$ respectively denote a two-place buffer with nothing in, with x in and with x and y in.) So we have shown that our original processes satisfy this guarded recursion and therefore equal its unique fixed point. It is quite irrelevant that the definition of the original processes involved hiding. There was, we should point out, no need to go through the intermediate step of discovering the C' recursion: it would have been just as good to prove that a vector of parallel/hiding combinations satisfy the B^2 recursion.

Note that what we actually proved here was that the parallel combination of two one-place buffers, placed in parallel with the middle channel hidden, behaves like a two-place buffer—clearly something we would expect.

Exercise 5.1 Take the dining philosophers network from pp. 53 and 58 with the *picksup* and *putsdown* events hidden (after the entire network has been combined). Can this system still deadlock? Do you think hiding can ever affect deadlock? *Think carefully and write down your conclusions—we will later develop theories that will answer this question definitively.*

Exercise 5.2 If $P = (a \rightarrow P) \square (b \rightarrow a \rightarrow P)$, we would expect that $P \setminus b$ is equivalent to $\mu p.a \rightarrow p$. Use ⟨hide-step⟩ (5.6) and an idempotence law of $\rhd$ to show that

$$P \setminus b = a \rightarrow (P \setminus b)$$

and hence that this equivalence is true by the UFP rule. *Make sure that you understand why the rule is valid here when it was invalid on the very similar equation $P = a \rightarrow (P \setminus a)$.*

Exercise 5.3 If $P = a?x \rightarrow b!x \rightarrow b!x \rightarrow P$ then it is possible to find a process Q such that

$$(P \ _{\{|a,b|\}} \| _{\{|b,c|\}} Q) \setminus \{|b|\} =_T COPY'(a, c)$$

(i.e., a one-place buffer). Find Q and use the UFP rule to prove the equivalence.

Exercise 5.4 Give a CSP expression defining the process equivalent to the one on the left-hand side of Fig. 5.1. Use the step law of hiding and laws and those about the choice operators to find a constructive context $F(\cdot)$ such that $P \setminus \{a\} = F(P \setminus \{a\})$.

Exercise 5.5 Use ⟨⊓-□-dist*⟩, ⟨□-dist⟩ and other standard laws to prove that

$$(Q \square R) \sqcap STOP = (Q \square R) \sqcap Q \sqcap R \sqcap STOP \quad \text{and hence}$$
$$(P \square Q \square R) \sqcap P = (P \square Q \square R) \sqcap (P \square Q) \sqcap P$$

5.2 Renaming and Alphabet Transformations

In the previous section we saw how to remove certain events from sight. A less drastic effect is achieved by *renaming*, which means applying a map that changes which (visible) member of Σ a process is performing.

While one can imagine that the alphabet transformation thus accomplished might change through the life of a process—perhaps event a maps to b if it appears before the 12th event and to c later—in practice we rarely want to do this. Thus the CSP renaming operator applies the same transformation throughout a process's life: in this section we see three increasingly general ways of doing this.[5]

5.2.1 Injective Functions

Suppose P is a CSP process and $f : \Sigma \to \Sigma$ is an injective, or 1–1, function (simply meaning that $f(x) = f(y)$ implies $x = y$) from Σ to itself. f can be a *partial* function provided its domain contains every event possible for P. Then $f[P]$ is the process which can communicate $f(a)$ whenever P can communicate a. The communications of P have been *renamed*, or equivalently P has been subjected to an *alphabet transformation*. The transition system of $f[P]$ is that of P with the function f applied to the arcs.

All of this works whether f is injective or not. The reason why we want to distinguish this case is because it is both simpler to understand and is used most often in CSP descriptions of real systems. The point is that, in this case, $f[P]$ works *exactly* like P except for the names of its events. (The sense in which this is not true when f is not 1–1 will be seen later.)

If f is the function that swaps the events *down* and *up*, then $f[COUNT_0]$ will behave like a counter through the negative numbers, since it will never allow any more *ups* than *downs*.

If g is a function that maps (for any $x \in T$) *left.x* to *a.x* and *right.x* to *b.x* then $g[COPY]$ is the same as the parameterised process $COPY'(a, b)$ (assuming, of course, that *left*, *right*, a and b are all channels of type T). One could similarly devise a renaming that would map a single $FORK_i$ from the dining philosophers to any other $FORK_j$, and likewise for the philosopher processes. In each case this is possible because, except for the names of their events, the target process always behaves identically to the original: evidently no renaming could make $FORK_i$ into $PHIL_i$!

Thus, renaming is an alternative to parameterisation as a way of creating many similar processes to put into a network. Which method is better depends on the example and the taste of the programmer.

Since injective renaming leaves the behaviour of a process unchanged except for the names of actions, it has an extremely rich set of laws—too many to write down conveniently! Essentially it distributes over all operators. We will give a list of laws that apply to any sort of renaming later, but three that apply specifically to this one

---

[5] It is possible to achieve the effect of variable renaming by combining one-to-many renaming with parallel combination with a process that chooses the appropriate image of an event for the current trace. See Exercise 5.10 below.

are

$$f[P \parallel_X Q] = f[P] \parallel_{f(X)} f[Q] \quad \text{if } f \text{ is } 1\text{–}1 \qquad\qquad \langle f[\cdot]\text{-}\parallel\text{-dist}\rangle \quad (5.9)$$

$$f[P \;_X\parallel_Y Q] = f[P] \;_{f(X)}\parallel_{f(Y)} f[Q] \quad \text{if } f \text{ is } 1\text{–}1 \qquad \langle f[\cdot]\text{-}_X\parallel_Y\text{-dist}\rangle \quad (5.10)$$

$$f[P \setminus X] = f[P] \setminus f(X) \quad \text{if } f \text{ is } 1\text{–}1 \qquad\qquad \langle f[\cdot]\text{-hide-sym}\rangle \quad (5.11)$$

The third of these is frequently used, in combination with the following, to change the name of hidden actions. This might be done to prevent a clash of names for the subsequent application of other laws.

$$f[P \setminus X] = P \setminus X \quad \text{if } f(y) = y \text{ for all } y \in \Sigma \setminus X \qquad \langle f[\cdot]\text{-hide-null}\rangle \quad (5.12)$$

5.2.2 Non-injective Functions

The most common use of renaming $f[P]$ when f is not injective on the events of P is when we want to forget about some level of detail in a process. Consider a splitting process which accepts inputs on channel *in* and, depending on what the input is, sends it either to *out1* or to *out2*.

$$SPLIT = in?x : T \rightarrow ((out1.x \rightarrow SPLIT) \triangleleft x \in S \triangleright (out2.x \rightarrow SPLIT))$$

For some purposes the composition of messages may be unimportant. If we forget that detail by using the renaming function *forget* which remembers only the channel name, the process *forget*[*SPLIT*] we get is equivalent to *SPLIT'*, where

$$SPLIT' = in \rightarrow (out1 \rightarrow SPLIT' \sqcap out2 \rightarrow SPLIT')$$

This has introduced nondeterminism because we have deliberately forgotten the information which allowed us to know whether *out1* or *out2* occurs. Though this might appear a retrograde step, this type of abstraction is frequently beneficial, for

- it allows us to demonstrate that some aspect of the correctness of the system does not depend on precisely how decisions are made, and
- in cases where this is true the details of decision making frequently clutter proofs.

Consider, for example, the routing algorithms from Sect. 4.2. The pieces of code we presented there all contained details of the sender, addressee and the contents of the message itself. While all of these details are vital if a routing algorithm is going to fulfil its purpose, none of them is in the least important for ensuring the deadlock freedom of any of our networks.

Some of the CSP files associated with this chapter show how this *forgetful renaming* both demonstrates this and allows FDR to gain an advantage by using compression functions.

Non-injective renaming becomes more dangerous when the alphabet transformation f in use maps an infinite set of events to a single one (i.e., f is not finite-to-one). This, like $\sqcap S$ for infinite S, and $P \setminus X$ for infinite X, is a construct which can introduce unbounded nondeterminism.

5.2.3 Relational Renaming

Various treatments of CSP have included a second sort of renaming, using *inverse* functions: $f^{-1}[P]$ can communicate a whenever P can communicate $f(a)$. This is equivalent in expressive power to the direct image renaming we have seen already when f is 1–1, but it can produce some interesting effects when f is many-to-one. For a single event in P can be transformed into the choice between many different ones—though all leading to the same place. What we will now describe here is a more general form of renaming that encompasses both direct and inverse functions, and at the same time corresponds most closely to the notation for renaming used in machine-readable CSP.

A function can be thought of as a set of ordered pairs: (x, y) is in the set if $f(x) = y$. A set of pairs is a (partial) function if no x is mapped to more than one y. A *relation* on the other hand, is any set of ordered pairs, with no restriction as to how many things a given object can be related to. If $(x, y) \in R$ we write $x\, R\, y$. If R is a relation, its *domain* and *range* are respectively

$$dom(R) = \{x \mid \exists y.x\, R\, y\}$$

$$ran(R) = \{y \mid \exists x.x\, R\, y\}$$

The composition of two relations $R \circ S$ is

$$\{(x, z) \mid \exists y.x\, R\, y \wedge y\, S\, z\}$$

(confusingly, because of a clash of conventions, this is the opposite way round to the way composition of functions works). The *relational image* $R(x)$ of x under R is $\{y \mid x\, R\, y\}$.

If R is a relation whose domain includes all the events of P, then $P[\![R]\!]$ is the process that can perform each event in $R(a)$ whenever P can perform a. If R is a function then this is identical to the renaming $R[P]$. If f is a function then its inverse f^{-1} is the relation $\{(y, x) \mid (x, y) \in f\}$. The operator $f^{-1}[P]$ is then identical to $P[\![f^{-1}]\!]$. For example, if D is the relation which relates a to both itself and b, then

$$(a \rightarrow STOP)[\![D]\!] = (a \rightarrow STOP) \,\square\, (b \rightarrow STOP)$$

If U is the universal relation $\Sigma \times \Sigma$, then $P[\![U]\!] = RUN$ if and only if the divergence-free process P is deadlock-free.

The following laws are thus all true (suitably translated from the forms below) for the functional form of renaming. Renaming distributes over both choice operators:

$$(P \sqcap Q)[\![R]\!] = P[\![R]\!] \sqcap Q[\![R]\!] \qquad\qquad \langle [\![R]\!]\text{-dist}\rangle \;(5.13)$$

$$(P \mathbin{\Box} Q)[\![R]\!] = P[\![R]\!] \mathbin{\Box} Q[\![R]\!] \hspace{3cm} \langle[\![R]\!]\text{-}\mathbin{\Box}\text{-dist}\rangle \; (5.14)$$

If the initials of P' are A, then those of $P'[\![R]\!]$ are $R(A) = \{y \mid \exists x \in A. (x, y) \in R\}$:

$$(?x : A \to P)[\![R]\!]$$

$$= ?y : R(A) \to \bigsqcap\{(P[z/x])[\![R]\!] \mid z \in A \wedge z \, R \, y\} \hspace{1.5cm} \langle[\![R]\!]\text{-step}\rangle \; (5.15)$$

This shows that renaming can introduce nondeterminism when more than one event in A maps under R to the same thing. This cannot happen when R is either an injective function or f^{-1} for any function: in these cases the nondeterministic choice is over a set of one process—no choice at all—as there is then only ever one z such that $z \, R \, y$.

Renaming by one relation and then another is equivalent to renaming by the composition of these relations:

$$(P[\![R]\!])[\![R']\!] = P[\![R \circ R']\!] \hspace{3cm} \langle[\![R]\!]\text{-combine}\rangle \; (5.16)$$

This law is one reason why relations are written on the right of a process rather than (as with functions) on the left. It implies the following law for functional renaming, where the opposite sense of composition is used

$$f[g[P]] = (f \circ g)[P] \hspace{3.5cm} \langle f[\cdot]\text{-combine}\rangle \; (5.17)$$

Renaming in this most general form is such a powerful operator that most of the useful distribution laws that held for 1–1 renaming are no longer true. (In most cases versions can be found, but these tend to come with an unfortunately complex set of side conditions.)

The traces of $P[\![R]\!]$ are just the images of those of P under the obvious extension of R to traces:

$$\langle a_1, \ldots, a_n \rangle R^* \langle b_1, \ldots, b_m \rangle \Leftrightarrow n = m \wedge \forall i \leq n.a_i \, R \, b_i$$

$$traces(P[\![R]\!]) = \{t \mid \exists s \in traces(P).s \, R^* t\}$$

A good way of defining relations for use as alphabet transformations is to use a notation like substitution: we can write $P[\![a/b]\!]$ to mean that the event or channel b in P is replaced by a. (Note that all others remain the same—including any a that is already there.) To modify more than one thing, or to send one thing to more than one place, we write something like

$$P[\![a, b/b, a]\!] \quad \text{or} \quad P[\![b, c/a, a]\!]$$

Note that the first of these *swaps* a and b and the second maps a to both b and c.

One-to-Many Renaming as a Magic Wand

Relational renaming gives us the ability to create a process that will offer several alternatives in place of a single event. On first encountering this possibility one is inclined to wonder what purpose it might serve, particularly since the result of performing any of these alternatives is exactly the same. However, there are two important uses for it that we meet regularly in practice.

The first is as an aid to creating processes that treat large numbers of events in the same way. Typically these are specification processes or simple components of larger systems. For example, you can define a process in which members of the sets A and B of events alternate by defining one $\mu p.a \to b \to p$ alternate, and then renaming a and b (respectively) to all members of A and B. One could define $Chaos_A$ as

$$(\mu p.((a \to p) \sqcap STOP))[\![^x/a \mid x \in A]\!]$$

By using this style it is sometimes possible to achieve greater clarity than without (since evidently any use in this style could be replaced by prefix-choice), and in some cases it results in a more efficient implementation for FDR.

An excellent example of this is provided by the approaches to modelling Sudoku that we saw in Sect. 4.1. For a 9×9 puzzle we need 81, and for a 16×16 puzzle, 256 different processes for the squares. See the Tools section below.

The second use is rather more interesting, not least since it produces results that do not seem possible using any other CSP construct. That is to create, in effect, a renaming operator that maps each event only to a single target, but one which varies with more than just the input event. Thus we might rename the event *apple* to either *Cox* or *Braeburn* depending on what has gone before it. This is achieved by first renaming the event to all its targets, and then designing a regulator process that is put in parallel with the resulting process and which selects which of the new events happens on each trace. For example, if Adam and Eve prefer the different varieties here we might define

$$Reg = Braeburn \to Reg$$
$$\Box \, Adam \to Reg$$
$$\Box \, Eve \to Reg'$$

$$Reg' = Cox \to Reg'$$
$$\Box \, Adam \to Reg$$
$$\Box \, Eve \to Reg'$$

The construct

$$P[\![^{Braeburn, Cox}/_{apple, apple}]\!] \quad\underset{\{Adam, \, Eve, \, Braeburn, \, Cox\}}{\|}\quad Reg$$

creates a process that will do one or other of *Braeburn* and *Cox* whenever P would have done *apple*, the choice being determined by which of *Adam* and *Eve* was most recently mentioned in the trace.

All sorts of weird and wonderful effects can be achieved with variations on this theme, such as hiding every other event a process does, or just the first one. Certainly when trying to achieve something unusual in CSP, it is one of the first things the author usually tries, and indeed we will see several indispensable uses of this idea in later chapters.

Exercise 5.6 Recall that $COPY = left?x \rightarrow right!x \rightarrow COPY$. Suppose we want, instead, a process $CELL_f$ which inputs values v on channel $left$ and immediately outputs $f(v)$ on $right$. Find an appropriate alphabet transformation g_f so that $CELL_f = g_f[COPY]$. Under what conditions is g_f injective?

Exercise 5.7 Use an alphabet transformation to connect the output channel of $COPY$ to the input channel of $CELL_f$ and *vice-versa* (i.e., there are two processes running in parallel). How does this process behave? How does it behave if $COPY$ is replaced by $right!x \rightarrow COPY$?

Add an extra channel in to $COPY$ so that the resulting process can be initialised along this channel and thereafter behaves as before, so achieving the effect of the second case in the last paragraph for any x.

Exercise 5.8 Find renaming relations R_i which, applied to the process $COUNT_0$, achieve the following effects:

(a) A process with events a, b and c, where the number of cs is always less than or equal to the total of the as and bs.
(b) A process that can always communicate either up or $down$.
(c) A process that has the same traces as $COUNT_0$ but may nondeterministically sometimes refuse to communicate $down$ when $COUNT_0$ would have accepted it.

Exercise 5.9 Find examples to show that the laws for distributing *injective* renaming over hiding and general parallel composition do not work when the function f is not injective.

What weaker restrictions on the renamings could you make so that these laws become valid again? *You might find thinking about the laws for distributing hiding over parallel helpful here.*

Exercise 5.10 Remember the possibility quoted at the start of this section of mapping a to b if it is before the 12th event and to c thereafter. Use a combination of a relational renaming and parallel composition with a process you define to achieve this effect. (Assume that the process P does not itself use events b and c.)

Exercise 5.11 Show how to hide the odd-numbered communications that a process performs, and how to hide just the first communication it performs. (Assume that the alphabet of your process is contained in A, and that Σ contains a disjoint set of events A' that are in natural correspondence with A via $a \mapsto a'$.)

Exercise 5.12 Show that every labelled transition system (LTS, see p. 41) can be represented as a CSP process using a combination of prefix-choice, hiding, renaming and recursion. [*Hint: use prefix-choice and recursion to set up the basic shape of the LTS, but with unique branching and no τ actions, and then use hiding and renaming to map this to the desired shape.*]

5.3 Linking Operators

As we said at the start of this chapter, it is very natural to expect the parallel composition of processes to hide the actions that are synchronised. It is as though by plugging a connecting wire between two systems we lose the ability and desire to see and control what goes down the wire.

While CSP contains many uses of the parallel and hiding operators individually that to not fit this pattern, it is so common in natural models of real parallel systems that it is good to be able to write them down succinctly.

The fact that processes are connected by their common use of events means that one has to give a good deal of thought to the design of the entire alphabet Σ before constructing the component processes, and that the component processes' designs already contain the details of the connections. All the examples in Chap. 4 illustrate this very well.

Fortunately we can create operators out of parallel, hiding and renaming that allow natural networks to be plugged together more conveniently. Both TPC and Hoare's book concentrated particularly on two of these forms, but we will be more general and follow the form used in CSP_M.

Suppose that a is a channel of the process P, and that b is a compatible channel of Q. By "compatible" we mean that either a and b are both simple events, or are channels along which the same type flows. In other words, $a.x$ is an event if and only if $b.x$ is. In many cases one each of a and b will be used for inputs and outputs respectively for the two processes. In this case, $P[a \leftrightarrow b]Q$ is the process in which P's communications on a are synchronised with Q's on b, and then hidden. There is nothing to stop P using b and Q using a, but these are neither synchronised nor hidden. If c is a fresh (i.e. not used in P or Q) channel name of the same type as a and b, then we can define

$$P[a \leftrightarrow b]Q = (P[\![^c/a]\!] \underset{\{|c|\}}{\|} Q[\![^c/b]\!]) \setminus \{|c|\}$$

We can extend this definition so that it applies to any number of pairs of channels (a_i, b_i) of P and Q (where a_i and b_i have the same type, but not necessarily the same type as other pairs, with all the a_i being different, and also all the b_i):

$$P[a_1 \leftrightarrow b_1, \ldots, a_n \leftrightarrow b_n]Q$$

Here, of course, we need fresh channel names $c_1, \ldots, c_n$ and rename a_i to c_i in P, b_i to c_i in Q, before synchronising these and hiding the result.

Here it is the parallel operator that does the linking, rather than the fact that we have used the same channel name in both processes. One of the benefits of this is that we can link together several different processes that use the same channel names, or even several copies of the same process. So

$$COPY[right \leftrightarrow left]COPY[right \leftrightarrow left]COPY$$

has the output channel of the left-hand $COPY$ connected to the input channel of the middle process, whose output is connected to the input of the third. Thus this process itself has external input channel *left* and output *right*. A little thought reveals that this system is a three-place buffer.

The fact that it can generate arbitrarily large chains using a fixed alphabet means that this *link parallel* operator can be used to build processes recursively. For example, the processes

$$B1 = left?x \rightarrow (B1 \, [right \leftrightarrow left] \, right!x \rightarrow COPY)$$

$$B2 = left?x \rightarrow (B2 \, [right \leftrightarrow left] \, right!x \rightarrow B2)$$

are both equivalent to the unbounded infinite buffer $B_{\langle\rangle}^{\infty}$.

These, and many other interesting recursive schemes in terms of two specialisations of link parallel are discussed in Chap. 4 of TPC. These two specialisations are *chaining*:[6]

$$P \gg Q = P[right \leftrightarrow left]Q$$

as used above, and *enslavement* $P \parallel_X Q$ in which the whole of Q's alphabet X is synchronised with P and hidden.

In past work on CSP chaining ($\gg$) was particularly associated with buffers: a series of laws relating $\gg$ and buffers was stated in Chap. 5 of TPC. All of these translate, with slightly improved generality, to laws involving link parallel. The most important of these are given below:

BL1. If P is an $(a \Rightarrow b)$-buffer, and Q is $(c \Rightarrow d)$-buffer, with $a \neq d$, then $P \, [b \Rightarrow c] Q$ is a $(a \Rightarrow d)$-buffer.

BL5. Suppose P uses events $\{|a, b|\}$ and Q uses $\{|c, d|\}$, with $a \neq d$. If x is free in neither P nor Q, which are such that

$$P \, [b \leftrightarrow c] \, Q \sqsupseteq a?x \rightarrow (P \, [b \leftrightarrow c] \, d!x \rightarrow Q)$$

then $P \, [b \leftrightarrow c] \, Q$ is an $(a \Rightarrow d)$-buffer.

Here, a $(p \Rightarrow q)$ buffer is a process that satisfies the buffer specification in which the input and output channels have respectively been relabelled p and q.

The two laws above are true either in the traces specification of a buffer that we have seen on p. 37, or the more complete one that we will see on pp. 122 and 122.

BL1 shows that we can combine buffers together to form bigger ones in a natural way. BL5 provides what is to all intents and purposes an inductive rule: it shows that if a linked system handles the first input correctly for a buffer, and then behaves as before, then it is a buffer.

We will use the notation $\gg$ occasionally in this book, particularly when the direction of the channel is important as in Sect. 17.4.

Enslavement has often been used to create dynamic, recursively defined networks as chains or trees in which all communications with the environment are centred on

---

[6]Chaining ($\gg$) is sometimes called *piping*.

a single node. Several examples of this can be found in TPC. The following example implements the Mergesort[7] algorithm using link parallel in an analogous way. In this implementation, sorting processes input a stream of values on one channel, followed by the special value *end*, and then output the same set of values sorted into ascending order on a second channel, followed by *end*. In this version of Mergesort a process manages the sorting of a list of length 1 or less itself, and otherwise partitions the list into two nearly equal length sublists which it sends to two slave Mergesort processes, which it expects to sort them into ascending order. To give the result it takes the output from the two slaves and sorts them into a single sorted list. The dynamic structure is created by the following recursion, which names the slaves *up* and *down*:

$$M = in.end \to out.end \to M$$
$$\square\, in?x : T \to M1(x)$$

$$M1(x) = in.end \to out!x \to out.end \to M$$
$$\square\, in?y : T \to$$
$$((upto!x \to downto!y \to Mu) \,[upto \leftrightarrow in, upfrom \leftrightarrow out]\, M)$$
$$[downto \leftrightarrow in, downfrom \leftrightarrow out]\, M)$$

Here *Mu* represents a node in "inputting" mode whose next input is to be sent to the *up* slave, with *Md* being the same for the *down* slave.

$$Mu = in.end \to downto.end \to upto.end \to O1$$
$$\square\, in?y : T \to upto!x \to Md$$

$$Md = in.end \to downto.end \to upto.end \to O1$$
$$\square\, in?y : T \to downto!x \to Mu$$

$$O1 = upfrom?x \to downfrom?y \to O2(x, y)$$

$$O2(x, y) = x = end \wedge y = end \& out!end \to Mu$$
$$\square\, x = end \wedge y \neq end \& out!y \to downfrom?y' \to O2(x, y')$$
$$\square\, x \neq end \wedge y = end \& out!x \to upfrom?x' \to O2(x', y)$$
$$\square\, x \neq end \wedge y \neq end \& (out!x \to upfrom?x' \to O2(x', y)$$
$$\mathbin{\triangleleft} x < y \mathbin{\triangleright}$$
$$out!y \to downfrom?y' \to O2(x, y'))$$

If *M* did not wait until the second input had arrived before starting up the slaves, this recursion would not work: it would diverge. But there is no need for a similar wait once the first sort is over and this process already has slaves.

The link parallel operator has many pleasant algebraic properties that can largely be derived from those of the operators it is built from. It is obviously symmetric if the pairs of channels swap as well as the processes, and is associative under natural conditions: see Exercise 5.16.

---

[7] A similar implementation of Hoare's Quicksort can be found in TPC.

Exercise 5.13 Re-program the Alternating Bit Protocol (Sect. 4.3) using link parallel. Note that there is no longer any need to use different channel names for the copies of the medium process.

Exercise 5.14 Suppose that a and d are channels of 4-bit "nibbles" (small bytes!), and that b and c are channels of bits. Devise processes T (inputting on a, outputting on b) and R (inputting on c, outputting on d) so that T unpacks nibbles $\langle b1, \ldots, b4 \rangle$ into bits, and R packs them back up into nibbles. Show that $T\ [b \leftrightarrow c]\ R$ is a buffer (of nibbles) using $BL5$. Is $R\ [d \leftrightarrow a]\ T$ a buffer (of bits) in the sense defined on p. 37?

Exercise 5.15 A variant on the Quicksort algorithm finds the kth smallest of a list of at least k elements. It inputs a stream of data followed by the event $in.(end, k)$, and then outputs the kth smallest one x via the communication $out.x$. During the input phase this program works exactly like Quicksort, except that the nodes remember how many elements d they have sent to their *down* neighbours as well as the number e equal to the pivot. So, on receiving (end, k) a node knows which of the three "piles" the kth belongs to, and if it is in the *down* or *up* piles which number it is in that pile.

Adapt the program Q so that it implements this algorithm, being careful not to leave nodes hanging when no $out.x$ is required from them.

Exercise 5.16 Show that if the alphabets of the processes P and Q that are left visible by $P[a \leftrightarrow b]Q$ are disjoint, then you can replace $\underset{\{|c|\}}{\|}$ by alphabetised parallel in its definition.

Formulate an associative law for link parallel: in what circumstances is the following true?

$$(P[a \leftrightarrow b]Q)[c \leftrightarrow d]R = P[a \leftrightarrow b](Q[c \leftrightarrow d]R)$$

5.4 Tools

The notation for hiding in machine-readable CSP is almost exactly the same as we have used already: $P \backslash X$, where X must be a *set of events*. While it is often convenient to have X a single event or channel, or a set of channels, in written text, you must convert it to the proper type for running. This is made easier by the $\{|a,b|\}$ notation, which corresponds to the notation $\{|a, b|\}$ we have already defined.

There is only one way of writing renaming, which (apart from the precise way it is written) is a simple extension of the 'substitution' style renaming we saw at the end of the section: you create a relation by using variations on the notation

```
P [[b <- a, d <- c]]
```

This relation maps b to a, d to c and leaves all other events alone. a,b,c,d can be simple events or channel names. If you want to map one event to many (as in inverse function renaming) this can be done by using the same event on the left-hand side of <- more than once: P[[a <- a, a <- b]] 'shadows' each a with the alternative of a b. More sophisticated forms of this notation exist, in which the renamed pairs are generated rather than explicitly listed: see Appendix B of TPC.

Now that we have this notation, we can come back the use of one-to-many renaming in Sudoku. We concentrate here on the last coding in Sect. 4.1: recall the definitions:

```
EmptyM2(p,X) =
card(X)>0 &
  (select.p?v:X -> FullM2(p)
  [] select?q:adj(p)?v -> EmptyM2(p,diff(X,{v}))
  [] select?q:diff(Coords,nhd(p))?v -> EmptyM2(p,X)

FullM2(p) = select?q:diff(Coords,{p})?v -> FullM2(p)
            [] done -> FullM2(p)
```

A very simple model of the same process forgets about its position p, and uses only a single channel for the three different classes of squares:

```
EM2(X) =
card(X) > 0 & (selhere?v:X -> FM2
              [] seladj?v -> EM2(diff(X,{v}))
              [] selother -> EM2(X)

FM2(p) = seladj?v -> FM2(p)
        [] selother?v -> FM2(p)
        [] done -> FullM2(p)
```

We can turn this into the corresponding process for position p by the renaming

```
Cell(p) =
let X0 = diff(Symbol,{init(q) | q <- adj(p)})
within
(if init(p)==0 then EM2(X0)
                else GF2(init(p)))
[[selhere.v <- select.p.v | v <- Symbol]]
[[seladj.v <- select.q.v | q <- adj(p), v <- Symbol]]
[[selother.v <- select.q.v |
               q <- diff(Coord,nhd(p)), v <- Symbol]]
```

A little thought reveals that the behaviour of this process is identical to that of an a Cell built using EmptyM2(p,X0) or FullM2(p). The real advantage comes when you run the file. FDR avoids a great deal of re-compilation relative to the un-named version. On a 256-square puzzle (the first one of this size in the files sudoku.csp and sudoku2.csp (the latter having the renaming), the author timed the respective versions at 40 and 130 seconds. The whole of this difference came from the saving in compilation time, which was 20 and 110 seconds respectively. (Almost all of the remaining time was spent loading the result of the compilation into the part of FDR that runs the refinement check. The check itself takes about a second.)

Link parallel is syntactically very like renaming, in that the operator is built out of a collection of ordered pairs. As for renaming, you can, in CSP_M, either write out these pairs explicitly [a <-> b, c <-> c] or use generators of the same type used in sets, for example [a <-> b | (a,b) <- conns].

Chapter 6
Beyond Traces

Though we have known it since Chap. 2, our exposure to the nondeterminism introduced by hiding and renaming, and the divergence caused by hiding has emphasised that traces alone give a far from complete picture of the way a process behaves. Whether or not you intend to study the details of the way these phenomena are modelled in detail—this is done in Chaps. 10, 11 and 12—you should at least gain a basic understanding of the two main tools that are used, in addition to traces.

We will find that these give us powerful new languages for specifying processes.

6.1 A Brief Introduction to Failures and Divergences

Traces tell us about what a process *can* do, but nothing about what it *must* do. The processes $\mu p.a \rightarrow p$ and $(\mu p.a \rightarrow p) \sqcap STOP$ have the same traces, even though the second is allowed to do nothing at all no matter what we offer it. In order to distinguish these processes we need to record not only what a process *can* do, but also what it can *refuse* to do. A *refusal set* is a set from which a process can fail to accept anything, however long it is offered. (It is *not* enough for it simply to be refused for a finite time.) *refusals*(P) is the set of P's initial refusals.

In fact, we need to know not only what P can refuse to do after the empty trace, but also what it can refuse after any of its traces. A *failure* is a pair (s, X), where $s \in traces(P)$ and $X \in refusals(P/s)$. (Recall that P/s represents process P *after* the trace s.) *failures*(P) is the set of all P's failures.

One can calculate the failures of a process P in the same way as we have already shown how to calculate the traces of P: a denotational semantics based on induction over P's syntax. For details of this you should see Chap. 10. But they can be calculated just as easily from the LTS of a process: you simply collect together all the routes through this diagram which (ignoring τs) result in a given trace. If the node you end up at is *stable*—i.e., has no τ action leading out of it—then this gives rise to a failure, since the node can (and must) refuse all actions which do not lead out of it. On the other hand, a node with one or more τs (an *unstable* node) does not give rise to a refusal since, if the environment offers no visible action that the node can

A.W. Roscoe, *Understanding Concurrent Systems*, Texts in Computer Science, DOI 10.1007/978-1-84882-258-0_6, © Springer-Verlag London Limited 2010

Fig. 6.1 The refusal sets of some transition systems

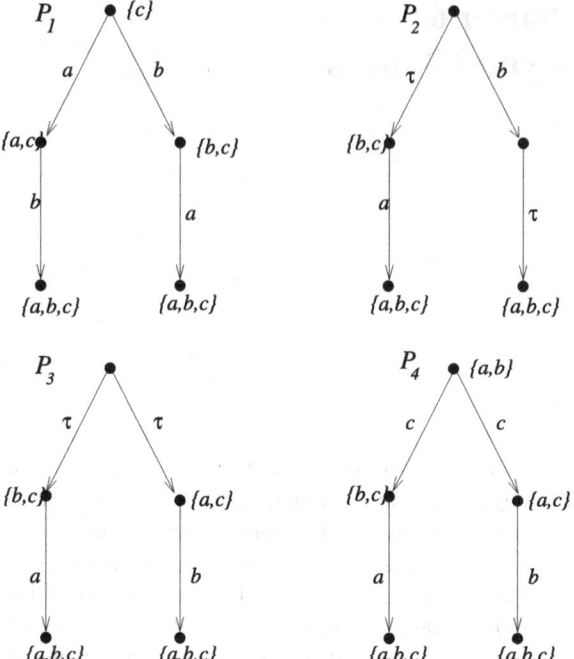

accept, then the internal action will eventually happen: as we cannot sit at this node for ever, it cannot give rise to a refusal. In other words, we have to wait for the τs to run out before we get refusals. In Fig. 6.1 we see how to calculate the failures of a few simple processes in this way. Assuming the alphabet is $\{a, b, c\}$, each stable node is labelled with its maximal refusal. (If a node can refuse X, then it can clearly refuse $Y \subseteq X$.)

P_1 is $(a \rightarrow b \rightarrow STOP)\ \square\ (b \rightarrow a \rightarrow STOP)$ (or equivalently $(a \rightarrow STOP)\ |||\ (b \rightarrow STOP)$). It has a *deterministic* transition system (as it has no τs, and no ambiguous branching on any visible actions). It follows that there is a unique path through the tree for any trace. Thus, there will be just one maximal refusal for any trace s: the complement of *initials*(P/s). Examples of this process's failures are $(\langle\rangle, \emptyset)$, $(\langle\rangle, \{c\})$, $(\langle a\rangle, \{a, c\})$ and $(\langle b, a\rangle, \{a, b, c\})$.

P_2 shows how internal actions can introduce nondeterminism. It could have arisen as $((c \rightarrow a \rightarrow STOP)\ \square\ (b \rightarrow c \rightarrow STOP)) \setminus c$. Its initial refusals are the subsets of $\{b, c\}$ but it can also accept b initially. Its complete failures are

$$\{(\langle\rangle, X) \mid X \subseteq \{b, c\}\} \cup \{(\langle a\rangle, X), (\langle b\rangle, X) \mid X \subseteq \{a, b, c\}\}$$

P_3 could be $(a \rightarrow STOP) \sqcap (b \rightarrow STOP)$. It has two initial τs to choose from. Its initial refusals are $\{X \mid \{a, b\} \not\subseteq X\}$. It can refuse either a or b separately but must accept something if $\{a, b\}$ is offered. Notice how this is different from the initial behaviours of both P_1 (which must accept either) and P_2 (which must accept a), even though all three have exactly the same initial events.

P_4 which could be $(c \rightarrow a \rightarrow STOP) \,\square\, (c \rightarrow b \rightarrow STOP)$ shows how ambiguous branching on a visible action can lead to nondeterminism. Its refusals after the trace $\langle c \rangle$ are $\{X \mid \{a, b\} \not\subseteq X\}$. The similarity to the initial refusals of P_3 is no accident: we know this process is equivalent to $c \rightarrow (a \rightarrow STOP \sqcap b \rightarrow STOP)$ and the equality simply reflects this fact.

One process *failures*-refines another: $P \sqsubseteq_F Q$ if and only if

$$traces(P) \supseteq traces(Q) \quad \text{and} \quad failures(P) \supseteq failures(Q)$$

or, in other words, if every trace s of Q is possible for P and every refusal after this trace is possible for P. Q can neither accept nor refuse an event unless P does. Among the processes of Fig. 6.1, P_2 and P_3 are trace equivalent and both trace-refine P_1. The only failures refinement that holds is that P_2 refines P_3. Make sure you understand why this is. We can define two processes to be *failures*-equivalent ($=_F$) if each failures-refines the other.

Failures allow us to distinguish between internal and external choice, something we could not do with traces alone. This is shown by the examples in Fig. 6.1, but comes across more clearly when we consider the failures of

$$Q_1 = (a \rightarrow STOP) \,\square\, (b \rightarrow STOP) \quad \text{and}$$
$$Q_2 = (a \rightarrow STOP) \sqcap (b \rightarrow STOP)$$

If $\Sigma = \{a, b\}$, the only refusal on $\langle \rangle$ of the first of these processes is $\emptyset$: the only time it will not communicate is if it is offered nothing at all! Q_2 can additionally refuse $\{a\}$ and $\{b\}$, but cannot refuse $\{a, b\}$ since whichever way the nondeterministic choice is resolved it has to accept one or the other. On the other hand, the process

$$Q_3 = STOP \sqcap ((a \rightarrow STOP) \,\square\, (b \rightarrow STOP))$$

can refuse any set of events, because it can behave like $STOP$. In general, a process can deadlock if, and only if, it can refuse the whole of Σ. The failures specification of deadlock freedom is thus that, for all traces s, $(s, \Sigma) \notin failures(P)$.

Full calculation of the failures of Q_1, Q_2 and Q_3 would reveal that

$$Q_3 \sqsubseteq_F Q_2 \sqsubseteq_F Q_1$$

As we will see in Chaps. 11 and 12, there are many different models one can use to judge whether two CSP processes are equivalent or refine each other, and traces is the simplest of these. So there is no simple answer to what the "right" sort of refinement is between processes. However, it is reasonable to ask that such a model:

(a) can tell us whether a process is nondeterministic or not, and
(b) allows us to specify that a process certainly *will accept* a given visible action from the environment.

The model consisting of a process's failures (calculated from stable states) and traces[1] in both its implementation in FDR and in our theoretical discussions in Chaps. 10 and 11 very nearly meets this bill, but it does not account for divergence properly. Consider the two processes

$$a \to STOP \quad \text{and} \quad (a \to STOP) \sqcap \mathbf{div}$$

where **div** is the process discussed earlier that performs τ actions for ever. These processes have identical failures and traces. It is clear that the left-hand process certainly will accept the event a when offered it, but that the right-hand one can respond by simply performing τs. The left-hand process is deterministic by any reasonable definition but, thanks to having the option of responding or not responding, the right-hand one is not.

Imagine that, having seen trace s, you are offering some process the set X of events. Three things can happen if you wait long enough:

- The process accepts some member of X: evidently this behaviour is reflected in its *traces*, so that if it is an undesirable behaviour we will see this from the set of traces.
- It becomes stable in a state that can perform no member of X. In that case we get the failure (s, X).
- It performs τs for ever and diverges.

Remember that the fewer recorded behaviours a process has, the more refined we consider it to be. It follows that, if our model is not recording a particular sort of behaviour that is an alternative to others we *are* recording, then it will be more refined if it makes that choice. It should therefore not surprise the reader to learn that the most refined process under failures refinement, where divergence is not recorded, is **div**: it has no failures and traces $\{\langle\rangle\}$.

It should also be unsurprising that the way to get a model that meets the requirements above is to add a component of *divergences* into the representation of a process. This can actually replace the set of traces from the model above, because if s is any trace of P and the environment (ungenerously) offers the process the empty set $\emptyset$ of events, P will certainly either diverge (meaning that s is a divergence trace) or become stable and refuse $\emptyset$ (meaning that $(s, \emptyset) \in failures(P)$).

There is an important choice to make in how to model divergence, and the choice we make is dependent on our attitude to the question of whether divergence is disastrous or not, already raised on p. 118.

Much of the mathematical theory of CSP works (considerably) more easily if we treat divergence as so catastrophic that once a process has reached a trace where it *might* diverge, we do not try to distinguish what else it might do. In fact, in such circumstances, it is helpful to assume in the mathematical model that the process can do absolutely anything! This assumption is called *divergence strictness*. One of the main advances in CSP theory since the publication of TPC is that we do now

---

[1]This is termed the *stable failures* model $\mathcal{F}$.

understand how to build working models of CSP that contain divergence but are *not* divergence-strict. These[2] are outlined in Sect. 12.4, but for the rest of this chapter we *will* assume divergence strictness.

Following this route to divergence strictness leads to what has become the standard model of CSP, the *failures-divergences model*, where a process is represented by $(failures_\perp(P), divergences(P))$. Here

- *divergences(P)* is the set of traces after which P can actually diverge, and all their extensions because of divergence strictness.
- $failures_\perp(P)$ means $failures(P) \cup \{(s, X) \mid s \in divergences(P), X \subseteq \Sigma\}$: the set of stable failures extended by all failures associated with the strict divergences.

More generally, we use notations analogous to $failures_\perp(P)$ for other types of behaviour. For example, $traces_\perp(P) = traces(P) \cup divergences(P)$: the divergence-strict set of a process's traces.

The representation $(failures_\perp(P), divergences(P))$ can either be extracted from the transition graph by simply recording which behaviours it can perform, as in Fig. 6.1, or via clauses like those seen earlier for $traces(P)$. In the former case, in a finite transition system, s is a divergence if and only if P can reach some state Q after some $t \leq s$ (perhaps with some τs mixed in), where Q can be reached from Q itself after some non-zero number of τs. In other words, Q is on a τ-*loop*. The latter can be found in Sect. 10.4, as can further details of the model, but for now it is quite sufficient for you to think primarily in terms of observing the transition graph. That is, after all, essentially how FDR works out the failures and divergences of a process. Your main aim in reading this section should, perhaps, be to understand what failures and divergence are, so that you know what it means when FDR does the calculations involving them for you.

Because of the closure under divergence, over this model *any* process that can diverge immediately (i.e., without any visible communication) is equivalent to **div**, no matter what else it may also be able to do.

It is important to understand just what the idea of divergence closure means. There is no suggestion that any process that can diverge after a given trace s really can perform all extensions of s and all associated failures. Rather, divergence strictness simply removes all distinctions between processes, based on what they do after a possibly divergent trace, by adding all such behaviour into what we record, whether it is really there or not. It is a bit like erasing black text by painting black ink over it.

One process *failures-divergences-refines* another, written $P \sqsubseteq_{FD} Q$ (or just $P \sqsubseteq Q$ when the context makes this model clear), if and only if

$$failures_\perp(P) \supseteq failures_\perp(Q) \land divergences(P) \supseteq divergences(Q)$$

---

[2]While the theory that allows us to build full CSP models without divergence strictness is complex, this does not mean that such models are hard to apply. In fact the difficulties only really appear for infinite-state processes rather than the finite-state ones that FDR can handle, and the model with failures and non-strict divergences could and should be implemented in FDR. The value given by this model to the token ring routing system with internal actions hidden is very natural: see Sect. 12.4.

div is the *least* refined process under $\sqsubseteq_{FD}$: **div** $\sqsubseteq_{FD} P$ for all P.

The corresponding notion $=_{FD}$ of equivalence in the failures-divergences model is the standard notion of equivalence for CSP processes in most of its literature.[3]

Even though most of the correct processes one ever writes are divergence-free, we often need to be able to demonstrate that this is indeed so for ones we have constructed. This is why we need to go to the trouble of including divergence in our model of refinement: if it were not there, we would have no way of telling if a process could diverge or not.

It is only when we know the failures and divergences of a process that we can definitively tell whether it is *deterministic* or not. A process P is defined to be deterministic if, and only if, *divergences*$(P) = \emptyset$ and $s^\frown\langle a\rangle \in traces(P) \Rightarrow (s, \{a\}) \notin failures(P)$. In other words, it cannot diverge, and never has the choice of both accepting and refusing any action. It turns out that the deterministic processes are exactly the maximal ones under $\sqsubseteq_{FD}$—the processes that have no proper refinements. $P \sqsubseteq_{FD} Q$ means, rather precisely, that Q is more deterministic than P. Of the processes in Fig. 6.1, only P_1 is deterministic (as any process with a deterministic transition system is, though the reverse is not true).

There is an important difference between deterministic and nondeterministic processes when it comes to *testability*. Suppose we have tested to be sure that process P will perform some trace s that was part of its design specification. If P is deterministic, then if we put P into use and feed it the events of s in turn, it will certainly accept them. But this is not true if P is nondeterministic. Exactly the same is true for requirements that P *does not* perform certain events after traces. In some sense, "deterministic" means the same as "reliably testable".

We will discover more about the class of deterministic processes in later chapters, particularly Sect. 10.5.

The unique fixed point (UFP) rule is valid with respect to both failures and failures-divergences equivalence.

We have referred to the *traces model* $\mathcal{T}$: a structure that contains all the sets of traces that are non-empty and prefix-closed. The traces model consists of all representations of CSP processes as sets of traces. It will not surprise the reader that there are also *stable failures* $\mathcal{F}$ and *failures-divergences* $\mathcal{N}$ models of CSP, respectively containing all the representations of CSP processes in these two forms. The structures of these models are not needed for an introductory course on CSP, and so we defer the more technical details of them to Part II. In the rest of this chapter we will confine ourselves to understanding some of the additional possibilities that the new notions of refinement offer us in specification and in running FDR.

6.2 Failures and Divergences in Specifications

The three levels of refinement that we have seen to date—traces, failures, and failures-divergences—were the only refinement options available in all pre-2009

---

[3]Though one needs to be careful with unboundedly nondeterministic ones.

versions of FDR, and remain the most important and intuitive for practical purposes.[4] Indeed, FDR stands for *Failures-Divergences Refinement*.

The two modes of refinement introduced in this chapter, $\sqsubseteq_F$ and $\sqsubseteq_{FD}$, allow us to formulate stronger specifications of processes than are possible with traces refinement, since we can now make assertions about what a process can refuse and when it must not diverge, as well as what traces it can perform. Just as with trace specifications, they can be formulated either as behavioural specifications or, directly, as their characteristic processes. Thus deadlock freedom (either as a failures or failures-divergences specification) becomes the behavioural specification

$$\forall s.(s, \Sigma) \notin failures(P) \quad \text{or} \quad ref \neq \Sigma$$

In other words, P can never refuse all events; so there is always something it can do. The right-hand form extends the convention seen on p. 36, that tr represents an arbitrary trace, to the assumption that (tr, ref) is an arbitrary failure (i.e., tr and ref are respectively identifiers used to represent a trace and a refusal within a logical expression, which thus becomes a predicate on failures). tr does not appear in the above simply because this specification is independent of traces. The characteristic process of the above deadlock specification is DF_Σ, where

$$DF_A = \sqcap\{a \to DF_A \mid a \in A\}$$

DF_Σ is, of course, the most nondeterministic deadlock-free process for, just as over the traces model, the characteristic process of any behavioural specification is equivalent to the nondeterministic choice of all processes that meet it. In similar vein, the most nondeterministic divergence-free process (in the failures-divergences model) is *Chaos*.

A specification can be general like the above, can be highly specific and attempt to define all the behaviour of one's implementation—for example if Q is a deterministic process such as B_0^2 on p. 101 then $Q \sqsubseteq_{FD} P$ is equivalent to $P =_{FD} Q$ and so P must be a complete description of intended functional behaviour—or can be somewhere in between. A good example of the latter is the *buffer* specification.

We have already stated the trace specification of a buffer: an $(a \Rightarrow b)$-buffer is a process with alphabet $\{|a, b|\}$, where the types of a and b are the same, where for all traces tr we have $tr \downarrow b \leq tr \downarrow a$: the outputs are an initial subsequence of the inputs. As with other trace specifications, this admits some unlikely processes such as

- *STOP* which does nothing
- $Sink = a?x \to Sink$ which accepts inputs but never produces an output.
- *COPY* $\sqcap$ *STOP* which can choose to be a well-behaved buffer or do nothing.

Every trace that these processes perform is a legitimate behaviour for another process that is obviously a well-behaved buffer; indeed they are all traces of the infinite buffer processes $B_{\langle\rangle}^\infty$. Where these processes fall down is that they may fail to perform actions we would expect of a reasonable buffer. We can therefore extend our specification to failures. In English:

---

[4]For details of the more advanced models now additionally supported, see Chaps. 11 and 12.

(a) All an $(a \Rightarrow b)$-buffer does is input on a and output on b. It correctly copies all its inputs to its output channel, without loss or reordering.
(b) Whenever it is empty (i.e., it has output everything it has input) then it must accept any input.
(c) Whenever it is non-empty, then it cannot refuse to output.

More formally:

(a) $s \in traces(B) \Rightarrow s \in \{|a,b|\}^* \wedge s \downarrow b \leq s \downarrow a$
(b) $(s, X) \in failures(B) \wedge s \downarrow b = s \downarrow a \Rightarrow X \cap \{|a|\} = \emptyset$
(c) $(s, X) \in failures(B) \wedge s \downarrow b < s \downarrow a \Rightarrow \{|b|\} \not\subseteq X$

Of the examples above, *STOP* and *COPY* ⊓ *STOP* both fail (b), since on the empty trace they can refuse to input. *Sink* fails (c), since after $\langle a.0 \rangle$ it refuses the whole of $\{|b|\}$.

Judged in stable failures, the above specification still has an obvious hole: it permits some divergent processes such as **div**. Judged in failures and divergences, it actually forbids all divergent processes as a side-effect of divergence strictness: since **div** has all traces, some of them necessarily fail (i), for example. However, it is certainly better to state the absence of divergence explicitly, so the specification of a buffer becomes a *failures-divergences* one with the addition of the condition $divergences(B) = \emptyset$. This can also be written in the slightly enigmatic form $false(div)$ where div stands for an arbitrary divergent trace in the same way that tr does for a trace. This is exactly equivalent to saying that $BUFF_{\langle\rangle} \sqsubseteq_{FD} B$ (see p. 12).

It is this specification that the buffer laws in Chap. 5 of TPC refer to. While BL1 and BL5 are true for the traces specification as well, several of the others are not.

It should be noted that $BUFF_{\langle\rangle}$ is an infinite-state process and therefore cannot be used as a specification in FDR. It is frequently possible, in a given implementation, to bound how much buffering a system provides. In these cases we can often use finite-state approximations to the buffer specification. In different cases it is useful to have either over-approximations or under-approximations. The following are under-approximations that are refined by $BUFF_{\langle\rangle}$:

$$WBUFF_{\langle\rangle}^N = left?x \rightarrow WBUFF_{\langle x \rangle}^N$$
$$WBUFF_{s^\frown\langle a\rangle}^N = ((left?x \rightarrow (WBUFF_{\langle x\rangle^\frown s^\frown\langle a\rangle}^N \lessdot \#s < N-1 \rhd \mathbf{div}))$$
$$\sqcap STOP)$$
$$\Box\, right!a \rightarrow WBUFF_s^N$$

This behaves like a buffer so long as it has never contained more than N items. As soon as it has contained $N + 1$ things it breaks. (This version is for $\mathcal{N}$; for $\mathcal{F}$ or $\mathcal{T}$ you should replace **div** by *Chaos*.)

Any process that is not a buffer will fail to refine one of these processes. The corresponding finite-state *over*-approximations are the processes $BUFF_{\langle\rangle}^N$ seen on p. 14. Any finite-state process that is a buffer will refine one of these.

Divergence checking uses a completely different search strategy (depth-first search, usually abbreviated DFS) from the one that FDR uses. It does not scale as well to very large checks. Therefore $\sqsubseteq_{FD}$ checks are sometimes slower, and need to be kept smaller, as explained in Sect. 16.3.1. In practice we often know that processes are divergence-free for independent reasons. The most common use of failures checks is for proving failures-divergences refinements $P \sqsubseteq_{FD} Q$ for processes P and Q that are already known (or are assumed) to be divergence-free. Indeed, at the time of writing, the author almost always structures a substantial failures-divergences check this way. We will see some more sophisticated circumstances where one has to check $\sqsubseteq_F$ rather than $\sqsubseteq_{FD}$ in Sect. 6.5 and later chapters.

The fact that divergence checking uses DFS can be useful when performing traces checks where we expect there to be a significant number of counter-example traces. See Sect. 8.6.

Exercise 6.1 What failures-divergences refinements hold between the following processes: div, $Chaos_{\{a,b\}}$, $Chaos_{\{a\}}$, $DF_{\{a,b\}}$, $RUN_{\{a,b\}}$, $RUN_{\{a\}}$, $STOP$, $a \to div$ and $a \to STOP$? Which of them are deterministic?

Exercise 6.2 Formulate a behavioural failures specification (using the variables tr and ref as discussed above) which asserts that a process must always accept the event a if the number of as in tr is less than that of bs in tr. What is the characteristic process (i) on the assumption that $\Sigma = \{a, b\}$ and (ii) on the assumption that it is larger?

Exercise 6.3 Repeat the last part of Exercise 5.14 using the buffer specification referred to in this section (namely whether the system that combines groups of bits into nibbles and then unpacks them is a buffer of bits).

Exercise 6.4 Create the failures-divergences specification of a *bag*: a process that inputs data on one channel and outputs it on another, like a buffer, but does not guarantee to preserve order.

6.3 Ungranted Requests and the Limits of Failures

If either the alphabet Σ is finite, or the processes we are considering are finitely nondeterministic, then every failure (s, X) can be extended to one with a maximal refusal: (s, X') where $X' \supseteq X$ and $X'' \supset X' \Rightarrow (s, X'') \notin failures(P)$. Maximal failures represent the smallest-possible offers that a process can make. In the case of a deadlocked process the maximal refusal is obviously Σ. Think about the problem of defining an *ungranted request* as described on p. 75: one process P asking another (Q) to communicate with it, and the latter refusing. The interface of P and Q is some subset I of Σ.

The strange thing is that, though this is an intuitively obvious idea, it is not that easy to discover how to describe it in failures. Life is easier if P and Q are deterministic, since then the refusals are of impossible events. An ungranted request from P to Q can then be identified with a maximum failure (s, X) of P such that $I \nsubseteq X$, and a failure (t, Y) of Q where $s \upharpoonright I = t \upharpoonright I$, and where $I \subseteq X \cup Y$. In other words, the unique set of events (because it is deterministic) that P offers after s has members in I, but Q is in a state where it refuses them all.

It is sufficient for the purposes of deadlock analysis to carry this definition over to the case of nondeterministic processes. This is true because extending all refusals to be maximal refusals certainly will not eliminate any deadlock.

However, in a wider sense, only looking at the potential for ungranted requests when P has a maximal refusal may be a bit limiting. It implies, for example, that the process $(?x : A \rightarrow P) \sqcap STOP$ cannot have an ungranted request (initially) to another process, because its unique maximal refusal Σ contains the interface I.

The fascinating answer to this conundrum is that it is possible to specify (absence of) ungranted requests properly for deadlock checking in failures, but that a more general specification requires a finer model. We will discuss this further in Sect. 11.2.3, but to get an idea of why we may need to go beyond the failures model, consider the process $(?x : A \rightarrow P) \rhd STOP$. This has identical failures to the process in the previous paragraph, but its offer (if any) of A is far weaker as it is from an unstable state—too weak to be regarded a *request*, perhaps?

Exercise 6.5 Recall the concept of a *strong conflict* from Sect. 4.2.1: a process P having an ungranted request to Q when P has now possible communications possible other than with Q. Give a maximal-failures-style specification of this.

6.4 Avoiding Divergence

We have already seen (in Sect. 4.2) a number of methods for avoiding deadlock in networks. It is interesting to examine whether we can find similar methods for avoiding livelock, in other words the sort of divergence that arises from an infinite sequence of hidden communications in a network. There seems little reason to suspect that the methods will be similar, since while deadlock arises from lack of activity, livelock represents an over-abundance of it.

We give a single technique here, which works in a large percentage of cases. It, like one of the rules given earlier for deadlock, assumes that there is a partial order on the nodes in our network such that any two processes that interact are related to each other. The rule is then both simple and obviously correct.

Order rule for divergence freedom   Suppose we have an ordered network as described above in which all internal communication (i.e. all events in the alphabet of at least two processes) is hidden, and no other. Suppose further that each component process is divergence free when all communications with processes less than it in the partial order are hidden. Then the network is divergence free.

This can be proved by mathematical induction. It is true for networks of size 1, and if we have a network S of size n, let S' be the same network but with an arbitrary node P that is maximal in the order removed (with the same alphabets for all processes, and all its internal communications not with P hidden). S' is divergence-free by induction, and so if there is a divergence in S there must be an infinite number of communications between S' and P in the pre-hidden behaviour of S that creates the divergence. All these communications are between P and processes less than it. The assumption we made about P in the rule means that if one of its infinite traces has an infinite number of such communications, then it also has an infinite number of external, unsynchronised communications because it is maximal. Thus the pre-hiding trace of S also contains these, contradicting the assumption that hiding the synchronised events gives a divergence.

Think of a chain of buffer processes connected together by link parallel. A buffer can input infinitely without outputting, but it cannot output infinitely without in-putting. Thus the obvious order in which the first member of the chain is *greatest* works for the above rule (proving divergence freedom), but the opposite order does not.

Exercise 6.6 Let S be a connected network in which no process can communicate infinitely without an infinite number of communications with *each* of its neighbours. Suppose (at least) one member of the network must communicate infinitely exter-nally in any infinite trace. Show that the network (with hiding as in the rule above) is divergence free.

6.5 Abstraction by Hiding

It is often useful to be able to understand what a process P looks like to a user who can only see a subset of P's alphabet. This can be because we want to understand—and specify—the interface that P offers to a given neighbour, or for a number of other reasons that we will see below.

We would like to form an *abstraction* of P into any subset A of its alphabet. There are two obvious ways of doing this, given what we have already seem: one prevents the process from doing any event in the complement of A, and the other lets them happen freely:

$$P \underset{\Sigma \setminus A}{\|} STOP \quad \text{and} \quad P \setminus (\Sigma \setminus A)$$

Naturally, these give very different answers, and so cannot both be correct all the time. What they actually represent are opposing views of how "concealed" users of P who interact with it in $\Sigma \setminus A$ behave while we are watching P in A. The first says that the concealed user never does anything: he prevents P from performing any action in $\Sigma \setminus A$. The second says that he is always happy to let P perform any action it likes in this set.

In reality the situation may well be somewhere in between: the concealed user can offer any selection of actions he likes to P, anywhere from offering none to offering all.

In trying to formulate what P looks like in A, the right answer is usually to bring in the *most nondeterministic* view of the concealed user. This corresponds to treating the concealed user as $Chaos_{\Sigma \setminus A}$, the most nondeterministic divergence-free process using the events $\Sigma \setminus A$. The resulting model of how P looks to a user only able to see A is

$$(P \parallel_{\Sigma \setminus A} Chaos_{\Sigma \setminus A}) \setminus (\Sigma \setminus A)$$

This is called the *lazy abstraction* of P: $\mathcal{L}_{\Sigma \setminus A}(P)$, because, while the concealed user can perform any action in its alphabet $\Sigma \setminus A$, it does not have to and can refuse anything. In the case where the concealed user interacts with the CSP process P in the standard way, this is the correct way to form the expected view.

For example, consider the processes $P1 = a \rightarrow b \rightarrow P1$ and $P2 = a \rightarrow P2 \,\square\, b \rightarrow P2$, and suppose we want to form the abstracted view of a user who can see only a. Intuitively we might think that the abstracted views of these two processes are the same, since in each case the process seems to be able to do an infinite sequence of as.

That is not, however, true since there is nothing to force the concealed user controlling b to allow any of them. This does not matter for $P2$, since this process can perform any number of as without a b, but

$$\mathcal{L}_{\{b\}}(P1) = a \rightarrow Chaos_{\{a\}}$$

Lazy abstraction is assumed not to introduce any divergence even if the formulation $(P \parallel_{X} Chaos_X) \setminus X$ can: in other words we assume that the concealed user really is lazy. For that reason, lazy abstraction is always calculated over $\mathcal{F}$ on FDR.

Under this assumption, we see that $\mathcal{L}_{\{b\}}(P2) = RUN_{\{a\}}$.

Lazy abstraction is highly relevant to the *controlled error model* for examining the effects of process misbehaviour on overall system behaviour. Recall that in Sect. 4.3 we showed that there were two choices for introducing explicitly faulty components into CSP models: we could either have the faults triggered by nondeterministic choice or by specific events under the imagined control of some demon.

This is a natural situation for process abstraction, since the normal users want to see the behaviour of the resulting system through their own alphabet, not the demon's.

If E is the set of demon events in such a system, then

- $\mathcal{L}_E(System)$ represents the users' view of the complete system on the assumption that the demons get to do whatever they like.
- $\mathcal{L}_E(System \parallel_{E} Limit)$ is, for any process $Limit$ which communicates only in E, the users' view if the demon is restricted to the traces allowed by $Limit$.
- $System \parallel_{E} STOP$ is how the system behaves when no errors are permitted.

So we can, in fact, gain understanding the effects of errors on the overall behaviour of our system with the refinement checks

$$System \parallel_E STOP \sqsubseteq_F \mathcal{L}_E(System)$$

$$System \parallel_E STOP \sqsubseteq_F \mathcal{L}_E(System \parallel_E Limit)$$

In particular, if one of them *succeeds*, then the presence of the errors does not affect the semantics of the process: it is truly *fault tolerant* (in the second case with respect to the given *Limit*). We can take this as the *definition* of fault tolerance.

The reader will find that the first holds for the Alternating Bit Protocol as described (in any of its several implementations) in Sect. 4.3.

We are now in a position to state the second of the two reasonableness criteria for a controlled error model. That is that for each component process with errors, the process $\mathcal{L}_E(C)$ must behave like a natural model of the component with the errors controlled by nondeterminism.

Lazy abstraction is also relevant to computer security, and indeed the first version of it [139] was devised for this application. Imagine that a process P is being used by two users, whom we will call Hugh and Lois. Hugh is working at a high security level, and Lois at a low one. Their alphabets are H and L, that partition Σ. It is natural to specify that Hugh must be unable to transmit information through P to Lois. This is the area known as *non-interference* in security.

If P provides a way in which Hugh *can* transmit information to Lois, this is called a *covert channel*. Covert channels often exist in real systems thanks to contention for resources such as CPU and memory.

Abstraction provides us with a very elegant way of specifying non-interference. If what Lois sees of P actually depends on what Hugh does with P outside her view, then the abstraction she sees must be nondeterministic. After all, if she sees the same deterministic process independent of what he does, he cannot be passing her any information. We can define P to be *lazily independent* with respect to H if and only if $\mathcal{L}_H(P)$ is deterministic.

To see why this specification works, consider the examples $P1$ and $P2$ above with $H = \{b\}$ and $L = \{a\}$. We have seen that $\mathcal{L}_H(P1)$ is nondeterministic. This is correct because here Hugh can send Lois a coded message based on the number of bs he allows. On the other hand $\mathcal{L}_H(P2)$ is deterministic: this again is correct since nothing Hugh can do will change Lois's view of this process – she always gets to perform an a if she wants to.

Suppose Hugh and Lois respectively want to send messages to Henry and Leah, who share their security levels. Consider the network

$$Comm_1 = ((SendH \parallel\!\parallel\!\parallel SendL) \underset{\{|in|\}}{\parallel} Medium) \underset{\{|out|\}}{\parallel} (RecH \parallel\!\parallel\!\parallel RecL)$$

where

$$SendL = send.lois?x \rightarrow in.lois.leah!x \rightarrow SendL$$

$$SendH = send.hugh?x \rightarrow in.hugh.henry!x \rightarrow SendH$$

$$RecL = out.leah?x \rightarrow rec.leah!x \rightarrow RecL$$

$$RecH = out.henry?x \rightarrow rec.henry!x \rightarrow RecH$$

$$Medium = in?s?t?x \rightarrow out!t!x \rightarrow Medium$$

Even though the high-level processes cannot send messages to the low-level ones through this system, it does not satisfy lazy independence. Despite the buffering provided at the two ends, it is possible for the high-level processes to block up the network if Henry refuses to accept the messages that arrive for him. This means that the low-level lazy abstraction is nondeterministic: the low-level processes can detect certain high-level activity via their own messages (including their first) being blocked.

The reader is invited to try out this check on FDR using the files provided. This is a classic example of how resource contention can create a covert channel.

There is a lot more material on abstraction in Chap. 12 of TPC, including:

- Methods for removing the covert channel from the example above.
- A form of abstraction that is more appropriate in cases where the concealed user is assumed not to be able to refuse *output* communications from P to it.
- The links between abstraction, security and *separability*: the property that a process P can be written $P_H \parallel P_L$ where P_H and P_L use only the events of H and L respectively.

One interesting feature of the lazy independence definition of security is that it does not distinguish between the sort of nondeterminism that H can introduce into L's view and the sort of nondeterminism that the process P introduces all by itself. This can mean that it can be over-cautious when P itself is nondeterministic— something that has been the subject of much debate and comment in the academic literature. There is a fascinating parallel with the discussion of ungranted requests above, in that here again is a property which can be specified using failures *exactly* for deterministic P and *approximately* for nondeterministic P. You can read more about this issue (for security) in Sect. 12.4 of TPC.

Exercise 6.7 Let P be any divergence-free process with alphabet $H \cup L$. Show that $P' = P \sqcap Chaos_L$ satisfies the definition of fault tolerance

$$P' \parallel_{H} STOP \sqsubseteq \mathcal{L}_H(P')$$

but need not be secure.[5]

---

[5] There are a number of definitions of 'security' in the literature which would define such P' to be secure for all P, even though if with $P = LEAK = hi?x \rightarrow lo!x \rightarrow LEAK$, for example, you can guarantee that if Hugh communicates anything with P', then Lois gets to hear it.

6.6 Tools

In a number of modes, FDR allows you to choose which model it is use when analysing a process or comparing two. We now understand the three most important ones: Traces, Failures, and Failures/divergences. Failures and failures-divergences can be used in `assert` statements claiming refinements by using [F= and [FD= rather than traces [T=.

FDR has modes for checking determinism, deadlock-freedom and divergence freedom. The corresponding `assert` statements are

```
assert P :[deterministic]
assert P :[deterministic [F]]
assert P :[deadlock-free]
assert P :[deadlock-free [F]]
assert P :[divergence-free]
```

where the two cases with [F] use the stable failures model rather than the standard failures-divergences.

Because the stable failures model does not have strict divergence, checking P and $P \setminus X$ for deadlock freedom with the [F] option will always give the same answer.

Before undertaking a large amount of security checking using the non-interference formulation, the reader is advised to read Chap. 8 and in particular Sect. 8.7.

Chapter 7
Further Operators

7.1 Termination and Sequential Composition

7.1.1 What is Termination?

In many programming languages there is a sequential composition operator: P; Q runs P until it *terminates*, and then runs Q. In CSP we would expect to see all of P's communications until it terminates, and for it then to behave like Q. There is no conceptual problem with this provided we understand just what termination means.

So far we have come across two sorts of processes which can communicate no more: on the one hand, a deadlocked process such as *STOP* or a deadlocked parallel network; on the other, the divergent process **div**. Neither of these can be said to have terminated *successfully*, since both represent error states. Indeed, divergence is in principle undetectable in a finite time in general, as a result of the unsolvability of the halting problem. It is natural to want to associate P; Q with a form of termination which happens positively rather than by default.

The process which terminates immediately will be written *SKIP*. We will think of the act of terminating as producing the special event $\checkmark$ (usually pronounced 'tick'). Thus, *SKIP* can be identified with the process $\checkmark \rightarrow STOP$. You can think of a process communicating $\checkmark$ as saying 'I have terminated successfully'. The identification of termination with an event is often convenient, but the analogy should not be taken too far—for example, $\checkmark$ is always the final event a process performs. $\checkmark$ is not (in this presentation of CSP) a member of Σ—emphasising that it is very special. It is not permitted to introduce $\checkmark$ directly: *SKIP* is the only way it arises; for example the syntax $\checkmark \rightarrow STOP$ used above is illegal because it mentions $\checkmark$. $\Sigma^{\checkmark}$ will denote the extended alphabet $\Sigma \cup \{\checkmark\}$ and $\Sigma^{*\checkmark}$ will denote the set of all possible finite traces that may include $\checkmark$, namely $\{t, t^\smallfrown\langle\checkmark\rangle \mid t \in \Sigma^*\}$. So we have to extend the traces model $\mathcal{T}$ to be all the non-empty, prefix-closed subsets of $\Sigma^{*\checkmark}$.

The trace semantics of these two new constructs are straightforward:

$traces(SKIP) = \{\langle\rangle, \langle\checkmark\rangle\}$

$traces(P; Q) = (traces(P) \cap \Sigma^*) \cup \{s^\smallfrown t \mid s^\smallfrown\langle\checkmark\rangle \in P, t \in traces(Q)\}$

A.W. Roscoe, *Understanding Concurrent Systems*, Texts in Computer Science,
DOI 10.1007/978-1-84882-258-0_7, © Springer-Verlag London Limited 2010

Notice that the $\checkmark$ of the *SKIP* in *SKIP*; *P* is hidden from the environment—this simply means that we cannot see where the join occurs from the outside, so that we do not confuse the occurrence of the first $\checkmark$ with overall termination. Because of this concealment parts of the theory of sequential composition bear some similarity to that of hiding and, in particular, it turns the final $\checkmark$ of the first process into a τ (invisible action).

We regard $\checkmark$ as an event that, while visible, is not controllable by the environment. So while events in Σ only happen when the environment is happy to perform them, $\checkmark$ is a signal from the process to the environment. It is therefore halfway in nature between a member of Σ and τ, which is neither controllable nor visible to the environment.

Over the traces model *SKIP*; $P = P = P$; *SKIP* for all P, and of course we would like this law to hold in general.

$$P; SKIP = P \qquad\qquad\qquad\qquad\qquad \langle ;\text{-unit-r}\rangle \;\; (7.1)$$

$$SKIP; P = P \qquad\qquad\qquad\qquad\qquad \langle ;\text{-unit-l}\rangle \;\; (7.2)$$

In contrast, *STOP*; $P = STOP$, since *STOP* does not terminate; it merely comes to an ungraceful halt. Similarly **div**; $P = \mathbf{div}$, and in fact $Q; P = Q$ whenever Q is a process that never communicates $\checkmark$.

A formal tabulation of the laws of these new constructs is delayed to later in this book. However, we would expect ; (sequential composition) to be associative

$$P; (Q; R) = (P; Q); R \qquad\qquad\qquad\qquad \langle ;\text{-assoc}\rangle \;\; (7.3)$$

and distributive, and

$$(?x : A \to P); Q = ?x : A \to (P; Q) \qquad (*)$$

This last 'law' brings up an interesting point in the interpretation of 'state' identifiers in CSP processes, the identifiers that represent objects input or used in parameterised recursions such as *COUNT* or B^∞. For consider the 'identity'

$$(?x : A \to SKIP); x \to STOP = ?x : A \to (SKIP; (x \to STOP))$$

In the right-hand side, it is quite clear that the second x must be the same event as the first, while on the left-hand side this would require the value of x communicated first to be remembered outside the prefix-choice construct that introduced it, and across the sequential composition ;. This raises the important question of how the values and scopes of identifiers are to be interpreted. The real question we need to resolve in order to decide this is whether CSP is an *imperative* language, where the value of an identifier can be modified (and the input $?x : A$ is taken to modify an existing value), or a *declarative* language, where it cannot. We take the declarative view that a construct like $?x : A \to P$ creates a new identifier called x to hold the input value in P and that this value is not remembered once P has terminated, since we have left x's *scope*. An identifier gets its value at the point where it is declared and keeps the same value throughout that scope. If there are any other identifiers called x created by input or otherwise within P, then these simply create a hole in scope in the same way as in many programming languages. Thus, the final x in the term

$$?x : A \to ((?x : A \to SKIP); (x \to STOP))$$

will always be the one created by the first input.

It is this decision which allows us to identify all terminations with the single event $\checkmark$, and also allows us to avoid the question of how an assignable state is shared over a parallel construct.

In conclusion, equation $(*)$ above is only valid if the term Q does not contain an unbound (i.e., free) reference to an identifier called x. If it does, then it would simply be necessary to change the name of the bound identifier so that it no longer clashes with ones free in Q. So the step law of sequential composition is

$$(?x : A \to P); Q = ?x : A \to (P; Q) \quad [x \notin fv(Q)] \qquad \langle ;\text{-step}\rangle \ (7.4)$$

In examples, sequential composition can be used to improve the modularity of descriptions – allowing one to separate out different phases of behaviour. It also permits us to express some definitions finitely which normally require infinite mutual recursion. Recall the infinite mutual recursion defining $COUNT_n$ for $n \in \mathbb{N}$. There is a very clear sense in which this describes an infinite-state system, for all the different values that n can take lead to essentially different $COUNT_n$. We can simulate this behaviour using sequential composition as follows:

$$ZERO = up \to POS; ZERO, \quad \text{where}$$
$$POS = up \to POS; POS$$
$$\qquad \Box \ down \to SKIP$$

The intuition here is that POS is a process that terminates as soon as it has communicated one more $down$s than ups. Thus $ZERO$, which is intended to behave like $COUNT_0$, initially only accepts an up, and returns to that state as soon as the number of subsequent $down$s has brought the overall tally into balance.

The algebraic laws of $;$ and $SKIP$ discussed above, together with $\langle\Box\text{-step}\rangle$, allow us to prove by UFP[1] that the process $ZERO$ defined earlier is equivalent to $COUNT_0$. To do this we prove that the vector of processes $\underline{Z} = \langle Z_n \mid n \in \mathbb{N}\rangle$, defined

$$Z_0 = ZERO \quad \text{and} \quad Z_{n+1} = POS; Z_n$$

(an inductive definition rather than a recursive one), has the property that $Z_n = COUNT_n$ for all n. We will demonstrate that $\underline{Z}$ is a fixed point of the constructive

---

[1]It was actually this equivalence, claimed but not proved by Hoare, that inspired the author to discover the principles of constructiveness and unique fixed points for CSP in 1979.

recursion defining the $COUNT_n$, proving this claim. Trivially $Z_0 = up \to POS$; $Z_0 = up \to Z_1$, and

$$Z_{n+1} = (up \to POS; POS$$
$$\square\, down \to SKIP); Z_n$$

$$= (up \to POS; POS; Z_n)$$
$$\square\, (down \to SKIP; Z_n)$$

$$= (up \to POS; POS; Z_n)$$
$$\square\, (down \to Z_n)$$

$$= up \to Z_{n+2}$$
$$\square\, down \to Z_n$$

Iteration

Now that we have a sequential composition operator it is natural to want ways of repeating a process. The simplest repetition operator is infinite iteration: P^* means the repetition of P for ever with no way of escaping. This is not a construct that makes sense in many programming languages, since in a standard language an in-finitely repeated program would simply send one's computer into a useless loop (divergence). In CSP, of course, a process is measured by what it communicates as it goes along, so that the definition

$$P^* = P; P^*$$

makes sense. For example, $(a \to SKIP)^*$ is simply a process that communicates an infinite sequence of as; it is indistinguishable from $\mu p.a \to p$. We can similarly write

$$COPY = (left?x \to right!x \to SKIP)^*$$

However, the declarative semantics of identifiers means that no information can be 'remembered' from an input in one P to a later one in P^*. Thus a two-place buffer cannot be written as neatly: the best we can do is to create a two-place temporary buffer that terminates when emptied:

$$TB = left?x \to TB'(x)$$
$$TB'(x) = right!x \to SKIP$$
$$\square\, left?y \to right!x \to TB'(y)$$
$$IterBuff_2 = TB^*$$

Because of the way the values x and y are intertwined in this definition, there is no hope of writing TB or $TB'(x)$ as an iteration. To do so we would require an external place to store values: see Exercise 7.2.

The declarative semantics also means that there can be no direct analogue of a WHILE loop: this depends on being able to evaluate a boolean whose value changes with the state of the process—something that makes no sense when an identifier's value does not change within its scope.

We can, however, use CSP to model WHILE loops, assignments and other imperative constructs by running the control state of a program (performing actions like reading and writing variables) in *parallel* with a separate process that holds the variable state—probably implemented as an interleaved set of processes holding the values of individual variables. In this model, the CSP ; operator can represent sequential composition within the control state, since no variable values need to be passed across the ;.

For example, the program *WHILE i > 0 DO i := i − 1* could be implemented as the parallel composition of the processes

$$VAR_i(x) = read.i!x \rightarrow VAR_i(x) \;\square\; write.i?y \rightarrow VAR_i(y)$$

$$S0 = read.i?x \rightarrow ((Ass; S0) \triangleleft i > 0 \triangleright SKIP)$$

$$Ass = read.i?x \rightarrow write.i!(x − 1) \rightarrow SKIP$$

with $VAR_i(x)$ initialised with any integer.

Chapter 18 shows just how far this idea can be taken, as it creates a compiler, actually written in CSP_M, that generates CSP implementations of multiple imperative programs interacting concurrently with a set of shared variables, implemented very like the simple example above.

Exercise 7.1 Define a process *PHOLE* representing a pigeon-hole: it can communicate *empty* when empty, when it will also accept *in?x* and become full. When full it can only accept *out.x* for the appropriate x, which empties it. You should give both a definition as an ordinary recursion and one as Q^*, where Q contains no recursion.

Show that the two processes you have defined are equivalent.

Exercise 7.2 Find a process P such that the two-place buffer equals

$$\left(P^* \underset{\{|in,out,empty|\}}{\|} PHOLE \right) \setminus \{|in, out, empty|\}$$

and P contains no form of recursion. [*Hint: P should, on each of its cycles, communicate first with its slave.*]

Exercise 7.3 The recursive definition of *POS* and *ZERO* can be modified easily to represent, instead, an unbounded *stack* process. The process S_x behaves like a temporary stack containing (only) the value x (i.e., it can have any value pushed onto it, or x popped off it) and terminates when all its contents are removed; while *Empty* is an empty stack which never terminates.

Define an unbounded, tail recursive, stack process $Stack_{\langle\rangle}$ as a parameterised recursion very like B_s^∞, which behaves like *Empty*. Prove $Empty = Stack_{\langle\rangle}$, modelling your proof on the one that *ZERO* is equivalent to $COUNT_0$.

·

7.1.2 Distributed Termination

Having introduced the concept of termination we have to understand how it relates to the other CSP operators, and in particular the parallel operators. If we treated $\checkmark$ like any other event, then we would say that $P\ {}_X\|_Y\ Q$ has the following cases for determining termination:

- If $\checkmark \notin X \cup Y$ then it can never terminate.
- If $\checkmark \in X \setminus Y$ then it will terminate whenever P does.
- If $\checkmark \in Y \setminus X$ then it will terminate whenever Q does.
- If $\checkmark \in X \cap Y$ then it terminates when both P and Q do.

The middle two of these are somewhat problematic, for they leave behind the question of what to do with the other process, which has not terminated. We might assert that it is closed down by some powerful mechanism which, if we are really expecting a distributed parallel implementation, seems to have to act instantaneously over a distance. On the other hand, the other process might continue, creating the embarrassment of a system which communicates after 'terminating'. Realising that termination is really something that the environment observes rather than controls, the first case (and the non-terminating halves of the second and third) cannot realistically prevent the arguments from terminating, but may fail to report this $\checkmark$ to the outer environment. Given this observation, there is really no sensible use of the first item ($\checkmark \notin X \cup Y$) above, since all that it can achieve is to turn what would have been termination into deadlock.

The route we take is to assert that the final clause always holds implicitly: there is no need to include $\checkmark$ in the alphabets X or Y, for after all $\checkmark$ is not a member of Σ, but the combination $P\ {}_X\|_Y\ Q$ always behaves as though it were in both. In other words, a parallel combination terminates when all of the combined processes terminate. This is known as *distributed termination*. This reading makes it sound as though the various processes have to synchronise on termination, as they do on normal events in $X \cap Y$. In fact, the best way of thinking about distributed termination is that all of the processes are allowed to terminate when they want to, and that the overall combination terminates when the last one does. The fact that termination is the last thing a process does means that these two views are consistent with each other: in $P\ {}_X\|_Y\ Q$, neither of P and Q can communicate when it has terminated but the other has not.

This means, for example, that if P is any process, $P\ {}_\Sigma\|_\emptyset\ SKIP = P$.

If A is a set of events which we wish to communicate in any order and then terminate, then this can be expressed

$$\big\|_{a \in A} (a \rightarrow SKIP, \{a\})$$

The principle of distributed termination is extended to all other parallel operators. The view that distributed termination means waiting for all processes to terminate, rather than actively synchronising $\checkmark$s fits far better with the notion that $\|\|$ has distributed termination than the view that has both sides synchronising on $\checkmark$.

Over the traces model, the definition of synchronous parallel is not changed by distributed termination, and the definition of $traces(P \, _X\|_Y \, Q)$ is the same as if $\checkmark$ were added to both X and Y, as we would expect from the definition above. The definition of $traces(P \parallel\!\!\parallel Q)$ becomes

$$\{interleave(s, t) \mid s \in \Sigma^* \cap traces(P), t \in \Sigma^* \cap traces(Q)\}$$

$$\cup \{u^\frown\langle\checkmark\rangle \mid s^\frown\langle\checkmark\rangle \in traces(P), t^\frown\langle\checkmark\rangle \in traces(Q) \wedge u \in interleave(s, t)\}$$

For $P \parallel Q$, the simplest definition is just to add $\checkmark$ to the set of synchronised events in the trace-level definition $s \underset{X}{\|} t$, though it is also possible to re-work that into an equivalent form that explicitly allows one process to terminate before the other.

The fact that $\checkmark$ is being interpreted differently from other events—for example in its finality—means that we must protect it from confusion with other events. This is helped by our assumption that $\checkmark \notin \Sigma$, but we should explicitly mention that $\checkmark$ may not be hidden by the usual hiding operator, and nor may it be affected by renaming. Any renaming affects only members of Σ, and implicitly maps $\checkmark$ and only $\checkmark$ to $\checkmark$.

If P is a $\checkmark$-free process then $P \underset{\Sigma}{\|} RUN_\Sigma = P$: this is because RUN_Σ is happy to agree with every event P performs. But $RUN_\Sigma = ?x : \Sigma \to RUN_\Sigma$ can never terminate, so its parallel composition with P does not. So the law $P \underset{\Sigma}{\|} RUN_\Sigma = P$ fails for every P that can perform $\checkmark$. We cannot fix this by replacing RUN_Σ with $\mu p.((?x : \Sigma \to p) \,\square\, SKIP)$ since, as discussed above, this process can at any time refuse any member of Σ by simply opting to terminate.

There is a straightforward, but not especially elegant, solution to the problem posed in the previous paragraph. Add an element $tick$ to Σ that does not appear in P. Then $P; tick \to SKIP$ is a process that behaves like P except that whenever P would have terminated, this process offers the controllable event $tick$ and terminates only after the environment accepts it. The process

$$PU = (?x : (\Sigma \setminus \{tick\}) \to PU) \,\square\, tick \to SKIP$$

then PU has the properties

$$P; tick \to SKIP = (P; tick \to SKIP) \underset{\Sigma}{\|} PU \quad \text{and}$$
$$P = ((P; tick \to SKIP) \underset{\Sigma}{\|} PU) \setminus \{tick\}$$

We will see this construction in action in Sect. 9.4 and Exercise 7.7.

7.1.3 Effects on the Failures-Divergences Model

The introduction of $\checkmark$ means that we have to look carefully at what a process can refuse (immediately) before and after this special event, and similarly at its effect on possible divergence.

The easy part is what goes on after $\checkmark$: nothing. We have already largely implied this in the revision of $\mathcal{T}$, since that says that no visible events can appear. Perhaps the best way of thinking about this is that once a process has communicated $\checkmark$, we are no longer interested in it. The logical conclusion is that we do not bother to record refusal and divergence information after $\checkmark$, but we can also choose any completely standardised treatment of them. Therefore, to avoid having a third component (terminated traces) in the failures-divergences model, we declare

- If $s^\smallfrown\langle\checkmark\rangle$ is a trace, then $(s^\smallfrown\langle\checkmark\rangle, X)$ is a failure for all $X \subseteq \Sigma^\checkmark$.
- $divergences(P) \subseteq \Sigma^*$.

We want to distinguish between the processes $SKIP$ and $SKIP \sqcap STOP$, even though they have the same traces. The first one certainly terminates successfully, the second one only might. If we put them in sequence with a second process P, the first one gives P, while the second might deadlock immediately whatever P is. The obvious way to make this distinction is to include $\checkmark$ in refusal sets: then the failure $(\langle\rangle, \{\checkmark\})$ belongs to $SKIP \sqcap STOP$ (because it belongs to $STOP$) but not $SKIP$, which cannot refuse to terminate. Thus, when recording a process's failures we will take note of when it can refuse to terminate as well as other events.

It turns out, however, that $\checkmark$ is not quite on a par with other potential members of refusal sets (i.e., ones that are members of Σ). This is because, as discussed earlier in this chapter, $\checkmark$ is not something a process needs its environment to agree to: it is simply a signal to the environment that it is terminating. Thus no process will ever offer its environment the choice of $\checkmark$ or events in Σ. In other words, any process that can terminate must be able (on the appropriate trace) to refuse every event other than $\checkmark$; if a process has the trace $s^\smallfrown\langle\checkmark\rangle$, it has the failure (s, Σ). This is discussed further in Chaps. 9 and 10.

The unnatural process $SKIP \,\square\, Q$—the subject of law $\langle\square\text{-}SKIP\text{ resolve}\rangle$ (13.17) which declares it to equal $Q \vartriangleright SKIP$—apparently offers its environment the choice of $\checkmark$ and the initial events of Q, in contravention of the above principle. In fact, since the environment's cooperation is not required for the event $\checkmark$, this process can decide to terminate whatever the environment. In other words, it can refuse all events other than $\checkmark$ despite the way it is built. For example, $SKIP \,\square\, a \to STOP$ (which $\langle\square\text{-}SKIP\text{ resolve}\rangle$ identifies with $(a \to STOP) \vartriangleright SKIP$) has failures

$$\{(\langle\rangle, X) \mid \checkmark \notin X\} \cup \{(\langle a\rangle, X), (\langle\checkmark\rangle, X) \mid X \subseteq \Sigma^\checkmark\}$$

The precise way in which failures are extracted from a process's transition system, allowing for possible $\checkmark$ actions, is described in Sect. 9.5.1. See Sect. 10.4 for full details of the way the failures-divergences semantics of processes composes, including taking account of the $SKIP \,\square\, Q$ issue.

7.2 Interrupting Processes

With our present range of operators, once a process has communicated with the external environment, it remains alive until it $STOP$s or terminates ($\checkmark$), although some or all of its Σ actions may get blocked by other processes. In this section we will see two ways in which one process can shut down and another one take over.

The first is called the *interrupt* operator: $P \bigtriangleup Q$ behaves like P except that at any time Q may perform one of its initial events and take over. You can think of this as being like $P \square Q$ except that when P performs an event from Σ the options of Q do not vanish. The only time that the options of Q vanish is if P performs $\checkmark$.

In practice, Q will almost always take the form $?x : E \rightarrow Q(x)$, where E is some set of events distinct from those used by P that the interrupting process is designed to handle. If, however, some event is possible both for P and Q, the choice of which occurs is nondeterministic, as it is with $\square$.

For example, if *reset* is not an event of P, then

$$resettable(P) = P \bigtriangleup (reset \rightarrow resettable(P))$$

behaves like P except that each time the event *reset* occurs, it moves back to its initial state.

$\bigtriangleup$ is a distributive operator whose step law is given

$$(?x : A \rightarrow P(x)) \bigtriangleup (?x : B \rightarrow Q(x))$$
$$= ?x : A \cup B \rightarrow ((P(x) \bigtriangleup Q) \sqcap Q(x)$$
$$\triangleleft x \in A \cap B \triangleright$$
$$(P(x) \bigtriangleup Q) \triangleleft x \in A \triangleright Q(x)) \qquad\qquad \langle \bigtriangleup\text{-step}\rangle \; (7.5)$$

where $Q = ?x : B \rightarrow Q(x)$.

It follows that $P \bigtriangleup STOP = STOP \bigtriangleup P = P$ for all P.

It is divergence-strict in both arguments, as $P \square Q$ is. This is a little counter-intuitive for the second (Q) argument, since it means that Q can run τs before performing a visible event. This can happen when Q is trying to compute what its initial events are! This gives one reason why the second argument is sometimes restricted (as it was in TPC) to the case where Q is of the form $?x : E \rightarrow Q(x)$ mentioned above.

Its traces are computed:

$$traces(P \bigtriangleup Q) = traces(P) \cup \{s\hat{\ }t \mid s \in traces(P) \cap \Sigma^* \wedge t \in traces(Q)\}$$

One of the most frequent uses of interrupt is to describe what happens when some problem or disaster strikes from the outside of a process. Rather than write the complete process description, bearing in mind that a lightning bolt $\frac{7}{7}$ can strike at any time, for example by adding $\square \frac{7}{7} \rightarrow STOP$ to every state of a process, it is much cleaner and easier to write $P \bigtriangleup \frac{7}{7} \rightarrow STOP$.

We can allow for several different sorts of faults: for example we might think that a smaller power surge $\S$ could leads to a more dangerous fault since it does not kill off the process completely, but lead to it behaving unpredictably: $P \bigtriangleup (\frac{7}{7} \rightarrow STOP \square \S \rightarrow Chaos)$.

Exceptions can occur not only outside a process but also inside it. Some P might have an event such as *error* that it performs when some run-time error such as divide-by-zero occurs. In this case also, we might wish to hand control over to some standard process rather than incorporate error-catching behaviour throughout P's code. The *throw* operator $P \, \Theta_{error} \, Q$ achieves this: whenever *error* occurs in P, P is shut down and Q is started. Clearly we can use any other event as well as *error*.

As a generalisation we can replace *error* by a set of events A, or even a named choice from some A as in $P \, \Theta_{x:A} \, Q(x)$. In the latter case we allow (as implied by the syntax) Q to be a process expression that depends on the identifier x. In the last two cases, P communicating any member of A starts up Q, with the actual value communicated being substituted for x in the last case, as in $?x : A \rightarrow Q(x)$. In describing the throw operator's properties below, we will consider just $P \, \Theta_A \, Q$: this can express the cases $P \, \Theta_a \, Q$ and $P \, \Theta_{x:A} \, Q(x)$.

The most general version can be used where the process P might throw a variety of different run-time errors, and Q's behaviour depends on which occurs.

The throw operator is not only used for error handling: in some sense it can be regarded as a generalised form of sequential composition, where a process P terminates on a choice of ordinary events rather than the signal $\checkmark$. Note, however, that events which trigger the change in control flow are not hidden by the operator, though of course the programmer can choose to hide them using $\setminus A$.

$P \, \Theta_A \, Q$ is a distributive operator that is divergence-strict only in its left-hand argument: it has no need to run Q before any event $a \in A$ occurs. Its step law is

$$(?x : A \rightarrow P(x)) \, \Theta_B \, Q$$

$$= ?x : A \rightarrow (P(x) \, \Theta_B \, Q \lhd x \notin B \rhd Q) \qquad\qquad \langle \Theta_B\text{–step}\rangle \; (7.6)$$

Its traces are calculated:

$$traces(P \, \Theta_A \, Q)$$

$$= \{s \in traces(P) \mid s \in (\Sigma \setminus A)^{*\checkmark}\}$$
$$\cup \{s^\smallfrown\langle a\rangle^\smallfrown t \mid s \in (\Sigma \setminus A)^* \cap traces(P) \wedge a \in A \wedge t \in traces(Q)\}$$

The throw operator is a relatively new addition to CSP. As shown above it has a natural role to play in expressing programming concepts. It also has an important role in CSP's theory, as we will see in Chaps. 9 and 12 (p. 290). An interesting use of it can be found on p. 342.

Exercise 7.4 A certain computer can be turned *on* and behave like the process *RUNNING* (which we do not specify, except that it can accept a software "off" event *soft_off* and turn off at any time). It may also generate *error* events, at which point it enters the state *Blue*, which can only accept the software event *blue*. Fortunately it will, at any time it is on, accept the actual button press *hard_off* and return to its initial *Off* state.

Describe this with an appropriate mixture of interrupt and throw operators.

Exercise 7.5 Suppose that the visible events of the processes P and Q are contained in $A \subseteq \Sigma$ and that neither ever terminates ($\checkmark$). Let $A' = \{a' \mid a \in A\}$ be a subset of Σ disjoint from A (with $a' \neq b'$ if $a \neq b$). Define renamings *prime* which maps a to a' and *unprime* which maps a' and a to a. Find a deterministic process *IntRegT* such that

$$traces(P \triangle Q) = traces(((P \parallel\!\parallel\!\parallel Q[\![prime]\!]) \underset{\Sigma}{\parallel} IntRegT)[\![unprime]\!])$$

This equivalence does not hold if we replace *traces* by (stable) *failures*; why not? How about *divergences* and (strict) *failures*$_\perp$?

Exercise 7.6 Repeat the last exercise for Θ_A: find a process *ThRegT* such that

$$traces(P \, \Theta_A \, Q) = traces(((P \parallel\!\parallel\!\parallel Q[\![prime]\!]) \underset{\Sigma}{\parallel} ThRegT)[\![unprime]\!])$$

and discuss whether this identity still holds for *failures*, *failures*$_\perp$ and *divergences*.

Exercise 7.7 Show that the special form $P \, \Theta_{x:A} \, Q(x)$ can be expressed in terms of other CSP operators including Θ_A and parallel. Do this first for the case where P and all the $Q(x)$ are $\checkmark$-free, and then adapt the construction seen on p. 137 to deal with the general case.

7.3 Tools

The translations of the operators described in this section to CSP_M are largely straightforward:

- *SKIP* and ; are just SKIP and ;.
- $\triangle$ becomes /\.
- Θ_A becomes [| A |>

There is no current support for the indexed form $P \, \Theta_{?x:A} \, Q(x)$, but an equivalent process, for the case where P and all Q(x) are $\checkmark$-free, is

```
(P [| A |> RUN(A)) [|A|] ([] x:A @ x -> Q(x))
```

This lets the member of A that P picks drive the choice of Q(x).

FDR originated before the author proposed the treatment of $\checkmark$ as a *signal* in TPC, as opposed to an ordinary refusable event as it was in earlier treatments of CSP. At the time of writing, FDR has never "caught up," in part due to problems of backwards compatibility. This means that FDR's treatment of termination at present coincides with Hoare's where the law $P = P; SKIP$ does not always hold. The difference between these two approaches is very rarely an issue, because

(a) The difference only shows up when the processes under consideration make an explicit external choice between *SKIP* and other alternatives, as in *SKIP* □ *P*. This is not usually considered good style.

(b) While the internal construction of systems checked with FDR involve SKIP and sequential composition fairly often in their definitions, it is less common for the complete system to have the option of terminating.

(c) There is no difference between the two approaches for the traces model, only for richer ones.

The author hopes that there will soon be an option to set either semantics of termination in FDR.

Even without this, it is still possible to achieve the effect of the √-as-signal semantics, since for all the standard CSP models the √-as-refusable semantics of *P*; *SKIP* are exactly the same as the √-as-signal semantics given in TPC and the present book. So checking Spec; SKIP [X= Impl; SKIP on FDR without such a switch will always give the correct answer as defined in these two books.

Chapter 8
Using FDR

FDR is, at the time of writing, the most important and useful tool for the automatic analysis of systems described in CSP. Indeed it is FDR that makes CSP such a practical tool for the specification, analysis and verification of systems.

This chapter covers, in its first four sections, the basics of understanding how FDR works and how to use it effectively in a straightforward way. It is intended that these sections are studied in parallel with the introductory section of this book: those studying CSP may well want to use FDR from day one, but will not be in a position to understand some of the basic functions of the tool until they have mastered failures and failures-divergence refinement (Chap. 6). Section 8.1 can be read together with Chaps. 1 and 2.

The remaining Sects. 8.5–8.8 cover some other interesting topics in the use of FDR. The last of these four, on compression, is essential for anyone wanting to use FDR seriously, and they all give insight both into how to use FDR successfully and into CSP itself.

The web-site for this book contains an extensive library of CSP scripts. To get to know FDR, the reader is recommended to try—and perhaps modify—some of these, and to implement his or her solutions to exercises. The web-site also contains a number of more extensive practical exercises, most of which have been used in courses at Oxford University.

The primary aim of the exercises in the present chapter is to re-inforce the reader's understanding of how FDR works and interacts with CSP's theory.

8.1 What is FDR?

FDR can be described as a *refinement checker* or *model checker*[1] for CSP. It is a tool for checking properties of processes written in CSP and, when these are not true, giving details of one or more counter-examples.

---

[1] A broad definition of a 'model checker' is any tool which automatically decides whether systems meet their specifications, by somehow exploring all relevant execution paths of the system,

A.W. Roscoe, *Understanding Concurrent Systems*, Texts in Computer Science,
DOI 10.1007/978-1-84882-258-0_8, © Springer-Verlag London Limited 2010

It does not allow you to "run" CSP programs in any conventional way, though there is an associated CSP animator ProBE which allows you to explore how a program behaves. Rather, FDR allows you to make assertions about processes and then explores (if necessary) every possible behaviour of the target process to see if the assertions are true.

FDR operates by loading a script written in the language CSP_M, which is an ASCII syntax for CSP with the addition of a functional programming language. We have already seen the CSP_M versions of the operators introduced in earlier chapters. All the CSP processes, and most objects derived from them, are presented in CSP_M in the present chapter, using this typeface.

Almost all CSP scripts define some processes, and FDR allows you to decide refinement relationships between them, and to check directly whether an individual process is deadlock-free, divergence-free or deterministic. These checks can be set up by choosing the appropriate mode of FDR and then selecting two processes (for refinement) or one (for the other checks) and sometimes a semantic model. Usually, however, checks are pre-loaded thanks to them being included in the CSP_M script via assert statements. The screen shot in Fig. 8.1, shows the main windows opened by FDR 2.91.[2] The one at the top is the controlling window that is opened up on starting FDR. Here it is in Refinement mode with a file loaded and the user has run a check.[3] This check has failed (in that a solution has been found for the puzzle that the script codes) and the debugger is showing some details of how a sub-process of the implementation behaved.

Aside from its Refinement, Deadlock, Divergence and Determinism modes, it will be apparent from the screen-shot that there is also Evaluate. This is not for processes, but allows the user to calculate the value of any non-process expression, from simple expressions such as $2 + 2$ and N (where a value of N is defined in the script) to testing complex pieces of non-process programming present in the script.

An optional[4] Graph mode is also available, which can be activated by setting the environment variable FDRGRAPH to any value. This allows the user to see a graphical representation of the states of a CSP process in the form that FDR explores. The graphs that are displayed would frequently be too large to understand if calculated for a full system implementation, so typically this mode is employed to help the user understand one of the smaller (typically either the specification or a component) processes he or she has created.

---

and exhibiting a counter-example behaviour if one of the states found does not meet the implied requirements. By a narrower definition, namely that the specification is cast in some, usually temporal, logic such as the one described in Sect. 16.4 and that the role of the tool is to check that the implementation is a *model* of the specification, FDR is not a model checker.

[2]It is likely that the GUI for FDR 3 will look rather different.

[3]This is, in fact, the solution to a 16×16 Sudoku puzzle taken from a newspaper. The fact that it has explored only 142 states—as you can see from the Status window—is testament to the great effectiveness of the coding for this sort of puzzle that is set as Exercise 20.2.

[4]The reason why this mode is optional at the time of writing is that it is, at present, less sophisticated than one might like. If it is subsequently improved it may well be present by default.

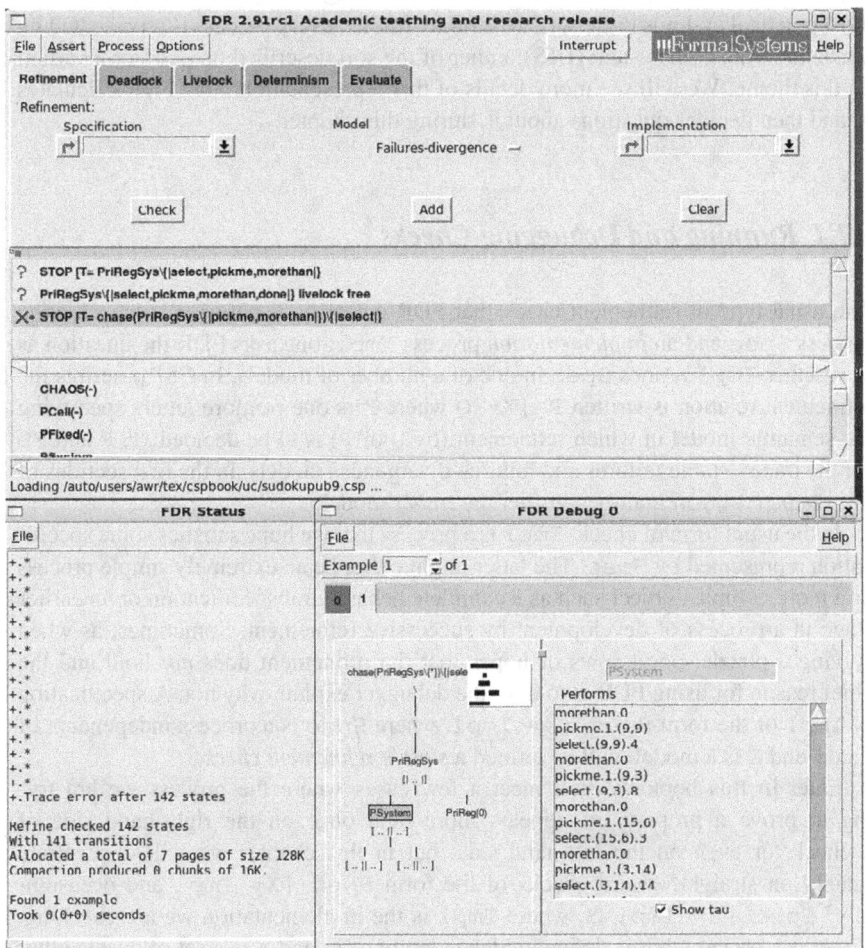

Fig. 8.1 The main FDR windows

All this is illustrated by the simple input script `intro_fdr.csp` which, like many other scripts associated with this book, can be down-loaded from the book's web-site. This script has three sections of definitions and numerous `assert` lines, which pre-load checks. It was deliberately created without any parallel operator, so it can be understood by readers who have not yet reached Chap. 3. In Sect. 8.2 we discuss how the use of parallel operators affects FDR. The script `fdr_oper.csp` does, however, refer to CSP concepts such as failures, divergence and determinism that are not described in Chaps. 1 and 2. We give cross-references and informal descriptions of these where relevant in the rest of Sect. 8.1.

It is important to understand how FDR represents processes. While almost every function it computes is based on one of CSP's semantic models, FDR never represents processes explicitly as sets of traces, failures, etc. This is just as well since for most practical systems these sets are infinite. Rather, every process is represented by a labelled transition system (LTS): either of the sort described on p. 41 or a variant on this theme. We will see more details of this representation, how FDR calculates it, and then decides questions about it, during this chapter.

8.1.1 Running and Debugging Checks

The usual type of refinement check that FDR performs is between a *specification* process Spec and an *implementation* process Impl: one asks FDR the question as to whether Impl refines Spec in one of a number of models. In CSP$_M$ scripts the refinement relation is written P [X= Q where X is one or more letters specifying the semantic model in which refinement (by Q of P) is to be decided: T, F and FD for the traces, stable failures and failures-divergences models. In the first sections of this chapter we will mainly consider the *traces* model.

In the usual form of check, Impl is a process that we hope satisfies some specification represented by Spec. The latter might either be an extremely simple process or a more complex object such as a complete behavioural specification or an earlier stage in a process of development by successive refinement. Sometimes, as when solving a puzzle, one knows or hopes that the refinement does *not* hold and the chief reason for using FDR is to have the debugger explain why not. A specification of Impl or the form Spec [X= Impl, where Spec is a process independent of Impl and X is a model, will be termed a *simple refinement check*.

Later in this book we will meet a few cases where the process we are trying to prove a property of appears more than once on the right-hand side of a check, or even on the left-hand side, but in this chapter we will concentrate mainly on straightforward checks of the form Spec [X= Impl and occasionally[5] Spec [X= Impl\Y, where Impl is the implementation we are checking, Spec is a process that is defined independently of it, and Y is a set of events other than those the specification cares about. For example, we can check that a process P never performs an event in Errors by either of

```
CHAOS(diff(Events,Errors))  [T= P
```

```
STOP [T= P\diff(Events,Errors)
```

The first section of fdr_intro.csp declares three simple events and defines four processes.

```
channel a,b,c
```

---

[5] P\X is the CSP *hiding operator* introduced in Chap. 5. It allows all of P's actions in X to happen, but conceals them from the environment.

```
P = a -> b -> P
Q = (a -> b -> Q) [] (c -> STOP)
R = (a -> b -> R) |~| (c -> STOP)
DIV = DIV |~| DIV

assert P [T= Q
assert Q [F= R
assert Q :[deterministic]
assert P :[deadlock-free]
assert DIV :[divergence-free]
assert DIV [FD= R
```

Many checks can be performed on FDR in examining and comparing these processes: the notation above shows some of those that fdr_intro.csp pre-loads.

DIV (which performs internal τ actions for ever) only has the empty trace <> and therefore trace-refines the other three. P trace-refines Q and R, which are trace equivalent (i.e. refine each other). P is deterministic and free of deadlock and livelock. Both Q and R can deadlock (by reaching the STOP state) and are divergence free. Q is deterministic[6] but R is not, since it can accept or refuse either of a and c on the empty trace (see Sect. 6.1). DIV, naturally, can diverge, since divergence is defined to be a process performing an infinite unbroken sequence of τ actions.

The notation P [F= Q creates the claim that Q *failures*-refines P. This is an extension of trace refinement described in Sect. 6.1 and says that if Q can ever *refuse* a set of events, then so can P after the same trace. Similarly P [FD= Q asserts that Q *failures-divergences* refines P—see p. 119, which additionally states that Q can only diverge when P can.

If you run an assertion, you will find that FDR prints a cross next to the check if it fails, and a tick if it succeeds. Double-clicking on a failed check will take you into the debugger, which shows you a behaviour of the implementation process that contradicts the refinement, or if appropriate finds a deadlock or finds a divergence. In the case of a determinism check that fails other than by finding a divergence, the debugger will show you two behaviours: one on which some event was accepted after a given trace, and one on which it was refused after the same trace.

The great simplicity of the processes P, Q, R and DIV means that the debugger has nothing to analyse more deeply. However, with more complex processes (generally speaking ones involving parallel, renaming and hiding operators) the debugger will (as illustrated in Fig. 8.1) allow you to analyse what the behaviours of component processes are.

---

[6]A process is deterministic (see Sect. 10.5) if it can never either diverge or have the option of performing an event or refusing it.

8.1.2 FDR's Settings

In this section we discuss the settings in running checks on FDR that are accessible through the range of buttons at the top of the GUI on FDR 2.91. (We anticipate a revised GUI for FDR 3, but most or all of the following options will still be there.)

The button FILE gives you the options to load and re-load a script, to edit the current script, to run all the asserts in the current script, and to quit FDR.

The button OPTIONS is more interesting. The tabs on it are listed here in roughly the order of interest to a relatively new user.

- Show Status creates a separate window in which you can see output from FDR's various functions. You should normally select this to be open. The output you will see reports progress on the various functions of running a check: on simple checks you are likely to see output from the compiler and the main run of the check. It also displays both parsing and compiling errors for your script, and statistics on any run you have just completed. This was illustrated in Fig. 8.1.
- Messages controls the level of detail printed out during a check into the Status window. It defaults to a moderate amount (auto) in which the amount of detail gradually decreases as a check proceeds. Setting it to high can be very useful if you are having problems getting a script to compile, because it gives you great detail on the terms it goes though, and so in particular you will know where the problem was encountered.
- Restart is used if FDR gets into some sort of bad state and is not responding: it is a more decisive version of the INTERRUPT button, and makes no attempt to retain state from previous checks.
- Examples determines how many counter-examples FDR will look for when running a check. This defaults to 1 so that a check halts as soon as one counter-example is found. If a higher number is selected then the tool will try to find more counter-example states until the limit is reached. Two counter-examples are reckoned to be different here if their final states are different, namely the ones that exhibit a particular behaviour such as an event, refusal or immediate divergence that violates the specification. It is possible that different counter-examples might have the same trace, and if there is only one counter-example state with lots of traces leading to it, only one trace will be reported. For instance, if you ask for more than one counter-example in the following:

```
P = a -> c -> STOP
    [] a -> a -> c -> STOP
    [] a -> c -> c -> STOP

Q = a -> Q

assert Q [T= P
```

you will find that FDR finds the errors on lines 1 and 3 of P, but not the one on line 2. This is because the processes c -> STOP from which c appears are the same on the first two lines, and the first has the shorter trace. The error on line 3 happens from state c -> c -> STOP which is different. Thus FDR reports the error trace <a, c> twice but <a, a, c> not at all. See Exercise 8.3 for some ways of discovering multiple traces to the same state.

One interesting application of this feature is to discover whether a Sudoku puzzle has one solution (which is usually the intention) or more. Interestingly, only one of PuzzleM and PuzzleB from Sect. 4.1 makes this possible. See if you can work out which before experimenting. We will see a further application in Sect. 14.6.

- Compact controls the way in which FDR stores large state spaces. The higher the level of compression, the less space it should use. There is no need to worry about this setting unless you are running very large checks.

  In general there is a trade-off between CPU time and memory bandwidth when you run large checks on FDR. You can roughly imagine FDR as a process that has to shovel large amounts of previously stored data through the CPU, while it generates more data in large quantities that have to be stored for later. Its algorithms are tuned to make maximal use of the data it brings in, but the sheer quantity of this information sometimes means that the memory systems (and backing store when necessary) cannot deliver data fast enough to the CPU to keep it busy. By storing the data in a compressed form, it can be delivered to the CPU faster, and the extra work the CPU has to do in expanding and re-compressing the data is often well worthwhile.

  The default on this setting is at present normal. This, instead of storing each successive state separately, only records those bytes of the next state that are different from the present one, along with a table showing which bytes are different. This is known as Δ-compression, since the Greek letter Δ (Delta) is often used to denote the difference between two things. With present computer architectures, this almost always seems to give better speed (as well as memory consumption) than none. The high setting uses gzip on blocks of states, using typically around 70% of the memory required by normal. This tends to win when running a check that extends into backing store (virtual memory) because it both defers the point where that happens and means that less data needs to be swapped when it is needed.

The INTERRUPT button stops whatever FDR is doing and attempts to retain information from previously completed checks if you ask it to Continue. HELP brings up an on-line version of the FDR manual, which contains a far more complete description of what the tool does than we have given in this section. Your attention is drawn to the appendices on *Direct Control of FDR* and *Configuration*, which respectively describe FDR's *batch mode*, in which it is directly driven from the command line rather than the GUI, and ways of configuring your system (e.g. through environment variables) to guide FDR in its work. Batch mode is invaluable to anyone wishing to write an alternative front end to FDR, for example to support a different input language than CSP. (It is used, for example, by the SVA front end described in Chap. 18.) The environment variable FDRPAGEDIRS is especially important at the time of writing: it tells FDR where to store the data structures of states it builds in a check. If it is not set then FDR just stores all its data inside a running process, which on large checks can quickly grow beyond the operating system's limit on the size of processes.

8.1.3 Defining Non-Process Objects

The second section of `fdr_intro.csp` is a brief illustration of some of the styles of programming that can be used on non-process values. In a normal script functions like these would be used to help build process descriptions.

As we said earlier, the basic style of programming in CSP_M is *functional* (or *declarative*): this means that a script consists of a series of definitions, frequently of functions, in which the value of a term can be evaluated by systematically *reducing* an expression. One of the great benefits of this style is that it allows one simply to write down the same sort of definitions of events, functions and sets in a CSP_M program as one would in writing CSP down with paper and pencil. It also brings with it a type discipline[7] that is invaluable in creating real system models, and which earlier versions of CSP notably lacked.

No special skill in creating functional programs is required for this style of use, but it makes CSP_M a hugely expressive language for those who do acquire expertise in it, as is illustrated, for example, by the way we write a compiler in CSP in Chap. 18. Readers interested in this aspect of CSP_M are advised to study a text on the programming language Haskell [66] such as that by Richard Bird [9], or any related language.

The following are the examples from `fdr_intro.csp` that illustrate some basic functional programming techniques, some of which are not available in Haskell.

```
factorial(0) = 1
factorial(n) = n*factorial(n-1)

nth(0,xs) = head(xs)
nth(n,xs) = nth(n-1,tail(xs))

reverse(<>) = <>
reverse(<x>^s) = reverse(s)^<x>

reverse'(<>) = <>
reverse'(t^<x>) = <x>^reverse'(t)
```

---

[7]There is a CSP type checker called *Checker* that, at present, is run independently of other tools like FDR. The reason for this is that the type rules relating to the infix dot "." as in *a.b.c* are problematic and can cause a lot of branching, meaning that Checker can take an unreasonably long time and give output that is less than clear. The author hopes that a revised, less generous, type-checker will be created soon, imposing assumptions on this sort of question. Nevertheless Checker can be invaluable, and it was used a great deal by the author in creating the compiler *written in CSP* described in Chap. 18.

```
qsort(<>) = <>
qsort(<x>^xs) =
let
p(<>,ls,es,gs) = (ls,es,gs)
p(<y>^ys,ls,es,gs) = if y < x then p(ys,<y>^ls,es,gs)
                    else if y == x then p(ys,ls,<y>^es,gs)
                                    else p(ys,ls,es,<y>^gs)
                    (lsx,esx,gsx) = p(xs,<>,<>,<>)
within
qsort(lsx)^<x>^esx^qsort(gsx)

qsort'(<>) = <>
qsort'(<x>^xs) = qsort'(<y | y<-xs, y<x >)^<x>^
        <y | y<-xs, y==x >^qsort'(<y | y<-xs, y>x >)

facs = {(x,factorial(x)) | x <- {0..9}}

fact(n) = pick({m | (n',m) <- facs, n'==n})

invfact(m) = {n | (n,m') <- facs, m'=m}

pick({x}) = x
```

The definition of the factorial function (the number of ways one can arrange n different objects into a list) given here is essentially what you will find in a mathematics textbook. The thing to notice here is that there are two lines of definition, which act together using a technique called *pattern matching*. If you call this function with argument 0 it will match the pattern in the first line (you can use any fixed integer as a pattern). If you call it with any other argument, that match will fail and it will go onto the second line, which in this case always succeeds. So, for example, the term factorial(3) reduces successively to 3*factorial(2), 3*(2*factorial(1)), 3*(2*(1*factorial(0))), 3*(2*(1*1)), 3*(2*1), 3*2 and 6.

As in most functional programming languages, lists are an important part of CSP$_M$. The notation used for them is based on that of traces in CSP. Thus lists are written <> (the empty list), <a,b,c> or using *list comprehensions*, for example <n*2 | n <- <1..10>, n != 4> (meaning twice each integer in the range 1..10 except for 4). In a list comprehension, the right-hand side consists of zero or more *generators* in which members are drawn from lists, and zero or more *predicates*, namely boolean expressions that allow us to select which of the generator values creates a member of the list. Of course the separator | is only used if there is at least one predicate or generator.

The order in which things appear in lists is important, as is the number of times they occur. <a,b>, <b,a> and <b,a,a> are all different. In a generated list, the second generator goes round once for each value of the first, the

third goes round once for each pair of values of the first two, and so on. Thus
`<10*i+j | i <- <0..9>, j <- <0..9>>` is the same as `<0..99>`.

Like many functional programming languages, CSP$_M$ permits the use of *infinite*
lists such as `rep(x) = <x>^rep(x)`, though infinite lists cannot, for example,
be used as parts of events.

The function `nth`, as defined above, allows you to extract a member of a list by
index, with 0 being the index of its first member. Note that this makes use of inbuilt
`head` and `tail` functions: for non-empty xs, `head(xs)^tail(xs)` is equal
to xs.

The next two definitions, `reverse` and `reverse'`, are two different ways of
defining the same function by pattern matching on lists. In CSP$_M$ you can pattern-
match on the last (or several last) members of a list, as well as on the first.

Probably the most practically important work Tony Hoare has done was not to
invent CSP but to invent the *Quicksort* sorting algorithm.[8] The next two definitions
(`qsort` and `qsort'`) both implement basic versions of this: to sort a nontrivial list
they use the first member of the list as the *pivot*, partition the list into those things
less than, equal to, and greater than, the pivot, and the result is then got by sorting
those less than the pivot, then writing down the pivot and any other things equal to
it, and finally sorting those greater than it. The only difference between qsort and
qsort' comes from the way the partitioning is done. qsort does this by creating
a locally-defined (i.e. using `let  .... within`) partitioning function p that goes
through the members of xs one at a time and adds them to the three lists `ls`, `es`
and `gs` as appropriate.

The amazingly concise definition of `qsort'` uses list comprehension to define
these three lists separately. This is less efficient in terms of the number of reductions because of the way it requires three separate passes along xs: one for each of
the analogues of `ls`, `es` and `gs` rather than a single pass using the function p (for
partition).

The final four definitions above illustrate that, unusually,[9] CSP$_M$ allows you to
program with sets. The language allows you to have infinite sets like `Int` (all integers), but in practice there is not much you can do with these finitely. So, in contrast
to lists, it is usually wise only to define finite sets in your scripts.[10] Sets have been

---

[8]See Note 1 at the end of this chapter for a salutary tale of how Quicksort's use in FDR gave an
unexpected result.

[9]CSP$_M$ is the only functional language known to the author in which sets are supported as first-
class objects. They were included because of the importance of sets to CSP as process alphabets,
sets to hide, etc. They have proved immensely useful in other contexts also. Probably the reason
why they are not seen elsewhere is that they do not fit entirely comfortably with the concept of lazy
evaluation: for example to compute the size of a set (as opposed to a list), all its members have to
be evaluated completely.

[10]In common with Haskell, the implementation of the CSP$_M$ language is based on *lazy evaluation*,
which is what allows it to compute with infinite lists. The need to determine which the distinct
elements of a set are means that much more evaluation is forced early when using sets as opposed
to lists.

included because they appear so much in CSP programs (for example as process alphabets and sets to be hidden). In a set, the order in which elements appear and the number of times each is put in are ignored: the sets {1,2}, {2,1} and {1,1,2} are all the same. This means that in order to do much with a set, the language implementation has to remove duplicates and to store the members in an order that depends only on their fully reduced forms. It is therefore not recommended to put potentially "infinitary" objects such as processes, functions and infinite lists into sets. These are just the same types of object that cannot be communicated over channels.

The first of the set-based definitions illustrates the standard way of turning a function (here factorial) into its *graph*: a set of pairs of function arguments and results. By taking a finite part of a function's graph, like this one, turns it into something that *can* sensibly be put into a set, or communicated across a channel.

We then see how set comprehensions, which follow the pattern of list comprehensions (though all the generators now range over sets rather than lists), can be used to achieve the effect of applying and inverting the graph of a function. Notice that the inverse used here takes a member m of the domain of a function and maps it to the *set* of all values that map to m. In this case there is one value, 1, that has more than one inverse, and there are many that have none.

The function pick uses pattern matching to take the unique element from a singleton set.

There is an in-built function set(xs) that converts a finite list xs into the set of its elements. There is no standard function that converts the other way, or indeed one that extracts an "arbitrary" element of a set S, because these processes are not *functional*: there are many ways to achieve them, so the language behaviour would be under-specified. See Exercise 8.1, however.

The final part of fdr_intro.csp illustrates user-defined data-types. The effect of a declaration like

```
datatype fruit = Banana | Apple | Pear | Lemon | Mango
datatype cheese = Cheddar | Brie | Stilton | Camembert
```

is to introduce some new constants into the program. Values like Pear and Stilton are now things that can, for example, be passed along channels that have types fruit or cheese. (An often-followed convention is to give the labels introduced by data-type definitions a capital letter, as here, but it is not compulsory.)

We can use types when constructing other types, as in

```
datatype item = Cheese.(cheese,Wt) | Fruit.(fruit,Wt)
              | Butter.Wt | Mustard | Crackers
```

where Wt is a numeric type of weights. So we can identify a shopping basket with List(item), the type of lists of item, each of which is either an item bought by weight (Wt might be a synonym for Int) or one bought as a unit (such as a jar of mustard). So a typical shopping basket is

```
<Mustard,Crackers,Crackers,Butter.1,
 Cheese.(Camembert.2),Cheese.(Brie.2)>
```

datatype definitions can be recursive. For example, the type

```
datatype fruitlist = EmptyFL | ConsFL.fruit.fruitlist
```

builds a type very similar to List(fruit): in fact the two types are naturally equivalent, though different notation is used for each of them. The labels introduced in datatype definitions need to be different from each other (so one cannot use the same one in different types) and from the other identifiers such as channel names and processes used in the script. For example, we could not have used labels Empty and Cons in both the above and

```
datatype chslist = EmptyCL | ConsCL.cheese.chslist
```

One can also construct structures that are more complex than simple lists, for example binary trees of integers and arbitrary trees of booleans

```
datatype bintreeI = LeafI.Int | NodeI.bintree.bintree
```

```
datatype treeB = LeafB | NodeB.Bool.Seq(treeB)
```

Notice that bintreeI has integers at its leaf nodes, whereas treeB has booleans at its non-leaf nodes. We will make major use of tree-like types in Sect. 8.8.1 and Chap. 18.

Functions of such data-types are frequently defined using pattern matching:

```
fringe(LeafI.n) = <n>
fringe(NodeI.t1.t2) = (fringe(t1))^(fringe(t2))
```

is a function from bintreeI to Seq(Int).

It is possible to use the type Proc, meaning processes, in defining a datatype, and we will see an example in Sect. 8.8.1 below. Members of such types cannot be communicated along channels and should not be used in sets.[11]

The user can also give names to types constructed straightforwardly, without the need for tags such as Banana or LeafI. For example

```
nametype MyInts = {MinI..MaxI}
nametype Basket = Seq(item)
nametype CountedItem = (item,MyInts)
```

---

[11]User-defined data-types that include the process type Proc have only been supported since FDR 2.90.

The last of these is the type of pairs whose first element comes from item and whose second comes from MyInts.

8.1.4 The Limits of FDR

The third and final section of fdr_intro.csp illustrates the boundary between what FDR can and cannot do.

FDR has a two-level approach to computing the operational semantics of CSP. The first thing FDR does is to identify a number of (usually sequential) component processes that it has to *compile* to *explicit state machines*, namely lists of states, where each state is marked with the initial actions (visible and τ) it can perform, together with the indices of the states that can be reached from the state under each action. It also identifies one or more ways in which these sequential machines are combined together into the whole system: usually this uses parallel, hiding and re-naming operators, in which case the high-level composition consists of a single *format* for composing the sequential processes. Sometimes, as in

$$a \rightarrow (P \parallel Q), \qquad \mu p.(P \parallel_A Q); R; p, \qquad (P \parallel_A Q) \Theta_B R$$

other operators get involved (here, respectively prefixing, sequential composition and throw) which results in there being more than one format: two in each of these examples.

Bear in mind that sometimes there are many states a process can reach under τ (e.g. P |~| Q) or a single visible action (e.g. (a -> P) [] (a -> Q)) actions. In exploring the state space of a process all these options need to be covered.

FDR cannot complete its task if any of these components are either infinite state or have too many states to compile in a reasonable amount of time and space. This is illustrated by the following processes:

```
Inf1(n) = a -> b -> Inf1(n+1)

Fin(0) = a -> b -> Fin(0)
Fin(n) = a -> b -> Fin(n-1)

Inf2 = a -> Inf2'(0,0)
Inf2'(n,0) = a -> Inf2'(n+1,n+1)
Inf2'(n,m) = b -> Inf2'(n,m-1)
```

Inf1(0) is compiled as an infinite-state process—because its parameter value increases unboundedly—even though it is actually equivalent as a CSP process to the finite-state process Fin(0). The parameter is causing the problem, even though it is irrelevant to behaviour. Every Fin(n) is equivalent to Inf1(0), but finite state. Inf2 is an infinite-state process with no finite-state equivalents.

Bound(0,m) below is infinite state, but Bound'(0,m) is finite state: it prevents the second parameter spiralling into regions that are irrelevant. Both processes allow b to occur when there have been at least m copies of a since the beginning or the most recent c. They are equivalent.

```
Bound(n,m)  = a -> Bound(n+1,m)
                [] (m<=n)& b -> Bound(n,m)
                [] c -> Bound(0,m)

Bound'(n,m) = a -> Bound'(if n==m then n else n+1,m)
                [] (m<=n)& b -> Bound'(n,m)
                [] c -> Bound'(0,m)
```

A different manifestation of this same problem is that FDR has difficulty in handling processes that use large data-types, particularly when many unrelated values of such a type can be held at the same time. Thus a process that inputs a member of a very large (or infinite) type may well be too large to compile. So while it can handle processes that hold quite a lot of binary or similar values, or one or two values from a moderate-sized type and (thanks to the sub-process language) do complicated things to these values, FDR is not a tool for analysing the correctness of programs' complex manipulation of a large data state.

There are some fairly advanced techniques that can allow us to extend results about small types to large ones: see Chap. 17, for example. However, all component processes that FDR actually compiles must use only small to moderate types (or similar sized parts of large or infinite ones), and furthermore must have all their parameters fully defined. One cannot, using a simple FDR check, verify a property of some process P(n) for *arbitrary* n, just for *particular* n such as 4 or 10. Again, we will look at the parameterised verification problem: proving a result for a parameterised collection of systems, in Chap. 17.

Integer types are not the only ones used in CSP_M programming that can get large or infinite. These include *lists* (there being n^k lists of length k over a type of size n) and *sets* (there being 2^n subsets of a set with size n). So, for example, while the following process, where X ranges over subsets of a finite set T,

```
SET(X) = add?x -> SET(union(X,{x})
           [] isin?x!member(x,X) -> SET(X)
           [] (card(X)==0) & isempty -> SET(X)
           [] remove?x -> SET(diff(X,{x}))
```

can be used provided the type T is reasonably small, by the time it has size approaching 20 the number of states will start to get slow to compile. FDR is much slower at compiling each state of a component process than it is at running the final check, so while most checks of size 1,000,000 will take just a few seconds on a modern computer, compiling a sequential component of that size will take much longer. We will see how this fact can be used to produce a better version of SET in Sect. 8.2.

Fig. 8.2 See Exercise 8.2

Exercise 8.1 If X is a set drawn from a type T that can be compared (i.e. either the inbuilt relation < is meaningful or you can define a similar linear comparison function yourself), then it is possible to turn X into a list by *sorting* into ascending order using the CSP_M language. Find a way of doing this. [*Hint: you can write a version of Quicksort based on sets provided you can find a way of choosing the pivot, which can be done by finding a subset of* X *with size* 1 *and applying* pick *to it. Note that you can count the size of a finite set with the function* card(.).]

Exercise 8.2 One of the author's favourite ways of using FDR is in solving combinatorial puzzles. Most of these require parallel processes for a reasonable model, but the following one is small enough that it can be solved with a sequential model. (We have already seen one of these in Exercise 4.3.)

Figure 8.2 shows a puzzle. It is defined for all $n > 0$ and the figure has $n = 3$. There are n black pegs (in holes), an empty hole, and then n white pegs. Black pegs can move to the left either by hopping one space into an empty slot, or can jump leftwards over a single white peg into an empty slot. White pegs move to the right in analogous ways (hopping one space or jumping over a black).

The puzzle is solved when the white and black pegs have been exchanged.

Write a CSP_M description of this puzzle. It should keep a parameter that is a list of length $2n + 1$ that describes the state of the puzzle, allowing just those moves that are possible in the current configuration. It should communicate done when the puzzle is solved.

Use the names right, left, jumpleft and jumpright for the four sorts of moves: you can choose to add a data field to each of these events denoting the target of the move, if you wish.

8.2 Checking Parallel Processes

While we can see the basic functionality of FDR in checking sequential processes, it is not until we start analysing parallel systems that it shows its power. That is both because understanding how parallel systems behave is inherently complex and because the number of states that a system has can grow exponentially with the number of parallel components.

If we want to understand a sequential program, all we have to do is follow the states that one process definition gets into. For example, a sequential program written in an imperative language like C is always at a single line in the program.

In a parallel process, on the other hand, there will be a number of processes, each *at* some separate control state, so a state of || i:{1..m} @ [A(i)] P(i) is

described by an m-tuple of states, the ith being a state of P(i). Understanding the
behaviour of a compound system like this may be far less clear, and it will probably
have many more control states than that of a similar-size sequential system.

This is one of the main reasons why we need a tool like FDR that is good at
analysing large numbers of these states.

SET({}) is a sequential process that really has only a single control state, but
it has a huge number of states thanks to the way its parameter varies. FDR finds it
much harder to compile this one sequential process than an equivalent representation
as a parallel composition of many processes: one for each potential member of the
set. SET(X) is thus equivalent to ParSet(X) described below, using parallel:

```
Present(x) = isin!x -> Present(x)
             [] add!x -> Present(x)
             [] remove!x -> Absent(x)

Absent(x) = isempty -> Absent(x)
            [] add!x -> Present(x)
            [] remove!x -> Absent(x)

ParSet(X) = [|{isempty}|] i:T @
  (if member(i,X) then Present(x) else Absent(x))
```

You can verify this equivalence for smallish T. ParSet(X) has exactly as many
states as SET(X), namely $2^{|T|}$. You can count the states of any CSP process P
by running CHAOS(Events) [T= P. This is certain to succeed, and the number of states reported in the Status window is always the number of distinct
states FDR finds in P. In some cases this may be smaller than you expect because of the way FDR automatically applies a simple compression operator to each
component process, but both versions of our set process give 2^k for k the size
of T.

So why do we say that the parallel implementation is better for FDR? The first
reason, as will be apparent from running the counting checks for appropriate sizes
of T, is speed. As remarked earlier, FDR is much faster at running checks than
compiling a similar number of states of component processes. The ParSet version
gives only 2*card(T) states to compile, so almost all the time spent counting
states for it is spent in the running (or model checking) phase of the check, whereas
the sequential version SET spends almost all its time compiling.

Unfortunately, so dire are the effects of the exponential explosion in state space
that this example brings, that ParSet does not increase the tolerable size of T by
very much: 30 would give it just over a billion states, which (at the time of writing)
takes far too much time and CPU to waste on such a pointless check!

It is, however, frequently possible to use ParSet and similar processes in contexts where there are very many more components than that. What matters in an
actual run is how many different subsets are encountered during a run, and making
a set process part of the state that other processes can use as a service may well
substantially limit the number of subsets that are actually explored.

As a simple example, consider the following program, which allows an ant to move around a rectangular board provided it never steps twice on the same square except the one where it started. This is enforced with a process based on `ParSet` that now only allows a `done` event in place of `isempty`, and an action that removes a member from the set, which is naturally identified and synchronised with the action by which the ant moves to the given place in the grid.

```
T = {(m,n) | m <- {1..M}, n <- {1..N}}

channel move: T
channel done

Ant((m,n)) = (n>1)& move.(m,n-1) -> Ant((m,n-1))
             [] (n<N)& move.(m,n+1) -> Ant((m,n+1))
             [] (m>1)& move.(m-1,n) -> Ant((m-1,n))
             [] (m<M)& move.(m+1,n) -> Ant((m+1,n))

Unused(x) = move!x -> Used(x)

Used(x) = done -> Used(x)

Board(X) = [|{done}|] i:T @
  (if member(i,X) then Unused(i) else Used(i))

System = Ant(start) [|{|move|}|] Board(T)
```

Notice that the ant crawls only to directly adjacent squares. The `System` process has many fewer states than `Board(T)` for the simple reason that most subsets of the grid are not the sets of points of some non-revisiting path starting from `start`.

So, for example, the 7×6 version of this system has 261 M (approximately 2^{21}) states which, though a lot, is hugely less than the 2^{42} states of `Board(T)` here. What we find, and this is typical of examples from many domains, is that only a small fraction of the potential states of this subprocess are required in the real system.

The way FDR works means that, when we use the `Board` representation, the extra states are never visited. However, if a single sequential component like `SET` is used, all the states are compiled, whether visited or not in the completed system.

For both these reasons it is almost always a good idea, if you have the choice, to factor what would otherwise be a large component process into a number of components running in parallel. In doing this you should, wherever possible, avoid introducing extra states. We will see an interesting but more advanced technique for dealing with this last issue—the "`chase`" operator—in Chaps. 16 and 20.

A *Hamiltonian circuit* is a path that visits every location in some graph exactly once and then ends up back where it started. The specification `NoHamiltonian` below says that there is no such circuit around our grid: the event move.start (which means that the ant has returned to its starting point) cannot immediately be followed by the done event that indicates that there are no squares left to visit. It is clear that whether this specification is true or not does not depend on which start location is chosen, but it does depend on the dimensions M and N.

```
NoHamiltonian = move?(i,j) -> if (i,j)==start
                                 then NoHamiltonian'
                                 else NoHamiltonian
              [] done -> NoHamiltonian

NoHamiltonian' = move?_ -> NoHamiltonian

assert NoHamiltonian [T= System
```

Exercise 8.3 Recall the example in Sect. 8.1.2 that showed how FDR only reports a single trace to each state that exhibits an erroneous behaviour. You can get more traces that lead to a single trace by putting your original system in parallel with a second or companion process that (i) does not change the behaviour of the system and (ii) changes its own state sufficiently on the trace to get FDR to observe different states of the compound system despite the main process being in the same state. The only real difficulty in doing this, provided the main implementation never terminates, is to ensure that the states of the companion process are not identified by the strong bisimulation the FDR automatically applies to compiled components. Perhaps the best way of doing this is to construct the companion so that it always accepts every event of the process it accompanies, but sometimes is able to communicate extra events too. The extra events are then prevented by the way the system is put in parallel, say Impl[|Events|]Companion)[|Extra|]STOP. Note that this technique will, by its very nature, increase the state-space of a check, and that the companion process needs to be finite state.

(a) Find a companion process with alphabet {a,b,c} that can find the counter-example trace <a,a,c> in the example set out on p. 148.
(b) Find one that can find multiple Hamiltonian paths (when they exist) when combined with the example above, noting that all such paths are necessarily the same length.

Exercise 8.4 Repeat Exercise 8.2 (p. 157), only this time make it a parallel composition with a single process per slot. In this version you will definitely need to attach data fields to the four move events so that you can define the alphabet of each of the $2n + 1$ slot processes correctly. (All should synchronise on *done*.)

Compare FDR's performance on the sequential and parallel versions.

8.3 The Structure of a Refinement Check

Having got this far through this chapter, you should already have run some large checks on FDR. If you open up the Status window you will see the stages of these checks being reported on. There are three phases to each refinement check.

Compilation (in which with the auto level of messages, what you see reported is the number of transitions calculated so far) is the stage at which, in the check of a parallel process, FDR identifies the parallel components and compiles these to explicit state machines, namely data structures where each state has a record that lists its actions: pairs of the label and the index of the target state. It also works out a set of rules, called *supercombinators* (see p. 212) by which the transitions of the parallel combination can be deduced from those of the components. It does this both for the specification and implementation processes.

Normalisation is the phase during which the specification process is transformed into a form that can efficiently be compared against the implementation. In essence this is a form such that, for every trace, there is a unique state that the specification is in. In the case of simple specifications this is so quick and easy that there is no evidence for this phase other than FDR reporting that it is starting and ending.

The user has to be aware, however, that if a complex specification is normalised this can take a long time, and in some cases can create normalised processes that are very much larger than the original specifications. In particular, before a process is normalised it is turned into an explicit transition system and so, even if normalisation goes very smoothly, one is still only able to handle specification processes that are very much smaller than implementations. Full details of the normalisation algorithm can be found in Sect. 16.1. In the untypical worst case, as demonstrated by the example file pathol.csp, it can generate a normal form representation that is exponentially larger than the original process (in terms of state space). Some techniques that can alleviate difficult normalisations are discussed in Sect. 16.1, which also has an analysis of the cases where this may be necessary.

The closer a specification is to being in normal form, namely having only a single execution path leading to each state, the easier it is to normalise. Complexity can increase dramatically when decisions made early in a trace can give rise to separate ways of performing it. Fortunately, almost all processes written as clear specifications have essentially only one way of performing each trace, and so cause no problems at all.

By the time normalisation is complete, we have efficient representations of both the implementation and a form of the specification that is efficient to check against.

The third and main *running* or "model-checking" phase of the check can now take place. What it does is to explore the pairs of states that can be reached on any trace by the normalised specification and the implementation. In each such pair the specification state imposes restrictions on what the implementation state can do: these will relate to the next events, and for richer models to things like refusal sets and divergence information. Usually each implementation state ends up paired with only one specification state, but there may be more. Consider the following:

```
AS = a -> AS

Spec = a -> a -> a -> Spec
       [] b -> b -> STOP
```

Clearly AS has only one state whereas Spec (presented here in what is already normal form) has five. The check Spec [T= AS naturally succeeds, and explores 3 state-pairs. After traces <a,a,...,a> with length divisible by 3, the implementation is allowed to perform either a or b, but on all other lengths it is not. Of course AS never performs a b , so the single implementation state is always paired with one of the top three states of Spec.

When a refinement check completes successfully, it actually represents a proof that, for each state-pair (SS,IS) explored (respectively the specification and implementation states), SS [X= IS where X is the relevant model.

In its standard mode of exploring a check, the running phase is performed as a breadth-first search in which each state-pair is considered separately. In other words, FDR first finds the successor states of the starting state (the pair of the initial states of specification and implementation), then their successor states, and so on. It explores all of the successors at level n (i.e., the pairs reachable in n actions but not in any fewer) before going on to explore those at level $n + 1$.

The information you see in the Status window at this stage is just a count of the number of state-pairs completed, which in the standard checking mode are broken down into the different levels of the search.[12] These levels always start off small, and then typically grow until they reach a peak and then shrink back until eventually no more new state-pairs are found and the check terminates. The rate at which this growth and shrinkage happens depends, of course, on the details of the CSP processes you are checking.

Usually, if a check fails, a counter-example will be found somewhere in the middle of the enumeration of the state-pairs, more often near the beginning than the end. The main exceptions to this rule are checks designed to search for a particular example, such as the solution to a puzzle. In these cases the counter-examples are frequently found at or near the end. This is true of the checks designed to search for Hamiltonian circuits since necessarily such a circuit cannot be found until all the points in the grid have been used up.

If a counter-example is found, the user is given the chance to examine the behaviour that caused it. In its standard debugging mode, a window will appear in which the trace leading to the error is displayed together with refusal or divergence information if relevant. For refusals, you have the option to view *acceptance* information, since this is frequently more concise and intuitive. (A minimal acceptance is the complement of a maximal refusal.)

---

[12]When performing a failures-divergences check, you may also see bracketed counts of the number of implementation states checked for divergence in the manner described on p. 169.

All this debugging information is about the implementation process. It is easy to attribute blame on its side of the refinement check, since it has performed a single behaviour that is to blame for violating the specification. Sometimes, however, when you look at the debugging information, you will come to the conclusion that the implementation behaved perfectly: you want to understand why the specification did not allow it. Working out why one process *did not* do something is a great deal harder, and a lot less systematic, than working out how the implementation *did* it. Unfortunately, therefore, FDR offers no direct support for the debugging of specifications.

There are many further advanced functions of FDR that we have not described here. For others (some implemented, some planned) see, for example, Chaps. 11, 12, 14, 16, and 20. Hopefully yet more will be devised after the publication of this book.

Exercise 8.5 This exercise is about the Hamiltonian circuit check. (See p. 159.)

(a) Why is it obvious that the value of start does not affect whether the check for such a circuit succeeds or not?
(b) Use FDR and different values of the grid dimensions M and N to formulate a conjecture about what values of these parameters allow a Hamiltonian circuit. Then use mathematical analysis to prove it. [*Hint: imagine that the grid has its nodes coloured black and white like a chess-board. If the starting square is black, what is the colour of the last member of the circuit before it returns to the start?*]

8.4 Failures and Divergences

All the refinement checks we have discussed to date involve the traces model: one process refines another if its set of traces is contained in that of the other. For various reasons a large percentage of practical FDR checks are trace checks, but richer models allow the tool to check more detailed properties.

The standard checks for deadlock and divergence freedom are in fact refinement checks performed in the richer models, and the determinism check implemented by FDR conceals such a check. In many cases users are content with establishing the first two of these properties, without delving more deeply into what other failures and failures-divergences properties hold of their implementations.

The way the failures-divergences model $\mathcal{N}$ treats divergence strictly suggests that any check performed in this model should regard divergence as an error to be eliminated. Usually, divergence in an implementation would indeed be an error. In such cases, the inbuilt divergence-freedom check is all one has to do in that model.

By and large it is better to follow this approach and then base subsequent checks in models that do not model divergence, for a purely pragmatic reason. That is because, every time FDR performs a refinement check in the failures-divergences model, it has to test each reached state for divergence. This is an additional, and sometimes expensive, piece of work, and it is better to do this once rather than each time a property of a given system is verified.

Divergence can sometimes be useful in formulating specifications. If we want to make a forcible *don't care* statement in a specification, namely that the implementation is allowed to do anything at all once it performs a particular sort of trace, a good way of doing this is by putting a divergent term in the specification on the left-hand side of the refinement check. So, for example, if we have a specification Spec and we want to transform it so that it allows the implementation to do anything at all after the event c, we can do this by using[13] Spec[|{c}|](c -> DIV) over $\mathcal{N}$. This particular example makes interesting use of the strict treatment of divergence in $\mathcal{N}$.

The use of DIV as "don't care" brings a real practical benefit in cases where we expect much of the implementation's behaviour to come into the category where this clause will apply. FDR recognises, when checking over $\mathcal{N}$, that a divergent specification state is refined by anything, and it does not pursue the search in the running phase of a check when a state-pair with a divergent specification state is reached. In such cases refinement can be proved without visiting all of the specification states. At the time of writing there is no similar optimisation for refinements not involving divergence, in part because the least refined process in such models is harder to recognise.

In understanding processes it is sometimes useful to ask whether a process with more than the "natural" set of events hidden can diverge. For example, if P is divergence-free but P\A is not, we know that P can perform an infinite sequence of actions from the set A. There is an example of this idea in Sect. 14.3.1.

We will now concentrate on failures checking [F=. The check P [F= Q says two different things depending on whether or not Q is known to be divergence free. If it is, then it implies P [FD= Q which says that whatever trace Q has performed, it will eventually reach a stable state in which it makes an offer acceptable to P. In other words, on the same trace P can reach a stable state where the set of events it offers is contained in the set now offered by Q. So P will definitely accept a member of any set of events that Q cannot refuse. So, for example, if P is a deterministic process and Q is divergence-free, P [F= Q says that P and Q behave identically.

Such a check allows us to draw positive inferences about the *liveness* of Q. If, on the other hand, we suspect that Q might diverge, then we can make no such inference; after all, P [F= DIV for every process P. If we know Q is divergence-free, then proving P [F= Q\X proves the traces of Q\X are contained in those of P, and that every stable state of Q *that is not offering any member of* X makes an offer acceptable to the corresponding state of P. So, for example, DIV [F= P\X says P never performs any event outside the set X *and* never deadlocks, and if AB = a -> b -> AB and C = diff(Events,{a,b}) then

---

[13]This version only allows those c events that are allowed by Spec. See Exercise 8.6 for an alternative version.

AB [F= (P [|C|] CHAOS(C))\C

AB [F= P\C

say two different things on the assumption that P is divergence free. The first says that a and b alternate (possibly interrupted by other events), and that P is *always* offering one of these two events. This is because if P reaches a stable state in which neither a nor b is offered, the synchronisation with CHAOS(C) means the right-hand side can refuse *everything* and deadlock. The second simply says they alternate and P is deadlock-free: here, the right-hand side only becomes stable when no event outside {a,b} is offered by P.

Variations on this theme can express many different properties.

Sometimes we might model a system where we know divergence is formally possible in a system P, at least with the CSP description we have given it, but we want to analyse the system on the assumption that this divergence never happens. We have already seen such a case with the modelling of lazy abstraction in Sect. 6.5.

Exercise 8.6 We showed above how to weaken a specification Spec so that it makes no assertion about the implementation at all when the implementation has performed a c that Spec allows. Show how to weaken it further so that it now always allows a c in addition to this. Your revised version should always allow the *event* c, but the revised specification should have identical refusal sets to the original after every trace s that does not include a c.

What refinement relations hold between the three versions of the specification (the original, the modification on p. 164, and your new one)?

Exercise 8.7 Recall how, on p. 162, we gave an example of a one-state implementation process AS that gets paired with three of the five states of a normal form during a successful trace refinement check. Use the additional expressive power of failures to find an N-state normal form Spec'(N) (for arbitrary N>0) which this same process [F= refines and where it gets paired with every single normal form state in the refinement check.

If M>1 is co-prime to N (i.e. their least common multiple is M*N), find an M-state process AS'(n) that cycles through its states using the action a and which is a *proper* stable failures refinement of AS but has the same traces.

If you check Spec'(N) [F= AS'(M) you may find that N*M state-pairs are reached. (If not, find an alternative AS'(M) that does have this property.) This is, of course, the greatest possible number given the sizes of the two processes. Explain why this happens and why it is helpful to assume that N and M are co-prime.

Exercise 8.8 Formulate refinement checks that test the following properties of divergence-free processes P:

(a) Every infinite trace of P contains a b.
(b) Every infinite trace of P contains an infinite number of bs.

(c) Every infinite trace of P contains the finite trace s as a (not necessarily consecutive) subsequence. [This part and the next are more difficult than they look.
Check that AS = a -> AS does not satisfy the specification you derive for
s = <a,b>.]

(d) Every infinite trace of P contains the infinite trace u as a (not necessarily consecutive) subsequence.

8.5 Watchdogs

As described in the last section, FDR runs checks by normalising the specification and searching through the state space produced when the normalised specification follows the traces that the implementation performs. It finds a counter-example
when the implementation does something that the specification cannot follow. Apart
from the last part of this, it is very like putting the specification and implementation
in synchronous parallel.

There is an alternative way of structuring this check on FDR that can sometimes give an advantage. For simplicity we will confine ourselves to traces checks
of non-terminating (i.e. $\checkmark$-free) processes. Imagine modifying the normal form of
the specification by adding to each of its states exactly those events that the state
cannot already perform, with each of these new transitions leading to the state
Woofing = *woof* $\rightarrow$ *Woofing*, where *woof* is some new event (i.e. not one the implementation ever uses) representing an "alarm".

The augmented normal form is a *watchdog* process: we will call it *TWD(Spec)*.
It watches everything that *Impl* does, and if *Impl* performs any trace not permitted
by *Spec*, it barks! The refinement *Spec* $\sqsubseteq_T$ *Impl* is equivalent to

$$STOP \sqsubseteq_T (TWD(Spec) \underset{\Sigma \setminus \{woof\}}{\|} Impl) \setminus (\Sigma \setminus \{woof\})$$

This approach can be applied to processes and specifications that can per-
form $\checkmark$ by a simple transformation: in general *Spec* $\sqsubseteq_T$ *Impl* holds if and only if
Spec; *Tick* $\sqsubseteq_T$ *Impl*; *Tick* where *Tick* = *tick* $\rightarrow$ *STOP*. Here *tick* is an event in Σ that
neither *Spec* nor *Impl* performs. So the watchdog version of *Spec* $\sqsubseteq_T$ *Impl* is

$$STOP \sqsubseteq_T (TWD(Spec; Tick) \underset{\Sigma \setminus \{woof\}}{\|} (Impl; Tick)) \setminus (\Sigma \setminus \{woof\})$$

Watchdogs can also be applied to stable failures and failures-divergences checks,
but these are much more complicated transformations and we will not describe them
here (see [46]).

8.6 Breadth versus Depth, Symmetry and Divergence

As we stated above, FDR's default method of searching through the state space is
breadth first search (BFS). It first checks through the successors of the root node,

then their successors, and so on, always eliminating states that have already been seen. These successors can either be found down visible or τ actions. BFS has two advantages:

(a) It finds the shortest path from the root to any counter-example, meaning that the reported counter-example is in some sense a simplest one. (It is not necessarily *the* simplest one, because there may be others with the same length.) These steps include τ actions, so it does not necessarily report the shortest possible *trace*.
(b) BFS and similar search methods scale better to very large checks: we will discuss this further in Sect. 16.3. On such examples BFS generally works significantly faster when the check succeeds (i.e. proves refinement).

In cases where there are counter-examples, particularly where there are significant numbers of paths to them, and they all take a relatively large number of actions to reach, DFS often works much faster. In DFS the first successor of any state is fully explored (through its own successors etc.) before the second. DFS tends to reach the area where counter-examples are to be found quickly, rather than having to enumerate all of the predecessor states first. This is amplified where the system under consideration has a lot of *symmetry*, in the sense that there are classes of states that behave essentially the same because of self-similarity in the system being considered.

For example, the dining philosophers in which all philosophers are right handed have *rotational symmetry*: it does not matter at what point we start numbering the philosophers as we go around the ring. So, for example, for every trace in which philosopher 1 picks up a fork first, there is a symmetric one in which philosopher 3 does so, after which the system behaves in the same way apart from the numberings of the action. In particular, if there is a deadlock reachable after any philosopher picks up a fork, there is one where philosopher 1 was the first to do this.

DFS will tend to look at more equivalence classes under symmetry early in a check than BFS does. This is because symmetries will often relate states reachable in the same number of steps from the root. In the dining philosophers it will see if there is any deadlock reachable after one first action before trying any others. Symmetry then means that if the system can deadlock, DFS will find this before it tries a second initial action.

An impressive illustration of DFS in action is provided by the *peg solitaire* puzzle as described in Sect. 15.1 of TPC. Recall that the rules of this puzzle, illustrated in Fig. 8.3, are:

- Initially all slots except the middle one are full.
- A peg may move by hopping over an adjacent peg into an empty slot in any horizontal or vertical direction, with the hopped-over peg being removed. Thus a move can happen only when three adjacent slots are respectively full, full and empty, and the move makes them empty, empty, and full.
- The puzzle is solved (necessarily in exactly 31 moves) when the middle slot is full and all the rest are empty.

The CSP description of this puzzle can be found in TPC and in an example file accompanying the present book.

Fig. 8.3 Peg solitaire

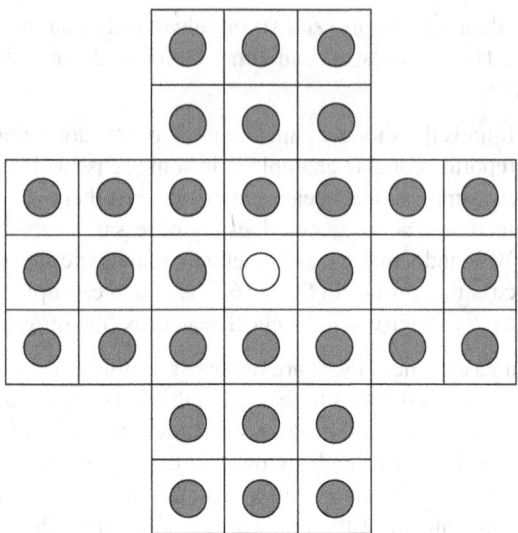

The standard BFS search of this puzzle encounters about 187 M states and takes (on workstations tried by the author) 40 or more minutes to run at the time of writing.[14] Almost the entire reachable state space is searched by the time a solution is found, since only five states of the puzzle have a only single peg remaining and none have less. On the other hand the puzzle has 8-fold symmetry (rotations and reflections), and a little thought reveals that there are a great number of states after (say) 16 moves from which the puzzle is solvable.[15] We only have to find one of these level-16 states in a DFS to be certain to find a complete solution beyond it. There is therefore every reason to believe that FDR would work much faster on solitaire using DFS.[16]

It is intended that an (optionally *bounded*) DFS search feature is included in FDR in the not-too-distant future, and this may be implemented by the time you read this. By bounded, we mean that the search is not permitted to reach more than a chosen number of steps from the root. The reason for the bound is so that counter-examples, when found, are not excessive in length: note that there will be no such problem with peg solitaire. The existence of a bound will mean that the failure to find a counter-example does not mean that refinement necessarily holds, merely that there is no counter-example with depth no greater than the bound. We expect that this mode will be used mainly for examples where counter-examples are thought probable.

---

[14]This is a considerable advance on the situation in 1997 when TPC was written: the unrestricted state space was then well beyond the reach of the workstations on which the author tried this example.

[15]Think of running the puzzle backwards from its final state for 15 moves.

[16]Although, as we will see, this is true, it does not invalidate solitaire as a benchmark for testing the efficiency of algorithms for searching through an entire state space by BFS or any other strategy.

There is, interestingly, a way of performing trace refinement checks by DFS in all earlier versions of FDR. This relies on the way in which FDR checks for divergence. One of the properties of the DFS strategy is that all the states which are only partially explored at any time form a chain from the root of the search to the most recently discovered node. This means that if there is a cycle in the graph that is being searched, then it will appear as one of the nodes in this chain being a successor of the current node. The graph therefore contains a cycle if and only if such a successor is ever found during the search. Most good algorithms textbooks contain a number of interesting algorithms exploiting this fact.

Since there is no similar property of BFS, the divergence checking function of FDR has always been performed by doing a DFS from each reachable node, through the set of nodes τ-reachable from it.

Suppose Impl is a divergence-free and $\checkmark$-free process. Consider the assertion that the trace check Spec [T= Impl has a counter-example trace of length no more than N. This is equivalent to Spec [T= Impl[|Events|]NEvs(N), where NEvs(N) performs any N events from Events and then STOPs.

Consider the watchdog version of this last check:

STOP [T= (TWD(Spec)[|Ev|](Impl[|Events|]NEvs(N)))\Ev

where Ev = diff(Events,{woof}). The process on the right-hand side never diverges, because it can only perform at most N non-woof events, and the latter are left visible. However, by the definition of TWD(Spec) in Sect. 8.5, once the right-hand side can perform one woof it can perform infinitely many. It follows that the above check is equivalent to

(TWD(Spec)[|Ev|](Impl[|Events|]Nev(N)))\Events

being divergence free. Both fail if and only if the watchdog ever barks.

FDR performs this check entirely as a DFS. It is straightforward to use the debugger to find the trace which Impl performed prior to a loop of hidden woofs. This will, of course, have length no more than N, but may well not be the shortest possible in general.

The CSP coding of solitaire is, like the Sudoku programs in Sect. 4.1, programmed so that it signals a solution with the event done and can from that point carry on communicating dones. This works exactly like the watchdog transformation of a general trace specification. There is, of course, no need to limit the length of a pre-done trace, since there are never more than 31 moves in any play. Thus, checking the process Puzzle\Events for divergence works exactly like the more general version above and has FDR do a DFS for a solution of peg solitaire. It finds a solution almost instantly.

While the proper DFS mode of checking for FDR will work for any form of refinement, this trick for doing a DFS traces check by means of a divergence check will only work for the traces model.

8.7 Determinism Checking

As described in Sect. 6.1, the question of whether or not a process is *deterministic* is important in understanding it, and in particular can be said to decide whether it is *testable*.

One cannot check the determinism of a process P by refinement checking it against some specification in any model X: Spec [X= P, since the deterministic processes are the maximal ones under refinement, and the nondeterministic choice of all deterministic processes is *Chaos* and very nondeterministic!

Nevertheless there are several ways of using refinement checking to decide if a process is deterministic. The FDR algorithm (i.e. the one invoked by asking FDR explicitly whether a process is deterministic) was invented by the author and proceeds as follows.

- Given a process P, extract a "pre-deterministic" refinement of it as follows, by choosing subsets of its states and transitions as follows:
  - Include the root node in the state subset.
  - If an included node Q has a τ transition, then in the subset it has only a single transition, namely τ to some node that is arbitrarily chosen amongst those reachable under τ from Q in the original system.[17]
  - If Q is stable, then choose, for each event a it can perform, a single (arbitrary) one of the states Q can reach under a.
  - In both the cases there is a practical advantage in picking an already-seen state if possible, but for the decision procedure this is not necessary.

  The result is a process that is deterministic on every trace except those on which it diverges. Such processes are called *pre-deterministic*.
- If divergence has been discovered then P is not deterministic.
- Otherwise, the subset (under the transitions picked above) represents a process P' that is deterministic and is a refinement of P. If the two are failures-divergences equivalent then P is deterministic; if they are not then it is nondeterministic (since a deterministic process has no proper refinements over $\mathcal{N}$).
- It follows that, when P' is divergence free, P is deterministic if and only if P'[FD= P or equivalently P'[F= P. Fortunately the way P' has been produced means it is trivial to normalise it.
- When P has been found not to be deterministic then, except in the case where a divergence is found, the FDR debugger reports both the behaviour of P that led to refinement failing, and the unique path of P' to a stable state after the same trace.

---

[17]If we wanted the algorithm to respect the $\checkmark$-as-signal model of termination we are using in this book, there would be a clause that said that if the node had no τ but a $\checkmark$, then the only action it has in the subset is that $\checkmark$. However, as remarked on p. 141, FDR does not at present follow that model, so it handles $\checkmark$ under the next clause. Replacing P by P; *SKIP* will here, as elsewhere, have FDR treat it as though it were in the $\checkmark$-as-signal model.

This algorithm works efficiently and, when the refinement check is successful, will always visit exactly as many state-pairs as there are states in P. This is because, by the time the refinement check is carried out, P' has been reduced to a normal form all of whose states are deterministic and therefore incomparable: it follows that each state of deterministic P refines exactly one of them.

Because the FDR algorithm relies on a special routine to extract P', you cannot reproduce this algorithm using its refinement checking function.

FDR actually gives you two options for determinism checking: you can pick the failures-divergence $\mathcal{N}$ or stable failures $\mathcal{F}$ model. The version above is the former, corresponding to the form of determinism described in Sect. 6.1. Formally speaking, determinism checking over $\mathcal{F}$ seeks to decide whether there is a deterministic process P' such that P' [F= P. Another way of saying that is to specify that P never has the combination of a trace $s^{\frown}\langle a \rangle$ and the failure $(s, \{a\})$. Notice that DIV is $\mathcal{F}$-*deterministic* (as we shall call this property) since it refines *all* deterministic processes. In practice, however, we only seek to decide $\mathcal{F}$-determinism for processes that are known to be divergence free, so that the two notions coincide. There are two cases we need to consider.

The first is where running the FDR check for divergence freedom on P gives a positive answer. There is not much to say about this since it is exactly in the spirit we discussed in Sect. 6.2 of establishing first that a process is divergence-free and doing all further checks over $\mathcal{F}$ or $\mathcal{T}$ as appropriate.

The second is when checking for divergence freedom does find a counter-example, but where (as discussed in the same place) we are making some fairness assumption that means we can ignore such behaviour. In such cases we cannot be sure the above algorithm works, since we do not know what to do when the routine that extracts P' finds a divergence. What often happens in this case is that FDR, instead of giving its usual tick or cross sign to show a positive or negative outcome to a check, instead displays a "dangerous bend" sign to show that it failed to find an answer.

Since this second style of checking for $\mathcal{F}$-determinism has a major practical use in computer security (see Sect. 6.5), this is not a happy position to be in. Fortunately there are two ways round it that can be used with FDR: one depends on the structure of the security checks and the second is to use Lazić's algorithm for determinism checking (introduced in [80]), which depends on running the target process in parallel with itself and a harness and refinement-checking the result against a simple specification.

The first method works whenever the process to be checked for $\mathcal{F}$-determinism takes the form $\mathcal{L}_H(P)$ for a divergence-free process P. Recall (Sect. 6.5) that this process is assumed to behave like $Q = (P \parallel_H Chaos_H) \setminus H$ except that it never diverges. When following the determinism-checking algorithm above, we can replace this process by any refinement Q' when picking the deterministic refinement P'. After all, a deterministic refinement of Q' is a deterministic refinement of Q. So, as $STOP \sqsupseteq Chaos_H$, we can restrict the choice of P' to ones that refine $P \parallel_H STOP$. This can be achieved by checking $P \parallel_H STOP$ for determinism or

$\mathcal{F}$-determinism (the same since this process is divergence-free) and then checking $P \parallel_{H} STOP \sqsubseteq (P \parallel_{H} Chaos_H) \setminus H$.

Note that this emphasises the connection between non-interference and fault tolerance as defined on p. 126.

Lazić's algorithm, modified slightly to make it easier to use on FDR, is described below.

- For any process, let `Clunking(P)` = `P [|E|] Clunker`, where `E` includes all events that `P` uses, but not the special event `clunk`, and

```
Clunker = [] x:E @ x -> clunk -> Clunker
```

`Clunking(P)` therefore behaves exactly like `P`, except that it communicates `clunk` between each pair of other events.

- It follows that `(Clunking(P) [|{clunk}|] Clunking(P))\{clunk}` allows both copies of `P` to proceed independently, except that their individual traces never differ in length by more than one.

- If `P` is deterministic, then, whenever one copy of `P` performs an event, the other one cannot refuse it provided they have both performed the same trace to date. It follows that if we run

```
RHS(P) = (Clunking(P)[|{clunk}|]Clunking(P))\{clunk}
         [|E|] Repeat
```

where `Repeat = [] x:E @ x -> x -> Repeat`, then the result will never deadlock after a trace with odd length. Such a deadlock can only occur if, after some trace of the form `<a,a,b,b,...,d,d>` in which each `P` has performed `<a,b,...,d>`, one copy of `P` accepts some event `e` and the other refuses it. This exactly corresponds to `P` *not* being $\mathcal{F}$-deterministic.

We can thus check determinism and $\mathcal{F}$-determinism by testing whether `RHSDet(P)` refines the following process, respectively over $\mathcal{N}$ and $\mathcal{F}$.

```
LHS = STOP |~| ([] x:E @ x -> x -> DetSpec)
```

Because it runs `P` in parallel with itself, Lazić's algorithm is at worst quadratic in the state space of `P`. (In other words, the number of states can be as many as the square of the state space of `P`.) In most cases, however, it is much better than this, but not as efficient as the FDR check.

Lazić's algorithm works (in the respective models) to determine whether a process is deterministic (i.e. over $\mathcal{N}$) or $\mathcal{F}$-deterministic.

The fact that this algorithm is implemented by the user in terms of refinement checking means that it is easy to vary, and in fact many variations on this check have been used when one wants to compare the different ways in which a process `P` can behave on the same or similar traces. There is an example of this in Exercise 8.11 below, and we will meet more in Chap. 16.

Exercise 8.9 Which of the following processes are $\mathcal{F}$-deterministic? You should try to decide which *without* FDR, and then try them out on FDR. (i) a -> DIV, (ii) (a -> DIV) |~| (a -> STOP), (iii) (a -> DIV) |~| (b -> DIV), (iv) (a -> DIV) ||| ABS, where ABS = a -> ABS [] b -> ABS. If any of them fails to give an answer using FDR's determinism check, use Lazić's algorithm.

Exercise 8.10 A further way of checking to see if a process is deterministic is to replace the arbitrary deterministic refinement P' by a specific one in the FDR algorithm. The most obvious one is the process with the same traces as P which never diverges and never refuses an event that P can perform after the current trace. Imagine this is achieved by embedding the $\mathcal{T}$ (traces) normal form of P, as the unique most deterministic process with that set of traces, within one of the richer models, though FDR does not offer a way of doing this at the time of writing. Compare this with the two algorithms offered above: does it work in general for $\mathcal{F}$-determinism? How does it compare in terms of worst case performance? How would you expect it to compare in the average case?

Exercise 8.11 Modify Lazić's check of determinism so that it checks the following property of a process: P cannot, after any trace s, allow the event b in B while also having the stable failure (s, {b}).

This is a weaker specification than determinism, since it allows P to show non-determinism in events outside B.

8.8 Compression

One of the ways in which FDR can help you overcome the state explosion problem is by attempting to reduce the number of states it has to visit by *compressing* some of the subcomponents of a system. Since the questions that FDR poses about processes are all formulated in terms of semantic models like $\mathcal{T}$, $\mathcal{F}$ and $\mathcal{N}$, it really does not matter how these processes are represented as transition systems. It follows that if, presented with the representation of some process as one transition system, we can find a smaller one with the same value in the relevant model, it is probably better to use the latter since it will be quicker to perform computations on.

FDR supplies a number of functions that try to compress a transition system in this way, most of them behaving slightly differently depending on which model we happen to be using. Three deserve a mention at this stage, and more will be described in more detail in Sect. 16.2:

1. Strong bisimulation sbisim identifies two nodes if their patterns of actions are equivalent in a very strong way. FDR automatically applies this to all the low-level component processes it compiles, so there is no point in applying it again to these processes. (All the compression functions have the property that applying them twice to a process is equivalent to applying them once.)

2. Normalisation normal is the process already discussed: the same function that is always applied to the specification. Its last stage is also strong bisimulation, so again there is no point in applying sbisim to its result. As described earlier, it may actually expand a process, so needs to be used carefully.

3. Diamond compression diamond can be viewed as a sort of half normalisation. It eliminates all τ actions and seeks to eliminate as many of the states of the original system as possible. In summary, this is by recording, if the state S has many states reachable by chains of τs, as few of these "down-τ" states as possible and adding all of their behaviours to S. As a preliminary, diamond applies a function called tau_loop_factor that identifies all pairs of states that are reachable by τ-chains from each other. diamond does not call sbisim automatically, and one frequently gets good results from applying sbdia(P) = sbisim(diamond(P)). diamond can only compress processes with τ actions, but it never expands the state space.

This last combination and normal are the two most used compression functions. Depending on the example, each may perform better than the other. As we will see in Sect. 16.2, sbdia and normal always give exactly the same result when applied to a deterministic process P.

There is no point (at least for speed) in applying a compression function to the complete right-hand side of a refinement check, or to a process being checked for deadlock, divergence or determinism (using the FDR algorithm). This is because it is much more difficult to apply any of these compressions to a process than it is to refinement check it. In fact, the first thing FDR does when applying any of the above functions is to turn the object process into an explicit state machine.

When working in models richer than $\mathcal{T}$, both normal and diamond can produce transition systems with more detail than an ordinary LTS: they are marked with *acceptance* and perhaps *divergence* information. This is because, without this, the compression would lose important details of how the object process behaves. In a *generalised* labelled system (GLTS, see also Sect. 16.1), nodes can be marked with information recording other sorts of behaviours. In the examples we will see, these markings are always either *"divergent"* or one or more acceptance sets—sets of actions that the state can offer stably. There are different rules for what markings states have, depending on which CSP model we are using. For the failures-divergences model $\mathcal{N}$, for example, divergent nodes have no actions, and every node that is not marked as divergent and has no τ or $\checkmark$ actions must be marked with one or more acceptances. Nodes with τ or $\checkmark$ actions can also have acceptances, and in any case acceptances are always subsets of the members of Σ the state can perform. If X and Y are two acceptances of the same state over $\mathcal{N}$ or $\mathcal{F}$, then $X \not\subseteq Y$, or in other words all the acceptances are *minimal*.

Fig. 8.4 The effects of compression on a small LTS

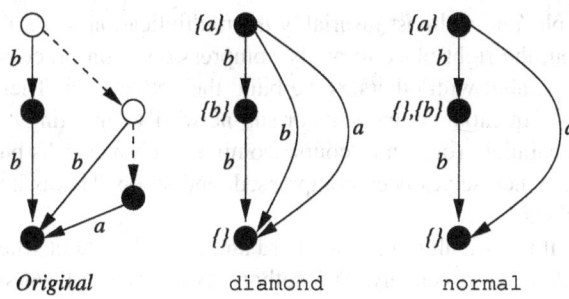

We then understand that a process implemented by such a GLTS starts at the initial node, and can follow any route of actions through the system. At any node marked as divergent it can diverge (as though that node had a τ action to itself), or it can become stable, accepting actions only from A, if A is one of its acceptances. Figure 8.4 shows the results of compressing (relative to either $\mathcal{F}$ or $\mathcal{N}$) the process on the left, the transition system of

```
(b -> b -> STOP)[> ((b -> STOP) [> (a -> STOP))
```

(in which τ actions are drawn with a dashed line and unstable states are drawn as circles rather than solid discs) under respectively diamond and normal. Notice that both, by eliminating τ actions, require acceptance marking to reveal that the only acceptance set in the initial state is {a}. normal gives a unique initial arc labelled by b whereas diamond gives two. There is a further graphical illustration of diamond compression in Sect. 16.2, and one of normalisation in Sect. 16.1.

The author has found that using the Graph mode of FDR to view the result of a compression is a good way of understanding how the various choices work, and how effective they are in particular examples.

To use non-CSP functions such as normal and diamond which are implemented directly by FDR and whose purpose is to transform one state-space representation of a process into another, equivalent one, they must be declared within the CSP_M scripts that use them. The form of the declaration is

```
transparent normal, sbisim, diamond
```

with the word transparent indicating that they are not intended to alter the meaning of the objects they are applied to.

8.8.1 Using Compression

The usual reason for using compression functions is to reduce the number of states explored when checking or normalising a complete system. Since the cause of state explosion is almost invariably the multiplication that arises from parallel composition, the right place to apply compression is on processes that yet have to be put in parallel with others as we build the network up. These might either be individual sequential components or sub-networks consisting of a number of components in parallel. You can of course compress sub-networks built up of smaller ones that have themselves been compressed, and so on. This is known as *hierarchical* compression.

It is difficult to give any hard and fast rules about when compression techniques will work effectively. The author has frequently been surprised both at how well they work on some examples and at how badly they work on others. Some examples are given below, further ones can be found in Chaps. 16–19 and the reader will find many more in this book's web-site. However, there is no real substitute for personal experience.

Broadly speaking, you have a reasonable chance of success when the following are all true:

(a) Part of the alphabet of the process you are compressing has been hidden, either because the hidden events are true internal actions or because they have been abstracted as irrelevant to the specification.

(b) It usually helps if these hidden actions represent progress within the process, as opposed to the resolution of nondeterminism. This is the case with the automated compressions we will see in Chap. 18, for example.

(c) It is not the case that a large part of the state space of the process you are compressing is never visited when it is put into the complete system. The danger here is that you will expend too much effort compressing irrelevant states, or that the irrelevant states will make the subsystems too large to compress. See Example 8.1 below for some ways to reduce or avoid this problem.

The following principles should generally be followed when you are structuring a network for compression:

1. Put together processes which communicate with each other early. For example, in the dining philosophers, you should build up the system out of consecutive fork/philosopher pairs rather than putting the philosophers all together, the forks all together and then putting these two processes together at the highest level.

2. Hide all events at the lowest possible level. $\langle$ hide-$_X \|_Y$-dist$\rangle$ (5.7) and other laws allow the movement of hiding inside and outside a parallel operator as long as its synchronisations are not interfered with. In general, therefore, any event that is to be hidden should be hidden the first time that (in building up the process) it no longer has to be synchronised at a higher level. The reason for this is that the compression techniques all tend to work much more effectively on systems with many τ actions.

The typical system one wants to apply compression to often takes the form

```
System = (|| i:I @ [A(i)] P(i))\H
```

The above principles suggest that you should distribute the hiding of the set H through the composition using $\langle$hide-$_X \| _Y$-dist$\rangle$ (5.7), moving it all to as low a level as possible. The only thing that prevents the hiding of an event being distributed across a parallel operation is when it is synchronised. This is a non-trivial calculation, particularly since one will frequently want to hide further events in System in order to get efficient representations of some specifications, and one might therefore have to do the job several times. For example, one could decide whether System can ever deadlock or communicate error via the checks

```
SKIP [F= System\Events
SKIP [T= System\diff(Events,{error})
```

By far the easiest way of dealing with this is to use utilities from an include file such as compression09.csp that does all these calculations for you. This particular file[18] supplies a number of functions that assume that the network is presented as a data structure involving *alphabetised processes*: in the above example these are the pairs (P(i),A(i)).

Depending on which function you want to use from compression09.csp, networks must be represented in one of two forms: a simple list of alphabetised processes < (P(i),A(i)) | i <- L> with L being some ordering of the indexing set I, or a member of the data-type

```
datatype SCTree = SCLeaf.(Proc,Set(Event))
                | SCNode.Seq(SCTree)
```

In the latter a tree of processes is defined to be either a leaf containing a single alphabetised process or a sequence of trees (with the file assuming that all such lists are non-empty).

The intention with the type SCTree is to put a parallel system together in a hierarchical fashion, combining individual processes into groups, those into larger groups and so on until the network is composed. This is most natural—and we might hope to get the best performance from compression—when the processes grouped together interact a lot with each other and less so with ones outside the group.

One can, of course, turn a list of processes into one of these trees in various ways. For example, given a branching factor K, we can define

```
btree(K,<p>) = SCLeaf.p
btree(K,ps) = SCNode.<btree(K,ps')| ps'<- split(K,ps)>
```

where split(K,ps) divides ps into K (or #ps if less) portions with sizes differing by at most one. This gives a nearest approximation to a K-branching tree that contains the same processes as a given list.

---

[18]compression09.csp is an extended version of compression.csp, which was one of the example files that accompanied TCP.

Each of the compression utilities is an operator that takes a compression function (or any other function from processes to processes that is intended to leave its argument's semantic value unchanged), a network in one of the two forms above, and the set of events that you wish to hide. So, for example,

```
LeafCompress(normal)(SysList)(H)
```

calculates the set of events from H that can be hidden in each P(i) (all those belonging to A(i) and no other A(j)). If H(i) is this set of locally hidden events, the function then applies normal (the chosen compression operator) to each A(i)\H(i), composes the rest in parallel, and then hides the events from H that belong to more than one of the A(i).

The version of the dining philosophers from Sect. 3.2 provides a very good illustration of leaf compression. In analysing deadlock over $\mathcal{F}$ we can hide all events. Each philosopher has four events that are not synchronised with any other process, namely thinks.i, sits.i, eats.i and getsup.i. Therefore these events get hidden and allow compression in Leafcompress(normal)(S)(Events) with S being either the symmetric or asymmetric version of the dining philosophers. In effect this reduces Phil(i) to the process

```
CP(i) = picksup.i.i -> picksup.i.(i+1)%N ->
        putsdown.i.(i+1)%N -> putsdown.i.i -> CP(i)
```

which can reasonably be regarded as the "essence" or skeleton of Phil(i) needed to examine deadlock. Compressing the Fork(i) processes has no effect, since all their events are synchronised. With 8 philosophers this reduces the asymmetric case's 6.4 M states to 11,780. It is reasonable to expect good results from leaf compression whenever the individual processes have a significant number of actions (and this includes τ actions) that can be hidden and are not synchronised.

One can, of course, put parallel combinations of processes in a list rather than just sequential ones, and the same goes for the leaves of an SCTree. The obvious thing to do with the dining philosophers is to combine Phil(i) and Fork(i), obtaining the list

```
ASPairList = <(PandF(i),APF(i)) | i <- <0..N-1>>

PandF(i) = ASPhil(i)[AlphaPhil(i)||AlphaFork(i)]Fork(i)
APF(i) =   union(AlphaPhil(i),AlphaFork(i)))
```

This, remarkably, reduces the 8-philosopher asymmetric check to 55 states, and the corresponding check of the symmetric system finds the deadlock in its initial state (i.e. the compressed hidden system deadlocks before any actions have occurred).

The above methods, namely attacking individual processes or natural small combinations of processes, usually work reliably. It is certainly worth experimenting with different compression functions and trying to formulate specifications so that as many events as possible can be hidden. The results obtained for the dining philosophers with this approach are exceptionally good, but we will see another, much more ambitious and practical, case where compression reliably produces excellent results in Chap. 18.

In some cases we might want to build up the network a process at a time, compressing as we go. The logical way to do this is to keep the size of the interface between the constructed parts of the system and the rest of the world as small as possible. Often this works well, but the following should be borne in mind:

- The time taken to do many large compressions can become significant.
- The size of system that FDR can compress is far less than the size it can handle on the right-hand side of a refinement check.
- As discussed earlier, a partial network may reach many more states when considered by itself as opposed to when it runs in the context of the whole network. Typically this is because the structure of the complete system imposes some invariant on the sub-network. Therefore much of the work involved in compressing the partial system may be wasted.

A good example of the third point is a token ring such as that in Sect. 1: the whole ring ensures that there is only one token present, but typically an open-ended section can allow any number of tokens in up to the number of nodes it contains. See Example 8.1 below, Exercise 8.16 and the practical entitled *A multi-dimensional puzzle* (which generalises the exercise) for examples of how one can sometimes eliminate this type of problem by imposing an invariant on sub-networks. See also Sect. 16.2.5, where an alternative to the use of invariants is discussed.

The function `InductiveCompress`, applied to a list of processes, builds up the network in this way, starting from the end of the list. In other words, it compresses the two right-hand processes together, composes and compresses the result, and then iteratively adds on further processes, individually compressed, each time applying the chosen compression function. One must therefore arrange the list so that the processes are added in an appropriate order: in building up a linear network one will follow the natural order, meaning that only one process's communications that are internal to the network remain visible at any time. This is well illustrated by the dining philosophers. It is clear that we should arrange the processes so that they follow the natural order round the table, as indicated in Fig. 8.5. The deadlock check is represented by

```
InductiveCompress(normal)(ASPairList)(Events)
```

This works exceedingly well, since each of the partially constructed lists with all but externally synchronised events reduces to only 4 states (with most being equivalent up to renaming). You can therefore check as many philosophers as you please on FDR, the only limit being the time it takes to compile the components. Leaving the {|eats|} or {|getsup|} events visible works similarly well, though the state space does grow with N if you leave {|sits|} or {|thinks|} visible since these events can prevent a philosopher being in contention with one of his or her neighbours. In Sect. 17.1 we will see how this compression can lead to inductive proofs of the dining philosophers for any size of network.

Fig. 8.5 Inductive
compression strategy applied
to the dining philosophers

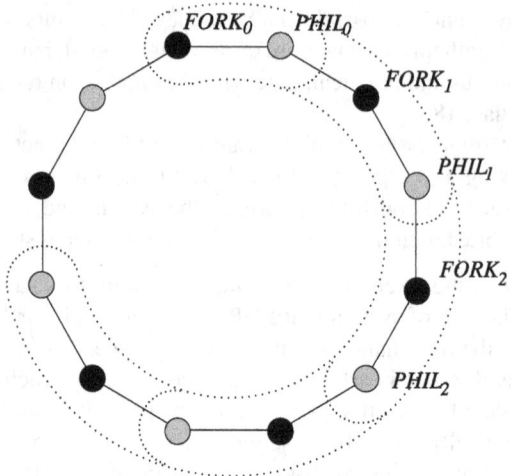

Inductive compression can also work well on two-dimensional grids. One such example is provided by the file matmul.csp in the directory of examples relating to Chap. 13 of TPC, which also contains some files with further one-dimensional examples. A further example can be found in the practical entitled *A class of puzzles*. In such cases it usually makes sense to start at a corner of the grid and add nodes in something like a "raster scan" order (namely adding all the nodes in one row one at a time before starting on the next row).

Example 8.1 (IMPOSING AN INVARIANT) This example illustrates how one can sometimes avoid the state space of one or more sub-networks, considered in isolation, expanding well beyond the limits that are imposed on them in the completed system.

In such cases, the whole network is imposing limits on the states the sub-network can reach. Sometimes the user can identify what these limits are and express corresponding *invariants* succinctly: in these cases one can often take advantage of them to prevent a compression strategy failing because of an explosion in the sizes of the compressed subcomponents.

A very simple N-node token ring (known as *Milner's scheduler*) is described by the processes

```
Nd(0)  = a.0 -> c.1 -> b.0 -> c.0-> Nd(0)

Nd(r)  = c.r -> a.r -> c.(r+1)%N -> b.r -> Nd(r)      (r>0)
```

The token is represented by the synchronisations on the channel c which rotate starting with c.1. Nd(r) performs a.r when it holds the token, and b.r when it does not.

The usual view of this ring is with { | c | } hidden, with { | a, b | } left visible so that the ring *schedules* their relative order—note these events are not synchronised within the ring. However, we will contemplate proving that the a.i rotate, repeating the sequence <a.0,a.1,...,a.N-1> for ever. We can establish this by additionally hiding {|b|} and showing that the result refines Rotate(0) where

```
Rotate(r) = a.r -> Rotate((r+1)%N)
```

We can therefore apply compression strategies to the ring of Nd(r)s hiding {|b,c|}.

You will find that applying InductiveCompress to these processes works poorly, and compares very badly to the 2*N states that the complete network has under leaf compression. This is because the partially constructed networks can contain many tokens whereas the complete network always holds exactly one. We can re-impose the invariant of there being only one as follows. The chain of processes Nd(0)...Nd(r-1) has "token passing" interface {c.0,c.r}. For each r>0 we know that the token emerges from this chain before re-entering it, so that when the chain is put in the context of the one-token ring these events cycle <c.r,c.0,c.r,c.0,...>.

We could *enforce* this invariant on the chain by putting the latter in parallel with the process EI(r)=c.r -> c.0 -> EI(r). We could add these enforcing processes (with alphabet {c.0,c.r}) to the network and they would not in fact change the behaviour of the complete network, but would avoid the compression of so many unvisited states.

The problem with this approach is that it builds in an assumption that our invariant holds without demonstrating that each of the chains does in fact remain within its constraints when the whole network runs. We can do better than this: the following process simply *assumes* that the invariant holds by saying that the process can behave however it likes if the invariant is violated.

```
AI(r) = c.r -> AI'(r) [] c.0 -> DIV
AI'(r) = c.0 -> AI(r) [] c.r -> DIV
```

For any √-free process P, we then have P[|{c.0,c.r}|]AI(r) [FD= P because AI(r) [FD= RUN({c.0.c.r}). This means that inserting these processes into the network creates an anti-refinement, and does not block any of the behaviour of the chains. However, when FDR performs the resulting checks $\mathcal{N}$ it avoids checking the unnecessary states. This is because the divergence of DIV in these states means that FDR prunes its search thanks to divergence strictness.

The network described

```
<Node(N-1)>^
<(AI(N-2-r),{c.0,c.N-1-r}),Node(N-2-r) | r<-<0..N-2>>
```

where the assumption processes have been placed appropriately, therefore behaves well under inductive compression over $\mathcal{N}$. The fact that the complete network is divergence-free (unlike most of the processes constructed *en route*) in fact proves that the exception clauses of the AI(r) are never encountered during a complete run.

Note how we have used strict divergence to our advantage here. The reader will find that using a model without strict divergence does not work in the same way if its refinement-least member replaces DIV in the definition of AI(r): while the overall model will still be accurate, there is no saving in states during inductive compression. A way of achieving a similar (though slightly less efficient) effect is to replace DIV by RUN({error.r}) within AI(r). This should prevent many states being explored following an error.r as it prevents the partial network from performing any further visible events. One should then ensure that no error event ever occurs in the complete system. See also Exercise 8.15 below.

TPC also discusses the compression of Milner's scheduler, but from a slightly different perspective.

The SCTree datatype referred to above has been introduced to make it easy for users to devise their own compression strategies, as well as to craft a hierarchy for a particular network:

```
StructuredCompress(compress)(t)(X)
```

builds up the network, first of all compressing all the leaves as in LeafCompress, and then combining each group of sub-networks implied by an SCNode. At every level of this tree except the topmost, as much hiding as possible is pushed to that level and compression applied. Thus the function from lists of process/alphabet pairs to SCTree defined

```
OneLevel(ps) = SCNode.<SCLeaf.p | p <- ps>
```

is such that applying StructuredCompress(compress) to the result is exactly equivalent to applying Leafcompress(compress) to ps.

We will find applications of this type in Chaps. 18 and 19.

Compression on the Left-Hand Side of a Refinement Check

It goes without saying that in cases where the process on the left-hand side of a refinement check has many states, compressions may also work well as pre-processing before normalisation. There are a number of special considerations in this.

The following two techniques can be used either in combination or separately:

- Use compression on proper sub-systems of the left-hand side but not the whole. In other words use the same compression strategy that you would on the right-hand side of a check. However, in this case it is often a good idea to use normal as the compression function, since (for obvious reasons) the type of compressed structure it produces is unlikely to cause problems in normalisation.
- Use compression on the whole left-hand side: this may well be worthwhile since normalisation is a considerable transformation of the target process. In this case there is no point in using normal, so you should use sbdia, the composition

of diamond and sbisim. Doing this may either increase or decrease the number of pre-normal form states FDR finds in the normalisation, but almost always makes normalisation faster when the uncompressed left-hand side has a significant number of τ actions.

See p. 363 for the description of an alternative approach to normalisation that FDR supports: instead of pre-computing a normal form, it just discovers those normal form states that are required by the complete check.

Exercise 8.12 Given a list ps of alphabetised processes, define functions that turn it into an SCTree such that applying StructuredCompress to the respective result has the effects of (i) InductiveCompress on ps, (ii) grouping the list into pairs of consecutive elements (and perhaps a singleton over) and composes and compresses these pairs, but applies no compression above this level, and (iii) dividing up the list into two pieces that differ in size by at most one, and applying inductive compression to each half, starting with the two processes at the ends of the original list—the same as inductively compressing to meet in the middle.

Exercise 8.13 Use FDR to discover a sequential process that is equivalent in $\mathcal{F}$ to to the parallel composition of ASPairList hiding all but { | eats | } for each N>2, where ASPairList represents the asymmetric dining philosophers as defined on p. 178. Note that this is bound to be a process that only uses the events { | eats | }. You might well find it helpful to apply InductiveCompress and use the Graph mode of FDR. Explain the asymmetry in your answer. *Of course the application of the compression strategy does not change the semantic value here, but it can help clarify the problem.*

Exercise 8.14 Modify both the definition of the token ring and the invariant processes IA(r) from Example 8.1 so that there are always 1 <= K < N tokens in the ring. What effect do you think the assumption process will have on the compression of the ring when K=2, K=N/2 and K=N-1? [Note that if, when you perform a check of the complete ring with all assumptions in, it is not divergence-free, then your assumption processes must be wrong!]

Exercise 8.15 The non-$\mathcal{N}$ approach to a checkable "assumed" invariant set out at the end of Example 8.1 introduces a separate state with an error event that is reached from the invariant process once the invariant *has been* breached. This is not as efficient in terms of the intermediate state spaces as the approach in which strictly interpreted DIV is reached, since the presence of divergence as soon as the invariant has been breached means that no further behaviour is examined, whereas the error.r approach takes one more step.

Show that it is possible to improve on this by turning the event that breaks the invariant into an appropriate error.r. [*Hint: use 1-to-2 renaming.*]

Exercise 8.16 Recall the puzzle solved in Exercises 8.2 and 8.4. Why would you not expect this to compress well under straightforward inductive compression? Find invariant processes which improve this performance by restricting the region under consideration to having one or no empty slots. Now compare the performance of the compressed and uncompressed parallel implementations.

8.9 Notes and Reflections

FDR originally came into being in 1991 for use in a hardware design project, at the instigation of Geoff Barrett, then of inmos (see Note 2 below). Between that date and 2007 it was a product of Formal Systems (Europe) Ltd. Since 2008 it has been the responsibility of a team at Oxford University Computing Laboratory (OUCL).

FDR underwent a major re-write in 1994/5, to become "FDR2", and from then on there has been a long series of incremental releases, of which the most recent one, as this book was written, is FDR2.91. That is the version which is described in this book. FDR2.91 is itself a major advance on FDR2.84 (the last release by Formal Systems). Hopefully the next year or two will see the release of FDR3, which we hope will be extended in various important directions, for example giving users the ability to address its functionality other than through CSP and the incorporation of further algorithms for checking based on ideas such as SAT checking [38, 102] and CEGAR (Sect. 17.5).

FDR's web-site can be located through this book's, and potential users should consult it for details of how to obtain the tool. At the time of writing, FDR is freely down-loadable for academic teaching and research, and most of the source code is also freely available for use by academic institutions, with use of that code being restricted by a licence. Most of FDR is written in C++.

FDR is the work of many people. While the author has designed much of its functionality and some of the algorithms that make this possible, he has not written a single line of its code. Those most important to its development include Michael Goldsmith, who designed and wrote much of it and managed the project for many years; Bryan Scattergood, who designed and implemented the CSP_M input language that is so important to FDR's usability as well as the compiler; David Jackson and Paul Gardiner, who played vital parts in the development of FDR in the 1990s; and Philip Armstrong, who both worked on it at Formal Systems for some years and now coordinates development of the code at OUCL.

The idea of transforming language containment (i.e. trace refinement) into the reachability of a single state (in our case, the one in which the watchdog *woof*s) is a standard concept in automata theory. It, and the harder versions for richer models, were developed for CSP in [46].

Some other model checkers use DFS as their default search method. The idea of using divergence checking to implement DFS searches using FDR arose in discussions between the author and James Heather. Some statistics on its effectiveness can be found in [102].

Lazić's determinism-checking algorithm was developed because he wanted a test for determinism expressed using ordinary refinement so that the theory of *data independence* could be applied to it. (See Sect. 17.2.) This algorithm is one of the keys to understanding what properties can be checked with CSP refinement, as discussed in Sect. 16.4.

The idea of compositional compression of state spaces was not original to the CSP/FDR model—see [47], for example—but some of the compressions it uses [135] are particular to CSP models.

Note 1: A Lesson About Quicksort   When FDR computes a strong bisimulation (sbisim) it works out a series of equivalence relations, each calculated from the previous one: see p. 364. The first relation is based purely on any marking of the nodes (as in a GLTS), and each subsequent one $\equiv_{n+1}$ is based on the marking plus the set of all pairs of the form (x, C) possessed by a node, where x is an action and C is a $\equiv_n$ equivalence class reachable under x from the node.

After performing this marking, FDR sorts a standardised representation of this information about the states so as to bring all nodes related under $\equiv_{n+1}$ together in the overall list. Since these lists may get quite long, it is important to use an efficient (i.e. $n \log n$) sorting algorithm. It is well known that Quicksort has this as its expected time, with the chance of getting a significantly slower performance being vanishingly small if the pivot is chosen well (and picking the first element of the list as in the functional programming (p. 152) implementation in this book does not usually qualify!) Imagine our surprise, therefore, when our first implementation, which used a library implementation of Quicksort, ran in what looked like deterministic n^2 time and was unacceptably slow.

The cause of this was that, instead of splitting the list into three parts: `<x | x <- X, x<p>`, `<x | x <- X, x==p>` and `<x | x <- X, p<x>`, the library routine split it into two, with the second and third of these combined to `<x | x <- X, p<=x>`. When sorting a list of objects that were equal in the order (for example any set of states that are all equivalent under $\equiv_{n+1}$ in our application), this version of Quicksort takes *deterministic* $O(n^2)$ time since everything apart from the pivot ends up in a single list which is then sorted recursively. Since there are, particularly for small n, often large numbers of equivalent states in our application, this explains why the library routine was completely unsuitable for FDR.

Note 2: Inmos, the Transputer and FDR   Inmos was an independent British company set up in the late 1970s to design and build microprocessors, and it was later taken over by SGS Thomson Microelectronics. Its main products were highly innovative. *Transputers* were the first microprocessors to have on-chip memory and communications hardware—creating a "computer-on-a-chip". Their communications hardware was designed, in essence, to implement a CSP-style handshake. The architecture not only envisaged transputers running in parallel and connected directly to one another, but gave excellent support—such as fast context switching—for multiple parallel threads on the same processor.

To support this concurrency, inmos introduced a language called OCCAM, itself a mixture of CSP and a simple imperative programming language. See [69, 72] for more details of OCCAM. The design process of later generations of transputers involved a significant amount of formal specification and verification, based on CSP, OCCAM and other notations.

Barrett identified the need for a tool like FDR for the analysis of the relatively sophisticated communications hardware on a later transputer (the T9000), and the basic algorithms of FDR were designed during a memorable meeting held in the summer of 1991 in the French town of Auch.

Reflections on Technology and Formal Verification   Perhaps the most striking thing about working with this tool for the last 19 years is the vast increase in the size of systems that it can handle now in comparison to then. This means FDR (in common with some other automated formal methods) is useful on a much greater percentage of developments than it was then. Such tools were frequently over-sold in their early days, but have now become invaluable.

I recall how impressed I was when the first version of FDR handled a check of about 30,000 states in an hour or two, and that the following year running a check of about 600,000 states (the constrained solitaire board described in Sect. 15.1 of TPC) took perhaps 5 hours. By the time I published TPC in 1997, the unconstrained solitaire board with 187M states was still out of range, whereas by 2000 and the revised edition it took 12–24 hours on a reasonably powerful workstation or 2.5 hours on a prototype (8 processor) parallel implementation. As I write this in 2009 my powerful laptop will run the same check in 40 minutes and I am confident that by the time this book appears in print a parallel implementation will run it in a few minutes on an 8-core PC. And this is in running the same model, visiting the same set of states once each using (at least since the mid-1990s) little-changed algorithms and code. An experimental way of finding FDR's counter-examples quickly using *bounded model checking*[19] based on SAT checking—a completely different way of examining the state space implemented by Hristina Palikareva—has already been able to solve the unconstrained board in under 4 minutes [102] on a single core. We have already seen (p. 167) how a DFS search through the state space can solve the puzzle far faster than that.

While programmers and algorithm designers might like to take credit for the vast increase in capability since then, in truth much, and possibly most, of the advance in power is due to the continuing application of Moore's Law both to the processing power and memory size of computers, as illustrated above. All we have to do is find ways of using this, and in particular the recent phenomenon by which the increase in single-CPU speed has been replaced by an increase in the number of cores. See Sect. 16.3.2.

This is not to say that advanced techniques such as compression and the SAT checking advance described above do not sometimes have a huge effect on what examples can be approached, and we will see many in this book. It is just that in practice the effect of these is only rarely on a par, at least reliably, with the spectacular basic computer advances detailed above.

---

[19]Bounded model checking means that, instead of searching through a process's complete state space, one looks only for errors that can be reached within some chosen N steps from the root. It is particularly appropriate for SAT checking because of the algorithms used for the latter, but the CSP notation makes it simple to limit any check in this way.

Though the human mind is no more capable than it used to be, the complexity of the systems it tries to design increases just about as rapidly as the computing power available. This is a splendid demonstration of *Parkinson's Law:* "Work expands so as to fill the time available for its completion.", which is a splendid complement to Moore's Law (one version of which is that the number of transistors on a chip doubles every two years). It follows that, though the size and complexity of components that can be formally verified have increased remarkably and hopefully this trend will continue, formal methods tools like FDR will probably never be powerful enough to verify all the systems that designers would like them to.

Part II
Theory

CSP has a highly distinctive theory based on behavioural models like $\mathcal{T}$ and $\mathcal{N}$. In the next five chapters we give an in-depth study of these models. We also present completely revised operational and denotational semantics for CSP, each of which is intimately connected with the hierarchy of behavioural models.

The first chapter is on operational semantics. We introduce a new style of presenting operational semantics that guarantees that all definitions make sense in CSP models. The middle three chapters are respectively an introduction to denotational semantics based on behavioural models, and detailed studies of the hierarchies of finite and infinite behaviour models. Finally, in Chap. 13, we show how to create an algebraic semantics based on transformation to normal form, and demonstrate that a small selection of optional laws such as $\langle \square\text{-idem}^* \rangle$ $(P = P \,\square\, P)$ tie in with the existence of a hierarchy of models.

In this part we restrict ourselves to the *untimed* interpretation of CSP that we saw in Part I. A little of the theory of Timed CSP can be found in Chaps. 14 and 15 in Part III.

Much of the material in Part II has appeared previously in TPC or in more recent academic papers. Therefore we are able to avoid giving some fine details and technical proofs, instead referring the reader elsewhere.

Throughout we look at the uses of the various models we discover, including the sorts of specifications they support.

Part II
Theory

Chapter 9
Operational Semantics

Of all the forms of semantics mentioned above, operational semantics is probably the easiest for a non-mathematician to follow and the most important for using existing tools. Many of the ideas underlying it have already been seen in earlier chapters, at a lower level of formality.

The main purpose of CSP is to describe communicating and interacting processes. But in order to make it useful in practice we have added quite a rich language of sub-process objects: as we saw in Chap. 8, CSP_M contains a functional programming language to describe and manipulate things like events and process parameters. Of course, any complete semantics of the language would have to take account of this other facet: in effect, we would need to give the sub-language a semantics too. But this would take a lot of extra space and take the focus off understanding the semantics of communication: it is complex in its own right. Thus, just as in the rest of this book we have focused on the main purpose of CSP, in this and the other chapters on semantics we will deliberately ignore exactly how the calculation of sub-process objects fits in.[1] Therefore we will tend to ignore the detailed syntax and evaluation of sub-process objects, just treating them as values. This 'glossing-over' is made a good deal less dangerous because CSP has a declarative (purely functional) semantics, meaning that values are never changed by assignment. The only real problem occurs when the evaluation of a sub-process object fails to terminate or produces some other sort of error. Error-handling is an important, if occasionally irritating, part of the construction of any formal semantics, but in the spirit of our simplified treatment of sub-process objects we will not deal with these types of CSP_M[2] error in this book. They are discussed in [144].

---

[1] Operational and denotational semantics taking these details into account can be found in Scattergood's thesis [144] and (in a more sophisticated form), in Lazić's work [80].

[2] In Chap. 18 we will give a semantics *in* CSP for another language, and give many of the details of how to handle run-time errors in that.

A.W. Roscoe, *Understanding Concurrent Systems*, Texts in Computer Science,
DOI 10.1007/978-1-84882-258-0_9, © Springer-Verlag London Limited 2010

9.1 Transition Systems and State Machines

We introduced the idea of *labelled transition systems* on p. 41 and used them in Part I to understand both the operational behaviour of processes and, in Chap. 8, the workings of FDR. The main subject of this chapter is how to give CSP a *formal* semantics in LTSs. In this section we investigate the behaviour of transition systems, whether or not derived from a process.

Recall that a *labelled transition system* (LTS) is a set of nodes and, for each event a in some set, a relation $\xrightarrow{a}$ between nodes. It is a directed graph with a label on each edge representing what happens when we take the action which the edge represents. Most LTSs have a distinguished node n_0 which is the one we are assumed to start from.

The operational interpretation of an LTS is that, starting from any node such as n_0, the process state is always one of the nodes, and we make progress by performing one of the actions possible (on outward-pointing edges) for that node. This set of the initial actions of node P will be denoted P^0. The only things that matter are the actions each node has: if the nodes do carry some annotation then this cannot be observed during a run.

In interpreting CSP we usually take the set of possible labels to be $\Sigma^{\checkmark,\tau} = \Sigma \cup \{\checkmark,\tau\}$. Actions in Σ are visible to the external environment, and can only happen with its cooperation. The special action τ cannot be seen from the outside and happens automatically. Thus, if the process is in a state with no actions outside Σ (a *stable* state) it might have to wait there for ever; when it is in an *unstable* state ($\tau \in P^0$) we assume that some action must occur within a short time. (The event that occurs may be visible or τ.)

$\checkmark$, as discussed in Chap. 7, is a special signal representing the successful termination. It is—as we saw in Chap. 7—different from other events, not least because it is presumably always the last event that happens. It is certainly visible to the environment, but it is better to think of it as an event that does not require the environment's cooperation: it is in one way like τ and in another like ordinary members of Σ. A state P that has $\checkmark \in P^0$ is not stable, because the environment cannot prevent it from happening. (Note that the previous discussion of stable states, in Sect. 6.1, was before we had met $\checkmark$.) As in TPC, we will give $\checkmark$ this intermediate interpretation, unlike some works where it was treated like a member of Σ. We will, however, define a state to be $\checkmark$-*stable* if it has no τ action, since we will find this useful when studying transition systems.

Where a state has a range of visible actions we assume, especially when the state is stable, that the environment has a free choice of which (if any) of the events (i.e., distinct labels) to choose. If there is more than one action with a given label a, the environment has no control over which is followed when it chooses a. In other words, this is a source of nondeterminism.

We assume that only finitely many actions (visible or invisible) can happen in a finite time.

To explain these ideas we will consider two LTSs. The one shown in Fig. 9.1 displays most of the possible types of behaviour without $\checkmark$.

Fig. 9.1 Example of a
labelled transition system

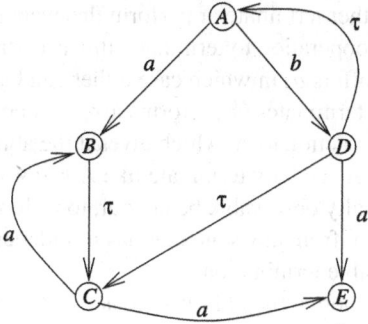

Fig. 9.2 A labelled transition
system with ✓ actions

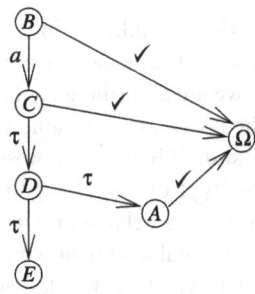

- In state A, the environment has the choice of either a or b, and since this is a stable state, nothing can happen until one of these is selected. The process then moves into state B or D, this being determined by which event is chosen.
- The only action available to state B is an internal one. Therefore the process takes this action and moves to state C.
- In state C, there is only one event available, a, and the process must wait until the environment communicates it. There are two possible states that can then arise, and the environment has no control over which one the process moves to.
- In state D, internal and external actions are both possible. The environment might be able to communicate the a action, but cannot rely on this. It can, however rely on the process moving to either A or C if a does not happen. As in the previous case, the environment has no control over which.
- State E has no actions: it is deadlocked. Once the process reaches this state it is doomed to remain there for ever.

Figure 9.2 enables us to see the effects of ✓. This transition system follows the obvious convention that ✓ is always the last event and leads to an end state Ω. (If forced to interpret a transition system where this was not true we would just ignore anything that could happen after ✓.)

- The easiest state to understand is A: the only thing it can do is terminate. It behaves like the process *SKIP*.

- B can either terminate or perform the event a. Since it does not need the environment's cooperation to terminate, this is certain to happen unless the environment quickly offers a, in which case either can happen (nondeterministically).
- C either terminates or performs a τ, the choice being nondeterministic.
- D has a τ action to A, which gives it the ability to terminate. Indeed a τ action to a state that can only terminate like A is *always* equivalent, from the point of view of externally observable behaviour, to its having a $\checkmark$ action of its own. Either can be chosen, from any state that has it, independently of the environment and leads to inevitable termination.

Even though the only visible action that can ever happen to a process in state D is $\checkmark$, its behaviour is different from A since it can follow the τ action to E and become deadlocked. In other words, D can refuse to terminate while A cannot.

An LTS can be finite or infinite (in terms of its set of nodes), and it is clearly the case that only those parts reachable from a node n (via finite sequences of actions) are relevant when we are describing the behaviour of n. In particular, we will usually assume that all the nodes are reachable from the distinguished node n_0. A process is said to be *finite state* if it can be represented by a finite LTS.

An LTS is not—by itself—a very good way to describe a process if you want to capture the essence of its behaviour, since there are many different ways of representing what any reasonable person would agree is essentially the same behaviour. For example, any LTS can be expanded into a special sort of LTS, a *synchronisation tree*, where there are no cycles and there is a unique route from the root to every other node, in the manner illustrated in Fig. 9.3. (The distinguished root nodes are indicated by open circles.) But notice that even two synchronisation trees can easily represent the same behaviour, as all the original LTSs—and hence all their different expansions—represent behaviours we might suspect are essentially the same. If one does want to use operational semantics as a vehicle for deciding process equivalence, some sort of theory is required which allows us to analyse which process descriptions as an LTS represent the same behaviour.

In CSP, the main mode of deciding process equivalence is via failures, divergences etc., which are not primarily based on transition systems. However, some other process algebras (most notably CCS) take the approach of defining the basic meaning of a process to be an LTS and then deciding equivalence[3] by developing some theory that decides which LTSs are essentially the same. Thus, getting this analysis right can be extremely important.

Many different equivalences over LTSs (and the nodes thereof) have been proposed, most of which are specific to a given view, but the most fundamental is valid in them all (in the sense that if it defines two nodes to be equivalent then so do the others). This is the notion of *strong bisimulation*, where to be equivalent two processes must have the same set of events available immediately, with these events leading to processes that are themselves equivalent. Another way of looking at it

---

[3]We can relate these two ideas either by the type of congruence theorem discussed in this book or via the idea of *testing equivalences* [35].

Fig. 9.3 Unfolding LTSs to synchronisation trees

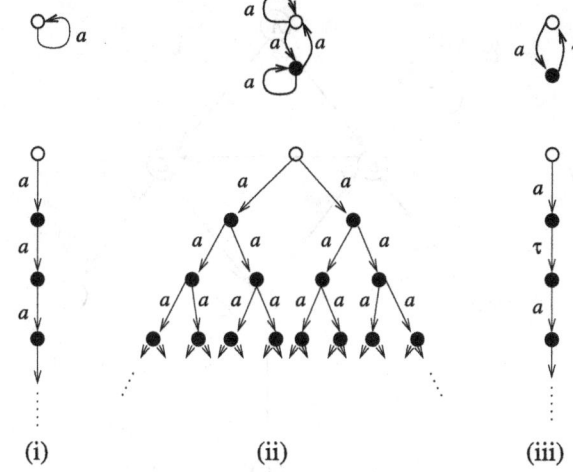

is that no experiment which is based on exploring the behaviour of two nodes by examining and performing available events (including τ and $\checkmark$ on an equal basis to all the others) can tell them apart.

Definition If S is an LTS, the relation R on the set of nodes $\hat{S}$ of S is said to be a *strong bisimulation* if, and only if, both the following hold:

$$\forall n_1, n_2, m_1 \in \hat{S}.\forall x \in \Sigma^{\checkmark,\tau}.$$
$$n_1 R n_2 \wedge n_1 \xrightarrow{x} m_1 \Rightarrow \exists m_2 \in \hat{S}.n_2 \xrightarrow{x} m_2 \wedge m_1 R m_2$$

$$\forall n_1, n_2, m_2 \in \hat{S}.\forall x \in \Sigma^{\checkmark,\tau}.$$
$$n_1 R n_2 \wedge n_2 \xrightarrow{x} m_2 \Rightarrow \exists m_1 \in \hat{S}.n_1 \xrightarrow{x} m_1 \wedge m_1 R m_2$$

(Note that, though there is no requirement that a bisimulation is symmetric, the above definition is symmetric so that R^{-1} is a bisimulation if R is.)

Two nodes in $\hat{S}$ are said to be *strongly bisimilar* if there is any strong bisimulation which relates them. It is a theorem (see Exercise 9.5) that the relation this defines on the nodes of an LTS is *itself* a strong bisimulation: the maximal one. This is always an *equivalence relation*: reflexive, symmetric and transitive—it partitions the nodes into the sets whose members' behaviours are indistinguishable from each other (see Exercise 9.3).

Consider the systems in Fig. 9.4, where for simplicity all the actions have the same label (a, say). In the left-hand system, it should not come as a surprise that E, F and G are all strongly bisimilar, since none of them can perform any action at all. All the others can perform the event a, and are therefore *not* strongly bisimilar to these three. This means that A cannot be strongly bisimilar to any of B, C, D, as all of these can become one of E, F, G after a and A cannot: the definition of strong bisimulation states that if A is bisimilar to B then it must be able to move under a to

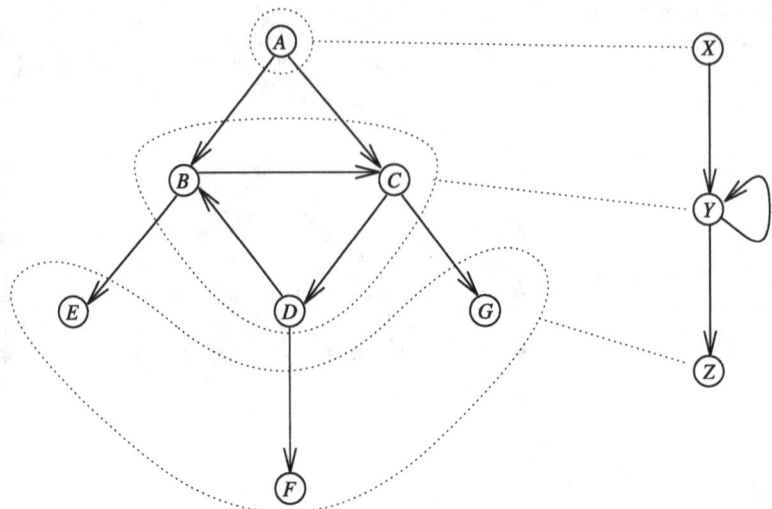

Fig. 9.4 Strong bisimulation equivalence

something bisimilar to E. On the other hand, all of B, C and D are bisimilar—each of them can perform an a either to a member of the same set or to one of E, F, G. The partition produced by the maximal strong bisimulation is shown in the figure.

It makes sense to say that two nodes in different LTSs (with the same underlying alphabet) are bisimilar, because we can embed the two systems in one larger one (whose nodes are the union of disjoint copies of the nodes of the two we are summing). In this sense all the nodes of both versions of systems (i) and (ii) of Fig. 9.3 are strongly bisimilar. They are not, however, strongly bisimilar to those in system (iii)—since the latter can perform τ actions. This shows the chief weakness of strong bisimulation as a technique for analysing process behaviour: its inability to distinguish between the different effects of visible and invisible actions.

Having found the maximal strong bisimulation on an LTS, we can produce another LTS with one node for each equivalence class, and an action a from class C_1 to class C_2 just when the nodes in C_1 have a actions to C_2 (they all will if and only if one does). This factoring process is shown in Fig. 9.4, with the system on the right being the one derived from the one we have already examined. It is always the case that the nodes of the new system are bisimilar to the members of the classes they represent, and that no pair of the new system's nodes are bisimilar.

Many other forms of bisimulation for LTSs have been devised over the years, almost all of which represent weaker (i.e. coarser) equivalence relations over nodes. The one which is more frequently seen is *weak* bisimulation. We do not use this for CSP since it does not distinguish between *STOP* and **div**, and therefore does not respect any CSP model other than finite traces. There is, however, a slight strengthening of weak bisimulation, *divergence-respecting* weak bisimulation, which does respect all such models: if two LTS nodes are bisimilar then they are identified in all CSP models. This is defined as follows, where the notation $P\!\Uparrow$ means that P is immediately divergent, namely there exist P_i (with $P_0 = P$) such that $P_i \xrightarrow{\tau} P_{i+1}$ for all i. $P \xRightarrow{s} Q$ means that there exist $P_0, \ldots, P_m$ with $P_0 = P$, $P_m = Q$ and events x_i such that $P_i \xrightarrow{x_i} P_{i+1}$ and the trace consisting of the non-τ x_i is s.

Definition If S is an LTS, the relation R on the set of nodes $\hat{S}$ of S is said to be a *divergence-respecting weak bisimulation* (which we will abbreviate to *DRW-bisimulation*) if and only if $n\,R\,m \Rightarrow (n\!\Uparrow\,\Leftrightarrow\,m\!\Uparrow)$ and

$$\forall n_1, n_2, m_1 \in \hat{S}.\forall s \in \Sigma^{*\checkmark}.$$
$$n_1 R n_2 \wedge n_1 \xRightarrow{s} m_1 \Rightarrow \exists m_2 \in \hat{S}.n_2 \xRightarrow{s} m_2 \wedge m_1 R m_2$$

$$\forall n_1, n_2, m_2 \in \hat{S}.\forall s \in \Sigma^{*\checkmark}.$$
$$n_1 R n_2 \wedge n_2 \xRightarrow{s} m_2 \Rightarrow \exists m_1 \in \hat{S}.n_1 \xRightarrow{s} m_1 \wedge m_1 R m_2$$

The definition of *weak bisimulation* is the same as this except that the requirement that $n\!\Uparrow\,\Leftrightarrow\,m\!\Uparrow$ is dropped.

As with strong (and weak) bisimulation, there is a maximal DRW-bisimulation. This makes equivalent any pair of nodes that are equivalent under any DRW-bisimulation. Such a pair of nodes are said to be *DRW-bisimilar*.

The following result tells us a lot about how DRW bisimulations treat stable states.

Lemma 9.1 *Every DRW-bisimulation has the following property, which is a direct strengthening of the main part of its definition above:*

$$\forall n_1, n_2, m_1 \in \hat{S}.\forall s \in \Sigma^{*\checkmark}.$$
$$n_1 R n_2 \wedge n_1 \xRightarrow{s} m_1 \Rightarrow \exists m_2 \in \hat{S}.n_2 \xRightarrow{s} m_2 \wedge m_1 R m_2$$
$$\wedge\ (m_1\ stable \Rightarrow m_2\ stable)$$

$$\forall n_1, n_2, m_2 \in \hat{S}.\forall s \in \Sigma^{*\checkmark}.$$
$$n_1 R n_2 \wedge n_2 \xRightarrow{s} m_2 \Rightarrow \exists m_1 \in \hat{S}.n_1 \xRightarrow{s} m_1 \wedge m_1 R m_2$$
$$\wedge\ (m_2\ stable \Rightarrow m_1\ stable)$$

Proof The proof of this result comes in two parts. The first is to establish it with "stable" replaced by "$\checkmark$-stable" (i.e. the state has no τ action, as opposed to τ or $\checkmark$ as in "stable"). If R is a DRW bisimulation, n is $\checkmark$-stable and $n\,R\,m$, then necessarily n, and hence (by definition of DRW-bisimulation) m are not immediately divergent. It follows that the set $\{m' \mid m \xRightarrow{\langle\rangle} m' \wedge m'\ \text{is}\ \checkmark\text{-stable}\}$ is non-empty. Since $m \xRightarrow{\langle\rangle} m'$ for each such m' it follows from R being a DRW-bisimulation that there is n' such that $n \xRightarrow{\langle\rangle} n'$ and $n' R m'$. However, $\{n' \mid n \xRightarrow{\langle\rangle} n'\} = \{n\}$ because n is $\checkmark$-stable. It follows that every m' in the set above is as required for the property.

That the property holds for "stable" then follows because if $n\,R\,m$ and both states are $\checkmark$-stable then clearly one has the initial action $\checkmark$ if and only if the other does. $\square$

Fig. 9.5 Example of DRW bisimulation

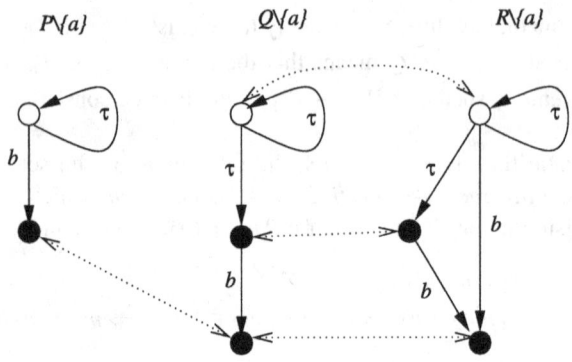

$P\backslash\{a\}$ $Q\backslash\{a\}$ $R\backslash\{a\}$

This lemma is extremely important, since it says that any behaviour (such as the stable failure (s, X) where m_1 refuses X) that n_1 has thanks to m_1's stability is also a behaviour of n_2.

It is a fairly easy consequence of the definitions that every strong bisimulation is a DRW-bisimulation. For example, it is straightforward to show that if n_1 and n_2 are strongly bisimilar then $n_1 \Uparrow \Leftrightarrow n_2 \Uparrow$.

DRW-bisimulation allows us to identify behaviours that are the same except for the presence or absence of some τ actions. For example, all the nodes in systems (i)–(iii) of Fig. 9.3 are DRW-bisimilar. However, *unlike* weak bisimulation, it does not allow a divergent node to be identified with a non-divergent one, and says that if in one process we can reach a stable node with a given behaviour, we can reach a stable one in the other. This is a weaker statement than saying that stable nodes can only match with stable nodes, since for example both nodes of the process $(a \rightarrow STOP) \backslash \{a\}$ are bisimilar to each other: the unstable initial node can reach a stable, deadlocking node under $\overset{\langle\rangle}{\Longrightarrow}$. To illustrate DRW-bisimulation, consider the processes

- $P \backslash \{a\}$, where $P = (a \rightarrow P) \,\Box\, (b \rightarrow STOP)$
- $Q \backslash \{a\}$, where $Q = (a \rightarrow Q) \,\Box\, (a \rightarrow b \rightarrow STOP)$
- $R \backslash \{a\}$, where $R = (a \rightarrow Q) \,\Box\, (b \rightarrow STOP) \,\Box\, (a \rightarrow b \rightarrow STOP)$

These are illustrated in Fig. 9.5. $P \backslash \{a\}$ and $Q \backslash \{a\}$ are not DRW-bisimilar, since $Q \backslash \{a\}$ can reach a non-divergent state on $\langle\rangle$ which can perform b whereas $P \backslash \{a\}$ can not. On the other hand $Q \backslash \{a\}$ and $R \backslash \{a\}$ are DRW-bisimilar. All the bisimulations between nodes are shown with dotted lines.

DRW-bisimulation is important in the theory of CSP because it respects every behavioural model of CSP. We will formalise this in Lemma 11.1 (p. 257).

As with strong bisimulation, we can factor a transition system by the maximal DRW-bisimulation. However, this time we have to be a bit more careful in the handling of τ actions. Suppose that $C1$ and $C2$ are two equivalence classes and that there are members $P1$ and $P2$ of these respectively, and that $P1 \overset{x}{\longrightarrow} P2$. Unless $C1 = C2$ and $x = \tau$ we will introduce the action $C1 \overset{x}{\longrightarrow} C2$. However, it is possible that introducing $C1 \overset{\tau}{\longrightarrow} C1$ when $C2 = C1$ and $x = \tau$ may be wrong. For example, consider $STOP$ and $\tau STOP$. These two processes are DRW-bisimilar, but it would be wrong to put a τ action from the single equivalence class $\{STOP, \tau STOP\}$ to itself, because neither of these processes can diverge. The action $C1 \xrightarrow{\tau} C1$ is only inserted when $C1$ contains a τ-loop: a cycle of states where each can take τ to the next. In fact we will generally assume that even these self-τs are excluded and replaced by a "divergent" marking in the resulting GLTS (see below).

This is, in fact, the general way to factor a transition system by an equivalence relation. It gives exactly the same result as the procedure on p. 196 in the case of the maximal strong bisimulation, simply because if there is a τ action from P_1 to P_2 where P_1 and P_2 are strongly bisimilar, it is easy to show that this sequence can be extended to P_3, P_4 and so on, all of which are strongly bisimilar to P_1 and where there is a τ from P_n to P_{n+1}.

In general, factoring an LTS by an equivalence relation produces a GLTS as described on p. 174 because different members of the class might have different stable acceptance or refusal sets; and one might diverge and another one not. Where we, in general, factor an LTS by an equivalence relation it is necessary to mark the nodes with all the acceptance, divergence and refusal information necessary for the model being used.

Of course, not all factorings by general equivalence relations make sense semantically, but there are general results we can prove about this process: for example given an arbitrary equivalence relation $\cong$ over the nodes of an LTS, and $\mathcal{M}$ any trace-plus model,[4] we always have $\overline{P} \sqsubseteq_M P$ for all nodes P, where $\overline{P}$ is the equivalence class of P considered as a member of the quotient GLTS.

Exercise 9.1 No pair of nodes in the LTS of Fig. 9.1 are strongly bisimilar. Prove this. Are any of the nodes DRW-bisimilar?

Exercise 9.2 Which pairs of nodes are strongly bisimilar in the LTS shown in Fig. 9.6?

Exercise 9.3 Draw an LTS describing a game of tennis between players A and B, with the alphabet $\{point.A, point.B, game.A, game.B\}$. (The intention is that the appropriate event $game.X$ occurs when player X has won.) Recall that successive points take either player through the scores $\langle 0, 15, 30, 40, game \rangle$ except that the game is not won if a player scores a point from 40-all (deuce), but rather goes to an 'advantage'–'deuce' cycle until one player is two points ahead. Which scores are strongly bisimilar?

Exercise 9.4 Show that every strong bisimulation is a DRW-bisimulation.

Exercise 9.5 Do this exercise twice. First time interpret "bisimulation" as "strong bisimulation", the second time as "DRW-bisimulation". Let V be any LTS and R

---

[4]The concept of a trace-plus model will be defined on p. 272. It includes all the CSP models we have seen to date.

Fig. 9.6 Which nodes are strongly bisimilar (see Exercise 9.2)?

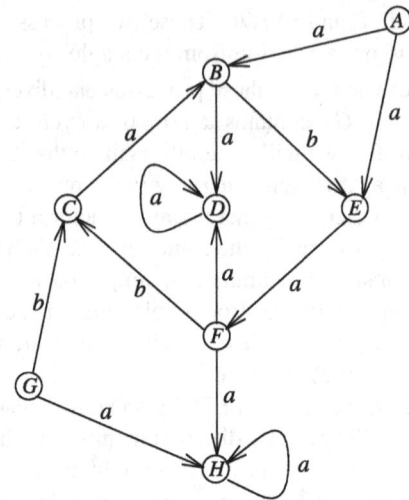

be a bisimulation. Show that its reflexive closure $R \cup I$ is a bisimulation, where I is the identity relation $\{(x, x) \mid x \in \hat{V}\}$.

Suppose R and S are both bisimulations. Show that the relation $(R \cup S)^*$ is a bisimulation which has both R and S as subsets.

The reflexive, transitive closure T^* of the relation T is

$$I \cup T \cup T \circ T \cup T \circ T \circ T \cup \cdots$$

Use this to prove that the relation on $\hat{V}$ defined

$$x \, R^{\sqcup} y \Leftrightarrow \exists \, \text{bisimulation} \, R . x \, R \, y$$

is an *equivalence relation* (i.e. is symmetric, transitive and reflexive).

Prove that $R^{\sqcup}$ is itself a bisimulation on V. By construction it is the *maximum bisimulation*: it contains all others.

A different way of proving the existence of the maximum bisimulation can be found by following Exercises 7.2.4–7.2.6 in TPC.

9.2 Firing Rules for CSP

The operational semantics of CSP treats the CSP language itself as a (large!) LTS. It allows us to compute the initial events of any process, and what processes it might become after each such event. By selecting one of these actions and repeating the procedure, we can explore the state space of the process we started with. The operational semantics gives a one-state-at-a-time recipe for computing the transition system picture of any process. It is traditional to present operational semantics as a logical inference system: Plotkin's SOS, or Structured Operational Semantics, style [108]. A process has a given action if and only if that is deducible from the rules given. The operational semantics of CSP have usually been presented in that style, for example in Chap. 7 of TPC, but in some ways it is *too general* for CSP. The approach we take in this book is first to give the rules for a few operators in SOS style, but later concentrate on a new notation, which we term the *combinator* style. This has the considerable advantage that any definition one can give in it makes sense in the world of CSP's semantic models.

In either style, there are separate rules for each CSP operator, to allow us to deduce what the actions of a process are in terms of its top-level operator (often depending on the actions of its syntactic parts).

The rules themselves all simply formalise our intuition of how and why processes perform actions, both visible and invisible.

9.2.1 SOS Style Operational Rules

Because the process *STOP* has no actions, there are no inference rules for it. It has no actions in the operational semantics because there is no possibility of proving it has any.

SKIP, on the other hand, can perform the single action $\checkmark$, after which it does nothing more.

$$\frac{}{SKIP \xrightarrow{\checkmark} \Omega}$$

The fact that there is nothing above the horizontal bar here means that no assumptions are required to infer the action described. The special process term Ω (which we are adding to the language/LTS for convenience) is intended to denote any process that *already has* terminated. The result state after a $\checkmark$ action is never important (its behaviour is never looked at) and it is sometimes helpful to have a standardised way (Ω) of representing the result of termination in the LTS of processes.

The main way communications are *introduced* into the operational semantics is via the prefixing operation $e \to P$. In general, e may be a complex object, perhaps involving much computation to work out what it represents. There is a choice in what to do about computations like this in an operational semantics. Clearly a real implementation would, in general, have to go through a procedure to work out this and other types of sub-process objects. One could include these steps (as τ actions or perhaps some other sort of invisible action) in the operational semantics, but this would make them much more complex both to define and to analyse. In the spirit of the discussion at the start of this chapter, we will ignore these computation steps (taking the values as given) and concentrate only on 'actions' which arise directly from CSP rather than from lower-level behaviour.

The prefix e may represent a range of possible communications and bind one or more identifiers in P, as in the examples

$$?x : A \to P, \qquad c?x?y \to P, \qquad c?x!e \to P$$

This leads to one of the main decisions we have to make when constructing an operational semantics for CSP (and many other languages): how do we deal with the identifiers in programs that represent data values, other processes, etc.? For it is clearly the case that the behaviour of a program with a free identifier (one whose value is not created within the program itself) might depend on the value of the identifier. The simple answer to this problem is to deal only with *closed* terms: processes with no free identifiers. Using this it is possible to handle most of the situations that can arise, making sure that each identifier has been substituted by a concrete value by the time we need to know it. Because of its simplicity, this is the approach we will take.

This simple approach does create some problems when handling some more advanced aspects of CSP, which means that another style would be preferable if one wished to give a complete operational semantics covering every nuance of the language. This is to introduce the concept of an *environment*:[5] a mapping from identifiers to the values (which might either be data or processes) they represent. Environments are then added to the state space of the LTS that we are defining with the operational semantics: instead of transitions being between processes, we now have transitions between process/environment pairs. This alternative style results in very few differences to the individual semantic clauses except where a value is being looked up in the environment. Full details can be found in [144].

To implement the simpler approach we will assume the existence of functions *comms* and *subs*.

- *comms(e)* is the set of communications described by e. For example, $d.3$ represents $\{d.3\}$ and $c?x{:}A?y$ represents $\{c.a.b \mid a.b \in type(c), a \in A\}$.
- For $a \in comms(e)$, $subs(a, e, P)$ is the result of substituting the appropriate part of a for each identifier in P bound by e. This equals P if there are no identifiers bound (as when e is $d.3$). For example,

$$subs(c.1.2, c?x?y, d!x \to P(x, y)) = d!1 \to P(1, 2)$$

The transition rule for prefix is then easy to state:

$$\frac{}{e \to P \xrightarrow{\ a\ } subs(a, e, P)} \quad (a \in comms(e))$$

It says what we might expect: that the initial events of $e \to P$ are *comms(e)* and that the process then moves into the state where the effects of any inputs in the communication have been accounted for. Note the way the limitation on events was introduced: via a *side condition* to the inference rule. A side condition simply means that the deduction is only valid under the stated restriction.

This is the only transition rule for prefixing, which means that the only actions of the process $e \to P$ are those deducible from it. The *initial* actions of $e \to P$ are thus independent of whatever P can or cannot do (in that $initials(e \to P) = comms(e)$ and this process is always stable). There are only two other operators of which this

---

[5]The word "environment", as used here, has an entirely different meaning to the idea of an environment that the process communicates with, discussed elsewhere.

can be said. One is nondeterministic choice, which is modelled by a choice of τ actions, one to each process we are choosing between:

$$P \sqcap Q \xrightarrow{\tau} P \quad , \qquad P \sqcap Q \xrightarrow{\tau} Q$$

This easily translates to the generalised notion of choice over a non-empty set of processes:

$$\frac{}{\sqcap S \xrightarrow{\tau} P} \quad (P \in S)$$

It is important to remember the restriction that S is non-empty: even though the above rule makes sense in itself when $S = \emptyset$, the value of $\sqcap \emptyset$ it predicts does not. (No value X makes sense in the failures-divergences model for this object, since it would have to (i) be a unit for $\sqcap$ in the sense that $P \sqcap X = P$ for all P, and (ii) refine every process even though, as we will see in the next chapter, the failures-divergences model does not have a greatest element.)

The final case where the initial actions are determined completely by the operator itself is recursion. It is a good idea to introduce a τ action to represent the 'effort' of unfolding a recursive definition via the following rule:[6]

$$\frac{}{\mu p.P \xrightarrow{\tau} P[\mu p.P/p]}$$

This τ action never causes any harm, since the externally visible behaviour of any process P is unchanged by the addition of an extra starting state with a τ action to P. The recursive process has no option but to take this invisible action and behave like P. The τ action in recursion is there to avoid the difficulties caused by under-defined recursions such as $\mu p.p$ and $\mu p.(p \square Q)$. The most natural symptom of this type of behaviour is divergence, and this is exactly what the introduction of the τ achieves. In fact, for well-constructed recursions, the τ is not really needed, though it still makes the mathematical analysis of the operational semantics a good deal easier.[7]

All the other operators have rules that allow us to deduce what actions a process of the given form has from the actions of its sub-processes. Imagine that the operators have some of their arguments 'switched on' and some 'switched off'. We will refer to these as **on** and **off** arguments respectively. The former are the ones whose actions are immediately relevant, the latter the ones which are not needed to

---

[6]The $\mu p.P$ style of recursion is the only one we will deal with in this operational semantics, since a proper treatment of the more common style of using names in a script to represent (perhaps parameterised, and perhaps mutual) recursive processes requires the introduction of environments. The rule we are introducing here extends simply to that context: it is then the act of looking up a process identifier that generates a τ.

[7]FDR does not introduce τ actions of this sort because the only effect they have on well-constructed definitions is to increase the size of the state space. If you are using a tool where such actions are not introduced, the result is likely to be that an attempt to use a recursion like $\mu p.p$ will make the tool diverge. Thus, if you need to create a representation of **div** in such a tool where it is not built in as primitive, it is necessary to use a term like $(\mu p.a \rightarrow p) \setminus a$ or $\mu p.P \sqcap p$.

deduce the first actions of the combination. (All the arguments of the operators seen above are initially switched off.) This idea comes across clearly in the construct $P; Q$ (whose operational semantics can be found below), where the first argument is switched on, but the second is not as its actions do not become enabled until after the first has terminated.

Both the arguments of external choice ($\Box$) are **on**, since a visible action of either must be allowed. Once an argument is **on**, it must be allowed to perform any τ or $\checkmark$ action it is capable of, since the argument's environment (in this case the operator) is, by assumption, incapable of stopping them. There is, however, a difference between these two cases since a τ action is invisible to the operator, which means that there are always rules like the following:

$$\frac{P \xrightarrow{\tau} P'}{P \Box Q \xrightarrow{\tau} P' \Box Q}, \qquad \frac{Q \xrightarrow{\tau} Q'}{P \Box Q \xrightarrow{\tau} P \Box Q'}$$

which simply allow the τ to happen without otherwise affecting the process state. (In some cases these rules are implied by more general ones.) These rules simply *promote* the τ action of the arguments to τ actions of the whole process. On the other hand, the $\checkmark$ event is visible, so (as with other visible actions) the operator can take notice and, for example, resolve a choice. With $\Box$, there is no difference in how $\checkmark$ and other visible events are handled:

$$\frac{P \xrightarrow{a} P'}{P \Box Q \xrightarrow{a} P'} \ (a \neq \tau), \qquad \frac{Q \xrightarrow{a} Q'}{P \Box Q \xrightarrow{a} Q'} \ (a \neq \tau)$$

9.2.2 Combinator Style Operational Rules

The SOS style of operational semantics that we have used above could reasonably be said to give *too many* choices for how to define an operator. It is easy, in this style, to define operators that make no sense in CSP. For example, there is nothing about it that forces one to promote the τ actions of **on** arguments, or to ensure that whenever an action $P \xrightarrow{x} P'$ sits on top of the bar, any process derived from P below the bar is P'.

The *combinator* style of presenting operational semantics concentrates on combining the visible actions of the **on** argument processes into the result actions, and gives the operator definer far less freedom about what to do with the process terms and τ actions.

We will illustrate it by giving the operational semantics of $P \Box Q$ once more. The first thing to do is to declare which of the process arguments are **on** (the rest being **off**). In the $\Box$ case both are relevant to the first step, so we declare $\{1, 2\}$ as **on**. Note that we are referring to the arguments by number. We will thus think of the operator term we are defining as $OP(1, \ldots, N)$, where $1, \ldots, N$ represent the N arguments of the operator OP.

The τs of **on** arguments are always promoted. There is therefore no need to include rules for this explicitly in combinator-style operational semantics for individual operators. Therefore there is no analogue of the rules for promoting τs that we saw in the SOS semantics of $\square$. The main part of the combinator description of an operator consists of triples of the form: (ϕ, x, R) where

- ϕ is a partial function from the indices of the **on** arguments to Σ. This is arbitrary (and can even be the empty function). It represents the actions that any number (from none to all) of the **on** arguments perform when contributing to an overall action.

  In other words, the action is enabled if and only if, for every $i \in \operatorname{dom}(\phi)$, the ith argument process can perform $\phi(i)$.

- x is any member of $\Sigma^{\tau\checkmark}$: the overall action that $OP(P_1, \ldots, P_N)$ performs. We allow it to be τ or $\checkmark$ even though none of the "input" actions are. Both of these possibilities occur in CSP operators: for τ in several operators such as hiding and $\sqcap$, and for $\checkmark$ in the semantics of *SKIP*.

- R defines the *format* of the result state: a piece of CSP syntax that has any selection of the argument indices (**on** or **off**) as free "process variables". We highlight these arguments in a bold typeface **1**, **2** etc.

  A number such as **1** denotes one of two things in R. If $1 \in \operatorname{dom}(\phi)$, the process P in argument 1 has participated in the action via some action $P \xrightarrow{y} P'$ and so **1** denotes P'. If $1 \notin \operatorname{dom}(\phi)$ then **1** denotes P.

  The syntax of R is subject to three rules. Firstly, if $x = \checkmark$, then $R = \Omega$. The second rule is that the index of no **on** argument can appear more than once in R. This says that **on** arguments cannot be copied: we will discuss this point further in Sect. 10.2. The third rule says that **on** arguments can appear (whether directly or indirectly) only as **on** arguments of the operators used to make up R. So for example R might be **1** (i.e. the result is simply the appropriate state of the first argument) or $(\mathbf{1} \square \mathbf{2}); (a \to SKIP)$. It cannot be $\mathbf{1} \square \mathbf{1}$ (because **1** appears twice), $a \to \mathbf{1}$ or $\mu p.\mathbf{1} \square (a \to p)$ (in each case because the argument appears in an **off** place—the argument of a recursion is deemed to be **off** for this purpose).

  There are no complex Rs required in the semantics of the operators of CSP. In fact in every case (except for handling termination) the result process will always be a single argument (**on** or **off**), or retain exactly the same structure or *format* as existed before the action.

  For convenience we will allow R to be omitted from a triple, with the understanding that if $x = \checkmark$ then $R = \Omega$ and that otherwise it is $OP(\mathbf{1}, \ldots, \mathbf{N})$, namely exactly the same format that we started with.

If there are M **on** arguments, we can represent the partial function ϕ as an M-tuple, whose components are members of Σ or $\cdot$, meaning that a component is not in the domain of this particular function. Thus the two rules of $\square$ based on visible actions are $((a, \cdot), a, \mathbf{1})$ and $((\cdot, a), a, \mathbf{2})$ for each $a \in \Sigma$. In other words, the result states are just the first and second arguments respectively. When there is only one **on** argument, we will omit the tuple brackets (see sequential composition below, for example); when there is no **on** argument, we will write $^-$ as the partial function.

As well as handling the Σ actions of the **on** arguments, we also have to set out how the operator responds when one of these terminates. Termination is, as discussed earlier, somewhere between a τ action and an ordinary visible one. It can be observed like a member of Σ but, like τ, it cannot be refused by a process's environment. This means that $\checkmark$s are not synchronised by any operator and cannot be turned into events that *can* be refused by the environment. It follows that each **on** argument i must have at least one rule for the event $\checkmark$, that the corresponding partial function ϕ is precisely $\{(i, \checkmark)\}$ (equivalent to the tuple $(\cdot, \ldots, \cdot, \checkmark\cdot, \ldots, \cdot)$ with the $\checkmark$ in the ith place) and that the result action is always τ or $\checkmark$. The result state R is restricted to terms that *do not* contain the terminated argument. R is Ω if and only if $x = \checkmark$.

Thus the two termination rules for $\square$ are $((\checkmark, \cdot), \checkmark, \Omega)$ and $((\cdot, \checkmark), \checkmark, \Omega)$. We use the convention mentioned above, so these become $((\checkmark, \cdot), \checkmark)$ and $((\cdot, \checkmark), \checkmark)$.

Of course, the place where $\checkmark$ is most important is in the sequential composition operator $P; Q$. Here, the first operand P is **on**, while the second is **off**. So we can declare the set of **on** arguments to be $\{1\}$. In $P; Q$, P is allowed to perform any Σ action at all, giving us the rule (a, a) for each $a \in \Sigma$ (which abbreviates $(a, a, \mathbf{1}; \mathbf{2})$ using the convention that we do not mention an unchanged process structure). The termination rule is $(\checkmark, \tau, \mathbf{2})$.

A combinator-style operational semantics easily translates into an SOS one: the implicit τ promotion, the Σ-rule and the $\checkmark$-rule respectively become

$$\frac{P_1 \xrightarrow{\tau} P_1'}{P_1; P_2 \xrightarrow{\tau} P_1'; P_2}, \qquad \frac{P_1 \xrightarrow{a} P_1'}{P_1; P_2 \xrightarrow{a} P_1'; P_2} (a \in \Sigma), \qquad \frac{P_1 \xrightarrow{\checkmark} P_1'}{P_1; P_2 \xrightarrow{\tau} P_2}$$

Another operator that has one argument **on** and one **off** is the (asymmetric) sliding choice operator $P \rhd Q$: only the first argument is **on**. There are three rules:

$$(a, a) \quad [a \in \Sigma], \qquad (\cdot, \tau, \mathbf{2}), \qquad (\checkmark, \checkmark)$$

The most interesting rule here is the second, since it enables an action (here τ) that is unrelated to any action of the **on** process.

The rules for hiding and renaming have much in common, since both allow all the actions of the underlying process but change some of the names of the events. There are three rules for the hiding operator $P \setminus B$: $(a, a) [a \notin B]$, $(a, \tau) [a \in B]$ and $(\checkmark, \checkmark)$.

The renaming operator $P[\![R]\!]$ has just two rules: $(a, b) [a \mathbin{R} b]$ and $(\checkmark, \checkmark)$. In both hiding and renaming the only operand is **on**.

Both arguments of the parallel operator $\|_X$ are **on** and it has the following three rules for its Σ actions:

$$((a, \cdot), a) \quad [a \notin X], \qquad ((\cdot, a), a) \quad [a \notin X], \qquad ((a, a), a) \quad [a \in X]$$

or, in other words, the two arguments progress independently when not communicating in X, but have to synchronise over X.

Recall that $P \|_X Q$ terminates when both P and Q do. Following the rules for termination above, however, it would not be proper to insist on the two $\checkmark$s synchronising. Therefore, isomorphic to the treatment in TPC, we make both the processes'

$\checkmark$s into τs and follow these with an externally visible one. In the following we regard the syntaxes $P \parallel_X \Omega$ and $\Omega \parallel_X P$ as separate unary operators on P. The termination rules are then

$$((\checkmark, \cdot), \tau, \Omega \parallel_X 2) \quad \text{and} \quad ((\cdot, \checkmark), \tau, 1 \parallel_X \Omega)$$

where the rules for both of the unary constructs $P \parallel_X \Omega$ and $\Omega \parallel_X P$ are

$$(a, a) \quad [a \notin X] \quad \text{and} \quad (\checkmark, \tau, SKIP)$$

We could also have given a semantics where the second $\checkmark$ is passed to the outside, rather than becoming a τ that leads to $SKIP$. That would not be isomorphic to TPC, though.

In interrupt, $P \triangle Q$, both arguments are **on**, and the rules are

$$((a, \cdot), a) \quad [a \in \Sigma], \qquad ((\cdot, a), a, 2) \quad [a \in \Sigma]$$
$$((\checkmark, \cdot), \checkmark), \qquad\qquad ((\cdot, \checkmark), \checkmark)$$

In other words, the first argument performing an event a does not change the format, but as soon as the second performs a visible event it throws away the first argument. However, if the first argument terminates before the second performs a visible event, this terminates the whole construct.

In throw, $P \Theta_A Q$, only the first argument is **on**, and the rules are

$$(a, a) \quad [a \notin A] \quad \text{and} \quad (a, a, 2) \quad [a \in A]$$

To complete the operational semantics, we now give the combinator-style equivalents of the operators that we presented only in SOS style. None of these: the constants $STOP$ and $SKIP$, nondeterministic choice $\sqcap$ and prefixing, have any **on** arguments, so we write "–" as the ϕ component of the rules, which are

- $STOP$: no rules
- $SKIP$: $(-, \checkmark, \Omega)$
- $P \sqcap Q$: $(-, \tau, 1)$ and $(-, \tau, 2)$
- $a \to P$: $(-, a, 1)$

Notice that we have only covered the binary form of $\sqcap$ and the simple form of prefix here. That is because general forms of each of them can have any number—even an infinite number—of **off** arguments.

To deal with this we have to extend our notation for **off** arguments beyond the one we have been using to date. All we need to do is use an arbitrary set to index them rather than include them amongst the natural numbers used for the **on** arguments. Thus the operator $\sqcap\{P_\lambda \mid \lambda \in \Lambda\}$, whose arguments are parameterised by Λ, will simply have the rules

$$\{(-, \tau, \lambda) \mid \lambda \in \Lambda\}$$

and the general prefix $e \to P$ has arguments parameterised by $comms(e)$ and rules[8]

$$(-, a, \mathbf{a}) \quad [a \in comms(e)]$$

in which the argument labelled **a** is $subs(e, a, P)$.

Notice that even when they are infinite in number, only one of the arguments ever becomes turned **on** in a run. It is not permissible to extend the notation so that there are an infinite number of **on** arguments for any operator. It seems plausible that we could introduce an infinite form of $\Box$, again parameterised by Λ, whose rules (choosing to represent the partial functions as sets of pairs rather than infinite tuples) would be

$$\{((\lambda, a)\}, a, \lambda) \, [a \in \Sigma] \mid \lambda \in \Lambda\} \cup \{((\lambda, \checkmark), \checkmark) \mid \lambda \in \Lambda\}$$

But promoted τ actions create a problem: imagine combining together infinitely many $STOP$ processes, and infinitely many $STOP \sqcap STOP$ processes. Since $STOP = STOP \sqcap STOP$ in every CSP model, the results ought to be the same. But they are not, since the τ actions at the start of the second process could all be promoted, one after another, through an infinite $\Box$, creating a divergence and eliminating stability. Thus if we were to allow this infinite form of $\Box$, it could not be congruent over either $\mathcal{F}$ or $\mathcal{N}$.

The reader might wonder why we have presented our operational semantics in the combinator form rather than the tried and tested SOS. As we said above, SOS allows one to express operational rules that are completely foreign to CSP, so it is far from certain that an operator that someone proposes to introduce to CSP by defining it in SOS will make sense: it may very well not behave compositionally with respect to the various CSP models. The reason—something we will justify in Sect. 9.4—is that if $\mathcal{L}$ is a language all of whose operators are defined using combinator operational semantics, then every operator in it can be simulated to a high degree of faithfulness by a CSP construction which is congruent to it over every CSP model.

In other words, any operator defined in this way that is not already a CSP operator is a natural extension to CSP: we will call such operators *CSP-like*. It is hoped that future versions of FDR will allow users to define any operators they choose using

---

[8]As with the SOS treatment of prefix, we would be able to handle general prefix much more elegantly if we were to add environments that bind free identifiers to their values in the combinator operational semantics. In fact doing so would give an even clearer distinction between **on** and **off** arguments, as an **on** one must already have its environment and an **off** one need not. There would still be the choice of whether to show the environment explicitly in the semantic term. Of course if we did so then the appearance of all the operational semantic clauses would change. However, at least for the purpose of giving a semantics to CSP, we can use an implicit notation where it is assumed that the environment given to each newly turned-**on** argument is the same as the "input" one unless we state a modification explicitly. In this, we might write the rule for prefixing as

$$(-, a, (\mathbf{1}, subs(e, a, \rho))) \quad [a \in comms(e)]$$

In other words, we now treat prefixing as a unary operator and use $subs(e, a, \cdot)$ in a modified form on a conventional name ρ for the surrounding environment. In this style we could have two different infinitary forms of $\sqcap$: one with an infinite set of processes, and the other with an infinite set of (perhaps tuples of) values to be substituted into the environment.

combinator-style operational semantics. It will then be possible to use these in conjunction with standard CSP in full confidence that all the refinements, compressions etc. of CSP will still be valid.

Example 9.1 To show the operational semantics in action we will see how to derive the transitions of a simple process, namely

$$COPY[right \leftrightarrow left]COPY = COPY \gg COPY$$

$$= \left(COPY[\![^{right,\, mid}/mid,\, right]\!] \underset{\{|mid|\}}{\|} COPY[\![^{left,\, mid}/mid,\, left]\!] \right) \setminus \{|mid|\}$$

where

$$COPY = \mu p.left?x \rightarrow right!x \rightarrow p$$

and the type of the various channels is $\{0, 1\}$, meaning that we can assume

$$\Sigma = \{left.x, mid.x, right.x \mid x \in \{0, 1\}\}$$

- Consider first the initial state $P_0 = COPY \gg COPY$. Since none of the rules associated with the operators $\|_X$, $\setminus B$ or renaming allows us to infer any action not produced by an action of an argument process, the only initial actions of P_0 are those associated with progress by the two *COPY* processes. These, in turn, can each perform only a τ action to become

$$COPY^\tau = left?x \rightarrow right!x \rightarrow COPY$$

This τ action is promoted by each of renaming, parallel (both arguments) and hiding, so two τ actions are possible for P_0, to the processes

$$P_1 = COPY^\tau \gg COPY$$
$$P_2 = COPY \gg COPY^\tau$$

- In P_1, the second argument has exactly the same τ available as it did in P_0 (because it was not used in the move to P_1), so this can still be promoted to a τ action from P_1 to

$$P_3 = COPY^\tau \gg COPY^\tau$$

$COPY^\tau$ has initial actions $left.0$ and $left.1$ leading respectively to the states

$$COPY(0) = right!0 \rightarrow COPY$$
$$COPY(1) = right!1 \rightarrow COPY$$

These are promoted unchanged by the renaming $[\![^{right,\, mid}/mid,\, right]\!]$. They are allowed by the parallel operator $\underset{\{|mid|\}}{\|}$ because they do not belong to $\{|mid|\}$, and by the hiding operator $\setminus \{|mid|\}$, so P_1 has actions $left.0$ and $left.1$ to

$$P_4(0) = COPY(0) \gg COPY$$
$$P_4(1) = COPY(1) \gg COPY$$

- In P_2, the first argument still has the same τ available as it did in P_0, so this can be promoted to a τ action from P_2 to P_3. The actions available to the right-hand argument are the same ones ($\{|left|\}$) as were available to the left-hand one in P_1. This time they are promoted to *mid* actions by the renaming operator, and prevented by the parallel operator since actions on *mid* require a synchronisation (which is not possible). Thus P_2 only has the single τ action.
- In $P_3 = COPY^\tau \gg COPY^\tau$, the actions of the two arguments are obviously the same. As in P_1, the two *left* actions of the left-hand one are promoted to actions with the same name leading to respectively

$$P_5(0) = COPY(0) \gg COPY^\tau$$
$$P_5(1) = COPY(1) \gg COPY^\tau$$

while the corresponding actions of the right-hand one are prevented as in P_2.
- In $P_4(x)$, the right-hand argument only has a τ action available, which is promoted by the rules to a τ action to $P_5(x)$. The left-hand argument has only the action *right.x*, which is renamed to *mid.x* and prevented by the parallel operator since the right-hand process cannot synchronise.
- The unique action of $COPY(x)$ is promoted by renaming, in $P_5(x)$, to *mid.x*. The two *left* actions of the right-hand argument are also promoted to *mid*. This time synchronisation is possible (under $\underset{\{|mid|\}}{\|}$) on the action *mid.x*, which becomes a τ action of the overall process because of the hiding operator. The resulting process is

$$P_6(x) = COPY \gg COPY(x)$$

- In $P_6(x)$, the left-hand process has a τ to $COPY^\tau$, which can be promoted to a τ action to

$$P_7(x) = COPY^\tau \gg COPY(x)$$

and the right-hand one has the action *right.x* to $COPY$, which promotes to the same action leading back to P_0.
- In $P_7(x)$, the right-hand process can communicate *right.x*, which again promotes to the same action, leading to $COPY^\tau \gg COPY$, in other words, P_1. The left-hand process can communicate *left.0* or *left.1*, which promote to the same events and the overall state

$$P_8(y, x) = COPY(y) \gg COPY(x)$$

for the chosen y.
- The final state we have to consider is $P_8(y, x)$, where both components can only output. The right-hand one's *right.x* communication promotes to the same action externally leading to $P_4(y)$. The reason why no more states have to be considered is simply that all the states discovered during our exploration have already been examined.

Taking account of all the variations in x and y, there are 16 states altogether in the resulting LTS, which is shown in Fig. 9.7. The states that the labels $a-p$ in the

Fig. 9.7 The full state space of *COPY* ≫ *COPY*

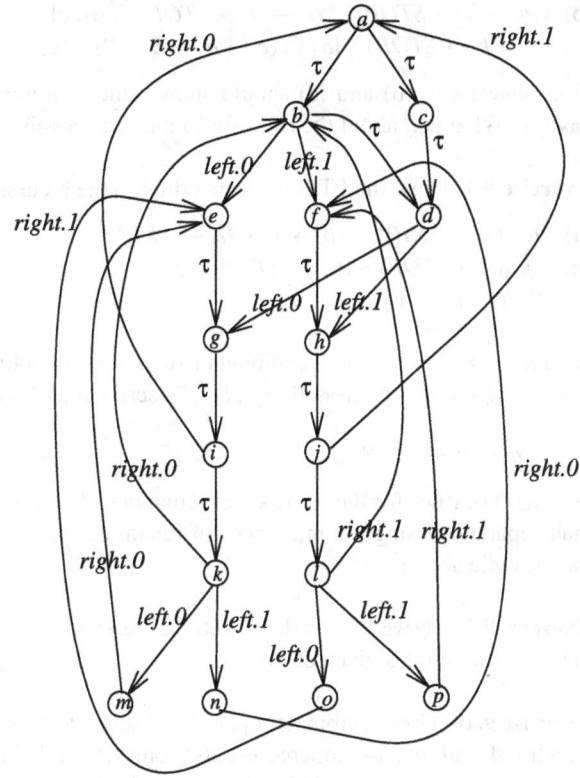

Table 9.1 States of Fig. 9.7

a	P_0	g	$P_5(0)$	m	$P_8(0,0)$
b	P_1	h	$P_5(1)$	n	$P_8(0,1)$
c	P_2	i	$P_6(0)$	o	$P_8(1,0)$
d	P_3	j	$P_6(1)$	p	$P_8(1,1)$
e	$P_4(0)$	k	$P_7(0)$		
f	$P_4(1)$	l	$P_7(1)$		

figure denote are shown in Table 9.1. You should compare the LTS derived carefully here with the one, for essentially the same system, described in Fig. 3.3 on p. 53. The only differences are hiding the intermediate communications, the presence of the τ actions produced by unfolding recursions, and the fact that we have taken individual account of the values held in the buffer rather than showing them symbolically. Evidently this creates considerably more complexity! (*End of example.*)

Exercise 9.6 Compute the LTSs resulting from evaluating the operational semantics of the following processes:

(a) $(a \rightarrow b \rightarrow STOP) \; \Box \; (c \rightarrow d \rightarrow STOP)$

(b) $((a \rightarrow b \rightarrow STOP) \,\square\, (c \rightarrow d \rightarrow STOP)) \setminus \{a, c\}$

(c) $(a \rightarrow b \rightarrow STOP) \setminus \{a\} \,\square\, (c \rightarrow d \rightarrow STOP) \setminus \{c\}$

Your answers to (b) and (c) should show rather different externally observed behaviour. What is it about the rules for $\square$ that causes this?

Exercise 9.7 Draw the LTSs corresponding to the recursively defined processes

(a) $(\mu p.(a \rightarrow SKIP) \,\square\, (b \rightarrow p)); (a \rightarrow SKIP)$

(b) $\mu p.(a \rightarrow STOP) \triangleright ((b \rightarrow STOP) \triangleright p)$

(c) *ZERO* (see p. 133)

Exercise 9.8 Give a set of combinator rules for computing the operational semantics of $P \,|||\, Q$, derived from those of $\,\|\,$. Describe the LTS resulting from the process

$$(a \rightarrow b \rightarrow SKIP) \,|||\, (a \rightarrow c \rightarrow SKIP)$$

Give a set of rules for the operational semantics of $P[right \leftrightarrow left]Q$ directly, rather than separately using the inferences of renaming, parallel and hiding illustrated in the example above.

Exercise 9.9 Derive SOS style operational semantics for $P \vartriangle Q$ and $P \,\Theta_A\, Q$ from the combinator ones given above.

Exercise 9.10 Give combinator operational semantics for an operator $althide(X, P)$ which hides all even-numbered events from the set X in P. Namely, it leaves the first event from X visible, hides the second, leaves the third visible and so on.

9.3 From Combinators to Supercombinators!

As already stated on p. 161, FDR actually runs high-level state machines using a technique called *supercombinators*. In this section we will see what these are and show how to compute them from the combinator style operational semantics.

In fact, supercombinators take exactly the same form as the combinators seen in the last section, only instead of combining the actions of one or two processes together, they combine an arbitrary collection. They treat a composition of CSP operators as a single operator. FDR computes the combinators for the compound operator by combining those $\square$ of its parts.

Consider, for example, the compound operator $((P \,\|\, Q) \,\|\, R) \setminus (X \cup Y)$. This combines three processes together, so the combinators that represent it have three process arguments **1, 2** and **3**. All of these are **on** because neither the hiding nor the parallel operator have any **off** arguments.

Recall (p. 155) that in general FDR compiles CSP_M into a form where there may be one or more formats that FDR uses to run them. Here we will consider for simplicity a one-format case in which FDR is combining together processes

$(P, Q$ and $R)$ that never terminate. Then it is not hard to see how we can feed the result event of the combinators for $\mathbf{1} \underset{X}{\parallel} \mathbf{2}$ into the first input of $\ldots \underset{Y}{\parallel} \mathbf{3}$, yielding the following "supercombinators" for $(P \underset{X}{\parallel} Q) \underset{Y}{\parallel} R$:

- $((\cdot, \cdot, a), a)[a \notin Y]$ derived solely from $((\cdot, a), a)[a \notin Y]$
- $((a, \cdot, \cdot), a)[a \notin X \cup Y]$ derived by composing $((a, \cdot), a)[a \notin X]$ and $((a, \cdot), a)[a \notin Y]$
- $((\cdot, a, \cdot), a)[a \notin X \cup Y]$ from $((\cdot, a), a)[a \notin X]$ and $((a, \cdot), a)[a \notin Y]$
- $((a, a, \cdot), a)[a \in X \setminus Y]$ from $((a, a), a)[a \in X]$ and $((a, \cdot), a)[a \notin Y]$
- $((a, \cdot, a), a)[a \in Y \setminus X]$ from $((a, \cdot), a)[a \notin X]$ and $((a, a), a)[a \in Y]$
- $((\cdot, a, a), a)[a \in Y \setminus X]$ from $((\cdot, a), a)[a \notin X]$ and $((a, a), a)[a \in Y]$
- $((a, a, a), a)[a \in Y \cap X]$ from $((a, a), a)[a \in X]$ and $((a, a), a)[a \in Y]$.

In other words—exactly as we would expect—there is one rule for each way in which events of the three arguments might synchronise doubly or triply or happen independently.

These rules can be composed with the combinators for $\setminus (X \cup Y)$ so that the first rule in the above list splits into two:

- $((\cdot, \cdot, a), a)[a \notin X \cup Y]$
- $((\cdot, \cdot, a), \tau)[a \in X \setminus Y]$

The next two rules are not changed by the composition, since in both cases $a \notin X \cup Y$, and all the others (where $a \in X \cup Y$) have the result event a converted to τ.

In any case we get a set of "large" or "super" combinator rules to cover the complete high-level composition of processes, so these can be implemented efficiently rather than needing, for each state we meet during a search, to calculate its available actions by recursion on high-level syntax.

In any network assembled using alphabetised parallel and top-level hiding, there is—if there are no $\checkmark$s—exactly one supercombinator for each member of the union alphabet.

Think of the saving this involves on a composition of many processes as in some of the case studies in Chap. 4, compared to having to work out all the transitions of intermediate syntax. FDR implements supercombinators using bit-vector calculations.

In general we construct a supercombinator for arbitrary syntactic constructs such as $OP_1(OP_2(P_1, P_2), OP_3(P_3, P_4))$ out of those for the three operators. There are two types of these: the first is when OP_2 or OP_3 has a rule that generates a τ. In this case, since the τ is just promoted by OP_1, we simply lift the combinator by adding two further arguments that are not in the partial function ϕ's domain. So if OP_2 had the rule $((a, b), \tau)$, we would get the supercombinator $((a, b, \cdot, \cdot), \tau)$. The other type of supercombinator arises when we can match all the input action requirements of one of OP_1's combinators using combinators for OP_2 and OP_3 that give visible results. So, for example, if OP_1 has the combinator $((a, b), c)$, OP_2 has $((\cdot, a), a)$ and OP_3 has $((b, d), b)$, then the composition will have $((\cdot, a, b, d), c)$.

FDR matches supercombinators against states by computing the initial actions of each component process in its current state, and testing each supercombinator against these as they range across all the components. It also, naturally, operates a τ promotion rule for each argument. It does these computations using bit vector representations to make them efficient.

There is one stylistic difference between the supercombinators implemented in FDR and the ones implied by the combinators described earlier. That is that the former do not have explicit **off** arguments, but instead make **off** arguments implicit in the supercombinator. Two different **off** arguments give two different FDR supercombinators, rather than a single one with different arguments. This makes no difference to the transition system produced, since whenever one of the combinators described earlier would have started up an **off** argument, an FDR-style supercombinator, which contains that argument in its definition, will start it up as a constant process. In the author's experience, most state machines run by supercombinators have an unchanging format. FDR does, however, also support systems that move between a finite set of formats. The supercombinators for these can also be calculated as compositions of the ones for the operators making them up.

9.4 Translating Combinators to CSP

While there are many operators that can be presented in SOS style that make no sense as CSP operators, the same is not true for the much restricted combinator style.

Theorem 9.1 *Suppose we have a CSP-like operator, namely one whose operational semantics is defined in our new combinator style. Then we can simulate the operator extremely accurately using standard CSP: in languages without $\checkmark$ this simulation can be as tight as possible, namely up to strong bisimulation. If termination and sequential composition using $\checkmark$ are used, we can simulate up to strong bisimulation a process equivalent to the original under the application of one of the laws of CSP.*

In either case it follows from this result that the translation accurately reflects the behaviour of the new operator over every CSP model. So the new operator can be added seamlessly to CSP. The *proof* of this statement is achieved by building a complex machine out of CSP that carries out the simulation. Necessarily this is a very complex CSP program. Readers prepared to take it on trust can proceed to the next section.

Readers who are interested in the details (perhaps because they are looking for ideas for achieving unusual effects with CSP) can find a reasonably complete sketch below. Full details of this work can be found in the paper [132].

First, consider the case of a CSP-like operator extending CSP *without* $\checkmark$ and sequential composition. It has a finite number of **on** arguments, and a family of **off** arguments. We can build an action-accurate simulation of the operator using a parallel composition whose components are

- The **on** arguments, subject to some renaming and mechanisms that allow them to be discarded.

- A process that is capable of turning **on** any (finite) selection of **off** arguments in response to communications of the form $turnon.S$ for S a function from the indexing set Λ to $\mathbb{N}$. (So if this function is ζ and $\zeta(\lambda) = k$, then this action turns on k copies of the λ-th **off** argument.)
- Rather elaborate renamings on the processes above so that they can take part in the various synchronisations that combinators might call for.
- A regulator process that ensures that the only visible actions and turning on/discarding of processes that happen are those allowed by the combinator operational semantics.

Before giving the details of these components, it helps to understand the way the complete simulation is put together: the actions that the parallel composition described above actually communicates are the combinators and supercombinators derived from (a) the operator being simulated and (b) the simulations of other operators reachable from this simulation. If PC is this parallel composition, then the complete simulation is $(PC[\![CR]\!]) \setminus \{tau\}$ where CR is a renaming that maps any combinator to its result event, except that it maps combinators whose result event is τ to the special visible event tau (not used by any of the processes involved).

It should not be difficult to see that if we can succeed in having the combinator events happening only when the combinator can fire in the operational semantics then:

- This structure (with all the **on** arguments running) will have all of the promoted τ events that happen because of one of the **on** arguments performing a τ.

  Furthermore the state of the simulation will only change through the particular **on** argument following the τ. The rest of the arguments and the overall structure will not change at all, which reflects our definition of how such τ actions are promoted as described on p. 204.
- The event the simulation produces in response to a given combinator firing is the correct one. It is, of course, our responsibility to ensure that the result state of the simulation is the correct one.

We arrange that the individual argument processes each have a fixed index in the composition: the **1**, **2**, etc. of the original set-up together with distinct indices for all the **off** arguments that may have been started up along the way. The alphabet of each (index **i**, say) is the set of all possible combinator rules with one of the following two properties:

- The rule involves an action from component **i**: $\mathbf{i} \in \mathrm{dom}(\phi)$.
- The rule starts off with **i** on, but discards it (i.e. **i** does not appear as an index in the resulting term). We can define the set of combinators that discard **i** to be $Discard(\mathbf{i})$. We can split $Discard(i)$ into two sets $IDiscard(i)$ and $XDiscard(i)$ which respectively are the members c of $Discard(i)$ that do, and do not, have $i \in \mathrm{dom}(\phi_c)$. In other words, they are the combinators that discard **i** where that argument respectively does and does not participate in the action.

If P is the ith **on** argument of our operator, then the process we use in the ith place in the simulation is $(P[\![ER(i)]\!] \bigtriangleup (?x : XDiscard(i))) \,\Theta_{IDiscard(i)}\, STOP$: think of this as

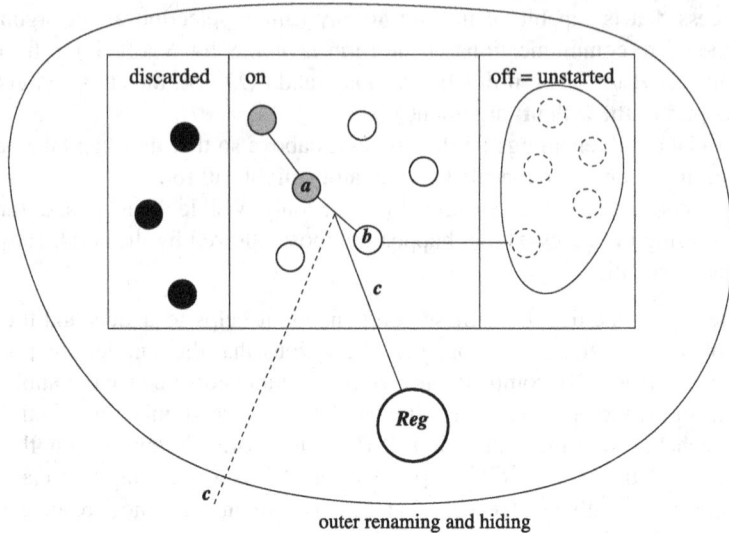

Fig. 9.8 Graphical representation of combinator simulation

putting P in a *harness*. Here $ER(i)$ is an *Expanding Renaming*, mapping all of P_i's visible actions to the possibly many ways this action can happen in the simulation. It is the counterpart to the *Converging Renaming CR* discussed above.

The regulator's role is to remember the current format of the term, which may well have evolved from the original one. It will remember which arguments are currently **on** and will allow just those combinators that apply to the current format. After performing such an event (which may in fact be a combinator with empty $\mathrm{dom}(\phi_c)$) it moves to the state appropriate to the next format.

Where one or more **off** arguments are turned on by a combinator, the process that contains copies of them all synchronises with the relevant combinator and becomes the parallel composition of the newly turned on processes (these are allocated the next unused indices) and a copy of itself "shifted" by the number of new indices. Figure 9.8 gives a graphical representation of our simulation. The rectangular box contains three sorts of processes running in parallel. The leftmost of these (black) are the arguments that have already been discarded and are therefore behaving as *STOP* in the parallel composition. The next group are the current **on** arguments. Finally there is a single process that is able to make copies of the **off** arguments and start them up. This process accepts instructions to do this, activating the **off** arguments themselves only when instructed to do so.

Outside the box we see the regulator, which has to participate in every action except the τs that are automatically promoted from the **on** arguments. The outer line represents the top-level renaming and hiding that turn the complex internal combinator events into the external ones they represent.

The figure illustrates a particular combinator firing: the nodes the edges join are the ones that participate: the regulator, an **on** node that simply performs an action,

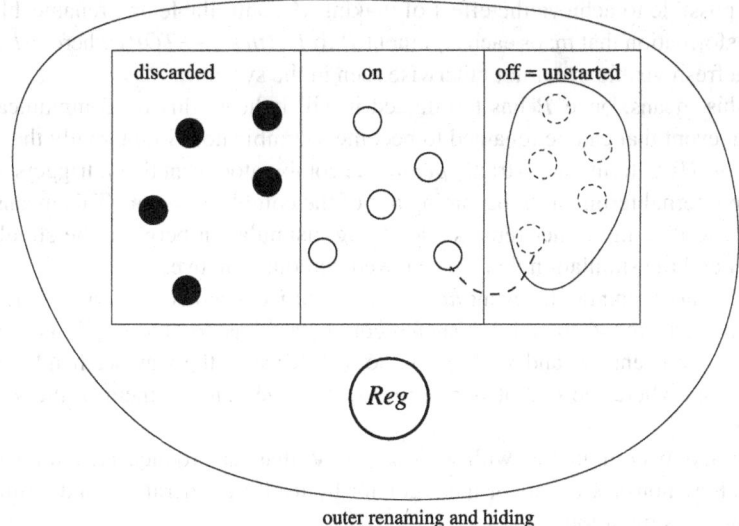

Fig. 9.9 Result of firing combinator in simulation

an **on** node that performs an action but will be discarded by the combinator (shaded gray) and one (also shaded gray) that will be discarded by the action but does not contribute to it. The process containing the **off** arguments is also taking part, indicating that one or more new processes will be joining the **on** arguments after this action. Figure 9.9 shows the state of our simulation after the firing of the combinator illustrated in Fig. 9.8: two more processes have been discarded and become *STOP* components of the parallel composition. A new active process (i.e. one in the middle section of the rectangle) is an **on** copy of the **off** one that is indicated by the dashed line, and *all* previous **off** arguments remain in virtual form in the process that can spawn them.

The **on** arguments participating in an action are those that are in the domain of the given combinator's ϕ plus any that are discarded by this action. It is necessary to keep careful note of *which* arguments have been discarded so that they can no longer contribute τ actions to the whole, which would for example have the danger of introducing an inaccurate divergence and would act contrary to our aim of strong bisimulation.

For full details of this extremely complex "machine" for simulating an operational semantics, see [132], which also contains some simpler versions for handling classes of operator that do not use the full generality offered by combinators.

We have yet to cover the possibility of termination ($\checkmark$). The reason for this is that, to have dealt with this in the same way as above, we would have had to rename $\checkmark$ to many events, and many events to $\checkmark$ (just as we did for other events). CSP forbids renaming to or from $\checkmark$, or hiding it.

It is possible to achieve the effect of making ✓ controllable and renameable by the transformation that maps each argument P to P; $(tick \rightarrow STOP)$ where *tick* (like *tau*) is a fresh visible event not otherwise seen in the system.

By this means, once P has terminated it will indicate this by communicating *tick*—an event that can be renamed to become a combinator. So internally the P of P; $tick \rightarrow STOP$ terminates strictly *before* the combinator event that it triggers does, with the internal termination becoming a τ of the complete system. This means we have to sacrifice the rather remarkable *strong* bisimulation between the simulated operator and the simulation that we achieved without ✓ above.

We can now rename the event *tick* in argument i to each combinator where that argument performs ✓: recall that such a combinator has $\text{dom}(\phi) = \{i\}$ and results in one of the events ✓ and τ. There is no difference in the way we handle these combinators where the output is τ from the way we handled them in the ✓-free case above.

It is not only combinators with some $\phi(i) = ✓$ that can produce a resulting event ✓: we allow non-*tick* events or the regulator by itself to generate ✓ and terminate the complete simulation.

We are not allowed simply to rename such combinators to ✓, so we put the complete simulation S (including the regulator but excluding the external renaming and hiding) in the context $S \ominus_T SKIP$ where T is the set of all combinators that have ✓ as an output event. We then have the outer renaming CR (around this context) map all such combinators to *tau* so they are hidden. As with the termination of the individual components, this introduces an extra τ. So, for an operator $OP(P_1, P_2, \ldots, P_n)$ where we make no distinction between the P_i being **on** and **off**, what we actually simulated up to strong bisimulation is $OP(P_1; SKIP, P_2; SKIP, \ldots, P_n; SKIP); SKIP$.

We can therefore simulate every CSP-like operator in CSP to a very high degree of accuracy when judged via the operational semantics. We can draw some important conclusions from this:

1. We do not need to add any further operator to CSP to express CSP-like operators.
2. Adding a CSP-like operator OP to CSP can cause no theoretical difficulty, because (just like the link parallel operator $[a \leftrightarrow b]$) OP can be translated into standard CSP.
3. Any language consisting of CSP-like operators will have semantics in any model for CSP, and a theory of refinement over any of the behavioural models for CSP we have met or are yet to meet.
4. We can add any CSP-like operator to the ones supported by FDR confident in the knowledge that FDR's refinement calculations, compressions etc. will still be valid. While this is clearly true if we use the simulation in terms of CSP operators, what we actually mean here is including the new operator via its operational semantics in the same way as the standard CSP operators are built into FDR.[9]

---

[9]At the time of writing it is proposed to add a function to FDR by which new operators can be described to it via combinator-style operational semantics.

This is an important theoretical result because, at least within the sphere of CSP-like operators, it shows both that CSP is a *universal* language and that the behavioural models of CSP have an important role beyond just CSP.

Example 9.2 (Angelic choice) Consider the following combinator semantics for an *angelic* choice operator $P \boxdot Q$. While $P \Box Q$ offers the environment the choice between P and Q on the first step, behaving nondeterministically if an event in the intersection of *initials*(P) and *initials*(Q) is chosen, $P \boxdot Q$ keeps on giving the environment the choice of actions of P and Q as long as the environment picks an event they both offer.

We have to define infinitely many different operators: $P_s \boxdot Q$ for s a non-empty member of Σ^* represents a state where Q has got ahead of P by the trace s. This will continue to allow Q to perform events and will also allow P to catch up. Symmetrically $P \boxdot_s Q$ has Q needing to catch up P by s. The combinator semantics of $P \boxdot Q$, $P_s \boxdot Q$ and $P \boxdot_s Q$ are given by the following terms. In each case both arguments are **on**.

- For $\boxdot$: $((a, .), a, \mathbf{1} \boxdot_{\langle a \rangle} \mathbf{2})$ and $((., a), a, \mathbf{1}_{\langle a \rangle} \boxdot \mathbf{2})$ for all $a \in \Sigma$, plus $((\checkmark, .), \checkmark)$ and $((., \checkmark), \checkmark)$.
- For $_{\langle b \rangle ^\frown s} \boxdot$: $((b, .), \tau, \mathbf{1}_s \boxdot \mathbf{2})$ and $((., a), a, \mathbf{1}_{\langle a, b \rangle ^\frown s} \boxdot \mathbf{2})$ for all $a \in \Sigma$, plus $((\checkmark, .), \tau, \mathbf{2})$ and $((., \checkmark), \checkmark)$.
- For $\boxdot_{\langle b \rangle ^\frown s}$: $((., b), \tau, \mathbf{1} \boxdot_s \mathbf{2})$ and $((a, .), a, \mathbf{1} \boxdot_{\langle a, b \rangle ^\frown s} \mathbf{2})$ for all $a \in \Sigma$, plus $((\checkmark, .), \checkmark)$, and $((., \checkmark), \tau, \mathbf{1})$.

In other words, both arguments of $\boxdot$ are always left **on** unless one of them terminates, to allow the one that has only completed part of the current trace to catch up. The termination of an argument that has "fallen behind" the present trace resolves the choice in favour of the other.

It is actually rather easier to give a failures semantics for this operator than to build the above operational semantics: see Exercise 9.11. The result above tells us that we can implement $\boxdot$ directly in CSP, with a rather complex implementation. In practice it is usually more elegant to pick just those features of the machine described above which a given operator requires rather than rolling the whole thing out. Things that *don't* appear for this operator are **off** arguments (or turning them on), synchronising actions of multiple arguments, or arguments discarding themselves except by terminating.

Following this principle, we will have five copies of the alphabet Σ in our implementation of $\boxdot$: Σ (what the environment sees) and $\Sigma \times \{1, 2\} \times \{h, v\}$, where 1 or 2 is the argument that performs the event, with v meaning the event will be visible to the outside and h meaning it is to be hidden. To implement $P \boxdot Q$ we run $(P; tick_1 \rightarrow STOP)[\![ER1]\!]$ and $(Q; tick_2 \rightarrow STOP)[\![ER2]\!]$ in parallel with *Reg*, where *ERi* maps each $a \in \Sigma$ to (a, i, v) and (a, i, h) and *Reg* is defined

$$Reg = \Box_{a \in \Sigma}(a, 1, v) \rightarrow Reg1(\langle a \rangle)$$
$$\Box \Box_{a \in \Sigma}(a, 2, v) \rightarrow Reg2(\langle a \rangle)$$

$$\Box \ tick_1 \to tick \to STOP$$
$$\Box \ tick_2 \to tick \to STOP$$

$$Reg1(\langle b \rangle\hat{\ }s) = \Box_{a \in \Sigma}(a, 1, v) \to Reg1(\langle a, b \rangle\hat{\ }s)$$
$$\Box \ (b, 2, h) \to (Reg \ \Downarrow s = \langle\rangle \Downarrow Reg1(s))$$
$$\Box \ tick_1 \to tick \to STOP$$
$$\Box \ tick_2 \to Reg1'$$

$$Reg1' = \Box_{a \in \Sigma}(a, 1, v) \to Reg1'$$
$$\Box \ tick_1 \to tick \to STOP$$

$$Reg2(\langle b \rangle\hat{\ }s) = \Box_{a \in \Sigma}(a, 2, v) \to Reg2(\langle a, b \rangle\hat{\ }s)$$
$$\Box \ (b, 1, h) \to (Reg \ \Downarrow s = \langle\rangle \Downarrow Reg2(s))$$
$$\Box \ tick_1 \to Reg2'$$
$$\Box \ tick_2 \to tick \to STOP$$

$$Reg2' = \Box_{a \in \Sigma}(a, 2, v) \to Reg2'$$
$$\Box \ tick_2 \to tick \to STOP$$

We then put the resulting combination S in the context

$$(S \ \Theta_{tick} \ SKIP)[\![CR]\!] \setminus \{tau\}$$

where CR renames (a, i, v) to i, and (a, i, h) and all the *tick* events to *tau*.

Note how *Reg* is based on the combinator operational semantics, just as in our construction of the machine, but that we have chosen a smaller alphabet that does not consist of combinators. Two example files accompanying this chapter illustrate both the above approach to implementing angelic choice, and an alternative one that does not use Θ_{tick}.

Exercise 9.11 Give semantics in $\mathcal{F}$ and $\mathcal{N}$ for the angelic choice operator ⊡ defined above. Compare the operators $\Box$ and ⊡ in terms of practicality and elegance. What algebraic properties does ⊡ have? What is its step law?

Exercise 9.12 Implement the following operators in CSP: do so first assuming there is no termination, and second assuming $\checkmark$ is allowed.

(a) *RemDups(P)* behaves exactly like P except that if two consecutive visible events of P are the same, the second is hidden.
(b) The parallel operator[10] $P|Q$ allows P and Q to perform any event they wish individually, but if P and Q can perform the same event other than $\checkmark$ they may synchronise, with the resulting event being τ.

---

[10]Many readers will notice that this is a slightly simplified version of the CCS operator |. Those familiar with that operator are welcome to represent it in CSP instead. In this, all events x have duals $\bar{x}$ (where $\bar{\bar{x}} = x$). The CCS operator | behaves just like the one described in this exercise except that x synchronises with $\bar{x}$ and not x.

CCS is not completely CSP-like in the sense described above because its $+$ operator, an analogue both of $\Box$ and $\sqcap$, is resolved by the occurrence of τ. We know that no CSP-like operator can react to a τ in one of its arguments. It is possible to model CCS in CSP, as shown in [131], by treating τ as a visible event until a syntactic level above all $+$ operators, and then hiding it. It is not possible to model CSP in CCS since the latter has no way of creating many-way synchronisations.

9.5 Relationships with Abstract Models

9.5.1 Extracting Failures and Divergences

It was pointed out in Sect. 6.1 that there are two quite separate ways to work out a process's traces, failures and divergences: either by using the inductive *denotational* semantic rules for piecing them together (which we will be studying in the next chapter), or by examining the process's transition system.

It is easy to formalise the extraction of these values from an LTS C.

We use two multi-step versions of the transition relation. The first just allows us to glue a series of actions together into a single sequence. If $P, Q \in \hat{C}$ and $s = \langle x_i \mid 0 \le i < n \rangle \in (\Sigma^\tau)^{*\checkmark}$ we say $P \overset{s}{\longmapsto} Q$ if there exist $P_0 = P, P_1, \ldots, P_n = Q$ such that $P_k \overset{x_k}{\longrightarrow} P_{k+1}$ for $k \in \{0, 1, \ldots, n-1\}$.

This first version includes τ actions (invisible to the environment) in the sequence shown. The second version, already used on p. 197, ignores τs: for $s \in \Sigma^{*\checkmark}$ we write $P \overset{s}{\Longrightarrow} Q$ if there exists $s' \in (\Sigma^\tau)^{*\checkmark}$ such that $P \overset{s'}{\longmapsto} Q$ and $s' \setminus \tau = s$. We sometimes write $\Longrightarrow$ for $\overset{\langle\rangle}{\Longrightarrow}$. The following properties of $\overset{s}{\Longrightarrow}$ and $\overset{s}{\longmapsto}$ are all obvious.

(a) $P \overset{\langle\rangle}{\Longrightarrow} P \wedge P \overset{\langle\rangle}{\longmapsto} P$

(b) $P \overset{s}{\Longrightarrow} Q \wedge Q \overset{t}{\Longrightarrow} R \Rightarrow P \overset{s \hat{} t}{\Longrightarrow} R$

(c) $P \overset{s}{\longmapsto} Q \wedge Q \overset{t}{\longmapsto} R \Rightarrow P \overset{s \hat{} t}{\longmapsto} R$

(d) $P \overset{s \hat{} t}{\Longrightarrow} R \Rightarrow \exists Q.P \overset{s}{\Longrightarrow} Q \wedge Q \overset{t}{\Longrightarrow} R$

(e) $P \overset{s \hat{} t}{\longmapsto} R \Rightarrow \exists Q.P \overset{s}{\longmapsto} Q \wedge Q \overset{t}{\longmapsto} R$

It is easy to extract the set of a node's finite traces using the above relations:

$$traces(P) = \{s \in \Sigma^{*\checkmark} \mid \exists Q.P \overset{s}{\Longrightarrow} Q\}$$

Suppose C is a transition system and $P \in \hat{C}$. We say P can *diverge*, written $P \Uparrow$, if there exist $P_0 = P, P_1, P_2, \ldots$ such that, for all $n \in \mathbb{N}$, $P_n \overset{\tau}{\longrightarrow} P_{n+1}$.

$$divergences(P) = \{s \hat{} t \mid s \in \Sigma^* \wedge t \in \Sigma^* \wedge \exists Q.P \overset{s}{\Longrightarrow} Q \wedge Q \Uparrow\}$$

Notice that we have said that $s \hat{} t$ is a divergence trace whenever s is. This is a reflection of the decision, discussed in Sect. 6.1, not to try to distinguish what can happen after possible divergence. It would, of course, be easy to avoid divergence strictness here, but, as we will see later, it is much harder to get things right in the denotational semantics without it. Notice that *minimal* divergences (i.e., ones with no proper prefix that is a divergence) do not contain $\checkmark$. This is because we are not concerned with what a process does after it terminates. Our exclusion of divergences of the form $s \hat{} \langle \checkmark \rangle$, where s is one, is simply a matter of taste as discussed on p. 138.

In Sect. 6.1, we said that the only states that give rise to refusals are stable ones, since a τ action might lead to anything, in particular to a state that accepts an action from whatever set is on offer. Since then the notion of a stable state has been complicated a little by the intermediate nature of $\checkmark$, and so, inevitably, are the criteria for extracting refusals.

- A stable state (one without τ or $\checkmark$ events) refuses any set of visible events (perhaps including $\checkmark$) that does not intersect with the state's initial actions.
- We are interpreting $\checkmark$ as an event that cannot be resisted by the environment. Thus *any* state with this event amongst its initial actions can decide to terminate, plainly refusing all events other than $\checkmark$. So any state with a $\checkmark$ action (even such a state with τ actions) can be held to be able to refuse any subset of Σ. To help understand this, remember the discussion of Fig. 9.2, where we commented that any state with a $\checkmark$ action is equivalent, so far as external observation is concerned, to one with a τ to state A (one with only a $\checkmark$ action). If we make this transformation, it will be the 'A' state that introduces this refusal.

We can formally define $P \; ref \; B$ (read "P refuses B" for $B \subseteq \Sigma^{\checkmark}$) if and only if *either* P is stable and $B \cap P^0 = \emptyset$ *or* there is Q with $P \xrightarrow{\checkmark} Q$ and $B \subseteq \Sigma$.

We can then extract the failures by combining this with the traces, taking account of the convention that a process refuses anything after $\checkmark$.

$$ failures(P) = \{(s, X) \mid \exists Q.P \xRightarrow{s} Q \wedge Q \; ref \; X\} $$
$$ \cup \{(s^\frown\langle\checkmark\rangle, X) \mid \exists Q.P \xRightarrow{s^\frown\langle\checkmark\rangle} Q\} $$

As we saw briefly in Chap. 5, and will study more in Sect. 10.4, it is sometimes necessary to ignore details of what a process does after possible divergence. Sets of traces and failures with post-divergence details obscured are given by the definitions

$$ traces_\perp(P) = traces(P) \cup divergences(P) $$
$$ failures_\perp(P) = failures(P) \cup \{(s, X), (s^\frown\langle\checkmark\rangle, X) \mid s \in divergences(P)\} $$

The following important result is an immediate corollary to Lemma 9.1.

Theorem 9.2 *If the nodes n and m are related by a DRW-bisimulation, then $traces(n) = traces(m)$, $failures(n) = failures(m)$ and $divergences(n) = divergences(m)$. Hence also $failures_\perp(n) = failures_\perp(m)$ and $traces_\perp(n) = traces_\perp(m)$.*

9.5.2 Infinite Traces and Infinite Branching

We will see other sorts of behaviour that can be extracted from LTSs in Chaps. 11 and 12, but there is one other type that is so important that we study it now. These are the *infinite traces*, the infinite sequences of communications a process can engage in—an obvious extension of the idea of finite traces. The notations $\xmapsto{u}$ and $\xRightarrow{u}$ can be extended to infinite u, though they now become unary rather than binary relations on the nodes in an LTS:

- If $u = \langle x_i \mid i \in \mathbb{N} \rangle \in (\Sigma^\tau)^\omega$ (the set of infinite sequences of members of Σ^τ), we say that $P \xrightarrow{u}$ if there exist $P_0 = P, P_1, P_2, \ldots$ such that $P_i \xrightarrow{x_i} P_{i+1}$ for all i.
- If $u \in \Sigma^\omega$ then $P \xRightarrow{u}$ if and only if there exists $u' \in (\Sigma^\tau)^\omega$ such that $P \xrightarrow{u'}$ and $u = u' \setminus \tau$.

$\checkmark$s, being final, play no part in infinite traces. Note that not all $u' \in (\Sigma^\tau)^\omega$ have $u' \setminus \tau$ infinite—the rest have the form $s^\frown \langle \tau \rangle^\omega$ and give rise to divergences.

Infinite traces have more in common with divergences than with finite traces, in the sense that both take an infinite amount of time to observe and result from the process performing infinitely many actions (in the case of divergence, all but finitely many being τs). This means that, as with the set of divergences, it is difficult to model, in the denotational semantics, what goes on in the infinite traces after potential divergence. The set of infinite traces we extract from an LTS therefore closes up after potential divergence, rather than offering a choice of two functions as with finite traces and failures.

$$infinites(P) = \{u \mid P \xRightarrow{u}\} \cup \{s^\frown u \mid s \in divergences(P) \cap \Sigma^* \wedge u \in \Sigma^\omega\}$$

An analogue of Theorem 9.2 also applies to infinite traces, though the proof is not quite so immediate.

Theorem 9.3 *If n and m are related by a DRW-bisimulation then $\{u \in \Sigma^\omega \mid n \xRightarrow{u}\} = \{u \in \Sigma^\omega \mid m \xRightarrow{u}\}$, and therefore, using Theorem 9.2, infinites$(n) = $ infinites(m).*

Proof Whereas the proof of the earlier theorem can look at the whole trace as a single step thanks to the formulation of DRW-bisimulation, here we need to break up the trace u into an infinite number of finite, non-empty parts $u = t_1^\frown t_2^\frown \ldots$ (the most obvious way of doing this is by putting a single member of Σ in each). By definition of $\xRightarrow{u}$, there is a sequence of nodes $n_0 = n, n_1, n_2, \ldots$ such that $n_i \xRightarrow{t_{i+1}} n_{i+1}$. Setting $m_0 = m$, we can construct a sequence m_i by induction such that n_i and m_i are bisimilar and $m_i \xRightarrow{t_{i+1}} m_{i+1}$. This proves that $m \xRightarrow{u}$. $\qquad\square$

It makes a lot of sense, of course, to combine finite and infinite traces into a single set

$$Traces(P) = traces_\perp(P) \cup infinites(P)$$

This set is, naturally, always prefix-closed like $traces(P)$ and $traces_\perp(P)$. Thus, every finite prefix of an infinite trace is also in this set. Studying infinite traces only conveys *extra* information about a process if the reverse of this can fail: if there can be u *not* in $infinites(P)$ all of whose finite prefixes are in $Traces(P)$, for otherwise

$$Traces(P) = \overline{traces_\perp(P)}$$

where $\overline{A} = A \cup \{u \in \Sigma^\omega \mid \{s \mid s < u\} \subseteq A\}$. We will say that $Traces(P)$ is *closed* when this happens.

There is a large and important class of LTSs where this identity always holds: ones with the following property:

Definition The LTS C is said to be *finitely branching* if, for all nodes P and each $x \in \Sigma^{\checkmark,\tau}$, the set $\{Q \mid P \xrightarrow{x} Q\}$ is finite.

This says that there are only finitely many nodes we can reach from a given one under a single action. This means that, if we know what action or sequence of actions have occurred, there is only finite uncertainty, or nondeterminism, about what state the process has reached. If Σ is infinite, because the above condition only restricts the size of the set that is reached after a single event, it is possible that a node of a finitely-branching LTS might have infinitely many successors.

The *proof* that nodes in finitely-branching LTSs have closed *Traces*(P) is a corollary of the following standard result, which we will need to use a number of times in the mathematical analysis of CSP.

Theorem 9.4 (König's Lemma) *Suppose X_i is, for each $i \in \mathbb{N}$, a non-empty finite set and that $f_i : X_{i+1} \to X_i$ is a (total) function. Then there is a sequence $\langle x_i \mid i \in \mathbb{N} \rangle$ such that $x_i \in X_i$ and $f_i(x_{i+1}) = x_i$.*

One proof of König's Lemma can be found in Sect. 7.2 of TPC.

This result is often stated in graph-theoretic terms: a finitely-branching tree with nodes at every (natural number) depth below a root r has an infinite path from r. The sets X_i just become the nodes reachable in i steps from r, and the functions f_i map each node to the one from which it was reached.

We can now use this result to establish the result about finitely-branching LTSs. What this shows, in essence, is that in divergence-strict models[11] like $\mathcal{N}$, the semantic value of a finitely branching process is determined by the combination of its finitely observable behaviours and its divergences.

Theorem 9.5 *If C is a finitely-branching LTS, and $P \in \hat{C}$, then Traces(P) is closed.*

Proof Let $u \in \Sigma^\omega$ be such that $\{s \in \Sigma^* \mid s < u\} \subseteq traces_\perp(P)$. We can assume that none of these ss is in *divergences*(P), for then $u \in infinites(P)$ by definition. The proof works by applying König's Lemma to the nodes reachable from P on traces that are prefixes of u. We can formally define sets and functions for the lemma as follows:

- $X_n = \{(Q,s) \mid Q \in C \land s \in (\Sigma^\tau)^n \land P \xrightarrow{s} Q \land s \setminus \tau < u\}$
- If $(Q, s^\smallfrown\langle x \rangle) \in X_{n+1}$ then there must be $R \in C$ such that $P \xrightarrow{s} R$ and $R \xrightarrow{x} Q$. Necessarily $(R, s) \in X_n$. Let $f_n(Q, s^\smallfrown\langle x \rangle)$ be any such (R, s). (R is not necessarily unique, but this does not matter.)

In later chapters we will meet some models where the proof below does not apply exactly, because they replace traces with richer structures. A modified version of the above argument always applies in these cases, giving an appropriate analogue of this result.

The sets X_n are all finite by induction on n, using the assumption that C is finitely branching: if $(Q, s) \in X_n$, then the set of its successors in X_{n+1} is contained in the finite set

$$\{(R, s^\frown\langle\tau\rangle) \mid Q \xrightarrow{\tau} R\} \cup \{(R, s^\frown\langle a\rangle) \mid Q \xrightarrow{a} R\}$$

where a is the unique element of Σ such that $(s \setminus \tau)^\frown\langle a\rangle < u$. That the X_n are all non-empty is an easy consequence of the assumption that $s \in traces_\perp(P)$ for all $s < u$.

König's Lemma then gives a sequence (P_i, s_i) such that $f_i(P_{i+1}, s_{i+1}) = (P_i, s_i)$. The structure of the X_i and the f_i imply that there is an infinite sequence $u' = \langle x_i \mid i \in \mathbb{N}\rangle \in (\Sigma^\tau)^\omega$ such that $s_i = \langle x_0, \ldots, x_{i-1}\rangle$ and $P_i \xrightarrow{x_i} P_{i+1}$. The fact that $s_i \setminus \tau < u$ for all i implies $u' \setminus \tau \le u$. In fact, $u' \setminus \tau = u$ since otherwise (contrary to our assumption) a prefix of u is in $divergences(P)$.

Figure 9.10 shows how a finitely nondeterministic system can (for the infinite trace $\langle a, a, a, \ldots\rangle$) depend on the divergence-closure of $infinites(P)$ to make this result true.   □

On the other hand, as soon as we allow infinite branching, the set of infinite traces does convey important information about $Traces(P)$. For example, consider the two systems in Fig. 9.11: they clearly have the same sets of failures, divergences and finite traces, but the one on the left has the infinite trace $\langle a\rangle^\omega$ while the other does not. We will study the consequences of distinctions like this, and the extra power infinite traces give us for specifications, in Chap. 12.

The above result makes it important that we understand which CSP terms produce finitely-branching operational semantics. Every one of the operators, if *applied* to a term that already has infinite branching, is capable of producing infinite branching itself. But fortunately only three operators are capable of *introducing* infinite branching, or *unbounded nondeterminism* as it is often called.

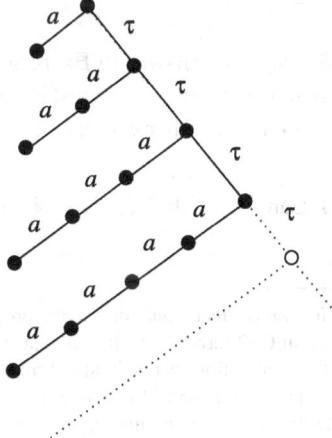

Fig. 9.10 The role of divergence in Theorem 9.5

Fig. 9.11 Infinite branching
makes infinite traces
significant. (All actions are a)

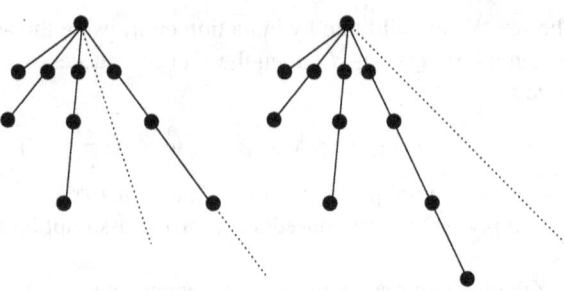

- The choice operator $\sqcap S$ clearly introduces infinite branching (of τ actions) when S is infinite.
- If the set X is infinite, then $P \setminus X$ can branch infinitely (on τ) even if P does not. For example, the process $Q = (?n : \mathbb{N} \to P(n)) \setminus \mathbb{N}$ is operationally equivalent to $\sqcap\{P(n) \setminus \mathbb{N} \mid n \in \mathbb{N}\}$.
- If the relation R is such that $\{x \mid x \mathrel{R} y\}$ is infinite for any y, then the renamed process $P[\![R]\!]$ can branch infinitely on y when P is finitely branching. For example, the functional renaming $f[Q]$ where $f(n) = 0$ for all $n \in \mathbb{N}$ introduces infinite branching.

The last two of these can only happen when Σ is infinite, but there is no such limitation on the first.

We could easily prove that avoiding these three constructs guarantees finite branching. The proof comes in two parts:

- Show by structural induction[12] that the initial actions of any CSP term not involving one of these three constructs are finitely branching.
- Show that if P does not involve them, and $P \xrightarrow{x} Q$, then neither does Q.

Exercise 9.13 Use your answer to Exercise 9.7 and the functions defined in this section to determine $traces(P)$, $failures(P)$ and $divergences(P)$ for each of the processes referred to in that earlier exercise. Is any of them infinitely nondeterministic?

Exercise 9.14 Can ($\sqcap\{COUNT_n \mid n \in \mathbb{N}\}) \setminus down$ diverge? What are its failures?

---

[12] *Structural induction* is a technique for proving properties of objects in syntactically-defined sets such as the set of all CSP terms **CSP**. It says that if you can prove a property R of each term T of a syntax on the assumption that R holds of all the immediate sub-terms that T is built from (e.g., assuming it holds of P and Q to prove it holds of $P \square Q$) then R holds for all members of the syntax. Over most programming languages one can justify this principle easily, because structural induction is implied by ordinary mathematical induction over the size of programs. But

9.6 Tools

The role of an animator like ProBE is to bring the operational semantics to life: it will let you carry out the actions of a process as derived from the operational semantics. It may well allow you to see how the rules of the operational semantics have derived each action of a compound process from the actions of its parts.

You can use a tool like this both to help you understand the operational semantics and to apply these semantics to allow you to experiment with complex process definitions.

FDR is heavily dependent on the operational semantics, since the way it understands any process is by using the operational semantics to expand it into a finite LTS. As already discussed, this is done at two levels, the *compilation* of component machines and the *exploration* a system built out of these using supercombinators.

9.7 Notes

Historically, the operational semantics of CSP was created to give an alternative view to the already existing denotational models rather than providing the intuition in the original design, as it has with some other process algebras such as CCS.

The style of presenting an operational semantics as an inference system (Structured Operational Semantics, or SOS) evolved at about the same time as CSP, the main influence being Plotkin's notes [108] which set out the general style used here. The operational semantics of CSP first appeared in something like its present form in Brookes's thesis [18], though essentially the same semantics in LTSs using different notations (more remote from Plotkin's) were present in [19, 117]. In providing

---

a careful examination of what we allow as CSP terms reveals that this argument does not work here, since we have infinite mutual recursion as well as the infinitary constructs $\sqcap S$ and $?x : A \rightarrow P$, meaning that there are terms with no finite 'size' in the ordinary sense. Structural induction can still be justified provided we assume that the syntax is *well-founded*, meaning that there is no infinite sequence of terms each of which is a sub-term of its predecessor. This means we cannot have terms like

$$a_1 \rightarrow a_2 \rightarrow \cdots \rightarrow a_i \rightarrow \cdots$$

actually in the language, though there is nothing wrong with achieving the same effect using an infinite mutual recursion $P_i = a_i \rightarrow P_{i+1}$.

Well-foundedness corresponds to the natural assumption that the language generated by a syntax is the smallest set of terms which is closed under all the constructs of the syntax. This leads to a trivial proof of the principle of structural induction: the assumptions of that rule imply that the set of terms in the language that satisfy R is itself closed under all the constructs, and therefore contains the smallest set.

Readers with the necessary mathematical background might like to note that, in order to make the infinitary syntax of CSP well defined, it is necessary to put some bound on the size of sets that can have $\sqcap$ applied to them. This can be any infinite cardinal number κ, which can be chosen to accommodate all the nondeterministic choices required for a given theory. (The necessity of this bound is tied up with Russell's paradox and the non-existence of a set of all sets.)

CSP with an operational semantics of this form we were certainly heavily influenced by the earlier work on CCS, the standard treatment of which is now [91].

The version in [18] did not use the τ-expansion rule for recursion unfolding. This first seems to have appeared in print in [97], though it had certainly been in use for several years by then. This rule is interesting because it shows up one of the major differences between CSP and those other process algebras which, like CCS, give semantic significance to a single τ action. If it were not the case that, for any node P, another node Q whose only action is $Q \xrightarrow{\tau} P$ is equivalent to P, then the unwinding rule would be much more controversial.

The combinator style of presenting an operational semantics, which is original as far as the author is aware, was jointly inspired by the supercombinators that FDR uses and the results of [132], some of which were discussed in Sect. 9.4. The idea of identifying the **on** and **off** arguments of an operator arose first in the author's thesis [117] (Chap. 8) together with much of the intuition behind combinator rules. There are close relationships between combinators and work reported in [11, 12], for example.

The name "supercombinator" was given to FDR2's technique for calculating operational semantics by analogy with the role of supercombinators in functional program implementation [67]. In that, John Hughes suggested that instead of using a one-size-fits-all set of combinators for representing and evaluating function programs, a program could be implemented more efficiently if it represented using a special set of *supercombinators* designed specifically for it. The supercombinators of FDR were designed to play essentially the same role there: avoid applying many rules for individual operators and instead give only rules for the complete construction. It is only very recently, however, that the author realised that *any* operator defined in terms of supercombinators could be implemented *in CSP* (see Sect. 9.4), and that it therefore it made sense to present all operators in this style.

While many of the ideas behind combinator operational semantics were present in [117], the author's recent development of them and the proof of the result that any combinator-style operational semantics can be simulated in CSP arose somewhat serendipitously. Having been forced to add the throw operator Θ_A to the language for theoretical reasons (see Sect. 12.3 and [129]), he felt the need to investigate whether one might ever have to add further operators. Combinator-style (CSP-like) operational semantics and the expressivity result represent the answer "no" to this question, at least within the normal confines of CSP.

The operational semantics presented in this book are (except from the extended set of operators) isomorphic to those presented in TPC, and differ from some earlier versions in the way $\checkmark$, and hence the distributed termination of parallel constructs, are interpreted.

Chapter 10
Denotational Semantics and Behavioural Models

10.1 Introduction

CSP has been given a number of denotational semantics, mainly based on sets of behaviours such as traces, failures and divergences. We will term this type of model *behavioural*. It is not necessary to understand a lot of difficult mathematics to use the behaviours as a tool for describing or specifying processes, especially when equipped with automated tools for evaluating which behaviours a process has. Indeed, the sets of behaviours of processes can equally and equivalently (thanks to congruence theorems that we will meet in this chapter) be extracted from operational semantics. However, it is possible to gain a much deeper insight into the language by investigating behavioural notions of equivalence and the properties of the models they generate. In this chapter we set out the main ideas and methods of denotational semantics, or at least the ones important to CSP, and start to investigate what behavioural models of CSP exist.

There are three chapters (8, 9 and 10) in TPC on this topic. The first two of these concentrate on the three models we have seen already: $\mathcal{T}$ (traces), $\mathcal{F}$ (stable failures) and $\mathcal{N}$ (failures-divergences). While we will use these models as examples, our aim in this book is to reveal more of the overall hierarchy of models that exist for CSP. An important part of this hierarchy are the options for including infinitely observable behaviours such as divergences and infinite traces into models which, like $\mathcal{T}$ and $\mathcal{F}$, are based on finite observations. Chapter 10 of TPC looks at one of these options, namely adding infinite behaviours in a divergence-strict way analogous to $\mathcal{N}$.

The present chapter—mainly a re-working and summary of Chaps. 8 and 9 of TPC—looks at what is expected of a denotational or behavioural model, and the sort of properties one can be expected to prove of them. Chapter 11 looks at the alternatives there are to $\mathcal{T}$ and $\mathcal{F}$ in the class of models built on finitely observable behaviour. Chapter 12 discusses the corresponding hierarchy of models that include infinite behaviour—looking both at divergence-strict models and the more recently discovered option of adding infinite behaviours without, or rather *almost* without, divergence strictness.

In this chapter and the following two we will assume that the reader has a basic knowledge of the mathematics of partial orders and metric spaces as typically used

A.W. Roscoe, *Understanding Concurrent Systems*, Texts in Computer Science, 229
DOI 10.1007/978-1-84882-258-0_10, © Springer-Verlag London Limited 2010

in programming language semantics. There is a tutorial introduction to these topics in Appendix A of TPC.

In building a denotational semantics—a function[1] $\mathcal{S}[\![\cdot]\!]$ from a programming language $\mathcal{L}$ into a mathematical model $\mathcal{M}$—there are a number of things we must always seek to do. The following paragraphs set out these aims.

Natural But Abstract Relationship Between Model and Language Ideally the construction of $\mathcal{M}$ should have a close relationship to a natural language for describing the 'essence' of programs in $\mathcal{L}$. This makes it easier to devise and justify the semantic clauses for the different operators and to use the semantic value of a program as a vehicle for specifying properties of it.

Natural Notion of Process Equivalence The equivalence over process terms induced by the semantics should be a natural one, in the sense that for all terms P and Q, $\mathcal{S}[\![P]\!] = \mathcal{S}[\![Q]\!]$ if and only if P and Q behave equivalently in some clearly defined sense. Depending on the way the model is built this may be obvious, or it may be rather more subtle. One of the best ways of demonstrating this is to identify a very few (rarely more than one or two) simple tests based on simple specifications (such as 'does not immediately deadlock', 'does not immediately diverge' or 'does not have the trace $\langle fail \rangle$') which are uncontroversial reasons for deciding two processes are different, and then showing that $\mathcal{S}[\![P]\!] = \mathcal{S}[\![Q]\!]$ if and only if, for all process contexts $C[\cdot]$, $C[P]$ and $C[Q]$ satisfy the same selection of tests. If one can prove a result like this we say that the semantics $\mathcal{S}[\![\cdot]\!]$ is *fully abstract* with respect to the chosen selection of properties. We will summarise the full abstraction properties of the various models we see. Chapter 9 of TPC has a detailed discussion of full abstraction, and contains a number of proofs.

Model Must Be a Congruence The semantics has to be a *congruence* in that, for each operator $\oplus$ in the language, it is possible to compute $\mathcal{S}[\![P \oplus Q]\!]$ in terms of $\mathcal{S}[\![P]\!]$ and $\mathcal{S}[\![Q]\!]$ (with obvious modifications for non-binary operators). It is quite possible to propose what looks like a good model for a language, only to discover that this property fails for some operator. For example, we might design a model for CSP in which a process was modelled by $(traces(P), deadlocks(P))$, where $deadlocks(P)$ is the set of traces on which P can deadlock, as a simplification of the stable failures model. We would then find it possible to give semantic clauses for $deadlocks(P)$ for most CSP operators, for example

$$deadlocks(STOP) = \{\langle\rangle\}$$

$$deadlocks(a \to P) = \{\langle a\rangle\hat{\,}s \mid s \in deadlocks(P)\}$$

$$deadlocks(P \,\square\, Q) = ((deadlocks(P) \cup deadlocks(Q)) \cap \{s \mid s \neq \langle\rangle\})$$
$$\cup (deadlocks(P) \cap deadlocks(Q))$$

---

[1]The special style of brackets $[\![\cdot]\!]$ is commonly used in denotational semantics to separate program syntax from abstract semantics. They have no formal significance, but give a useful visual signal. In fact we will not generally use them when it comes to dealing with CSP except in places where a clear distinction between syntax and semantics is vital.

$$deadlocks(P \sqcap Q) = deadlocks(P) \cup deadlocks(Q)$$

$$deadlocks(P; Q) = (deadlocks(P) \cap \Sigma^*)$$
$$\cup \{ s^\frown t \mid s^\frown \langle \checkmark \rangle \in traces(P) \wedge t \in deadlocks(Q) \}$$

But this breaks down for parallel operators involving synchronisation, such as $\parallel_X$. If, for example

$$P = (a \rightarrow P) \sqcap (b \rightarrow P)$$

$$R = (a \rightarrow R) \,\square\, (b \rightarrow R)$$

P and R have exactly the same sets of traces ($\{a, b\}^*$) and deadlock traces ($\emptyset$). But, while $R \parallel_{\{a,b\}} R$ still cannot deadlock, the process $P \parallel_{\{a,b\}} P$ can (on any trace) because the left-hand P can opt only to accept a and the right-hand one can opt only to accept b. Thus it is impossible, in general, to predict the semantics of $S \parallel_X T$ from those of processes S and T, so our proposed semantics is not a congruence and must be rejected.

There are many arguments for a model being a congruence, over and above the fact that it is needed to construct a denotational semantics. It is crucial to support the concept of hierarchical compression described in Sect. 8.8. It is also needed for the idea of an algebraic law to make sense, since (like compression) that relies on us being able to substitute one semantically equivalent program for another in a CSP *context* $C[\cdot]$: a process definition with a hole for a process value.

10.1.1 Fixed-Point Theory

Just as we need to be able to combine semantic values accurately under all of the basic operators of our language, we also need to be able to compute the values of recursively defined processes. While you can think of recursion as just another operator that is applied to process terms (turning P into $\mu p.P$), it is conceptually a quite different thing to operators like $a \rightarrow$, $\square$ and $\parallel_X$. What $\mu p.P$ represents is a solution to the equation

$$A = P[A/p]$$

Since the denotational semantics is a congruence, the semantic value $\mathcal{S}[\![P[A/p]]\!]$ is a function of the value $\mathcal{S}[\![A]\!]$, in the sense that if $\mathcal{S}[\![A]\!] = \mathcal{S}[\![B]\!]$, then $\mathcal{S}[\![P[A/p]]\!] = \mathcal{S}[\![P[B/p]]\!]$. Thus $\mathcal{S}[\![\mu p.P]\!]$ is a *fixed point* of this function. You can think of the term P as a context in which the identifier p represents the process argument.

Giving a denotational semantics to recursively defined processes thus reduces to finding fixed points of the functions from $\mathcal{M}$ to itself that are generated by process contexts. This means that every appropriate function over $\mathcal{M}$ must have a fixed point—not something that is true for most mathematical structures. Even if there is a fixed point, there may be several, and we need to find a way to select the right one.

Sometimes (see p. 283) it turns out there is *no* sensible way to pick the right one, so a model that otherwise makes sense must be discarded.

We make a distinction between CSP *models*, which must have a way of extracting the correct fixed point from the function represented by evaluating $\mathcal{S}[\![P]\!]$ where the identifier p is bound to the argument, and *congruences*. A congruence is an equivalence relation on closed CSP terms (ones with no free process identifiers) which is preserved by every non-recursive operator: if $P \cong P'$ and $Q \cong Q'$ then $P \oplus Q \cong P' \oplus Q'$ for every CSP operator $\oplus$.

Just as the semantics of recursion is stylistically very different from the semantic clauses of more ordinary operators, so too are the methods available for proving properties of recursively defined process. We need ways of proving properties of the objects extracted by whatever mechanism is chosen to pick fixed points. Such proof methods, such as the UFP rule, are inevitably tied up with whatever mathematical theory is used to prove the existence of the fixed points.

10.2 Analysing Traces Semantics

In this section we will examine the traces model $\mathcal{T}$ as an example of a behavioural model, and more specifically a behavioural model in which all the recorded behaviours can be observed in a finite time.

When a model like $\mathcal{T}$ is a congruence, it is possible to define each CSP operator over the model itself: a function that takes one member of the model for each argument, and returns the value of the composition. Thus the parallel operator $P \parallel_X Q$ takes the value of P, the value of Q, and returns the value of the parallel composition. We have, of course, already seen this for all the operators of the traces model in Sect. 2.2.1 and later chapters.

The reader will have seen that every behaviour computed for $P \parallel_X Q$ (see p. 30 for traces) arises because of a single behaviour of P and a single behaviour of Q (where, for $\mathcal{T}$, you can read "behaviour" as "trace"). This is true with variations for all the other operators over $\mathcal{T}$, in the sense that every "output" behaviour always depends on a single[2] behaviour of each of a subset of the arguments of an operator.

Note we said *subset* here: you can expect this subset to be the set of arguments that have been **on** during the execution that led to the output behaviours being observed. For example, the prefix operator creates $\langle\rangle$ without looking at its process argument(s), and $P \sqcap Q$, $P; Q$ and $P \Theta_A Q$ have behaviours generated by P alone.

---

[2]The fact that only a single behaviour of each argument is used is closely related to the "no copying" requirement we placed on combinator operational semantics in Chap. 9. That requirement implies that no operator can use more than one behaviour of an **on** argument as it progresses. There is nothing of a similar nature that prevents *off* arguments being used multiple times; but all the standard, non-recursive, CSP operators with *off* arguments happen to obey the no-copy rule for them also.

Over T, and every other model we will meet, which is *either* based on finitely observable behaviours *or* is divergence-strict, the intuition above can be formalised by showing that all CSP operators can be represented as a set of *relations* on behaviours. In other words, the result of applying our operator to a tuple of arguments has a given behaviour if and only if that behaviour is an image, under one of a family of relations representing the operator, of behaviours belonging to its arguments.

So for example sequential composition over T is represented as two relations: one (binary) between traces of P and output traces and one (ternary) between traces of P, traces of Q and output traces. These are described

$$s[;]_1 u \Leftrightarrow s \in \Sigma^* \wedge u = s$$
$$(s,t)[;]_{1,2} u \Leftrightarrow \exists s_0.s = s_0\hat{}\langle\checkmark\rangle \wedge u = s_0\hat{}t$$

Thus, we get one relation describing the overall behaviours that the first argument can produce without the help of the second, and one describing the behaviours in which both arguments are active. There are two further relations we might need for a binary operator $\oplus$: $[\oplus]_2$ for the second argument acting alone and $[\oplus]_\bullet$ for the set of behaviours that can be produced without either playing a part; but in the case of ';' these are both empty. In general we then get

$$\begin{aligned}
traces(P \oplus Q) = \{u \mid &\exists s \in traces(P), t \in traces(Q).(s,t,u) \in [\oplus]_{1,2}\} \\
&\cup \{u \mid \exists s \in traces(P).(s,u) \in [\oplus]_1\} \\
&\cup \{u \mid \exists t \in traces(Q).(t,u) \in [\oplus]_2\} \\
&\cup [\oplus]_\bullet
\end{aligned}$$

This representation of operators is discussed in detail in Sect. 8.2 of TPC. It has a number of useful consequences.

Theorem 10.1 *Any operator $\oplus$ over T definable as the lifting of a family of trace relations is fully distributive in each of its arguments, in the sense that $F(\sqcap S) = \sqcap\{F(P) \mid P \in S\}$ for each non-empty S (where $F(\cdot)$ represents any unary function produced by fixing all arguments of $\oplus$ other than the one we are studying).*

For the proof of this result, which applies equally to other models, see TPC.

This gives another view of the distributive laws that hold of CSP operators and also proves (i) that they are all monotonic with respect to the refinement order and (ii) that under the subset order (i.e., the reverse of refinement) they are all continuous. The former is because we know $P \sqsubseteq Q$ is equivalent to $P \sqcap Q = P$, and so $F(P) \sqcap F(Q) = F(P)$ for distributive $F(\cdot)$. The latter is because continuity under that order is equivalent to distributivity over directed sets.

It is also informative to consider continuity in the other direction. Now, it turns out, not all operators are continuous. An example that fails is hiding an infinite set $X = \{a_1, a_2, \ldots\}$, since, if we pick $b \notin X$, the processes

$$P_n = STOP \sqcap \sqcap\{a_i \to b \to STOP \mid i \geq n\}$$

form an increasing sequence under $\sqsubseteq_T$ with limit $STOP$. However, for every n,

$$P_n \setminus X = STOP \sqcap b \to STOP$$

so that the limit of applying $\setminus X$ to the sequence:

$$\bigsqcup \{P_n \setminus X \mid n \in \mathbb{N}\}$$

equals this value, which of course is not equal to $STOP \setminus X$.

The key to which operators are continuous lies in the relations that represent them. The crucial feature of $\setminus X$ (whether or not X is infinite, though it may not be empty) is that for any trace u not including a member of X, the set $\{s \in \Sigma^{*\checkmark} \mid (s, u) \in [\setminus X]_1\}$ is infinite: if we are told that $s \in traces(P \setminus X)$, there are infinitely many potential reasons for this, and as we go through an infinite refining sequence of processes these reasons can disappear just as in the example above until there are none left in the limit.

We say that the operators representing a given operator $\oplus$ are *finitary* if each behaviour that the result might perform has only finitely many pre-images.

The following result (proof in TPC) shows the importance of these ideas to continuity.

Theorem 10.2 *If $\oplus$ is any operator of finite arity, which can be represented by a family of relations all of which are finitary, then it is $\sqsubseteq_T$-continuous in each argument.*

$\mathcal{T}$ can be given a metric structure based on the system of restriction functions

$$P \downarrow n = \{s \in P \mid \#s \leq n\}$$

We can define a metric (distance function) between members of $\mathcal{T}$ as follows:

$$d(P, Q) = inf\{2^{-n} \mid P \downarrow n = Q \downarrow n\}$$

If the sequence

$$\langle P_0, P_1, P_2, \ldots \rangle$$

satisfies $P_{n+1} \downarrow n = P_n$, then it is easy to see that $P^* = \bigcup\{P_n \mid n \in \mathbb{N}\}$ satisfies $P^* \downarrow n = P_n$. It follows easily from this that $\mathcal{T}$, with the metric defined above, is complete. These ideas extend simply to any product space of $\mathcal{T}$, as used in mutual recursions, and to the other finite-behaviour models we will see later.

This metric structure is at the heart of the theory of guardedness/constructiveness that we first met in Chap. 2. For we can now precisely define what it means for a function F to be constructive with respect to $\mathcal{T}$: for all processes P, Q and $n \in \mathbb{N}$

$$P \downarrow n = Q \downarrow n \Rightarrow F(P) \downarrow (n+1) = F(Q) \downarrow (n+1)$$

It is useful to define a corresponding concept of *non-destructive* function:

$$P \downarrow n = Q \downarrow n \Rightarrow F(P) \downarrow n = F(Q) \downarrow n$$

A function is constructive if and only if it is a contraction mapping with respect to the associated metric and is non-destructive when it is non-expanding in the metric space.

This immediately means that a constructive function has a unique fixed point (thus justifying the UFP rule for analysing recursions that we have used frequently in this book).

All standard operators of CSP except hiding are non-destructive, and prefixing is constructive (and see Exercise 10.3).

Because not all functions are guarded, the fixed point theory used to define the meaning of recursions is always based on partial orders (often Tarski's Theorem, see Appendix A for TPC, but we will see there are notable exceptions in the world of infinite traces). Except in one advanced case (see Sect. 12.4) and Timed CSP (see Chap. 15) we will always use the *least* fixed point in an order. Sometimes, however, there is a choice of which order to use and $\mathcal{T}$ is a good example of this since we have the choice of the refinement order $\sqsubseteq_T$ and the subset order. These are of course the opposite of each other, so by calculating the least $\subseteq$-fixed point we get the $\sqsubseteq_T$-greatest fixed point, and vice-versa.

The correct choice for $\mathcal{T}$ is to identify every recursion $\mu p.F(p)$ with its $\subseteq$-least fixed point which, because of the continuity of all operators with respect to this order, is just the set of all traces which some $F^n(STOP)$ can perform. In other words it is $\prod_{n=0}^{\infty} F^n(STOP)$. This is remarkably easy to justify, provided we keep in mind that F is monotonic.

Certainly $STOP \sqsubseteq_T \mu p.F(p)$, and applying F n times to both sides of this gives $F^n(STOP) \subseteq F^n(\mu p.F(p)) =_T \mu p.F(p)$ (the last equivalence holds because $F(\mu p.F(p)) =_T \mu p.F(p)$). Hence every trace of each $F^n(STOP)$ is a trace of $\mu p.F(p)$. This just says that any trace we can get by unwinding the recursion a finite number of times is a trace of $\mu p.F(p)$, which is scarcely surprising since in running the recursion you are allowed to unfold it arbitrarily often.

On the other hand any finite trace a process performs can be observed in a finite time, and the recursion can only have been unfolded a finite number of times n in that period. It follows that the trace must be one of $F^n(STOP)$.

The reader can find a mathematically precise version of this argument in Sect. 9.4 of TPC. Those familiar with versions of Tarski's Theorem will realise that the formula (looking at the natural number iterations of the function F from the subset-least element $STOP$) coincides with the continuity of CSP operators under the $\subseteq$ order. With monotone but discontinuous operators we would in general require a more complex formula.

Exercise 10.1 Find sequences of processes of the form $P_0 \sqsubseteq_T P_1 \sqsubseteq_T P_2 \sqsubseteq_T \cdots$ illustrating failures of $\sqsubseteq_T$-continuity of (i) hiding a single event $\setminus \{a\}$ and (ii) infinite-to-one renaming.

Exercise 10.2 Prove that the relation $[\|]_{1,2}$ is finitary.
X

Exercise 10.3 Recall that we said above that all non-hiding operators are non-destructive and that prefixing is constructive. There is another operator that is always constructive in one of its arguments: which is it?

Exercise 10.4 Suppose Σ is infinite. Use renaming to find a CSP-definable function that is constructive but not continuous with respect to $\sqsubseteq_T$.

10.3 The Stable Failures Model

We met the idea of failures refinement $P \sqsubseteq_F Q$ in Sect. 6.1. It was defined there to mean that $failures(P) \supseteq failures(Q)$ and $traces(P) \supseteq traces(Q)$. Given that $failures(P)$ is the set of *stable failures* of P, it should not come as a surprise, therefore, that $(failures(P), traces(P))$ is the representation of P in a CSP model, the *stable failures model*, written $\mathcal{F}$.

We have already seen in Sect. 6.1 that failures give us the language to distinguish between processes on the basis of what they can refuse as well as actively communicate, so that we can (for example) distinguish between $P \sqcap Q$ and $P \;\square\; Q$, and specify deadlock-freedom. In other works it lets us see certain sorts of nondeterminism. In this section we will concentrate mainly on the construction of $\mathcal{F}$ as a behavioural semantic model.

It is obvious that $\mathcal{F}$ refines $\mathcal{T}$ in the sense that every two processes distinguished by $\mathcal{T}$ are also distinguished by $\mathcal{F}$. We will write this relation $\mathcal{T} \preceq \mathcal{F}$. $\mathcal{F}$ also shares the property with $\mathcal{T}$ that all its behaviours are finitely observable: this is because if a process comes into a stable state (one without a τ or $\checkmark$) and refuses the set X, then this happens at some finite time.

Every CSP model has its own *healthiness* conditions: a set of properties that sets of behaviours representing a real process must have. The healthiness conditions of $\mathcal{T}$ are that the set of traces is non-empty and prefix-closed. The role of healthiness conditions is partly to be a sanity check on operator definitions: if we give them arguments satisfying the conditions, then the result ought to satisfy them as well. But they also allow us to investigate other properties of the space of "realistic" processes describable in a particular language of behaviours, for example completeness under limits.

The picture we are painting in this book is one in which the operational, denotational and algebraic semantics of CSP can be regarded as an integrated whole. In that setting there is another way of viewing healthiness conditions: they show which sets of behaviours are the images of LTSs under functions of the sorts described in Sect. 9.5.1.

The healthiness conditions of $\mathcal{F}$ are as follows. They assume a pair (F, T) where $T \subseteq \Sigma^{*\checkmark}$ and $F \subseteq \Sigma^{*\checkmark} \times \mathcal{P}(\Sigma^{\checkmark})$.

T1 T is non-empty and prefix-closed.

T2 $(s, X) \in F \Rightarrow s \in T$. Every trace associated with a failure is a trace.

F2 $(s, X) \in F \wedge Y \subseteq X \Rightarrow (s, Y) \in F$. When a process refuses X it refuses any subset of X.

F3 $(s, X) \in F \wedge Y \cap \{x \mid s^\frown\langle x\rangle \in T\} = \emptyset \Rightarrow (s, X \cup Y) \in F$. When a process refuses X it also refuses all events that the process can *never* perform after the same trace.

F4 $s^\smallfrown\langle\checkmark\rangle \in T \implies \{(s, \Sigma), (s^\smallfrown\langle\checkmark\rangle, \Sigma^\checkmark)\} \subseteq F$. When a process can terminate it can refuse to do anything else, and it is formally assumed to refuse everything after $\checkmark$.[3]

The numbering above is the same as that used in TPC except that the two properties quoted there for refusal behaviour associated with $\checkmark$ are amalgamated here. There is an obvious gap, namely F1. In TPC, where the failures-divergences model $\mathcal{N}$ was introduced before $\mathcal{F}$, this is the property that the traces associated with failures are non-empty and prefix-closed, analogous with T1 here. That property is not true for $\mathcal{F}$: for example $(a \to STOP) \rhd \mathbf{div}$ is a process that has no failures of the form $(\langle\rangle, X)$ at all since it can never become stable on $\langle\rangle$. However, it does have the failure $(\langle a \rangle, X)$ for all X.

We said that the touchstone of a set of healthiness conditions is that they define exactly the set of "processes" (i.e. tuples of sets of behaviours) that are the images of LTSs under the natural abstraction maps. As in most cases, it is easy to show that every LTS node is mapped (by the functions $traces(\cdot)$ and $failures(\cdot)$ defined in Sect. 9.5.1) into $\mathcal{F}$.

Lemma 10.1 *For each $(F, T) \in \mathcal{F}$, there is an LTS node that maps to it.*

Proof To construct our LTS we exploit the curious transparency that $\mathbf{div}$ has over $\mathcal{F}$ and other finite-behaviour models. For any member T of $\mathcal{T}$, and in particular our T, we can build an LTS representing it in which the nodes are

- Ω (representing the terminated process)
- $(s, T/s)$ where $T/s = \{t \mid s^\smallfrown t \in T\}$ for each member s of $T \cap \Sigma^*$
- $\mathbf{div}$

and where the action $\checkmark$ leads from $(s, T/s)$ to Ω when $s^\smallfrown\langle\checkmark\rangle \in T$; a leads from $(s, T/s)$ to $(s^\smallfrown\langle a \rangle, T/(s^\smallfrown\langle a \rangle))$ whenever $s^\smallfrown\langle a \rangle \in T$; and τ leads from $(s, T/s)$ to $\mathbf{div}$ for all $s \in T$.

It should be easy to see that this has no stable states at all other than Ω, and therefore only the failures implied by F4. We can, however, add whatever failures we like to this set within the constraints of F2 and F3 by adding, from $(s, T/s)$, a τ action to the stable state described in CSP by $?x : (\Sigma \setminus X) \to \mathbf{div}$. F3 means we can

---

[3]The effect of F4 is, in combination with F2, to make the failures behaviour of a process standardised in line with the assumption discussed in Sect. 7.1.1 that $\checkmark$ is a non-controllable *signal*. We could have achieved the same effect by (i) removing $\checkmark$ from refusal sets, and (ii) not having any failures with terminated traces. A stable failure (s, X) would then be interpreted as coming from a stable state (without τ or $\checkmark$) rather than allowing it to come from any $\checkmark$-stable state. This would represent exactly the same equivalence over LTSs and CSP processes as the representation above: see Exercise 10.7.

Stylistically, it would probably be cleaner to take the option described in the previous paragraph, but we have used the representation above for two reasons. Firstly, it is obviously desirable that the notation of $\mathcal{F}$ should be consistent with $\mathcal{N}$, and using this alternative approach for $\mathcal{N}$ would require the addition of an extra component to the model that told us the terminated traces. Secondly, the version in which $\checkmark$ can be a member of refusal sets is consistent with TPC.

assume $\Sigma \setminus X$ only contains members of $\{a \mid s^\frown \langle a \rangle \in T\}$, so this extra state adds no traces.

The overall LTS we have constructed has exactly the behaviours seen in (F, T).   □

It is reasonably straightforward to convert the construction of the LTS described above into a CSP process that has the same value over $\mathcal{F}$.

Recall that refinement over $\mathcal{F}$ is defined by reverse containment in both components. With respect to this, $Chaos_\Sigma$, defined

$$Chaos_A = SKIP \sqcap STOP \sqcap ?x : A \rightarrow Chaos_A$$

is the refinement-least process, and $\mathbf{div} = (\emptyset, \{\langle\rangle\})$ is the refinement-greatest member. Note that $STOP$, which is identical to $\mathbf{div}$ over T, is no longer equivalent to it since it has the failures $(\langle\rangle, X)$ for all X.

The interesting thing about $\mathbf{div}$ is that it has no finitely observable behaviour at all except the empty trace $\langle\rangle$. It follows that it is bound to represent not only the refinement-greatest member of T and $\mathcal{N}$, but of *every* behavioural model based on finite observations!

So the right formula for the meaning of a recursive term over $\mathcal{F}$ is $\bigsqcap_{n=0}^{\infty} F^n(\mathbf{div})$, because $\mathbf{div}$ is the process that has no recorded behaviours not belonging to all processes. The argument for the validity of this formula—i.e. that is gives the correct fixed point—is exactly the same as that on p. 235, again depending crucially on the finite observability of all the behaviours used in $\mathcal{F}$.

The essence of a denotational semantics is giving clauses for calculating the semantics of each program in terms of its sub-components. The argument above deals with recursion, so we need clauses for handling all the other operators. We have already given the definitions for traces, of course, so what we need are ones for the failures component of each operator. These are as follows:

$$failures(STOP) = \{(\langle\rangle, X) \mid X \subseteq \Sigma^\checkmark\}$$

$$failures(SKIP) = \{(\langle\rangle, X) \mid X \subseteq \Sigma\} \cup \{(\langle\checkmark\rangle, X) \mid X \subseteq \Sigma^\checkmark\}$$

$$failures(a \rightarrow P) = \{(\langle\rangle, X) \mid a \notin X\}$$
$$\cup \{(\langle a \rangle^\frown s, X) \mid (s, X) \in failures(P)\}$$

$$failures(?x : A \rightarrow P) = \{(\langle\rangle, X) \mid X \cap A = \emptyset\}$$
$$\cup \{(\langle a \rangle^\frown s, X) \mid a \in A$$
$$\wedge (s, X) \in failures(P[a/x])\}$$

$$failures(P \sqcap Q) = failures(P) \cup failures(Q)$$

$$failures(\sqcap S) = \bigcup\{failures(P) \mid P \in S\}$$
$$\text{for } S \text{ a non-empty set of processes}$$

$$failures(P \triangleleft b \triangleright Q) = \begin{cases} failures(P) & \text{if } b \text{ evaluates to } true \\ failures(Q) & \text{if } b \text{ evaluates to } false \end{cases}$$

$$failures(P \square Q) = \{(\langle\rangle, X) \mid (\langle\rangle, X) \in failures(P) \cap failures(Q)\}$$
$$\cup \{(s, X) \mid (s, X) \in failures(P)$$

$$\cup\, failures(Q) \wedge s \neq \langle\rangle\}$$
$$\cup\, \{(\langle\rangle, X) \mid X \subseteq \Sigma \wedge \langle\checkmark\rangle \in traces(P) \cup traces(Q)\}$$

$$failures(P \rhd Q) = failures(Q) \cup \{(s, X) \mid s \neq \langle\rangle \wedge (s, X) \in failures(P)\}$$
$$\cup\, \{(\langle\rangle, X) \mid \langle\checkmark\rangle \in traces(P) \wedge X \subseteq \Sigma\}$$

$$failures(P \parallel_X Q) = \{(u, Y \cup Z) \mid Y \backslash (X \cup \{\checkmark\}) = Z \backslash (X \cup \{\checkmark\})$$
$$\wedge\, \exists s, t.(s, Y) \in failures(P)$$
$$\wedge\, (t, Z) \in failures(Q) \wedge u \in s \parallel_X t\}$$

$$failures(P \setminus X) = \{(s \setminus X, Y) \mid (s, Y \cup X) \in failures(P)\}$$

$$failures(P[\![R]\!]) = \{(s', X) \mid \exists s.s \, R \, s' \wedge (s, R^{-1}(X)) \in failures(P)\}$$

$$failures(P; Q) = \{(s, X) \mid s \in \Sigma^* \wedge (s, X \cup \{\checkmark\}) \in failures(P)\}$$
$$\cup\, \{(s\hat{\,}t, X) \mid s\hat{\,}\langle\checkmark\rangle \in traces(P)$$
$$\wedge\, (t, X) \in failures(Q)\}$$

$$failures(P \triangle Q) = \{(s, X) \mid (s, X) \in failures(P) \wedge (\langle\rangle, X) \in failures(Q)\}$$
$$\cup\, \{(s\hat{\,}t, X) \mid s \in traces(P) \wedge (t, X) \in failures(Q)$$
$$\wedge\, t \neq \langle\rangle\}$$

$$failures(P \, \Theta_A \, Q) = \{(s, X) \mid (s, X) \in failures(P) \wedge s \in (\Sigma \backslash A)^{*\checkmark}\}$$
$$\cup\, \{(s\hat{\,}\langle a\rangle\hat{\,}t, X) \mid s\hat{\,}\langle a\rangle \in traces(P) \cap (\Sigma \backslash A)^*$$
$$\wedge\, a \in A \wedge (t, X) \in failures(Q)\}$$

All of these can be re-written in terms of relations in the style shown on p. 233, which gives them the same distributivity and continuity properties seen there. Notice that in some cases, for example $\square$ and $\triangle$, the calculation of the failures set depends not only on the failures of the arguments to the operators but also on their traces. We might write such relations in notation like $[\triangle]^F_{T1, F2}$, meaning the relation producing failures of $P1 \triangle P2$ that uses traces of $P1$ and failures of $P2$.

We can define a process's restriction up to n steps by $(F, T) \upharpoonright n = (F \upharpoonright n \cup \{(s\hat{\,}\langle\checkmark\rangle, X) \mid s\hat{\,}\langle\checkmark\rangle \in T \upharpoonright n\}, T \upharpoonright n)$ where $T \upharpoonright n$ means the same as it did over T and

$$F \upharpoonright n = \{(s, X) \in F \mid \#s < n\}$$

In other words, $(F, T) \upharpoonright n$ behaves exactly like (F, T) except that after performing precisely n actions, unless the last was $\checkmark$, it diverges. This turns $\mathcal{F}$ into a complete metric space in exactly the same way as the corresponding restriction operators do over $\mathcal{T}$.

10.3.1 Applications

Whenever we introduce a model other than $\mathcal{T}$ and $\mathcal{N}$, we will briefly indicate its applications in a section like this one.

The main application for $\mathcal{F}$, as already indicated in previous chapters, is as a substitute for $\mathcal{N}$ in cases where divergence is known not to be an issue. This is simply because FDR has to do less work on checks of the form P [F= Q than with the corresponding P [FD= Q.

A second application is in connection with the form of abstraction seen in Sect. 6.5. The lazy abstraction $\mathcal{L}_H(P)$ is, for divergence-free P, *defined* to be divergence-free, even though its CSP representation $(P \parallel_X Chaos_H) \setminus H$ may well diverge. For this reason, FDR analysis using lazy abstraction is always performed using $\mathcal{F}$.[4] The same applies to the *mixed* abstraction defined in Chap. 12 of TPC, where there is further discussion of the relationship between abstraction and $\mathcal{F}$.

The third application arises in the area of specifications. Suppose there is some set of actions A which are irrelevant to the traces a given specification will accept, in the sense that the specification accepts the failures (s, X) if and only if it accepts $(s \setminus A, X)$, and secondly, any refusal set that the specification rejects must include the whole of A. Then the divergence-free process P satisfies the specification if and only if $P \setminus X$ does, over $\mathcal{F}$.

The best-known example of this is the specification of deadlock freedom. The process P is deadlock free if and only if $P \setminus \Sigma \sqsupseteq_F SKIP$ (usually *SKIP* is replaced by **div** when P cannot terminate).

The main advantage of using hiding like this is that it tends to enable effective compression (see Sect. 8.8).

Exercise 10.5 Give three failures specifications that say that a process P can never refuse to communicate in the set B. They should work in the checks (a) $SPEC_1 \sqsubseteq_F P$, (b) $SPEC_2 \sqsubseteq_F P \setminus B$, and (c) $SPEC_3 \sqsubseteq_F \mathcal{L}_{\Sigma \setminus B}(P) \setminus B$.

Exercise 10.6 If you were to give relational representations of the *failures*$(P \oplus Q)$ clauses above, what relations would be required for the following operators: $\setminus X$, $\parallel_X$, ; and Θ_A?

Define the relations for ; .

Exercise 10.7 Consider the alternative version of $\mathcal{F}$ envisaged in the footnote on p. 237. As stated there, this induces the identical equivalence as the one we have adopted. Why does this imply that there is a refinement order preserving bijection between the two? Find this bijection, and define the modified function *failures'*(P) (analogous to *failures*(P) defined on p. 222) from LTSs to the failures component of this alternative model.

---

[4]There is no reason why one could not use a richer finite-behaviour model of the form we will see in Chap. 11 provided one was careful with the definition of $Chaos_H$. However, the author has never found cause to do so.

10.3.2 Channel-Based Failures

Throughout this book we will, by default, think of refusal sets and acceptance sets as being constructed from events in Σ or $\Sigma^{\checkmark}$. Certainly that is the right decision for the full version of the CSP language.

Sometimes, however, when modelling some other notation (examples being OCCAM [118] and the π-calculus [131] one discovers that it is natural to use channel names rather than events in refusal sets etc. This is almost always in cases (as in these two examples) where channels have a definite direction from output to input, and where one never attempts to synchronise two outputs.

Another necessary feature of such notations is that they do not allow *selective* inputs over channels: if a process is willing to accept one input over a channel, then it must accept any alternative.

Naturally all hiding, synchronisation and renaming of such channels must also respect this type of principle.

It is always worth bearing this possibility in mind when using CSP models or restricted versions of the CSP language to model some other notation. We will not be going into it more deeply, however, because in some sense it tends to be a straightforward idea when it applies, and because most of the time we will be studying models for *the whole of* CSP.

10.4 The Failures-Divergences Model

As we have already specified in Sect. 6.1, in the failures-divergences model each process is modelled by the pair $(failures_{\perp}(P), divergences(P))$, where, as formally set out in Sect. 9.5.1,

- $divergences(P)$ is the (extension-closed) set of traces s on which P can diverge, in the sense that an infinite unbroken sequence of τ actions can occur after some $s' \leq s$.
- $failures_{\perp}(P)$ consists of all stable failures (s, X) (where s is a trace of P and X is a set of actions P can refuse in some stable (unable to perform a τ or $\checkmark$) state after s, or results from a state after s which can perform $\checkmark$ and $X \subseteq \Sigma$), together with all pairs of the form (s, X) and $(s^{\frown}\langle\checkmark\rangle, X)$ for $s \in divergences(P)$.

This model has long been taken as the 'standard' equivalence for CSP, and with good reason. It allows us to describe safety properties (via traces) and to assert that a process must eventually accept some event from a set that is offered to it (since stable refusal and divergence are the two ways it could avoid doing this, and we can specify in this model that neither of these can happen). Although it is possible to reason about either (stable) failures or divergences in the absence of the other, neither alone provides a sufficiently complete picture of the way processes behave.

It is important to notice that if s is a trace that process P can perform then certainly either P diverges after s, or reaches either a stable state or one that can perform $\checkmark$. Thus, the failure $(s, \emptyset)$ always belongs to $failures_{\perp}(P)$, either because of the closure under divergence or because any stable (or $\checkmark$) state obviously refuses the empty set of events. It is, therefore, in general true that $traces_\perp(P) = \{s \mid (s, \emptyset) \in failures_\perp(P)\}$, and we will use this identity without comment in what follows.

We require healthiness conditions for this model, as we did for $\mathcal{T}$ and $\mathcal{F}$. Processes take the form $P = (F, D)$, where $F \subseteq \{(s, X) \mid s \in \Sigma^{*\checkmark}, X \subseteq \Sigma^{\checkmark}\}$ and $D \subseteq \Sigma^*$. As above, we can identify $traces_\perp(P)$ with $\{s \mid (s, X) \in F\} \cup D$. With this set replacing $traces(P)$, the healthiness conditions are F2, F3 and F4 as on p. 236, as well as F1 which, thanks to the identification above, is equivalent to T1:

F1 $traces_\perp(P)$ is non-empty and prefix-closed.

We now need the following healthiness conditions on $(failures_\perp(P), divergences(P))$ to impose divergence strictness[5]

D1 $s \in D \wedge t \in \Sigma^* \Longrightarrow s\hat{\ }t \in D$

This ensures the extension-closure of divergences as discussed briefly above.

D2 $s \in D \Longrightarrow (s, X) \in F$

Just as with $\mathcal{F}$, it is straightforward to show that every member of $\mathcal{N}$ can be implemented as an LTS and as a CSP process, demonstrating that the above are the correct healthiness conditions. See the example file `failsim.csp`.

Recall that refinement is defined over this model by reverse containment:

$$(F, D) \sqsubseteq_{FD} (F', D') \equiv F \supseteq F' \wedge D \supseteq D'$$

Any immediately divergent process such as **div** is identified with the bottom element of $\mathcal{N}$:

$$\perp_{\mathcal{N}} = (\Sigma^{*\checkmark} \times \mathbb{P}(\Sigma^{\checkmark}), \Sigma^*)$$

Notice that, thanks to conditions D1 and D2, $\langle\rangle \in divergences(P)$ implies that all of these behaviours are present.

The greatest lower bound for any non-empty subset of $\mathcal{N}$ is just given by component-wise union:

$$\sqcap S = (\bigcup\{F \mid (F, D) \in S\}, \bigcup\{D \mid (F, D) \in S\})$$

which is naturally identified with the nondeterministic choice over S and easily shown to be a member of $\mathcal{N}$.

Clearly **div** $\sqsubseteq_{FD} P$ for all P, so this process is the least refined under failures-divergences refinement. There is no single *most* refined process, unlike $\mathcal{T}$ and $\mathcal{F}$ where **div** was most refined.

The fact that there is no top element under refinement should be regarded as a *good thing*. After all there is not really a best-of-all program that will work in all

---

[5]The observant reader of this book and TPC will notice that D1 is slightly different from the version in TPC, and that we have dropped condition D3 from there. Both these changes are consequences of our decision here to drop terminated traces $s\hat{\ }\langle\checkmark\rangle$ as possible members of D. This change makes no difference to the equivalence the model induces over processes. The modification was, in fact, suggested in an exercise in TPC.

circumstances, as is implied by there being a most refined complete semantics for processes.

$\mathcal{N}$ allows us to specify that a process *must* perform a specific action if offered it: it may neither diverge nor have the failure (s, X) for relevant traces. This was impossible over $\mathcal{F}$.

The maximal processes of $\mathcal{N}$ are those that cannot diverge and can only refuse those sets implied by condition F3. These are the divergence-free processes that never have the option to accept or refuse any communication: the *deterministic* processes that we met in Sect. 6.1. We will discuss these further in Sect. 10.5.

In order to extend the notions of constructiveness and non-destructiveness to $\mathcal{N}$ we need to define restrictions $P \downarrow n$ with the same properties as those already studied over other models. The following definition is in exactly the same spirit as the one over $\mathcal{F}$. $(F, D) \downarrow n = (F', D')$, where

$$D' = D \cup \{s\hat{\ }t \mid (s, \emptyset) \in F \wedge s \in \Sigma^n\}$$
$$F' = F \cup \{(s, X) \mid s \in D'\}$$

In other words, $P \downarrow n$ behaves exactly like P until exactly n events have occurred, at which point it diverges unless it has already terminated. The different treatment of divergence in $\mathcal{F}$ and $\mathcal{N}$ means that, in general, $P \downarrow m \sqsubseteq_{FD} P$ as opposed to $P \downarrow m \sqsupseteq_F P$. The complete metric that the restriction operators define over $\mathcal{N}$ behaves in exactly the same way as over the previous models when it comes to defining and analysing guardedness.

A difference between $\mathcal{F}$ and $\mathcal{N}$ is that in the latter there are observed behaviours, namely divergences, which take an infinite amount of time to happen. This has a much greater effect on the mathematics of $\mathcal{N}$ than you would probably expect. The most obvious effect is on the calculation of fixed points required for the semantics of recursion. To see this problem clearly it helps to move to a slightly simpler model, the *divergence-strict traces model*, which we will write $\mathcal{T}^{\Downarrow}$: any finite-behaviour model $\mathcal{M}$ can be turned into a divergence-strict one in a way we will discuss in Chap. 12, and we will call the result $\mathcal{M}^{\Downarrow}$. Thus, in fact, $\mathcal{N} = \mathcal{F}^{\Downarrow}$. (The notation $\mathcal{M}^{\Downarrow}$ will also be explained in Chap. 12.)

A process's value in $\mathcal{T}^{\Downarrow}$ has two components, $(traces_{\perp}(P), divergences(P))$ and is identical to its representation in $\mathcal{N}$ except that all failures are replaced by the corresponding traces. This model has a top element,[6] $STOP = (\{\langle\rangle\}, \emptyset)$. On the basis of what we saw for $\mathcal{T}$, you might expect that the right value for the recursion $\mu p.F(p)$ would be $\bigsqcap_{n=0}^{\infty} F^n(STOP)$. But this is not the right answer. Consider the recursions $\mu p.a \rightarrow (p \setminus \{a\})$, $\mu p.p \sqcap STOP$ and $\mu p.p$. The first of these clearly diverges after performing an a, as will be apparent from calculating its operational semantics. The second diverges immediately thanks to the τ actions used to implement nondeterministic choice in the operational semantics. As remarked in Sect. 9.2.1, in order to give an operational semantics to the third term we need to use the version in which unfolding a recursion yields a τ: that certainly makes it diverge also.

---

[6]This is because it models what processes communicate and when they diverge but not when they refuse things stably. So the top element is the one that does no diverging and no communicating, and refuses everything instead.

But the formula above gives these three recursions, respectively, the values $a \rightarrow STOP$, $STOP$ and $STOP$. The reason why the formula works over $\mathcal{T}$ is that every finite trace appears finitely, and so must be present in some $F^n(STOP)$. Divergence, on the other hand, takes an infinite amount of time to appear and there is no corresponding argument we can make for it.

In fact the correct formula is to start from the other end of the model, identifying these recursions with $\bigcap_{n=0}^{n} F^n(\mathbf{div})$ (as in $\mathcal{N}$, $\mathbf{div}$ is the refinement-least member of $\mathcal{T}^{\Downarrow}$). These give the values $a \rightarrow \mathbf{div}$, $\mathbf{div}$ and $\mathbf{div}$, which are operationally correct.

Intuitively this corresponds to starting with the assumption that a recursive process has absolutely any behaviour, and looking at successive iterations of the recursion to reduce this set. The formula $\sqcap_{n=0}^{\infty} F^n(STOP)$, on the other hand, means we start with the belief that the recursion has the smallest set of behaviours, and using iterations to add further ones.

Thus the correct fixed point semantics for $\mathcal{T}^{\Downarrow}$, and also for $\mathcal{N}$, is the refinement-least fixed point.[7] Notice that divergence strictness is vitally important to the correctness of this fixed point, since none of the three recursions above can *actually* perform any traces other than those in their $\mathcal{T}$ fixed points. The many other traces in the refinement-least fixed points are only present in these processes' $\mathcal{T}^{\Downarrow}$ representations thanks to divergence strictness.

The reader might well wonder why the $\subseteq$-least fixed point is correct for $\mathcal{T}$, but the $\sqsubseteq$-least fixed point is correct for $\mathcal{T}^{\Downarrow}$, even in cases where the recursion in question does not diverge at all. If these can ever be different then one of them must be wrong.

There is an interesting answer to this question, versions of which apply to all models $\mathcal{M}^{\Downarrow}$, but we state here for $\mathcal{T}^{\Downarrow}$ and $\mathcal{N}$:

Lemma 10.2 *Suppose s is not in* $divergences(\mu p.F(p))$ *and that P and Q are two fixed points of F. Then $s \in traces(P) \Leftrightarrow s \in traces(Q)$, and, for $\mathcal{N}$, $(s, X) \in failures_{\perp}(P) \Leftrightarrow (s, X) \in failures_{\perp}(Q)$.*

In other words, once we know that a particular finite trace s is not a divergence of $\mu p.F(p)$, then all fixed points of $F(\cdot)$ agree about their behaviour on s.

This result is proved by introducing a new order on the models that implies, but is not implied by, refinement: $P \leq Q$ if and only if $divergences(Q) \subseteq divergences(P)$, and for all $s \notin divergences(P)$ the behaviour of P and Q is identical. It turns out (see [121]) that all CSP operators are monotonic with respect to this order and that the $\sqsubseteq$ and $\leq$ fixed points of CSP-definable functions are always the same. The above result follows since we then have that $\mu p.F(p) \leq Q$ for every fixed point of $F(\cdot)$. $\leq$ is called the *strong order*.

Of course to complete our denotational semantics for CSP over $\mathcal{N}$ we need to show how each of the CSP operators acts over this model. We first consider divergences, since they are new to us. Most of the operators are straightforward, and are tabulated below:

---

[7]The formula $\bigcap_{n=0}^{n} F^n(\mathbf{div})$ is correct whenever F is a continuous function with respect to $\sqsubseteq$, or the recursion is guarded, but in general the fixed point might be a proper refinement of this value.

$$divergences(STOP) = \emptyset$$

$$divergences(SKIP) = \emptyset$$

$$divergences(a \rightarrow P) = \{\langle a \rangle^\frown s \mid s \in divergences(P)\}$$

$$divergences(?x : A \rightarrow P) = \{\langle a \rangle^\frown s \mid a \in A \wedge s \in divergences(P[a/x])\}$$

$$divergences(P \sqcap Q) = divergences(P) \cup divergences(Q)$$

$$divergences(\sqcap S) = \bigcup\{divergences(P) \mid P \in S\}$$

$$divergences(P \square Q) = divergences(P) \cup divergences(Q)$$

$$divergences(P \triangleright Q) = divergences(P) \cup divergences(Q)$$

$$divergences(P[\![R]\!]) = \{s^\frown u \mid \exists t \in divergences(P).t \, R \, s\}$$

$$divergences(P \triangle Q) = divergences(P)$$
$$\cup \{s^\frown t \mid s \in traces_\perp(P) \cap \Sigma^*,$$
$$t \in divergences(Q)\}$$

$$divergences(P \ominus_A Q) = \{s^\frown t \mid s \in divergences(P) \cap (\Sigma \setminus A)^*\}$$
$$\cup \{s^\frown \langle a \rangle^\frown t \mid s^\frown \langle a \rangle \in traces_\perp(P),$$
$$s \in (\Sigma \setminus A)^*, a \in A, t \in divergences(Q)\}$$

Notice that in two of these cases (renaming and $\ominus_A$) we have had to adjust what might be seen as the natural definitions to allow for healthiness condition D1.

The parallel operator also requires this, and is a little more complex since *either* of the two arguments diverging will cause $P \parallel_X Q$ to diverge:

$$divergences(P \parallel_X Q) = \{u^\frown v \mid \exists s \in traces_\perp(P), t \in traces_\perp(Q).$$
$$u \in (s \parallel_X t) \cap \Sigma^*$$
$$\wedge (s \in divergences(P) \vee t \in divergences(Q))\}$$

The most important, and most subtle, $divergences(\cdot)$ definition is that for hiding. While all the definitions above simply say that the respective operators treat existing divergences much as the corresponding clauses for traces treat them, hiding can actually introduce divergence. This happens when an infinite consecutive sequence of hidden actions occurs. This immediately gives us a problem, because we are only recording *finite* traces in this model. The solution to this is to try to *infer* infinite traces from finite ones: the infinite trace u is deemed to be present if all of its finite prefixes are, leading to the definition

$$divergences(P \setminus X) = \{(s \setminus X)^\frown t \mid s \in divergences(P)\}$$
$$\cup \{(u \setminus X)^\frown t \mid u \in \Sigma^\omega \wedge (u \setminus X) \text{ finite}$$
$$\wedge \forall s < u.s \in traces_\perp(P)\}$$

We need to ask the question whether this inference is always accurate. Certainly the presence of the infinite trace implies the existence of the finite prefixes, so we can be sure that every real divergence is included by the definition above. Unfortunately there are processes where the reverse is not true: if A_n is the process that performs n copies of the event a and then *STOP*s, $A^* = \sqcap_{n=0}^\infty A_n$ can perform any finite trace of as but not the infinite trace a^{ω}. It follows that the definition above will incorrectly diagnose $A^* \setminus \{a\}$ as divergent.

In fact, the definition above is only accurate when we can guarantee that P is finitely nondeterministic. The fact that it is accurate then is a consequence of Theorem 9.5. We have to conclude the following:

$\mathcal{N}$, $\mathcal{T}^{\Downarrow}$ and all other models in which infinite traces are inferred from finite ones are only accurate for that fraction of the CSP language which either (i) is finitely nondeterministic or (ii) excludes hiding.

Naturally, the solution to this problem is to add a component of infinite traces to our models, as will be discussed in Chap. 12.

Having established the semantic clauses for $divergences(P)$, which depend solely on the $traces_{\perp}(\cdot)$ and $divergences(\cdot)$ of the sub-processes, you can create the semantic clauses for $failures_{\perp}(P)$ by

(a) starting with the clauses for $failures(P)$ (p. 238),
(b) replacing each use of a $failures(Q)$ by the corresponding $failures_{\perp}(Q)$,
(c) replacing each use of a $traces(Q)$ by the corresponding $traces_{\perp}(Q)$,
(d) adding $\{(s, X), (s^\frown\langle\checkmark\rangle, X) \mid s \in divergences(\Delta)\}$ to each clause, where Δ represents the construct that is being defined. In a number of cases such as prefix and nondeterministic choice this is not necessary.

So, for example,

$$failures_{\perp}(P \setminus X) = \{(s \setminus X, Y) \mid (s, X \cup Y) \in failures_{\perp}(P)\}$$
$$\cup \{(s, Y) \mid s \in divergences(P \setminus X)\}$$

You can, of course, modify the traces definitions of operators for $\mathcal{T}$ in the same way to obtain clauses for $traces_{\perp}(P)$ to use in conjunction with $divergences(P)$ for $\mathcal{T}^{\Downarrow}$.

It is interesting to note that the models $\mathcal{T}$ and $\mathcal{T}^{\Downarrow}$ are incomparable in the sense that there are processes identified by each model but not by the other. For example, $(a \rightarrow STOP) \sqcap \mathbf{div}$ and $\mathbf{div}$ are identified by $\mathcal{T}^{\Downarrow}$, but not by $\mathcal{T}$. The same happens for $\mathcal{F}$ and $\mathcal{N}$, and all the similar pairs of models that we will meet in the next two chapters. See Exercise 10.10 for more insight into this.

Exercise 10.8 List all the members of $\mathcal{N}$ whose traces are $\{\langle\rangle, \langle a\rangle, \langle b\rangle\}$, and find a CSP process corresponding to each.

Exercise 10.9 Show that component-wise union of any non-empty subset S of $\mathcal{N}$ is a member of $\mathcal{N}$.

Find an example to show that the intersection of two members of $\mathcal{N}$ need not be in the model. What can you say about the intersection of two processes with the same traces?

Exercise 10.10 Comment on the following statement: "Both $\mathcal{T}$ and $\mathcal{T}^{\Downarrow}$ are models for CSP. Therefore their Cartesian product, which represents a process by

$$(traces(P), traces_{\perp}(P), divergences(P))$$

is also a model."

Show that this model is in fact equivalent to one in which a process is represented by $(traces(P), divergences(P))$, and that it gives an equivalence over CSP processes that is strictly finer than either of T or $T^{\Downarrow}$.

What, in each of these representations, is the right order to use for computing the fixed points of recursions?

10.5 Determinism, Confluence and Proof

We defined what it means for a process to be deterministic in Sect. 6.1 and introduced methods for verifying both this property and the related (though less important) property of $\mathcal{F}$-determinism in Sect. 8.7. Recall that a process P is deterministic if it is divergence free and for all traces s,

$$\neg \exists x.s^{\smallfrown}\langle x \rangle \in traces(P) \wedge (s, \{x\}) \in failures(P)$$

Now that we know the precise structure of $\mathcal{N}$ we can justify our earlier claim that the deterministic processes are precisely its refinement-maximal elements. This essentially depends on healthiness condition F3. The definition of determinism above actually says that our process P has no more refusal sets for the trace X than those *demanded* by F3 for the given set of traces. Equally it says that a trace $s^{\smallfrown}\langle x \rangle$ cannot be removed from P without adding the failure $(s, \{x\})$. A full proof can be found in TPC.

It is tempting to think that if a CSP process is deterministic then it must be implemented as a deterministic LTS by the operational semantics. We might define the latter to be one in which (i) no state has both Σ actions and one in $\{\tau, \checkmark\}$, (ii) no state has multiple actions with the same label, (iii) no state has both τ and $\checkmark$ actions. But this is not so: consider, for example $STOP \sqcap (a \rightarrow STOP) \setminus \{a\}$. Here the initial τ branch leads to two different operational behaviours with the same failures and divergences.

This phenomenon, whereby a process that has internal nondeterminism can look deterministic from the outside, is at the core of the definition of noninterference seen in Sect. 6.5: recall that this is expressed by saying that the process $(P \parallel_{H} Chaos_H) \setminus H$ is deterministic (or $\mathcal{F}$-deterministic if this process diverges). In other words, none of the nondeterministic behaviour exhibited by $Chaos_H$ may be seen from the outside.

The form of determinism defined over $\mathcal{N}$ (or, indeed, $\mathcal{F}$) is therefore an *extensional* characterisation whereas the one defined over LTSs is *intensional*. In other words the former is defined in terms of the externally visible behaviour of a process, whereas the latter is defined in terms of the precise details of how it is implemented. In the context of CSP, "deterministic" always means the sort judged over $\mathcal{N}$ unless further qualified. For clarity, in this section we will sometimes refer to intensional or extensional determinism.

It is easy to show that a divergence-free (intensionally) deterministic LTS maps to a deterministic member of $\mathcal{N}$, and that every deterministic LTS maps to a *predeterministic* member of $\mathcal{N}$, namely one that satisfies the definition of determinism displayed above on every non-divergent trace.

There are two distinct sub-languages of CSP that generate deterministic processes. One consists of those operators that usually create deterministic LTSs in the sense described above: *SKIP*, *STOP*, guarded recursion, prefix-choice, injective renaming (i.e. under relations that never map two different events of the process to the same externally visible ones), external choice $?x : A \rightarrow P \,\square\, ?x : B \rightarrow Q$ provided $A \cap B = \emptyset$, sequential composition $P; Q$, the throw operator $P \,\Theta_A\, Q$, and alphabetised parallel composition $P \,_X\|_Y\, Q$. All of these non-recursive operators (with some careful analysis[8] in the case of $P; Q$ because of the restriction on the use of *SKIP*) have the property that when we know what trace a compound process such as $P \,_X\|_Y\, Q$ has performed, we know what trace the arguments (P and Q) have performed, relative to the traces semantics of the operators.

The only way in which the above syntax can fail to create a deterministic LTS in the sense defined above is through the mechanics of distributed termination of parallel combinations. That, however, never introduces extensional nondeterminism since we have ensured that when a process in our syntax performs $\checkmark$, that is the only event it can perform.

In the above syntax, we are allowing processes to branch provided we can always see in the trace which way they have branched. Hiding is forbidden because any τ action with another action as an alternative can create extensional nondeterminism: note that both

$$((b \rightarrow STOP) \,\square\, (a \rightarrow STOP)) \setminus \{a\}$$

$$((a \rightarrow STOP) \,\square\, (b \rightarrow c \rightarrow STOP)) \setminus \{a, b\}$$

are nondeterministic. In these examples hiding causes nondeterminism because it is allowed to resolve choices.

Notice, however, that applying hiding to a process in which there is no choice—the only operators used are guarded recursion, single-event prefix, 1–1 renaming, *STOP*, *SKIP* and sequential composition[9]—creates no nondeterminism unless it causes divergence. The resulting LTS is (intensionally) deterministic. Adding alphabetised parallel $P \,_X\|_Y\, Q$ to this list clearly introduces branching into the LTS, so the LTS produced by hiding the result may no longer be intensionally deterministic. Therefore it may be surprising to learn that the result, if divergence-free, is always extensionally deterministic. This is because of a property called *confluence*.

Definition 10.1 An LTS is *confluent* if, whenever $P \stackrel{s}{\Longrightarrow} Q$ and $P \stackrel{t}{\Longrightarrow} R$, then there exists T such that $Q \stackrel{t-s}{\Longrightarrow} T$ and $R \stackrel{s-t}{\Longrightarrow} T$ where $s - t$ is the sequence s in which all elements in t have been deleted as many times as they appear in t, starting from the beginning.[10]

---

[8]Each process this syntax can create has the property that if $s\hat{\,}\langle\checkmark\rangle$ is a trace, then (for $a \in \Sigma$, $s\hat{\,}\langle a\rangle$ is not.

[9]One could add Θ_A into this list, but it does not preserve the property of confluence described below.

[10]Therefore $\langle a, b, a, c, a, d\rangle - \langle a, d, a, d\rangle = \langle b, c, a\rangle$, with the first two as and the only d being deleted from the first trace.

See Exercise 10.13 for a formulation in terms of $\mathcal{N}$ rather than LTSs.
Each of the clauses of the following result is easy to prove.

Lemma 10.3 *Each of single prefix, 1–1 renaming, sequential composition, $P \; {}_X\|_Y \; Q$ and $P \setminus X$ has the property that if its arguments are confluent then so is the result of applying it to them.*

For example, if $P \; {}_X\|_Y \; Q \stackrel{s}{\Longrightarrow} P_1 \; {}_X\|_Y \; Q_1$ and $P \; {}_X\|_Y \; Q \stackrel{t}{\Longrightarrow} P_2 \; {}_X\|_Y \; Q_2$ then $P \stackrel{s\upharpoonright X}{\Longrightarrow} P_1$ and $P \stackrel{t\upharpoonright X}{\Longrightarrow} P_2$. It follows that there is P_3 such that $P_1 \stackrel{(t-s)\upharpoonright X}{\Longrightarrow} P_3$ and $P_2 \stackrel{(s-t)\upharpoonright X}{\Longrightarrow} P_3$. By symmetry there is Q_3 such that $Q_1 \stackrel{(t-s)\upharpoonright Y}{\Longrightarrow} Q_3$ and $Q_2 \stackrel{(s-t)\upharpoonright Y}{\Longrightarrow} Q_3$. It follows that $P_1 \; {}_X\|_Y \; Q_1 \stackrel{t-s}{\Longrightarrow} P_3 \; {}_X\|_Y \; Q_3$ and $P_2 \; {}_X\|_Y \; Q_2 \stackrel{s-t}{\Longrightarrow} P_3 \; {}_X\|_Y \; Q_3$.

The reason why this is so interesting is that any divergence-free member of a confluent LTS is always extensionally deterministic. This follows because if it were not there would have to be a divergence free node P, a trace s and event a such that $P \stackrel{s\frown\langle a\rangle}{\Longrightarrow} Q$ for some Q and $P \stackrel{s}{\Longrightarrow} R$ for some stable R which refuses a, in contradiction to the fact that there must be some T with $R \stackrel{\langle a\rangle}{\Longrightarrow} T$. Every confluent process is pre-deterministic, and is also $\mathcal{F}$-deterministic. In fact, no divergent trace of a confluent process, or any extension of that trace, can have any stable refusals at all.

An interesting class of confluent processes is provided by the *cyclic communication networks* of Sect. 13.2.2 of TPC (see also [37]): networks of nodes, each of which communicates with each of its neighbours in turn and then starts over again. These can be generalised in various ways as discussed in TPC, including putting groups of the communications on each cycle in parallel as in the *matrix multiplication* example given there: it is composed of a rectangular array of processes with the communication pattern:[11]

$$Node = (left \to SKIP \; ||| \; up \to SKIP);$$
$$(right \to SKIP \; ||| \; down \to SKIP);$$
$$Node$$

Here, the use of interleaving is equivalent to ${}_X\|_Y$ for processes with disjoint alphabet, and the channels $\{up, down, left, right\}$ are renamed to the appropriate events that link adjacent processes.

So hiding some or all of the internal communications of the rectangular grid is guaranteed to result in a confluent, and therefore deterministic, process. (We can be sure that the network is divergence free by the rule quoted on p. 124.)

Notice that in both the syntactic classes of processes we have discussed in this section, the confluent ones and the ones that excluded hiding and ambiguous branching, we stated that it was safe to include guarded recursion in the syntax for the

---

[11]Readers who compare this definition with that in TPC will see that this one is abstracted. The one in TPC is not in fact confluent because the nodes input data over *left* and *up*, which is prefix-choice not single prefix. Networks like that one, where communication patterns are confluent even though the unabstracted networks are not, are themselves of interest. See [127] for example.

subset of CSP they define. The reason why we are able to include this is because of *fixed-point induction*. There are a number of formulations of fixed-point induction, and we have seen two of these already. One is the UFP rule, and the other is the rule quoted on p. 38 for proving **sat** properties of recursive terms.

Fixed-point induction can be paraphrased "Suppose that, by assuming property R of P, you can infer it true of $F(P)$. Then you may infer that R holds of $\mu p.F(p)$." This rule is not always true: we have to place conditions on R and F. The applications on the classes of processes above can be read "If F is a constructive function that maps deterministic (resp. confluent) processes to deterministic (confluent) processes, then $\mu p.F(p)$ is deterministic (confluent). That is a consequence of the following result:

Theorem 10.3 *If $\underline{P} = F(\underline{P})$ is any recursive definition of a vector of processes which is guarded (i.e. F is constructive), with indexing set Λ and R is a property that is* closed *in the usual metric on $\mathcal{N}^\Lambda$. In other words, every limit of a convergent sequence $\underline{Q}_n$ of values that satisfy R also satisfies it. Then if there is any $\underline{Q}$ satisfying R, so does $\underline{P}$.*

This has a remarkably simple proof: the sequence $F^n(\underline{Q})$ all satisfy R, and can easily be shown to converge to $\underline{P}$. There are many other variants on fixed-point induction; further ones are described in TPC and in [117, 120, 121]. It is possible to give a theoretical justification for the refinement proofs performed by FDR in terms of fixed-point induction: the state exploration of a finite-state system may be viewed as calculating a (usually large) mutual recursion.

We conclude this section by stating an elegant generalisation of the UFP rule. Recall that when we stated it we said that the recursion had to be guarded. In fact, thanks to the existence of the strong order ($\leq$) (see p. 244), we can state that for any CSP recursion $\mu p.F(p)$, if its least fixed point over $\mathcal{N}$ is divergence-free, then it is the *only* fixed point. This is because all divergence-free values are maximal with respect to $\leq$, just as the deterministic ones are with respect to $\sqsubseteq_{FD}$. This is an easy consequence of the definition of $\leq$ and the fact that all CSP operators are monotonic with respect to it. (NB It is not in general legitimate to replace constructiveness with divergence-freedom in the statement of the theorem above.)

Exercise 10.11 Which of the following statements are true?

1. If P is nondeterministic, then so is $a \to P$.
2. If P is nondeterministic, then so is $P \parallel_{\Sigma} P$.
3. If P and Q are nondeterministic, then so is $P \parallel_{\Sigma} Q$.
4. If P and Q are nondeterministic, then so is $P \,\square\, Q$.

Exercise 10.12 Show by example that if P and Q are both confluent then $P \,\Theta_A\, Q$ need not be.

Exercise 10.13 Consider the following specification of divergence-free confluence: P is divergence-free, and $s, t \in traces(P) \wedge t - s = \langle x \rangle\hat{} u \Rightarrow (s, \{x\}) \notin failures(P)$.

(a) Show that this specification implies that P is deterministic.
(b) Show that if $s, t \in traces(P)$ then $s^\frown(t - s) \in traces(P)$. [*Hint: use induction on the length of $t - s$.*]
(c) Deduce that if $s, t \in traces(P)$ then $traces(P/(s^\frown(t - s))) = traces(P/(t^\frown(s - t)))$.

Note that, since a deterministic process's value in $\mathcal{N}$ is completely determined by its traces, (a) and (c) imply that $P/(s^\frown(t - s)) = P/(t^\frown(s - t))$ holds over $\mathcal{N}$.

Exercise 10.14 Fixed-point induction, stated informally, might be 'if a recursive process meets some specification R on the assumption that all recursive calls do, then it meets the specification unconditionally'. There are, however, three conditions that are required of the recursion/specification pair to make this valid: the specification must be satisfiable, the specification must satisfy some continuity condition, and the recursion must satisfy some well-formedness condition (such as being constructive).

The first of these is trivially necessary: without it, the rule would prove the predicate '*false*' true of any recursion! Find examples to show that the other two are needed as well.

10.6 Full Abstraction and Congruence

The concept of full abstraction addresses the question of how well suited a semantic model is to the language it is designed for and the type of specifications we want to be able to verify. The definition sometimes takes the form A below, and sometimes incorporates B in addition.

A. The semantics $\mathcal{S}[\![\cdot]\!]$ should distinguish two programs P and Q if, and only if, they are distinguished by some natural criterion. Usually this criterion is the existence of some context such that one of $C[P]$ and $C[Q]$ passes, and the other fails, some simple test.
B. The model $\mathcal{M}$ being used should not contain large classes of elements that are not in the image of $\mathcal{S}$. Specifically, the aim is usually to show that the expressible elements of the model are *dense*, in the sense that every element is the limit of a directed set of expressible ones, or of a convergent sequence in metric settings. Sometimes this condition is called *no junk*.

In CSP, the statement B essentially says that the healthiness conditions have been chosen correctly. We have already seen that *every* member of the models $\mathcal{T}$, $\mathcal{F}$ and $\mathcal{N}$ is denoted by an LTS and a CSP process, though of course for the latter we need to use infinite mutual recursions.

In TPC it is shown[12] that these three models are respectively fully abstract with respect to the tests:

---

[12]The proof of the $\mathcal{N}$ result in the printed version of TPC is faulty: the reader should consult the on-line version.

$\mathcal{T}$: P has the trace $\langle fail \rangle$ (where *fail* is any fixed member of Σ).

$\mathcal{F}$: P can deadlock immediately (i.e. it has the failure $(\langle\rangle, \Sigma^{\checkmark})$).

$\mathcal{N}$: P can either diverge or deadlock immediately (i.e. it has the divergence $\langle\rangle$ or the failure $(\langle\rangle, \Sigma^{\checkmark})$).

Though these results remain interesting, it turns out that they are all corollaries to new structural results (Theorems 11.3 and 12.2–12.4) that we will meet later in this book. We do not, therefore, give details of the proofs here.

We have two methods of working out the representations of CSP processes in our abstract models: either following the route of Chap. 9 and calculating the operational semantics and then extracting behaviours via abstraction functions, or the denotational semantics highlighted in the present chapter. There is a claim implicit in this, namely that both ways calculate the same value. We are, in other words, claiming that the operational semantics is *congruent* with each of the denotational ones.

Congruence proofs come in three parts:

- The overall result is formulated in such a way that we can prove it by structural induction. This always means that we have to consider *open* terms (ones with free process identifiers) as well as closed ones. These are evaluated, in the denotational semantics, in the context of an *environment* that maps these identifiers to members of the semantic model. In the operational semantics we carry around *substitutions* for process identifiers: closed terms to evaluate whenever an identifiers is encountered.

- Each individual CSP operator requires a lemma to show that the operational and denotational semantics coincide for it. For example, if $\Phi_{\mathcal{N}}$ is the function that maps an arbitrary LTS to $\mathcal{N}$, we should show that

$$\Phi_{\mathcal{N}}(P \,\Box\, Q) = \Phi_{\mathcal{N}}(P) \,\Box\, \Phi_{\mathcal{N}}(Q)$$

  where P and Q are closed CSP terms, the $\Box$ on the left-hand side is CSP syntax to which the operational semantics are applied, and the one on the right-hand side is the operator from $\mathcal{N} \times \mathcal{N}$ to $\mathcal{N}$ defined earlier in this chapter.

- A proof is provided that the fixed-point method used to define the denotational semantics of recursion gives the same value as applying the relevant function $\Phi_{\mathcal{M}}$ to the recursive term.

Fortunately for them, few *users* of CSP ever need actually to prove such a theorem. There is a reasonably detailed introduction to the proofs of congruence in TPC, but for full details the reader should consult [122]. The natural congruence results hold for all the models we have seen so far, provided that in the case of the two divergence-strict models ($\mathcal{T}^{\Downarrow}$ and $\mathcal{N}$) the language is restricted to finitely nondeterministic CSP.

10.7 Notes

Most of this chapter is a summary of Chaps. 8 and 9 of TPC. The only major topic that did not appear there is the material on *confluence*. Confluence has long been studied in the context of CCS: see [91], for example: what is presented here is simply a translation into CSP of what has long been understood elsewhere.

The traces model of CSP was discovered by Tony Hoare [59]. The failures model, with an imprecise treatment of divergence, was presented in [19, 61]. The failures-divergences model was first presented in the author's and Stephen Brookes's theses [18, 117] and later in [20]. The stable failures model was conjectured by Albert Meyer and Lalita Jagadeeshan to the author, who worked out the details. The use of confluence in process algebra is due to Milner [90, 91].

Extensional determinism as presented here has been an integral part of CSP theory since [19, 61].

Two rather different proofs of the congruence between CSP's operational and denotational semantics can be found in [21, 154] and [122].

Chapter 11
Finite Observation Models

In this chapter we ask ourselves the question: what does a general behavioural model of (untimed) CSP look like? As discussed in the previous chapter, it is natural to differentiate between those behaviours that can be seen completely in a finite time such as finite traces and those that cannot. In this chapter we look at the hierarchy of models such as $\mathcal{T}$ and $\mathcal{F}$ that only contain finitely observable behaviours.

We will be introducing quite a large number of different models in this chapter and the next. To help cope with this complexity we adopt the following convention: if P is a CSP process or LTS node, and $\mathcal{M}$ is a CSP model, then $\mathcal{M}[\![P]\!]$ represents the value in $\mathcal{M}$ of P. Thus $\mathcal{T}[\![P]\!]$ means exactly the same as $traces(P)$ and $\mathcal{N}[\![P]\!]$ means $(failures_\perp(P), divergences(P))$.

11.1 What is a Behavioural Model?

The tradition in CSP is to record only *linear* behaviours of a process: collections of observations that can be made on a single interaction with no back-tracking. This is crucial for a number of familiar "truths" about CSP, including the principle that all CSP operators distribute over $\sqcap$.

In defining the class of finite-behaviour models we will postulate:

- A process can only perform a finite number of actions in a finite time, whether these are visible or invisible. This means, for example, that neither divergence nor infinite traces are finite observations.
- While an observer can potentially see when a process becomes stable, it is impossible to conclude by observation that a visible action happened from an *unstable* state. This is because to know that the state was unstable, the observer would have to be able to copy the state and see lack of stability in one of the two and the action from the second—this is not a linear observation. So, while we can see that an action occurred from a stable state, or that it came from a state that had not been observed to be stable, we cannot *know* (and therefore record) that an action definitely came from an unstable state.

A.W. Roscoe, *Understanding Concurrent Systems*, Texts in Computer Science,
DOI 10.1007/978-1-84882-258-0_11, © Springer-Verlag London Limited 2010

- The most that an observer can see directly in a stable state is the set of actions it can perform: its *acceptance* or *ready* set.

It follows that the most our observer can see of a process in a finite time is a sequence of visible actions and acceptance sets. Since once a process has one acceptance set it cannot have a different one until after a further visible action has occurred, we can assume that there is at most one acceptance set between any two of the beginning of the behaviour, the observed visible actions, and the end of the behaviour.

We can represent any such observation in the formats

$$\langle A_0, a_1, A_2, \ldots, A_{n-1}, a_n, A_n \rangle \quad \text{and} \quad \langle A_0, a_1, A_2, \ldots, A_{n-1}, a_n, \bullet, \checkmark \rangle$$

possible for a process, where all $a_i \in \Sigma$ and each A_i is either an acceptance ($\subseteq \Sigma$) set or the marker $\bullet$ that indicates that no acceptance, and hence no stability, was observed here. When A_{i-1} is *not* $\bullet$, necessarily $a_i \in A_{i-1}$ because A_{i-1} is precisely the menu of visible actions possible at this point. We will use Greek letters β, γ, $\delta, \ldots$ to represent these *FL-behaviours* and sections of them. FL stands for Finite Linear.

Notice from the second sort of observation that we do not regard a state able to do a $\checkmark$ action as stable for reasons discussed on p. 192, and that because $\checkmark$ is the end of a process's behaviour when it happens, there is no acceptance to observe afterwards.

The interpretation of the behaviour $\langle A_0, a_1, A_2, \ldots, A_{n-1}, a_n, \bullet, \checkmark \rangle$ is that we successively see the events a_i and the A_i that are proper acceptance sets. $\bullet$ itself represents the lack of an observation. In the world of traces we are accustomed to the idea of a prefix and to prefix-closure. For these more complex behaviours a *prefix* will mean an initial subsequence which is either the entire behaviour or ends in one of the A_i, or such a subsequence where an A_i that is not $\bullet$ has been replaced by $\bullet$.

In other words $\langle \bullet \rangle$, $\langle A \rangle$, $\langle A, a, \bullet \rangle$ and $\langle A, a, B \rangle$ are the prefixes of $\langle A, a, B \rangle$: these are the successive observations that the environment will have seen along the way.

In the traces model $\mathcal{T}$, if a process P has the trace t we know that P also has all the prefixes of t: these are the only implications of one behaviour by another. In a model based on FL-observations, we will clearly expect a process with behaviour β to have all β's prefixes as defined above. But these are not now the *only* such implications. Exactly the same path through the operational semantics that gives rise to β will also allow the observation of any of the prefixes of β in which any or all non-bullet As have been replaced by $\bullet$. There is no compulsion to observe a stable acceptance. We will write $\beta' \leq \beta$ for all β' whose presence is implied by β in this way.

11.1.1 The Finest Model of Them All

It will not be too much of a surprise to the reader to learn that the set of finite linear observations of a process provides another finite-behaviour model of a process. As with $\mathcal{T}$ and $\mathcal{F}$, a process's value in this model can be determined either by observing the operational semantics or by a denotational semantics. The resulting model, which we will call $\mathcal{FL}$, has the following healthiness conditions (which already take into account the fact that $a_i \in A_i$ if $A_i \neq \bullet$) for a set of FL-behaviours S.

FL1 $\beta \in S \wedge \gamma \leq \beta \Rightarrow \gamma \in S$, where $\gamma \leq \beta$ as defined above.

FL2 $\beta^\frown \langle A \rangle \in S \wedge a \in A \neq \bullet \Rightarrow \beta^\frown \langle A, a, \bullet \rangle \in S$. This simply says that whenever a stable offer is made then it can be taken up.

There is no particular problem in devising the various clauses that calculate each operator's effects on this model. For example:

- $S \square T = \{\langle A \cup B \rangle^\frown \alpha, \langle A \cup B \rangle^\frown \beta \mid \langle A \rangle^\frown \alpha \in S, \langle B \rangle^\frown \beta \in T\}$ where $\bullet \cup A = \bullet$: no initial stable offer is made unless both processes are stable.
- $S \setminus X = \{\beta \setminus X \mid \beta \in S\}$ where $\langle A_0, a_1, A_2, \ldots, A_{n-1}, a_n, A_n \rangle \setminus X = \langle A_{i-1} \setminus X, a_i \mid i \in \langle 1 \ldots n \rangle \wedge a_i \notin X \rangle^\frown \langle A_n \setminus X \rangle$. Here $A \setminus X = \bullet$ if $A = \bullet$ or $A \cap X \neq \emptyset$, and A if $A \cap X = \emptyset$. And similarly for β ending in $\checkmark$.

Since this is a finite-behaviour model, we know (thanks to discussion in the previous chapter) that **div** is the refinement maximum process and that the correct way of computing the value of a recursive process $\mu p.F(p)$ is $\bigcup_{n=0}^{\infty} F^n(\mathbf{div})$.

$\mathcal{FL}$ records absolutely everything about a process that we have postulated can be observed finitely about CSP processes. It follows that $\mathcal{FL}$ is the finest possible such model: any two processes that it identifies are identified in every finite-behaviour model.

It follows that if an algebraic law is true in $\mathcal{FL}$ then it is also true in all such models, and if $P \sqsubseteq_{FL} Q$ then $P \sqsubseteq_F Q$ etc.

It is straightforward to prove the following result:

Lemma 11.1 *If P and Q are nodes in an LTS that are DRW-bisimilar, then their values in $\mathcal{FL}$ are equal.*

This is because any sequence of visible actions and stable acceptances in P can be shown to exist in Q, and vice-versa.

Applications

At the time of writing the author has not applied the model $\mathcal{FL}$ other than theoretically, and nor is refinement over it implemented in FDR. He would expect that it is too precise for the convenient expression of most abstract specifications, though it (and the variants of it we will see in the next chapter) may well have a role in modelling appropriate *temporal logics*.

When refinement checking is done to highlight the differences between two implementations, or in related applications such as the specification of fault tolerance on p. 128, there may be good reason to use a highly discriminating model like $\mathcal{FL}$.

11.1.2 Clouding the Glass

We know that a process's value in $\mathcal{FL}$ contains all the information that can be observed finitely of it. It follows that every other finite behaviour model must, at least for some processes, throw away some of this information.

We cannot necessarily predict how another model will represent a behaviour: note for example that a refusal set is a rather different creature from an acceptance set. What we can say is that each recorded behaviour comes from a single observation of the process, and can therefore be deduced from the existence of a single FL-behaviour. It also seems reasonable to restrict ourselves to models that have only finitely many components.

We therefore state that the members of each finite-behaviour model consist of a finite number of components, each of which is a subset of some fixed set. So for example the stable failures model $\mathcal{F}$ has two components, one of which is a subset of $\Sigma^{*\checkmark} \times \mathbb{P}(\Sigma^{\checkmark})$ and the other of which is a subset of $\Sigma^{*\checkmark}$. The value of a given process P in this model may be obtained from applying a separate relation for each component to that process's value in $\mathcal{FL}$. So for example the failures component is obtainable from the following relation:

- $(\beta\hat{\ }\langle A\rangle, (trace(\beta), X))$ whenever $A \neq \bullet$ and $X \cap A = \emptyset$. Here, $trace(\beta)$ is just β's sequence of visible actions.
- $(\beta\hat{\ }\langle\checkmark\rangle, (trace(\beta), X))$ whenever $\checkmark \notin X$.
- $(\beta\hat{\ }\langle\checkmark\rangle, (trace(\beta)\hat{\ }\langle\checkmark\rangle, X))$ for unrestricted X.

The traces component is obtained by applying $trace(\cdot)$ to each member of the $\mathcal{FL}$ representation.

The model may then be *defined* to be the values of this "multi-relation" applied to all members of $\mathcal{FL}$. (Healthiness conditions, if defined, would be expected to come up with the same answer.)

Most importantly, the proposed model must be a *congruence* in the sense defined on p. 230. Recall, for example, that in the previous chapter we had to reject the "model" $(traces(P), deadlocks(P))$ because it is not a congruence for the parallel operator.

When we say "*the* traces model $\mathcal{T}$" we are in fact ignoring an important fact: that the definition of this model depends on a particular alphabet Σ. In this case it is clear how the family of models gives rise to a single natural equivalence for CSP. It follows that the relations that extract process values from $\mathcal{FL}$ depend also on Σ, and that we should *require* such relations to be defined for every Σ. In general we need the following principle:

- If P and Q are two processes over alphabet Σ, and $\mathcal{M}$ is a model, then P and Q are equivalent for the Σ interpretation of $\mathcal{M}$ if and only if they are for every Σ' interpretation, $\Sigma' \supseteq \Sigma$.

In every naturally defined model that the author is aware of, it is the case that the relations extracting a process's value for Σ are the *restrictions* of those for larger Σ' to the smaller domain and co-domain.

Note that over $\mathcal{T}$ and $\mathcal{FL}$, the value of a given process does not change as we increase Σ. The same is not true for $\mathcal{F}$. For example, the value of the process $a \rightarrow STOP$ gains the additional failure $(\langle\rangle, \{b\})$ as we increase the alphabet from $\{a\}$ to $\{a, b\}$.

The principle above is important for the results we will be establishing about the hierarchy of models in this chapter and the next. This is usually because, to prove a result about what congruences exist for CSP, it is necessary to add additional events, extending the alphabet Σ to some larger Σ'. Clearly we would not expect this to change the equivalence between processes defined over Σ.

It is possible to derive some surprisingly strong results about what CSP models look like, based on the above definitions. We will reserve the most powerful results until Sect. 11.3, but can now see some simpler ones.

Theorem 11.1 *The coarsest non-trivial CSP model is $\mathcal{T}$. In other words, if such a model $\mathcal{M}$ does not identify all processes, then $\mathcal{T} \preceq \mathcal{M}$.*

The proof of this result, taken from [130], will be discussed in Sect. 11.3.

Theorem 11.2 *Every CSP model is completely symmetric in the alphabet Σ. In other words, for every injective functional renaming f, P and Q are equivalent in a model $\mathcal{M}$ if and only if $f[P]$ and $f[Q]$ are.*

This is a corollary of the facts that $\mathcal{M}$ is a congruence for renaming, and that $f[\cdot]$ has the inverse $f^{-1}[\cdot]$.

11.2 A Tour through the Hierarchy

The best-known examination of the hierarchy of congruences for concurrency was compiled by Rob van Glabbeek [152, 153]. That covers a much wider range of congruences than we do, since it studies branching-time congruences as well. Van Glabbeek does, however, make an important simplifying assumption that we do not: he only looks at τ-free transition systems and so cannot support the hiding operator. There are therefore no distinctions in the congruences he describes based on phenomena that can only arise thanks to τ. For example, there is no distinction between visible actions that happen from stable states and ones that can only occur from unstable states.

The model $\mathcal{FL}$, which roughly corresponds to the *ready traces* model described in [152, 153], does make such distinctions. For example, $(a \rightarrow STOP) \rhd STOP$ has no behaviour in which a happens from a stable state, and is different in $\mathcal{FL}$ from the process $(a \rightarrow STOP) \sqcap STOP$, where a is offered stably. We will be seeing a lot more of this pair of processes.

Apart from the ready-traces, failures and traces semantics, van Glabbeek studies two other finite linear observation models. (In the absence of τ actions, finite-observation means there is nothing like an infinite trace considered.) These are the "readiness model" and the "failure trace semantics". We will discover that both lead to analogous models of CSP below, and that each them has to become a little more subtle to deal with unstable actions.

11.2.1 The Ready Sets, or Acceptances Model $\mathcal{A}$

The structures in this model look almost the same as those for $\mathcal{F}$. A process is modelled by its finite traces and a set of pairs of the form (s, X), where s is a trace and X is a subset of Σ. The difference is in the interpretation of X: in $\mathcal{F}$ it is a set of events that the process can refuse after s. Here, however, it is the actual set of offers in a stable state, corresponding to the acceptance sets in $\mathcal{FL}$. In this model, for historical reasons, we will call the acceptance sets *ready sets*. So if we refer to an "acceptance set" it will usually be in the context of $\mathcal{FL}$, and a "ready set" will be something that is seen after a trace in $\mathcal{A}$.

This model was first studied by Hoare and Olderog in [97]. It is strictly more discriminating than $\mathcal{F}$, since the only ready sets that are definitely revealed by the latter are the minimal ones: if $(s, X) \in failures(P)$ and $Y \supset X$ implies $(s, Y) \notin failures(P)$ then we can be sure that P has the actual ready set $\Sigma \setminus X$ possible after s, but there is no way of telling whether any $Y \supset (\Sigma \setminus X)$ such that $Y \subseteq initials(P/s)$ can be stably offered or not. So, for example,

$$(a \rightarrow STOP) \rhd STOP \quad \text{and} \quad (a \rightarrow STOP) \sqcap STOP$$

are a pair of processes equated over $\mathcal{F}$ but not over the *stable ready sets*, or *stable acceptances* model $\mathcal{A}$. The left-hand process's only initial ready set is $\emptyset$, whereas the right-hand one also has $\{a\}$.

It is easy to construct the healthiness conditions of this model: clearly the traces component must be a member of $\mathcal{T}$, every trace associated with a ready set must be in the trace component, and whenever (s, X) is a *ready pair*, each $s^\frown\langle a \rangle$ for $a \in x$ is a trace.

Just as with failures, there are two possible ways to treat termination. We can assume that $\checkmark$ is never a member of a ready set and no ready sets get paired with $s^\frown\langle\checkmark\rangle$, or we can state that whenever $s^\frown\langle\checkmark\rangle$ is a trace, then $(s, \{\checkmark\})$ is a ready pair, and possibly also $(s^\frown\langle\checkmark\rangle, \emptyset)$. As before these would give isomorphic models, so it is just a matter of taste. Here, consistently with $\mathcal{FL}$, we adopt the minimalist approach, restricting ready sets to traces in Σ^* and to be subsets of Σ.

It is in fact easy to see that the behaviours recorded in this model are isomorphic to a subset of those recorded for $\mathcal{FL}$, namely those in which all non-final acceptance sets are $\bullet$.

We said above that unstable actions play an important role in all CSP models stronger than $\mathcal{F}$. Consider the process $(a \rightarrow STOP) \rhd STOP$. This has ready pairs $\{(\langle\rangle, \emptyset), (\langle a \rangle, \emptyset)\}$, from which we can deduce that is can perform a initially, but cannot do so from a stable state. Over $\mathcal{F}$ this only happens on traces where the process can *never* become stable.

We can conclude that there is no process written using only prefix-choice and nondeterministic choice that is equivalent to $(a \to STOP) \vartriangleright STOP$ over $\mathcal{A}$. We will see important consequences of this in Chap. 13.

To the author, the single most interesting thing about this model is an algebraic property it does *not* have: the law $\langle \Box\text{-idem}^* \rangle$ (2.1): $P = P \Box P$. The name of this law is starred because it is not true in all models, and here is why. Consider $P = (a \to STOP) \sqcap (b \to STOP)$. This clearly has initial ready sets $\{a\}$ and $\{b\}$. $P \Box P$, on the other hand, has the additional ready set $\{a, b\}$ because the two Ps can make different choices. We will explore this further in Sect. 13.5.

We know that $\mathcal{F} \prec \mathcal{A} \prec \mathcal{FL}$. Whenever (for behavioural models) $\mathcal{M} \prec \mathcal{M}'$ and $P \in \mathcal{M}$, we can construct the set $n(P) = \{P' \in \mathcal{M}' \mid P =_{\mathcal{M}} P'\}$, namely the values in $\mathcal{M}'$ of the processes that are equivalent to P in $\mathcal{M}$. Let $\hat{P}$ be the nondeterministic choice over this set. Since every behaviour of $\hat{P}$ is that of a member of $n(P)$, we can deduce that $\hat{P} \in n(P)$, meaning that there is a refinement-minimum member of $\mathcal{M}'$ subject to being $\mathcal{M}$-equivalent to P.

Applications

One might think that having a finer model than $\mathcal{F}$ is better for specification purposes, because we can identify more precise properties. If S is any member of $\mathcal{F}$, then $\hat{P}$ defined as above from the models $\mathcal{F} \prec \mathcal{A}$ has the property that $\hat{P} \sqsubseteq_A Q$ if and only if $P \sqsubseteq_F Q$.

The problem with this way of thinking is that it leads to more complex specifications than are needed for properties that can be expressed in $\mathcal{F}$. For example, where the natural deadlock-freedom specification over $\mathcal{F}$ has $|\Sigma| + 2$ states: $DF_F = \sqcap\{a \to DF \mid a \in \Sigma\} \sqcap SKIP$, the corresponding specification over $\mathcal{A}$ requires $2^{|\Sigma|} + 1$:

$$DF_A = \sqcap\{?x : X \to DF_A \mid X \subseteq \Sigma, X \neq \emptyset\} \sqcap SKIP$$

The least refined member of $\mathcal{A}$, $\mathcal{FL}$ and every other finite behaviour model is given by the process definition

$$CHAOS_3 = (\sqcap_{A \subseteq \Sigma} ?x : A \to CHAOS_3) \sqcap SKIP$$

This definition is given in contrast to the usual definition of *Chaos*, which we now relabel

$$CHAOS_1 = STOP \sqcap SKIP \sqcap ?x : \Sigma \to CHAOS_1$$

and $CHAOS_2$, which we will see shortly. $CHAOS_1$ and $CHAOS_3$ are equivalent over $\mathcal{F}$.

In reality, we only need to use $\mathcal{A}$ when we want to be very precise about what members of Σ are to be offered together. If a design mandates a fixed set of "menus" (i.e. ready sets) from which a process may not deviate, then this is the right model.

Exercise 11.1 Find a pair of processes that are identified by $\mathcal{A}$ but not by $\mathcal{FL}$.

Exercise 11.2 Demonstrate that $CHAOS_3$ is the refinement-least member of $\mathcal{FL}$.

11.2.2 The Stable Refusal Testing Model $\mathcal{RT}$

While the stable failures model $\mathcal{F}$ records what processes refuse at the ends of traces, $\mathcal{RT}$ records refusals before, during and after traces. Intuitively, it is in the same relationship to $\mathcal{F}$ as $\mathcal{FL}$ is to $\mathcal{A}$—but see Sect. 11.2.3.

Refusal testing was discovered by Iain Phillips [107] and the (divergence-strict) refusal testing model for CSP was developed in [95].[1] This is the model that corresponds to the *refusal traces* model in the van Glabbeek hierarchy.

It is, of course, easy to extract refusal information from knowledge of ready sets: a set X can be refused if there is a ready set A with $A \cap X = \emptyset$. In particular this means that it is easy to create relations that map FL-behaviours respectively to failures and interleaved traces of refusal sets or • and events.

One could argue that refusal is a much easier thing to observe than ready sets: the process does not have to show us the actual range of events *it* is offering, only that it is stable and not accepting anything *we* are offering.

In $\mathcal{RT}$, a process is represented as a set of behaviours of the two forms

$$\langle X_0, a_1, X_1, \ldots, a_n, X_n \rangle$$

$$\langle X_0, a_1, X_1, \ldots, a_n, \bullet, \checkmark \rangle$$

in which X_i is a refusal set $\subseteq \Sigma$ or •, and $a_i \notin X_{i-1}$. It is governed by the healthiness conditions:

RT1 $\rho \in P \wedge \sigma \leq \rho \Rightarrow \sigma \in P$. Here, $\sigma \leq \rho$ means that it is obtained from an initial subsequence of ρ by mapping each refusal set X_i to either a subset or •.

RT2 $\rho\hat{\ }\langle X \rangle\hat{\ }\sigma \in P \wedge X \neq \bullet \wedge \forall a \in Y.\rho\hat{\ }\langle X, a, \bullet \rangle \notin P \Rightarrow \rho\hat{\ }\langle X \cup Y \rangle\hat{\ }\sigma \in P$. This corresponds to condition F3 from $\mathcal{F}$: it says that in any state that refuses a set of actions, any Σ events that the state cannot perform are certainly refused.

As you might expect, $\mathcal{RT}$ is strictly more discriminating than $\mathcal{F}$ and strictly less discriminating than $\mathcal{FL}$. For example, the processes

$$P = (a \rightarrow a \rightarrow STOP) \rhd (a \rightarrow STOP)$$

$$Q = (a \rightarrow STOP) \rhd (a \rightarrow a \rightarrow STOP)$$

are identified by $\mathcal{F}$ but not by $\mathcal{RT}$: in the first one, the second a can only be observed after an initial •. In the second, it can be observed after the initial refusal of $\emptyset$. So $\langle \emptyset, a, \bullet, a, \bullet \rangle \in \mathcal{FL}[\![Q]\!] \setminus \mathcal{FL}[\![P]\!]$.

---

[1]It was in helping with this work that the author first recognised the importance of allowing actions to occur after no refusal and suggested the • alternative.

Applications

The main applications of refusal testing occur when we want to change the standard execution model of CSP in subtle ways. The theory of operational semantics that we developed in Chap. 9 was based on the idea that operators' actions can depend on individual actions which their arguments can perform, but not on multiple actions (of the same argument) or the absence of actions.

There are sometimes (as we will see in Chaps. 14 and 20) good reasons to want to interpret *prioritised execution* in CSP: to specify that one action cannot occur unless a second one is absent. For priority to be well behaved in CSP we need to be more specific: we can specify that the first action cannot occur except in *stable* states where the second is absent.

Such ideas cannot be expressed in any model weaker (i.e., coarser) than $\mathcal{RT}$. As a simple example, consider the operator $stable(P)$. This process runs like P except that, with the exception of $\checkmark$, visible actions only occur in stable states. Thus its SOS-style operational semantics are

$$\frac{P \xrightarrow{x} P'}{stable(P) \xrightarrow{x} stable(P')} \quad [x \in \{\tau, \checkmark\}]$$

$$\frac{P \xrightarrow{a} P', \, P \xrightarrow{\tau}\!\!\!\!/ \; \cdot, \, P \xrightarrow{\checkmark}\!\!\!\!/ \; \cdot}{stable(P) \xrightarrow{a} stable(P')} \quad [a \in \Sigma]$$

This is beyond the range of what can be expressed in combinator-style operational semantics, since all such operators make sense over $\mathcal{T}$ and all other CSP models. It can, however, be expressed over $\mathcal{RT}$:

$$stable(P) = \{\sigma \mid \exists \rho \in P.\sigma \leq \rho \wedge \rho \text{ has no non-final } \bullet\}$$

This means, for example, that inside such an operator it is safe to apply FDR compression operators such as DRW-bisimulation that respect $\mathcal{RT}$, but not ones such as *diamond* that do not. See Sect. 16.2.

We will see applications of these ideas in Sect. 14.5 where we see that prioritised execution is sometimes necessary for timed processes, and in Sect. 20.2, where we study priority in a more general setting.

Exercise 11.3 Show that the pair of processes used above to show that $\mathcal{RT}$ is more discriminating than $\mathcal{F}$ are also identified by $\mathcal{A}$. Find a pair of processes identified by $\mathcal{RT}$ but not by $\mathcal{A}$.

Exercise 11.4 The operator $delay_A(P)$ prevents actions in $A \subseteq \Sigma$ from occurring when P has a τ or $\checkmark$ action possible. Give the SOS operational semantics of this and give a definition of it over $\mathcal{RT}$.

11.2.3 *The Stable Revivals Model*

The ready sets, refusal testing and failures models of CSP have all been known for many years. Now we have seen the three, it seems as though $\mathcal{RT}$ and $\mathcal{A}$ are both natural extensions of $\mathcal{F}$ in different directions: each adding a completely different sort of additional information. It seems likely that $\mathcal{F}$ records exactly that information about a process which is in *each* of the other two. That is what the author implicitly assumed for years, but it is not true.

In studying termination conditions for networks of CCS processes, Jakob Rehof and Sriram Rajamani discovered a new way of looking at processes: to examine a trace s, followed by a stable refusal X, followed by a visible event $a \notin X$ that the process can perform after the refusal has been observed.

They and Hoare asked how this new idea related to CSP models. The author was surprised to discover (in about 2003) that it led to a completely new model intermediate between, on the one hand, $\mathcal{RT}$ and $\mathcal{A}$, and $\mathcal{F}$ on the other. There is a thorough investigation of this model and its divergence-strict analogue in [130], including complete descriptions of CSP semantics over these models. The author termed (s, X, a) a *revival*, since it in some sense represents a process recovering from refusing to accept X. The corresponding CSP model was therefore called the *stable revivals model*. In addition to revivals we need to record both a process's finite traces and the finite traces on which it can deadlock: since one cannot perform any event in a deadlocked state, these do not give rise to any revivals.

This model thus consists of triples $(Tr, Dead, Rev)$, where $Tr \subseteq \Sigma^{*\checkmark}$, $Dead \subseteq \Sigma^*$ and $Rev \subseteq \Sigma^* \times \mathcal{P}(\Sigma) \times \Sigma$, satisfying the following healthiness conditions:

Tr1 Tr is non-empty and prefix-closed: $\langle\rangle \in Tr$, and if $s \hat{\ } t \in Tr$, then $s \in Tr$.

Dead1 $Dead \subseteq Tr$. Every deadlock trace is a trace.

Rev1 $(s, X, a) \in Rev \Rightarrow s \hat{\ } \langle a \rangle \in Tr$. This simply says that every trace implied by a revival is recorded in Tr.

Rev2 $(s, X, a) \in Rev \wedge Y \subseteq X \Rightarrow (s, Y, a) \in Rev$. This says that the state which refuses X and accepts a also refuses any subset of X.

Rev3 $(s, X, a) \in Rev \wedge \forall b \in Y.(s, X, b) \notin Rev \Rightarrow (s, X \cup Y, a) \in Rev$ This is an analogue of F3, but note that the final event a is factored into it in a subtle way.

Since the combination of *Dead* and *Rev* allows us to calculate all a process's failures, it is easy to see that $\mathcal{F} \preceq \mathcal{R}$. That they do not give the same equivalence is illustrated by the familiar pair of processes

$$(a \rightarrow STOP) \rhd STOP \quad \text{and} \quad (a \rightarrow STOP) \sqcap STOP$$

which are equated by $\mathcal{F}$ but not by $\mathcal{R}$: the right-hand process has the revival $(\langle\rangle, \emptyset, a)$ but the left-hand one does not.

Notice that, just as when we discussed the issue of unstable actions above, we can tell from the left-hand process's value in $\mathcal{R}$ that the a it can perform can only happen from an unstable state. In general, the event a is only possible unstably after s if $s \hat{\ } \langle a \rangle \in Tr$ and $(s, \emptyset, a) \notin Rev$.

$CHAOS_1$ is not the refinement-least element of $\mathcal{R}$ since it has no revival of the form (s, X, a) when X is non-empty. $CHAOS_3$ is clearly the refinement-least element since it is least in finer models. As you might guess from the numbering, we can define an intermediate $CHAOS_2$ that works in $\mathcal{R}$ (and also $\mathcal{RT}$) but not in $\mathcal{A}$:

$$CHAOS_2 = STOP \sqcap \sqcap\{a \to CHAOS_2 \mid a \in \Sigma\} \sqcap SKIP$$

As we would expect, $CHAOS_2$ has all possible traces, deadlock traces and revivals, the latter coming from the middle component above.

Note that it is possible to compute the set of revivals either from ready sets or refusal-testing behaviours. If P has the ready pairs (s, A), $a \in A$ and $X \cap A = \emptyset$ then it has the revival (s, X, a). And we can identify the revival (s, X, a), where $s = \langle b_1, \ldots, b_n \rangle$, with the refusal testing behaviour $\langle \bullet, b_1, \bullet, \ldots, \bullet, b_n, X, a, \bullet \rangle$. So we can deduce that $\mathcal{R} \preceq \mathcal{A}, \mathcal{RT}$.

So $\mathcal{RT}$ actually allows us to deduce not only refusals information after each trace (i.e. failures), but also revivals. It is probably truer, therefore, to say that $\mathcal{FL}$ is to $\mathcal{A}$ as $\mathcal{RT}$ is to $\mathcal{R}$ rather than $\mathcal{F}$ as suggested earlier.

There is no analogue of $\mathcal{R}$ in [152, 153], because this model remained undiscovered when that paper was written.

Applications

As we have seen, $\mathcal{R}$ has its origins in the study of termination in a CCS-like language. [41] sought to distinguish between configurations in which all component processes had reached a state equivalent to $STOP$ and deadlocked ones where some components were unfinished. CSP already distinguishes between these sorts of states if $SKIP$ is used for a completed process.

Nevertheless, $\mathcal{R}$ finds some interesting applications in areas where we want to specify that processes interact correctly. One class of applications can be found in [113], where this model is used to specify the property of *responsiveness*: P *responds to* Q in the parallel composition $P \underset{X}{\|} Q$ if, whenever Q makes a stable offer to P (i.e., Q has a revival $(s, \emptyset, a)$ where $a \in X$), P and Q can agree on some communication.

Another application comes in specifying properties such as *freedom from strong conflict* as defined on p. 76. Recall that this was defined to mean that two processes $P \underset{X}{\|}_Y Q$ each request communication from each other, and at least one of them cannot communicate outside their interface. This property can be specified very naturally in $\mathcal{R}$, while over $\mathcal{F}$ it has to be confined to maximal refusals. Given that P and Q are themselves known to be deadlock free, this can be specified by choosing new event req and checking if

$$P[\![x, req/x, x \mid x \in X \cap Y]\!] \underset{X \cup \{req\}}{\|}_{Y \cup \{req\}} Q[\![y, req/y, y \mid y \in X \cap Y]\!]$$

has any revival of the form (s, Y, req) or (s, X, req), where req does not appear in s. When req can occur from a stable state, each process is making a stable request to the other, but the refusal of X or Y means that one of the processes is completely blocked.

A further use for $\mathcal{R}$ in specification allows you to specify properties such as "whenever any event from A is offered, so is the whole of B". This simply says that there is no revival of the form (s, X, a), where $a \in A$ and $X \cap B \neq \emptyset$, which can be turned into the CSP

$$BwhenA(A, B) = STOP \sqcap \sqcap\{x \rightarrow BwhenA(A, B) \mid x \notin A\}$$
$$\sqcap (\sqcap\{a \rightarrow BwhenA(A, B) \mid a \in A\} \,\Box?x : B \rightarrow BwhenA)$$
$$\sqcap SKIP$$

In both these examples we are using $\mathcal{R}$ to specify finer properties of ready sets than we can with $\mathcal{F}$. Of course these could also be expressed in either $\mathcal{A}$ or $\mathcal{RT}$, but with a loss of succinctness.

Exercise 11.5 Express strong conflict freedom as a refinement check over $\mathcal{R}$. In other words, find the most nondeterministic process over this model that has no revival with either of the forms (s, Y, req) or (s, Y, req).

A pair of processes is *conflict free* (TPC, Chap. 13) if they can never reach a stable state in which each is asking the other for a communication, but they cannot agree on any. Express conflict freedom as a refinement check over $\mathcal{R}$.

11.2.4 Other Models

We will term the 6 finite-behaviour models that we have seen to date the *principal* ones. We know that in $\mathcal{FL}$ we have the finest such model, and as we will find in the next section the coarsest three ($\mathcal{T}$, $\mathcal{F}$ and $\mathcal{R}$) are unique in the sense that all others refine $\mathcal{R}$. However, there are actually infinitely many models sitting between $\mathcal{R}$ and $\mathcal{FL}$, of which $\mathcal{A}$ and $\mathcal{RT}$ are two. Here are a few examples.

- Notice that $\mathcal{R}$ gives you partial information about the ready set of a stable state: an arbitrary subset of its complement (the refusal set) and a single member (the "reviving" event that is possible after the refusal). We could have chosen to represent a process by its finite traces and triples (s, X, A) where s is a trace, X a stable refusal, and A is a set of events with size ≤ 1 offered by the same state.

  For any integer k it is possible to generalise this and record triples (s, X, A) where now A (necessarily disjoint from X) has size $\leq k$. A is again a subset of the events offered by the state that exhibits the refusal. This will give a different equivalence for all $k < |\Sigma|$.

- You cannot extend the revivals model by turning the last event into a trace of any bounded length other than 1. This is because it would not be possible to compute the semantics of hiding (where a trace of length 2, say, can result from one of length 4).[2] You do, however, get a model by recording behaviours that are traces, deadlock traces, and triples of the form (s, X, t) where (s, X) is a failure and t is a trace seen after X.

- The refusal set in the previous model can be replaced by a ready set. The resulting model then records traces with at most one ready set arbitrarily placed in a trace.
- The "least upper bound" of $\mathcal{A}$ and $\mathcal{RT}$ is not $\mathcal{FL}$, but rather the Cartesian product of these two models, equivalent to one where the behaviours recorded are just the union of those recorded for $\mathcal{A}$ and $\mathcal{RT}$.

  Another model, strictly between this Cartesian product and $\mathcal{FL}$, can be formed with the same behaviours as $\mathcal{RT}$ except that the final refusal set (i.e. the one after the least visible event) is replaced by a ready set.

It is not clear to the author whether any of the above models has a role in the study or application of CSP. Indeed the way in which algebraic laws allow us to jump in Sect. 13.5 between the principal models may help to convince the reader that the above are really just curiosities.

Possible Futures: A Study in Linearity

We will, however, look a little harder at one of these additional models: the one in which the behaviours are traces and (s, A, t) for A a ready set. It is clear that, for any particular ready pair (s, A) of a process P, the set of traces t such that (s, A, t) belongs to the process is a member $P_{(s,A)}$ of $\mathcal{T}$, and that its traces of length 1 are precisely $\{\langle a \rangle \mid a \in A\}$.

It would indeed be perfectly reasonable for the user of P, having observed (s, A), to view the process as one that will now behave like $P_{(s,A)}$.

This seems very similar to the *possible futures* model as described in [152, 153]: namely a process is identified with triples (s, A, V) where V is a member of $\mathcal{T}$ that can occur after the observation of (s, A). Possible futures, discovered by Brookes and Rounds, was one of the first models proposed for CSP [22]. Van Glabbeek characterises it as a forerunner of the ready sets model.

The possible futures model is not, however, a linear observation model. Consider, for example, the pair of processes

$$a \rightarrow a \rightarrow (a \rightarrow STOP \sqcap b \rightarrow STOP)$$

$$(a \rightarrow a \rightarrow a \rightarrow STOP) \sqcap (a \rightarrow a \rightarrow b \rightarrow STOP)$$

Notice that in the first process the decision as to which event to perform after $\langle a, a \rangle$ has definitely *not* been made after $\langle a \rangle$, whereas in the second process it definitely has.

---

[2]This does not happen for the final event seen in a revival because that event is always possible from the *same* state as the refusal. The revivals of $P \setminus X$ only arise from those states that refuse the *whole* of X.

These processes are related by the law ⟨prefix-dist⟩ (2.9) and equivalent in $\mathcal{FL}$. They are not, however, equivalent in the possible futures model since the first process's only possible future after the observation $(s, \{a\})$ is the trace set $\{\langle\rangle, \langle a\rangle, \langle a, a\rangle\langle a, b\rangle\}$, whereas the second process has only the two smaller ones $\{\langle\rangle, \langle a\rangle, \langle a, a\rangle\}$ and $\{\langle\rangle, \langle a\rangle, \langle a, b\rangle\}$.

The possible futures model is not the coarsest non-linear finite-behaviour model of CSP. Depending on how we choose to characterise the class of such models, that distinction might well go to the *binary futures model*, in which a process is modelled as a set of triples (s, t, u) where all of s, t, u belong to $\Sigma^{*\checkmark}$. The meaning of (s, t, u) is that P can reach a state, after s, where both t and u are possible traces. Naturally, if s ends in $\checkmark$, then t and u are empty. It has the healthiness conditions

BF1 $(\langle\rangle, \langle\rangle, \langle\rangle) \in P$
BF2 $(s, t, u) \in P \Rightarrow (s\hat{\ }t, \langle\rangle, \langle\rangle) \in P \wedge (s\hat{\ }u, \langle\rangle, \langle\rangle) \in P$
BF3 $(s\hat{\ }s', t\hat{\ }t', u\hat{\ }u') \in P \Rightarrow (s, s'\hat{\ }t, s'\hat{\ }u) \in P$

BF3 is a combination of a prefix-closure condition on the second and third components and a statement that anything that is observable with a late branching point is also observable with an early one. The latter is true because if we start to observe the branched traces after s rather than $s\hat{\ }s'$, both copies are free to follow s' for their first events and then go the respective ways of the other triple. This implication cannot be reversed, as illustrated by the example below.

This model distinguishes the pair of processes above that we used to show the difference between the acceptance-trace model and possible futures. The first has the triple $(\langle a\rangle, \langle a, a\rangle, \langle a, b\rangle)$, but the second does not: after the trace $\langle a\rangle$ it is always committed to its third event.

Neither the possible futures nor the binary futures model fits into our hierarchy because they require branching observations. This hints, of course, at a richer hierarchy of branching models that one could choose to study that are nevertheless still based on finite observations. Some of that is revealed in [152, 153].

11.3 The Big Picture

From the preceding sections, the reader will see that we have established the existence of an initial sequence of three models, $\mathcal{T} \prec \mathcal{F} \prec \mathcal{R}$, which are refined by a variety of other models including $\mathcal{A}$ and $\mathcal{RT}$, and finally by $\mathcal{FL}$, the finest finite-behaviour model.

Recent results have shown that this really is the picture:

Theorem 11.3 *If $\mathcal{M}$ is a finite-behaviour model of CSP other than $\mathcal{T}$ and $\mathcal{F}$ (and ones giving the same equivalence as one of these) then $\mathcal{R} \preceq \mathcal{M}$. Furthermore, $\mathcal{T}$, $\mathcal{F}$ and $\mathcal{R}$ are the only three models that both $\mathcal{A}$ and $\mathcal{RT}$ refine.*

The hierarchy implied by this result is illustrated in Fig. 11.1. The shaded part indicates the area where there are more models including the additional linear ones described in Sect. 11.2.4.

Fig. 11.1 The hierarchy of
finite-behaviour models

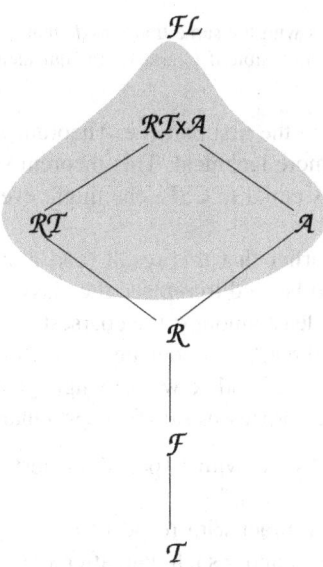

The proof of this result (of which Theorem 11.1 is a corollary) can be found in [130]. It is in fact a collection of four results: one to prove that $\mathcal{T} \preceq \mathcal{M}$ for any finite-behaviour CSP model; one to prove that any model making any distinction not made by $\mathcal{T}$ satisfies $\mathcal{F} \preceq \mathcal{M}$, one showing that every other model satisfies $\mathcal{R} \preceq \mathcal{M}$, and finally one showing that any pair of processes identified by both $\mathcal{A}$ and $\mathcal{RT}$ are also identified by $\mathcal{R}$. The easiest of these is the second, which is argued as follows.

Suppose $\mathcal{M}$ is a finite-behaviour model (as defined earlier) which distinguishes two members of $\mathcal{FL}$ that are identified in $\mathcal{T}$. Then we can assume that these are P and Q, with $P \sqsubseteq_{FL} Q$. This is because if P and Q are incomparable we can replace one of them by $P \sqcap Q$. Suppose further that U and V are two members of $\mathcal{FL}$ that have different values in $\mathcal{F}$ but the same value in $\mathcal{M}$. By the first part of our theorem [not proved here] we know that U and V have the same value in $\mathcal{T}$, since $\mathcal{T} \preceq \mathcal{M}$. So $traces(U) = traces(V)$.
Without loss of generality we can therefore assume that there is some failure (s, X) with $(s, X) \in failures(U) \setminus failures(V)$ and $s \in \Sigma^*$.
We can build a context $C_{(s,X)}[\cdot]$ that tests for this failure:

$$T_{(\langle\rangle,X)} = ?x : \Sigma \setminus X \to \mathbf{div}$$

$$T_{(\langle a\rangle^\frown t,X)} = (a \to T_{(t,X)}) \,\Box\, \mathbf{div}$$

$$C_{(s,X)}[W] = ((W; \mathbf{div}) \parallel_{\Sigma} T_{(s,X)}) \setminus \Sigma$$

In general $C_{(s,X)}[W]$ always equals $STOP$ or $\mathbf{div}$ over the model $\mathcal{FL}$ and hence over all finite-behaviour models. This is because it clearly never communicates or terminates, and these are the only two values of this sort. Furthermore it can only become stable (i.e., is $STOP$) if W has the failure (s, X).
Assuming P is $\checkmark$-free (for the case where it is not, see [130]), we can now define the context

$$C[W] = (C_{(s,X)}[W] \,|||\, P) \sqcap Q$$

If W has the failure (s, X) this equals P over $\mathcal{FL}$, and otherwise it equals Q. This uses the facts that $P \sqsubseteq_{FL} Q$, that these two processes have the same trace set, and that $\mathbf{div} \,|||\, P$

is the process with the same traces as P that never becomes stable. Thus $C[U] = P$ and $C[V] = Q$, impossible if U and V are equivalent in $\mathcal{M}$, and thus contradicting our initial assumption.

The proof of the first part (i.e. Theorem 11.1) is similar to this. The third part is surprisingly more technical. This theorem shows that the first three models are in some sense essential to CSP: one might even compare them to the *Platonic solids* in geometry.

We said earlier that this result (and a similar one we will discuss in the next chapter) could be said to replace the classical idea of full abstraction in CSP. This is because, at least amongst the coarsest models, we now know *exactly* what is the weakest model that can model any finitely observable[3] phenomenon: the first one in the sequence $\mathcal{T}$, $\mathcal{F}$ and $\mathcal{R}$ whose language of process observations can answer the question which processes satisfy a particular test. So we can see immediately that

- $\mathcal{T}$ is fully abstract with respect to the tests "P has a non-empty trace" and "P can perform the event a".
- $\mathcal{F}$ is fully abstract with respect to the tests "P can deadlock immediately" and "There exist s and a such that, after s, P can either accept or refuse a".
- $\mathcal{R}$ is fully abstract with respect to "P can stably offer $\{a\}$" or "P can stably offer some non-empty subset of Σ on the empty trace" (respectively corresponding to revivals of the form $(s, \Sigma \setminus \{a\}, a)$ and $(\langle\rangle, \emptyset, x)$ for arbitrary x and s.

11.4 Tools

At the time of writing the models $\mathcal{RT}$ and $\mathcal{R}$ have been implemented in FDR alongside the two finite-behaviour models that we have already seen there, namely $\mathcal{T}$ and $\mathcal{F}$. There is no reason in principle why $\mathcal{FL}$ and $\mathcal{A}$ could not be implemented there also.

Revivals refinement ($\mathcal{R}$) is written P [V= Q, and refusal testing refinement ($\mathcal{RT}$) is written P [R= Q.

---

[3]This is important, because tests that require more cannot be decided in the class of finite-behaviour models. By "finitely observable properties", we mean ones that the process's representation in $\mathcal{FL}$ can answer. We should notice that the class of divergence-strict models provides no competition because such models can never decide non-trivial finitely observable properties: if P satisfies some such property and Q does not, then the same is respectively true of $P \sqcap \mathbf{div}$ and $Q \sqcap \mathbf{div}$. But these last two processes are identified in any divergence-strict model.

Chapter 12
Infinite-Behaviour Models

There is no such thing as a CSP model based *only* on infinite observations. All models, such as $\mathcal{N}$ and $\mathcal{T}^{\Downarrow}$ that include them are based on a mixture of finite and infinite observations. We will be able to show, for example, that $\mathcal{T}^{\Downarrow}$ is the coarsest possible divergence-strict model, just as $\mathcal{T}$ is the coarsest finite-behaviour model. $\mathcal{T}^{\Downarrow}$ is based on finite observations (traces) and infinite ones (divergences).

It is therefore natural to consider how finite-behaviour models can be extended by giving the observer the power to see and record infinite things as well.

It is natural to start off by considering the model $\mathcal{FL}$. We can extend the observations β that go to make it up in two ways. The first is to add the observation of divergence (written $\Uparrow$) at the end of the sequence of acceptances and events. Thus, as well as perhaps seeing $\langle \bullet, \checkmark \rangle$, A or $\bullet$ at the end of such a β, we can additionally have $\Uparrow$. The second option is to allow the observed behaviours β to be infinite and have no right-hand end. We will call the collection of all these sorts of behaviours the FL*-behaviours.

Just as the FL-behaviours form a model for CSP, so it is natural to expect the FL*-behaviours to do the same. But we have a question to ask: are we treating divergence as strict, or not? In other words, if $\beta^{\smallfrown}\langle\Uparrow\rangle$ belongs to a process, do all $\beta^{\smallfrown}\beta'$s? It is reasonably straightforward to define the effect of every CSP operator over these behaviours in either case, but it is another matter entirely once one starts to study what fixed point theory we might use for recursion—this is in sharp contrast to the finite-behaviour models, where the choice of fixed point theory was automatic and easy.

In this chapter we first study the relatively easy case of divergence-strict models before trying to address the general case.

It is sensible to break up the finite-behaviour models into two categories as far as adding infinite behaviour information is concerned. On the one hand there are $\mathcal{T}$, $\mathcal{F}$, $\mathcal{R}$ and $\mathcal{A}$, in which the behaviours recorded are either (potentially incomplete) traces or are completed observations of what can happen at the end of a trace. The only infinite behaviours we can add to these without adding more finite behaviours are (i) divergence at the end of a finite trace and (ii) infinite traces. This means that exactly the same information about a process's behaviour is added by moving from each of these models $\mathcal{M}$ when we add in infinite behaviour. If the models are correct

A.W. Roscoe, *Understanding Concurrent Systems*, Texts in Computer Science, DOI 10.1007/978-1-84882-258-0_12, © Springer-Verlag London Limited 2010

we will certainly get the same sets of divergent traces and infinite traces in each. We can call these the *trace-plus* models.

On the other hand the models $\mathcal{FL}$ and $\mathcal{RT}$ have incomplete behaviours (all those ending in •) that have extra information in, respectively, acceptance and refusal. It follows that we will want to add divergence information by replacing the final • by ⇑, and to include infinite interleaved sequences of acceptances/refusals and events from Σ in the style envisaged above for FL*-behaviours. We can call these models, and any other where divergences are attached to richer structures than traces, the *rich-trace* models.

12.1 Divergence-Strict Models for Finite Nondeterminism

We are already familiar with two divergence-strict models, namely $\mathcal{T}^{\Downarrow}$ and $\mathcal{N} = \mathcal{F}^{\Downarrow}$, and the fact that these only work for finitely nondeterministic CSP.

We would naturally expect the finest such model to be $\mathcal{FL}^{\Downarrow}$. In this, a process is represented as a set of the finite FL*-behaviours, namely all except the infinitely long ones. That set of behaviours is its value in $\mathcal{FL}$, together with all $\beta\hat{\ }\beta'$ such that $\beta\hat{\ }\langle\Uparrow\rangle$ is observable.

Therefore its healthiness conditions are those of $\mathcal{FL}$ together with

FLD1 $\beta\hat{\ }\langle\Uparrow\rangle \in P \Rightarrow \beta\hat{\ }\beta' \in P$ whenever this is well formed.
This imposes divergence strictness. Notice that, in particular, it implies that $\beta\hat{\ }\langle\bullet\rangle \in P$.

FLD2 $\beta\hat{\ }\langle A\rangle\hat{\ }\beta'\hat{\ }\langle\Uparrow\rangle \in P \Rightarrow \beta\hat{\ }\langle\bullet\rangle\hat{\ }\beta'\hat{\ }\langle\Uparrow\rangle \in P$. In other words, if divergence can occur when stability and an acceptance set are observed, it is also possible when these are not observed.

FLD3 $\beta\hat{\ }\langle\bullet\rangle \in P \wedge \beta\hat{\ }\langle\Uparrow\rangle \notin P \wedge \beta\hat{\ }\langle\bullet, \checkmark\rangle \notin P \Rightarrow \exists A \subseteq \Sigma.\beta\hat{\ }\langle A\rangle \in P$. In other words, if we watch a process for long enough it will do one of (i) diverge, (ii) terminate and (iii) become stable with some acceptance set.

In the literature of concurrency, ⇑ is frequently used as a label for divergence, exactly as we have used it here. ⇓, on the other hand, is used to represent the absence of divergence. It may therefore seem strange that we use it to denote models "with added divergence"! The key to this notation, however, is the use of *strict* divergence: in fact these models serve the purpose of identifying those parts of a process where divergence certainly is absent. They do not attempt to give any detail at all when divergence is present.

As we have already discussed in Sect. 10.4, $\mathcal{T}^{\Downarrow}$ and $\mathcal{N}$ fail for infinitely nondeterministic processes because they do not handle hiding properly. We cannot then use König's lemma to deduce that if a process can exhibit all finite approximations to an infinite behaviour, then that whole behaviour is possible. Specifically, there are no congruence theorems between denotational and operational semantics in these cases.

The same is true for all models $\mathcal{M}^{\Downarrow}$, simply because to know whether $P \setminus X$ can diverge we need to know whether P can perform an infinite sequence of X events, something not decidable from the $\mathcal{FL}^{\Downarrow}$ behaviours of an unboundedly nondeterministic process.

As with $\mathcal{N}$ and $\mathcal{T}^{\Downarrow}$, the correct partial order for calculating the values of recursions in $\mathcal{M}^{\Downarrow}$ is always refinement, so that the convergence to the fixed point always starts from the least refined process **div**. Under the restriction to finitely nondeterministic CSP, we can specifically say that the value of the recursion $\mu p.F(p)$ is always given by

$$\bigsqcup_{r=0}^{\infty} F^r(\mathbf{div})$$

where $\bigsqcup$ is the least upper bound operator with respect to the refinement order.

$\mathcal{FL}^{\Downarrow}$ and $\mathcal{N}$ are *complete partial orders* (cpos) under refinement if Σ is finite, but both fail to be when Σ is infinite. The following example[1] works for both. Suppose $\Sigma = \mathbb{N}$ and let $P_n = \sqcap\{m \to STOP \mid m \geq n\}$. Clearly $P_n \sqsubseteq P_{n+1}$ in all CSP models because P_{n+1} is the nondeterministic choice over a smaller set than P_n. It is clear that any upper bound (which would necessarily exist for the chain in a cpo) to this increasing sequence can have no trace other than $\langle\rangle$. But nor can such a process diverge, terminate or deadlock on $\langle\rangle$, which is inconsistent with the healthiness conditions of $\mathcal{FL}^{\Downarrow}$ and $\mathcal{N}$.

Fortunately, all CSP-definable recursions still have least fixed points, it is just that we cannot rely on Tarski's Theorem over our chosen order to find them.

There are a number of alternative ideas we can use instead. One is to develop a version of the *strong order* for each model $\mathcal{M}^{\Downarrow}$: $P \leq Q$ if and only if Q's divergent behaviours are contained in those of P's, and the only change between the finite observations of P and Q comes in those places where P is constrained by divergence strictness but Q is not. The author believes it will be possible to do this for any CSP model $\mathcal{M}^{\Downarrow}$ in such a way that all CSP operators are monotone, and this order calculates the same fixed points as $\sqsubseteq$ as in [121]. In particular, we can define the strong order over $\mathcal{FL}^{\Downarrow}$:

$$P \leq Q \equiv Q \subseteq P \wedge (\beta \in P\backslash Q \Rightarrow \exists \beta' \leq \beta.\beta'^{\frown}\langle\Uparrow\rangle \in P\backslash Q)$$

This trick does not work, however, once infinite non-divergent behaviours are included in a model. We will later discuss two methods that do work for the more general models as well as this one.

Divergence-strict models work (i.e. are compositional) because no CSP operator can ever depend on a behaviour β of one of its arguments without having previously allowed the argument to pass through all the states it needs to perform it. If one of those states has the alternative of diverging, then (remembering that every CSP operator whose actions depend on an argument can simply promote at τ) the operator applied to the argument can diverge at that point too. Thus the post-divergence

---

[1] The observant reader might notice that this example uses unbounded, or infinite, nondeterminism, which is not generally allowable over these models. However, all we are doing here is defining members of the models themselves. There is no difficulty about interpreting these processes because they involve no hiding.

behaviour of the argument is never needed to deduce the pre-divergence behaviour of the whole.

To form $\mathcal{M}^{\Downarrow}$ for general $\mathcal{M}$ we need to identify which divergent behaviours to add to $\mathcal{M}$. Each $\mathcal{M}$ will—because of the need to be compositional under Θ_A and because it is at least as fine as $\mathcal{T}$—have behaviours representing a process's state at those points where it has just performed an action from Σ, or has just started and may not yet have become stable. In the cases of the trace-plus models these are the finite traces, and in the cases of $\mathcal{FL}$ and $\mathcal{RT}$ they are those ending in •.

These are the behaviours which can be marked as divergent to construct $\mathcal{M}^{\Downarrow}$, because these are just the points in a process's evolution where it can diverge.

The healthiness conditions for such an $\mathcal{M}^{\Downarrow}$ would then just parallel those of $\mathcal{FL}^{\Downarrow}$: every behaviour included in this divergence component is in the set of ordinary observations; every extension of a divergence is a divergence; and if β is a divergence, and if β' is an observation of the same trace implied by the presence of β, then β' is a divergence also.

Note that in the rich trace models $\mathcal{RT}^{\Downarrow}$ and $\mathcal{FL}^{\Downarrow}$ it is natural to extend the language used for finite behaviours/observations by a representation of divergence (i.e. ⇑ instead of the final •) rather than having an explicit separate component of divergences.

12.1.1 Determinism amongst the Richer Models

In this section we will study how the deterministic processes, and more generally *pre-deterministic* processes, which we touched on p. 170, behave in the divergence-strict models that give more details than $\mathcal{N}$. Recall that *deterministic* processes (defined over $\mathcal{N}$) are those that are divergence-free and satisfy

$$(s, \{a\}) \in failures_\perp(P) \Rightarrow (s\hat{}\langle a\rangle, \emptyset) \notin failures_\perp(P)$$

Pre-deterministic processes, on the other hand, are processes that behave deterministically until they diverge:

$$(s, \{a\}) \in failures_\perp(P) \wedge (s\hat{}\langle a\rangle, \emptyset) \in failures_\perp(P) \Rightarrow s \in divergences(P)$$

Therefore the deterministic processes are precisely those that are divergence free and pre-deterministic.

It is easy to deduce from this that if $s \notin divergences(P)$ then $s\hat{}\langle\checkmark\rangle \in traces(P)$ implies that P has no stable states after s, for these would refuse $\{\checkmark\}$. We can therefore deduce that if $s = \langle a_1, \ldots, a_n\rangle \in traces(P)\backslash divergences(P)$ then *either* $\langle \bullet, a_1, \bullet, \ldots, \bullet, a_n, \bullet, \checkmark\rangle \in \mathcal{FL}^{\Downarrow}[\![P]\!]$ *or* $\langle \bullet, a_1, \bullet, \ldots, \bullet, a_n, B, \rangle \in \mathcal{FL}^{\Downarrow}[\![P]\!]$ where $B = \{a \mid s\hat{}\langle a\rangle \in traces(P)\}$, *but not both.*

Furthermore, in either case, any • except one immediately before $\checkmark$ can (uniquely) be increased to the set of events possible after this partial trace. Similarly, s is a minimal divergence trace of P if and only if $\langle \bullet, a_1, \ldots, \bullet, a_n, \Uparrow\rangle \in \mathcal{FL}[\![P]\!]$ is a minimal divergence behaviour in $\mathcal{FL}[\![P]\!]$ and the same is true when the •s are increased to the acceptance after the partial trace.

The conclusion is that there is a unique member of $\mathcal{FL}^{\Downarrow}$ that corresponds to each pre-deterministic process in $\mathcal{N}$, so no more distinctions are made amongst these processes by moving to the finest divergence-strict model than are made in $\mathcal{N}$.

We can therefore conclude that the only extra distinctions made by the finer models are between processes that are nondeterministic. There is one interesting conclusion: that the definition of security (lack of information flow) in terms of *lazy independence* given in Sect. 6.5 does not depend on which model at least as fine as failures is chosen.

There is, nevertheless, one important distinction between the way pre-deterministic processes relate to $\mathcal{N}$ and the richer models. It has long been known that if P is any $\checkmark$-free process then, over $\mathcal{N}$,

$$P = \sqcap\{Q \mid Q \sqsupseteq_{FD} P \wedge Q \text{ is pre-deterministic}\}$$

This is not true over richer models, because of their ability to capture behaviour that is only possible after visible events that have occurred from unstable states. For example, the process $(a \to STOP) \rhd STOP$ has, over any richer model than $\mathcal{N}$, only the single (pre-)deterministic refinement $STOP$, whereas over $\mathcal{N}$ it additionally has $a \to STOP$.

Nevertheless, over these models, the deterministic processes are exactly the maximally refined processes, and every process has deterministic refinements.

12.1.2 Applications

The failures-divergences model is often thought of as *the* standard model for CSP, and it has been written about in many places in this book and elsewhere.

Proving divergence freedom in any model proves it in all others too. As mentioned above, all the trace-plus models carry exactly the same divergence information as each other.

$\mathcal{FL}^{\Downarrow}$ and $\mathcal{RT}^{\Downarrow}$ allow you to make more distinctions between the divergence behaviour of processes relative to the other four (and $\mathcal{FL}^{\Downarrow}$ more than $\mathcal{RT}^{\Downarrow}$). This is because they can detect cases when the observation of some refusal or acceptance earlier in a trace can guarantee that the process does not now diverge. For example

$$(a \to \mathbf{div}) \rhd (a \to a \to STOP) \quad \text{and} \quad a \to \mathbf{div}$$

are different in these two models, but not the other four, because no divergence is possible after $\langle a \rangle$ in the left-hand process when stability has been observed on $\langle \rangle$.

In almost every case, therefore, the choice of a divergence-strict model will be governed by which of them is the right one to characterise or specify the finitely observable properties of processes correctly.

Divergence-freedom is a natural condition to want to prove of prospective implementations, and we have already discussed a way of proving it in Sect. 6.4. Quite aside from the rather strange use we illustrated in Sect. 8.6, it can also be used to establish other properties of systems. It can be used to prove the *termination* of distributed algorithms where this may not be obvious. A good example of this is provided by the distributed database consistency algorithm described in Sect. 15.2 of TPC (15.3 in the on-line version), where an important part of the algorithm's correctness is that the network will settle after a finite time.

When we hide more than just the natural internal events of a system, we can use divergence freedom to understand the patterns of actions it performs. Recall the rule we established in Sect. 6.4, that a network is divergence-free if there is an order on its nodes such that no node can communicate infinitely with lesser neighbours without communicating either with a greater neighbour or externally. We actually expressed this by stating that, for each node P, $P \setminus X$ is divergence-free where X is its interface with lesser neighbours. This illustrates that divergence-freedom can easily be used to specify that a process cannot perform infinitely many of one type of event without performing one of another type.

Exercise 12.1 Write down the healthiness conditions of the models $\mathcal{RT}^{\Downarrow}$ and $\mathcal{R}^{\Downarrow}$.

Exercise 12.2 Recall Exercise 6.6. Show how to check the main precondition of this result with a series of checks for divergence freedom.

12.2 Strict Divergence for General CSP

It is unfortunate that the $\mathcal{M}^{\Downarrow}$ models are restricted to the finitely nondeterministic subset of CSP. This is both because it prevents us from reasoning about things like *fairness* and *eventuality* within CSP and because it means that we can no longer form characteristic processes for specifications. For example, there is no most general process in which every trace contains both an infinite number of as and an infinite number of bs.

To deal with the semantics of hiding in unboundedly nondeterministic CSP in a world where we are recording divergence means that we need to see behaviours with infinite sequences of visible actions. The extension of $\mathcal{T}^{\Downarrow}$ and $\mathcal{N}$ by infinite traces were the subject of Chap. 10 of TPC. Here we give a summary of the general principles that relate to building divergence-strict models for unbounded nondeterminism.

12.2.1 Healthiness Conditions

Imagine you have a divergence-free process whose finitely observable behaviours are, in any model at least as strong as $\mathcal{F}$, the same as those of the process

$$C = a \to C \sqcap b \to C$$

It is obvious that this process must have an infinite trace, because if you offer it $\{a, b\}$ for ever then it will certainly perform one. On the other hand it need not have *every* infinite trace composed of these two events. The definition C above will indeed create every such trace, but there are other processes with the same finite behaviours that only have proper subsets. Consider, for example, B where

$$B = \sqcap_{n=0}^{\infty} B_n \quad \text{where}$$

$$B_0 = A$$

$$B_{n+1} = a \rightarrow B_n \sqcap b \rightarrow B_n$$

$$A = a \rightarrow A$$

Plainly the only infinite traces of B are those that eventually consist only of as, but with a finite number of bs sprinkled in at the beginning.

So we need to ask which sets of infinite traces, or infinite behaviours in the case of the rich trace models, are allowable with this set of finite behaviour. At first sight this is going to require a much more complex healthiness condition than any we have seen to date, and this is an accurate assessment if we attempt to use the normal language of logic. There is an interesting study of the possible presentations of the necessary healthiness condition for the failures-divergences-infinite traces model in [10].

But fortunately there is another way of looking at this problem. If we unfold the operational semantics of a process P into a tree, any observed behaviour b will follow a (finite or infinite) path through that tree. We can prune the tree, starting from the root, as follows. For each node N reached, select exactly one arc with each action label (τ, $\checkmark$ or a member of Σ) that N can perform, subject to the condition that if N is a non-final node in b's path then the arc to the next node of b is included. The prunings are thrown away. Once this procedure has been performed at all depths, what remains is a finitely nondeterministic process P' that refines P in all models. (The only remaining nondeterminism can come from divergence and from nodes that have the choice of more than one of (i) a single τ, (ii) $\checkmark$ and (iii) a choice of visible actions.) Furthermore P' has the behaviour b.

It follows that $P = \sqcap \{P' \mid P' \sqsupseteq P \wedge P'$ is finitely nondeterministic$\}$. We call this the **CC** or *closed covering* principle. At a deep level, it is related to distributivity laws of CSP and especially that of prefixing, since both allow us to bring nondeterministic choice up to the front of a process. CC can be read as saying that all infinite nondeterminism in any CSP process can be resolved on the very first step.

If P is a finitely nondeterministic process in a divergence-strict model, the set of its infinite behaviours is precisely the ones all of whose finite prefixes are behaviours of P, as demonstrated for traces in Sect. 9.5.2. The argument is exactly the same as used there: examine that part of the synchronisation tree representing P where the behaviours are prefixes of an infinite behaviour b, all of whose finite prefixes belong to P. Then this tree has an infinite path because of König's Lemma, and that path must exhibit the whole of b or a prefix on which P can diverge.

We therefore know exactly how each finitely nondeterministic process embeds into the model where $\mathcal{M}^{\Downarrow}$ is extended by infinite behaviours: the infinite behaviours are precisely the *closure* of the finite ones. The closure $\overline{B}$ of a set of finite behaviours is B together with all infinite behaviours that have infinitely many prefixes in B. For the trace-plus models $\mathcal{M}$ this means that the representation of a finitely nondeterministic process is the same as that in $\mathcal{M}^{\Downarrow}$ plus all the infinite traces whose finite prefixes are all traces of the process.

This, of course, explains the word "closed" in the name "closed covering". This principle states that each process has sufficient infinite behaviour to be consistent with what is recorded of its finite behaviour. If we look at the set of finite behaviours of the process C quoted above, we know that it contains every finite trace composed of a and b. If P is a process with this set of finite behaviours, it follows that there is some closed $P' \sqsupseteq P$ that has such a trace t. As P' cannot diverge and cannot refuse $\{a, b\}$, it follows that P' has arbitrarily long traces $t' > t$. König's Lemma then tells us that the (closed) process P' necessarily has an infinite trace that extends t. It follows that, for every $t \in \{a, b\}^*$, P has an infinite trace that extends t.

Another way of stating CC is to say that every process is the nondeterministic choice of all the closed processes that refine it.

All this applies to any divergence-strict model, and so shows us exactly how to build a model $\mathcal{M}^{\Downarrow\omega}$ for any $\mathcal{M}$.

It is not obvious from the statement of the property, but it can be shown that CC imposes no upper bound on the infinite behaviours of a process P other than that the infinite behaviours are contained in the closure of the finite ones (in the case of C over $\mathcal{F}^{\Downarrow\omega}$, the infinite traces $\{a, b\}^\omega$). A proof of this that is valid in $\mathcal{F}^{\Downarrow\omega}$ (there termed $\mathcal{U}$) can be found in [122], and readily adapted to the other $\mathcal{M}^{\Downarrow\omega}$ models.

12.2.2 Fixed Point Theories for Unbounded Nondeterminism

For all such models other than $\mathcal{T}^{\Downarrow\omega}$, the refinement order (as usual, component-wise superset) is incomplete. This is true for any alphabet of size at least two.

Recall the example B above, and rename it $B(\langle a, a, \ldots \rangle)$ after the trace that represents the tail of all infinite traces. Consider the infinite traces u_n which consist of repetitions of $\langle a, a, \ldots, a, b \rangle$ (n as). No finite number of additions or deletions of events in u_n can turn it into another u_m.

Define $D_n = \bigsqcap_{m=n}^{\infty} B(u_m)$. Much as with the P_n on p. 273, these form an increasing sequence with no upper bound. Note that it is only the infinite traces that vary through this sequence, and that any upper bound contains no infinite trace at all. This is inconsistent with the fact demonstrated above that, over any finite-behaviour model other than $\mathcal{T}$, any closed divergence-free process that refines the finite behaviours of the D_n has an infinite trace.

Whereas this situation can be fixed for the models $\mathcal{M}^{\Downarrow}$ by use of the strong order, that does not work for the $\mathcal{M}^{\Downarrow\omega}$: in [122] it is shown that no cpo structure with respect to which CSP operators are monotonic can give the operationally correct fixed points for $\mathcal{F}^{\Downarrow\omega}$.

There are two known solutions to this problem. The author, in [122], established the existence of least fixed points for every CSP defined recursion by proving this in parallel with the congruence theorem with operational semantics. In essence, the fact that the abstraction into $\mathcal{F}^{\Downarrow\omega}$ of the operational semantics of $\mu p.F(p)$ is a fixed point of the mapping over $\mathcal{F}^{\Downarrow\omega}$ created by F means that F has *a* fixed point. It easily follows that F has a *least* fixed point (though one that may take a good deal longer than the ordinal ω to reach[2]). The proof that the least fixed point equals the operationally derived one is then complex, using "transfinite induction" (i.e., induction through the ordinals).

The advantage of this approach to proving the existence of fixed points is the substantial by-product: the proof of congruence. However, it is long and difficult when all the details are filled in. One might also regard it as strange that, to prove a result that is purely about how CSP behaves over an abstract model, one needs to move over to the operational semantics and back again. An alternative proof, lying purely within the denotational world, was discovered by Geoff Barrett [4, 5].

His insight was to concentrate on the *pre-deterministic* processes $\mathcal{P}$ as discussed earlier in this chapter. Operationally, a pre-deterministic process is one where each node takes one of three forms: it has a single τ action; it has a single $\checkmark$ action; or it has a range of actions labelled by members of Σ with at most one action per label. We have already met this concept on p. 170. This operational condition implies pre-determinism as was exploited in Sect. 8.6, but it is not *necessary* that a process be operationally pre-deterministic to be a member of $\mathcal{P}$.

In all divergence-strict CSP models other than $\mathcal{T}^{\Downarrow}$ the only refinements between the values of pre-deterministic processes are ones that are true in the strong order: if $P \sqsubseteq Q$ then Q can only refine P in places where P could have diverged. Indeed, the pre-deterministic processes form an unvarying "core" of processes that remain invariant as we look at models at least as fine as $\mathcal{N}$.

Barrett created monotonic analogues $\oplus'$ of all the CSP operators $\oplus$, that map $\mathcal{P}$ to $\mathcal{P}$ and such that $P \oplus Q \sqsubseteq P \oplus' Q$ for all $P, Q \in \mathcal{P}$ (and similarly for operators with different arities).

For example, we can define

- $P \sqcap' Q = P$

- $P \rhd' Q = Q$

- $\mathbf{div} \,\square'\, Q = P \,\square\, \mathbf{div} = \mathbf{div}$

- $SKIP \,\square'\, Q = P \,\square\, SKIP = SKIP \ (P, Q \neq \mathbf{div})$
- $?x : A \to P \,\square'\, ?x : B \to Q = ?x : A \cup B \to (P \,\llcorner\! x \in A \!\lrcorner\, Q)$
- $\mathbf{div} \setminus' X = \mathbf{div} \quad SKIP \setminus' X = SKIP$

- $(?x : A \to P) \setminus' X = \begin{cases} ?x : A \to (P \setminus X) & \text{if } X \cap A = \emptyset \\ P[c(X \cap A)/x] & \text{otherwise} \end{cases}$

---

[2]In other words, we cannot rely on reaching the fixed point using the usual interpretation of $\bigsqcup_{n=0}^{\infty} F^n(\mathbf{div})$. If that value is not a fixed point we carry on the iteration from there, and so on until the fixed point is eventually reached. This is the general construction given by Tarski's Theorem. A proof of this that does not require ordinals can be found in Appendix A of TPC.

In the last case $c : \mathbb{P}(\Sigma)\backslash\{\emptyset\} \to \Sigma$ is a *choice function* satisfying $c(X) \in X$ for all X.

The pre-deterministic processes form a complete partial order of closed processes within each $\mathcal{M}^{\Downarrow\omega}$. The structure of this cpo is, as we have already noted, independent of which model other than $\mathcal{T}^{\Downarrow\omega}$ we choose.

It follows that for every CSP recursion $\mu p.F(p)$ we have a corresponding recursion $\mu p.F'(p)$ over $\mathcal{P}$ that does have a least fixed point (we simply replace each CSP operator making up F by its primed version to get F'). It is easy to show that $F(\mu p.F'(p)) \sqsubseteq \mu p.F'(p)$. The fact that there is a process value such that $F(P) \sqsubseteq P$ guarantees that F has a least fixed point (one formula for which is $\bigsqcap\{P \mid F(P) \sqsubseteq P\}$.)

This argument works for every one of the models $\mathcal{M}^{\Downarrow\omega}$ except $\mathcal{T}^{\Downarrow\omega}$, which does not need it because the model itself is a cpo.

These arguments are not easy, but fortunately the user of the infinite behaviour models does not need to worry about this, because the existence of fixed points can be taken on trust, as can congruence with operational semantics.

There is, however, one major practical problem that does arise with the fixed points in models of the form $\mathcal{M}^{\Downarrow\omega}$: the UFP principle, and all other methods that depend on the idea of *constructiveness* or *guardedness* no longer apply. Guardedness works by showing that all behaviours associated with finite traces are uniquely defined. This is not enough over models like $\mathcal{F}^{\Downarrow\omega}$ because there is nothing similar to constrain the infinite traces. Remember the guarded recursion

$$C = (a \to C) \sqcap (b \to C)$$

The operational semantics give this all infinite traces from $\{a, b\}^{\omega}$, and indeed that set of infinite traces are a fixed point when combined with the appropriate set of failures. But equally all of the processes B_m as defined on p. 278 are fixed points of this recursion, as are many more.

We can nevertheless say that this particular recursion is finitely nondeterministic and so will have a unique *closed* fixed point. More generally, if a closed process P is a fixed point of the guarded function $F(\cdot)$ (whether F is finitely nondeterministic or not) then it equals $\mu p.F(p)$ because it is necessarily F's *least* fixed point.

12.2.3 Applying Infinite-Behaviour Models

Many natural specification processes are written using $\sqcap$ over infinite sets of processes. For example, we can define the process that acts like the most general buffer which never accepts more than $n \geq 1$ objects:

$$Buff_n(\langle\rangle) = in?x \to Buff_n(\langle x\rangle)$$
$$Buff_n(s^\smallfrown\langle y\rangle) = \#s < n - 1 \& (STOP \sqcap in?x \to Buff_n(\langle x\rangle^\smallfrown s^\smallfrown\langle y\rangle))$$
$$\square\ out!y \to Buff_n(s)$$

These are of course finitely nondeterministic and satisfy $Buff_{n+1}(\langle\rangle) \sqsubseteq_{FL} Buff_n(\langle\rangle)$. We can create a nondeterministic buffer that cannot perform an infinite trace without an infinite number of outputs:

$$Buff^*(\langle\rangle) = \textstyle\prod_{n=1}^{\infty} Buff_n(\langle\rangle)$$

Although it has the same finite behaviours as $Buff_{\langle\rangle}$ as defined on p. 12, and refines that process, it is very different. For example, $Buff^*(\langle\rangle) \setminus \{|in|\}$ is divergence-free. $Buff^*(\langle\rangle)$ is *fair* between inputs and outputs: it is impossible to have infinitely many of one without the other.

We can also state that $Buff^*(\langle\rangle)$ will *eventually* output because the deadlock-free process $Buff^*(\langle\rangle) \setminus \{|in|\}$ is not immediately divergent, and that it will *always eventually* output because this term is divergence-free.

Recall our construction of the *characteristic* process of any behavioural specification on p. 39. This construction is not valid over the $\mathcal{M}^{\Downarrow}$ models, but is over $\mathcal{M}^{\Downarrow\omega}$.

In Sect. 6.5 we defined *lazy abstraction* and in order to avoid the consequences of strict divergence chose to *define* that $\mathcal{L}_H(P)$ is always divergence free when P is. Nevertheless, we used the construction $\mathcal{L}_H(P) = (P \parallel_H Chaos_H) \setminus H$ which can formally introduce divergence. (Recall that P was assumed to be a $\checkmark$-free process whose alphabet is partitioned into $H \cup L$.) Using the model $\mathcal{F}^{\Downarrow\omega}$, we can define it in a way that does no have this apparent contradiction. Define processes as follows:

$$Rest(n, m) = (m < n)\&(STOP \sqcap \textstyle\prod\{x \to Rest(n, m + 1) \mid x \in H\})$$
$$\square ?x : L \to SKIP$$

$$Rest1^* = \textstyle\prod\{Rest(n, 0) \mid n \in \mathbb{N}\}$$
$$Rest^* = Rest1^*; Rest^*$$

$Rest1^*$ may allow a finite sequence of H events, but always allows an L event, which makes it terminate. Therefore $Rest^*$ always allows L events, and can choose whether not to accept one from H, but never accepts an infinite sequence of events in H. We can therefore define

$$\mathcal{L}_H(P) = (P \parallel_{H \cup L} Rest^*) \setminus H$$

and achieve exactly the effect that we want, without any "double think" about models.

The definition of $Rest^*$ is itself interesting: it would be tempting to define processes that allow up to n members of H for each member of L, and take the nondeterministic composition of these. This would not have given the same result, since it would not have allowed a trace in which there are exactly n members of H between the nth and $n + 1$th members of L. Our definition above does allow this since it permits a different limit on the Hs every time.

Exercise 12.3 If you compare the definitions of $Buff^*$ and $Rest^*$ carefully, you will discover that $Buff^*$ is not the *most* nondeterministic buffer that cannot perform an infinite unbroken sequence of inputs. Explain why it is not. Create a CSP definition for the process that is.

12.3 The Hierarchy of Divergence-Strict Models

It is vital to understand that, while $\mathcal{M}^{\Downarrow}$ and $\mathcal{M}^{\Downarrow\omega}$ are different models, they represent the same equivalence for finitely nondeterministic CSP processes and LTSs. So in understanding the hierarchy of divergence-strict models for CSP we can treat the two as being the same.

This hierarchy is analysed in [129], where the proofs of the results quoted in this section can be found. That paper also *defines* a divergence-strict model in terms of relational images of $\mathcal{FL}^{\Downarrow}$ and $\mathcal{FL}^{\Downarrow\omega}$ in much the same way as we defined a finite-behaviour model in the previous chapter.

In general, the way one can extend a finite-behaviour model to a divergence strict one is not unique. For example, it is possible to extend either $\mathcal{FL}$ or $\mathcal{RT}$ by divergence *traces* rather than richer behaviours, thereby getting slightly coarser equivalences. However, this extension is unique for the trace-plus models because the *only* available choice is to add divergence *traces*.

Just as the $\mathcal{M}^{\Downarrow}$ are uniquely defined for the trace-plus models, so are the $\mathcal{M}^{\Downarrow\omega}$. The following result is taken from [129].

Theorem 12.1 *Suppose that $\mathcal{M}$ is any one of $\mathcal{T}$, $\mathcal{F}$, $\mathcal{R}$ and $\mathcal{A}$ (i.e. the trace-plus principal models) and $\mathcal{M}'$ is a divergence-strict model for full CSP, that induces the same equivalence on finitely nondeterministic CSP as $\mathcal{M}^{\Downarrow}$. Then $\mathcal{M}'$ induces the same equivalence as $\mathcal{M}^{\Downarrow\omega}$, the extension of $\mathcal{M}$ by strict divergence traces and infinite traces.*

What this means is that, by proving uniqueness results for $\mathcal{T}^{\Downarrow}$, $\mathcal{F}^{\Downarrow} = \mathcal{N}$ and $\mathcal{R}^{\Downarrow}$ analogous to Theorem 11.3 amongst the divergence-strict models of finitely nondeterministic CSP, you automatically get one for general CSP. After all, every model for general CSP is one for finitely nondeterministic CSP too.

This uniqueness is presented in [129] as the following series of theorems.

Theorem 12.2 *If $\mathcal{M}$ is a non-trivial divergence-strict model for CSP, then $\mathcal{T}^{\Downarrow} \preceq \mathcal{M}$.*

The proof of this result is similar to that given for the second part of Theorem 11.3 on p. 269 and is relatively straightforward. However, the following results both have very technical proofs.

Theorem 12.3 *Any divergence-strict model $\mathcal{M}$ of finitely nondeterministic CSP that is not $\mathcal{T}^{\Downarrow}$ is a refinement of $\mathcal{N}$: in other words if $\mathcal{N}$ distinguishes a pair of processes then so does $\mathcal{M}$.*

Theorem 12.4 *Every divergence-strict model $\mathcal{M}$ of finitely nondeterministic CSP that is a proper refinement of $\mathcal{N}$ is in turn a refinement of $\mathcal{R}^{\Downarrow}$.*

Just as for the finite-behaviour models, this set of results defines the coarsest end of the hierarchy of divergence-strict models very precisely, and establishes, for example, that

- $\mathcal{T}^{\Downarrow\omega}$ is fully abstract with respect to the test "P can diverge".
- $\mathcal{F}^{\Downarrow\omega}$ is fully abstract with respect to the tests "P can diverge or deadlock immediately" and "P is deterministic".

12.4 Seeing Beyond Divergence

One of the most remarkable facts about FL*-behaviours is that, if we want to model CSP processes by the behaviours of this form that they can *actually* perform, unfettered by any form of obscuration such as divergence strictness, then there is no conventional fixed point theory that will give the correct value (i.e. the observable behaviours of the operational semantics). By "conventional" here, we mean a procedure that determines the fixed point purely from the function that the recursion represents over the model. This is shown by the following argument, which was discovered independently by the author [126] and Paul Levy [85], in each case for the model with finite and infinite traces, and divergence traces.

> Let *FinCh* be the set of all FL*-behaviours other than the infinitely long ones over the alphabet $\Sigma = \{a\}$. It is straightforward to define (using infinite nondeterministic choice) a CSP process with this set of behaviours: see Exercise 12.4. Now consider the recursions
>
> $$P = (\mathbf{div} \parallel_{\Sigma \setminus \{a\}} a \to P) \sqcap FinCh$$
> $$Q = (\mathbf{div} \parallel_{\Sigma \setminus \{a\}} Q) \sqcap FinCh$$
>
> Thanks to the parallel composition with **div** there is only one possible infinite FL*-behaviour possible for the right-hand sides of each these recursions, namely an infinite trace of as with no stable states (so all •s between the as). Since *FinCh* contains every finite behaviour and divergence, it follows that the right-hand sides take only two possible values: *FinCh* itself and with the addition of this single infinite one. In each case the right-hand side contains this extra behaviour if and only if the recursive call to P or Q does. *We can conclude that the two right-hand sides denote exactly the same function from sets of FL*-behaviours to themselves.* This means that any conventional way of giving denotational semantics to P and Q would necessarily identify them.
> However, while the operational semantics of Q cannot perform $\langle \bullet, a, \bullet, a, \ldots \rangle$, those of P can perform it by following the left-hand option of the nondeterministic choice every time. It follows that either P or Q must disagree, operationally, with the fixed point generated by the hypothetical denotational fixed point process.
> There is nothing vital in this example about the fact that the critical infinite trace is unstable throughout. See Exercise 12.5 below.

Notice that in both this example and the one in Exercise 12.5, every finite behaviour can be followed by divergence. It turns out that the infinite behaviours that confuse fixed point processes are just those that have infinitely many divergent prefixes:

$$\{\beta \mid \{\beta' < \beta \mid \beta'^\frown\langle\Uparrow\rangle\} \in P\} \text{ is infinite}\}$$

We therefore need to adopt a weak form of divergence strictness if we are to get a working fixed point theory for recursion, so we will add an additional healthiness condition to such models: that if a process *does not* contain a given infinite behaviour β, then divergence is observable directly after at most *finitely many* prefixes of β.

The finest model that we will envisage for CSP is therefore $\mathcal{FL}^{\sharp}$, which consists of sets P of FL*-behaviours that are subject to the following *weak divergence strictness* healthiness condition, which replaces the divergence strictness condition of $\mathcal{FL}^{\Downarrow}$, namely FLD1. (FLD2 and FLD3 are still required.)

WDS If $\{\gamma \mid \gamma^\frown\langle\Uparrow\rangle \in P \wedge \exists\delta.\gamma^\frown\delta = \beta\}$ is infinite, then $\beta \in P$. In every case the healthiness conditions of $\mathcal{M}^{\sharp}$ are the same as those of $\mathcal{M}^{\Downarrow\omega}$ except that those imposing divergence strictness are replaced by a suitable version of WDS.

The notation $\sharp$ (the musical "sharp" symbol) is just a pun: $\mathcal{M}^{\sharp}$ is the "sharpest" (i.e. most detailed) way in which we can add infinite behaviours to $\mathcal{M}$ and get a CSP model. We should note that WDS makes no difference in the case where P is a closed process, such as when it is finitely nondeterministic.

Whereas with $\mathcal{M}^{\Downarrow}$ and $\mathcal{M}^{\Downarrow\omega}$ we had the choice of finite nondeterminism *or* recording infinite behaviours, with $\mathcal{FL}^{\sharp}$ there is no choice. This is because, if we are to see beyond potential divergence, we *have* to handle unbounded nondeterminism, as is illustrated by the following example, closely related to the one illustrated in Fig. 9.10 on p. 225.

Consider the deterministic process $P(0)$, defined:

$$P(n) = (a \rightarrow P(n+1)) \,\square\, (b \rightarrow C(n))$$
$$C(n) = n > 0 \,\&\, c \rightarrow C(n-1)$$

It performs any number of as, a b, and then the same number of cs as as.

It is clear that $(P(0) \setminus \{a\}) \setminus \{c\}$ can diverge on the empty trace, but when it succeeds in performing b it will not diverge as it is limited to some finite number of hidden cs. If we record the infinite traces of $P(0) \setminus \{a\}$ there is no problem in deducing this—actually it does not have any infinite traces. However if, as over $\mathcal{N}$, we try to deduce the presence of an infinite trace from its finite prefixes, there is no difference between $P(0) \setminus \{a\}$ and $P(0) \setminus \{a\} \sqcap b \rightarrow CS$ where $CS = c \rightarrow CS$. And of course, hiding c in this second process should record $\langle b\rangle$ as a divergence.

What we are seeing here is exactly the same phenomenon in a finite-branching process that necessitated infinite traces with infinite nondeterminism in divergence-strict models. The reader will see that the infinite chain of states $P(n) \setminus \{a\}$ as n varies is effectively becoming a single state, and a single b from each of them becomes the same as infinite branching from a single state. This cannot happen in a finite-branching, divergence strict model since, in such a system, if there are infinitely many nodes τ-reachable from a node P, then P is divergent by König's Lemma.

In other words: *Beyond potential divergence, the effect of unbounded nondeterminism can arise even in finitely branching systems. The divergence-strictness of models like $\mathcal{N}$ prevents this from causing problems there.*

There is therefore no option about the $\mathcal{M}^{\sharp}$ models: they consist of the same sorts of behaviour as $\mathcal{M}^{\Downarrow\omega}$, but replacing divergence strictness with a version of WDS. In each case, except $\mathcal{T}^{\sharp}$ the allowable sets of infinite behaviours are governed by the closed cover (CC) principle, just as in the $\mathcal{M}^{\Downarrow\omega}$ models.

With the exception of recursion, there is no problem defining the action of every non-recursive CSP operator over the model $\mathcal{FL}^{\sharp}$ or any of the other principal models' $\mathcal{M}^{\sharp}$. You can find full details that apply to each of the trace-plus models in [126]. In the case of some operators (for example $\sqcap$) it is necessary to apply a weak divergence closure operator that adds in the infinite limits of divergences.

We will defer discussion of the fixed point theory until after looking at applications.

12.4.1 Applications of $\mathcal{M}^{\sharp}$

Divergence has had such a bad press in the literature of CSP that one might wonder why we need a model that can see beyond a potential divergence and detect further possible divergences that could lurk there. After all we know that we can see the minimal divergences through models like $\mathcal{N}$, and we can see all of a process's finitely observable behaviour (whether before or after possible divergences) via models like $\mathcal{F}$.

When talking of things happening beyond *potential* divergence we need to be clear what this means. Divergence itself is always the last thing a process does: after all divergence takes an infinite amount of time. There is thus no question of anything happening after divergence. It is, however, entirely possible for a process that is able to perform some infinite sequence of τs to escape from this. There are three ways this could happen:

- There is some visible action possible from the same state as one of the τs, the environment offers it and it happens.

  $$(\mu p.(a \to p \,\square\, b \to STOP) \setminus \{a\}$$

- There is, in one of the states on the possible divergence, a choice of τs; and one is picked that leads to a stable state.

  $$(\mu p.(a \to p \sqcap b \to STOP) \setminus \{a\}$$

- Suppose a particular behaviour (trace or rich trace) has been observed up to the point where a divergence might or must happen. The process might have a different way to perform the same behaviour that leads to a non-divergent state.

  $$(a \to \mathbf{div}) \sqcap (a \to a \to STOP)$$

In other words to see things beyond potential divergence means to see what a process might do if it gets beyond, or avoids diverging, on some observed behaviour.

Suppose you are part of a team designing an operating system and it is your responsibility to program the *off* button. If a user presses this button, the system is supposed to terminate gracefully. It will be your responsibility to ensure that the system behaves like *SKIP* after *off*, and is therefore unable then to deadlock, diverge or communicate anything else, but it is not your responsibility to ensure that it does not diverge beforehand.

An appropriate $\mathcal{F}^{\sharp}$ specification you might wish to aim for is

$$\textit{OffOK} = \textit{DIV} \sqcap ((\textit{off} \rightarrow \textit{SKIP}) \,\square\, (\textit{STOP} \sqcap ?x : \Sigma \backslash \{\textit{off}\} \rightarrow \textit{OffOK}))$$

which says that *off* must be offered unless the process diverges, that it never terminates until after *off*, and that it certainly terminates once *off* has occurred.

What we might conclude is that models like $\mathcal{F}^{\sharp}$ allow us to make specifications that say that processes behave in restricted ways (including absence of divergence) after particular behaviours b, even when we do not care if divergence could happen on proper prefixes of b.

As a second example, consider the token ring described on p. 82. If we hide the internal events $\{|\textit{ring}|\}$ this system can diverge, because when there are no current messages the empty tokens can pass round and round the ring for ever. This is in a sense necessary because otherwise a message inserted into the ring might never meet an empty token that it can ride on. This is a *busy wait*. A specification for this ring-with-hiding would have to permit divergence in states where the ring is empty, but can specify divergence freedom for other states.

The above examples persuade the author that the model $\mathcal{F}^{\sharp}$ is worth implementing in FDR. There will be no particular challenge in doing this. The problems relating to calculating fixed points, and issues of infinite traces and WDS will be irrelevant because FDR works by interpreting the *operational* semantics of *finite-state* processes.

An interesting topic for future work would be whether such models add usefully to the theory of lazy abstraction $\mathcal{L}_H(P)$ as defined in Sect. 6.5 and discussed earlier in this chapter, and to its applications in fault tolerance and security.

Exercise 12.4 Use CSP syntax to create the following processes, where $\Sigma = \{a\}$:

(a) *FinCh* as described above.
(b) *NAStable*, which has every possible FL*-behaviour except for $\langle \{a\}, a, \{a\}, a, \ldots \rangle$: an infinite succession of stable offers of a followed by the event a itself.

Both will require an unboundedly nondeterministic construction.

Exercise 12.5 By using *NAStable* in place of *FinCh*, and making other adjustments, modify the pair of recursions above for P and Q so that instead of clashing on the unstable trace of as, they now have the same paradoxical behaviour on the infinite trace of stably offered as.

12.5 The Fixed Point Theory of $\mathcal{M}^{\sharp}$

We have signalled rather clearly that models like $\mathcal{F}^{\sharp}$ have difficult fixed point theories, not least through the pair of examples that illustrated the need for the WDS condition.

The difficulty is not in calculating a fixed point of CSP recursions over these models, but in finding the one that correctly predicts the value we can extract from the operational semantics. This value can easily be calculated from the LTS the operational semantics produce, though that value will in general need to be closed under the WDS property.

Consider the model $\mathcal{T}^{\sharp}$. This has both refinement least and greatest values. The first is the one with all traces, divergences and infinite traces; the second is *STOP*. Now consider the recursion

$$P = a \rightarrow (P \setminus \{a\})$$

If the correct approach to finding the semantics of recursion was to find the refinement *least* fixed point, we would get the process that could not diverge on the empty trace, whose only length-1 trace is $\langle a \rangle$, and which can perform any trace at all after that (finite or infinite), diverging after any finite one, provided the rest of the trace contains no a.

That is clearly incorrect: the operational semantics say that P performs $\langle a \rangle$ and then diverges "deterministically": $a \rightarrow \mathbf{div}$. So we might consider the refinement *greatest* fixed point. But that is $a \rightarrow STOP$, which is not correct either. So while the operational value is a fixed point of $F(Q) = a \rightarrow (Q \setminus \{a\})$, it is neither the least nor the greatest one, the two we have used for all CSP models up to now.

Interestingly the solution to this problem, which is presented in full in [126], uses the intuition of both these fixed points to find a third one: suppose we have a CSP recursion $\mu p . F(p)$.

- We know that the refinement-least fixed point computes the operationally correct fixed point Ω of F over each of the $\mathcal{M}^{\Downarrow\omega}$ models. That means it agrees with the operationally correct fixed point Θ of F in $\mathcal{M}^{\sharp}$ *up to and including the first point in any behaviour where divergence is possible*.

- Consider the map Π from $\mathcal{M}^{\sharp}$ to $\mathcal{M}^{\Downarrow\omega}$ in which processes have divergence strictness imposed. This gives the correct value in the second model corresponding to each value in the first. Clearly $\Omega = \Pi(\Theta)$ is itself in $\mathcal{M}^{\sharp}$ and is the refinement-least member of $\mathcal{M}^{\sharp}$ with the same image under Π as Θ.

- There is also a refinement-greatest such member $\tilde{\Omega}$, obtained by *deleting* all behaviours from P that are implied by divergence strictness, though not the minimal divergences. So for example in one of the trace-plus models we delete all divergence traces and traces $s\hat{\ }t$ where $t \neq \langle \rangle$ and s is a divergence; and we would delete all failures, ready pairs, deadlock traces and revivals which are associated with a minimal divergence trace s and any extension of it. Necessarily $\Omega \sqsubseteq \Theta \sqsubseteq \tilde{\Omega}$ and the three are all equal only if P is divergence free.

  Note that $\Pi^{-1}(\Theta)$ is then precisely the "interval" $I = [\Omega, \tilde{\Omega}] = \{Q \mid \Omega \sqsubseteq Q \sqsubseteq \tilde{\Omega}\}$.

- The fact that Ω is a fixed point of F over $\mathcal{M}^{\Downarrow\omega}$ then means that whenever $Q \in I$, $F(Q) \in I$ also.

- The interval is a complete lattice (and so is a cpo in both directions). We can therefore deduce that F has both refinement-least and refinement-greatest fixed points in I. It should not be too hard to see that the refinement-least one is actually

Fig. 12.1 Illustration of the
reflected fixed-point
calculation

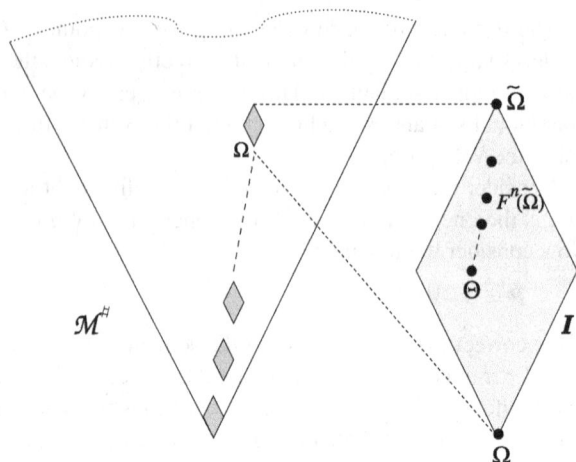

the least fixed point of F on the whole of $\mathcal{M}^\sharp$. We already know that this is not
always the operationally correct one over $\mathcal{M}^\sharp$.

- Give the refinement-greatest fixed point in I the name $\mathit{\Xi}$. We know that $\Theta \sqsubseteq \mathit{\Xi}$
  since Θ is a fixed point of F in I. In fact the two are equal. The proof of this (for
  the model $\mathcal{T}^\sharp$) can be found in [126]. It depends crucially on a consequence of
  WDS, namely that for any member P of $\mathcal{M}^\sharp$, if u is an infinite behaviour in the
  closure of P that is not in P itself, there is a finite prefix s of u such that neither
  s nor any longer prefix of u is a divergence.
- Thanks to the continuity of all CSP operators in the $\subseteq$ order (as opposed to $\sqsubseteq$),
  as discussed on p. 233, $\Theta = \mathit{\Xi}$ is always given by the formula $\bigsqcap_{n=0}^{\infty} F^n(\tilde{\Omega})$.

We term this the *reflected fixed point* for obvious reasons. As illustrated in
Fig. 12.1, the fixed point calculation runs in two stages: the first one goes upwards
to find an upper bound for Θ that agrees with it up to and including the first divergence. We then reflect back off that and iterate towards the correct fixed point. The
diamonds in the left-hand part of the figure are the inverse images under Π of the
iterations towards the least fixed point in $\mathcal{M}^{\Downarrow\omega}$ under the standard Tarski's Theorem
construction: $F^\alpha(\mathbf{div})$ as α varies over the ordinals.

Returning to the example $\mu p.a \rightarrow (p \setminus \{a\})$ we find that $\Omega = a \rightarrow Bottom$,
where *Bottom* is the refinement-least member of $\mathcal{M}^\sharp$, and that $\tilde{\Omega} = a \rightarrow \mathbf{div}$. In
this particular example $\tilde{\Omega}$ is a fixed point of the recursion and so equals $\mathit{\Xi}$. It is, of
course, the operationally correct value.

Now consider the recursion $\mu p.a \rightarrow (p \setminus \{a\} \sqcap b \rightarrow STOP)$. This has the same
Ω and $\tilde{\Omega}$ as the previous ones, but $\tilde{\Omega}$ is now no longer a fixed point since

$$F(\tilde{\Omega}) = a \rightarrow (\mathbf{div} \sqcap b \rightarrow STOP)$$

This is in fact the fixed point, but see Exercise 12.6.

As a further example consider the recursion

$$Q = ((a \rightarrow Q; b \rightarrow SKIP) \sqcap SKIP) \setminus \{a\}$$

This can diverge immediately, and so its Ω and $\tilde{\Omega}$ are respectively the refinement-least member of $\mathcal{M}^{\sharp}$ (i.e. the one with all possible behaviours) and **div**. The iterations from **div** are

> **div** $\sqcap$ *SKIP*
> **div** $\sqcap$ *SKIP* $\sqcap b \rightarrow$ *SKIP*
> **div** $\sqcap$ *SKIP* $\sqcap b \rightarrow$ *SKIP* $\sqcap b \rightarrow b \rightarrow$ *SKIP*
> and so on.

It is easy to see therefore that the reflected fixed point here is

> **div** $\sqcap \sqcap_{n=0}^{\infty} B_n$

where $B_0 = SKIP$ and $B_{n+1} = b \rightarrow B_n$.

Exercise 12.6 Suppose we change the second example recursion to $\mu p.a \rightarrow (p \setminus \{a\} \sqcap b \rightarrow p)$ (replacing the *STOP* by a recursive call p). What is now its value in $\mathcal{T}^{\sharp}$?

12.6 The Hierarchy

For finite behaviour and divergence-strict models we have established quite strong results about which CSP models exist, particularly at the coarse end of the spectrum.

Since, in any case, $\mathcal{M} \prec \mathcal{M}^{\sharp}$ and $\mathcal{M}^{\Downarrow \omega} \prec \mathcal{M}^{\sharp}$ (whereas $\mathcal{M}$ and $\mathcal{M}^{\Downarrow \omega}$ are incomparable), it is harder to characterise the models $\mathcal{T}^{\sharp}$, $\mathcal{F}^{\sharp}$ and $\mathcal{R}^{\sharp}$ as the coarsest three of anything simple.

Besides this, it is possible to create strange models in which more detail is recorded before the first divergence than after, which means that beyond the finite-behaviour and divergence-strict hierarchies things get more complex.

In addition, many extra models can be created by taking Cartesian products of others.

What we can definitely say is that the finest of all CSP models, at least under the postulates we made earlier, is $\mathcal{FL}^{\sharp}$. We will find this fact very useful in Chap. 13.

At the end of the previous chapter we defined the six principal finite behaviour models of CSP. What we can say now is that each of them has a divergence-strict analogue $\mathcal{M}^{\Downarrow \omega}$, which can be simplified to $\mathcal{M}^{\Downarrow}$ for finitely nondeterministic processes; and each of them has a "seeing beyond divergence" extension: a model that allows divergences and infinite behaviours to be added without almost all the obfuscation of divergence strictness.

18 models is obviously far too many. In practice the usual $\mathcal{T}$ and $\mathcal{N}$ will serve the great majority of practical purposes, with $\mathcal{F}$ playing a bridging role. But many of the others will have more specialised roles in modelling, specification and theory, as we have highlighted in these last two chapters.

12.7 Tools

At the time of writing there are three infinite-behaviour models built into FDR, namely $\mathcal{F}^{\Downarrow} = \mathcal{N}$, $\mathcal{R}^{\Downarrow}$ and $\mathcal{RT}^{\Downarrow}$. Checks in $\mathcal{T}^{\Downarrow}$ can easily be carried out: $Spec \sqsubseteq_{TD}$ $Impl$ is equivalent to $Spec \parallel_{\Sigma} Chaos_{\Sigma} \sqsubseteq_{FD} Impl$ since the left-hand side in this second refinement always permits any refusal set.

The author hopes that this range will increase, though there is a strong argument for ensuring that this is done in such a way that the extra functionality does not confuse the user.

12.8 Notes

The author developed most of the theory explained in this chapter in the late 1980s, at least as it applies to the traces and failures models. (Not the results of Sect. 12.3, which are recent.) While the results about divergence-strict models were published at that time [122], he did not get around to publishing those about "seeing beyond divergence" until much later [126], after he had finally summoned up the energy to prove the associated congruence theorem.

By this time there had been two interesting streams of work done by others which were closely related. The first, already mentioned, was Paul Levy's independent discovery of the inadequacy of traditional fixed points over models like $\mathcal{T}^{\sharp}$ without WDS.

The second was the work on congruences for CSP and CCS-like languages by Antti Valmari and his co-workers, including Antti Puhakka. Their work did not concern itself with fixed-point theories, but did hit upon many *congruences* closely related to those in this chapter, at the levels of traces, failures and divergence traces. These included CFFD (Chaos-Free Failures-Divergence) [151], which corresponded to the model $\mathcal{F}^{\sharp}$ without WDS, and another: *Tr-DivTr-Enditr* where the equivalence, though not[3] the representation, corresponded precisely to $\mathcal{T}^{\sharp}$. This was characterised as the weakest congruence that could accurately determine the divergence traces of a process.

The presence of the new Θ_A operator in CSP, and therefore the new expressivity results in Chap. 9 which rely on it, owes a lot to Theorem 12.3. This theorem is not true without Θ_A in the language. Notice that $(a \rightarrow \mathbf{div}) \Theta_a P = a \rightarrow P$ in general. This means that the left-hand argument is performing the action a without the combination diverging, even though a leads the left-hand argument into a divergent state. No other CSP operator can have this effect: if an argument is allowed to perform an action leading to divergence, the other operators all have this action lead to a divergent state of the whole construct.

---

[3]They chose to exclude, rather than include, the traces with an infinite number of divergence prefixes. We chose to include them because it gives smoother definitions of refinement and closed processes.

In trying to prove the theorem without Θ_A, the author was forced to rediscover a model which is identical to $\mathcal{N}$ except that it does not record which of the events that lead immediately to divergence are refused (see [129]). This model had previously been discovered by Puhakka [109].

The author's reaction to discovering this model, and the reason for its existence, was to search for something like the Θ_A operator in the CSP literature. On failing to find it, he added it to the language. It was embarrassment at having had to add an extra operator that led him to try to discover if any *further* operator might have to be added: this investigation led to the expressivity results. These say, of course, that within certain parameters no further operators are needed.

The author's construction of the reflected fixed point was influenced by a similar two-stage construction by Manfred Broy in [23]. Broy's use of closure under the Egli-Milner ordering is replaced by our use of divergence strictness.

Chapter 13
The Algebra of CSP

13.1 Introduction

Throughout the introductory chapters we used algebraic laws to help explain the meanings of the various operators of CSP. Laws of this type have historically played an important role in the field of process algebra (the very name of which suggests this).

In this chapter we will show how algebraic laws can be used to develop a third type of semantic framework to add to operational semantics and behavioural models, and how algebraic laws can be used to explain the differences between operational and model-based semantics. This *algebraic semantics* gives much extra insight into the differences between the finitely nondeterministic versions of the main models in the hierarchy developed in Chaps. 11 and 12.

An algebraic semantics for a programming language is one where the notion of process equivalence is derived from a set of laws. Some authors proposing process algebras have regarded algebraic semantics as the most basic means of defining process equality, in that they propose a given set of laws and set about investigating what equivalence they produce. The theory most closely associated with this approach is ACP (see, for example, [7, 8]). This gives a remarkable degree of freedom, since essentially any set of laws will create an equivalence on the set of process terms. There is no constraint on one's choices that is nearly as sharp as the requirement that a denotational model induce a congruence.

Simply quoting a set of laws does bring the dangers of not identifying processes that you had intended to be equal, or, more worryingly, identifying far too many. See Exercise 13.1 for an example of the latter. Therefore the equivalence induced by a proposed set of laws must be thoroughly investigated to make sure it has the intended effect.

However, we have *already* developed a hierarchy of equivalences for CSP. Our approach in this chapter will be to try to understand how algebraic laws correspond to these models. We will find ourselves building a framework for deciding the equality of programs algebraically. That framework is relatively complex to develop, but once we have it the differences between the models will be characterised remarkably easily in terms of a few laws that may or may not hold depending on the model.

A.W. Roscoe, *Understanding Concurrent Systems*, Texts in Computer Science,
DOI 10.1007/978-1-84882-258-0_13, © Springer-Verlag London Limited 2010

We will find ourselves introducing quite a large number of laws in this chapter in addition to ones seen earlier in this book. Recall the convention that all laws not true in all CSP models have some suitable superscript on their reference numbers. In some cases this indicates the class of models where a law is true. In cases where it is an asterisk $*$ the reader should refer to this chapter to discover where the law is valid. All the laws introduced in the present chapter have a particular purpose in a transformation strategy, and a number are calculated directly from the underlying operational semantics.

There is a corresponding chapter (11) in TCP, which studies in detail how to create an algebraic semantics congruent to the failures-divergences model $\mathcal{N}$. The approach used in that chapter corresponds at a high level to the one we use in the present one:

- An algebraic strategy is developed which allows us to prove any pair of *finite* programs equal if they are equivalent in a chosen model. This comes in two stages:
  - Firstly we develop a way of unfolding an arbitrary finite CSP program into a form that reflects the structure of how the process's operational semantics creates a tree of states linked by visible and invisible actions. There should be no reason why this has to vary from one CSP model to another. We can think of this stage as being an *algebraic operational semantics* (or AOS): a strategy for reducing a program by algebraic laws to reveal its initial actions and the behaviour that follows each.

    The result of applying this strategy to a finite program will be one in a restricted syntax that we will refer to as AOS form.
  - Secondly, we develop a way of converting programs in AOS form into a true normal form for each model, namely a program structure where any pair of syntactically different programs are semantically different. Inevitably this will have to be different for each model, since the normal forms of different models must be different.

    The normal forms themselves, of course, give considerable insight into the structure of the models.
- Finally, rules are developed that allow us to decide the equivalence of arbitrary programs via relationships between their respective finitary *approximations*.

As in Chap. 11 of TPC, we will assume in this chapter that the alphabet Σ is finite, since this makes the concept of a finite program easier to define and manipulate. With this assumption, a finite program is one with no recursion in its definition (or derived operators or constants such as *RUN* and *Chaos* which require the use of recursion to define them). We do, however, allow the constant **div**, representing a divergent process.

Thus all finite programs only have a finite number of traces, other than ones implied by divergence in divergence-strict models.

Readers have two choices for studying this chapter. In either case they should study the next section, which shows how to define an AOS form into which the LTS representation of every finite CSP program can be mapped in a way that preserves semantics in every behavioural model. The choice comes in whether or not to study the details of Sect. 13.3, in which we develop a detailed strategy for applying algebraic laws to reduce every finite program to AOS form. This is the most technical part of the chapter, and of course we already know that every finite program is equivalent to one in this form thanks to the operational semantics from Chap. 9. The remaining sections make sense in either case.

Exercise 13.1 A certain text [56][1] proposes the following laws for CSP (amongst many others)

(1) $P \parallel \bot = \bot$
(2) $P \parallel STOP = STOP$
(3) $P \parallel Q = Q \parallel P$
(4) $\bot \triangle Q = \bot$
(5) $STOP \triangle Q = Q$

Which of these are true, and which false, over $\mathcal{N}$ on the assumption that $\bot$ is identified with **div**? Show that these laws alone (and hence any super-set) are sufficient to prove that $P = Q$ for all processes P and Q.

Exercise 13.2 Prove that the following laws are all valid in the semantics of CSP over $\mathcal{N}$:
   (a) $\langle$;-assoc$\rangle$ (7.3), (b) $\langle$hide-step$\rangle$ (5.6), (c) $\langle$hide-combine$\rangle$ (5.3).

13.2 AOS Form

The choice of an AOS form turns out to be something of a compromise. In order to be tractable, the AOS form we pick has to have relatively few top-level formats for processes. In an ideal world, given what we said above, the AOS form would make it easy for us to represent the initial state of every LTS in a convenient way whose own operational semantics was exactly the same. Unfortunately, it proves to be too complex in the CSP language to solve this problem in such a way that the algebraic semantics remains tractable. We therefore pick an AOS form that can easily be created from a finite process's operational semantics so that it is equivalent to that process in all CSP models, but is not always strongly bisimilar to it.

In Chap. 11 of TPC, this approach was taken for the failures-divergences model $\mathcal{N}$ alone. In $\mathcal{N}$, every program that cannot communicate $\checkmark$ on its first step is equivalent to one which is in one of the two forms **div** or $\sqcap\{?x : A_i \to P(i, x) \mid i \in S\}$ for S non-empty. The AOS form (there called head normal form) used in TPC is based on that observation.

---
[1] An amazing proportion of the 'laws' stated in [56] are false, and it is possible to find many distinct combinations which prove all processes equal. Some of the laws given in that book make even less sense than simply being false: for example '$P \parallel Q \wedge Q \parallel R \Rightarrow P \parallel R$' which is trivially ill-typed since processes are not truth values.

Consider the program $UA = (a \rightarrow P \ \Box \ b \rightarrow c \rightarrow Q) \setminus \{b\}$. It certainly has the trace $\langle a \rangle$, and certainly cannot diverge after the empty trace. If this program were equivalent to one in the above form, we can conclude that $a \in A_i$ for some $i \in S$. This cannot happen in the revivals models $\mathcal{R}$ and $\mathcal{R}^{\Downarrow}$. This is because, if $a \in A$, the revival $(\langle \rangle, \emptyset, a)$ belongs to $?x : A \rightarrow P(x)$, but it does not belong to UA. Since the revivals models are, thanks to the results of Sect. 11.3, contained in *all* models stronger than those based on failures, it follows that UA can only be transformed to the TPC AOS form in very few of the models that exist for CSP. We therefore conclude that the said form is too restrictive to be the core of an algebraic OS that is consistent with all behavioural CSP models.

The problem, of course, is that the initial action a only happens from an *unstable* state in UA: one that cannot give rise to a stable revival. This issue is the same as the one which forced us to adopt the symbol • in the refusal testing and acceptance traces models, to represent a non-final refusal or acceptance that was not observed.

It follows that whatever AOS form we choose to transform programs into for our algebraic OS, it needs to have a way of representing unstable visible events: ones that occur only from unstable states. This is because it has to be equivalent to the original program in all models, including those richer than $\mathcal{R}$. Note that the non-divergent nodes in the TPC form described above all have only τ actions or only visible actions.

We need a syntactic form equivalent in all CSP models to an operational state which has both τ and visible actions, including possibly $\checkmark$. Our solution to this problem is to use the sliding choice operator $\rhd$: the initial actions of $(?x : A \rightarrow P(x)) \rhd Q$ are $A \cup \{\tau\}$. Adding this form to the **div**, $?x : A \rightarrow P(x)$ and nondeterministic choice used in TPC allows us to represent nodes of the forms shown in Fig. 13.1.

Adding *SKIP* as an allowed constant process in AOS form (along with **div**) permits us to represent, via $(?x : A \rightarrow P(x)) \rhd SKIP$, and $(?x : A \rightarrow P(x)) \rhd (SKIP \sqcap Q)$, processes $\mathcal{FL}^{\sharp}$-equivalent to ones that have $\checkmark$ amongst their initial actions. These particular forms do not have $\checkmark$ amongst their initial actions, instead allowing the τ of $\rhd$ and perhaps that of $\sqcap$ to commit to *SKIP*. To understand why this is a valid representation, think of the law $P = P; SKIP$ ($\langle ;$-unit-r$\rangle$ (7.1)) which says that any process is equivalent (in all CSP models) to the process in which each $\checkmark$ action is replaced by a τ to a state with only a $\checkmark$.

In formally defining AOS form we generalise the binary nondeterministic choice $Q \sqcap R$ to choice over an arbitrary non-empty finite set S. We therefore say that a process is in AOS form if it is **div**, *SKIP* or takes one of the forms $\sqcap S$, $?x : A \rightarrow P(x)$

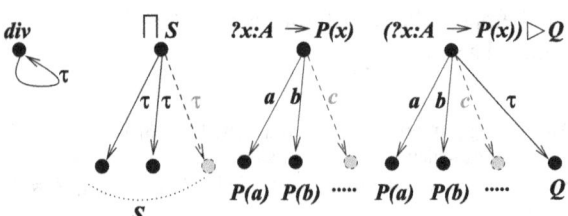

Fig. 13.1 LTSs of AOS nodes other than *SKIP*

and $(?x : A \to P(x)) \rhd Q$ where all $P(x)$, Q and all members of S are themselves in AOS form. We will see shortly how every finite CSP program is equivalent to one in this form with respect to every linear observation CSP model discussed in Chaps. 11 and 12.

The operational semantics of finite CSP programs, as defined above, all have the following properties:

- They have a finite number of nodes (states).
- The only cycles are trivial ones caused by the presence of **div** in the syntax of the node: a τ action from a state to itself. [Such nodes can have other actions apart from these τs.]

We can transform such LTSs into ones equivalent to AOS form by the following procedure:

1. If a node is divergent in the way detailed above and it has any further actions, then the self loop is replaced by a τ action to the simply divergent process **div**.[2]
2. If a node has a $\checkmark$ action and it has any further actions, then the $\checkmark$ is replaced by a τ action to *SKIP*.
3. If a node n has multiple actions with any label x, and the node has any action labelled a from Σ (whether or not $x = a$), then all the x actions are replaced by a single x to a node that has τs to all the targets of n's x-actions.

None of these transformations ever changes a node's value in any linear observation model. We can therefore conclude both that every finite CSP program is equivalent to one in AOS form, and furthermore that this can actually be derived directly from its standard operational semantics. This is because, after applying the above transformations to any LTS derived from a finite CSP program, it is trivial to translate the result into an AOS form with exactly these operational semantics.

Example 13.1 Consider the finite program *PB*, where

$$PB = Q \,\triangle\, (b \to (SKIP \,\Box\, \textbf{div}))$$

$$Q = (a \to STOP) \sqcap (b \to (\textbf{div} \,\Box\, a \to STOP))$$

This is deliberately contrived so that it contains different examples of the transformations discussed above. Its LTS operational semantics is illustrated in Fig. 13.2. Two of its nodes have multiple actions with the same label: the initial node has two τs and the node equivalent to $(b \to a \to STOP) \,\triangle\, (b \to \textbf{div})$ has two bs. Fig. 13.3 shows the effect of introducing two extra nodes as described above (labelled A) and introducing τ actions into the nodes labelled B and C to split off divergence and a *SKIP*.

---

[2]The fact that this transformation preserves equivalence over all our CSP models gives an interesting insight into the way in which the models without strict divergence treat **div**.

Fig. 13.2 LTS of *PB*

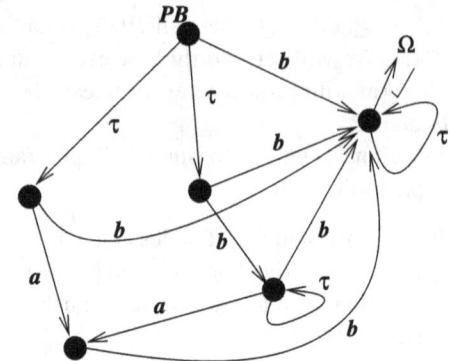

Fig. 13.3 LTS of *PB* after transformation

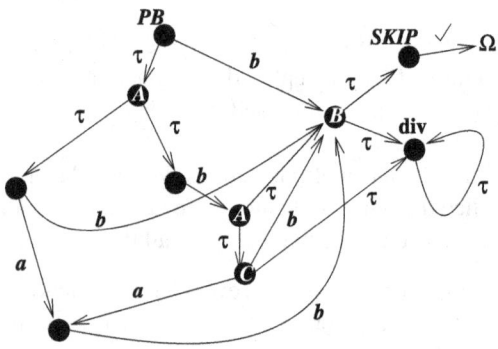

The AOS form derived from this second figure is:

$$PB = (b \rightarrow B) \rhd A1$$
$$B = SKIP \sqcap \mathbf{div}$$
$$A1 = P1 \sqcap P2$$
$$P1 = (a \rightarrow P3) \,\Box\, (b \rightarrow B)$$
$$P2 = b \rightarrow A2$$
$$P3 = b \rightarrow B$$
$$A2 = B \sqcap C$$
$$C = (a \rightarrow P3 \,\Box\, b \rightarrow B) \rhd \mathbf{div}$$

where $?x : \{a, b\} \rightarrow P(x)$ has been written $(a \rightarrow P(a)) \,\Box\, (b \rightarrow P(b))$.

In the next section we will see that an AOS form for every finite program can be derived by applying an algebraic reduction strategy which to some extent is based on the operational semantics.

13.3 Algebraic Operational Semantics

While the discussion above shows the close connection between AOS form and operational semantics, it is not what we mean by an algebraic operational semantics. For this we need to be able to reduce an arbitrary finite CSP program into AOS form using a systematic procedure based on laws true in all models. The laws we use will be a mixture of the ones introduced in Part I and ones we introduce here. Most of the latter will be ones devoted to understanding how the various operators of CSP interact with the unstable actions introduced by $\rhd$.

Of course the processes **div** and *SKIP* do not need to be reduced to AOS form, because they are already in it. Thanks to $\langle STOP$-step$\rangle$ (2.15), *STOP* reduces to $?x : \emptyset \to$ **div** (where what follows the prefix is immaterial). To reduce a program of the form $?x : A \to P(x)$ all we need to do is to reduce each of the $P(x)$s. If our program has the form $(?x : A \to P(x)) \rhd Q$ we need to reduce the $P(x)$ and Q. Similarly for all $P \in S$ in $\sqcap S$. Bear in mind that, thanks to the assumptions we made earlier, S and A here are finite.

The rest of the procedure has similarities to the more traditional operational semantics seen in Chap. 9. We need a way of computing the first-step behaviour (in our case the top-level structure of the AOS form) of the result of applying any other operator in terms of the first-step behaviour of its **on** arguments.[3]

Apart from handling termination, all of this work in TPC was done by the laws of distributivity, the *step* laws for handling arguments of the form $?x : A \to P(x)$ and divergence strictness laws for **div** (bearing in mind that we were concentrating on the divergence-strict model $\mathcal{N}$).

The situation is a little more complex in the general setting we present here. This is both because we can no longer rely on divergence strictness and because we have to deal with arguments of the form $(?x : A \to P(x)) \rhd Q$.

As an example, let us consider the operator $P \setminus X$. Since its argument is **on**, we need to be able to handle all cases P can give when reduced to AOS form. The easiest case (and this applies to all operators) is when it is a nondeterministic choice, since then we can apply the distributive law.[4] So $(P_1 \sqcap P_2) \setminus X$ is reduced to $(P_1 \setminus X) \sqcap (P_2 \setminus X)$. This gives the top-level behaviour; to get the next level the processes $P_1 \setminus X$ and $P_2 \setminus X$ are reduced recursively.

The next case is when $P = ?x : A \to P(x)$. Then the relevant step law ($\langle$hide-step$\rangle$ (5.6)) always computes something of the correct form, here

$$?x : A \to (P(x) \setminus X)$$

if $A \cap X = \emptyset$ and otherwise

$$(?x : A \setminus X \to (P(x) \setminus X)) \rhd (\sqcap \{P(x) \setminus X \mid x \in A \cap X\})$$

---

[3] See Chap. 9.

[4] Because all standard CSP operators other than recursion are fully distributive, we have not enumerated all such laws in this book.

We need a law each to handle the AOS form cases of *SKIP* and **div**. For hiding these are very simple:

$$SKIP \setminus X = SKIP \qquad\qquad \langle SKIP\text{-hide-Id}\rangle \quad (13.1)$$

$$\mathbf{div} \setminus X = \mathbf{div} \qquad\qquad \langle\text{hide-zero}\rangle \quad (13.2)$$

Finally, we need a law to handle the case of $P = (?x : A \to P(x)) \rhd Q$. The laws required for this form are a new class, not given in TPC, needed to understand how CSP operators handle unstable actions of the form discussed above. We can calculate the law of this form for hiding from the operational semantics of $((?x : A \to P(x)) \rhd Q) \setminus X$. This process certainly has an initial τ action (the one from $\rhd$) and more if $X \cap A \neq \emptyset$. It therefore always makes sense to express this process in the form $(?x : B \to R(x)) \rhd R'$:

$$((?x : A \to P) \rhd Q) \setminus X$$
$$= (?x : A \setminus X \to (P \setminus X))$$
$$\rhd \sqcap(\{Q \setminus X\} \cup \{P[a/x] \setminus X \mid a \in X \cap A\}) \qquad \langle \setminus X\text{-slide}\rangle \quad (13.3)$$

Note how in each of these cases we have revealed the initial actions and options of $P \setminus X$ by applying an algebraic transformation that depends on which of the five types of AOS form P takes.

Precisely the same approach works in each other case of an operator with a single **on** argument. The distributive laws all follow exactly the same pattern, and all the step laws were provided in Part I of this book. The laws for *SKIP*, **div** and the "slide" laws for the relevant operators are collected below:

$$SKIP[\![R]\!] = SKIP \qquad\qquad \langle SKIP\text{-}[\![R]\!]\text{-Id}\rangle \quad (13.4)$$

$$\mathbf{div}[\![R]\!] = \mathbf{div} \qquad\qquad \langle \mathbf{div}\text{-}[\![R]\!]\text{-Id}\rangle \quad (13.5)$$

$$((?x : A \to P) \rhd Q)[\![R]\!]$$
$$= (?y : R(A) \to \sqcap\{P[a/x][\![R]\!] \mid a \in A \wedge a\, R\, y\}) \rhd (Q[\![R]\!])$$
$$\langle [\![R]\!]\text{-slide}\rangle \quad (13.6)$$

$$SKIP; P = P \qquad\qquad \langle ;\text{-unit-l}\rangle \quad (7.2)$$

$$\mathbf{div}; P = \mathbf{div} \qquad\qquad \langle ;\text{-zero-l}\rangle \quad (13.7)$$

$$((?x : A \to P) \rhd P'); Q = (?x : A \to (P; Q)) \rhd (P'; Q) \quad [x \notin fv(Q)]$$
$$\langle ;\text{-slide}\rangle \quad (13.8)$$

$$SKIP \Theta_A P = SKIP \qquad\qquad \langle \Theta_A\text{-termination}\rangle \quad (13.9)$$

$$\mathbf{div}\Theta_A P = \mathbf{div} \qquad\qquad\qquad \langle \Theta_A\text{-zero}\rangle \quad (13.10)$$

$$((?x : A \to P) \rhd P') \Theta_B Q$$
$$= (?x : A \to (Q \mathbin{\ast} x \in B \mathbin{\ast} (P \Theta_B Q)))$$
$$\rhd (P' \Theta_B Q) \quad [x \notin fv(Q)] \qquad\qquad \langle \Theta_B\text{-slide}\rangle \quad (13.11)$$

The final instance of an operator with a single *on* argument is $\rhd$. The case when this (the left-hand) argument is $?x : A \to P(x)$ is already in AOS form. The case where it is $(?x : A \to P(x)) \rhd Q$ is covered by the associative law of $\rhd$, and we need laws to cover the cases of **div** and *SKIP*:

$$P \rhd (Q \rhd R) = (P \rhd Q) \rhd R \qquad\qquad \langle\rhd\text{-assoc}\rangle \quad (13.12)$$

$$\mathbf{div} \rhd Q = \mathbf{div} \sqcap Q \qquad\qquad\qquad \langle\mathbf{div}\text{-slide}\rangle \quad (13.13)$$

$$SKIP \rhd Q = SKIP \sqcap Q \qquad\qquad\qquad \langle SKIP\text{-slide}\rangle \quad (13.14)$$

The situation with those operators with two **on** arguments (namely $\square$, $\underset{X}{\|}$ and $\triangle$) is more complex, simply because instead of 5 options for each there are now 25: one for each way the two arguments can take each of the 5 sorts of AOS form.[5]

If we wanted fully to reflect, algebraically, the first step behaviour of each operator so that it essentially agreed with the standard operational semantics, we would need laws that calculate, for example, the initial visible actions of the combinations $(?x : A \to P(x)) \triangle (Q \sqcap R)$ and $(?x : A \to P(x)) \underset{B}{\|} (Q \sqcap R)$ when $A \not\subseteq B$. In each of these cases the combination can perform an initial visible action and defer the resolution of the nondeterministic choice by at least one step.

We can, however, get away with a smaller set of, on average, simpler laws if we are prepared to reduce each combination in a way that might give a smaller set of initial actions but still gives an AOS form equivalent to the original finite program. So whenever one of the arguments is a nondeterministic choice we can always use the appropriate distributive law and give the result process only initial τ actions. Thus the first step of the reductions of the two examples above will respectively give

$$((?x : A \to P(x)) \triangle Q) \sqcap ((?x : A \to P(x)) \triangle R)$$
$$((?x : A \to P(x)) \underset{B}{\|} Q) \sqcap ((?x : A \to P(x)) \underset{B}{\|} R)$$

In each case the initial visible actions arising from the left-hand argument are still possible, but deferred behind the τs of the nondeterministic choice.

---

[5]In the case of the symmetric operators $\square$ and $\underset{X}{\|}$ this reduces to 15 essentially different pairings.

We will use this strategy in every case where one of the two arguments is a nondeterministic choice. The case where both are prefix-choices $?x : A \rightarrow P(x)$ and $?x : B \rightarrow Q(x)$ is always handled by the step law.

The remainder of the reduction strategy for $\square$ uses the following three laws and their symmetric counterparts. The first says that $\triangleright$ and $\square$ have an associative property.

$$(P \triangleright P') \,\square\, Q = P \triangleright (P' \,\square\, Q) \qquad\qquad \langle\square\text{-slide}\rangle \quad (13.15)$$

This is used to reduce the remaining cases where either argument of $\square$ takes the form $(?x : A \rightarrow P(x)) \triangleright P'$.

The second and third laws allow us to reduce the remaining cases where one of the arguments of $\square$ is $?x : A \rightarrow P(x)$ and the other is **div** or *SKIP*.

$$P \,\square\, \mathbf{div} = P \triangleright \mathbf{div} \qquad\qquad \langle\square\text{-}\mathbf{div}\rangle \quad (13.16)$$

$$P \,\square\, SKIP = P \triangleright SKIP \qquad\qquad \langle\square\text{-}SKIP \text{ resolve}\rangle \quad (13.17)$$

The intuition behind these two laws is that if a process has the capability of diverging or terminating immediately, then there is nothing that the environment can do to prevent it: the process can just take the respective option nondeterministically.

The only remaining cases we have to consider for $P \,\square\, Q$ are those where both arguments are **div** or *SKIP*. These are reduced using the principles:

$$SKIP \,\square\, SKIP = SKIP$$

$$\mathbf{div} \,\square\, \mathbf{div} = \mathbf{div}$$

which are provable using the laws above, the idempotence principle of $\triangleright$:

$$P \triangleright P = P \qquad\qquad \langle\triangleright\text{-id}\rangle \quad (13.18)$$

and the following law

$$\mathbf{div} \,\square\, SKIP = \mathbf{div} \sqcap SKIP \qquad\qquad \langle\square\text{-}\mathbf{div}\text{-}SKIP\text{-red}\rangle \quad (13.19)$$

Note that the first two of these identities can be replaced by $\langle\square\text{-idem}^*\rangle$ (2.1) in those models where it is true.

We can organise the strategy for $\square$ into the table shown in Fig. 13.4: this represents the transformation to carry out on $P \,\square\, Q$ when P and Q take the forms indicated. Only the part of the table on or above the diagonal is populated because $\square$ is symmetric. The top row of this table displays the options for Q, and the left column the options for P.

We can collect the laws for $P \parallel_X Q$ into the similar table in Fig. 13.5. More, and more complex laws are required to handle cases of $((?x : A \rightarrow P(x)) \triangleright P') \parallel_X Q$ than for $\square$. The reason for this is that Q might perform a visible action and leave

$P \Box Q$	$\sqcap S_Q \overset{(?x:B \to Q(x))}{\triangleright Q'}$	$?x:B \to Q(x)$	**div**	*SKIP*
$\sqcap S_P$	Distributive law			
$(?x:A \to P(x)) \triangleright P'$		$(?x:A \to P(x)) \triangleright (P' \Box Q)$		
$?x:A \to P(x)$		$\langle\Box\text{-step}\rangle$ (2.14)	$(?x:A \to P(x)) \triangleright \textbf{div}$	$(?x:A \to P(x)) \triangleright \textit{SKIP}$
div			**div**	$\textbf{div} \sqcap \textit{SKIP}$
SKIP				*SKIP*

Fig. 13.4 The reduction strategy for $P \Box Q$

$P \parallel_C Q$	$\sqcap S_Q \overset{(?x:B \to Q(x))}{\triangleright Q'}$	$?x:B \to Q(x)$	**div**	*SKIP*
$\sqcap S_P$	Distributive law			
$(?x:A \to P(x)) \triangleright P'$	$?x:(A \cup B)\backslash C \cup (A \cap B \cap C) \to (P(x) \parallel_C Q(x)) \ {+}x \in C{+} \ (P(x) \parallel_C Q) \ {+}x \in A{+} \ P \parallel_C Q(x))) \triangleright (P' \parallel_C Q \sqcap P \parallel_C Q')$	$?x:(A \cup B)\backslash C \cup (A \cap B \cap C) \to (P(x) \parallel_C Q(x)) \ {+}x \in C{+} \ (P(x) \parallel_C Q) \ {+}x \in A{+} \ P \parallel_C Q(x))) \triangleright P' \parallel_C Q$	$?x:A\backslash C \to P(x) \parallel_C \textbf{div} \triangleright P' \parallel_C \textbf{div}$	$?x:A\backslash C \to P(x) \parallel_C \textit{SKIP} \triangleright P' \parallel_C \textit{SKIP}$
$?x:A \to P(x)$		$\langle\Box\text{-step}\rangle$ (2.14)	$(?x:A\backslash C \to P(x) \parallel_C \textbf{div}) \triangleright \textbf{div}$	$?x:A\backslash C \to P(x) \parallel_C \textit{SKIP}$
div			**div**	**div**
SKIP				*SKIP*

Fig. 13.5 The reduction strategy for generalised parallel

the $\triangleright$ choice within P unresolved until a subsequent action, something not possible in $P \Box Q$.

The required laws can be calculated from the operational semantics.

Since $\triangle$ is not symmetric, we need to populate its entire table: see Fig. 13.6.

Example 13.2 It is this last table that we need to reduce the process PB (p. 297) to AOS form. Note that the processes on either side of the top-level $\triangle$ are themselves

$P \triangle Q$	$\sqcap S_Q \dfrac{(?x : B \to Q(x))}{\triangleright Q'}$	$?x : B \to Q(x)$	**div**	*SKIP*
$\sqcap S_P$	Distributive laws			
$(?x : A \to P(x))$ $\triangleright P'$	$(?x : A \to (P(x) \triangle Q)) \triangleright (P' \triangle Q)$			
$?x : A \to P(x)$	$(?x : A \cup B \to$ $(P(x) \triangle Q$ $\sqcap Q(x))$ $\llcorner x \in A \cap B \lrcorner$ $(P(x) \triangle Q$ $\llcorner x \in A \lrcorner$ $Q(x)))$ $\triangleright$ $P \triangle Q'$	$\langle \triangle\text{-step} \rangle$ (7.5)	$?x : A \to$ $(P(x) \triangle \textbf{div})$ $\triangleright \textbf{div}$	$?x : A \to$ $(P(x) \triangle SKIP)$ $\triangleright SKIP$
div	$\textbf{div} \sqcap Q$			
SKIP	$SKIP \sqcap Q$			

Fig. 13.6 The reduction strategy for $P \triangle Q$

in AOS form and the one on the left is a nondeterministic choice. It follows that the reduction strategy in the table above first reduces PB to the nondeterministic composition of the following two processes

$$PB1 = (a \to STOP) \triangle P3$$

$$PB2 = (b \to (\textbf{div} \,\square\, a \to STOP)) \triangle P3$$

where $P3 = b \to (SKIP \sqcap \textbf{div})$ as above. These can both of the be reduced by $\langle \triangle\text{-step} \rangle$ (7.5), and the reductions give

$$PB1' = a \to (STOP \triangle P3) \,\square\, b \to (SKIP \sqcap \textbf{div})$$

$$PB2' = b \to (((\textbf{div} \,\square\, a \to STOP) \triangle P3) \sqcap (SKIP \sqcap \textbf{div}))$$

The step law is applied to $STOP \triangle (b \to (SKIP \sqcap \textbf{div}))$ to give $b \to (SKIP \sqcap \textbf{div})$, so the derived AOS form of $PB1$ is

$$(a \to ((b \to (SKIP \sqcap \textbf{div}))) \,\square\, (b \to (SKIP \sqcap \textbf{div}))$$

Turning to $PB2$, we can apply the $\square$ table to $\textbf{div} \,\square\, a \to STOP$ to obtain its AOS form $(a \to STOP) \triangleright \textbf{div}$. So $PB2'$ equals

$$b \to ((((a \to STOP) \triangleright \textbf{div}) \triangle P3) \sqcap (SKIP \sqcap \textbf{div}))$$

Applying the $\triangle$ table to $((a \to STOP) \triangleright \textbf{div}) \triangle (b \to (SKIP \sqcap \textbf{div}))$ then gives

$$(a \to (STOP \triangle P3)) \triangleright (P3 \triangleright \textbf{div})$$

Fig. 13.7 LTS of *PB* after
algebraic transformation to
AOS form

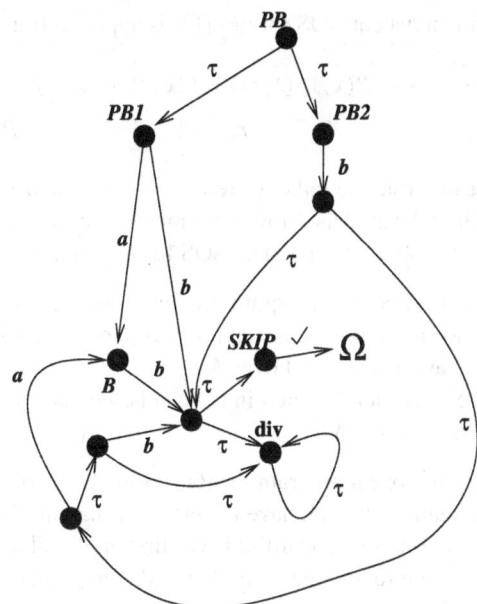

which reduces in one further step to the AOS form

$$(a \rightarrow P3) \rhd (P3 \rhd \textbf{div})$$

We can therefore collect together the derived AOS form of *PB2* as

$$b \rightarrow (((a \rightarrow P3) \rhd (P3 \rhd \textbf{div}))$$
$$\sqcap (SKIP \sqcap \textbf{div}))$$

The conventional operational semantics for this algebraically derived AOS form for
PB is shown in Fig. 13.7, which should be compared with Fig. 13.2, *PB*'s original
operational semantics.

We have gained a new perspective on operational semantics in this section, but it
is reasonable to conclude that the algebraic style of operational semantics is a good
deal more complex to present because instead of being able to deal with argument
processes an action at a time (and τ actions implicitly) we now have to deal with
multiple cases for their top level structure.

13.4 Normal Forms

Just like the LTS representations it is based on, converting two programs to AOS
form does not give us a way of deciding if they are equivalent or not in any CSP
model. This is because, even in the most discriminating models, any program has

many inequivalent AOS forms. This is apparent from the laws

$$?x : A \rightarrow (P(x) \sqcap Q(x)) = (?x : A \rightarrow P(x)) \sqcap (?x : A \rightarrow Q(x)) \quad \text{and}$$

$$P = (?x : \emptyset \rightarrow \mathbf{div}) \rhd P$$

quite aside from the rather different Figs. 13.3 and 13.7.

Each of the models $\mathcal{M}$ we have mentioned earlier in this book has a *normal form*, namely a restricted version of AOS form with the following properties:

(1) Every AOS form program is equivalent to one in normal form, over $\mathcal{M}$.
(2) If two normal form programs have more than trivial syntactic differences then they are inequivalent over $\mathcal{M}$.
(3) The equivalence stated in (1) can be proved by algebraic transformation using laws valid for $\mathcal{M}$.

We can move a program in AOS form closer to a normal form by the following transformations that all have the effect of making the way a particular behaviour is represented more standardised. We first apply all the transformations below to all the syntax up to and including the first communication $?x : A \rightarrow P(x)$, in order to standardise the process's syntax up to its first communication.

- Firstly, all nondeterministic composition which occurs syntactically outside first-step communications is moved to the top level using the right distributive law of $\rhd$, and combined into a single nondeterministic choice using the associative property of $\sqcap$:

$$\sqcap(S \cup \{\sqcap T\}) = \sqcap(S \cup T) \qquad\qquad \langle\sqcap\text{-assoc}\rangle \;\; (13.20)$$

- Each subterm of the form $?x : A \rightarrow P(x)$, representing first visible step communication, that is not a left-hand argument of $\rhd$ is converted to $(?x : A \rightarrow P(x)) \rhd (?x : A \rightarrow P(x))$ using the law $\langle\rhd\text{-id}\rangle$ (13.18).
- Any subterm P' of the form $SKIP$ or $\mathbf{div}$ is converted to $(?x : \emptyset \rightarrow \mathbf{div}) \rhd P'$ using the laws $\langle STOP\text{-step}\rangle$ (2.15), $\langle\Box\text{-unit}\rangle$ (2.16) and $\langle\Box\text{-}SKIP \text{ resolve}\rangle$ (13.17) or $\langle\Box\text{-}\mathbf{div}\rangle$ (13.16).
- The top-level choice $\sqcap S$ now consists of terms of the form $(?x : A \rightarrow P(x)) \rhd P'$ where P' is either of this same form or is $SKIP$, $\mathbf{div}$ or $?x : A' \rightarrow P'(x)$. We eliminate the first of these cases by (possibly repeated) use of the law

$$(?x : A \rightarrow P(x)) \rhd (?x : B \rightarrow Q(x)) \rhd R$$
$$=?x : A \cup B \rightarrow$$
$$((P(x) \sqcap Q(x)) \mathbin{\triangleleft} x \in A \cap B \mathbin{\triangleright} (P(x) \mathbin{\triangleleft} a \in A \mathbin{\triangleright} Q(x)))$$
$$\rhd R \qquad\qquad\qquad \langle\rhd\text{-combine}\rangle \;\; (13.21)$$

so that now all members of the nondeterministic choice that are not $(?x : A_i \rightarrow P_i(x)) \rhd SKIP$ and $(?x : A_i \rightarrow P_i(x)) \rhd \mathbf{div}$ take the form $(?x : A_i \rightarrow P_i(x)) \rhd P'$, with $P_i' = (?x : A_i' \to P_i'(x))$. By our construction $A_i' \subseteq A_i$ and $P_i(x) \sqsubseteq P_i'(x)$ for $x \in A_i'$.

- The laws

$$((?x : A \to P(x)) \rhd P') \sqcap Q = (?x : A \to P(x)) \rhd (P' \sqcap Q)$$

$$\langle \rhd\text{-}\sqcap\text{-ext} \rangle \quad (13.22)$$

and $\langle \rhd\text{-combine} \rangle$ (13.21), plus standard laws of nondeterministic choice enable us to convert our program of the form described above into

$$(?x : \textstyle\bigcup_{i=1}^{n} A_i \to \sqcap \{P_i(x) \mid x \in A_i\}) \rhd \sqcap S'$$

where S' is the set of all processes P_i' appearing as the second argument of $\rhd$ before this final transformation. S' therefore consists of a non-empty set of processes all of which are *SKIP*, **div**, or the $?x : A' \to P'(x)$ discussed above.

- If any pair of the latter have $A_i' = A_j'$ then they can be reduced to one by $\langle$input-dist$\rangle$ (2.11).

Then, having performed this standardisation on the first-step behaviour, we carry on by recursively standardising the behaviours of all the $P(x)$ and $P_i(x)$. This procedure will certainly terminate since there is an upper bound on the lengths of trace in a finite program, and will result in a program in the following form:

Definition 13.1 An AOS form program is said to be in linear normal form (*LNF*) if it takes the form defined above for its first step behaviour, and furthermore all the processes $P(x)$ and $P_i(x)$ are themselves in LNF.

Example 13.3 We can see in Fig. 13.8 the effect of the first-step transformation on the LTS of Fig. 13.7. The unstandardised part relevant to later steps is shaded. Note, for example, that the initial node T is of the form $(?x : \{a, b\} \to P(x)) \rhd P'$.

Completing the transformation of the process *PB* to LNF gives the following process:

$$PBNF = (a \to PBNF1 \,\square\, b \to PBNF2)$$
$$\rhd ((a \to PBNF1 \,\square\, b \to PBNF2) \sqcap (b \to PBNF2))$$

$$PBNF1 = (b \to PBNF3) \rhd (b \to PBNF3)$$

$$PBNF2 = (a \to PBNF1 \,\square\, b \to PBNF3)$$
$$\rhd (SKIP \sqcap \mathbf{div})$$

$$PBNF3 = (?x : \emptyset \to \mathbf{div}) \rhd (SKIP \sqcap \mathbf{div})$$

For the human reader it is clearer if we remove the unnecessary $\rhd$ operators from three of these four states, provided we broaden the definition of LNF (and the cor-

Fig. 13.8 Result of applying
algebraic standardisation to
first step of Fig. 13.7

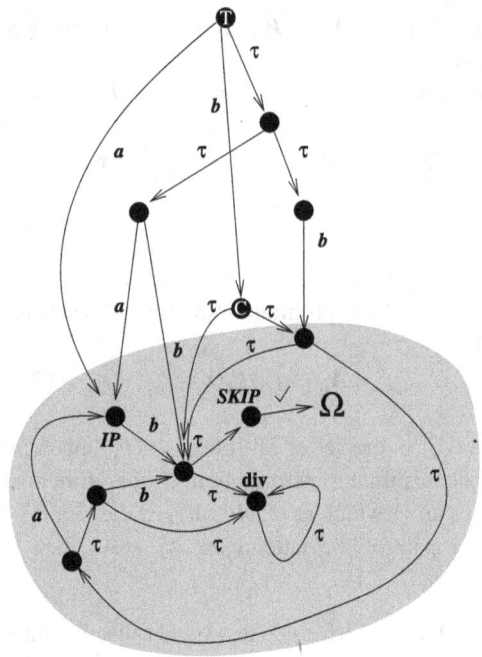

responding idea of trivial syntactic equivalence) a little:

$$PBNF = (a \to PBNF1 \,\square\, b \to PBNF2) \sqcap (b \to PBNF2)$$

$$PBNF1 = b \to PBNF3$$

$$PBNF2 = (a \to PBNF1 \,\square\, b \to PBNF3)$$
$$\quad\quad \triangleright (SKIP \sqcap \textbf{div})$$

$$PBNF3 = SKIP \sqcap \textbf{div}$$

This simply says that PB is a process that initially makes the stable offer of $\{a, b\}$
or $\{b\}$. If a is accepted then subsequently it stably offers b and then either diverges
or terminates.

If b is accepted (which could come from either side of $\triangle$) then the process can
immediately diverge or terminate, but it can also communicate a or b (but not stably
offer either), *and so on...*

The interesting thing about this is that LNF is the normal form for the finest CSP
model, $\mathcal{FL}^{\#}$. (This explains the use of the word *linear* in its name.) This is easily
proved by using the following result recursively through a LNF program's branching
structure.

Lemma 13.1 *Suppose that the two programs* $(?x : A \to P(x)) \triangleright \sqcap_{i=1}^{n} P_i$ *and*
$(?x : B \to Q(x)) \to \sqcap_{i=1}^{m} Q_i$ *are both in LNF and are equivalent in the model* $\mathcal{FL}^{\#}$.
Then

(a) $A = B$ and, for all $x \in A$, $P(x)$ is equivalent to $Q(x)$ in $\mathcal{FL}^\sharp$.
(b) $n = m$ and there is a permutation π of $\{1 \ldots n\}$ such that, for all $i \in \{1 \ldots n\}$, P_i and $Q_{\pi(i)}$ are equivalent in $\mathcal{FL}^\sharp$.

Proof $A = B$ follows by construction, since the set A of the LNF P is $\{a \in \Sigma \mid \langle \bullet, a, \bullet \rangle \in \mathcal{FL}^\sharp[\![P]\!]\}$, the set of all P's FL^*-behaviours and its representation in $\mathcal{FL}^\sharp$.

Because $a \in A_i$ implies that $P_i(x) \sqsupseteq P(x)$ in the syntactic sense described above, the same relation holds in every CSP model including $\mathcal{FL}^\sharp$. It follows that

$$\{s \mid \langle \bullet, a \rangle ^\frown s \in \mathcal{FL}^\sharp[\![P]\!]\} = \mathcal{FL}^\sharp[\![P(a)]\!]$$

and therefore that $P(x)$ and $Q(x)$ are equivalent in $\mathcal{FL}^\sharp$. This completes the proof of (a).

For (b), it is clear that the P_i and Q_i each contains *SKIP* (respectively **div**) if and only if the value in $\mathcal{FL}^\sharp$ contains the behaviour $\langle \Uparrow \rangle$ (respectively $\langle \bullet, \checkmark \rangle$), and therefore if and only if the other does. It is also clear that these sets of processes contain one of the form $?x : C \to R(x)$ if and only if $\langle C \rangle$ (i.e. the observation that the process can be stable on the empty trace and offer C) belongs to this same value, and that then (by the construction above) each contains exactly one. We can conclude that $m = n$ and that there is a unique permutation π on $\{1 \ldots n\}$ such that

- $Q_{\pi(i)}$ is *SKIP* if and only if P_i is.
- $Q_{\pi(i)}$ is **div** if and only if P_i is.
- $Q_{\pi(i)}$ takes the form $?x : A \to R(x)$ if and only if P_i does, for the same A.

In the last case we can conclude that the two $R(x)$s are equivalent in $\mathcal{FL}^\sharp$ for all $x \in A$ since each has exactly the observations

$$\{s \mid \langle A, x \rangle ^\frown s \in \mathcal{FL}^\sharp[\![P]\!]\}$$

This completes the proof of (b). □

What this means is that we have demonstrated a way of transforming any finite CSP program into a normal form for $\mathcal{FL}^\sharp$, and therefore found a way of deciding the equivalence of such programs algebraically.

13.5 A Tour through the Hierarchy

Linear normal form removes all uncertainty about how a program branches as it evolves, relative to the set of FL^*-behaviours that a process has.

- All nondeterministic choice $\sqcap$ is between processes that can be seen to be different on their very first steps, either because they have different sets of initial actions or are *SKIP* or **div**. Thus all branching that can be deferred is deferred.

- By ensuring that *all* actions from Σ can be taken unstably as well as perhaps stably, we have fixed the principle (discussed on p. 255) that we cannot observe positively that a state was unstable when one of its visible actions occurred.

The normal form for every other standard model is just a restricted form of LNF: in other words the other normal forms are LNF programs with additional constraints. While the transformation to LNF from an arbitrary finite process is quite complex, it is remarkably simple to characterise the difference between the standard models in terms of variations on this normal form and a few extra laws.

   For example,

- The normal form for the divergence-strict model $\mathcal{FL}^{\Downarrow}$ is the same as LNF except that instead of allowing **div** as an option in the nondeterministic choices, it becomes an alternative to such choices. The LNF of any finite program can be transformed to the $\mathcal{FL}^{\Downarrow}$ one by applying the law

$$\mathbf{div} \sqcap P = \mathbf{div} \qquad\qquad \langle\sqcap\text{-zero}^{\Downarrow}\rangle \ (13.23)$$

   which holds in all divergence-strict models and no other (as the notation here indicates).
- For the divergence-ignoring model $\mathcal{FL}$ (which is based on finite observations only), we can use the law

$$P \sqcap \mathbf{div} = P \qquad\qquad \langle\sqcap\text{-unit}^{*}\rangle \ (13.24)$$

   which holds precisely in finite-behaviour models, to transform to a $\mathcal{FL}$-normal form in which **div** is present in *all* nondeterministic choices.[6]

Furthermore it is clear that these two laws will make the difference between $\mathcal{M}^{\sharp}$ and respectively $\mathcal{M}^{\Downarrow}$ and $\mathcal{M}$ for any finite-behaviour model $\mathcal{M}$. See Exercise 13.3.

   The model $\mathcal{FL}$, of course, is based on acceptance traces. Two of our standard models simplify it without any other standard models in between, namely $\mathcal{RT}$ based on refusal traces and $\mathcal{A}$ based on pairs (s, A) where A is an acceptance set or $\bullet$, and s a trace.

   The law that characterises the difference between $\mathcal{RT}$ and $\mathcal{FL}$ is $\langle\Box\text{-idem}^{*}\rangle$ (2.1): $P = P \Box P$. This law is easily seen to be true over the first of these models, but it is not over $\mathcal{FL}$ and even $\mathcal{A}$: the process $P = a \rightarrow STOP \sqcap b \rightarrow STOP$ does not have the $\mathcal{FL}$ observation $\langle\{a, b\}\rangle$, but $P \Box P$ does.

   If we take any process

$$P = P^1 = (?x : A \rightarrow P(x)) \rhd \textstyle\prod(\{?x : A_i \rightarrow P_i(x) \mid i \in \{1 \dots m\}\} \cup S)$$

with $S \subseteq \{\mathbf{div}, SKIP\}$ in LNF over a finite alphabet and apply this law once and then simplify using the laws of $\Box$ above and $\langle\rhd\text{-combine}\rangle$ (13.21), the result can be

---

[6]An alternative is only to have **div** in those choices with no other members.

written

$$P^2 = (?x : A \rightarrow P(x))$$
$$\rhd \sqcap (\{?x : A_i \cup A_j \rightarrow P_{i,j}(x) \mid i \neq j\}$$
$$\cup \{?x : A_i \rightarrow P_i(x) \mid i \in \{1 \ldots m\}\} \cup S)$$

where $P_{i,j}(x) = P_i(x) \sqcap P_j(x)$ if $x \in A_i \cap A_j$ and otherwise $P_i(x)$ or $P_j(x)$ as appropriate. In other words, we now get a process with both the original acceptance sets of P and all pairwise unions. We can repeat this procedure again, calculating $P^3 = P^2 \,\square\, P^1$, $P^4 = P^3 \,\square\, P^1$ and so on until (at P^m) we have a process with every possible union of the A_i as an acceptance set. Of course some of the resulting acceptance sets may well be identical: just as in the original transformation to LNF we can use ⟨input-dist⟩ (2.11) to combine them.

And of course all these P^i are equivalent to P in any model, such as $\mathcal{RT}^\sharp$, where ⟨□-idem*⟩ (2.1) is true.

The result will take the form

$$P^* = (?x : A \rightarrow P(x)) \rhd \sqcap (\{?x : A_i^* \rightarrow P_i^*(x) \mid i \in \{1 \ldots n\}\} \cup S)$$

where $\{A_1^* \ldots A_n^*\}$ is an enumeration of the closure of $\{A_1, \ldots, A_m\}$ under $\cup$ (i.e. the smallest set that contains every A_i and $B \cup C$ for all members B and C), and each $P_i^*(x)$ is the nondeterministic composition of all those $P_j(x)$ such that $A_j \subset A_i^*$.

Note that whenever $A_i^* \supset A_j^*$ and $x \in A_j^*$ we get

$$P_j^*(x) \sqsupseteq P_i^*(x) \sqsupseteq P(x)$$

where the refinement holds in all models by the properties of LNF and the construction of the $P_j^*(x)$.

To complete the transformation to the $\mathcal{RT}^\sharp$ normal form, we simply apply the same transformation to each of the $P(x)$ and to each of the $P_i^*(x)$ after transforming the latter to LNF.

The conclusion of this is the following definition:

Definition 13.2 A program is in $\mathcal{RT}^\sharp$ normal form if it is in LNF, and every range of acceptance sets $\{?x : A_i \rightarrow P_i(x) \mid i \in \{1 \ldots m\}\}$ has the properties that $\{A_i \mid i \in \{1 \ldots m\}\}$ is closed under union, and $a \in A_j \subset A_i$ implies $P_i(x) \sqsubseteq P_j(x)$.

We have demonstrated that every finite program can be reduced to this form by the combination of laws true in all models plus ⟨□-idem*⟩ (2.1). It is not hard to show that two programs in this form which are different apart from the indexing of the A_i are semantically different in $\mathcal{RT}^\sharp$: see Exercise 13.5.

The normal forms for $\mathcal{RT}$ and $\mathcal{RT}^\Downarrow$ have exactly the same relationship to that of $\mathcal{RT}^\sharp$ as for the three $\mathcal{FL}$ models, using the same extra laws.

Example 13.4 The process PB that we have used for illustrative purposes so far in this chapter is only of limited use at this juncture, since actually its $\mathcal{RT}^\sharp$ normal form is the same as its LNF: the acceptance sets associated with each trace are already closed under union.

So consider the process

$$MT = (?x : \{a, b, c\} \rightarrow (STOP \sqcap a \rightarrow STOP)$$
$$\rhd ((a \rightarrow STOP) \sqcap (b \rightarrow STOP))$$

which is already, to all intents and purposes, in LNF.

Converting this into $\mathcal{RT}^\sharp$ normal form gives

$$MTRT = (?x : \{a, b, c\} \rightarrow (STOP \sqcap a \rightarrow STOP)$$
$$\rhd ((?x : \{a, b\} \rightarrow STOP) \sqcap (a \rightarrow STOP) \sqcap (b \rightarrow STOP))$$

where there is an additional acceptance set formed as the union of $\{a\}$ and $\{b\}$.

The difference between $\mathcal{RT}$ and $\mathcal{FL}$ (the rich-trace models), on the one hand, and $\mathcal{T}$, $\mathcal{F}$, $\mathcal{R}$ and $\mathcal{A}$ on the other, is that in the first group we are allowed to record refusals or acceptances at multiple points in a trace, whereas in the second group this sort of thing is only recorded at the end of a trace.

We can re-phrase this as follows: in the second group of models (the trace-plus models as defined in Chap. 11) it does not matter what might have been accepted or refused before some event a that has occurred. We can re-write this as the following law:

$$(?x : A \rightarrow P(x)) \rhd (?x : A \rightarrow Q(x))$$
$$= ?x : A \rightarrow (P(x) \sqcap Q(x)) \qquad\qquad \langle \rhd\text{-nohist}^* \rangle \ (13.25)$$

This law is true in all of the second group of models, and indeed can be said to characterise the idea of a trace-plus model.

In combination with other laws of $\rhd$ such as $\langle \rhd\text{-combine} \rangle$ (13.21), this law allows us to transform any program in LNF into one in which every $P_i(x)$ is the same as $P(x)$, so that the state we reach after any trace is independent of what acceptance sets we may have passed through.

This turns LNF into a normal form for the acceptance sets model $\mathcal{A}^\sharp$, and $\mathcal{RT}^\sharp$ normal form into a normal form for $\mathcal{R}^\sharp$, the revivals model in which we can see beyond divergence. Another way of looking at the normal forms for trace-plus models is as lists of what traces from Σ^* our finite program can perform, together with a record after each trace of whether it can terminate and/or diverge; plus either an arbitrary record of what sets of events can be accepted or, in the case of $\mathcal{R}$, a $\cup$-closed record.

Example 13.5 Returning to the process MT, we can therefore construct its $\mathcal{A}^\sharp$ and $\mathcal{R}^\sharp$ normal forms:

$$MTA = (?x : \{a, b, c\} \to MT')$$
$$\rhd (a \to MT' \sqcap b \to MT')$$

$$MTR = (?x : \{a, b, c\} \to MT')$$
$$\rhd (?x : \{a, b\} \to MT' \sqcap a \to MT' \sqcap b \to MT')$$

where $MT' = STOP \sqcap a \to STOP$.

We have thus found two laws (respectively $\langle \rhd\text{-nohist*}\rangle$ (13.25) and $\langle \square\text{-idem*}\rangle$ (2.1) which, when added to the set that determines LNF, respectively allow us to transform any finite program into the normal form for acceptance sets ($\mathcal{A}^\sharp$) or for refusal testing ($\mathcal{RT}^\sharp$). It is pleasing, given that we stated in Sect. 11.3 that the revivals model is the weakest model below this pair, that these two laws together allow us to transform into $\mathcal{R}^\sharp$ normal form.

Widening the picture to encompass the treatment of divergence, we can freely add $\langle \sqcap\text{-zero}^\Downarrow\rangle$ (13.23) or $\langle \sqcap\text{-unit*}\rangle$ (13.24) (but not both) to any of the sets characterising a $\mathcal{M}^\sharp$ model to move to either the divergence-strict $\mathcal{M}^\Downarrow$ or finite-observation $\mathcal{M}$ version, obtaining a natural $3 \times 2 \times 2$ lattice of some of our standard models. The first dimension represents the choice between $\mathcal{M}$, $\mathcal{M}^\Downarrow$ and $\mathcal{M}^\sharp$, the second between unrestricted and union-closed acceptance sets, and the third between rich traces and trace-plus models. Each of these dimensions is characterised by one or two laws. But this lattice does not yet include failures and traces models.

We can turn the revivals normal form into one for failures by adding the law[7]

$$P \rhd Q = (P \square Q) \sqcap Q \qquad\qquad \langle \rhd\text{-failures*}\rangle \ (13.26)$$

This law easily (though with a little care in the case that $SKIP$ or **div** is in S) converts any LNF from one in which the basic structure is $(?x : A \to P(x)) \sqcap \sqcap S$ rather than $(?x : A \to P(x)) \rhd \sqcap S$.

This same law, in conjunction with $\langle \rhd\text{-combine}\rangle$ (13.21), proves that

$$(?x : A \cup B \cup C \to P(x)) \sqcap (?x : A \to P(x))$$
$$= (?x : A \cup B \cup C \to P(x)) \sqcap (?x : A \cup B \to P(x)) \sqcap (?x : A \to P(x))$$

and will therefore turn the revivals normal form into the form

$$\sqcap(\{?x : A \to P(x) \mid A \in ACCs\} \cup S)$$

where either $S \subseteq \{\mathbf{div}, SKIP\}$ or $ACCs$ is non-empty, and if $ACCs$ is non-empty it has the properties (a) and (b) or (c) below.

---

[7]Note that in some presentations of CSP based on failures models only, this has sometimes been given as the *definition* or $\rhd$.

(a) $\bigcup ACCs \in ACCs$.

(b) If $A \subset A' \subset A''$ and $A, A'' \in ACCs$, then $A' \in ACCs$ (convexity).

(c) If $A \subset A'$ and $A, A' \in ACCs$, then $A' = \bigcup ACCs$ (anticonvexity).

(b) and (c) respectively correspond to two different ways of representing the normal form of a program over failures. In the first, the acceptance sets are *saturated*: every such set between the minimal acceptances and the process's initial events is offered. In the second, the set of initial events is offered, and apart from that only the minimal acceptances. The latter approach was used in TPC and is also used by FDR when representing failures-based normal forms.

The saturated failures-style normal form for the example MT additionally has the initial acceptances $\{a, b, c\}$ (replacing the left-hand side of $\rhd$), $\{a, c\}$ and $\{b, c\}$. In this we can no longer tell that c is only ever available from an unstable state.

Lastly, there is the traces model $\mathcal{T}$ and its variants. Its normal form is fairly obvious even without all the foregoing work: a finite program is in traces normal form if it is any of $?x : A \rightarrow P(x)$, or $(?x : A \rightarrow P(x)) \sqcap (\sqcap S)$ for S an non-empty subset of $\{SKIP, \mathbf{div}\}$. And of course this is exactly what we get if we apply the law

$$P \,\square\, Q = P \sqcap Q \qquad\qquad\qquad \langle \text{trace-equiv}^{\mathcal{T}} \rangle \quad (13.27)$$

often enough to the failures normal form, together with standard laws to collapse the result.

Exercise 13.3 Calculate the normal forms of the process PB in the models $\mathcal{FL}^{\Downarrow}$ and $\mathcal{FL}$.

Exercise 13.4 The usual specification over the stable failures model $\mathcal{F}$ of deadlock freedom is the process

$$DF = \sqcap\{a \rightarrow DF \mid a \in \Sigma\} \sqcap SKIP$$

This is not, of course, a finite process, so consider a one-step version

$$DF1 = \sqcap\{a \rightarrow SKIP \mid a \in \Sigma\} \sqcap SKIP$$

which says that a process terminates successfully after at most one step.

What is the normal form of this process over the acceptances and revivals models $\mathcal{A}$ and $\mathcal{R}$? Is DF the correct specification of deadlock freedom over these models? If not, give the correct one.

Exercise 13.5 Recall Definition 13.2 in which we defined the normal form for $\mathcal{RT}^{\sharp}$ and, implicitly, normal forms for $\mathcal{RT}^{\Downarrow}$ and $\mathcal{RT}$. We know that every finite program can be transformed into $\mathcal{RT}^{\sharp}$ normal form by universally valid laws plus $\langle \square\text{-idem}^* \rangle$ (2.1). To complete the proof that this normal form is appropriate, we need to show that any two normal form programs which are different (other than simply by re-ordering members of lists) have different values in $\mathcal{RT}^{\sharp}$. Do this by induction on the maximum length of trace $s \in \Sigma^*$ in a process P as follows.

Suppose that $P = (?x : A \to P(x)) \triangleright \sqcap S$ and $Q = (?x : B \to Q(s)) \triangleright \sqcap T$ are two such normal forms with the same value in $\mathcal{RT}^{\sharp}$.

(a) Prove that $A = B$ and that $P(x)$ and $Q(x)$ are equivalent in the model for all $x \in A$.
(b) Show that $A = B = \emptyset$ if and only if the traces of the processes are contained in $\{\langle\rangle, \langle\checkmark\rangle\}$, and that in this case $S = T$.
(c) Let $accs(S)$ and $accs(T)$ be the $\cup$-closed sets of initial stable offers of the form $?x : A'$ on the first steps of the processes in S and T. Show that if $accs(S)$ and $accs(T)$ are different then so are the $\mathcal{RT}$ semantics of P and Q, contrary to our assumption. [*Hint: show that we can assume without loss of generality that either $\emptyset \in accs(S) \backslash accs(T)$ or there is a $a \in A' \in accs(S)$ such that there is no $B' \in accs(T)$ with $x \in B' \subseteq A'$.*]
(d) Use (a) and (c) and the inductive assumption that the result holds for all P and Q with shorter maximal traces in Σ^{*} to prove the result for the given P and Q.

Exercise 13.6 Comment on the following statement: "The laws $\langle\sqcap\text{-}\square\text{-dist*}\rangle$ (2.13) and $\langle\triangleright\text{-failures*}\rangle$ (13.26) are true in all failures and traces models and no others. Therefore either, together with laws true in *all models*, must be able to transform LNF to $\mathcal{F}^{\sharp}$-normal form." Is this a correct inference? What can either of these laws actually achieve without $\langle\triangleright\text{-nohist*}\rangle$ (13.25) and $\langle\square\text{-idem*}\rangle$ (2.1)?

13.6 General Programs

Everything above has been done in terms of finite programs. There is no prospect of a terminating algebraic strategy that can transform one of any pair of equivalent general programs into the other. Such a strategy would provide a solution to the halting problem, which we could re-phrase $STOP =_{FD} P \setminus \Sigma$.

It would be natural, therefore, to draw the line for algebraic semantics here, observing that, with the exception of the subtleties arising from infinite nondeterminism, just about all interesting semantic issues arise in the class of finite programs.

Those subtleties are in fact perhaps too challenging for anything resembling a straightforward algebraic approach. Just contemplate using some sort of standard algebraic approach to try to distinguish

$$\sqcap\{A_n \mid n \in \mathbb{N}\} \quad \text{from} \quad \sqcap\{A_n \mid n \in \mathbb{N}\} \sqcap A_{\omega}$$

where A_n performs n as before stopping, and A_{ω} performs as for ever.

We will therefore assume for the rest of this section that all the programs we consider are finitely nondeterministic. Even that is not good enough for the "seeing past divergence" models $\mathcal{M}^{\sharp}$, since we have seen that finitely nondeterministic processes can simulate infinitely nondeterministic ones (see p. 284) and in particular can lead us into something remarkably like the example above. For this and other reasons we will not attempt here to discover a method of deciding the equality of non-finite programs over such models.

There is a discussion of how to devise the necessarily infinitary rules for completing the algebraic semantics for $\mathcal{N}$ in Chap. 11 of TPC, including the relationship with the normal forms used for FDR.

One approach mentioned, but not emphasised in TPC, is that of "finite syntactic approximations" [48].

Definition 13.3 Suppose P is a finitely nondeterministic CSP program and P' is a finite CSP program. Then $P' \preceq P$, meaning that P' is a finite syntactic approximation to P, if this relationship is provable from the following rules (where equality means syntactic equivalence):

1. $P' = \mathbf{div}$
2. $P' = P$ if P involves no recursion.
3. $P' = C[P'_1, \ldots, P'_n]$ and $P = C[P_1, \ldots, P_n]$, C is a recursion-free CSP context and $P'_i \preceq P_i$ for all i.
4. $P = \mu p.F(p)$, $P' = F'(P'')$, $P'' \preceq \mu p.F(p)$ and $F'(p) \preceq F(p)$.

Informally, $P' \preceq P$ if P' is obtained from P by unfolding any finite number of recursions, and then replacing any chosen parts of the resulting syntax *including all recursions* by **div**.

div is, of course, the refinement-least member of all $\mathcal{M}^{\Downarrow}$ models, and the refinement-maximal member of all finite-behaviour models. This immediately means that over the first sort of model $P' \preceq P$ implies $P' \sqsubseteq P$, and $P' \sqsupseteq P$ over the second.

Because of our assumptions about the programs being finitely nondeterministic, and the alphabet being finite, these two sorts of model have the following properties:

Lemma 13.2 *Suppose that $\mathcal{M}$ is any of the standard finite-behaviour models of CSP, that Q' is a finite process and that $P \sqsubseteq Q'$ for the finitely nondeterministic process P. Then there is $P' \preceq P$ such that $P' \sqsubseteq Q'$, both refinements being over $\mathcal{M}$.*

Lemma 13.3 *Suppose that $\mathcal{M}$ is any of the standard finite-behaviour models of CSP, that P is a finite process and that $P \sqsubseteq Q$ for the finitely nondeterministic process Q. Then there is $Q' \preceq Q$ such that $P \sqsubseteq Q'$, both refinements being over $\mathcal{M}^{\Downarrow}$.*

This pair of results gives a corresponding pair of rules. Their preconditions are provable algebraically because of $P \sqsubseteq Q \equiv P = P \sqcap Q$.

Infinite Rule 1 Over any standard finite-behaviour model $\mathcal{M}$, the two finitely nondeterministic CSP processes P and Q are in the relation $P \sqsubseteq Q$ if and only if, for all $Q' \preceq Q$, there is $P' \preceq P$ such that $P' \sqsubseteq Q'$.

Infinite Rule 2 Over any standard divergence-strict model $\mathcal{M}^{\Downarrow}$, the two finitely nondeterministic CSP processes P and Q are in the relation $P \sqsubseteq Q$ if and only if, for all $P' \preceq P$, there is $Q' \preceq Q$ such that $P' \sqsubseteq Q'$.

13.7 Notes

Algebraic laws have played an important part in the definition of CSP from its earliest beginnings, and many of those presented here can be found in [19]. Building a theory that satisfied "the right" laws was immensely important to Hoare when he first designed the process algebra version of CSP: see [71] for details.

The first algebraic semantics for CSP was given in Brookes's thesis [18], and the version given in TPC extends that one to handle further operators, and deals with recursion differently. Each of these treatments was based exclusively on failures models. The version in this chapter is significantly different because we have shown how each of the principal models of CSP has its own algebraic semantics in a closely linked hierarchy, with the normal forms often linked by a single law.

Part of the intention here has been to show how essential the concept of an *unstable* action is to the hierarchy of CSP models. It is natural to think of our models as representing the bottom part of the van Glabbeek hierarchy [152, 153] modified to take account of these actions.

The OCCAM language [69], a parallel language based on CSP with the added complexity of assignable state, was given an algebraic semantics in [137], also based on a failures-divergences model. Algebraic approaches to other process calculi may be found in [2, 7, 8, 54, 90] (amongst many other works).

The concept of algebraic reduction as an operational semantics has its origins in the λ-calculus and similar. Hoare and He have advocated their use on more general languages, see [50, 51, 62].

The idea of extending an algebraic semantics based on finite terms to general ones using syntactic approximation is quite standard: see [48]. Lemmas 13.2 and 13.3 work because of the simple partial order structures of CSP models of the two given types over a finite alphabet. In particular, finite programs always map to the so-called finite elements of these two order structures. This, in conjunction with the fact that the finite syntactic approximations to a given process P form a *directed set* whose limit is P, is what proves this pair of lemmas.

We have not attempted in any sense to create a *minimal* set of laws to reduce programs to the most discriminating normal form LNF. However the author finds it most satisfying and elegant how the addition of a single law such as ⟨□-idem*⟩ (2.1) can transform one normal form into another. In some sense the existence of these "optional" laws go a long way to explaining the hierarchy of models that we studied in Chaps. 11 and 12.

Part III
Using CSP in Practice

In Chaps. 14–17 we mirror the structure of TPC by including in-depth material on the practical use of CSP. In TPC there were three chapters in Part III: deadlock, time, and case studies. The case studies in the printed version of TPC were peg solitaire to show how CSP can be used to model combinatorial systems, a distributed memory to introduce the topic of data independence, and a cryptographic protocol to model a system with complex data.

Chapter 13 of TPC is an extensive study of design rules by which deadlock-free systems can be developed. Some of the more basic material from it was introduced in Sect. 4.2 of the present book. The reader is advised to look at TPC for further details.

Timed systems had already become one of the main practical application areas of FDR when TPC was published, but no real theoretical understanding existed of the relationship between the continuous Timed CSP language of Reed (Oxford University D.Phil. Thesis, 1988), Schneider (Concurrent and Real-Time Systems: The CSP Approach, Wiley, New York, 2000) and the discrete-time dialect introduced in Chap. 14 of TPC. Since that time there have been considerable advances both in the theoretical understanding of what can be done with discrete time in CSP, and in the support for time provided by FDR. Our Chaps. 14 and 15 bring this topic up to date.

In using FDR one usually concentrates on checks of the form Spec [X= Imp where Spec is a finite-state process representing a specification, X is one of the CSP models, and Imp is another finite-state process representing the implementation. Much has been discovered in recent years about what can be achieved by looking at the more general model LHS(Imp) [X= RHS(Imp), namely applying two different contexts to the same process and comparing them. Chapter 16 looks at this topic, gives details of FDR's compression algorithms, and discusses other advanced techniques in the use of FDR.

Anyone who has experimented with FDR to a significant extent will realise that what one can do with it is limited by the *state explosion problem*, by which the number of states a system has tends to grow exponentially with the numbers of parallel components and parameters involved in its definition. There is no real doubt that in some cases this increase in complexity is genuine in the sense that the verification problem truly is a lot harder as the system grows. But equally there are many cases where one has the strong feeling that no significant new issues arise as the system grows, so checks really should not become so much harder. Chapter 17 looks at some techniques that can be used to counter this problem in the context of CSP. These include data independence, induction and a study of buffered systems.

Chapter 14
Timed Systems 1: *tock*-CSP

14.1 Introduction

All of the modelling we have done so far has been done without measuring the passage of time. We have cared about the order events happen in, but not about how long there is between them or at what times they happen. When our correctness criteria are independent of time (as have been all we have seen to date, of course) and our implementations do not rely on internal timing details to meet their specifications, this abstraction is very useful since it simplifies both the description of, and reasoning about, processes. Nevertheless, it is in the nature of the sort of interactive systems we describe using CSP that sometimes it is desirable to be able to reason about their timed behaviour.

This is the first of two chapters on modelling timed systems in CSP. In this chapter we will review the options for describing real-time systems in CSP and study one of the options.

14.2 A Brief History of Time in CSP

A number of approaches have been proposed for modelling timed systems in CSP. The first to be developed, and probably the most elegant, is Timed CSP [110–112]. In this notation all of the operators of CSP (though not the constants **div**, *RUN* and *Chaos*) are reinterpreted in a timed context with the addition of a single new construct *WAIT t*, a process that terminates after t units of time. In Timed CSP time is traditionally recorded *exactly* as a non-negative real number (for example 0, 33, $\frac{22}{7}$ or π), so a trace becomes something like $\langle (1, a), (1, b), (\sqrt{2}, a) \rangle$: the times of events increasing, though not necessarily strictly. Steve Schneider's book [146] introduces Timed CSP in some detail.

Theoretically speaking, Timed CSP is very different from ordinary "untimed" CSP. The addition of times to events, and the presence of the *WAIT t* statement, means that everything becomes much more infinite. This, for obvious reasons, makes automatic verification a lot more problematic.

A.W. Roscoe, *Understanding Concurrent Systems*, Texts in Computer Science,
DOI 10.1007/978-1-84882-258-0_14, © Springer-Verlag London Limited 2010

One of the most important principles that applies in timed concurrency is that of *maximal progress*. This, in essence, says that as soon as an action becomes available to a process, it will perform an action (though not necessarily the same one). By "available", we mean here that everyone who has to agree to the action does so, including the external environment if the action is in Σ. So the process $a \rightarrow STOP$ in Timed CSP can wait arbitrarily long to perform a, but as soon as the environment offers this event it happens.

In particular, maximal progress means that as soon as a process can perform τ, it must either perform the τ or some other action. For example, $(a \rightarrow STOP \,\Box\, b \rightarrow STOP) \setminus \{a\}$ has a τ available immediately, and so if b occurs it can only happen at time 0. This has a striking consequence for the mathematical models of Timed CSP: there is no traces congruence or traditional failures one. In fact, the weakest possible model is one in which we observe what a process refuses at each instant through its trace, and it is called the *timed failures model*. To see why there is no traces model, consider $P1 = a \rightarrow STOP \sqcap b \rightarrow STOP$ and $P2 = a \rightarrow STOP \,\Box\, b \rightarrow STOP$. These have the same timed traces:

$$\{\langle\rangle\} \cup \{\langle(a,t)\rangle \mid t \geq 0\} \cup \{\langle(b,t)\rangle \mid t \geq 0\}$$

However, if we apply the operator $\setminus\{a\}$ they do not. As discussed above, $P2 \setminus \{a\}$ can only perform b at time 0, but $P1 \setminus \{a\}$ can do it at any time, since it does not have b and the τ from hiding a available at the same time.

This means we cannot always calculate the timed traces of $P \setminus X$ from those of P, something we would have to be able to do if timed traces were a model.

The observant reader may have noticed a similarity between ideas of the timed failures model and those of the *refusal testing* model of CSP $\mathcal{RT}$ (see Sect. 11.2.2). We will return to this topic later.

Historically, the second main style of modelling timed systems in CSP was introduced by the author into the practical FDR-using community in the early 1990s, and it was first properly described in Chap. 14 of TPC. In this, we write processes in standard CSP without any inbuilt timing assumptions, but add our own timing constraints by using a special event conventionally written *tock*. The idea is that, just as in standard CSP one defines the possible orders of ordinary events, in the "*tock*-CSP" style one can specify the order of ordinary events amongst an infinite regular sequence of *tock*s, which of course tells us, but not precisely, *when* the ordinary events happen.

This second style has been very widely used, as have variants in which there are multiple clocks: either running together with some drift, or with a faster clock for "small steps" running between the main *tock* actions: see Sect. 20.2.1, for example. It gives great flexibility in the modelling of time, since one can either regard the *tock*s as events that are visible to the actual implementation, or as tokens that allow *us* to judge how fast a program is running relative to some global clock.

This last issue has an important consequence for modelling. If the advance of time, as visible to a process, is marked by the event *tock*, then it makes sense for an external event to be available before a *tock* event and not after it, as in $TOCKS \,\Box\, a \rightarrow TOCKS$, where the standard process $TOCKS$ is defined to be $\mu p.tock \rightarrow p$.

Note that in this example *a* is never refused before the first *tock*, but never happens after it.

On the other hand, *tock* might represent a measurement of time that is not directly accessible to the underlying implementation. Then, even if the fact that a particular time has been reached makes a τ time-out action available in the implementation, any action that was available up to that *tock* is still possible *at that time*.

This applies equally in Timed CSP, where there is no explicit *tock* action. It follows that in models where, like Timed CSP, the clock is assumed to be external and not directly visible to the implementation, we adopt the rule that *if a particular event has been offered up to a particular time, it is also possible at that time*. We can call this the *no instantaneous withdrawal* principle: we will see it again on p. 350.

When TPC was written, the author knew of no formal connection between Timed CSP and *tock*-CSP. Close connections were, however, discovered by Joël Ouaknine in his doctoral thesis [98] (2000), in which he developed a theory of *digitisation* for CSP. In suitable cases this is capable of showing that a (continuous) Timed CSP program meets its specification if a discretely (*tock*-) timed version does.

To do this, Ouaknine produced a semantics for the *language* of Timed CSP (restricted so that waits are for integer times only) in the same semantic space as *tock*-CSP: namely in which regular *tock*s appear in traces to represent the passage of time.

In the rest of this chapter we study *tock*-CSP. We give an introduction and a case study before looking at the interaction of hiding, priority and maximal progress. In the next chapter we will show how to interpret Timed CSP discretely using the models of *tock*-CSP, give an example, and introduce the theory of digitisation.

14.3 *tock*-CSP

As described above, *tock*-CSP is ordinary CSP in which *tock* is treated as an ordinary visible event, and included in prefixes, choices, parallel alphabets and interface sets. Except for achieving very particular effects this event is not hidden or affected by a renaming.

This model assumes that *tock* happens regularly for ever, or at least until a process terminates with $\checkmark$—and usually the overall system is built so that it does not terminate. It follows that the usual CSP concept of deadlock, where an unterminated process reaches a state where no event ever happens again, is worse in this model than hitherto. It is not only useless but unbuildable: doing so would breach the laws of nature by preventing time from progressing. Exactly the same is clearly true of a diverging process.

It follows that we are moving to a rather different universe, even though the constructs we use in the CSP language are the same.

14.3.1 Expressing Timing Constraints

Having taken the decision to include the *tock* event in a process's alphabet, one is
forced to make detailed decisions about what its actions mean and how they occur
in time. This is illustrated by a timed version of *COPY*. Suppose it takes one unit
of time for a data value to pass through this one-place buffer, and that a further unit
of time is required between the output and the next input. The obvious definition,
given this, is

$$TCOPY1 = left?x \rightarrow tock \rightarrow right!x \rightarrow tock \rightarrow TCOPY1$$

But there is a big difference between this process and the original *COPY*, because
this one *insists* on performing an action each unit of time: it does not allow time to
pass until it has done something on each and every cycle. The original *COPY* will
wait as long as you like either to input or output. It is reasonable to say that *TCOPY1*
becomes *urgent* one time unit after performing any action: it insists on doing some
visible action before time can progress. The correct translation of *COPY* (with the
same assumptions about how long it takes for one communication to enable another)
is actually

$$TCOPY2 = left?x \rightarrow tock \rightarrow TCOPY2'(x)$$
$$\square\ tock \rightarrow TCOPY2$$

$$TCOPY2'(x) = right!x \rightarrow tock \rightarrow TCOPY2$$
$$\square\ tock \rightarrow TCOPY2'(x)$$

since this process says that there has to be *at least* one time unit between input
and output events, without expressing an upper bound. The states *TCOPY2* and
TCOPY2(x) might be said to be *idling*, in that the passage of time has no effect on
them.

An interesting hybrid between these processes is one which will wait to input,
but not to output—it idles on input but is urgent about outputting:

$$TCOPY3 = left?x \rightarrow tock \rightarrow right!x \rightarrow tock \rightarrow TCOPY3$$
$$\square\ tock \rightarrow TCOPY3$$

We can conclude that *tock*-CSP is a good deal more flexible in the way it
handles the interaction between process and environment than the standard assumptions about untimed CSP. We are able to express more or less arbitrary constraints about the times at which events happen, both absolutely and relative to each
other.

The problem with this flexibility is that, particularly when we conjoin timing
specifications by placing them in parallel, it is possible to impose inconsistent constraints that have no solution. To illustrate this idea, we can modify *TCOPY3* so
that it is parameterised by the channels it uses and, more importantly, by the delay
between the input and output of a datum:

$$TCOPY4(\mathit{left}, \mathit{right}, D) = \mathit{left}?x \rightarrow TCOPY4'(\mathit{left}, \mathit{right}, D, D, x)$$
$$\square\, \mathit{tock} \rightarrow TCOPY4(\mathit{left}, \mathit{right}, D)$$

$$TCOPY4'(\mathit{left}, \mathit{right}, D, N, x) = \mathit{tock} \rightarrow TCOPY4'(\mathit{left}, \mathit{right}, D, N - 1, x)$$
$$\{\!\!\{N > 0\}\!\!\}$$
$$\mathit{right}!x \rightarrow \mathit{tock} \rightarrow TCOPY4(\mathit{left}, \mathit{right}, D)$$

Let us think about what happens if we connect two of these together:

$$TCOPY4(a, b, D_1) \underset{\{|b, tock|\}}{\parallel} TCOPY4(b, c, D_2)$$

If $D_2 \leq D_1$, all is fine: we can guarantee that the right-hand process will not be expected to make its $(n + 1)$th input until at least $D_1 + 1$ time units after its nth, and it is therefore ready. On the other hand, if $D_2 > D_1$, then if (though it need not) the left-hand process makes its second input as soon as it can, this will lead to a *time-stop* when it needs to output D_1 units later and the right-hand process is not ready. This is exactly the type of contradictory state discussed in the preceding section. If, on the other hand, the environment is sufficiently slow in putting inputs into the combination, the problem will not arise.

Notice that processes like $TCOPY4$ have states that are neither urgent nor idling: in other words they allow *tock* but are not unchanged by it. It is as well to have a name for this type of state too, so we will call them *evolving*. Every state of a timed system falls into one of the three categories of urgent, idling and evolving, and it is a most helpful distinction to bear in mind when designing programs for this style of CSP system.

In most examples it would be ridiculous to have infinitely many ordinary actions between two *tock*s, since this would mean that infinitely many actions occur in a finite time interval. This is easy to check for, all we have to do is look for divergence in

$$P \setminus (\Sigma \setminus \{\mathit{tock}\})$$

Indeed, the most basic 'sanity check' on this sort of model of a timed system is to verify

$$TOCKS \sqsubseteq_{FD} P \setminus (\Sigma \setminus \{\mathit{tock}\})$$

where $TOCKS = \mathit{tock} \rightarrow TOCKS$. This is the same as an equivalence check because $TOCKS$ is deterministic and therefore maximal. This says both that there are no time-stops in P and that there are never infinitely many events without a *tock*. We term this a *timing consistency check*. If there were any possibility of our process terminating ($\checkmark$) we would have generalised this to proving refinement of

$$TOCKS^{\checkmark} = (\mathit{tock} \rightarrow TOCKS^{\checkmark}) \sqcap SKIP$$

though this will never be necessary for any of the examples we deal with in this chapter.

A process can satisfy this check when, in order to let time pass, it is necessary for the environment to engage in suitable communications with the process. Both *TCOPY*1 and *TCOPY*3 satisfy it, for example. It may well be that we need the process to be tolerant of not receiving some or all communications instantly—the most obvious distinction here being between *input* and *output* events. It may well be reasonable to assume that the environment is always willing to accept an output, but it may be unreasonable to assume that the environment is always waiting to send an input.

If there is a set of events D which the environment is assumed to be able to delay indefinitely, but may still allow, the above test should be modified to showing

$$TOCKS \sqsubseteq_{FD} (P \underset{D}{\|} Chaos_D) \setminus (\Sigma \setminus\{tock\})$$

If $D = \{|left|\}$, we will have that *TCOPY*3 satisfies this but that *TCOPY*1 does not. The point is that $Chaos_D$ may either allow or prevent actions from D, so the process can neither discount the occurrence of these events nor rely on them happening. Setting D equal to $\Sigma \setminus\{tock\}$ would correspond to *all* normal events being arbitrarily delayable by the environment—the conventional CSP view of communication.

In the above checks, using failures-divergences refinement will ensure that only finitely many events happen between *tock*s, whereas using failures refinement would check only for time-stops. It might well be the case that you want to relax the condition that only finitely many events can happen between *tock*s, but only as regards delayable events. In some circumstances it may be more appropriate to rely on the external process instigating these events not to send infinitely many in a finite time, and so putting in restrictions into our process P might seem unnecessary and over-complex. A good example of this will be found in the case study of the bully algorithm (Sect. 14.4). One appropriate check to use in this case is that

$$P \setminus (\Sigma \setminus(D \cup \{tock\}))$$

failures-divergences refines

$$TOCKS \|\| Chaos_D$$

This says that events in D are never required to enable *tock* to happen, and that only finitely many other events happen between each pair of events that are either *tock* or in D. If you intend to join a pair of processes together, with each process's signal events being the delayable ones of the other, then this weaker check ought only to be used at one end of the interface.

It would also be possible to allow for an environment that will guarantee intermediate levels of acceptance of communication, such as guaranteeing to accept any communication in a set B if offered for at least N units. There might well be a role for such tests when we know that the component in hand will ultimately be put in a system that makes such guarantees (because, for example, of scheduling). But in specifying a 'complete' system, events will tend to come into the category that are simply observed by the environment and which it cannot delay, and those which the environment can delay indefinitely.

Exercise 14.1 Define a version of *TCOPY* which outputs at a time it nondeterministically chooses between *A* and *B* time units from the corresponding input. It is then ready to input again *C* units later. What might happen when two of these are connected together?

Exercise 14.2 Give trace specifications for the following: (i) no more than *N* ordinary events occur between any two *tock*s, (ii) no more than *M* *tock*s occur between consecutive occurrences of the event *a*. Give definitions for the characteristic processes of these specifications.

14.4 Case Study: Bully Algorithm

In this section we show how to model a time-dependent distributed algorithm. In Chap. 14 of TPC there is a case study of a level crossing gate which achieves both timing and basic safety properties through the timed behaviour of a system. The following case study is slightly more complex, so some readers might find it helpful to look at the level crossing before the one below. The result below is, however, rather more *interesting*!

In books such as [27] you will find clear but relatively informal presentations of a wide variety of distributed algorithms for things like clock synchronisation, transaction processing, database management and communication. These algorithms are sometimes presented as a sequence of messages each node has to send to other nodes, and their reactions to the messages they receive. Sometimes an algorithm is described via the overall pattern of communications that arise in the system. Many, and probably most, of these use time in one way or another. The purpose of this section is to take a specific example and to show how, unless one is exceptionally careful, this style of description can contain dangerous imprecision. The example we use is of a leadership election algorithm—distributed algorithms frequently depend on there being an agreed node which can play some coordinating role—called the *bully algorithm* (for reasons that will become apparent).

The following description of an algorithm introduced in [43] is paraphrased from one on p. 306 of [27].

The Bully Algorithm This is used to allow a group of *N* processors to have an agreed *coordinator* from amongst them. It is intended to work despite processors failing and reviving from time to time.[1] The objective is always to have them agree that the coordinator is the highest indexed processor that is working. We assume that communication is reliable, but processors can fail at any time (including during the election procedure that the algorithm represents).

There are three types of message that the algorithm description refers to explicitly:

---

[1] The algorithm is therefore intended to be fault tolerant.

```
channel election:Proc.Proc
channel answer:Proc.Proc
channel coordinator:Proc.Proc
```

where `Proc={0..N-1}`, say, and all these represent synchronisations between a sender process (the first index) and a receiver.

An `election.n.m` message is used to announce an election (from `n` to `m`); an `answer` message is sent in response to an election message; and a `coordinator` message is sent to announce the identity of the new coordinator. A process begins an election when it notices that the coordinator has failed.

This statement lacks detail about the mechanism by which failure of the current coordinator is noticed. We use the two channels `test` and `ok` that are declared here: any process can decide to send a `test` message to its coordinator, who only sends `ok` back if it is a properly working coordinator. This raises the question of what happens if a process tests its coordinator but the latter, though working, does not think it *is* the coordinator!

```
channel fail, revive:Proc
channel test, ok:Proc.Proc
```

The first two are communicated when a process fails or revives (allowing us, as external observers, to see what the current status of each process is). The last two are used by one process to test another, and to give a positive response to such a test. It might be natural to have each live node test the coordinator regularly.

To begin an election, a process sends an `election` message to all those with a higher index. It then awaits an `answer` message in response. If none arrives within time `T1`, the processor considers itself the coordinator (as it thinks all the higher ones must be dead), and sends a `coordinator` message to all processes with lower identifiers announcing this fact. Otherwise, the process waits a further limited period (`T2`), expecting to receive a coordinator message as described in the next paragraph, before beginning another election (if no such message is received).

If a process receives a coordinator message, it records the identifier of the coordinator contained within it (i.e., the sender of that message) and treats that process as the coordinator.

If a process receives an `election` message, it sends back an `answer` message and begins another election, unless it has begun one already.

When a failed process is `revived`, it begins an election. If it has the highest live process identifier, then it will eventually decide that it is the coordinator, and announce this to the other processes. Thus it will become the coordinator, even though the current coordinator is functioning. It is for this reason that the algorithm is called the *bully* algorithm.

For example, consider the case where there are four nodes 1–4, all initially working so that the initial coordinator is node 4.

If this node fails, and node 2 tests it, then an election will be started by node 2. It sends `election` messages to 3 (who answers and starts its own election) and to 4, who does not answer. Node 3 will get no answer to its *election* message to

4, and will therefore send everyone a `coordinator` message. When 4 eventually revives it will realise that it ought to be coordinator (since there is no process with higher index) and bully all the others into accepting it.

The intention, it would seem, is that except when the coordinator has failed and has not been tested since, the nodes *either* all agree on the correct coordinator (i.e., the live one with highest index) *or* are in the process of an election which will, in the absence of any further process failures or revivals, result in such a state of agreement in a bounded time. It is that which we will test in this section.

14.4.1 Part 1: Specification

It is good practice to design your specification before your system. In the present case the specification is also rather easier.

Assume that all the actions described above, except for `fail`, `revive` and `test` have been hidden as internal, and do not therefore play a part in our specification. Assume, furthermore, that the additional channel `leader.i` where

```
channel leader:Proc.Proc
```

is one on which the processor i is prepared to communicate its view of who the coordinator is whenever it is neither failed nor in mid-election.

Basically, what we have to do is to translate the English specification above into CSP. This will require us to interpret some of its parts, such as the concept of 'agree', in CSP terms and to give concrete interpretation to things like time bounds.

We can capture the intended specification in terms of traces or (more strongly) in terms of failures.

(a) Whenever no process has revived for TS time units, and each `fail` has been followed by some `revive` or `test` event (the two sorts that could set an election going) at least TS time units before the present, then if any node believes there is a coordinator (i.e., communicates `leader.m.n`) then n is the highest "living" node.

There are three basic states to this specification: one in which the condition is enforced, and two where it is not because either the system is being allowed time to settle, or an untested coordinator failure has occurred. All three are parameterised by the set of live processes (ones that have revived since last failing).

The first case is when the condition is being enforced.

```
AGREEBY(0,alive) =
        alive != {} & leader?m:alive!max(alive) ->
                                        AGREEBY(0,alive)
        [] tock -> AGREEBY(0,alive)
        [] fail?k -> AGREEBY'(diff(alive,{k}))
        [] revive?k -> AGREEBY(TS,union(alive,{k}))
        [] test?n?k -> AGREEBY(0,alive)
```

In the second we are waiting n > 0 tocks before enforcing it. Note that in each case we allow failures other than the natural leader to reset the timer since they might well disrupt an in-progress election. The reader is invited to modify this specification so only the failure of the current leader resets the timer. Various "bugs" that are clearly correct behaviour will be found.

```
AGREEBY(n,alive) =
        leader?m:alive?k -> AGREEBY(n,alive)
        [] tock -> AGREEBY(n-1,alive)
        [] fail?k -> AGREEBY'(diff(alive,{k}))
        [] revive?k -> AGREEBY(TS,union(alive,{k}))
        [] test?m?k -> AGREEBY(n,alive)
```

Finally, we have the state in which the leader has failed but has not yet been tested. Since either a test or a process revival ought to start an election, either implies leaving this state.

```
AGREEBY'(alive) =
        leader?m:alive?k -> AGREEBY'(alive)
        [] tock -> AGREEBY'(alive)
        [] fail?k -> AGREEBY'(diff(alive,{k}))
        [] revive?k -> AGREEBY(TS,union(alive,{k}))
        [] test?n?k -> AGREEBY(TS,alive)
```

The above is, of course, a trace specification. Assuming that all processes start off working properly, the natural starting state of this specification is `AGREEBY(Proc,0)`.

(b) It is, however, easily turned into a failures(-divergences) specification that says that under the same conditions all live processes definitely do believe in the correct leader process. Simply replace the first lines of the second two cases above by themselves nondeterministically composed with STOP, and put the entire specification in parallel with

```
CHAOS({|tock,fail,revive,test|})
```

the set of all events that the specification uses other than {|leader|}.

In addition to these functional specifications, we would obviously like our implementation to be deadlock-free and to satisfy the appropriate timing consistency check (see p. 325).

14.4.2 Part 2: Implementation

Given the freedom with which the nodes potentially run, it seems to be necessary, for the avoidance of deadlock, to make the nodes continually receptive of almost all the messages that might be directed at them by another node. This even applies when the node has failed, since we would expect a dead node to ignore things that are directed at it rather than prevent them from happening. In other words this is a case where the handshaken communication of CSP is being used to model a somewhat freer form of interaction.

In programming the nodes you soon realise that, because of the necessity set out in the above paragraph, you have to deal with cases not directly catered for in the English description of the protocol. This is a very common experience in translating from English to formal specifications. The situations we have in mind here are ones in which a node is doing what it has to do to perform its role in one run of the protocol when it gets interrupted by a message from another run.

For example, if node n receives an `election` message in the middle of distributing its own `coordinator` signal, then we might think we ought to abandon the distribution and get on with the election, after `answering` the election message. That, however would be a mistake, especially because the `coordinator` message may well have arrived after (and therefore have overridden) the `election` message elsewhere, including at its origin. If, on the other hand, it ignored an election message from node m in a situation where this was sent subsequent to m having received its own `coordinator.n` (e.g., because m has revived) this could also lead to problems. The right solution to this particular conundrum appears to be that since nothing has happened to shake n from its belief that it is the rightful coordinator, the appropriate thing is for it to re-start its `coordinator` distribution so that the `election` sender will definitely receive it again.

We take a minimalist approach to introducing timing into our system. In particular we always assume that any response that the protocol calls for from node n without it having to wait for anything else, happens immediately (i.e., before the next `tock`). One could perhaps get a slightly more accurate model by introducing small delays here. However, this would get a more complex model with more states, and it does not appear to influence the outcome greatly. What the author did have to do to avoid some oddities and failures of timing consistency was to assume that no process generates more than one `test` of the coordinator in any time interval, and that at least one `tock` occurs between any process failing and reviving.

The following definitions set up the number of nodes, and some time delays. We will find later that this particular number of nodes is important.

```
N=4
Proc = {0..N-1}
T1 = 1
T2 = 2
TS = 5
above(n) = {k | k <- Proc, k>n}
below(n) = {k | k <- Proc, k<n}
```

The last two of these definitions are useful because all communications are directed to the processes with larger or smaller index than the sender.

Each process can be in one of a number of states. Let us begin with the one in which it is just starting an election:

```
BeginElection(n) = SendElections(N-1,n)
```

which results in it sending successive election messages to the appropriate nodes. Note how it can handle the receipt of any message it might receive, with varying results...

```
SendElections(k,n) =
(if k<=n then AwaitAnswers(T1,n)
        else election.n.k -> SendElections(k-1,n))
[] election?k':below(n)!n ->answer.n.k' ->
                                SendElections(k,n)
[] answer?k:above(n)!n -> AwaitCoordinator(T2,n)
[] ok?k':above(n)!n -> SendElections(k,n)
[] coordinator?c:above(n)!n -> Running'(n,c)
[] fail.n -> Failed(n)
[] test?m:below(n)!n  ->  SendElections(k,n)
```

Below, it is waiting for answers from its election messages, with the time-out making it the coordinator if it has not had one within T1:

```
AwaitAnswers(t,n) =
if t==0 then BecomeCoordinator(n)
else tock -> AwaitAnswers(t-1,n)
    [] answer?k:above(n)!n -> AwaitCoordinator(T2,n)
    [] ok?k:above(n)!n -> AwaitAnswers(t,n)
    [] election?k:below(n)!n -> answer.n.k ->
                                AwaitAnswers(t,n)
    [] coordinator?c:above(n)!n -> Running'(n,c)
    [] fail.n -> Failed(n)
    [] test?k:below(n)!n  ->  AwaitAnswers(t,n)
```

After it has had an answer message, it sits and waits to be sent a coordinator message (or any of a number of others), before starting another election if nothing significant has happened.

```
AwaitCoordinator(t,n) =
if t==0 then BeginElection(n)
else tock -> AwaitCoordinator(t-1,n)
    [] coordinator?c:above(n)!n -> Running'(n,c)
    [] answer?k:above(n)!n -> AwaitCoordinator(t,n)
    [] ok?k:above(n)!n -> AwaitCoordinator(t,n)
    [] election?k:below(n)!n -> answer.n.k ->
                                AwaitCoordinator(t,n)
    [] fail.n -> Failed(n)
    [] test?k:below(n)!n  ->  AwaitCoordinator(t,n)
```

The following represents the state when it has decided, for want of life above it, that it is the current coordinator

```
BecomeCoordinator(n) = SendCoords(n-1,n)
```

It distributes a coordinator.n message to all below it. Note that since it is the coordinator, it sends a positive response to the test message, unlike earlier states

```
SendCoords(j,n) =
if j<0 then RunAsCoord(n)
else coordinator.n.j -> SendCoords(j-1,n)
   [] election?k:below(n)!n -> BecomeCoordinator(n)
   [] coordinator?c:above(n)!n -> Running'(n,c)
   [] fail.n -> Failed(n)
   [] test?k:below(n)!n  -> ok.n.k -> SendCoords(j,n)
```

All the above states represent stages in the election protocol. Obviously we also need states in which a process is running, or has failed. When a node is coordinator it takes the following state:

```
RunAsCoord(n) =
tock -> RunAsCoord(n)
[] test?k:below(n)!n -> ok.n.k -> RunAsCoord(n)
[] coordinator?k:above(n)!n -> Running'(n,k)
[] election?k:below(n)!n -> answer.n.k
                         -> BeginElection(n)
[] fail.n -> Failed(n)
[] leader.n.n -> RunAsCoord(n)
```

and one in which it thinks some other node k is coordinator

```
Running(n,k) =
test.n.k -> Testing(n,k)
[] tock -> Running(n,k)
[] coordinator?k:above(n)!n -> Running'(n,k)
[] answer?j:above(n)!n  -> Running(n,k)
[] leader.n.k -> Running(n,k)
[] election?k:below(n)!n -> answer.n.k
                         -> BeginElection(n)
[] test?j:below(n)!n  -> Running(n,k)
[] fail.n -> Failed(n)
```

When it has sent a test message to the node it believes is coordinator, it waits until one time unit has passed before deeming the coordinator to have failed and beginning an election. Yet again, it is necessary to allow for anything else that might arrive in the meantime.

```
Testing(n,k) =
ok.k.n -> Running'(n,k)
[] tock -> BeginElection(n)
```

```
[] answer?j:above(n)!n   -> Testing(n,k)
[] coordinator?k:above(n)!n -> Running'(n,k)
[] election?k:below(n)!n -> answer.n.k
                                -> BeginElection(n)
[] fail.n -> Failed(n)
[] test?j:below(n)!n  -> Testing(n,k)
[] leader.n.k -> Testing(n,k)
```

After performing one test successfully, it goes into the following state in which it has to wait a time unit before performing another one (thereby avoiding a potential divergence):

```
Running'(n,k)  =
tock -> Running(n,k)
[] coordinator?k:above(n)!n -> Running'(n,k)
[] answer?j:above(n)!n   -> Running'(n,k)
[] election?j:below(n)!n -> answer.n.j
                                -> BeginElection(n)
[] fail.n -> Failed(n)
[] leader.n.k -> Running'(n,k)
[] test?j:below(n)!n  -> Running'(n,k)
[] ok?j:above(n)!n -> Running'(n,k)
```

A failed process just absorbs messages sent to it until

```
Failed(n) =
tock -> Failed'(n)
[] coordinator?k:above(n)!n -> Failed(n)
[] election?k:below(n)!n -> Failed(n)
[] test?k:below(n)!n  -> Failed(n)
[] ok?k:above(n)!n  -> Failed(n)
[] answer?k:above(n)!n  -> Failed(n)
```

it is revived, which is not until at least one time unit has passed

```
Failed'(n) =
tock -> Failed'(n)
[] coordinator?k:above(n)!n -> Failed'(n)
[] election?k:below(n)!n -> Failed'(n)
[] test?k:below(n)!n  -> Failed'(n)
[] ok?k:above(n)!n  -> Failed'(n)
[] answer?k:above(n)!n  -> Failed'(n)
[] fail.n -> Failed(n)
[] revive.n ->
        (if n==N-1 then BecomeCoordinator(n)
                        else BeginElection(n))
```

Note that if the highest-index process revives it has no need to carry out an election to know it should be coordinator.

We can then give each process its obvious alphabet and run them in parallel as a network.

```
Alpha(n) =
union(
{|tock, fail.n, revive.n, election.n, test.n
coordinator.n, answer.n, leader.n, ok.n|},
{election.k.n, coordinator.k.n,
    test.k.n, answer.k.n, ok.k.n| k <- Proc})

Node(n) = if n==N-1 then RunAsCoord(n)
                    else Running(n,N-1)

Network = || n:Proc @ [Alpha(n)] Node(n)
```

The first thing to try with any timed example is a timing consistency check along the lines set out on p. 325. The following events are all deemed 'delayable' because we do not want to have to rely on them happening urgently for time to pass. (The inclusion of test here serves the purpose of showing that the individual nodes can be 'lazy' about instigating tests if they want to be, though we will later be forced to re-think this in some circumstances.)

```
Delayable = {|fail, revive, leader, test|}
Urgent = diff(Events,union({tock},Delayable))
```

The following is the timing consistency check where we do not want to show that Delayable events are limited to finitely many in a finite time.

```
TOCKS ||| CHAOS(Delayable) [FD=  Network \ Urgent
```

14.4.3 Analysis

With the values of the parameters given, the timing consistency checks succeed, meaning that our model makes sense as a timed system. Fascinatingly, however, the others fail, even though we have done our best to implement the algorithm described in the literature. A typical error trace follows (though it is far from unique):

```
<fail.2, fail.3, test.1.3, tock, election.1.3,
 election.1.2, revive.2, revive.3, coordinator.3.2,
 fail.3, test.0.3, tock, coordinator.1.0,
 tock, tock, tock, tock, leader.2.3>
```

This can be interpreted as follows:

1. Nodes 2 and 3 fail.
2. Node 1 tests node 3; when it gets no response an election is started.
3. Both 2 and 3 revive shortly after they miss (through being failed) the election messages they get from 1.
4. 3 manages to tell 2 it is the coordinator before failing again.

5. 0 begins a test of 3.
6. By this time, 1 decides that, since it has not had any response to the election it started, it is the rightful coordinator. It therefore tells 0, which pre-empts the test the latter is doing.
7. The specification then gives the system time to settle (the `tock` events towards the end of the trace), though nothing of significance actually happens in this time.
8. We are left in a state where 0 and 1 believe 1 is the coordinator, and 2 believes that 3 is (though 3 has failed). Actually, of course, 2 ought to be agreed as coordinator since it is the highest indexed live process.

It is the way various elections get mixed up, and the way in which processes can fail in the middle of broadcasting a message to the others, that causes the problem. These two themes are common to about every error found by FDR in developed bully algorithm implementations and examined by the author. Indeed, if process failure is prevented during the `SendCoords` phase of broadcasting `coordinator` messages, all the specifications succeed.

It might or might not be regarded as a reasonable to assume that this type of failure never happens. This would be dangerous if the messages really do get sent out one after another rather than being broadcast all at once. If we do not assume this, the fact that the protocol appears to work when we do gives a clue as to how we might correct the program. We need to guard against only some of the nodes that ought to be informed about n's coordinator status getting this message. The dangerous scenario following this appears to be that one of the nodes who has *not* heard the `coordinator.n` message, tests who it thinks is the coordinator, which is sufficient for the specification to think that the network ought to settle to a correct state. One way to avoid this is to ensure that each node m that gets a `coordinator.n` tests n long enough after so that if this succeeds then it knows the broadcast has not been interrupted, for if the test fails then a new election will be started, and the inconsistent state will be cleared up.

This might get confused if process n were to fail and revive very quickly. In our modified implementation below we ensure that a reviving process waits sufficiently long to avoid this problem.

It is straightforward to adapt our program to encompass these extra tests and this delay. One slight complication arises from the timing model: in the first model it was helpful to think of the `test` events as delayable, since we did not want to rely on them happening simply to allow time to progress. We would still like to take this view of the tests that arise 'optionally', but it does not fit with the compulsory tests that happen after being sent a `coordinator` event. To solve this we make `test.n` events urgent, and guard each optional test with a new delayable event `dotest.n`.

Thus the following state can perform `dotest`, which takes it

```
Running(n,k) =
    dotest.n -> Testing1(n,k)
    [] tock -> Running(n,k)
    [] coordinator?k:above(n)!n -> Running''(n,k)
```

```
[] answer?j:above(n)!n  -> Running(n,k)
[] leader.n.k -> Running(n,k)
[] election?k:below(n)!n -> answer.n.k ->
                               BeginElection(n)
[] test?j:below(n)!n  -> Running(n,k)
[] fail.n -> Failed(n,TR)
```

to the Testing1 state, which actually starts the test proper.

```
Testing1(n,k) =
  test.n.k -> Testing2(n,k)
  [] answer?j:above(n)!n  -> Testing1(n,k)
  [] coordinator?k:above(n)!n -> Running''(n,k)
  [] election?k:below(n)!n -> answer.n.k ->
                                 BeginElection(n)
  [] fail.n -> Failed(n,TR)
  [] test?j:below(n)!n  -> Testing1(n,k)
  [] leader.n.k -> Testing1(n,k)
```

```
Testing2(n,k) =
  ok.k.n -> Running'(n,k)
  [] tock -> BeginElection(n)
  [] answer?j:above(n)!n  -> Testing2(n,k)
  [] coordinator?k:above(n)!n -> Running''(n,k)
  [] election?k:below(n)!n -> answer.n.k ->
                                 BeginElection(n)
  [] fail.n -> Failed(n,TR)
  [] test?j:below(n)!n  -> Testing2(n,k)
  [] leader.n.k -> Testing2(n,k)
```

Here, Running'(n,k) is a state like Running(n,k) except that it will not instigate a further test until after a tock. Running''(n,k) is a state that moves to state Testing1(n,k) after one tock, thereby testing the coordinator one time unit after coordinator.k is received.

With this amendment, the protocol meets its specification for all the cases (with reasonable timing parameters) that we have tried.

14.4.4 Conclusions

There are a number of observations we might make about this case study. During the process of creating the program for the bully algorithm set out above, there were far more problems encountered than is obvious from the way we have described it. Specifically, a number of iterations of the program failed deadlock or timing consistency checks, usually because the author had not allowed for various sorts of messages arriving at nodes who (one might have thought) were not really expecting them. The fact that these messages had to be handled, and the decisions about how to handle them, impressed on him that the English description of the protocol left more unanswered than one might think on first reading it.

Having ironed out these problems, we were left with an apparently working model (the uncorrected one presented above). Indeed, for three nodes all the specifications of it succeed, though as we have seen four is sufficient to find problems. It doesn't seem likely that many humans would find the ways in which four nodes have to interact in order to find the subtle problems FDR discovered. Indeed, the author had taught the bully algorithm in tutorials for several years without spotting them. It was only the feeling that there were stones left unturned in the arguments we constructed annually as to why the algorithm worked that led to this FDR analysis.

It is hard to say that the problem we encountered with inconsistent states for four or more nodes represents a definite error in the algorithm itself. What it does show is that a highly plausible implementation of the algorithm can fail what looks like an equally plausible formalisation of its specification. The author once used this example as an end-of-course assessment for Masters students, giving them the English description and a few hints on how to create the necessary CSP specifications and implementations. A majority of the students found essentially the same problem, and in at least one case a different problem that occurs when the order in which broadcast messages are sent out is changed. This might be taken as evidence that, at least for this algorithm, simply implementing what you find described in English in a book is far from being a guarantee of correctness.

This example thus displays both the strengths of the automated approach—since it found errors a human was unlikely to discover and allowed us to correct these at least to the bounds of FDR's capabilities for handling the resulting system—and one of its main weaknesses, namely that FDR is only able to verify relatively small implementations of the corrected system.

Exercise 14.3 Observing that it is node n−1 who is the first recipient of any batch of coordinator messages from node n, it is plausible to suggest that only node n−1 needs to instigate the test of node n that was introduced in the correction. Is this correct? (You should first attempt to solve this problem without using FDR on a modified file, but can of course use FDR should you not be sure of your answer.)

Exercise 14.4 Are the answer.n.m messages a necessary part of the protocol? If so, why, and if not can you suggest any pragmatic arguments as to why they are nevertheless there?

Exercise 14.5 Consider the following modification to the algorithm. There are now two sorts of election message. Elections caused by someone noticing coordinator failure use one sort, and follow exactly the same path as before. Elections caused by a node reviving use an election′ channel, with the property that when a node who is running normally receives it, it simply tells the sender who the coordinator is via a channel coordinator′.n.m.c (n telling m that the coordinator is c). If a reviving node has not been sent such a message or an answer (sent by nodes receiving election' when they are in the process of an election themselves) within a reasonable time, it deems itself to be the coordinator and broadcasts this fact as before.

Does this work (a) when the uncorrected program is modified accordingly, and if not, (b) when the corrected one is modified so that only coordinator as opposed to coordinator' messages force a test, and if not (c) when the corrected one is modified so that both sorts force a test? What advantages and disadvantages do you see for this new approach?

14.5 Maximal Progress and Priority

The link parallel operator in the form described in Sect. 5.3 does not work for *tock*-CSP, because in virtually every parallel composition we want to synchronise *tock* without hiding. It is easy to define a timed version of this operator that does exactly that: $P[a \leftrightarrow b]_{tock} Q$ synchronises P and Q on *tock* and the renamed channels a and b, but only hides the latter.

How should $TCOPY2[right \leftrightarrow left]_{tock}TCOPY2$ behave? If we interpreted this combination in ordinary CSP we would get a strange answer. A data item can enter the left-hand $TCOPY2$ and, after one *tock*, be available for output to the right-hand side, which is able to accept it. At this point, however, both processes are in an idling state and can perform any number, or even an infinite number, of *tock*s. So two things can happen, and there is no reason in a standard view of CSP to suppose that the data will *ever* pass over the hidden channel between the two nodes. Time can just drift on via repeated *tock*s.

This is neither particularly realistic and nor does it correspond to our intuition about the way $COPY[right \leftrightarrow left]COPY$ behaves. In the latter process, once the τ that takes data across from left to right becomes available, it certainly happens quickly if we are to believe the operational interpretation of LTSs that we have been explaining in the rest of this book.

Therefore, if we accept the model of $TCOPY2[right \leftrightarrow left]_{tock}TCOPY2$ in which the transfer can be delayed by an infinity of *tock*s, this is neither obliged to make any progress and nor is it a reasonable timed model of the process we are trying to simulate.

The solution is to use a different operational interpretation of LTSs for *tock*-CSP: if a state can perform both a *tock* and a τ, then it is the τ which happens. We can justify this as follows: once the state is entered, the τ is available immediately whereas the *tock* does not happen until the appropriate time. Examining this statement more closely implies that if any other events happen *at the same time* as *tock*, then the *tock* is always the first in the trace. We therefore have to give τ events *priority* over *tock*. This is known as the principle of *maximal progress*.

Under maximal progress, $TCOPY2[right \leftrightarrow left]_{tock}TCOPY2$ always transfers a datum from left to right one time unit after it is input on the left, provided of course that the right-hand process is empty at the time.

In any case where the LTS performs $\checkmark$ events, these are similarly given priority over *tock* under maximal progress.

The overall effect is that of applying the operator $delay_{tock}(\cdot)$, described in Exercise 11.4, to the timed system. Because *tock* is not renamed or hidden, this operator can *also* be applied at inner levels of the system.

Note that it would make no sense to write $(tock \rightarrow P) \rhd Q$ when running this model: the τ of the $\rhd$ would *always* preclude the *tock*. In general, particularly when writing specification processes, you should be careful that prioritising τ is not, as here, changing the meaning of a process in an undesired way.

When running the timing consistency check on some process *System*, the prioritised model can bring both benefits and problems. The main benefits are that it reduces the size of the state space and might well avoid FDR finding counter-examples that cannot in fact occur because they are unrealistic. You should, however be careful not to give the externally visible events of *System* priority over *tock* as would occur if we ran the whole right-hand side of $TOCKS \sqsubseteq_{FD} System \setminus (\Sigma \setminus \{tock\})$ in the priority model: here, more τs are getting priority over *tock* than should be.

Imagine in general that *System* has three sorts of external events: the first two are *Delayable* that the environment can delay indefinitely, and *Urgent* events that always happen as soon as the process can perform them. The third, are the *Constrained* events where it is assumed that the process makes them available for some interval where we want to explore all possibilities. On the assumption that, as previously, we do not want to force *System* only to perform finitely many *Delayable* events in a finite time, the correct formulation of timing consistency is then

$$TOCKS \,|||\, Chaos_{Delayable} \sqsubseteq_{FD} (System \setminus Urgent) \setminus Constrained$$

run in such a way that $System \setminus Urgent$ is run in the prioritised model, but where the τs created by hiding *Constrained* are not prioritised. See Sect. 14.7 below for the way to do this.

Consider what happens with $TCOPY_3[right \leftrightarrow left]_{tock}TCOPY2$. If we assume here that the overall *right* channel (i.e. *TCOPY2*'s output) is urgent then this satisfies the above specification, but if (as is implied by the definition of *TCOPY2*) this channel is delayable, then it does not.

14.5.1 Case Study: Timed Routing

The time priority model allows us to analyse timing behaviour of parallel systems with internal actions conveniently because it calculates when these actions happen. This is clear, for example, with a chain of processes like *TCOPY2* or *TCOPY3*: we can see exactly how long data takes to travel from one end to the other.

More interesting examples can be found in the routing algorithms described in Sect. 4.2. For example, we can compare the performance of both sorts of ring, namely token ring and non-blocking ring, when timing is built in and the internal `ring` communications are hidden under the timed priority model. The following is a timed version of the token ring:

```
NodeE(n) =
  ring.n.Empty -> tock ->  NodeET(n)
[] ring.n?Full.(a,b,m) -> tock -> NodeF(n,a,b,m)
[] tock -> NodeE(n)

NodeET(n) =
  send.n?b:diff(Nodes,{n})?m -> tock -> NodeF(n,n,b,m)
[] tock -> NodeET'(n)

NodeET'(n) =
  send.n?b:diff(Nodes,{n})?m -> tock -> NodeF(n,n,b,m)
[] ring.(n+1)%N.Empty -> tock -> NodeE(n)
[] tock -> NodeET'(n)

NodeF(n,a,b,m) =
if b==n then receive.n.a.m -> tock -> NodeET(n)
     else (ring.(n+1)%N.Full.(a,b,m) -> tock -> NodeE(n)
          [] tock -> NodeF(n,a,b,m))
```

Here, NodeET(n) and NodeET'(n) are two states in which the node contains an empty token. The second of these appears after one time unit in this state: the author found this necessary to avoid nodes being prevented from putting their messages on the ring by traffic on the channel ring, the latter being *prioritised* τs after hiding. CSP_M files for both examples can be found on this book's web-site. These files are designed to find the longest the rings can take to deliver a set of messages.

With equal message input from all nodes, the non-blocking ring easily outperformed the token ring (which is most effective when there are roughly half as many tokens as nodes) under light loading conditions, and was found still to outperform it under heavier conditions, but not by nearly as much. As one might expect, the time taken for the token ring to convey M messages is roughly linear in M, whereas the non-blocking ring works more slowly when it gets congested. These statements are based on only a small set of experiments and one timed implementation of each ring.

14.6 Specifying and Metering *tock*-CSP

As discussed in Chap. 14 of TPC, a curious feature of the *tock*-CSP model is that *liveness* properties frequently become *traces* specifications. This is because of the inevitable flow of time (established by the timing consistency property, itself requiring the failures-divergences model). We *know* that an infinite series of *tock* events will happen, so, for example, establishing that the nth *tock* cannot happen before the event b proves that b always happens before n time units are complete.

Consider, for example, the ring networks discussed above. The author tested their timing properties by queueing some small number c of arbitrarily addressed messages for posting at each node. This means that there are $c \times N$ messages in all to pass through the network. It is clear that in any reasonable network there will be an upper bound on how long it takes to deliver these messages, and that this is one possible measure of the network's performance.

An elementary way of discovering this bound is to try the following trace specification for enough values of N to discover when $Bound(N+1)$ holds as a trace specification but not $Bound(N)$:

$$Bound(0) = tock \rightarrow Bound(0)$$

$$Bound(n+1) = tock \rightarrow Bound(n)$$
$$\square \, ?x : \Sigma \setminus \{tock\} \rightarrow Bound(n+1)$$

This specification simply says that no events other than *tock* happen after the Nth *tock*.

It can be a little tedious to search for the boundary value. An interesting way of getting around this is to use an unusual combination of CSP operators. Suppose we have a process P where we want to calculate the smallest N such that $Bound(N) \sqsubseteq_T P$, and that we know this holds for some large M.

Add new events *nontock* and $\{ctock.n \mid n \in \{1 \ldots M-1\}\}$ to the alphabet. Let $TC(M) = STOP$ and $TC(n) = ctock.n \rightarrow TC(n+1)$ for $n < M$. Then

$$ctocks(P) = TC(1) \quad \underset{\{|ctock|\}}{\|} \quad P[\![ctock.n/tock \mid n \in \{1 \ldots M-1\}]\!]$$

is a process which behaves like P up to but not including the Mth *tock*, except that the *tock*s are now numbered in sequence.

Let the non-*tock* alphabet of P be A, then

$$crn(P) = P[\![a, nontock/a, a \mid a \in A]\!]$$

behaves like P except that every non-*tock* event is allowed to appear as either itself or as *nontock*. This means that in

$$trip(P) = crn(P) \Theta_{nontock}(flag \rightarrow STOP)$$

the state *flag* $\rightarrow$ *STOP* can be entered after P has performed *any* non-*tock* event, not just the first.

The crucial thing we have achieved here is that, if we check for absence of the event *flag*, every single error state is the same: FDR will only find one error even if you ask it for many, as discussed on p. 148.

We can make this into one different state for each number of *tock*s that have occurred by running the same specification on $ctocks(trip(P))$: the parallel component $TC(0)$ has one state for each number of tocks that have occurred. It follows that if you check this process for absence of *flag*, with FDR set to find multiple counter-examples, you will find a single counter-example for each number of tocks after which a non-*tock* event can occur in P. Furthermore, inspecting the trace will tell you (thanks to the use of the *ctock.n* events) how many *tock*s P has performed.

Without the use of $\Theta_{nontock}$ here, it is quite likely that far too many counter-examples would be produced if an otherwise similar approach were followed.

The above construction could be said to be one that *meters tock*-CSP: we can extract a numerical answer rather than a simple yes or no from a single refinement check.

Traces specifications can only ensure liveness when we demand that events will definitely have occurred by a particular time. If we want to ensure that events are accepted without saying they must occur, then failures specifications are still needed. Ways of turning failures specifications into their timed analogues are discussed in depth in Sect. 14.4 of TPC.

Timing consistency eliminates divergences that happen within a finite number of *tock*s. Divergence that happens over an infinite time-frame is not flagged as an error because *tock*-CSP concentrates on what happens between consecutive *tock*s rather than over an infinite time-frame.

14.7 Tools

FDR will provide two ways of running the model in which τ has priority over time. The first is to change the way it runs an entire check:

```
assert P [T= Q :[tau priority over]: {tock}
```

runs both P and Q giving τ priority over all events in the final set. At present this is implemented over trace checks [T= only, but it is expected that this will be extended to all models.

The second is to use the operator delay(P,{tock}) which runs P in such a way as to give τ priority over tock or whatever events sit in the set argument. This operator[2] is more flexible since it allows other operators to be applied outside it. This is useful, for example, when running the timing consistency check in the way recommended in Sect. 14.5 when we want to give τs generated by internal actions priority over *tock*, but not ones that are created by the timing consistency check itself. We might run the check

```
assert TOCKS|||CHAOS(Delayable) [FD=
    (delay(System\Urgent,{tock})\Constrained
```

where the sets of events are as described on p. 340.

delay's implementation is more like the chase operator (Sect. 16.2.5) than any other well-established FDR construct: like chase it builds a "wrapper" around the process so that it appears much like an explicit state machine on the outside, while maintaining a record of the explored state space of its process argument that only this wrapper needs to access.

---

[2]This operator is not released at the time of writing, but it will be included in a future release.

Chapter 15
Timed Systems 2: Discrete Timed CSP

15.1 Modelling Timed CSP

As mentioned in the previous chapter, Timed CSP is the usual language of CSP (but without the constants **div**, *RUN* and *CHAOS*, which all cause problems) with the addition of a *WAIT t* statement that terminates ($\checkmark$) exactly t time units after it has started. In this chapter we will restrict our attention to cases where t is a non-negative integer.[1]

We observed at the start of the last section that the accurate *tock*-CSP analogue of *COPY* is

$$TCOPY2 = left?x \to tock \to TCOPY2'(x)$$
$$\square \, tock \to TCOPY2$$

$$TCOPY2'(x) = right!x \to tock \to TCOPY2$$
$$\square \, tock \to TCOPY2'(x)$$

In Timed CSP this same process (with appropriate timing assumptions about events) is simply written $COPY = left?x \to right!x \to COPY$. In other words all the timing details become implicit rather than being included directly in the program.

The *advantages* of this approach are that this style of process is easier to write, and there is no need to write a timing consistency check since Timed CSP programs always satisfy them (e.g. it is impossible to write a time-stop). The *disadvantage* is that it is much less flexible in describing timing models; so for example it is impossible in Timed CSP to assert that a process *must* make some communication by some stated time.

Historically, Timed CSP used the set of non-negative reals as its time domain. However, work in the last ten years by Ouaknine and others has shown that it can be interpreted over a discrete time domain also.

---

[1] It has often been pointed out that this model in fact encompasses rational delays that are expressed as constants in the program, because one can always multiply the time domain by an integer.

A.W. Roscoe, *Understanding Concurrent Systems*, Texts in Computer Science, DOI 10.1007/978-1-84882-258-0_15, © Springer-Verlag London Limited 2010

In this section we show how this interpretation can be done by translation into an extended *tock*-CSP. In other words we will break time up into equal-sized intervals, each one starting either at the beginning of the trace or at a *tock* and ending just before the next *tock*. So if any non-*tock* event happens *at the same time* as a *tock*, that event follows the *tock* in the trace.

We will define a function $time(\cdot)$ that maps Timed CSP syntax into *tock*-CSP. The timed analogue of *STOP* is *TOCKS*, the process that just lets time pass: $time(STOP) = TOCKS$.

On the other hand, *SKIP* does not have to let time pass since $\checkmark$ is, as usual, treated like a signal: $time(SKIP) = SKIP$.

The *WAIT n* command is just an extended *SKIP*:

$$time(WAIT\,0) = SKIP \qquad time(WAIT\,(n+1)) = tock \rightarrow time(WAIT\,n)$$

The constants *CHAOS* and *RUN* are more interesting, since their natural interpretations, namely

$$RUN^t = tock \rightarrow RUN^t \,\Box\, ?x : \Sigma \setminus\{tock\} \rightarrow RUN^t$$

$$CHAOS^t = SKIP \sqcap (tock \rightarrow CHAOS^t \,\Box\, (STOP \sqcap ?x : \Sigma \setminus\{tock\} \rightarrow CHAOS^t))$$

violate the principle that only finitely many events can happen in a finite time. In a strong sense *there are no* useful finitely nondeterministic processes which might plausibly fill their roles that *do* satisfy this principle.[2] An analogue of *RUN* is simply impossible, whereas one of *CHAOS* requires unbounded nondeterminism and infinite traces models.

Similarly divergence (**div**) causes problems, since (a) a process that diverges in a finite time contradicts the idea that processes perform finitely many events in a finite time and (b) a process that diverges over an infinite time (i.e. with infinitely many *tock*s on the way) is indistinguishable from *STOP* in our timed theories.

In this simple treatment we will assume that, when introduced by prefixing or prefix-choice, each visible event takes a single time unit to complete, in the sense that (as in *TCOPY*2) the sequential process does not start whatever follows the event until one time unit after that event. It would be easy to adapt this so that the time becomes a function of the event. So

$$time(a \rightarrow P) = \mu p.(a \rightarrow tock \rightarrow time(P))$$
$$\Box\,(tock \rightarrow p)$$

$$time(?x : A \rightarrow P) = \mu p.(?y : A \rightarrow tock \rightarrow time(P[y/x])$$
$$\Box\,(tock \rightarrow p)$$

---

[2]This topic has been much discussed in the literature of Timed CSP. Schneider [94, 145] pointed out for continuous Timed CSP that the solution to the problem is to use infinitely long behaviours: you can then specify that only finitely many things can happen in a finite time without expressing a uniform bound on how many. The same is undoubtedly true for discrete models and if proposing a pure mathematical model we would be following this route. However, the rationale for moving to discrete models of Timed CSP here is primarily a practical one: to make Timed CSP accessible to FDR. This would be made far more difficult if we allowed unboundedly nondeterministic basic constants.

where $P[y/x]$ means the syntactic substitution of the event y chosen from A for the identifier x. This, of course, exactly mirrors the style of *TCOPY2* and expresses a process's indefinite willingness to communicate from the given choice. Indeed, *time*(*COPY*) is precisely *TCOPY2*.

We can simply define $time(P \sqcap Q) = time(P) \sqcap time(Q)$ since there is no reason why nondeterministic choice should not be resolved immediately.

The most challenging operator to translate is external choice $\Box$, because *tock* is not an event that resolves $P \Box Q$. Rather, P and Q should run lockstep in time until one or other of them performs any other visible event. We now give the combinator operational semantics[3] for the operator $\Box_T$ that we need.

Recall that the rules of $\Box$ are $((a, \cdot), a, \mathbf{1})[a \in \Sigma]$, $((\cdot, a), a, \mathbf{2})[a \in \Sigma]$, $((\checkmark, \cdot), \checkmark)$ and $((\cdot, \checkmark), \checkmark)$. The rules for $\Box_T$ are exactly the same except that the first pair of rules are restricted to $a \neq tock$ and augmented by $((tock, tock), tock)$.

The fact that $\Box_T$ is therefore CSP-like means, by Theorem 9.1, that it can be translated into ordinary CSP. This is left as an exercise, but no translation that the author has found is particularly practical for use in FDR, chiefly because when P or Q has taken over in $P \Box_T Q$, the state of the simulation is not (as one would hope) the corresponding state of P or Q, but rather a construct involving putting that state in parallel and renaming it.

Therefore, to make translation practical, it would be much better if this operator were implemented directly in FDR. In any case $time(P \Box Q) = time(P) \Box_T time(Q)$.

For the parallel operator $P \parallel_X Q$ we need to synchronise *tock* as well as manage distributed termination. For the latter we need to let time pass after the first process has terminated, and so define the process

$$TDT = (tock \to TDT) \Box (tick \to SKIP)$$

to run in sequence with *time*(*P*) and *time*(*Q*).

$$time(P \parallel_X Q) = ((time(P); TDT) \parallel_{X \cup \{tick, tock\}} (time(Q); TDT)) \setminus \{tick\}$$

The time priority model set out in the previous chapter is required for this treatment of termination. It is also required for the following rather obvious translation of hiding: $time(P \setminus X) = time(P) \setminus X$.

The rule for renaming is similar, bearing in mind that *tock* is not an event directly mentioned in Timed CSP and is therefore never renamed: $time(P[\![R]\!]) = time(P)[\![R]\!]$.

The translation of the sliding choice operator $P \rhd Q$ is also trivial: $time(P \rhd Q) = time(P) \rhd time(Q)$. The fact that, under the time priority model, the left-hand argument will never be allowed to perform *tock* is completely correct since the *tock* event is not (in Timed CSP) an event that P performs but rather an artifact of our modelling in *time*(*P*).

The translations of Θ_A and sequential composition; are similarly trivial.

---

[3] See Chap. 9.

The interrupt operator can be expressed in terms of the other ones but again, like $\Box_T$, requires parallel combinations and renamings that make it somewhat impractical. Therefore the best solution again is to define a time-specific version $\triangle_T$ of this operator, whose combinators are the same as those for $\triangle$ except that the only rule for *tock* events is $((tock, tock), tock)$.

The conditional choice $P \lessdot b \gtrdot Q$ translates as the obvious $time(P) \lessdot b \gtrdot time(Q)$, noting that there is no construct in Timed CSP that allows the conditional b to have access to any identifier that is influenced by time once the execution of the conditional has started.

The author hopes that $\Box_T$ and $\triangle_T$ will shortly be implemented in FDR to enable this translation to create scripts that can run easily on that tool. Of the two, the more inconvenient not to have is $\Box_T$, since $\Box$ is much more used in CSP than $\triangle$. We can provide two partial solutions that cover most practical cases, however.

The first is the observation that, in both Timed and untimed CSP, the step law of $\Box$ applies:

$$(?x : A \to P) \Box (?x : B \to Q)$$
$$= ?x : A \cup B \to ((P \sqcap Q) \lessdot x \in A \cap B \gtrdot (P \lessdot x \in A \gtrdot Q)) \quad \langle \Box\text{-step}\rangle \ (2.14)$$

We can use this rule, and the transparency of $time(\cdot)$ for conditional and nondeterministic choice as discussed above, to say that if P is an *idling choice construct*, namely a piece of syntax built from one level of prefix-choice, $\Box$, $\sqcap$ and conditionals, then we can define (alternatively to the above)

$$time(P) = \mu p.(tock \to p) \Box P'$$

where P' is the same syntax as P except that every process Q following one of the top-level prefixes is replaced by $time(Q)$.

Thus $((a \to Q_1) \Box ((b \to Q_2) \sqcap (c \to Q_3)))$ would map to

$$\mu p.((tock \to p) \Box ((a \to time(Q_1)) \Box ((b \to time(Q_2))$$
$$\sqcap (c \to time(Q_3)))))$$

The above actually covers the great majority of uses of $\Box$ in practical untimed CSP. There is one further common construct in Timed CSP, namely

$$timeout(P, t) = P \Box WAIT\ t$$

where we give a process P a fixed amount of time to begin communicating or be forced to terminate. In the case where P is an idling choice construct, we can adjust the construction above by maintaining a parameter recording how many *tocks* have occurred:

$$time(timeout(P, t)) = PT(0)$$
$$\text{where } PT(n) = (SKIP \lessdot n = t \gtrdot tock \to PT(n + 1))$$
$$\Box P'$$

where P' is exactly as above.

15.1.1 Semantics

The principle of maximal progress is as valid in Timed CSP as in *tock*-CSP. Indeed this principle (though not the name) was discovered as part of the development of (continuous) Timed CSP by Mike Reed and the author. It follows that the translated code must be run under the time priority model. Just as the refusal testing model $\mathcal{RT}$ is necessary to model general priority operators as described in Sect. 20.2, it is possible to use a more abstract model in which refusals only have to be recorded before *tock* events. The *timed failures* model for continuous Timed CSP was discussed briefly on p. 322: it associates a refusal set with every time during a trace, though (i) this refusal set only varies finitely often in a finite time and is constant through some half open interval $[t1, t2) = \{x \mid t1 \leq t < t2\}$ *beginning* at one time $t1$ up to but not including the time $t2$ and (ii) there are no refusals recorded *between* events that happen at the same time.

One way of describing the timed traces that make up the timed failures model is as a separate untimed failure for each non-negative real number. These are restricted to only finitely many having a non-empty trace, and the refusal set only changes finitely many times as time increases.[4] In other words, at each time there is a finite sequence of visible events followed by the refusal set that applies after this trace is finished.

We can use exactly the same insight for discrete time: a discrete timed trace is a sequence of (untimed) failures, followed by a trace. The intuition is that the first failure is what the process does and refuses up to the first *tock*, then between the first and second, and so on. The final trace is what happens after the *tock* following the last failure, and might, for example, end in $\checkmark$. Equivalently, we can say that a timed trace consists of a sequence of events from $\Sigma^{\checkmark}$ (where $tock \notin \Sigma$) in which (as usual) $\checkmark$ is always final, interleaved with *tock*s that are paired with the subset of Σ refused by the stable state from which the *tock* occurs. (The time priority model means that *tock* only occurs from stable states.)

So *time(COPY)* would have timed traces such as

$$\langle left.0, (\{|left, right|\}, tock),$$
$$(\{|left, right|\} \setminus \{right.0\}, tock),$$
$$right.0, (\{|left, right|\}, tock),$$
$$(\{|right|\}, tock)\rangle$$

We will call the model built from such traces the *Discrete Timed Failures* model $\mathcal{F}_{\mathbf{DT}}$.

In discussing *tock*-CSP it is on balance better to think of *tock* as being a special member of the set Σ of visible events. However, in modelling Timed CSP *tock* does not appear in the process description and it is easier to think of it as *not* being in Σ, but being a distinct value like $\checkmark$ and τ.

---

[4]In addition, if X is the refusal set at time t, then X must apply over some interval $\{x \mid t \leq x < t'\}$ for some $t' > t$.

The precise healthiness conditions to place on this model depend on exactly what language is being interpreted, with Timed CSP having strong conditions since it contains no urgent actions or time-stops.

In every case the discrete timed failures are closed under prefix and under subsets of the refusal sets.

For example, if we take the language of Timed CSP but restrict the use of recursion to instances where no recursive call can occur before at least one unit of time (i.e. *tock*) has elapsed (i.e. recursions are *time guarded*), then we get the following additional healthiness conditions:

NIW $s^\smallfrown\langle(X, tock)\rangle \in P \wedge s^\smallfrown\langle(X, tock), a\rangle \notin P \Rightarrow s^\smallfrown\langle(X\cup\{a\}, tock)\rangle \in P$. This is the *No Instantaneous Withdrawal* condition. It says that any event that is not refused before a *tock* is still possible after it. We discussed this principle briefly on p. 323.

NU $s \in P \Rightarrow s^\smallfrown\langle(\emptyset, tock)\rangle \in P \vee s^\smallfrown\langle\checkmark\rangle \in P$. This is the *No Urgency* condition. It says that every process will, even if the environment communicates nothing at all, either terminate or come into a state where it is stable and lets time pass. In effect this says that every process satisfies a timing consistency property with *all* events deemed delayable (see p. 335, for example).

This condition would not be true if we were to add urgent events into Timed CSP, as we would need to model examples such as the bully algorithm or the level crossing from Chap. 14 of TPC in the same style as we did in those presentations. However, see Example 15.1 for a different approach below.

UB $\forall n.\exists m.\#(s \downarrow tock) < n \Rightarrow \#(s \upharpoonright \Sigma) < m$. This *Uniform Bound* condition says that there is a bound on how many events can happen up to each finite time. It is a consequence of our time-guarded recursion assumption and is closely related to the fact that there are no good analogues for *RUN* and *CHAOS* in the discrete timed world.

This model is a congruence for the Timed CSP language with integer delays, a fact that depends heavily on the restriction that the event *tock* is never used explicitly in the language in any of prefixing, sets of events or renamings. Some example clauses are given below:

- $\mathcal{F}_{\mathbf{DT}}(STOP) = \{\langle(X_1, tock), (X_2, tock), \ldots, (X_n, tock)\rangle \mid n \in \mathbb{N}, X_i \subseteq \Sigma\}$
- $\mathcal{F}_{\mathbf{DT}}(P; Q) = \{s \in \mathcal{F}_{\mathbf{DT}}(P) \mid \checkmark \notin events(s)\} \cup \{s^\smallfrown s' \mid s^\smallfrown\langle\checkmark\rangle \in \mathcal{F}_{\mathbf{DT}}(P)$
  $\wedge s' \in \mathcal{F}_{\mathbf{DT}}(Q)\}$
- $\mathcal{F}_{\mathbf{DT}}(SKIP) = \{\langle\checkmark\rangle\}$
- $\mathcal{F}_{\mathbf{DT}}(a \to P) = \{u \mid u \leq \langle(X_1, tock), (X_2, tock), \ldots, (X_n, tock)\rangle^\smallfrown\langle a, (X, tock)\rangle^\smallfrown s,$
  $n \in \mathbb{N}, X_i \subseteq \Sigma \backslash\{a\} \wedge s \in \mathcal{F}_{\mathbf{DT}}(P)\}$
- $\mathcal{F}_{\mathbf{DT}}(P \mathbin{\square} Q) = \mathcal{F}_{\mathbf{DT}}(P) \cap \mathcal{F}_{\mathbf{DT}}(Q)$
  $\cup \{s^\smallfrown\langle a\rangle^\smallfrown s' \in \mathcal{F}_{\mathbf{DT}}(P) \mid a \in \Sigma^\checkmark \wedge s \upharpoonright \Sigma^\checkmark = \langle\rangle \wedge s \in \mathcal{F}_{\mathbf{DT}}(Q)\}$
  $\cup \{s^\smallfrown\langle a\rangle^\smallfrown s' \in \mathcal{F}_{\mathbf{DT}}(Q) \mid a \in \Sigma^\checkmark \wedge s \upharpoonright \Sigma^\checkmark = \langle\rangle \wedge s \in \mathcal{F}_{\mathbf{DT}}(P)\}$

The values of recursions are, as in many timed models, calculated using the metric spaces in which the distance between two different processes is 2^{-t} where t is the largest time during which the two processes are indistinguishable, or in other words the least number of tocks in a timed trace that one of them has and the other does not. Our assumption that recursions are time guarded means they all have unique fixed points as first discussed in Sect. 2.2.3.

15.2 Examples

The restriction to programs that only have time guarded recursions is not in the least serious if we assume (like the above semantics) that all visible events take a non-zero amount of time to complete in a sequential process. For then, not to be time guarded, they would need not to have any prefix before a recursive call. Whereas, as we know, hiding kills off ordinary guardedness of the sort used in Sect. 2.2.3, it has no effect on time guardedness: a hidden event takes just as much time after it has been hidden as before.

This means that every useful CSP program that does not involve one of the non-UB constants *CHAOS* and *RUN* can be given timed interpretations.

Like *tock*-CSP processes we can subject them to specifications that are either untimed or defined over the *tock*-time model. We can measure the amount of time these programs take to do things using the same techniques as in Sect. 14.6. Or we can check refinements between Timed CSP processes—a topic we will examine in the next section.

The most interesting Timed CSP examples are ones that make explicit use of time in the way they work. The following two examples illustrate this.

Example 15.1 (Urgent events in a non-urgent calculus) As discussed above, you cannot write a process in Timed CSP that will certainly perform an event in Σ within some finite time limit. This is what is meant by an *urgent* event.

You can, however, get a reasonable approximation in Timed CSP from the point of view of analysis, by using the *timeout*$(n, P) = P \square WAIT(n)$ construct discussed above. *timeout*$(n, a \to P); OOT(x)$, where $OOT(x) = oot.x \to STOP$ expresses the assertion that if no *a* has happened before time *n* then we are in an error state: *oot* stands here for "out of time".

If the *a* is eventually hidden (and therefore subject to maximal progress), the occurrence of an *oot.x* would be equivalent to a time-stop: *a* has not been allowed to happen when it must. If *a* is not hidden then you should check that it can always occur before it expires by hiding it and checking for *oot.x*. You can then assume the environment always lets it happen on time (as in the bully and level crossing examples) by ignoring implementation traces that include an *oot.x*. The label *x* allows you to distinguish between different "urgencies" within the system.

So an analogue of the process *TCOPY*4 on p. 325 (with implicit channel parameters) might look like

$$TCOPY4^{tcsp}(D, x)$$

$$= left?x \to WAIT\ D; timeout(1, right.x \to TCOPY4^{tcsp}); OOT(x)$$

and behaviour corresponding to the time-stop that occurs when two of these (with *oot* labels 1 and 2 and delays $D1$ and $D2$) are piped together with $D1 < D2$ would appear as the occurrence of *oot*.1. If, on the other hand, $D1 \geq D2$, then *oot*.1 will not occur. Though *oot*.2 will still be possible when the external $\{|right|\}$ channel is not hidden, which is not an error, it will never occur when it is hidden.

Example 15.2 (Timed ABP) The implementations of the Alternating Bit Protocol seen in Sect. 4.3 lacked the idea of a time-out. Instead of being sent only when an expected acknowledgement is not received, our implementations sent them in an uncontrolled way. There is a *tock*-CSP analysis of a timed version of ABP in TPC. Here we look briefly at how one might do this in Timed CSP.

The sender process of the ABP can be re-implemented as the following Timed CSP process that waits time T between retransmissions.

$$S(s) = AC(1 - s) \, \triangle \, in?x \rightarrow S'(s, x, 0)$$
$$S'(s, x, n) = AC(1 - s) \, \triangle \, S''(s, x, n)$$
$$S''(s, x, n) = d.s \rightarrow S(1 - s)$$
$$\square \, (WAIT(n); a.s.x \rightarrow S'(s, x, T))$$
$$AC(s) = d.s \rightarrow AC(s)$$

This continuously handles the acknowledgement signals arriving on channel d. The process $AC(s)$ is used to absorb redundant acknowledgements before a more useful communication comes along and causes it to be interrupted. We contemplated two different models of the receiver process in Sect. 4.3: one in which the numbers of received messages on b and sent acknowledgements are unrelated, and one (Exercise 4.12) in which there is one acknowledgement per message.

The simpler to implement in Timed CSP is the second, since there is no reason to introduce timing features into the CSP syntax, for example:

$$R(s) = b?x!(1 - s) \rightarrow c.(1 - s) \rightarrow R(s)$$
$$\square \, b?x!s \rightarrow out!x \rightarrow c!s \rightarrow R(1 - s)$$

The same is true of the media processes with faults. However, there is much to be said for not making the error-controlling events consume time, and in fact it is not too hard to see that this causes no problem with the definition below since there is never an infinite sequence of these events that could happen in a finite time.

$$CE(in, out) = in?x \rightarrow CE'(in, out, x)$$
$$CE'(in, out, x) = out!x \rightarrow CE(in, out) \quad \text{(correct transmission)}$$
$$\square \, dup \rightarrow out!x \rightarrow CE'(in, out, x) \quad \text{(potential duplication)}$$
$$\square \, loss \rightarrow CE(in, out) \quad \text{(loss of message)}$$

Once the resulting system is put together, we can test what effects errors have on it. We can construct timed regulators that allow different patterns of errors. For example, the process

$$ER(N) = ?x : E \rightarrow WAIT(N); ER(N)$$

allows at most one error from the set E in any N time units, and so interleaving k copies of this allows at most k errors in any N units. Thus, running versions of this and similar processes in parallel with the protocol (synchronising on the error events) will allow us to test the effects of different error patterns on the protocol. There are two different forms these effects might take:

- If there are enough errors for a given retransmission interval T then they might stop messages from getting through at all.
- Otherwise, any rate of errors will reduce the minimum rate at which the protocol can transmit data reliably. Fortunately we know by the untimed properties of this protocol that it can never transmit data in the wrong order: it is certainly a trace buffer.

Exercise 15.1 Translate the processes $S(b)$ and $R(b)$ defined above into *tock*-CSP.

Exercise 15.2 Create an alternative $R(b)$ which acknowledges each *new* message immediately and then sends acknowledgements every T time units.

Note that when this is coupled with $S(b)$ a stream of acknowledgements continues even when there is no message in the system, in part thanks to the fact that $S(b)$ continues to accept these acknowledgements when it is waiting for the next message on *in*. The fact that what would be divergence in an untimed model is spread over an infinity of *tock* time steps means that this is not problematic in the discrete timed failures model.

Do you think it is better for the state $S(b)$ to accept these redundant acknowledgements or not?

15.3 Digitisation

As explained earlier, the usual semantics of Timed CSP are in the Timed Failures model $\mathcal{F}_\mathbf{T}$, in which we record the exact real-number time at which each event occurs, and have a refusal set that says when each event is refused and varies finitely through time consistent with the idea that the process being observed only passes through a finite number of states in a finite time. These are usually written $(s, \aleph)$ with s a sequence of timed events such as $\langle (a, 0), (a, 0.5), (a, 0.5), (b, \sqrt{2}) \rangle$ and $\aleph$ (the Hebrew letter aleph) a finite union of sets of the form $A \times [t, t + t')$ where $A \subseteq \Sigma$. The semantics of a Timed CSP term in $\mathcal{F}_\mathbf{T}$ will be written $\mathcal{F}_\mathbf{T}(P)$, corresponding to the notation for the discrete semantics used above.

The continuous semantics does not lend itself easily to automated verification, and in the case where this is possible (when all delays in $WAIT(t)$ statements are integers and the specifications are sufficiently simple) the algorithms for deciding satisfaction are very different from those for untimed or discrete Timed CSP.

It is, however, sometimes possible to prove properties of Timed CSP processes interpreted in the continuous Timed Failures model by proving an analogous property of the same term interpreted in discrete Timed CSP. The theory that supports this is known as *digitisation*, which was adapted to CSP by Joël Ouaknine, whose work provides the main references [98, 99].

Digitisation is a way of describing a set of mappings from continuous models to discrete behaviour: the digitisation $[P]_\epsilon$ for $0 \le \epsilon \le 1$ maps each number attached to an event or refusal to either the integer immediately below it or the one immediately above it depending on whether its fractional part is $< \epsilon$ or $\ge \epsilon$. You can think of this either as a map from timed refusals $(s, \aleph)$ to discrete timed failures, or to timed refusals in which all events and refusal boundaries are integral. These two views are equivalent, but it is the latter which serves to define the idea of a process $F \in \mathcal{F_T}$ in the timed failures model being *closed under digitisation*:

$$[F]_\epsilon \subseteq F \quad \text{for all } 0 \le \epsilon \le 1$$

It turns out that the $\mathcal{F_T}$ semantics of all Timed CSP processes with integer delays have this property. This depends crucially on the no instantaneous withdrawals property.

Note that $[P]_\epsilon$ will frequently have multiple events happening at the same (integer) time in a trace, even where all traces of P have all events happen at different times. In fact both discrete and continuous versions of Timed CSP support this idea.

In this world a specification is a set of timed failures S that may or may not be a member of the timed failures model: so $F \in \mathcal{F_T}$ satisfies it if and only if $F \subseteq S$ (corresponding to process refinement). Such an S is *closed under inverse digitisation* if, whenever $[(s, \aleph)]_\epsilon \in S$ for all $0 \le \epsilon \le 1$ then $(s, \aleph) \in S$.

Not every Timed CSP process is closed under inverse digitisation, but a number of common classes are:

- Any specification that is independent of time, such as "the event a never occurs".
- *Bounded response* properties: every occurrence of an event a is followed, within t time units, by the inability to refuse b until b has occurred, for t an integer.

We get the following result [98]:

Theorem 15.1 *If S is closed under inverse digitisation and $F \in \mathcal{F_T}$ is closed under digitisation then $S \subseteq F \Leftrightarrow Z(S) \subseteq Z(F)$, where $Z(X)$ means all the $(s, \aleph) \in X$ such that all the events happen at integer times and all the discontinuities in $\aleph$ are also at integer times.*

Since, for all integer-wait Timed CSP programs P, $Z(\mathcal{F_T}(P)) = \mathcal{F_{DT}}(P)$, it follows that P satisfies the $\mathcal{F_T}$ specification S if and only if it satisfies $Z(S)$ judged over the discrete model. So for example we can infer that the continuous Timed CSP implementation of the description of ABP in Sect. 15.2 is a traces buffer, and that, conditionally on the number of error events, it satisfies bounds on how long transmission takes, by proving these properties in $\mathcal{F_{DT}}$. Concrete examples of this type of reasoning can be found in [98].

15.4 Notes for Chapters 14 and 15

Timed CSP was originally created by Mike Reed and the author in the mid 1980s [110–112]. It was developed by them and others including Jim Davies and Steve Schneider [32–34, 146]. All of this work was done on the assumption of a continuous time domain, specifically the non-negative real numbers. There was much work on the manual verification of Timed CSP programs, including the idea of *time-wise refinement*, whereby appropriate properties proved of untimed processes could be inferred of the timed analogues of these processes.

David Jackson wrote his doctoral thesis [70] on the prospects for the automated verification of Timed CSP with integer delays using *action timed graphs*. The idea of these, in common with some successful modern timed verifiers such as Uppaal [6] is to divide the very infinite state space of a continuously timed system into a hopefully finite set of regions. In some treatments these regions are based on an equivalence relation in which states (typically a control state plus a number of timers) are judged by (i) the control state they are in and (ii) the order relationship of the timers and their values relative to some (hopefully finite) set of constant values. No actual automated verification tool for Timed CSP has been created based on these principles.

The author therefore created the *tock*-CSP style in about 1992 when challenged to address the railway crossing problem, as reported in [52]. This specific example appeared in Chap. 14 of TPC, the first proper exposition of this style, which had in the meantime become very popular amongst users of FDR.

Maximal progress has been recognised as necessary for sensible timed semantics of hiding since the first work on Timed CSP. It was therefore recognised early on that to handle hiding in *tock*-CSP required the priority of τ over *tock*. While "undocumented" versions of this model have been present in FDR for many years, it has only recently (FDR 2.90) been included as an "official" feature of the tool.

The idea of a discrete-time interpretation of Timed CSP using the *tock* event is due to Joël Ouaknine, whose thesis [98] showed the formal connections between continuous and discrete Timed CSP that we outlined in Sect. 15.3. Ouaknine presented his digitisation work in [99]. The concept of digitisation itself has its origins in [55].

The discrete timed failures model proposed in the present chapter is essentially the same as the one proposed by Ouaknine in [99]. A number of variants have been proposed, for example [100], in which more refusal sets are included (that paper looks both at dense and discrete time, through digitisation).

Huang [65] shows how the information flow specifications described in Sect. 6.5 can be extended to *tock*-CSP and both continuous and discrete Timed CSP.

Chapter 16
More About FDR

In this chapter we look in some more detail at some of the algorithms that FDR uses, and study some advanced ways of specifying properties for checking on it.

We first look at the process of normalisation, then compression in general. Next we look at the management of search strategy and how it relates to memory usage, and at prospects for parallelising various functions of FDR. In the final two sections we study what can be specified using FDR's refinement model, and in particular look at the prospects for using specification languages like LTL.

16.1 Normalisation

In Sect. 8.3, where we first discussed the inner workings of FDR, we stated that the process on the left-hand side of a refinement check had to be *normalised*, namely transformed into a structure where all nondeterminism is delayed until as late as possible. For example, over many models there is effectively only one way to perform any given trace in a normal form process.

We saw the structure of normal forms for the first time in Chap. 13. In each case there was a clear relationship between the syntactic structure of a normal form and the behaviours that are observed to make up the model under consideration. Furthermore there is always a natural node in any normal form to represent exactly the behaviour that the observer can expect to see after any observation that is not complete.

The normal forms used by FDR for understanding specifications and for compression are the same as the algebraic ones except that (i) they can contain cycles and therefore infinite traces and (ii) they are represented as transition systems rather than CSP syntax. These normal forms are always finite-state systems in their own right, because they are formed by normalising the finite-state processes that FDR can enumerate.

We now study the procedure for normalising a finite-state process P over any of the *trace-plus* models, as defined in Chaps. 11 and 12, namely models in which every incomplete observation of a process is a finite trace. The principal trace-plus

A.W. Roscoe, *Understanding Concurrent Systems*, Texts in Computer Science,
DOI 10.1007/978-1-84882-258-0_16, © Springer-Verlag London Limited 2010

models are $\mathcal{T}$, $\mathcal{F}$, $\mathcal{R}$ (the stable revivals model), $\mathcal{A}$ (the stable acceptances, or ready-sets, model) and the various ways of adding infinite behaviours to these that are described in Chap. 12. Of the latter we need not consider the models $\mathcal{M}^{\Downarrow\omega}$ since these are only required for infinitely nondeterministic, and therefore infinite-state, processes.

The normalisation algorithm that FDR uses for these models comes in two stages.

Stage 1   Given a finite labelled transition system $L = (V, E, v_0)$ with nodes V, edges E and initial node v_0, we form a graph $\mathcal{P}_L$ whose nodes are members of $\mathbb{P}(V)$ as follows.

- The initial node is $\tau^*(v_0)$, where $\tau^*(v)$ is defined to be $\{w \mid v \Longrightarrow w\}$, the nodes reachable under some sequence of τs from v_0.
- For each node generated we have (if using a $\mathcal{M}^{\Downarrow}$ or $\mathcal{M}^{\sharp}$ model) to decide whether it is divergent: this is so if and only if it contains a divergent node of L. Techniques for deciding this are discussed below.
- A divergent normal form node over a $\mathcal{M}^{\Downarrow}$ model has no successors. In the other cases N we determine the set of non-τ actions possible for $v \in N$. For each such action a we form a new node, the set $\bigcup\{\tau^*(w) \mid \exists v \in N.v \xrightarrow{a} w\}$, the set of all nodes reachable after action a and any number of τs from members of N.
- The search is completed when all 'new' nodes generated are ones that have been previously expanded.

The resulting graph will be termed the *pre-normal form* of L.

This graph has, by construction, the property that there is a unique node reachable under each finite trace of the original process. This is because there are no τ actions and no node has more than one action with any given label. It may well contain different nodes that are equivalent to each other under the chosen semantic model. We need to eliminate these before we have a true normal form.

Each node has to be decorated with information that allows us to determine its refusals, revivals and ready sets as necessary. Note that it is already decorated with divergence information if relevant.

No additional information is required for $\mathcal{T}$, the traces model, and its infinitary extensions.

For failures models we need to add all *minimal acceptances* for nodes not marked as divergent in $\mathcal{N}$ and for all nodes for $\mathcal{F}$ and $\mathcal{F}^{\sharp}$. In other words, we need to look at all the stable states of L that are contained in the pre-normal form node, and record just those acceptances that have no subset also present. These, of course, correspond to the maximal refusals.

For revivals models such as $\mathcal{R}$ we similarly record the closure under union of all the stable acceptances present, and for variants on $\mathcal{A}$ we record precisely the stable acceptances. (The rules for what is recorded for divergent nodes are exactly as in the failures case.)

We now compute the maximal strong bisimulation over the pre-normal form that respects whatever labelling with divergences and/or sets of acceptances is relevant to the given model. Two pre-normal form nodes with different labellings are always distinguished by the bisimulation.

In other words, the pre-normal form is a GLTS as described on p. 174 with a marking appropriate to the model being used.

The true normal form is then found (**Stage 2**) by factoring the pre-normal form by this bisimulation, with the labelling on each node being that common to all its members.

If we are computing the normal form over $\mathcal{T}$ then there is no labelling, so the normal form is an ordinary LTS. In every other case there may well be nodes labelled with divergence information or with acceptance information that is different from just the set of initial actions of the normal form node. In these cases there are two choices about how to represent the normal form as a transition system.

The first is to add extra nodes that implement the divergence and the given acceptance sets for a given normal form node n. We can add a τ action either to the simply divergent process **div**, or to a stable node (a) that has precisely the range of actions for a chosen acceptance and (b) where the target of each labelled action is the same as the corresponding labelled action from N.

The second is to generalise the idea of a labelled transition system to a *Generalised LTS* or *GLTS* as discussed above. These are transition systems where the nodes have labellings that are taken account of when computing the behaviours of these systems or ones built out of them. The markings are always behaviours that the node exhibits such as divergence and/or collections of acceptance sets, with the latter representing the refusals, revivals or ready sets of the node. The markings on a GLTS depend on the trace-plus model being used.

The first is conceptually easier, since normal forms are represented in the same sort of LTS that we are already very familiar with. The second has the advantage that a node's allowable behaviours are immediately recorded—useful when it is a specification—and that it has less states. In fact, FDR supports GLTSs and uses this approach.

GLTSs as described here make sense over the trace-plus models but not over the rich trace models. This is because over $\mathcal{RT}$, $\mathcal{FL}$ and similar models (see Chap. 11) it is relevant which set of events was refused or stably accepted before a visible event happens—and this is not recorded in GLTS nodes. See the description of the normal forms for these models below.

Example 16.1 Consider the process $(P \,|\!|\!|\, Q) \setminus \{c\}$, where $P = a \to b \to c \to P$ and $Q = a \to ((b \to STOP) \,\Box\, (c \to Q))$. The explicit LTS of this system is shown in Fig. 16.1. In this the states are labelled with the notation XY where $X \in \{P0, P1, P2\}$ (the three states of $P = P0$) and $Y \in \{Q0, Q1, S\}$ (the three states of $Q = Q0$ where S is $STOP$). XY is equivalent to $X \,|\!|\!|\, Y$. A solid disc represents a stable state while a circle represents an unstable one.

The fact that this process has nondeterminism caused both by τ and by the ambiguity between actions performed on either side of $|\!|\!|$ means that we can expect its normalisation to be relatively complex, and that is exactly what happens, as we shall now see.

In Fig. 16.2 we have replaced these labels with briefer index numbers and indicated the first three levels of the pre-normalisation procedure:

Fig. 16.1 $(P \parallel Q) \setminus \{c\}$
before normalisation

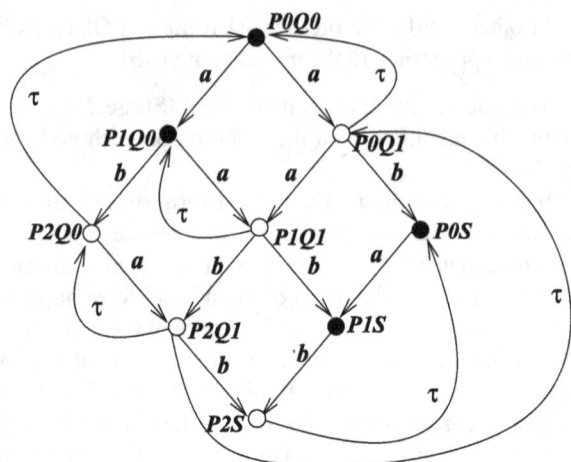

Fig. 16.2 $(P \parallel Q) \setminus \{c\}$
partly normalised

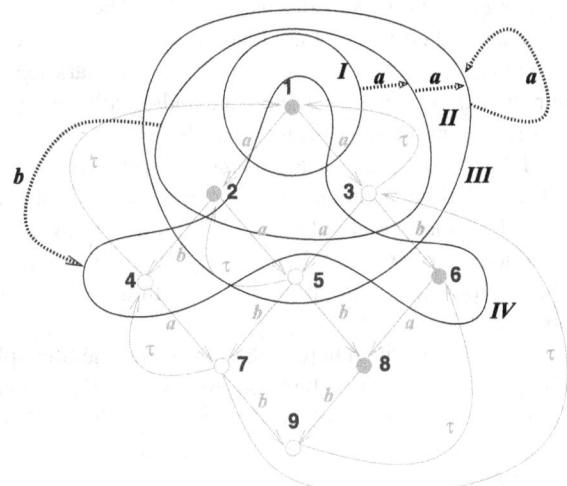

- The initial state I equals $\{1\}$: just the initial state. The only initial action this can perform is a which leads to
- $II = \{1, 2, 3\}$. This can perform either a which leads to
- $III = \{1, 2, 3, 5\}$ (whose a action leads to itself) and II can perform b which leads to
- $IV = \{1, 4, 6\}$.

This does not complete the procedure, since III can perform b leading to $V = \{1, 3, 4, 6, 7, 8\}$ and IV can perform a leading to $VI = \{1, 2, 3, 4, 7, 8\}$. V has a to $VII = \{1, 2, 3, 4, 5, 7, 8\}$ and b to $VIII\{6, 9\}$; VI takes a to $IX = \{1, 2, 3, 4, 5, 7\}$ and b to $X = \{1, 4, 6, 9\}$.

Fig. 16.3 The pre-normal form

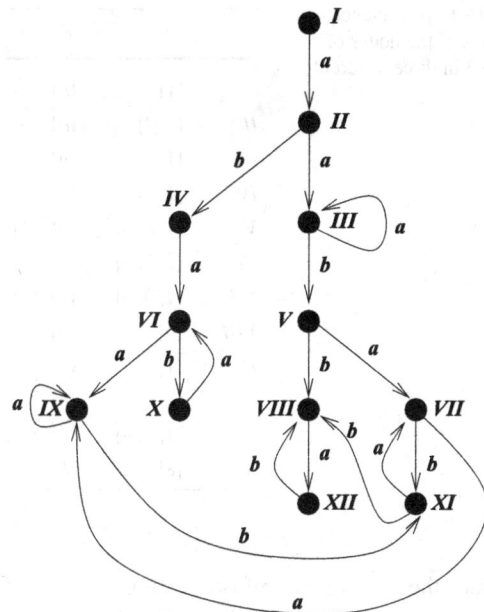

VII takes *a* to *XI* and *b* to $XI = \{1, 3, 4, 6, 7, 8, 9\}$. *VIII* takes *a* to $XII = \{8\}$ which in turn takes *b* to *VIII*. *IX* takes *a* to itself and *b* to $\{1, 3, 4, 6, 7, 8, 9\} = XI$. *X* takes *a* to $\{1, 2, 3, 4, 7, 8\} = VI$. *XI* takes *a* to $\{1, 2, 3, 4, 5, 7, 8\} = VII$ and *b* to $\{6, 9\} = VIII$. The transition diagram of these pre-normal form states is shown in Fig. 16.3. Notice how it has the desired property of having no τ actions and no branching on any visible action.

The traces ($\mathcal{T}$) normal form is found by factoring this machine by strong bisimulation, which gives the equivalence classes $\{I, IV, X\}$, $\{II, VI\}$, $\{III, VII, IX\}$, $\{V, XI\}$, $\{VIII\}$ and *XII*: a 6-state machine.

The markings for the twelve pre-normal form nodes for $\mathcal{F}$, $\mathcal{R}$ and $\mathcal{A}$ are as set out in Table 16.1. The second column is the set of stable nodes that belong to the given pre-normal form node.

Note that the $\mathcal{F}$ markings of the states *III* and *VI*, which are trace equivalent, are different. The $\mathcal{F}$ normal form in fact has 9 states, in which only the pairs $\{III, IX\}$, $\{V, XI\}$ and $\{IV, X\}$ are bisimilar/equivalent.

Since these pairs have the same markings in both $\mathcal{R}$ and $\mathcal{A}$, it follows that the normal forms in these models also have nine states.

In general you should be able to see how, moving from left to right (from an implicit left-hand column for $\mathcal{T}$ with no markings), more and more distinctions are made. Note in particular how *I* and *II* with identical minimal acceptances have different revivals, and how *V* and *VI* with identical revivals have different ready sets.

Normalisation in models where the incomplete behaviours are more complex than traces is more involved because actions are not simply labelled with events.

Table 16.1 Acceptance
markings of the nodes of
Fig. 16.3 in three different
models

		$\mathcal{F}$	$\mathcal{R}$	$\mathcal{A}$
I	$\{1\}$	$\{a\}$	$\{a\}$	$\{a\}$
II	$\{1,2\}$	$\{a\}$	$\{a\},\{a,b\}$	$\{a\},\{a,b\}$
III	$\{1,2\}$	$\{a\}$	$\{a\},\{a,b\}$	$\{a\},\{a,b\}$
IV	$\{1,6\}$	$\{a\}$	$\{a\}$	$\{a\}$
V	$\{1,6,8\}$	$\{a\},\{b\}$	$\{a\},\{b\},\{a,b\}$	$\{a\},\{b\}$
VI	$\{1,2,8\}$	$\{a\},\{b\}$	$\{a\},\{b\},\{a,b\}$	$\{a\},\{b\},\{a,b\}$
VII	$\{1,2,8\}$	$\{a\},\{b\}$	$\{a\},\{b\},\{a,b\}$	$\{a\},\{b\},\{a,b\}$
VIII	$\{6\}$	$\{a\}$	$\{a\}$	$\{a\}$
IX	$\{1,2\}$	$\{a\}$	$\{a\},\{a,b\}$	$\{a\},\{a,b\}$
X	$\{1,6\}$	$\{a\}$	$\{a\}$	$\{a\}$
XI	$\{1,6,8\}$	$\{a\},\{b\}$	$\{a\},\{b\},\{a,b\}$	$\{a\},\{b\}$
XII	$\{8\}$	$\{b\}$	$\{b\}$	$\{b\}$

Consider the case of the refusal testing model $\mathcal{RT}$. Here, from each pre-normal form node there is an arc labelled by each combination of a visible action a and set from which a might be offered. In keeping with the normal form for $\mathcal{RT}$ discussed in Chap. 13, we need to couple a with • (no stable offer observed) and each union of acceptance sets from the node that includes a.

If we were calculating the $\mathcal{RT}$ normal form of the process $(P \parallel Q) \setminus \{c\}$ as above, we would start with I, which would have actions $(a, \bullet)$ and $(a, \{a\})$ to II where things start to get more interesting. This has the actions $(a, \bullet)$ and $(b, \bullet)$ respectively to III and IV, $(a, \{a\})$ to II itself, $(a, \{a, b\})$ to III since anyone observing the refusal of $\{b\}$ can also observe the refusal of $\emptyset$; and $(b, \{a, b\})$ to $\{4, 1\}$.[1] Thus there may be more pre-normal form states as well as more actions. We will not elaborate further on these more complex normal forms.

Since the pre-normal form states of a process P are non-empty subsets of the set of states of P itself, there can potentially be $2^N - 1$ of them where N is the number of states of P. This is a potentially catastrophic blow-up in complexity, and lies behind a result of Paris Kannellakis and Scott Smolka [75] that the problem of deciding equivalence between two processes P and Q in any of the CSP models is PSPACE-complete, which is worse than NP-complete.

A class of process with this pathological behaviour on normalisation is described in Appendix C of TCP: here, $P(n)$ with $n + 1$ states has 2^N states in its normal form. This state explosion on normalisation only happens when—as in the $P(n)$ referred to here and in the $P \parallel Q$ example discussed above—there is much nonde-

---

[1]Recall from Chap. 13 that over this model we expect there to be a refinement relation amongst the results of the actions (a, A) in that the more we see refused (with • being least), the more refined the result.

terminism about which state our process will be in on particular traces and where nondeterministic decisions taken early may not be observable for some time.

In most cases, processes with poor normalisation behaviour will also be very confusing to humans and will therefore make poor specification processes to use with FDR. Mostly, specification processes will be very clear about what behaviour they allow after given traces by only having a single execution path for each trace: such processes never show pathological normalisation.

Sometimes it is not possible to be so confident. We might simply be comparing two implementations against one another in the natural spirit of refinement and have designed neither to be a specification in the ordinary sense. We might be using a specification of the sort we will see in Sect. 16.4 where the process under consideration may appear on both sides of the refinement symbol. Or the specification might be constructed as though with a high-level existential quantifier. A good example of this comes in the area of distributed databases operated on by multi-part transactions where we might demand that the result of several processes carrying out transactions in parallel is equivalent to executing the same transactions in some sequential order that is consistent with the orders of the transactions in the sequential processes. This is usually referred to as *serialisability* and is most naturally expressed as the nondeterministic choice over all allowable sequential choices.

Two approaches that can be taken in cases like these are

- Use hierarchical compression on the left-hand side of the refinement check as discussed on p. 182.
- Use FDR's `lazynorm` function on the left-hand side of the check (having declared it as `transparent`), thus

```
assert lazynorm(Spec) [M= Imp
```

does not attempt to normalise `Spec` completely before carrying out the refinement check. Rather, it does just enough pre-normalisation of `Spec` to cover the traces performed by `Impl`. We can therefore expect this to give a big gain in cases where `Impl` has only a small subset of the traces of `Spec`, since it may avoid calculating unnecessary normal form states of the specification. This has a good chance of working well with an existentially quantified specification if the implementation is a good deal more concrete.

16.2 More About Compression

In Sect. 8.8 we saw how compression can reduce the work required to carry out some large checks, when functions like `sbdia(P) = sbisim(diamond(P))` or `normal(P)` are applied to partially constructed systems. In this section we look at the definitions of those compression operators that have not been defined elsewhere, and the question of which can be used in the various models of CSP. We also look at the `chase` operator, which seeks to cut down the state space in a rather different way from the other compression operators, but which does not guarantee to preserve semantics.

There is a detailed description of `normal` in the previous section. Note that the number of states it produces can depend on the model in which it is computed. As we have said elsewhere, `normal` is risky because it can *increase* the number of states as well as reduce it.

16.2.1 Strong Bisimulation

The idea of the *strong bisimulation* as implemented in `sbisim` is described in Sect. 9.1. The maximal strong bisimulation is an equivalence relation on the nodes of an LTS L (or GLTS when the node markings are taken into account, as they were in the previous section for the second phase of normalisation). In other words, it partitions the nodes into groups where the behaviour of the members of each group is indistinguishable. The compression operator forms the *quotient* of the original LTS by the strong bisimulation relation as set out on p. 196 and more generally on p. 199. When quotienting GLTSs, we generalise this further so that the marking on a quotient node is derived from the union of the markings on its members, reduced by any healthiness conditions that apply in the chosen model such as removing non-minimal acceptances for $\mathcal{F}$.

Strong bisimulation respects all CSP models: the node x is equivalent in an arbitrary CSP model, of the types defined in Chaps. 11 and 12, to its equivalence class in the quotient space.

FDR calculates all bisimulation relations by computing a series of ever finer equivalence relations over the original state space. The first makes all nodes, or all nodes with the same marking, equivalent. When it has one relation it calculates the next by applying a functional derived from the definition on p. 195, and stops when this does not change the relation: the iteration has then reached the greatest fixed point of the functional. When FDR is calculating strong bisimulation over largish machines, you sometimes see the number of equivalence classes of the successive equivalence relations printed in the Status window.

16.2.2 DRW-Bisimulation

Recall how we defined *DRW-bisimulation* on p. 197: this is naturally converted into a compression function for LTSs. It is valid over all CSP models, a consequence of the following pair of results.

Lemma 16.1 *If x is a node in an LTS, then x is DRW-bisimilar to its equivalence class in the quotient LTS derived from the relation "is DRW-bisimilar to".*

Lemma 16.2 *If β is any FL^*-behaviour (as defined on p. 271) observable of an LTS node x, and x and y are DRW-bisimilar, then β is also observable of y.*

The second of these is proved by looking at the sequence of states that witnesses the observable components of β starting from x: $x = x_0' \Longrightarrow x_1 \xrightarrow{a1} x_1' \Longrightarrow x_2 \xrightarrow{a2} x_2' \ldots$ where, if required by β, the x_i are stable with the correct acceptance, and this sequence ends in one of the following ways

- a divergent state x_k' if β ends in $\Uparrow$;
- a stable state x_k with acceptance $A \neq \bullet$ if β ends in A;
- any state x_k if β ends in $\bullet$;
- $x_k \xrightarrow{\checkmark} \Omega$ if β ends in $\checkmark$;
- goes on for ever if β is infinite.

We can show—similarly to and using Lemma 11.1—that if x has such a sequence, then so does any y that is DRW bisimilar to x.

The result of quotienting an LTS by its maximal DRW-bisimulation is itself an LTS (i.e. no GLTS-style marking is required). For we know by its divergence-respecting quality that if one node of an equivalence class is divergent then they all are, and we know by Lemma 11.1 that if an equivalence class contains a stable node ms with acceptance set A then (i) all other stable nodes have the same acceptance and (ii) every unstable n in the class has some stable ms' bisimilar to ms such that $n \Longrightarrow ms'$.

DRW bisimulation is not implemented in FDR at the time of writing, but the author hopes it will be soon. It will be interesting to see how it compares with `sbdia`, particularly given limitations to the latter's use that we will see shortly.

16.2.3 τ-Loop Elimination

It should be clear that, if n and m are two nodes of an LTS or GLTS that are mutually reachable under sequences of τ actions (i.e. $n \Longrightarrow m$ and $m \Longrightarrow n$) then every behaviour visible of one is also visible of the other. It is also clear that they can both diverge, meaning that this equivalence is not interesting in any divergence-strict model. Over LTSs, the relation that relates every node n to itself and to all mutually τ-reachable m is a DRW-bisimulation, though not necessarily the maximal one.

The compression function `tau_loop_factor(P)`, implemented in FDR, forms the quotient by this relation. It is occasionally used by itself, but is mainly present because of a property that it creates in transition systems:

Lemma 16.3 *After applying `tau_loop_factor(P)` to a transition system, no node P has an infinite sequence $P_0 \xrightarrow{\tau} P_1 \xrightarrow{\tau} P_2 \xrightarrow{\tau} \cdots$ where P_{i+1} and P_i are always different.*

Fig. 16.4 The state space of
a small token ring

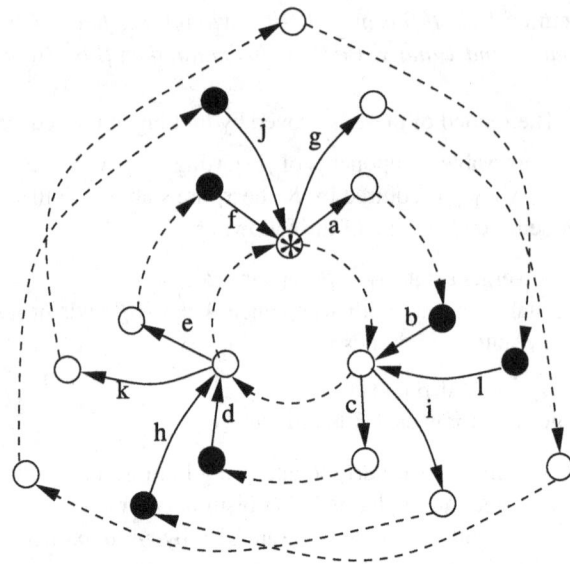

Fig. 16.5 Small token ring
after τ loop elimination

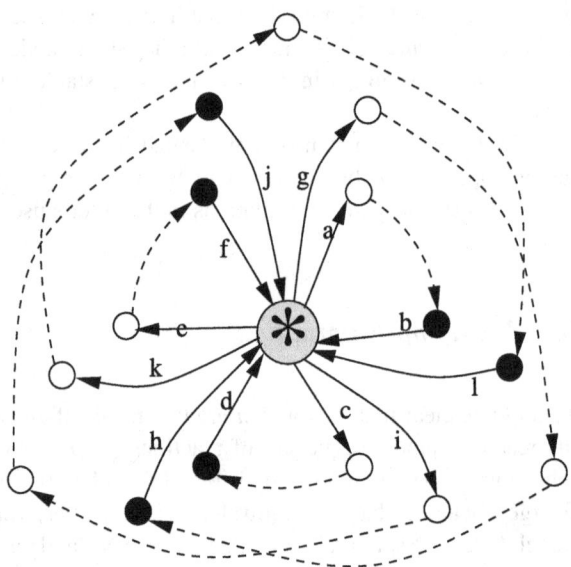

Another way of reading this is to say that the relation $n \Longrightarrow m$ is a partial order: it is reflexive, transitive and has no loops.

The effect of `tau_loop_factor(P)` is illustrated in Figs. 16.4 and 16.5. These illustrate the state space of the message-passing token ring network from Sect. 4.2.2 before and after this compression is applied. The ring illustrated has three nodes and only one message value. τ actions have been drawn with broken lines and the 12 different visible events have been renamed with the letters a–l for brevity. The three groups of six states (top, bottom-right and bottom-left) represent the alternative states the ring can be in when the token is in the three nodes. The inner ring shows the empty token moving round the ring (with the *-ed state being the initial one). The middle ring shows the three ways messages can pass from one node to the next one in ring order (with a dashed τ showing the message being passed one step round the ring). The outer nodes show messages moving two steps round the ring, using two τs per transmission.

The only τ loop in this is the inner ring, and the second figure shows this collapsed into a single node (which would be marked as divergent).

16.2.4 Diamond Elimination

The compression function diamond was designed specifically for failures and traces models. It does not respect the semantics of processes in revivals or richer models. Versions could be designed for other traces-plus models, but the one implemented in FDR (and described here) should not be used for models richer than failures-based ones.

It calls tau_loop_factor automatically, since it requires that its input satisfies the property set out above in Lemma 16.3.

Under this assumption, diamond reduction can be described as follows, where the input state-machine is S (which may be an LTS or GLTS for a failures model). The output is a new GLTS T each of whose nodes corresponds to one of S (its behaviour in the chosen CSP model is equivalent to the node it corresponds to), and there is one output node for each node explored in the following search:

- Begin a search through the nodes of S starting from its root n_0. At any time there will be a set of unexplored nodes of S; the search is complete when there are no unexplored nodes remaining.
- To explore node n, collect the following information:
  - The set $\tau^*(n)$ of all nodes reachable from n under a (possibly empty) sequence of τ actions.
  - Where relevant (based on the equivalence being used), divergence and minimal acceptance information for n: it is (thanks to the assumed property of the input) divergent if any member of $\tau^*(n)$ is either marked as divergent or has a τ to itself. The minimal acceptances are calculated by first taking the union of those of the members of $\tau^*(n)$, and then removing any non-minimal acceptances from the set that results. This information is used to mark n in T.
  - The set $V(n)$ of initial visible actions: the union of the set of all non-τ actions possible for any member of $\tau^*(n)$.
  - For each $a \in V(n)$, n_a is defined to be the set of all nodes reachable under a from any member of $\tau^*(n)$.
  - For each $a \in V(n)$, the set $min(n_a)$ which is the set of all τ-minimal elements of n_a. Here, m is τ-minimal in a set X if there is no $m' \in X$ which is distinct from m and such that $m' \Longrightarrow m$.

- A transition (labelled a) is added to T from n to each m in $\min(m_a)$, for all $a \in V(N)$. Any nodes not already explored are added to the search.

This creates a transition system where there are no τ-actions but where there can be ambiguous branching under visible actions, and where nodes might be labelled as divergent. The reason why this compresses is that we do not include in the search nodes where there is another node similarly reachable but demonstrably at least as nondeterministic: for if $m \in \tau^*(n)$ then n is always at least as nondeterministic as m. The hope is that the completed search will tend to include only those nodes that are τ-*minimal*: not reachable under τ from any other. Notice that the behaviours of the nodes not included from n_a are nevertheless taken account of, since their divergences and minimal acceptances are included when some node of $\min(n_a)$ is explored.

The reason why we can restrict the a actions from n to the τ-minimal members of n_a is that, if $m \Longrightarrow m'$ are two distinct members of n_a then $m \sqsubseteq m'$, meaning that removing the action $n \xrightarrow{a} m'$ does not change the semantic value of n.

In other words, whenever $n \xLongrightarrow{a} m$, we know there is at least one $m' \in \min(n_a)$ such that $m' \sqsubseteq m$. If we could create any other subset of n_a with this property, it could replace $\min(n_a)$ in the algorithm. You can view $\texttt{diamond}$ as a sort of half-normalisation: τ actions are removed exactly as in normalisation, but instead of giving each node n a single action with a given label a to a set of nodes of the original system, this new compression seeks to find a minimal set of such actions to individual nodes.

The effect of $\texttt{diamond}$ on the transition system in Fig. 16.5 is illustrated in Fig. 16.6. In this particular case it removes all states that have a τ into them. In effect the states that remain are the central one and ones corresponding to the τ-closures of the results of inserting any one of the six possible packets into the ring

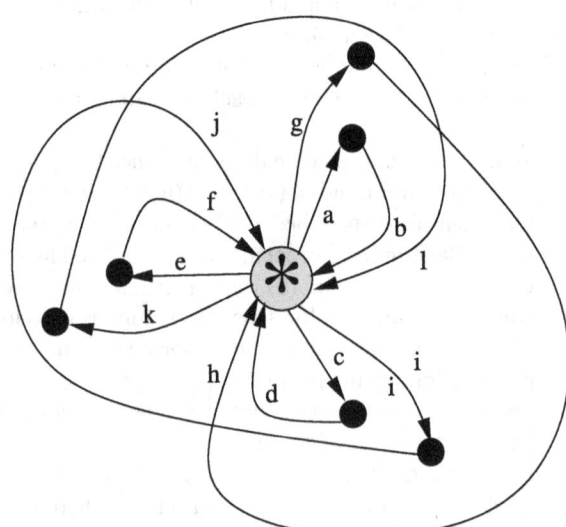

Fig. 16.6 Small token ring after τ loop elimination and diamond elimination

(i.e. a message from any one of three nodes to the two others). Naturally the only actions left are visible ones.

Just as with pre-normalisation, diamond can generate a transition system with nodes that are equivalent to each other. It is therefore a good idea to apply strong bisimulation to the result of diamond: hence our recommending the combination sbdia. It is difficult to predict in advance which of this and normal will produce the better (i.e. smaller) state machine output, but sbdia is generally faster to run and is more reliable since it never expands a system: the worst case is that it produces an output with the same number of states as its input.

The nodes of Fig. 16.6 are not further reduced by bisimulation. If, however, we were to alter the definition of the ring processes so that the receivers of messages are not told who they came from, strong bisimulation reduces 7 states remaining after diamond to 4.

The following interesting result shows that the two main existing methods of compression at the time of writing, and the prospective one DRW-bisimulation all agree on an important class of process.

Theorem 16.1 *Suppose that the LTS S consists of all nodes reachable from $P \in S$, and P is deterministic in the sense described in Sect. 6.1. Then the results of applying* sbdia, normal (*over any traces-plus model*) *and DRW-bisimulation are all isomorphic in the sense that there are bijections between them that exactly preserve all transitions.*

Proof By construction we know that every node of S represents a deterministic process which is P/s for one or more members s of $traces(P)$. Deterministic processes have the property (see Sect. 12.1.1) that they are equivalent in any CSP model if and only if they are equivalent over $\mathcal{T}$. It follows that the traces normal form is the same as those over other traces-plus models, and is the same as factoring S by the relation of trace equivalence. Furthermore, the relation on S in which two nodes are equivalent if and only if they are trace equivalent is a weak bisimulation, and is necessarily divergence-respecting since no node of S is divergent. Since two nodes that are not trace equivalent cannot be weakly bisimilar it follows that factoring by DRW-bisimulation gives the same system as factoring by trace equivalence.

It is straightforward to show that each node n of diamond(P) is, in general, trace equivalent to the corresponding node of the original system and, in S, has a unique minimal acceptance equal to its initial actions. In other words, we can think of it as another, but τ-free, LTS in which each node is equivalent to one of S. Factoring it by DRW-bisimulation is exactly the same as factoring it by strong bisimulation, since there are no τs. This therefore gives the $\mathcal{T}$ normal form. We know (by the semantic validity of diamond) that this is the same as that of the original P. The result follows.   □

16.2.5 *Laziness and* chase

We have just seen that compression operators tend to coincide on deterministic processes. Much of this argument was based on the fact that it does not matter how one resolves any apparent nondeterminism in such a process that arises either through the choice between a τ and a visible action, or a choice of targets for a given visible action.

The various compression strategies discussed above still look at the whole of a deterministic process's state space while compressing it. If the process is relatively small this may well not be a great burden, but if it is large it seems like too much work. It would be entirely legitimate, for a process known in advance to be deterministic, to compress it by simply extracting an arbitrary deterministic refinement as in the FDR algorithm for deciding determinism (p. 170) and then applying any one of the three compressions above to remove any remaining τ actions.

At the time of writing this particular compression is not accessible in FDR, but a similar and arguably more useful function is: chase. We will discuss this shortly.

All the compressions defined so far are "eager" in the sense that the process P has its compressed form calculated in full before anything else is done with it. A "lazy" compression is one that only works out its own state space as demanded by the context it is run in—typically when run as a component process in a refinement check. We have already seen one example of this: the lazynorm function described on p. 363. *In theory* we could use this function as a compression, thereby avoiding the need to invent an invariant of the sort seen in Sect. 8.8.1 since it will compress sub-processes on the fly, looking only at states reached in context. However, in *practice* the use of lazynorm as a compression as opposed to the use outlined on p. 363 does not work well at the time of writing since it does not integrate with the supercombinator-based implementation of state machines described in Sect. 9.3. While this difficulty could be overcome, and indeed a lazy version of diamond developed, both would suffer the disadvantage that no bisimulation would be applied to the output, as is done for the corresponding non-lazy operators (the latter in sbdia).

chase is, despite its name, a lazy operator in the sense described here. It works by forcing τs: if it encounters a state n with one or more τ actions available it simply selects one of them and follows it. Either it will find a stable state m or the function itself diverges. The latter possibility is an error: chase should not be applied to divergent states. In the first case the behaviour of n is replaced by that of m, which is in general a refinement.

There is therefore no sense in which chase looks at the whole state space of the argument process, or at all transitions. If applied to a divergence-free process P it is guaranteed to deliver a refinement (though not necessarily a deterministic refinement) of P. We can guarantee that the result is equivalent to P in the case where P is known to be deterministic. It is possible to generalise this a little, but not in any particularly useful way.

You will generally want to apply chase in cases where P is too large to compress using sbdia (which, thanks to bisimulation, may well produce a better result). P will therefore be too large to check for determinism using the algorithms discussed in Sect. 8.7. It follows that you will normally apply chase to processes that are known to be deterministic *by construction*. P will usually involve hiding in its definition since we need τ actions to make chase worthwhile. Two sorts of processes discussed in Sect. 10.5 are known to be deterministic by construction, but only one sort—the *confluent* processes—allows hiding. Indeed, most of the practical applications of the use of chase that the author is aware of are either confluent or closely related to confluent systems.

The use of chase to avoid looking at the complete state space of a system is a type of *partial order method*, as discussed in [150], for example.

The best-known application is to the *intruder*, or *spy* in the CSP model of cryptographic protocol as described in [136, 142] and Chap. 15 of TPC. In this example we want a process equivalent to Spy(IK), where

```
Spy(X) = say?x:inter(X,Messages) -> Spy(X)
         [] learn?x -> Spy(Close(union(X,{x})))
```

where X varies over subsets of a sizable finite set KnowableFacts, Messages is the subset of this that can be communicated over a channel and IK is the initial knowledge of the intruder. learn is a channel over which the intruder collects information from the network, and say is one over which it inserts messages into the network.

In this example, Close(X) applies the rules of encryption to deduce which other facts the intruder can know, given that it knows X. For example, if it knows a key k and encrypt(dual(k),f) then it knows f. The essential property we need for the following application of chase is that, if X is a subset of Y, then Close(X) is a subset of Close(Y).

The same model could also handle other cases in which a process behaves rather like one of the *Set* processes already discussed in Sect. 8.2 except that there is also some sort of inference rule that it applied to the set each time something new is collected. For example, the members of X could be points inside some geometric figure, with *Close* adding knowledge from the known structure of that figure (perhaps convexity).

Spy(X), as defined above, is not only deterministic but confluent in the semantic sense studied in Exercise 10.13 (p. 250). It follows that any parallel implementation of it is guaranteed to be safe for the application of chase. The natural conclusion of Sect. 8.2 is that we should model Spy(X) as a parallel composition of one two-state process for each member of KnowableFacts. That is in fact what we do, but the implementation is more complex than the one in Sect. 8.2 since members of sets are not only inserted and reported on, but also *inferred* using the rules that make up Close.

The type of such inferences is (X,f), where X is a set of KnowableFacts from which it is possible to deduce some f not in X. We declare a channel of this type for internal communication, and define two states:

```
Ignorant(f) = member(f,Messages) & (learn.f -> Knows(f)
              [] ([] X:precs(f) @
              infer.(X,f) -> Knows(f)))

Knows(f) = (member(f,Messages) &
           (say.f -> Knows(f) [] learn.f -> Knows(f)))
         [] ([] (X,f'):deds(f) @
           infer.(X,f') -> Knows(f))
```

where precs(f) is the set of Xs such that (X,f) is an inference and deds(f) is the set of inferences (X,f') such that f is in X.

The complete system is put together by choosing one or other of these processes for each fact based on initial knowledge, synchronising on appropriate infer.(X,f) events, and hiding the channel infer.

These processes are not quite confluent because we only allow each fact to be deduced once. However, it is clear that the complete parallel spy is equivalent to the sequentially defined Spy, and therefore deterministic. We can therefore apply chase safely, and indeed this is completely crucial to the efficiency of the standard CSP models of cryptographic protocols.

This model of the intruder [136] in cryptographic protocol models has been exploited in relatively recent developments in this topic. For example, [17, 76] have each built on this model by including trustworthy agents as well as the conventional intruder into one inference model so as to make possible proofs of a protocol in general rather than just a specific small model of it.

A completely different use of chase is shown in Exercise 16.2, and a further one is shown in Exercise 20.2 where we deliberately use it to explore only part of the reachable behaviour of a process.

It is crucial, however, to remember that any use of chase is carefully justified by showing either that it does not change the semantics of the process it is applied to, or that it has whatever other effect was intended.

Exercise 16.1 Consider networks made up of the components *Add* and *In(c)* where

$$Add = (in1 \rightarrow out \rightarrow Add) \,\square\, (in2 \rightarrow out \rightarrow Add)$$

$$In(c) = c \rightarrow out \rightarrow In(c)$$

The network is constructed using link parallel in which the output of all but one component is connected to an *in*1 or *in*2 of another one. Each *in*1 or *in*2 is connected to an *out*. The "input" events *c* in the *In(c)*s are all distinct. Thus a network represents an arithmetic expression built using binary + operators, with the various *c* inputs being "variables"; the one remaining *out* channel gives the output. The numbers, of course, are represented by the number of times the given events happen.

Show that all such networks are ones where chase is applicable.

For a few sample networks, compare the effectiveness of chase against other compression strategies (including no compression at all).

Exercise 16.2 Recall Milner's scheduler from Example 8.1. In Appendix C of TPC it was shown that attempting to prove the specification defined on p. 180 of the present book as `Rotate(0)` by inductive compression fails because partial networks have too many states. In Example 8.1 we showed how to solve this with invariants. Two alternatives suggested by the present section are[2]

(a) Showing that *Scheduler* is confluent, meaning that *chase* is semantically valid on *Scheduler* \ {|b|}.
(b) Lazy compressions such as `lazynorm` in inductive compression.

How effective are these?

16.3 Handling Large Checks

In this section we will briefly look at some strategies for executing large explicit checks efficiently, when we actually have to look at a very large number of states individually. They complement methods discussed in other parts of this book (for example Sects. 8.8, 16.2, 8.9, 17.5 and 17.2) that permit smaller numbers of states to be checked or use different algorithms.

As we have seen in Sect. 8.6, it is sometimes beneficial to use a search strategy deliberately designed to move quickly to areas where it is thought likely that possible counter-examples will lie. That is, if it is believed likely that counter-examples of a particular type exist. We will concentrate here, however, on strategies to complete checks that are expected to succeed.

We will look at two issues: memory locality and parallelism.

16.3.1 Memory Locality

One of the main problems of model checking is the amount of data that has to be stored and accessed during a check. One of the state-pairs used in a typical FDR check might take 10 words to store, once we take account not only of the specification and implementation states but also of housekeeping information, for example to allow debugging. (This figure can vary significantly depending on the number of parallel components in the process and the size of each.)

We need to store details of all the states we have discovered to date during a conventional check, simply so that we know when we are visiting a state we have seen before. Without this we would never know when we had covered all the states of a system unless the system in question has some special property.[3]

---

[2] TPC demonstrated a third: using leaf compression instead of inductive compression.

[3] For example, the transitions of one of our models of a Sudoku or Solitaire puzzle have no loops, meaning that they could be exhaustively searched without remembering all previous states. However, since the same state is often reached in multiple ways, there would still be the danger of covering the same state many times.

We will look successively at three different models for storing and accessing this information. Perhaps the most obvious way (and the one that was followed in early versions of FDR and other checkers) is to store the successively discovered states in a hash table. In other words, some randomising function is chosen from the values to be hashed into an array of pointers, each of which stores the list of state-pairs that hash to the given value.

The advantage of this approach is that it places no restriction on the search strategy, namely the order in which the various discovered states are visited. In particular it supports DFS, where we need to know whether or not a given state-pair is new the instant it is generated—for on that hangs the decision about whether the search should move there next. As previously discussed, FDR uses DFS for divergence checking.

DFS works well precisely when everything can be stored in fast, randomly accessible memory. When this is not so, we will assume the memory model where the main memory acts as cache for virtual memory, which might be stored on a disc. The crucial feature of this model is that data is swapped in and out of memory in large blocks of consecutive addresses, probably thousands of times larger than the memory required for a single state. So, while each transfer takes far longer than a fetch from main memory, the overall bandwidth can be high.

In fact, of course, modern computers have a number of levels of caching, but for simplicity we will consider only how algorithms work with a single level over disc-style storage. Certainly, based on experience, it is that barrier that poses the main challenge to FDR.

This a problem for model checking in general, but especially a problem for the hash table model of storing states. The random nature of hash functions—vitally important for getting good performance from a hash table in normal circumstances—means that the number of locations from a single block of virtual memory that are accessed before the block is replaced will frequently be very small. This is because the locations in the hash table that are accessed consecutively are likely to be widely spread. This means that one gets little "value for money" from these large transfers: we are wasting most of the bandwidth of the swapping.

FDR does not use hash tables for storing large bodies of states, but rather structures based on B-trees. B-trees store states in sorted order together with indexing. This sorted structure makes possible the Δ-compression algorithm discussed briefly in Sect. 8.1.2, and breaking the B-trees up into blocks enables the alternative use of gzip discussed in the same place. Therefore not only the memory transfers but also the amount of work devoted to compressions and decompressions depend on making use of as much of each these blocks as we can at a time.

There is little or no opportunity to be clever in the execution of a DFS as used for identifying divergent states, since it is necessary to check states for membership of the already-searched body as soon as they are generated. DFS executed in the B-tree model might, however, gain something if we could organise data structures so that a successor state is *usually* close to the one from which it was generated. We will return to this topic later.

With BFS there is considerably more opportunity, since the interval between a successor state being generated and the need to check it for newness is long on average, namely the length of time that it takes to complete a full level of the search. We can gain considerable locality in the use of memory by the following method.

- The BFS is divided explicitly into levels, or *plies*, where the 0th level consists of the root state and the $n + 1$th consists of all state-pairs reachable from ones in the nth layer that are not in layers $0 \ldots n$.
- All the plies are stored in the same sorted data structure S, which might be a list or a B-tree.
- The $n + 1$th ply is computed from a sorted list of all the successor state-pairs reached from the nth. These are inserted into S in order: if S is a list this is performed by merging the two lists together, and if a B-tree, by the normal insertion algorithm. In either case the insertion reveals whether each item is new. If so, its successors are calculated and added to the list that contains candidate members for ply $n + 2$.

  In either case we have the advantage that both S and the candidate state list are accessed in sorted order, meaning that we should not have to fetch a given disc-block of this storage more than once in each ply.
- The search is finished when no new state-pairs are discovered on a layer.

FDR has used variants on this approach since the introduction of FDR2 (1994/5). Computers, of course, have improved remarkably since that date in all of processing power, amount of main memory and sizes of disc. We are always, naturally, happy to accept the increases in power that such improvements bring. The author's perception over the years has been that the time it takes a CPU can fill up the memory in a typical workstation when running FDR has gradually reduced to about an hour. Also, the relative slow-down in speed between phases where a check runs in main memory and in virtual memory has increased with time to the point where improvements are once again clearly necessary.

The best solution to this problem, naturally, is to find a computer with enough memory to run your check. These, unfortunately, are not always available.

At the time of writing we are experimenting with an alternative search strategy specifically devised to reduce the amount of transfer between memory and disc.

Local search [133] seeks to break up the search space into pieces of the right size to fit into physical memory and which interact with other pieces as little as possible:

- It begins using the same BFS strategy as at present, with a parameter set for how much physical memory FDR is supposed to use.
- We monitor the position at the end of each ply of the BFS, and when the memory used by the combination of the accumulated state space $X(n)$ and the unexplored successors $S(n + 1)$ exceeds the defined limit, these two sets are each split into a small number (at least two) *blocks* by applying some *partitioning function*.
- This partitioning might either be done as a separate exercise, or be combined with the next ply of the search.
- From here on the search always consists of a number of these blocks, and a partitioning function Π that allocates states between them. Each such block $B(i)$ will

have an explored state space $EB(i)$ and a set of unexplored states $UB(i)$, which may intersect $EB(i)$.

- At any time FDR pursues the search on a single block $B(i)$ only, as a BFS, but the successors generated are partitioned using Π. The successors belonging to $B(i)$ are pursued in this BFS. Those belonging to other blocks are added to $UB(j)$ in a way that does not require operations on the existing body of $UB(j)$ to be brought into memory.
- The search on $B(i)$ might terminate because after some ply $UB(i)$ becomes empty. In this case we begin or resume the search on some other block with a non-empty $UB(j)$: if there is none, the search is complete and in FDR the refinement check gives a positive result. If there is another block to resume we must realise that $B(i)$ may not be finished for all time since other $B(j)$ might create a new $UB(i)$ for the block that has just terminated.
- On the other hand the size of the search of $B(i)$ might grow beyond our limit. In this case Π is refined so that $B(i)$ is split as above. After that a block which may or may not be one of the results of this last split is resumed.
- On resuming a block $B(i)$ the set $UB(i)$ might have grown very large thanks to input from other blocks, and furthermore it is possible that $UB(i)$ has much repetition. There is therefore a strong argument for (repetition removing) sorting of $UB(j)$ before assessing whether to split $B(i)$ at this stage.

At present we are experimenting with developing keys for state-pairs that have locality in the same sense as we discussed for DFS above. This is done by identifying specific components of the description of a state that do not change frequently under the actions that states perform. The chosen components are used as the primary sort key for the sorted lists and B-trees used in the implementation. Furthermore the partitioning algorithm Π is then just to split the state space using that same order. So each block consists of the state-pairs p that lie between two limits (state-pairs, $-\infty$ or $+\infty$).

One of the interesting questions at the time of writing is how critical the choice of this sorting key will be. If it is critical, should we always rely on an automated construction of the key or should we allow users to design their keys if they want to? (This might be by nominating one or more components of the implementation process that is to be used.)

There are other choices to be made in this strategy, such as the order in which to handle unfinished search blocks.

The author expects that a version of local search will soon be included in FDR releases.

16.3.2 Parallel Implementation

It is tempting to think that the fact that CSP is a notation for describing concurrent (i.e. parallel) systems will make it easy to *verify* it on a parallel computer. In other words, we might ask whether the parallel structure of the program under consideration will be reflected in the way we might parallelise its verification. In fact, at least for algorithms we now understand, the two are usually completely independent. (The only exception is one possibility discussed for compilation below.) What we actually do is break up the searches that verifications involve into parts that different processors can execute separately.

A parallel implementation of FDR was reported in [45]. This worked on a PC cluster and showed (for up to 8 processors—the size of the cluster used by the authors) that at least for the main search through state-pairs, an approximately linear speed up was obtained. The implementation reported there never became part of the general release of FDR, thanks in part to the variety of PC cluster architectures that might have had to be supported.

In the last few years, Moore's Law of ever-increasing microprocessor and computer capability has manifested itself almost entirely through the development of multi-core processors. This means that if we are to continue to see the power of tools like FDR increasing, we need to use the power of these systems as standard.[4]

There seems little doubt that the best way of parallelising the main search phase of FDR will be to split the state space using a partitioning algorithm such as that seen in the previous section. We will allocate one partition to each processor/core at the start. Every time a successor state-pair is generated, its destination partition is calculated and it is sent to the corresponding processor. The way this is done will depend on the communication model of the parallel system.

We could choose to run this in two ways: either have the same number of partitions as we have processing cores or more. In the second case the extra partitions may exist from the start or may be generated dynamically as the search progresses in similar ways to those described in the previous section.

Of course, with lots of processor cores working at the same time, we can expect that the search will fill up the main memory of the computer a lot faster. In this case we will *need* to use more partitions than there are cores.

In that case in particular there will be an advantage to be gained from (a) using a partitioning method designed for locality as in the previous section and (b) ensuring that the particular partitions in memory at any one time are close together.

Having more partitions carries the disadvantage that more communication will almost inevitably be needed. It has the advantage that it should be easier to balance the load between different cores: when one core has nothing left to do it can move to a different partition.

While FDR typically spends most of its time in the main "running" phase of the check discussed above, it is certain that we will wish to parallelise other parts of its activities as well. Below we discuss how we might parallelise other things it does.

---

[4]On a positive note, everyone else will have to do this too, which should mean that expertise in concurrency will be at a premium!

DFS As seen elsewhere, FDR uses the DFS search strategy for determining divergence information and sometimes for seeking counter-examples. DFS is an essentially sequential algorithm, but there is no reason why different processing cores should not carry out DFS searches on different parts of a state space at the same time, synchronising the information they have discovered from time to time.

Compilation There are various possibilities for dividing up the compilation of CSP processes into independent parts, such as addressing separate parallel components and partitioning the sets of supercombinator rules that have to be generated. This is likely to prove one of the more challenging parallelisation exercises, however.

Normalisation The main normalisation activity is the collection of the pre-normal form states. The search itself can be parallelised in exactly the same way as the main search through hashing: now of sets of states rather than state-pairs. It is harder to see, however, how to create localising partitioning functions on these.

Compression When using compression, FDR will frequently generate a list of processes whose individual state spaces have to be calculated and compressed. We may then have the choice of farming these sub-tasks out to separate cores or performing sub-tasks in sequence, parallelising each. Of course if we have many cores, it may be possible to use both sorts of parallelism at the same time.

Bisimulation FDR calculates bisimulations by calculating a series of ever finer equivalence relations, as described earlier in this chapter. One natural way of parallelising this is to make each core responsible for calculating the successive equivalence relations on its own subset of the overall state space. The calculation of each successive relation would need to be completed by a phase in which a global reconciliation of the calculated equivalence classes was done.

Diamond This is, once more, a search and can be parallelised using the same approach as for the main check.

Chase The chase function has two alternative sequential implementations in FDR. In one it gradually caches an explicit state machine representation for the chased system, so that when it encounters the same state to chase a second time it can simply look it up in this cache. In the other implementation (written chase_nocache) it does not do this, which is more economical in memory. Assuming that the running of chase on each state is the responsibility of the core that is working out the successors of a given state, we could perform the second of these without needing to coordinate the chasing procedure at all. If we were building up the table of an explicit representation then there would need to be quite a lot of synchronisation between cores to allocate and look up the names of the state indices of the chased machine. Therefore the chase_nocache version looks more attractive for parallel execution.

16.4 Generalising the Specification Model

The most familiar use of FDR is to carry out refinement checks of the form $Spec \sqsubseteq Impl$. Here, $Impl$ represents the process under consideration and $Spec$ represents the specification we want to prove of it. This is called a *simple* refinement check, and always tests for a *behavioural* specification (see p. 36). Sometimes we have modified $Impl$ by hiding or lazy abstraction, or by parallel composition with some process that restricts the behaviours it can perform (as in some uses of the controlled error model). But in all cases there is a single copy of $Impl$ running on the right-hand side of the check, and an independently described specification on the left-hand side. It is straightforward to show that every such case also checks a behavioural specification, and a result of [128] shows that there is an equivalent simple check.

In two particular cases we have used refinement in a more general way:

- In the check

$$Impl_E \parallel_E STOP \sqsubseteq \mathcal{L}_E(Impl_E)$$

where E is the set of error events (see p. 126) in the controlled-error process $Impl_E$, we have the implementation on both sides of the refinement symbol.
- In Lazić's determinism-checking algorithm (p. 172) we ran the implementation in parallel with itself on the right-hand side.

The most general question we can answer about a process $Impl$ with a single FDR refinement check is whether $F(Impl) \sqsubseteq G(Impl)$ in any one of the supported models, where F and G are both CSP-defined functions with the property that if $Impl$ is finite-state then so are $F(Impl)$ and $G(Impl)$. Both the examples above fall within this category.

For many years the question of what sorts of specifications could be formulated as $F(Impl) \sqsubseteq G(Impl)$ (without the additional finite-state requirement) remained unanswered. In the last few years there have been a number of interesting papers on this topic.

- The author, in [128], concentrated on the failures-divergences model $\mathcal{N}$, though modified versions of that paper's results are almost certainly true for the other CSP models. It looks at the case of finite Σ and does not restrict itself to finite-state processes or functions that map finite-state to finite-state. Its main result is that if $R(P)$ is any *closed* predicate on $\mathcal{N}$ then

$$R(P) \equiv F(P) \sqsubseteq G(P)$$

for a pair F and G of *uniformly continuous* CSP functions F and G.

Here, *closed* means that if P_i is a sequence of processes such that $R(P_i)$ for all i, and P_i converge to P in the usual restriction-based metric topology on $\mathcal{N}$, then $R(P)$ holds also. One way of understanding this concept is that a property R is closed if and only if, whenever $\neg R(P)$, then we can tell that this is so from some $P \downarrow n$: how P behaves up to some length of trace. Here, n can vary with P.

A function F is *uniformly continuous* if for all n there exists $m(n)$ such that $F(P) \downarrow n = F(Q) \downarrow n$ whenever $P \downarrow m(n) = Q \downarrow m(n)$. (This is a well-understood concept in the mathematics of metric spaces.)

It is also shown that every property that is expressed as a refinement using uniformly continuous F and G is closed.

Here is a trivial example: normally it would take two refinement checks to prove that P is equivalent to some given Q in one of our models. But we can achieve this with the single check

$$(a \rightarrow P) \,\square\, (b \rightarrow Q) \sqsubseteq (a \rightarrow Q) \,\square\, (b \rightarrow P)$$

The equivalence between closed properties and things expressible via refinement, using a restricted class of functions, was an unexpectedly powerful result. The paper also shows how, for restricted classes of property R, we can assume more about F and G.

- If R is *refinement closed*, so that $R(P)$ and $P \sqsubseteq Q$ implies $R(Q)$, then F can be a constant function (i.e. $F(P)$ can be a constant process independent of P). Lazić's determinism check is an example of this.
- If R is *distributive*— if P satisfies R for all $P \in S$ then so does $\sqcap S$—then G can be a distributive function, as in fact F *always* can be.

It is also shown in [128] that any property $R(P)$ that is both refinement-closed and distributive can be expressed as a *simple refinement check Spec $\sqsubseteq P$*: this should be unsurprising since *Spec* is (as in the construction of the characteristic process on p. 39) just the nondeterministic composition of all processes satisfying R.

- Gavin Lowe and Toby Murray pick up the theme of refinement-closed specifications in [89, 96]. Recall that in Lazić's determinism check we run two copies of the object process P in parallel with itself, and explicitly compare one behaviour from each to ensure they are consistent with each other. This is exactly in line with the specification of determinism (p. 120) which fails when a process has a pair of inconsistent behaviours.

  Lowe [89] shows this correspondence is exact, at least for properties that insist on divergence-freedom, which is all that paper considers. We can express such a closed and refinement-closed property $R(P)$ as *Spec $\sqsubseteq G(P)$* in which P appears in parallel with itself in $G(P)$ no more than N times if and only if there is some predicate $T(f_1, \ldots, f_N)$ on N-tuples of failures such that

$$R(P) \equiv \forall f_1, \ldots, f_N \in failures(P).T(f_1, \ldots, f_N)$$

The paper goes on to discuss cases in which this construction can be converted from an infinitary one to one that can be run on FDR, and to look at various specifications that can be handled by this type of specification.

- The author, in [125], showed how it is sometimes possible to transform checks of the form $Spec \sqsubseteq Impl$, where $Impl$ is finite-state and $Spec$ is infinite-state but has some sort of recursive quality, into a check of the form $F(Impl) \sqsubseteq G(Impl)$ where both left- and right-hand sides are finite-state. This is demonstrated for the specifications of being a counter (in effect a data-less bag or buffer), a stack, bag and some forms of buffer.

  So for example a process P is a trace counter (satisfying the **sat**-style trace specification $tr \downarrow down \leq tr \downarrow up$) if

$$Counter_L(P) \sqsubseteq_T Counter_R(P) \quad \text{where}$$

$$Counter_R(P) = P[\![up, up'/up, up]\!] \underset{\{up,up'\}}{\|} Reg$$

$$Reg = up \to Reg \,\square\, up' \to STOP$$

$$Counter_L(P) = (P \,\|\, up' \to down \to STOP) \underset{\{up,up',down\}}{\|} UpFirst$$

$$UpFirst = ?x : \{up, up'\} \to RUN(\{up, up', down\})$$

  This says, in a convoluted way, that if, by deleting the last up and perhaps a later $down$ from an arbitrary $tr \in P\langle P \rangle$, we obtain another trace of P, *and* if every trace of P begins with up, then P is a counter.

  The reader can discover more about this specification and related ones from [125].

  While this type of specification is interesting, its complexity in use suggests it will not find many practical applications. In particular many of the cases where one might want to use it for bags, stacks and buffers might well be susceptible to the use of `lazynorm` (p. 363) in conjunction with a large but finite specification process.

- Two papers, one by Michael Leuschel, Thierry Massart, and Andrew Currie [84] and the other by Gavin Lowe [88] have addressed the relationship between LTL specification and CSP refinement checking.

  LTL (Linear Temporal Logic) is a popular alternative view of specification to the usual CSP style where a specification is a process. Instead of specifying a process in terms of its observable actions, LTL [25] assumes that there are atomic propositions which may or may not be true at the states of a process. Because we are observing communicating processes, Lowe assumes that the atomic propositions are

  - a, meaning that the event a happens.
  - available a, meaning that a is not refused.
  - deadlocked with the obvious meaning.
  - live meaning the opposite of deadlocked.
  - true and false with the obvious meanings.

  These are propositions that are true or not of the first step behaviour of a (by assumption) divergence-free CSP process.

LTL also contains the propositional connectives $\wedge$, $\vee$ and $\neg$ with their usual meanings, and the following *temporal operators*. Here ϕ and ψ represent arbitrary LTL formulae.

- $\bigcirc \phi$ ("next ϕ"): in the next state, ϕ will hold.
- $\Box \phi$ ("always ϕ"): ϕ is true at all times through the execution.
- $\Diamond \phi$ ("eventually ϕ"): ϕ holds at some state in the execution.
- $\phi \mathcal{U} \psi$ ("ϕ until ψ"): ϕ holds in every state until ψ holds at some point.
- $\phi \mathcal{R} \psi$ ("ϕ releases ψ"): this means the same as $\psi \mathcal{U} \phi$ except that ϕ need never become true.

The LTL language that Lowe considers consists of just the atomic propositions and other constructs listed above.

For the formula ϕ to hold of a process P we mean informally that ϕ holds of every *complete* behaviour of P, namely a run to a deadlock or a run with an infinite number of visible actions. (Lowe does not consider $\checkmark$ and has assumed lack of divergence.) So, for example, the vending machine

$$VM = coin \rightarrow (coffee \rightarrow VM \,\Box\, tea \rightarrow VM)$$

satisfies the specification

$$\Box(coin \rightarrow \bigcirc(\text{available } coffee \wedge \text{available } tea)$$

or in other words "whenever a coin is inserted both coffee and tea are available on the next step".

This is equivalent to the failures specification:

$$CTC = STOP \sqcap (?x : \Sigma \setminus \{coin\} \rightarrow CTC) \sqcap coin \rightarrow C$$

$$C = ?c : \{coffee, tea\} \rightarrow CTC$$
$$\Box \, (STOP \sqcap ?x : \Sigma \setminus \{coffee, tea, coin\} \rightarrow CTC)$$
$$\Box \, (STOP \sqcap coin \rightarrow C)$$

Lowe shows that failures models are inadequate to interpret this logic, and instead uses $\mathcal{RT}$, the refusal testing model. He goes on to show how to decide the *bounded, positive* fragment of his LTL using simple refinement checks over $\mathcal{RT}$. This is the set of formulae that do not use $\Diamond$, $\mathcal{U}$ or negation.

Leuschel et al. [84] consider only traces properties of CSP processes since they do not use anything like the proposition available a. They are, however, able to handle a wider range of other constructs than Lowe by using a different model of satisfaction. Instead of looking at specifications of the form $Test(\phi) \sqsubseteq P$, they move P to the left-hand side of refinement:

$$(P \parallel_{\alpha P} Tester(\phi)) \setminus (\alpha P \cup X) \not\sqsubseteq_T SUC$$

where $SUC = success \rightarrow SUC$.

In practice that is a high price to pay because of the greater complexity of FDR in the left-hand sides of refinement.

Exercise 16.3 Devise LTL specifications which express the following:

(a) P is deadlock-free;
(b) every a is followed immediately by a b ;
(c) every a is followed by a b within 4 steps.

Exercise 16.4 Find an LTL specification that cannot be expressed within the stable failures model $\mathcal{F}$.

Chapter 17
State Explosion and Parameterised Verification

In this chapter we meet some techniques that either contribute directly to coping with the state explosion problem or which can be used to transform a check into a form where other methods are applicable.

Any reader who has used FDR on anything other than small examples will have experienced the state explosion problem, something we described in Sect. 3.6. This can be explained in two parts:

(a) If a network consists of N processes, each of which has k states, then the network can have as many as k^N states.
(b) If a process has M control states and k identifiers, each of which varies over a type of size N, then the process can have as many as $M \times N^k$ states.

While in many cases these bounds are not actually reached, in most cases a sufficiently large fraction *are* reached to make the use of many parallel components or large data-types impractical if we are to model check explicitly: one state at a time.

You can view this problem from two angles. In the first you might have a concrete system with large data-types, many parallel components, or both, that you want to verify. In the second you might have a parameterised family of systems, perhaps variably sized networks or fixed networks over varying data-types. You might then want to establish a given property for *all* (typically infinitely many) members of the family. In this, the *parameterised verification problem*, we not only have the problem of encountering rapidly growing state spaces but also of proving results about an infinite number of concrete systems at the same time.

The first sort of problem can be divided into two. There are those concrete systems that have (perhaps impossibly large) finite state spaces, and there are those that have infinite state spaces, perhaps because they have some identifiers ranging over infinite types or because they can grow to have any number of parallel components. In this chapter we will look at techniques that apply to each of these issues separately, and at them together.

There have been many very elegant theories proposed for analysing the model checking problem for different sorts of infinite-state systems over the past two decades. Many classes of problem are formally undecidable and many sit in complexity classes that suggest they *may* be as good as undecidable for all but the most

A.W. Roscoe, *Understanding Concurrent Systems*, Texts in Computer Science,
DOI 10.1007/978-1-84882-258-0_17, © Springer-Verlag London Limited 2010

trivial of examples.[1] Little of this work has been devoted to the question of refinement that is central to FDR and CSP. The idea of *Watchdogs* (Sect. 8.5) is useful for adapting such theories to CSP, namely how some notions of FDR refinement can be reduced to properties such as *reachability* and *deadlock* that are more often addressed in these other approaches.

We have already seen one approach to large concrete systems, namely hierarchical compression (Sects. 8.8 and 16.2), and discussed others such as partial order methods (p. 371) and SAT checking (p. 186).

There has been a vast amount of work devoted to the state explosion problem over the past two decades, with a large proportion of the papers in conferences such as CAV and TACAS being devoted to it. The following sections are brief essays on how a number of methods other than the ones mentioned in the previous paragraph can be applied in the context of CSP. Some of these—induction, data independence and CEGAR—were originally used for other notations. Data independent induction was developed for CSP, while buffer tolerance is a CSP idea that draws on the large body of work on asynchronous systems.

It is certainly impossible to create techniques that can perform all large checks quickly, or can resolve all instances of the parameterised verification problem. Some problems really are very complex. The best we can hope to do is to find methods that give us a good chance of capturing the essence of *why* a property does or does not hold of a system. When that essence is much simpler than a complete enumeration of its states, we want to find a way of capturing it, just as we did in some of the examples of compression in Sect. 8.8.

17.1 Induction

Most readers will be familiar with the principle of mathematical induction: if a property P holds of an integer N, and it can be shown that whenever $P(k)$ holds then $P(k+1)$ does, then P holds for all integers $k \geq N$.

There are many variants on induction, and one that has been used in this book already is *structural induction* (see p. 226). We can restate that: suppose we have defined a class of objects **L** by saying that it contains a set of basic objects $\mathbf{L}_0$ and a number of constructs for building others: whenever $x_1, \ldots, x_{r(C)}$ are in **L** then so is $C[x_1, \ldots, x_{r(C)}]$. Suppose further that **L** is the *smallest* set that contains $\mathbf{L}_0$ and is closed under the rules. This smallest set always exists, because it is the intersection of *all* the $\mathbf{L}'$ that satisfy these conditions. Then if

(a) some property R holds for all members of $\mathbf{L}_0$ and

---

[1]In fact, as discussed on p. 362, CSP refinement over any of the models we have seen also has a high complexity: PSPACE-complete in the number of states of the specification process. In this case, and possibly also some of the cases alluded to above, the worst case behaviour is only rarely seen. However, in the literature on infinite-state decision problems the complexity classes involved are often very much higher than PSPACE-complete. See [101], for example.

(b) for each construct C, if R holds of $x_1, \ldots, x_{r(C)}$ then it holds of $C[x_1, \ldots, x_{r(C)}]$,

then R holds of all members of **L**. There is no mystery about why this principle is valid: consider the set $\mathbf{L}' = \{x \in \mathbf{L} \mid R(x)\}$. $\mathbf{L}'$ contains $\mathbf{L}_0$ and is closed under applications of all the relevant constructs C. It follows that $\mathbf{L}' = \mathbf{L}$ because **L** is the smallest such set.

What we are going to explore in this section is the idea that **L** defines a set of networks: $\mathbf{L}_0$ is a set of "basic" members of this set, and the constructs C provide ways of building larger networks out of one or more smaller ones.

Proving that a whole class of networks has some property is immediately more general than one can prove directly with FDR, since that only addresses one concrete process at a time. And of course if one proves a property for arbitrary-sized networks it is likely that this will encompass networks that would be too large for FDR to handle comfortably or at all, that is unless an inductive or similar compression strategy works so well that any size of network compresses to the same size.

Interestingly enough, such cases usually signal the possibility of proving results of the given networks by induction. A good case in point is the dining philosophers (see pp. 53 and 58, for example).

Example 17.1 (Induction and the dining philosophers) Consider a sequence of n consecutive fork-and-philosopher pairs as defined on p. 53 with all those actions hidden that are not needed for synchronisation with others. This is, as in the inductive compression discussed on p. 179, ideal for deciding if the complete ring is deadlock free.

The *thinks*, *sits*, *getups* and *eats* actions of these philosophers will always be hidden, and in order to compare different length chains we will need to use the same unhidden alphabets for any length. We therefore define a generic *FORK* process and three different sorts of generic *PHIL* process that omit the events that are always hidden: left-handed, right-handed and ambidextrous.

```
FORK = left.Up->left.Down->FORK
       [] right.Up->right.Down->FORK

LHPHIL = left.Up -> right.Up->
            left.Down->right.Down-> LHPHIL

RHPHIL = right.Up->left.Up->
            left.Down->right.Down-> RHPHIL

AMBIPHIL = ((left.Up -> SKIP)|||(right.Up -> SKIP));
            (left.Down -> SKIP)|||(right.Down -> SKIP));
           AMBIPHIL
```

The use of ||| in AMBIPHIL is simply for succinctness. These three sorts of philosopher are designed to be joined with the link parallel operator, and so we can create fork/philosopher pairs

```
FRP = FORK [right <-> left] RHPHIL
FLP = FORK [right <-> left] LHPHIL
FAP = FORK [right <-> left] AMBIPHIL
```

If there are at least two philosophers of any sort in a chain, it is clear that the Up/Down cycles of the events at either end can happen independently of each other when all the philosophers that are not directly connected to the outside world (i.e. all but the rightmost) do nothing. Thus any such chain is bound to have the traces of CDD where

```
CDD = left.Up -> CUD [] right.Up -> CDU

CUD = left.Down -> CDD [] right.Up -> CUU

CDU = left.Up -> CUU [] right.Down -> CDD

CUU = left.Down -> CDU [] right.Down -> CUD
```

which is equivalent to the interleaving of processes that cycle the left and right events. It is easy to prove that by induction: first show that all two-unit chains have this set of traces (by two-way trace refinement) and then show that each CDD[left<->right]FxP is trace equivalent to CDD. This is very easy on FDR.

Of course this says nothing about deadlock behaviour: we need an inductive hypothesis formulated in the stable failures model for this. There are many inductive hypotheses that can be established for different mixtures of the three units. Here we will look at one for a chain of FLPs. Experimentation on FDR shows that length 1, 2 and 3 chains are all different, but that lengths 3 and 4 are equivalent over $\mathcal{F}$.

This *in itself* represents the core of an inductive proof that all such chains of length at least 3 are equivalent, since if a chain of length $n > 3$ is equivalent to one of length 3, so is one of length $n + 1$ (which induction proves is equivalent to one of length 4).

You might be satisfied with this result or you might want a form of the inductive hypothesis that explains more clearly how these chains behave. You can do this by finding a sequential process—a variant on CDD—that is equivalent to the length-3 chain. The author found the following using a few iterations of the FDR debugger:

```
CDDL = left.Up -> CUDL [> right.Up -> CDUL
CUDL = left.Down -> CDDL [] right.Up -> CUUL
CDUL = left.Up -> CUUL [] right.Down -> CDDL [] DIV
CUUL = left.Down -> CDUL [] right.Down -> CUDL [] DIV
```

The behaviour of a complete ring of philosophers can be discovered by completing the ring. We do not need to use the same unit or units for the completion. To complete using a single unit, given that all sufficiently long chains are equivalent to CDDL, all we have to do is form CDDL[left<->right, right<->left]FxP. As one might have expected, this deadlocks in the cases where x is L or A, but is deadlock free when it is R because this is the same as the asymmetric dining philosophers as on p. 55.

The dining philosophers work unusually well: we are able to get a fixed-size process such that an arbitrary-length chain is *equivalent* to it for the purposes of deadlock analysis. It is much more common to find that the processes considered during an induction are not equivalent and increase in state-space size for bigger networks. In these cases we have two options. The first, illustrated in Exercise 17.2, is to formulate a finite-state specification *Spec* that is properly refined by the actual networks but which is sufficient for the result you need, and then show that *Spec* is refined by all the base processes in L_0 and by $C[Spec, \ldots, Spec]$ for each construct C of the language L.

A second possibility is to place each network in the language in some context that tests it. For example, if we have class of networks that broadcast or route messages from a fixed origin that is also the base case of the language, then we might add a source that sends a particular combination of signals to check how all the networks in the language respond to those signals. We might then prove inductively that all networks respond in a particular way.

As an example, suppose we are given a finite set S of buffers (as specified over $\mathcal{N}$ on p. 122) that all operate over channels with a type containing $\{0, 1, 2\}$. Consider the chains that can be created by linking these together.

We can test these by connecting the input to

$$TOZ = in.2 \to out.2 \to TOZ$$
$$\square\, in.1 \to out.1 \to ZEROS$$
$$ZEROS = in.0 \to out.0 \to ZEROS$$

It should be clear that the result will be a process that failures refines the finite-state process

$$TOZB = (in.2 \to TOZB \,\square\, in.1 \to TOZB')$$
$$\sqcap\, out.2 \to TOZB$$
$$TOZB' = in.0 \to TOZB'$$
$$\rhd (out.2 \to TOZB') \sqcap (out.1 \to ZS)$$
$$ZS = in.0 \to ZS \sqcap out.0 \to ZS$$

and this can be proved by verifying that $TOZB \sqsubseteq_{FD} TOZ$ and that $TOZB \sqsubseteq_{FD} TOZB[out \leftrightarrow in]B$ for all $B \in S$.

You should think about what this says about these chains, putting to the back of your mind the fact that thanks to BL1 (p. 110) we already know that they are all buffers themselves. We will return to this subject at the end of Sect. 17.3.

A further example of induction can be found in the Millipede practical on this book's web-site: as you might expect from the name, this is about combining many sections of a many-legged robot together and proving properties of the result.

17.1.1 The Limitations of Induction

When it works, induction is wonderful because it proves results not only of very large networks but also of many different ones. Unfortunately there are several problems that mean its use is neither as easy nor as widespread as we might like.

(a) If we are to verify the inductive step(s) on FDR, the property we want must be refined to one that is finite state and actually inducts: it must be refined by various combinations of itself as we saw in examples above. In many cases there may well be no adequate finite-state description of the behaviour we want, and even if there is, one often has to be creative to find it. It is unusually lucky to find an example like the dining philosophers that creates its own inductive hypothesis.
(b) Any class of networks that is susceptible to this form of induction is necessarily built out of a finite set of different processes that do not vary at all from network to network. So in particular the processes cannot know the set of names of the other processes in the network, or the topology of the network. For, since these details change from network to network, including them in the component process definitions would mean that the components of one network would be different from the components of another.

We will show how to resolve the second of these issues, at least in some cases, in Sect. 17.3.

Exercise 17.1 Formulate processes CDDR and CDDA that are equivalent to sufficiently long chains of respectively FRP and FAP combinations.

Exercise 17.2 Recall Exercise 4.4 in which we studied the deadlock properties of a small road network. Imagine a grammar of road networks each describing a one-way path from entrance to exit. The grammar allows a simple one-car segment $Seg = in \rightarrow out \rightarrow Seg$, it allows us to place the "narrow" combination of two spaces from Exercise 4.4 at the entrance and exit of an existing network, and it allows us to join two existing networks in sequence $N1[out \leftrightarrow in]N2$. An example of a large network that can be constructed using these rules is shown in Fig. 17.1.

Formulate and prove an induction that establishes that all networks constructed using these rules are deadlock free (i.e. refines $DF = in \rightarrow DF \sqcap out \rightarrow DF$).

Try adding some other road construct into the grammar (e.g. based on the roundabouts we considered on p. 80).

17.2 Data Independence

Informally, a program is said to be *data independent* in one of its types T if its control structure does not depend at all on the members of T that it holds, or in some very limited ways like testing for equality between two members of T. It is always

Fig. 17.1 Complex road
network: see Exercise 17.2

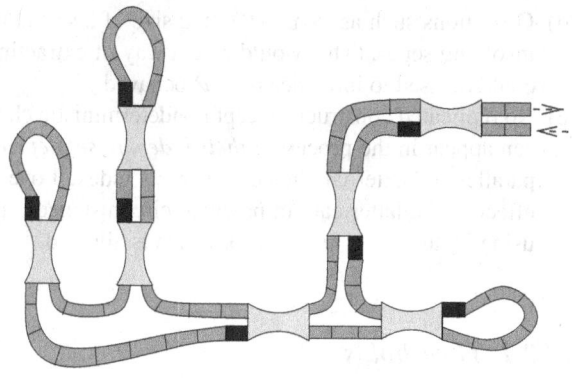

clear, looking at a data independent program, that its behaviour does not depend on the nature of members of T (such as whether they are numbers or sequences) or the assignment of them to the program's identifiers. So, for example, $COPY = in?x \rightarrow out!x \rightarrow COPY$ behaves essentially the same whatever type is passed over *in* and *out*, and whatever value it inputs.

It is intuitively clear that $COPY$'s behaviour for one type is very closely related to that for another. We might reasonably hope that, for many properties that we want to prove of it, establishing this property for one size would establish it for all others. *Before reading on, think about what size of type would prove that COPY satisfies* (i) *deadlock freedom,* (ii) *being a buffer* (iii) *being capable of outputting five different values consecutively.*

A data-type T used in a program P can fairly be said to be a parameter if P treats it *data-independently*: it can input and output values of type T along its channels, store them for later use, but never perform any 'interesting' computations on them that constrain what T might be. (For example, if members of T were added to each other, they would have to be numbers, ...) With one or two exceptions, the criteria for deciding whether a type is data-independent are identical to those for deciding whether it is a free *polymorphic* type variable in the sense of languages such as ML. Precise criteria for this, which are readily automatable, can be found in [80], but the following are the main principles:

(a) Concrete values from T (such as 0, *true*, etc.) may not appear in the program text of P, though abstract constant symbols can appear.

(b) You may use basic polymorphic operations on T such as tupling, list formation and suitable operations for extracting members of structures built out of T in these ways. Intuitively these can be thought of as operations which pass members of T around without looking inside them *at all*. No other functions which involve T either in the types of their arguments or result may be used.

(c) Equality and inequality may be tested between members of T, and the program can contain unary predicate symbols representing arbitrary subsets of T. Apart from this, no conditional or other control-flow in the program may be decided by any operation on one or more members of T.

(d) Operations such as `card(S)` (the size of a set) may not be applied to any set involving set T. (This would give a way of extracting information from T that could be used to influence how P behaved.)

(e) No replicated constructs except nondeterministic choice ($| \tilde{} | \; x : S \; @ \; Q(x)$) can appear in the process *if their indexing set depends in any way on* T. Thus, parallel and external choice constructs indexed over T are banned, though the effect of the latter can, in practical circumstances, almost always be recovered using input ($c \ldots ?x : S \ldots$), which is allowed.

17.2.1 Thresholds

A data-independent program over type T makes sense whatever non-empty set is substituted for T. If `Spec` and `Impl` are two of them, then it makes sense to ask questions such as

- `Spec` $\sqsubseteq_T$ `Impl`?
- `Spec` $\sqsubseteq_F$ `Impl`?
- `Spec` $\sqsubseteq_{FD}$ `Impl`?
- is `Impl` deterministic?

for any specific T. Anybody performing many checks of this sort quickly comes to the conclusion that there must be a strong relationship between the answers to these questions for different sizes of T (it being relatively easy to see that the answer for any pair of Ts of the same size *must* be the same). Fortunately this intuition is true and in almost all cases there is a *threshold*: an integer N such that the answer to one of the above questions for a type of size $M \geq N$ is independent of M. In other words, one can prove or refute a result for all sufficiently large[2] T via one check on FDR.

It is obviously of great practical importance to determine when these thresholds exist, and to find as small a threshold value as possible for each question we are presented with. There is a theory, too complex to present here, which allows the computation of thresholds by extension of the theory of *logical relations* (or *parametricity*) to processes, by augmenting the operational semantics and CSP normalisation to encompass terms with free variables as symbols for members of the independent type.

There are four main factors which influence the size (and in some cases the existence) of a threshold for a given refinement check. These are

- the extent to which the specification constrains which members of T are communicated,
- the kinds of equality checks between members of T that are present in the specification and implementation,

---

[2]Where there is such a threshold N the answer for sufficiently large finite T also applies to all infinite T.

- the subtlety of any nondeterminism in the specification, and
- the extent to which any values of type T which the specification uses are recorded in its traces (rather than only having some 'behind the scenes' effect).

Lazić proved a wide variety of results for calculating thresholds for refinement and determinism checks. The following sections present some of these results. Often the result presented can be improved (e.g., by weakening its assumptions or strengthening its conclusions) if, for example, we are interested only in traces refinement: the interested reader should consult [80].

In the following two sections we will assume that the programs under consideration have no constant symbols or unary predicate symbols. To handle the former you need to add the number of distinct values of the constants to each threshold. This assumes that you are allowed to test for equality and inequality with a constant. To handle predicate symbols you need to multiply each threshold by the number of distinct regions possible in the Venn diagram represented by the predicate symbols. For a single predicate symbol $R(\cdot)$ this means multiplication by 2; 3 for two predicates when one implies the other; 4 for two independent predicates. For the combination of predicates and constants you will need a custom calculation depending on which constants are known to satisfy or not to satisfy the predicates. We will see examples of this type of check in Sect. 17.3.

One way to think of constants and predicate symbols is that they divide up T into a number of subtypes: one-member subtypes in the case of constants. We can then regard it as legitimate to test for membership of these subtypes either in writing a program or drawing up a specification.

When $|T| = 1$ is Enough

One frequently wants to prove specifications of data-independent processes that do not say anything of significance about how they are permitted to handle members of T. Examples are deadlock and divergence freedom and any trace specification that is always happy to allow any member of T in an event when it allows one. It turns out that in many cases it is sufficient to prove such specifications for the simplest possible T: a one-element type. In other words, the threshold is just 1.

Equality tests over T are banned altogether from both the specification and implementation.[3]

It should be pointed out that there are ways of introducing 'hidden equality tests' into CSP programs via some operations and predicates on sets and sequences, and via communication. The communication effect appears when we synchronise on two output events: c!x -> P [|{|c|}|] c!y -> Q contains an implicit equality check between x and y and therefore violates **NoEqT**. These problems do not appear in the great majority of practical programs and can be avoided provided the

---

[3]In the case where there are constant symbols and the allowance discussed above has been made for these in the threshold (so this is no longer 1), you may test for equality and inequality with these values.

only set constructs used involving T are taking unions of straightforward channel alphabets (for synchronisation and hiding), and each synchronisation over channels of type T only has one output. If you are in doubt about the legitimacy of some construct you should consult [80].

NoEqT A data-independent process P satisfies this when it contains *no* test of equality between members of T.

COPY, all the other buffers and weak buffers we have defined in this book, as well as all the routing algorithms in Sect. 4.2, satisfy **NoEqT**.

To ensure that the specification basically ignores T we assert that the only way a member of T can occur in a communication of the specification process Spec is via a *nondeterministic selection* of the form a$x:T -> P which is introduced as an abbreviation for

```
|~| x:T @ a.x -> P
```

(For the purpose of trace specification, this is equivalent to a?x:T -> P.) In other words, Spec can never specify *which* member of T is communicated or that any more than one arbitrary member of T is offered. We will only use the $ form on the specification side of refinement, since it will always be permissible to re-write ones in the implementation using the more general | ~ | as above.

The characteristic processes DF of deadlock freedom and $Chaos_\Sigma$ of divergence freedom satisfy these criteria, as do processes like

```
ALT = a$x:T -> b$x:T -> ALT
```

This particular example just says that communications over a and b alternate without placing any constraint on which members of T appear.

We can now state the first of a number of results establishing exact criteria for data-independent reasoning.

Theorem 17.1 *Suppose we have processes* Spec(T) *and* Impl(T), *each data-independent with respect to the type parameter T and additionally satisfying condition* **NoEqT**. *Suppose further that* Spec *is restricted to nondeterministic selections over T as described above. Then, with $\sqsubseteq$ representing any of $\{\sqsubseteq_T, \sqsubseteq_F, \sqsubseteq_{FD}\}$ the result of the refinement check*

$$\text{Spec}(T) \sqsubseteq \text{Impl}(T)$$

is independent of which non-empty T is used. In particular, the answer for all T is given by the check when $T = \{0\}$ is a one-element type.

What this result says, in essence, is that if we have a program whose control-flow does not depend on which members of T it holds, and a specification which ignores how it handles members of T relative to each other, then we can collapse T to a single value without affecting the result of a refinement check. Obviously this will usually give a significant advantage in state space size.

When $|T| = 2$ is Enough

If we build a system which is data-independent in some type T then it is likely that we will want to prove things about the way it handles members of T as well as specifications that ignore T like those dealt with above. It turns out that, provided we make the same assumptions about the implementation as in the previous section (i.e., it is data-independent and satisfies **NoEqT**), and follow a set of conditions on the specification designed to remove ambiguity about what state it is in after a given trace, then we can assume that T has just two elements. In other words, the threshold is then 2.

The following condition states, in essence, that the specification is already nearly in the normal form for CSP used in the algebraic semantics and in refinement checking (see Chaps. 13 and 16).

Norm A process Spec meets this condition if

(a) its definition contains no hiding or renaming;
(b) the only parallel operators allowed are alphabetised parallel P [X||Y] Q and its replicated version;
(c) other than the nondeterministic selection construct[4] a$x:S -> P described above, no indexed nondeterministic choice is used whose indexing set depends on T;
(d) all internal and external choice constructs (Q |~| R, Q [] R, indexed versions of these, and [> (the sliding choice operator)) have the initial events of each argument disjoint (i.e., once one event has occurred we must know which branch was chosen), and
(e) any uses of the operators ; and /\ ($\triangle$, the interrupt operator) conform to some technical conditions given in [80] which essentially ensure that (d) is not broken implicitly.

The main role of this condition is to avoid the introduction of any nondeterminism except when its effects are immediately apparent. Almost all natural specification processes one ever builds satisfy this condition, or could easily be transformed to ones that do, since in order for us to know what a specification says it should be clear what state it is in after a given trace. In other words, **Norm** can be regarded almost as a well-formedness condition on specifications in a wider sense.

Theorem 17.2 *Suppose* Spec *and* Impl *are data-independent processes, both satisfy **NoEqT** and* Spec *satisfies **Norm**. Let $\sqsubseteq$ be any of* $\{\sqsubseteq_T, \sqsubseteq_F, \sqsubseteq_{FD}\}$.

- *If* Spec(2) $\sqsubseteq$ Impl(2) *holds (i.e., for T of size 2) then* Spec(m) $\sqsubseteq$ Impl(m) *holds for all finite and infinite $m \geq 1$.*

---

[4]It is legitimate to use complex prefixes such as cxy?z, but for technical reasons (see [80]) you may not mix (either here or anywhere else the nondeterministic selection construct is used in the study of data-independence) nondeterministic selections over T with inputs over types other than T.

- *If the refinement* $\text{Spec}(2) \sqsubseteq \text{Impl}(2)$ *fails then* $\text{Spec}(m) \sqsubseteq \text{Impl}(m)$ *fails for all finite and infinite* $m \geq 2$.

The difference between this result and the previous one is that here there is nothing to prevent the specification restricting which of the values of T it knows about is communicated after a given trace. Also, in the case of failures and failures-divergences specifications, it can specify much more about which refusal sets involving members of T are acceptable. Thus, for example, the processes $BUFF_{\langle\rangle}^N$ from Sect. 1.2.3 and $WBUFF_{\langle\rangle}^N$ (p. 122) would be acceptable for Spec in this result but not for Theorem 17.1.

Intuitively, this result says that if we have both an implementation and a specification which pass members of T around without letting them determine the control-flow, then in order to check whether a refinement holds it is sufficient to look at T of size 2. What you have to check in these cases is that each value input into an implementation is output in just the right places. In [80] it is shown that in many cases you can restrict the state space of the check further: although it still requires a data-type of size 2, one can assume that all but one of the values input into the implementation are equal. These references also contain (i) significant strengthenings of Theorem 17.2 which depend on definitions we have not had space for here, and (ii) a discussion of the extent to which specifications that do not satisfy the condition **Norm** can be transformed into ones that do via an equivalent of the normalisation procedures described in Sect. 13.4 and 16.1.

There is an important generalisation of this case. This is that many of the results *for the traces model* T in this subsection continue to hold if we relax our insistence that there be *no* equality tests and replace it with conditions that permit equality tests but only allow progress when equality is true. In other words, we allow the tests in contexts like

```
if e1 == e2 then P else STOP
```

where e1 and e2 are expressions of the data-independent type.

A process description is said to satisfy **PosConjEqT** when it contains no equality tests (explicit or implicit) which can result in some behaviour on inequality that is not possible on equality (other than on tests for equality with constant symbols). For a formal definition see [80].

The General Case

The definition of data independence quoted at the start of this section allowed for equality tests between members of T. Thus the process

```
RemDups = left?x -> right!x -> RemDups'(x)

RemDups'(x) = left?y -> if x==y then RemDups'(x)
                        else right!y -> RemDups'(y)
```

which removes adjacent duplicates from a stream of values, is data-independent even though its control-flow depends on the values of T it uses. Evidently, however, this does not satisfy the conditions **NoEqT** and **PosConjEqT**, and so neither of the earlier results applies to it. In cases like this it is still, under appropriate conditions, usually possible to find thresholds, but they vary with the complexity of the processes under consideration. For example, a process which inputs N values and then communicates a only if they are all different plainly needs a threshold of at least N in order to show that it can sometimes communicate a.

Lazić has shown how to compute thresholds for such checks: the details can be found in his work and in Chap. 15 of TPC.

Returning to the italicised question on p. 391, it is clear that the threshold for the refinement check $\mathbf{div} \sqsubseteq COPY \setminus \Sigma$ (i.e. deadlock freedom) is 1 since Theorem 17.1 applies. Similarly the refinement check that it is an N-bounded buffer for any N is 2, as Theorem 17.2 applies. The final question about it being capable of outputting 5 different values consecutively is rather different, since this represents the failure of a refinement check rather than one succeeding. To do this in the obvious way, one would specify that as soon as we have seen four values output all subsequent ones are the same: this can be written as a data-independent program with equality tests.

However, if you think about it carefully, you will realise that knowing $COPY$ is itself a buffer implies it has this capability, so perhaps the answer is just 2!

17.2.2 Beyond Thresholds

It is sometimes possible to use data independence to address some verification problem without the explicit calculation of a threshold. In some of these cases it is still possible to use FDR to perform the resultant checks, and in some it is not.

The main practical example in CSP has been in *proving* cryptographic protocols for arbitrarily large implementations. The coding of such a protocol in Chap. 15 of TPC is only for a very small implementation: two trustworthy participants who can run the protocol once each. In that example this is of no importance, since a counter-example is found that would plainly work in any reasonable implementation. However, if we had found no error (and there are such protocols!) it would have prompted the question of whether we might have found an attack on a larger implementation.

It was this problem that originally inspired the author's interest in data independence in CSP, and yet the process models involved are far more complex than can be handled by the threshold theorems with or without equality testing. The main problems are that the attacker model has an unbounded memory, that the models assume that many values are always generated fresh and different from all previous ones, and that there are usually multiple data-independent types (names, keys, nonces etc.) that are intertwined in complex structured data-types (of encryptions, messages, etc.).

It has nevertheless been possible [24, 76, 134] to develop highly practical methods for protocol proof using data independence and incorporate them into Gavin

Lowe's Casper security protocol analyser (a front end for FDR). The crucial facts that have allowed this are:

- The inference systems (as described in TPC and as alluded to on p. 371) that are programmed into intruder processes are always (in standard examples) positive in the sense that they never make any deduction from inequality, only from equality. For example, from k and $encrypt(k', m)$ we can deduce m if $k = k'$, where $encrypt$ is a symbolic representation of symmetric encryption.

   This means the intruder processes satisfy **PosConjEqT**, and in fact (apart from equality testing with constants) trustworthy agents invariably satisfy this too.
   All this means that the name-space of virtually any two-party protocol can be reduced to three: two trustworthy and one not.

- Performing active memory management on the values of non-name types so as to ensure that there are never more than a small number in play. So instead of remembering an unbounded number of messages containing different keys in, the intruder's memory is adjusted so that these keys are all mapped to a few (typically one or two: say one key that the intruder knows, and one that it does not). This is safe because of **PosConjEqT**: identifying the keys in two different pieces of information can only allow the intruder extra information and therefore make it more likely for him to succeed. It follows that if we can prove that the new intruder cannot succeed, the original one could not have either.

- One of the most difficult problems to solve was how to deal with situations where the trustworthy agents can run many sessions of the protocol at the same time (in parallel). The solution to this proved to be to include all or part of these agents as "oracles" within the intruder model.

A separate development [81–83, 138] has been the broadening of data independence to incorporate such constructs as arrays (indexed by data-independent types and containing either a finite type or a *different* data-independent one). A wide variety of results have been proved about the decidability of questions about programs involving these, depending *inter alia* on the number of arrays and what can be done to them—for example whether whole-array operations are allowed or only single-component ones.

In trying to decide questions of this type one sometimes (though by no means always) encounters very high complexity classes and verification techniques that go well beyond what is supported by FDR.

We will see further examples of how to reason using data independence in the next section.

17.3 Data-Independent Induction

One of the main limitations of the style of induction seen in Sect. 17.1 is that the processes that make up the arbitrary-sized networks must be ignorant of each others' existence. If they used a type *Names* representing the names of the processes in the network they would not fit into this. You could not extend a small network to a larger one by adding a few processes since the former would be unaware of the names of the processes we would be adding.

In order to cope with this we need to do a separate induction for every network. The nodes in each are indexed over some finite type T. Each step of the induction adds the node(s) indexed by one member of T, creating larger and larger subnetworks until T, and therefore the network, are complete. Normally we would expect only to be able to do this one induction, and therefore one network, at a time. Furthermore we might expect this to be costly for large *Names*.

Both these problems can be solved by using data independence results: we can prove the base and inductive steps of infinitely different inductions with a finite amount of work! A prerequisite, naturally, is that each of the node processes must be data independent in T. This method is called Data Independent Induction (DII) and was developed by the author and Sadie Creese [28, 30].

We will introduce it by means of an example. Consider the deadlock-free tree routing network from p. 77. A property we might want to prove of this is that, between any two fixed nodes, it represents a buffer if we make reasonable assumptions about how the users handle messages between other pairs of nodes. There are two data-independent types[5] in such a network, namely the messages that are passed around and the names of the nodes. Since the network satisfies **NoEqT** in the message type, we can expect to be able to use a type of size 1 or 2 for it depending on the specification. Actually, as far as the complete network is concerned, the latter is not very data independent since each node has a fixed set of neighbours. However, each individual node can be regarded as data independent in that type, provided there is an upper bound on the number of neighbours an individual node can have. We can then treat a node's neighbours as constant symbols (like its own name) and use predicate symbols to assign the correct route for any message.

In this particular case study we will assume that the tree is in fact a chain. This allows us to consider only two types of node: ones with one neighbour and ones with two; but it is straightforward to generalise the following argument to allow for more interesting trees.

The DII proof builds up an arbitrary length chain one node at a time. It builds a data-independent model of what a part chain looks like: in our proof we follow the obvious strategy of building the chain from one end. The partial chain is represented as a predicate symbol S: a name satisfies S if and only if it is in that part of the chain we have built up so far. The boundary between the chain constructed so far and the rest can be represented by two constant symbols `last` and `next`. This is an example: the particular proof we give below does not use any analogue of `last`, and in general there might be more constants involved. There are two further constants `inp` and `outp` that represent the arbitrary pair of nodes considered by

---

[5]It is, at least in this case, straightforward to justify the simultaneous use of data independence theorems on two types at once. Since the type of messages is **NoEqT** data independent we know, for the refinements we are checking, that establishing them for a message type of size 2 is equivalent to establishing them for a large type *with an arbitrary type of Names*. It follows that we can fix the message type as {0, 1}, say, before we start inducting over *Names*.

the specification. Without loss of generality we can assume that inp comes first in the chain, since we can choose the starting end for induction. The induction will go through the three phases where neither inp nor outp is in S, where only inp is, and both. The specification we will seek to prove of the complete chain C, for any fixed N, is as follows:

- When all inputs to the chain other than that at inp are lazily abstracted, all inputs at inp to nodes other than outp are hidden, and all outputs from the chain other than that at outp from inp are hidden, the chain represents a *weak buffer* of length N from inp to outp. Weak buffers $WBUFF_{\langle\rangle}^N$ (see p. 122) are used here to make the processes we use finite state.
- Or, in CSP_M notation, using the $\mathcal{F}$ version of $WBUFF^N$ with its channels adjusted to send.inp.outp and receive.outp.inp:

```
WBuff(N,<>) [F= Abs(C)

Abs(P) = (P [|LA|] CHAOS(LA))\H
LA = {|send.i | i <- diff(Names,{inp})|}
H = Union({{|send.i <- diff(Names,{inp})|},
            {|send.inp.j | j <- diff(Names,{outp})|}
            {|receive.i | j <- diff(Names,{outp})|}
            {|receive.outp.j |
               j <- diff(Names,{inp})|}})
```

Our aim is to prove this by induction as we build up the chain starting from a single end node $S = \{e\}$, and finishing up with $S = Names$.

Unfortunately the above specification is not true of any partial chains: some of them will not have the two channels we are particularly interested in and all will have external communications over the pass and swap channels (to be precise, between the last node in S and the first outside it). We therefore generalise it into what we term a *superstate* process, namely an abstraction of how the combination of the nodes in S behaves. It must satisfy three things:

- It must be true of the initial one-process case.
- When $S = Names$ it must satisfy the specification above.
- It must induct: adding the next node to a process satisfying it must create one that satisfies itself, perhaps with changed constant symbols and with a one-larger S.[6]

It is convenient in most cases, and certainly in this one, only to consider, in the induction, cases of Superstate(S) when S is a *proper* subset of the complete type. This is because, for example, the last node in the chain behaves differently to all but the first since it only has one neighbour rather than two.

There are two ways in which we can build up a chain via data-independent induction. One, described in [31] uses the constant symbols last and next discussed

---

[6]In purely formal terms, we replace the test $S(x)$ for satisfaction of the predicate symbol S by $S(x) \vee (x = c)$ where c is a constant symbol representing the name of the added node.

above. We can then use the type of channel labelling used in the original definition
of our network on p. 77.

An easier alternative is to use link parallel in a style analogous to the recursions
using it in Sect. 5.3: use the same "in chain" channels for all nodes. The following
definition also moves from the two-message swap mechanism seen on p. 77 to the
single message one as suggested in Exercise 4.5. (This latter transformation makes
the construction of the Superstate easier.)

```
NodeE5(n) =
  ([] d:nbrs(n) @ passin.d?(a,b,m) -> NodeF5(n,a,b,m))
  [] send.n?b?m -> NodeF5(n,n,b,m)

NodeF5(n,a,b,m) =
  if b==n then receive.n.a.m -> NodeE5(n)
  else let d = if b<n then Dn else Up
  within
  passout.d!(a,b,m) -> NodeE5(n)
  [] swap.d!(a,b,m)?(a',b',m') -> NodeF5(n,a',b',m')
```

Here, the directions d are from {Dn,Up} and nbrs(n) is {Up}, {Up,Dn} and
{Dn} respectively for the first, non-end and last nodes of the chain.

The above definition is not data independent in the type of names because it
performs a comparison. But it could easily be converted to a data-independent one
if we were to give it an additional parameter so it becomes DINodeE(D,n) where
D is a predicate symbol representing the set of addresses to which a message is
routed Dn: in other words D={0..n-1}. Note that if a data-independent program
only compares data with a constant symbol (e.g. its own name) then this can always
be achieved data independently using a predicate symbol. For brevity we will use
the NodeE5(n) version below, confident that if we had to we could convert all our
networks into fully data-independent form. Thus both chains take the form

```
C(r) = (..(NodeE5(0) [J] NodeE5(1)) [J] ..) [J] NodeE5(r)
```

where J represents the set of links between one process's Up channels and the next's
Down's.[7]

Superstate(S) must be refined by Abs(C(r)) when S={0..r}, and we
prove this by induction, helped by the fact Abs(P[J]Q) = Abs(Abs(P)[J]Q).

The first phase of the induction represents a section of the chain that does not
yet include either inp or outp, has its internal channels hidden and its send and
receive channels abstracted as set out above. So the only channels that remain
visible are those that connect it to the next member of the chain. The following
says that this section is deadlock free, and that whenever it offers an addressed

---

[7]In our implementation below we will rename each action of the form swap.Up.x.y in the
lower process to swap.Up.y.x: this is easier to set out than separately linking all these pairs
of channels. This "swapping of swap" is necessary so that the swapping of messages actually
happens on a synchronisation.

message it also offers to swap it. Because it is an *initial* segment of the chain it
only communicates Up.

```
SS1(S) =
(|~| a:S, b:diff(Names,S), m:Mess @
     passout.Up.(a,b,m) -> SS1(S)
[] swap.Up.(a,b,m)?(a',b',m') -> ok(a',b',S,SS1(S)))
|~| passin.Up?(a,b,m) -> ok(a,b,S,SS1(S))

ok(a,b,S,P) = if (member(a,S) or not member(b,S))
                  then CHAOS(Events) else P
```

The predicate ok says that an input message from the members of the chain not
in S is only acceptable if it comes from some a outside S and is addressed to b,
some node in S. Of course we would expect that in our actual chain no such message will be sent. So what the use of CHAOS achieves is to say that if a "bad"
message is sent we *do not care* what happens, or alternatively that our segment can
do anything it likes. These "don't care" clauses are extremely important to keep
Superstate processes relatively succinct. It is more elegant if we can use DIV
rather than CHAOS for this thanks to strict divergence, but in this case we cannot use
failures-divergences checks because of the way that the communications between
other pairs of nodes are abstracted.

Almost invariably, as here, "don't care" clauses in Superstate(S) processes
represent cases that we believe are possible in the partially constructed networks
these processes represent. This should be compared with the idea of invariants discussed in Sect. 8.8.1 as a way of dealing with this phenomenon.

We can establish this first phase of the induction by proving the base case

```
SS1({0}) [F= Abs(NodeE5(0))
```

and proving that for any non-empty S not containing inp or outp, and any n
distinct from all three,

```
SS1(union(S,{n})) [F= Abs(SS1(S) [J] NodeE5(n))
```

where S is precisely the set of nodes to which NodeE(n) routes Dn.

These two refinements can both be proved data independently, for *all* allowed
sizes of Names and S, with a small number of checks. The two verifications each
use 5 *Names* and a set of messages with size 2 as discussed above. For example, we
establish the second refinement *in general* by showing

```
SS1({0,1}) [F= Abs(SS1({0}) [J] NodeE5(1)
```

For the *Names* type we use Theorem 17.1 extended to deal with the three constant
symbols and one predicate symbol used in the model: we need one value for each
constant plus two other values, one inside and one outside S. We use Theorem 17.2
for the message type.

We now come to the crux of DII. Because we have established these results independently of the sizes of Names and S, we have actually proved the base and

step cases of infinitely many different inductions: one for each chain based on an ordering of some finite set Names.

The individual inductions then proceed on the size of the partially constructed chain. Each base case is established by the first data independent result, and assuming SS1(S) [F= Abs(C(n-1)) (where C(n-1) denotes, as above, the first n members assembled) we know the first line below by monotonicity of refinement. The second line follows from this and the second data independence result:

```
Abs(SS1(S)[J]NodeE(n))  [F=Abs(Abs(C(n-1))[J]NodeE(n))
 Abs(SS1(union(S,{n}))  [F=Abs(C(n))
```

This is what we want. Of course these particular inductions only work on the parts of our chains that fall short of the interesting nodes that actually do the work of sending messages from inp to outp.

Perhaps the most interesting stage of the induction is when inp is in S and outp is still outside it. This state of the Superstate has two parameters: the subset of Names included and the sequence s of messages from inp to outp that Superstate currently contains. We distinguish carefully between messages between the pair (inp, outp) and the rest, since only the former are seemingly relevant to the main property we are trying to prove. Note that this is legal in data independence because it is equality testing with the constants inp and outp. The following definition says, *inter alia*, that when there are messages in this chain it cannot refuse to output to the next process Up, and when it is empty it must either accept a message on send.inp.outp or one from the next process Up. These two things are expressed using the [> operator.

```
SS2(S,s) =
let
Others = diff({(a,b) | a<-S, b<-diff(Names,S)},{(inp,outp)})
PoS(a,b,s) = if (a,b) == (inp,outp) then
                    passout.Up.(a,b,head(s)) -> SS2(S,tail(s))
                [] swap.Up.(a,b,head(s))?(a',b',m')
                                -> ok(a',b',S,SS2(S,tail(s)))
                else |~| m:Mess @
                    passout.Up.(a,b,m) -> SS2(S,s)
                [] swap.Up.(a,b,m)?(a',b',m')
                                -> ok(a',b',S,SS2(S,s))
within
    if #s==0 then
        (passin.Up?(a,b,m) -> ok(a,b,S,SS2(S,<>)))
        [> ((send.inp.outp?m -> SS2(S,<m>))
            |~| (|~| (a,b):Others, m:Mess@ PoS(a,b,s))))
    else
        ((send.inp.outp?m -> (if #s<MaxB then SS2(S,s^<m>)
                            else CHAOS(Events))
        [] passin.Up?(a,b,m) -> ok(a,b,S,SS2(S,s)))
        [> (PoS(inp,outp,s)
            |~| (|~| (a,b):Others, m:Mess@ PoS(a,b,s))))
```

Fig. 17.2 A diagrammatic
representation of DII

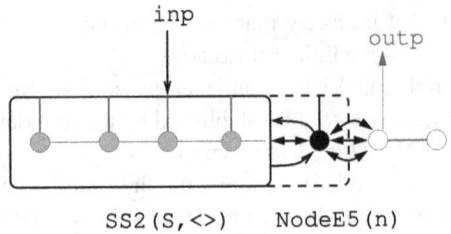

SS2(S,<>)   NodeE5(n)

Note that this process acts like WBuff(MaxB,s) regarding the sequence s. Without this assumption it would not be finite state.

The reader will have noticed that this is much more complex than the first phase. The author developed the above using an iterative process: starting with a rough outline of the above, he tried out the various obligations it has to satisfy (namely the various inductive refinement checks which involve it) and when these did not work, "refined" the program into the above form. In the author's experience there are few better ways of getting to know exactly how a network works than by developing a Superstate inductive hypothesis. Usually it teaches you more than you wanted to know! It is highly desirable that automated, or at least more automated, solutions to superstate development are found.

We can enter the second phase of the induction in one or two ways: either from the first one or directly (the case where inp is the first node in the chain). We therefore need to establish that, when inp=0,

SS2({0},<>) [F= Abs(NodeE(0))

and proving that for any non-empty S not containing inp or outp, but with inp the node immediately above S:

SS2(union(S,{inp}),<>) [F= Abs(SS1(S)[J]NodeE(inp)

These respectively need 3 and 4 Names to check. The second phase of the induction is then carried on by proving, when inp but not outp is in S and n is not outp that

SS2(union(S,{n}),<>) [F= Abs(SS2(S,<>)[J]NodeE(n)

which requires 5 names. This particular step is illustrated, with the channels slightly simplified, in Fig. 17.2: we see NodeE(n) attached to SS2(S,<>), and n thereby being added into S. The faint nodes and channels are not really in this model, but are in the chain it is partly modelling. Note that all of the external channels except two are abstracted.

The third inductive phase is entered at the point we add outp into S *but only if* outp *is not the top of the chain: we will deal with this below.*

SS3(union(S,{outp}),<>) [F= Abs(SS2(S,<>)[J]NodeE(outp)

where SS3(S,w) represents the way an incomplete chain that contains the sequence w from inp to outp behaves when these are both in S.

SS3(S,s) =
let

```
Others = diff({{(a,b) | a<-S, b<-diff(Names,S)},{(inp,outp)})
PoS(a,b,s) = |~| m:Mess @
                    passout.Up.(a,b,m) -> SS3(S,s)
               [] swap.Up.(a,b,m)?(a',b',m')
                                 -> ok(a',b',S,SS3(S,s))
within
   if #s==0 then
        (passin.Up?(a,b,m) -> ok(a,b,S,SS3(S,<>)))
        [> ((send.inp.outp?m -> SS3(S,<m>))
             |~| (|~| (a,b):Others, m:Mess@ PoS(a,b,s))))
   else
       (((send.inp.outp?m -> (if #s<MaxB then SS3(S,s^<m>)
                                        else CHAOS(Events)))
        [] passin.Up?(a,b,m) -> ok(a,b,S,SS3(S,s)))
        [> ((receive.outp.inp.head(s) -> SS3(S,tail(s)))
             |~| (|~| (a,b):Others, m:Mess@ PoS(a,b,s))))
```

We then have to be able to add further nodes beyond `outp`

```
SS3(union(S,{n}),<>)  [F= Abs(SS3(S,<>) [J]NodeE(n)
```

The chain can be completed in two distinct ways. To deal with the possibility that `outp` is at the very end of the chain we must show that, when `nbrs(outp)` equals `{Dn}`,

```
WBuff(MaxB,<>)  [F= Abs(SS2(S,<>) [J]NodeE(outp))
```

where the channels of `WBuff` are `send.inp.outp` and `receive.outp.inp`. For the case when the last member of the chain is not `outp` we must show that

```
WBuff(MaxB,<>)  [F= Abs(SS3(S,<>) [J]NodeE(n))
```

for n such that `nbrs(n) = {Dn}`.

Establishing all of these things by data-independent checks sets up a proof of the proposed property for any length of chain with any distinct `inp` and `outp` (by the symmetry argument quoted earlier). CSP scripts accompanying this book contain all the details.

We could not have done this using either induction or data independence alone.

The reader can find further examples of DII in the papers [28, 30, 31], and in particular [29] contains an industrial case study of a fault diagnosis and management protocol.

We used the weak buffers above for two reasons: first, they are finite state, and secondly

$$WBUFF(N, in, out) \sqsubseteq_F WBUFF(N, in, out)[out \leftrightarrow in]B(in, out)$$

when B is any buffer at all. The latter is why induction works: it would not have done if we had used size-N buffers instead.

Nevertheless our result about chains is a good deal weaker than we might have wished since it only proves they represent *weak* buffers between each two points rather than proper ones, the size being determined by how large we can make the constant `MaxB` before the model checking takes too long.

There is a very interesting way of correcting this problem. Recall the example on p. 389 where we set a test that any buffer must satisfy: namely linking TOZ to it creates a process that trace-refines TOZB. Suppose that B is any **NoEqT** data-independent process which passes that same test. Then B satisfies the trace specification for being a buffer. This is because any error that it could commit in reordering, losing or duplicating data from an arbitrary data-stream could also be committed on any stream of the form $2^n.1.0^m$ for $m, n \geq 0$, for example 222100, and if we arrange the 1 to be the data that is lost, duplicated or reordered it will not produce an output stream of the same form.

In fact, showing that the same refinement holds over $\mathcal{F}$ actually proves that B satisfies the failures specification of a buffer: we give an outline argument here. It cannot refuse an input when *empty* because the traces specification says that B cannot output and TOZB establishes that it must always input *or* output. It cannot refuse to output when *non-empty* because (thanks to data independence) we could ensure that the 1 was in B at the time, and TOZB says that the process can never refuse to output when it contains 1. It must be emphasised that this argument depends crucially on the **NoEqT** data independence of B without anything like a constant symbol or predicate symbol for this type.

A different coding of this can be found in [125]; both are based on an original argument of Pierre Wolper [157] for a slightly different buffer specification.

It should not be hard to show by DII (adapting our earlier argument) that linking a renamed analogue of TOZ to the input channel send.inp.outp creates a process which refines TOZB, again suitably renamed. We can then have Superstate processes, all of which are finite state, that prove that our chain represents a buffer between two arbitrary points, rather than the weak buffer result above. This is left as an exercise.

It is interesting that two completely different theories built on top of data independence—one of each of two types—have been used to prove this result.

Exercise 17.3 Modify the data-independent induction above so that instead of proving a result in $\mathcal{F}$ about Abs(C) it proves one in $\mathcal{N}$ about C, where C is the complete chain. You will therefore need to revise the superstate processes so that they can communicate over all the external channels that Abs(.) removes: you will have to be careful about the distinction between the lazy abstraction of input channels and the hiding of outputs.

You should be able to prove Spec [FD= C, where Abs(Spec) failures-refines

```
WBuff(N,send.inp.outp,receive.outp.inp,<>)
```

Exercise 17.4 Devise analogues of TOZ and TOZB that test to see if a data-independent process is a Bag: the same specification as for a buffer except that it allows one piece of data to overtake another. (There is still no divergence, message loss or duplication, and it never refuses any input when empty nor refuses to output when non-empty.) You should be able to do this using two values {0,1} rather than three.

17.4 Buffer Tolerance

In CSP, two processes that communicate do so by *handshaking*: neither does anything until both are willing to proceed. We said "two" here because of course two-way communication is the most obvious model for interaction between practical concurrent processes. The choice of handshaken communication matches some classes of application very well, but equally many practical applications use channels between processes that do not use handshaking. Typically one process outputs to the channel which holds the communication until the receiving process accepts an input from the other end.

These channels might be unbounded buffers, or they might in some cases allow overtaking. They might be bounded buffers, and when full they might either have a way of stopping further outputs from the processes feeding them or they might simply throw further data away. In this section we will concentrate on the case where there is buffering (so no reordering, duplication or message loss) on channels, and where this is nondeterministic.

You can model just about any variant in CSP, but any sort of buffering or asynchrony can contribute enormously to the state explosion problem. This is because (most obviously) the buffered channels will usually have many states and (less so) they will leave the component processes free to enter more combinations of states since they are less synchronised.

By *buffer tolerance* we mean the desirable property that the correctness of a network might be independent of the amount of buffering it contains. We want to understand when we can prove a network correct by analysing it with no buffering, or at least a minimum. We want to find a way of studying the effect of transforming a handshaken channel into one where there *might* be any amount of buffering added, and where this can vary in size or disappear as the network progresses.

Throughout this section all channels that are candidates for buffering will be point-to-point and have an obvious direction, with one process outputting and the other inputting. The external environment can play the role of outputting to or inputting from any such channel. Although we could terminate modified buffer processes by sending them a signal, for simplicity we will assume that the processes we put buffers between never communicate $\checkmark$.

There was a brief section on buffer tolerance (Sect. 5.2) in TPC. At the time that was written there was not a great deal more to say about it. In the meantime the author has engaged in a major study of this topic [127]. The present section is a summary of the main results from that paper.

Other process algebras tend to follow CSP and CCS in having handshaken communication, but there are other theories of concurrent systems that take different views. For example, in *data-flow* theory [73] it is assumed that an output is never blocked: there is an infinite buffer on each channel.

In practice communication over high latency media such as the Internet is best treated as buffered, but it may well be most accurate to model it over some nondeterministic amount of buffering rather than assume the ease of infinite buffering.

Unfortunately buffering can change the behaviour of a system significantly, and multiply exponentially (in total buffer size) the state space or make it infinite if the buffers are.

Therefore model checking significantly buffered systems requires special methods, typically by finding regular language abstractions and/or using advanced decision procedures [13, 14, 44]. Buffer tolerance, allowing us to infer results about buffered systems from unbuffered analogues, provides an alternative.

17.4.1 Definitions, Basics and Tree Networks

We will assume:

- that all communication in networks is point-to-point along directed channels (from output to input);
- that inputting processes never select (*No Selective Input*);
- that outputting processes never offer a choice (*Output Decisive*);
- that component processes are divergence free and do not terminate ($\checkmark$).

In looking at the semantics of networks we will assume that communications on internal channels are hidden. The purpose of these assumptions is to concentrate on networks where buffers are appropriate.

Recall from p. 12 that the process $BUFF_{\langle\rangle}$ is the most nondeterministic buffer process. Therefore $P \gg BUFF_{\langle\rangle} \gg Q$ puts the most nondeterministic buffer on the channel, but this always adds at least one slot and so is not a good generalisation of Q so that it *perhaps* exhibits buffering on its input channel. Even $(P \gg BUFF_{\langle\rangle} \gg Q) \sqcap (P \gg Q)$ is not right since once buffering has been observed we can always get at least one place. What we need is a way of adding buffering that is maybe there and maybe not, potentially varying through time. So define the zero-buffer

$$ZB_{\langle\rangle} = (thru?x \rightarrow ZB_{\langle\rangle})$$
$$\sqcap (in?x \rightarrow ZB_{\langle x\rangle})$$

$$ZB_{s^\smallfrown\langle y\rangle} = (out!y \rightarrow ZB_s)$$
$$\square (STOP \sqcap in?x \rightarrow ZB_{\langle x\rangle^\smallfrown s^\smallfrown\langle y\rangle})$$

Note that this is the same as $BUFF_{\langle\rangle}$ except for the use of *thru* in the empty state. $ZB_{\langle\rangle}$ either passes data without buffering through the channel *thru*, which is both an input and an output channel, or buffers inputs on *in* before sending them on *out*. Of course it can only use *thru* when empty, as to do otherwise would re-order the data stream.

It seems odd to have two different input channels and two different output ones, but this confusion can be eliminated by renaming when we plug $ZB_{\langle\rangle}$ into either an input or output channel of P.

$$(ZB_{()} \quad \underset{\{|thru,out|\}}{\|} \quad (P[\![^{thru,\,out}/c,c]\!])) \setminus \{|out|\})[\![^{c,\,c}/thru,in]\!]$$

$$((P[\![^{thru,\,in}/c,c]\!]) \quad \underset{\{|thru,in|\}}{\|} \quad ZB_{()}) \setminus \{|in|\})[\![^{c,\,c}/thru,out]\!]$$

This achieves exactly the effect we were looking for.

We can easily build a version $ZB_{()}^n$ for $n \geq 0$ that adds buffering of 0 to n items.

We will denote the addition of arbitrary buffering to an output channel by $P \diamond c>$, with $\diamond c> P$ doing the same to an input channel. Thanks to our construction of $ZB_{()}$, P refines both $P \diamond c>$ and $\diamond c> P$.

In general $\diamond$ will mean the addition of buffers to networks:

- $P > \diamond > Q$ is an arbitrarily buffered version of $\gg$. One could also create a similar generalisation of the link parallel operator.
- $N^\diamond$ puts buffering on all internal channels of N.
- $N^{\diamond\diamond}$ puts buffering on *all* channels.
- $\diamond> P$, $P\diamond>$ and $\diamond> P\diamond>$ respectively put buffering on all input, output and input/output channels of a process or the external channels of a network.

There are a number of different flavours of buffer tolerance:

- The network is *strongly buffer tolerant* if the introduction of arbitrary internal buffering does not change the overall semantics of the system. Namely, $N = N^\diamond$.
- It is *leftwards buffer tolerant* if $N^{\diamond\diamond}$ refines $\diamond> N$, and *rightwards buffer tolerant* if $N^{\diamond\diamond}$ refines $N\diamond>$.
- It is *weakly buffer tolerant* if $N^\diamond$ refines $\diamond> N\diamond>$.
- It is *strongly buffer tolerant relative* to a specification S if adding arbitrary internal buffering cannot make N fail to satisfy S, namely $N \sqsupseteq S \Rightarrow N^\diamond \sqsupseteq S$.
- It is *weakly* buffer tolerant relative to a specification S if $N \sqsupseteq S \Rightarrow N^\diamond \sqsupseteq \diamond> S\diamond>$. It is *leftward* or *rightward* buffer tolerant relative to S if, after adding the buffers, it refines $\diamond> S$ or $S\diamond>$.

Some of these definitions make sense for a single process, for example leftward buffer tolerance:

$$\diamond> P \sqsubseteq \diamond> P\diamond>$$

All the above definitions imply buffering on all relevant channels. It also makes sense for a process or network to have most of the above properties with respect to any set of channels: these are the ones on which buffering is placed.

The following result shows that, in a straightforward case, joining buffer tolerant processes together gives a buffer tolerant network. While this is not surprising, it is welcome. A slightly more general version can be found in [127].

Theorem 17.3 *Suppose N is a network in which the directed graph of channels is acyclic. Then if each individual process of N is leftward buffer tolerant, or each is rightward buffer tolerant, then N has the same property.*

However, buffering can change the behaviour of a system significantly, even one in which there are no cycles amongst the directed channels. Imagine that in some network N the process P sends a number of messages to Q in consecutive communications, and they follow a number of different routes. It is easy to imagine that the order in which these arrive may be greatly liberalised if buffering is placed on N's channels. If Q depends on a particular order *not* happening, then the buffered network might have some severe misbehaviour. For example, P might send messages with tags that increment *modulo N* (as with *modulo 2* in the alternating bit protocol in Sect. 4.3). In the unbuffered network it may be possible to rely on no message overtaking as many as N others, so that Q can reconstruct the sequence. (The messages with each index must arrive in order.) The introduction of buffering could then cause message reordering.

The alternating bit protocol itself is strongly buffer tolerant in the sense defined below, at least over finite-behaviour models: putting a finite-capacity buffer on any or all of its internal channels leaves its external behaviour unaffected. Adding one with infinite capacity can, depending on the version of ABP we are using, create the potential for divergence. Buffer tolerance is particularly desirable in applications which, like the ABP, are designed to be used in asynchronous networks. We will return to this topic in Sect. 17.4.2.

We might expect buffer tolerance to be easier in networks with no alternative paths between any A and B. These are networks where there are no cycles in the graph with an *undirected* edge for each directed channel. As we will see in the next few results, this is true.

The following fact was quoted as Buffer Law 6 (**BL6**) in TPC: *If P and Q are processes with one output and one input channel each, and satisfy the no-selective-input assumption we make, then*

$$P \gg Q \text{ is a buffer} \Rightarrow P \mathbin{>}\!\diamond\!\mathbin{>} Q \text{ is a buffer.}$$

In other words, every chain (of any length) is strongly[8] buffer tolerant relative to the specification of *being a buffer*.

It is natural to ask with respect to what other properties chains are always buffer tolerant. We certainly cannot expect the word "strongly" to apply with any sort of generality, since it is natural to expect the insertion of buffers in the middle of a chain to add buffering to the external view. A positive answer to the following question would be a natural generalisation of BL6.

Question Suppose $C = P_1 \gg P_2 \gg \cdots \gg P_n$ where each P_i has precisely the two channels $\{in, out\}$ and each P_i is deadlock-free and has the finite output property. Then is C weakly buffer tolerant in respect of all its channels simultaneously, meaning that, if $C^\diamond$ is a process obtained by adding arbitrary buffering to each channel,

---

[8]In fact this is equivalent to saying it is weakly buffer tolerant with respect to being a buffer since, you cannot make a non-buffer into a buffer by adding further buffering (see BL2 and BL3 in TPC).

$C^{\circ} \sqsupseteq \diamond\!\!\!> C\!\!\diamond\!\!>$? Here, the finite output property (FOP) means that P is divergence-free when all its output channels are hidden: it cannot output infinitely without also inputting infinitely.

The answer to this question in the traces model $\mathcal{T}$ is usually *yes*:

Theorem 17.4

(a) *If P is any process with a single output and a single input channel, then P is leftward buffer tolerant in the traces model.*

(b) *If P is any deadlock-free process with the finite output property, a single input channel and a single output channel, then P is rightward buffer tolerant in the traces model.*

(c) *Any chain of processes, each with a single input and a single output channel, is leftward buffer tolerant, and is also rightward buffer tolerant if all the component processes are deadlock-free and FOP.*

Unfortunately the above result does not apply in failures or richer models, as shown by the following example:

Example 17.2 Let P be the deterministic buffer which can reject an input only when both the following two conditions are met.

- It is non-empty, and
- it has output at least two items.

And let Q be the deterministic buffer which refuses input only when it has one item in and has never output.

$P >\!\!\diamond\!\!> Q$ can input three items (with no output), then refuse to input.

$P \gg Q$ can never refuse to input—so neither can $\diamond\!\!> P \gg Q$.

So internal buffering can introduce genuinely new behaviour!

Some positive results for chains over $\mathcal{F}$ can be found in [127]. This also contains buffer tolerance results about more complex forms of tree. For example, the reachability of a state in one of the components of a tree network is unaffected by the introduction of buffers.

17.4.2 Functional and Confluent Processes

Imagine a process whose channels are divided into inputs and outputs, and where the stream of data on each output channel is always a prefix of a monotonic function applied to the inputs. By "monotonic" we mean that if the sequence on each input is extended (in the sense of prefix) then the same is true on each output.

If we assume that this process never refuses to input, or if there are infinite buffers on its input channels, and that it never refuses to output when one is pending, then it is a basic component of a *data-flow* or *Kahn-MacQueen* network [74].

It is intuitively clear that such a network with no cycles in the directed graph of its channels computes the composition of the functions represented by the nodes. One of the classic results of computer science is the *Kahn principle* that generalises this to a network with a general topology.

> Any network N consisting of processes of this type calculates the least solution to the fixed-point equation on the contents of channels that it represents.

If we relax the assumption that there is infinite buffering on all these channels then we enter interesting territory for buffer tolerance. In general such networks of *functional* processes always output prefixes of what the corresponding data-flow network would calculate. These networks are investigated in [127], which shows that they are frequently buffer tolerant.

Networks of confluent processes are shown in [127] to be buffer tolerant with respect to deadlock freedom. We can generalise this: if applying the forgetful renaming that removes all data passed along channels makes each component process confluent (as is true, for example, of cyclic communication networks as defined on p. 249), then the original network remains buffer tolerant with respect to deadlock freedom.

Furthermore, confluence can be characterised in terms of buffer tolerance: a process P is confluent (in the sense defined on p. 250) if and only if it is deterministic after placing an inward-pointing one-place buffer on each event, or on every event separately.[9] While this result is of no practical use that the author can think of, it illustrates how related confluence and buffer tolerance are.

It is also possible to characterise functional behaviour in terms of buffer tolerance in several ways. It is shown in [127] that under assumptions defined there, a process P is functional if and only if $\diamond\infty> P$, in which deterministic infinite buffers are placed on all the input channels, is itself deterministic. (This is true even when the functional process P is nondeterministic.)

Exercise 17.5 Implement the processes from Example 17.2 (noting that it is not necessary to use infinite buffering to show the misbehaviour) and demonstrate the lack of buffer tolerance on FDR.

Exercise 17.6 Find an example of a pair of processes P and Q, composed in parallel with two separate channels from P to Q, which is not *trace* weakly buffer tolerant.

Exercise 17.7 Consider the various solutions to deadlock-free routing in Sect. 4.2. Which of them is still deadlock free when a *COPY* process on each internal channel. For which of the networks N is $N^\diamond$ deadlock free. [The answer is not the same.]

---

[9]In other words, we can check one process with many added buffers, or many processes each of which has a single added buffer.

17.5 Approximation Based Methods

One of the most successful techniques for overcoming the state explosion problems in recent years has been CEGAR: *Counter-Example Guided Abstraction Refinement* [26]. This is a systematic approach to something that is very natural in CSP: rather than attempting to prove a property of a complete and detailed description of a system, see first if it is true of a simpler, *abstracted* version.

The use of forgetful renamings (p. 104) is a good example of this since by losing the details of the data that a node carries we are likely to be able to compress it to a much smaller state machine than if we kept them.

Using a particular abstraction like this one, a number of things can happen. The system might still be too large to check (bad). The check might succeed and therefore prove the desired result of the unabstracted system (good). The check might fail and the resulting counter-example might be valid of the original system (good, in the sense that it resolves the original question). Or the check might fail but the resulting counter-example might not be valid in the original case (bad).

CEGAR performs repeated checks in an attempt to work around the bad cases. In the description below we will assume that the system S being analysed is a parallel combination (with maybe hiding and renaming) of reasonably simple finite-state processes P_i—exactly the sort of single-format system that represents a typical FDR check (see p. 155). We will also assume that we are trying to prove that it refines a specification *Spec* with a smallish number of states.

For us, then, an abstraction of the complete system will be formed by applying exactly the same parallel operator to abstractions of the P_i. (Namely P_i' such that $P_i' \sqsubseteq P_i$.)

We need a flexible abstraction mechanism for the P_i that can produce a finite set of different approximations $Aprx(P_i)$ where

(a) $P \in Aprx(P)$
(b) $Q \in Aprx(P) \Rightarrow Q \sqsubseteq P$
(c) $Q \in Aprx(P) \wedge Q \sqsubset P$ implies that Q has fewer states than P.
(d) $Aprx(P)$ has a member $P^\perp$ with a single state that is refined by all others.

CEGAR is then an iterative loop which starts from the system $S^0 = S^\perp$ where every P_i has been replaced by $P_i^\perp$. $S^\perp$ has only one state and its refinement check against *Spec* can result in no more state-pairs than *Spec* has states.

- The first step in the nth iteration is to perform the refinement check $Spec \sqsubseteq S^n$.
- If this succeeds then we have proved $Spec \sqsubseteq S$ since $S^n \sqsubseteq S$. So the iteration can terminate.
- If it fails then we analyse whether the counter-example behaviour b generated is valid for the original system S. The easiest way to do this is to calculate the behaviour b_i (in the relevant semantic model such as $\mathcal{F}$) that each component process P_i should have contributed to b if it followed the behaviour in S^n. We can then test if P_i actually does exhibit b_i. If this is true for all i then we have shown that $Spec \not\sqsubseteq S$ and can terminate.

- If at least one b_i fails to belong to P_i then we have to pick at least one such P_i^n to refine. To do this we pick some $P_i' \in Aprx(P_i)$ that does not have b_i and such that $P_i' \sqsupseteq P_i^n$.

    If there are several i where b_i fails to belong to P_i then we do not necessarily have to refine them all since taking away a single process's contribution may well be enough. In this case there are several heuristics we might want to follow, including refining the one where the ratio in states between P_i' and P_i^n is the smallest.

    In any case the system S^n with one or more of the P_i^n refined to avoid b_i becomes S^{n+1}, which becomes the subject of the next iteration.

We hope that this iteration terminates before the refinement check $Spec \sqsubseteq S^n$ becomes too big to handle.

The theory of CSP offers a number of abstraction mechanisms that we might apply to the P_i. Many of these involve calculating an equivalence relation over P_i's state space and then factoring by this relation: treating each equivalence class as a single state. The factorisation algorithm, namely how to treat equivalence classes as states, is set out for the traces-plus models on p. 199: it is always the case that the result of factoring is refined by the original.

The result of factoring P by the universal relation (where all states are deemed equivalent) is the process that can always perform any action that P ever can, can always refuse or accept any set that P ever can, and can always diverge if P ever can. (What is recorded depends on the model, of course.) This is the best candidate for the one-state abstraction $P^\perp$, whatever abstraction mechanism is used for later abstractions.

Suppose that the abstraction $\overline{P}$ that results from an equivalence relation $\cong$ over P's states has a behaviour b that P itself does not, and that we are operating over one of the trace-plus models. Then the way that $\overline{P}$ performs b can be expressed

$$\overline{P_0} \xrightarrow{x_1} \overline{P_1} \xrightarrow{x_2} \ldots \overline{P_{n-1}} \xrightarrow{x_n} \overline{P_n}'$$

where $P_0 = P$ and in each case P_{r+1} is the unabstracted state that can be reached from a member P_r' of $\overline{P_r}$, and P_n' exhibits whatever final behaviour such as a refusal set is needed for b. We can re-write this

$$P_0 \cong P_0' \xrightarrow{x_1} P_1 \cong P_1' \xrightarrow{x_2} \ldots P_{n-} \cong P_{n-1}' \xrightarrow{x_n} P_n \cong P_n'$$

By the way the quotient is formed, we may assume that some of the x_i may be visible and some τ, but that there is no τ from any state $\overline{P_r}$ to itself. The trace of b comprises all the x_i that are not τ.

Since b is not a behaviour of P, it follows that for at least one r we have that P_r' is not τ-reachable from P_r. We can remove at least this particular run of b from the abstraction by refining the equivalence class containing P_r and P_r' into two or more pieces, ensuring that, in the new equivalence $\cong'$, if $P_r \cong' Q$, $P_r \cong R$ and $Q \xrightarrow{\tau} R$, then $P_r \cong' R$, and of course that $P_r \not\cong' P_r'$.

So we could, for example, divide the equivalence class $\overline{P_r}$ into two parts: those of its nodes that are reachable in zero or more τs from P_r, and those that are not.

There are many choices of heuristics we could use in this process. The complications arising from τs could be eliminated, of course, by applying a τ-eliminating compression such as diamond to each of the processes P_i before the CEGAR procedure begins.

It is possible to modify either the normalisation algorithm for LTSs (see Sect. 16.1) or diamond compression so that they generate approximations to the original process rather than something equivalent. Recall our normalisation example on p. 359. From a nine-state process we got twelve pre-normal form states, each identified with a set of the states of the original process. In this example no less than 10 of the pre-normal-form states are supersets of the root state. Thus the process each of these represents is an anti-refinement of the root state meaning, that we could use them as approximations in examples like CEGAR. For example, we can use state VII as an approximation to I (which is equivalent to the process $(P \| Q) \setminus \{c\}$ that is the subject of this example). Figure 16.3 and the accompanying table allow us to calculate the value of VII in $\mathcal{F}$:

$$VII = (a \rightarrow IX) \sqcap (b \rightarrow XI)$$

$$VIII = a \rightarrow XII$$

$$IX = (b \rightarrow XI) \triangleright (a \rightarrow IX)$$

$$XI = (a \rightarrow VII) \sqcap (b \rightarrow VIII)$$

$$XII = b \rightarrow VIII$$

Intuitively we might expect that this is often a sensible abstraction of the original process provided that this is, as a component of the overall system, permitted to perform the trace that allows the normal form to get into the normal form state that becomes its new root.

CEGAR is not implemented in FDR at the time of writing, though an experimental implementation will shortly be created as part of a doctoral project.

17.6 Notes

The inductive theorem that underlies Exercise 17.2 is due to Sadie Creese [28], who (as noted above) was jointly responsible with the author for developing data-independent induction.

The idea of testing data independent s by sending defined streams of data, and of using these as part of an induction, is due to Pierre Wolper [157], who was probably the first to suggest data independence as a reasoning technique.

The author's work on buffer tolerance has benefited from discussions with Michael Goldsmith.

Part IV
Exploring Concurrency

In the final three chapters we will try to understand types of concurrent systems for which CSP is not generally thought appropriate, and at the same time see how it is often possible to translate automatically from these other notations into CSP.

We will spend most time studying the model of concurrency that the invention of CSP was a reaction against, namely *shared-variable* concurrency. In this, processes communicate by writing to and reading from shared variables rather than via explicit communication. Chapter 18 shows how we can both understand this type of concurrency and develop an automated verification engine called SVA for it using CSP and FDR.

Chapter 19 then examines shared-variable concurrency more deeply, for example by looking at how to define refinement over shared-variable programs and examining how to prove results about certain sorts of unbounded systems using SVA. Much of this is done through examples.

We have already studied timed concurrency in Chaps. 14 and 15. Chapter 20 looks at two other ways of extending the expressive power of CSP, namely to *prioritised* systems, where we can express a preference for which actions happen (e.g. *b* only if *a* is not available), and to *mobile* systems, in which processes and channel names can migrate.

Not only are shared variables, priority and mobility interesting in their own right, the fact that we can express and reason about these concepts in CSP and FDR may inspire others to explore further types of concurrent systems. For example, we can handle systems with a mixture of these ideas, as in Statecharts, (Sect. 20.2.1) which use time, priority, ordinary communication and shared variables.

Further work of interest includes incorporation of CSP and FDR into integrated tool sets. For example see Anderson et al. (An environment for integrating formal methods tools, 1997), the work of Verum (www.verum.com) (Hopcroft and Broadfoot, Automated Software Engineering, 2004) on integrating CSP/FDR with the Box Structure Development Method, and the integration of CSP and the B-method (Schneider and Treharne, Integrated Formal Methods, Springer, Berlin, 2004).

Chapter 18
Shared-Variable Programs

This is the first of two chapters devoted to the topic of *shared-variable* programming. They can be viewed in several ways: as a substantial case study in writing practical CSP, as a lesson in how to build simulators and compilers in CSP for another notation, as a guide to a new tool for assisting in analysing shared-variable programs, and as an introduction to shared-variable programming.

In this chapter we will build a CSP model of running shared-variable programs. Since this model takes the form of a compiler written in CSP, it enables us to analyse the behaviour of shared-variable systems; we show how FDR's compression functions work particularly well on the resulting CSP processes and are therefore integrated into the compiler; and we give two substantial case studies. We also describe how the compiler has been given a front end GUI, giving rise to a tool called *SVA* which is available from this book's web-site. In Chap. 19 we will examine the semantics of shared-variable programs in more detail, and describe various advanced features of the compiler, illustrating them by expanding on our case studies.

In these two chapters we will consider programs that consist of a number of *thread* processes that do not communicate directly with each other, but rather interact by writing to and reading from variables that they share.

We will study a simple shared-variable language in which each thread is written in a small sequential language, and the shared variables are of either integer or boolean type, including one-dimensional arrays. For the time being[1] we will assume that all variables and constants are declared *and initialised* at the outermost level (i.e. for all parallel threads): this is clearly necessary for all shared variables, and adopting a uniform approach makes compilation easier.

We deliberately concentrate on the model where the only modes of interaction between the threads is via shared variables, with the optional addition of declaring

---

[1] We will be studying two forms of the language: first a somewhat unconventional one that is closer to implementation and then a more conventional one that is what most users will actually write. We will allow locally defined variables in the latter.

A.W. Roscoe, *Understanding Concurrent Systems*, Texts in Computer Science,
DOI 10.1007/978-1-84882-258-0_18, © Springer-Verlag London Limited 2010

parts of programs to be atomic: executed as though at one time, with no other thread performing actions simultaneously.

Here are two types of thread process that are intended to implement mutual exclusion (mutex): in each case we run two processes in parallel with $i \in \{1, 2\}$, and both are supposed to ensure that the two critical sections never run at the same time. Mutual exclusion is an important aspect of practical concurrent programming, since it is used to prevent processes from accessing resources simultaneously when this could lead to an error.

```
H(i) = {iter {b[i] := true;
              while !(t = i) do
                {while b[3-i] do skip;
                 t := i};
              {CRITICAL SECTION}
              b[i] := false;}}

P(i) = {iter {b[i] := true;
              t := 3-i;
              while b[3-i] && (t = 3-i) do skip;
              {CRITICAL SECTION}
              b[i] := false;}}
```

H stands for Hyman's algorithm [68] and P stands for Peterson's algorithm [104]: both were proposed as solutions to the mutual exclusion problem. In both algorithms, t and i are integers (with i being treated as a constant since it is the parameter) and b is an array of two booleans. In both, b[i] is a flag that process i sets to indicate that it wants to perform a critical section, and they use these and the variable t to negotiate who goes first in the case that processes 1 and 2 both want to perform a critical section.

The only feature of the above programs that might be unfamiliar is iter, which is an abbreviation for while true do.

In trying to understand how these two algorithms work in practice it is important to realise that the various actions of the two threads are *arbitrarily interleaved*: the threads are completely unsynchronised, so shared variables can give a model of asynchronous communication. A thread may have to access several variables during an expression evaluation: we assume that accesses by the other process might well occur between these, and between an expression being evaluated and the value being used. Our language also contains a construct atomic C that ensures that the execution of the command C is not interleaved with any actions by another thread. Not only has atomic not been used in the above thread, but mutual exclusion is needed in practice to implement atomic execution: after all the code inside an atomic is given exactly the same privilege that mutual exclusion is meant to provide. It follows that one should not normally use atomic in implementing it!

In fact, only one of the two algorithms above succeeds in guaranteeing mutual exclusion: one of them can allow both processes to perform their critical sections simultaneously. See if you can work out which.[2]

Mutual exclusion is a fundamental building block of concurrent programming, and indeed many practical implementations of CSP-style handshaking depend on it. We will see both further mutual exclusion algorithms and applications of them in the case studies and exercises later in this chapter.

The rest of this chapter is devoted to a compiler called SVA (shared variable analyser) for shared-variable programs of this sort, which is actually written in CSP$_M$. It is primarily intended as a case study of how to compile other languages into CSP, but also provides interesting lessons on how to write CSP$_M$ and use FDR's compression functions effectively. The author hopes that SVA will prove to be useful in its own right.

SVA, with a front end that provides a parser, GUI and counter-example interpreter, is available from this book's web-site. Before going further in this chapter (but after applying some thought to the two mutual exclusion algorithms above) the reader is advised to try both the raw compiler (by running FDR on the files hyman.csp and peterson.csp) and SVA (by checking the two corresponding .svl files). Notice in particular the far clearer debugging output from SVA.

18.1 Writing a Compiler in CSP$_M$

CSP, and even CSP$_M$, which is extended by functional programming, seems a most unlikely language to write compilers in. At the time of writing it still has no type of strings, and nor does it have a conventional `write` or other command to save the result of compilation into a file. It certainly was not designed with this style of application in mind.

The compiler we will be describing overcomes the first of these objections by starting from a "source" program written as a member of a CSP$_M$ data-type. Such programs can be written by the user, or more usually created from an ASCII syntax for the language by the parser in SVA.

Our compiler does not have to output the resulting CSP in the conventional sense, since it is the combination of it and the source file (itself in CSP syntax) that is input to FDR. It would perhaps be more accurate to call it a simulator, since what it does is to build a CSP model that behaves as the source program does. It is, however, fairly accurate to think of the combination of it and the CSP compiler within FDR as a true compiler from the source language to FDR's internal notations: by the time a shared variable program is checked on FDR it has been compiled to an efficient state machine representation.

---

[2]This was an exercise set for a number of years by Oxford lecturers, originally by David Walker. This exercise and the paper [155] on which it was based inspired the creation of the compiler described in the present chapter.

The compiler described in this section is the CSP$_M$ back end used by SVA, simplified to remove the support for a few advanced features that we will describe in the next chapter.

18.1.1 Data Types

The compiler is a CSP program `svacomp.csp` that is included in the source file, and which itself includes the compression utilities `compression09.csp`.

To use the compiler, the source program must define various constants which we will introduce gradually. First, we will concentrate on how to describe a thread process and how the compiler deals with these.

There are three types that are fundamental to the description of a thread process: those of *Commands* `Cmd`, *Integer Expressions* `IExpr` and *Boolean Expressions* `BExpr`.

The integer expressions are as follows:

```
datatype BinIOps = Plus | Times | Minus | Div | Mod |
                   Max | Min
datatype UIOps = Uminus

datatype IExpr = IVar.ivnames | IArc.(ianames,IExpr) |
                 Const.{MinI..MaxI} |
                 BIOp.BinIOps.IExpr.IExpr |
                 UIOp.UIOps.IExpr | ErrorI
```

In other words, an integer expression is formed from integer variables, array components and constants using binary and unary operations and, for technical reasons that will be explained later, we need special syntax denoting an error. The boolean expressions are similar:

```
datatype BinBOps = And | Or | Xor
datatype CompOps = Eq | Neq | Gt | Ge | Lt | Le

datatype BExpr = BVar.bvnames | BArc.(banames,IExpr) |
                 True | False | Not.BExpr |
                 BBOp.BinBOps.BExpr.BExpr |
                 CompOp.CompOps.IExpr.IExpr | ErrorB
```

In this syntax there is an asymmetry because boolean expressions may include integer ones, but not vice-versa.

The syntax of commands is as follows:

```
datatype Cmd = Skip |
               Sq.(Cmd,Cmd) | SQ.Seq(Cmd) |
               Iter.Cmd | While.(BExpr,Cmd) |
               Cond.(BExpr,Cmd,Cmd) |
```

```
Iassign.(IExpr,IExpr) |
Bassign.(BExpr,BExpr) |
Sig.Signals | ISig.(ISignals,IExpr) |
Atomic.Cmd | ErrorC
```

Here, Skip is a command that does nothing, Sq and SQ are respectively binary and list forms of sequential composition, Iter runs its argument over and over for ever and While.(b,C) evaluates b and then runs C followed by the loop again, and Skip. Cond(b,C,D) is a conditional equivalent to if b then C else D. There are separate commands for integer and boolean assignments, each evaluating their second argument, determining what location the first represents, and performing a write. Sig.s and ISig.(sc,e) both cause the thread process to send a CSP-like communication to the environment; the first is the simple event s, the second outputs the value of expression e along the integer channel sc. These two constructs are included in the language to make specification easier: there is no mechanism for synchronising the signals produced by different threads, and in fact the signals used by different threads must be distinct. Atomic.C is as described earlier, and ErrorC is again included for technical reasons.

The data-types above are the main ones that someone writing a program that uses svacomp.csp directly needs to understand, since they are the ones in which programs are written.

18.1.2 Variable Names

In contrast to the complex types above, the types used within the programs are simple: just integer and boolean. Because FDR only supports finite-state component processes, and each variable process we will use has a state for every value it might take, in practice we can only handle programs using comparatively small ranges of integers—how small depends on the rest of the program—and two important constants MaxI and MinI that have to be defined in each program. Each integer variable or array is declared to contain members of any subtype of {MinI..MaxI} and the index type of any array is also a subtype. Each program contains a number of constants that allow the compiler to compute, for each array name a, its index type itype(a) and, for each integer variable or array component v, its content type ctype(v). These types are always subsets of {MinI..MaxI}.

The name of each variable or array component used in programs is drawn from the following datatype:

```
datatype namestype = IV.Int | IA.Int.Int
                   | BV.Int | BA.Int.Int | NonVar
```

Thus each integer variable takes the form IV.n, each integer array has the form IA.m where the jth component (starting from 0) is IA.m.j, and similarly for booleans.[3]

The introduction of a string type into CSP$_M$ would mean that the Int in each of these clauses could be replaced by String in future versions of SVA. The principal advantage of this would be making the debugger output directly from FDR more readable.

NonVar is a constant used to handle errors.

Each program using svacomp.csp defines sets ivnums, ianums, bvnums and banums: the variable and array numbers it uses. We can now define the sets of the arrays that are used in the program on the one hand, and the variables and array components on the other:

```
ianames = {IA.j | j <- ianums}
banames = {BA.j | j <- banums}

ivnames = union({IV.j | j <- ivnums},
                {IA.j.k | j <- ianums, k <- itype(IA.j)})
bvnames = union({BV.j | j <- bvnums},
                {BA.j.k | j <- banums, k <- itype(BA.j)})
```

Notice that these are used in the definitions of IExpr and BExpr.

In the rest of this chapter and the next we will refer to members of these sets as *locations*, namely slots where values are stored.

18.1.3 Compilation Strategy

A program consists of the declarations and initialisations of the variables and arrays it uses, together with a collection of thread processes (members of Cmd) that use them.

We build a network that consists of one process for each thread, and (usually) one process for each location. The thread processes do not communicate directly with each other at all. They just read and write the variable processes and communicate externally via their signals and, if they need to start and then end an atomic section, communicate with the processes that govern these.

An individual location (i.e. variable or array component) is a very simple process, particularly in the absence of any atomic constructs:

```
IVAR(x,v) = iveval?_!x!v -> IVAR(x,v)
         [] ivwrite?_!x?w -> IVAR(x,w)
```

---

[3]The SVA front end allows more conventional names for variables, and builds up a table associating each such name with one derived from namestype.

```
BVAR(x,v) = bveval?_!x!v -> BVAR(x,v)
          [] bvwrite?_!x?w -> BVAR(x,w)
```

Each thread will be allocated a distinct index, and the first parameter of ivwrite etc. is the thread that the variable is being accessed by. The second is the name of the location (variable or array component) and the final one is the value being read or written.

When a program does include atomic execution, the variable processes help implement this. While a thread runs atomically, we require that no other thread accesses variables, or itself enters an atomic section. Both these requirements are met by modified variable processes. We give only the boolean version here.

```
BVAR_at(x,v) = bveval?_!x!v -> BVAR_at(x,v)
             [] bvwrite?_!x?w -> BVAR_at(x,w)
             [] start_at?j -> BVAR_inat(j,x,v)

BVAR_inat(j,x,v) = bveval.j!x!v -> BVAR_inat(j,x,v)
                 [] bvwrite.j!x?w -> BVAR_inat(j,x,w)
                 [] end_at.j -> BVAR_at(x,v)
```

In other words, once some process enters an atomic section, only it is allowed to read and write the location until the atomic section ends, and no other process can enter an atomic section during this period.

An atomic section is uninterrupted; it behaves as though everything in it happens in an instant as far as the other threads are concerned. That last analogy will be very useful to us later (see Sect. 19.3, where we consider refinement between shared-variable programs), but it breaks down when more than one signal event can occur during a single atomic section. We will therefore regard it as good practice to ensure that no atomic section can output two or more signals; the results of that section are restricted to that case.

18.1.4 Compiling a Thread

Apart from the evaluation of expressions, the reduction of a thread process into CSP is remarkably straightforward. The complete translation for the Cmd type is given below. The first few clauses do not involve evaluating expressions:

```
MainProc(Skip,j) = SKIP

MainProc(Sig.x,j) = x -> SKIP

MainProc(Sq.(p,q),j) = MainProc(p,j);MainProc(q,j)
MainProc(SQ.<>,j) = SKIP
MainProc(SQ.<p>^Ps,j) = MainProc(p,j);MainProc(SQ.Ps,j)

MainProc(Iter.p,j) = MainProc(p,j);MainProc(Iter.p,j)
```

Expression evaluation is incorporated into the following definitions in *continua-tion* style: to calculate the value of an expression in a program, we use functions `BExpEval(b,P,j)` and `IExpEval(e,P,j)` where

* b and e are the expressions to be evaluated;
* P is a continuation: a function that expects a boolean or integer as appropriate, and behaves like the rest of the program after it has been given such a value;
* j is the index of the thread. This is included so that any error signal that occurs during the expression evaluation can be labelled properly.

So the local definition in the following pair of constructs defines a continuation which expects a boolean, and the controlling expression b is then evaluated with this continuation.

```
MainProc(While.(b,p),j) =
let
P(x) = if x then MainProc(p,j);MainProc(While.(b,p),j)
          else SKIP
within BExpEval(b,P,j)
```

```
MainProc(Cond.(b,p,q),j) =
let P(x) = if x then MainProc(p,j) else MainProc(q,j)
within BExpEval(b,P,j)
```

The effect of a boolean write statement is to generate a communication `bvwrite.j.lv.rv` where j is the thread index, lv is the location to which the write will be made, and rv is the value to be written. These cases make use of additional functions that supply continuations with respectively a boolean and integer *location* when applied to a suitably structured expression. Thus, below, `BLvEval(el,Q,j)` is a function that evaluates the BExpr el as a boolean *left value*: a boolean location that naturally sits on the *left* of an assignment. To evaluate successfully in this way the expression either has to be a variable or an array component a[e] where e is an integer-valued expression.

```
MainProc(Bassign.(el,e),j) =
           let Q(lv) =
           let P(rv) = bvwrite.j.lv.rv -> SKIP
               within BExpEval(e,P,j)
           within BLvEval(el,Q,j)
```

```
MainProc(Iassign.(el,e),j) =
           let Q(lv) =
           let P(rv) = if member(rv,ctype(lv)) then
                             ivwrite.j.lv.rv -> SKIP
                       else error.j -> STOP
               within IExpEval(e,P,j)
           within ILvEval(el,Q,j)
```

The effect of these definitions is to do the calculations necessary for working out the location (or *left value*) lv before those for the assigned value (or *right value*) rv. It is straightforward to achieve the opposite order (see Exercise 18.1). Which order is chosen makes a real difference, because it alters the order in which variables are read, in an environment where other threads may be writing to them at the same time as the assignment is being executed.

For integer locations, we need to check that the integer written is within the correct range. If not, a run-time error occurs.

The Eval functions can generate an execution error, for example through division by zero or array index out-of-bounds. In such cases these functions just generate an appropriate error message and stop: the continuation argument is not used.

The final three clauses of the definition of MainProc are straightforward, given what we have already seen.

```
MainProc(ISig.(c,e),j) = let P(x) = c!x  -> SKIP
                             within IExpEval(e,P,j)

MainProc(Atomic.p,j) =
start_at.j -> MainProc(p,j);end_at.j -> SKIP

MainProc(ErrorC,j) = error.j -> STOP
```

18.1.5 Evaluating an Expression

The evaluation methods for integer and boolean expressions are very similar. Because integer expressions are self-contained, we will concentrate on these here and define IExpEval. svacomp.csp evaluates an expression in two stages: first, it instantiates any free variables and array components in the expression one at a time until there are none left; then it reduces the resulting expression to a single value.

Because of the way we are structuring our model, each fetch from a location generates a communication of the form iveval.j.v?x, where j is the index of the process and v is the name of a variable or array component.

The order in which these fetches are performed is important, since other threads may be writing to the locations used at the same time. svacomp.csp orders them left-to-right, subject to any expression representing an array index needing to be evaluated in full before the array component can be fetched. This order is implemented through the function ffetchi(e) whose definition, together with that of the datatype fetch it returns, is given below.

```
datatype fetch =  NoF | ISV.ivnames | BSV.bvnames
                | ErrorX

ffetchi(IVar.n) = ISV.n
ffetchi(IArc.(v,e)) =
```

```
          let f = ffetchi(e)
          within
          (if f == NoF then
               (let k=evaluatei(e) within
                    if ok(k) then
                         let n=num(k) within
                              (if member(n,itype(v)) then ISV.v.n
                                                     else ErrorX)
                         else ErrorX)
               else f)

ffetchi(Const.k) = NoF

ffetchi(BIOp._.ea.eb) = let ffe = ffetchi(ea) within
                        if ffe==NoF then ffetchi(eb)
                                    else ffe

ffetchi(UIOp._.e) = ffetchi(e)

ffetchi(ErrorI) = NoF
```

The type `fetch` gives the result of a search for the first fetch required to evaluate an expression. `NoF` means that no fetch is required: the variables (including array components that appear in the expression) are fully instantiated. `ISV.v` or `BSV.v` denote an integer or boolean location.

The function that actually evaluates an expression is then

```
IExpEval(e,P,j) =
let
IXEF(NoF) = let k=evaluatei(e) within
      if ok(k) and num(k)>=MinI and num(k) <=MaxI then
                    P(num(k))
           else error.j -> STOP
IXEF(ISV.v) = iveval.j.v?x -> IExpEval(subsi(v,x,e),P,j)
IXEF(_) = error.j -> STOP
within IXEF(ffetchi(e))
```

The two additional functions used here are `evaluatei` which turns a fully substituted integer expression into an integer, and `subsi`, which substitutes the integer value v for location x in the integer expression e. We omit these (long but straightforward) definitions here: the reader can find them in `svacomp.csp`.

We now know how to compile a thread process, and how to create a process modelling a location. These are the only components of our model of a program. In the case where there are no `Atomic` constructs, an accurate simulation can be produced by interleaving (|||) all of the thread processes, interleaving all the location processes, and synchronising these two collections:

```
Threads {|iwrite,bwrite,ieval,beval|}|] Variables
```

It should be clear that any `Atomic` construct nested inside another has no effect on the intended execution of processes. On the other hand such constructs make compiler writing more difficult and add extra actions into the CSP simulation. `svacomp.csp` therefore removes all nested `Atomic`s using the function `One_at` before compilation (only outermost ones remain).

If we put the system together more carefully we can, however, gain considerable scope for applying FDR's compression operators, and that is the subject of the next section.

Pros and Cons of Compiler Writing in CSP

There are clearly three languages involved in any compiler: the *source* one that is being compiled, the *target* language, and the one in which the compiler itself is written.

The inability of CSP$_M$ to handle strings at the time of SVA's creation meant not only that the compiler has to input programs represented in CSP data-types such as `Cmd`, but that it is incapable of outputting the text of the CSP program that is the result of the translation. Therefore, the compiler itself has to interpret the source program as a CSP program each time we want to "run" the former.

This seems to work well in conjunction with FDR, but it would be unsatisfactory if we wanted to inspect the CSP result of the translation, or to input it into a tool that did not have a full understanding of the functional part of CSP$_M$.

It would be straightforward to adapt `svacomp.csp` so that instead of generating actual process behaviour, as it does now, it created a representation of a CSP process in a syntactic datatype analogous to `Cmd`. Thus, for example, we might write

```
SMainProc(Atomic.p,y) =
   SSeq.((SPfx.start_at.j,SMainProc(P,j)),
          (SPfx.end_at.j,SSKIP))
```

rather than the definition that begins on p. 425, where `SSeq`, `SPfx` and `SSkip` are the constructors representing the CSP syntax for prefix and *SKIP*.

We might notice that the result of the translation would be a fully laid-out CSP program, with no use of the functional constructs in CSP$_M$. So, for example, each parallel process would have a separate existence in the syntax.

Our compiler would then be a pure functional program that does not use the CSP features of CSP$_M$ at all. That version could be translated very easily into functional languages such as Haskell, or, given appropriate string additions to CSP$_M$, its output could be "pretty printed" into the text of a CSP program.

We conclude that it is very much a matter of personal taste, when compiling a language into CSP, whether to write the translation in CSP or in some other language. The author has tended to follow the former approach, whereas others have tended to follow the latter [63, 87]. The main reasons why we have used the former in this chapter are firstly that it provides an excellent illustration and case study of just how expressive the CSP$_M$ language is, and secondly that it should be more accessible to readers of this book.

Exercise 18.1 The order in which SVA assumes a thread reads the various slots it may require to evaluate an expression is somewhat arbitrary. Experiment with some different orders and find a case where changing the order changes the result of a check.

How much of a penalty would we pay for picking this order nondeterministically?

Construct a version of the compiler where the left value of an assignment is computed before the right value. Again, find an example where this makes a difference.

Exercise 18.2 What changes to the data-types and compiler would be necessary to encompass the program construct `for i=a to b do C` for `i` an integer variable, `a,b` integer expressions and `C` a `Cmd`?

18.2 Applying Compression

The simple way of composing the system as `Threads [|X|] Locations` leaves all synchronisation until the very last moment. This is exactly like interleaving all the philosophers and all the forks in the dining philosophers (see Sect. 8.8.1), and, like that example, leaves no prospect for compression other than any that might be available on the individual nodes.

Just as in that example, we must aim to get many of the interactions between the processes established early in the composition tree of our network. The main technique that `svacomp.csp` uses to achieve this is to associate each location process with a well chosen thread and then compress the combinations of the individual threads and the associated locations. It therefore has to choose *which* thread. There are two options for this:

- The user may specify that some location is associated with a specific thread. To allow this, a thread is coupled with a pair of sets when it is compiled: the integer and boolean locations that the user wishes to attach to it. Thus our descriptions of networks are built not from `Cmds` but from `Threads`, a type synonym for `(Cmd,(Set(ivnames),Set(bvnames)))`.
- If the above does not apply, then `svacomp.csp` chooses a thread automatically for each location.

We will concentrate on the second case. To make a sensible choice, we need to work out which threads use a given location for reading, and which for writing. In the case of ordinary variables this is simple textual analysis, but things are harder in the case of array components.

While one can imagine more sophisticated analysis, what svacomp.csp does is to work out which array indexing expressions are actually constant because they contain no variable or array component. This is common because, just as in the Hyman and Peterson cases above, many examples have a parameterised family of threads, in which the parameter (i in the cases mentioned) is treated as a constant (Const.i) "thread name". The compiler reduces these expressions to their values and replaces (for example) IArc.(IA.1,BBOp.Plus.Const.2.Const.1) by IVar.IA.1.3. Where an array index is not constant, the thread is assumed to be able to access any component.

The function ConstC is applied to each thread before compilation to carry out this reduction of constant expressions, supported by CBEx(b) and CIEx(e), which respectively determine whether a boolean or integer expression is constant.

It is this reduction that accounts for many of the error elements in types. For the reduction may produce an array index out-of-bounds or other "run time" error, so the result is an error expression or Cmd as appropriate.

Similarly, when evaluating an integer or boolean expression, the result type is one of

```
datatype EInt = Ok.AllInts | NotOk
datatype ExtBool = BOk.Bool | BNotOk
```

The NotOk elements in these types permit errors to propagate smoothly: this allows such errors to cause run-time error events in the compiled program, rather than compilation errors in FDR that stop the program being modelled.

The decisions about which locations are associated with which threads are made by a function Analyse, which is applied to a list of processes coupled with user-declared sets of local variables and returns many pieces of information about each thread in the context of the network:

- IW, IR, BW and BR give the integer and boolean locations each thread can write and read (most of the returned parameters are, like these, functions from the thread's index to its value).
- LIV and LBV give the integer and boolean locations that are to be grouped with each thread.
- ROI and ROB give the variables that each thread can read and *nobody* can write.
- Alpha and Alpha_at give, in the cases without and with Atomic constructs, the alphabets of each thread/location combination when all of these are combined in parallel.
- LI gives the interface between each thread and its own associated locations.
- SEv gives the set of signal events used by each thread. These sets of signals must be disjoint from each other.
- UseAtomic is a flag that is true when any of the threads have an Atomic construct.

The automatic allocation of locations to threads (i.e. where no overriding allocation applies) is done as follows:

- If at least one thread is able to write to the location, then such a thread is chosen. In the common case where only one thread can write to a location, this means that all writes to that variable can be hidden immediately. In the case where there is more than one writer, the locations are, at the time of writing, allocated in a round-robin manner.
- If no thread can write to the location, then that location has a constant value through each run. There are a number of ways in which we could optimise this. What svacomp.csp does is to give each thread that can read the location a separate read-only variable process, meaning that all reads of that variable are hidden immediately.[4]

The main reasons why one might want to use manual allocation of locations are:

- If the automated allocation process gives so many locations to a thread that the enumeration and compression operations for the combined process become problematic.
- If the uses of array indices produce natural allocations that are not spotted by the algorithm described above.

The function CompileList turns lists of threads into a list of CSP processes. Each of these is the parallel combination of MainProc applied to the Cmd representing the thread, and the processes implementing this thread's local variables, with the read and write actions linking these hidden. It chooses two options depending on whether UseAtomic is true or not. If not, then (except for the peculiarities relating to read-only locations) the result is just a re-arrangement of the Threads [|X|] Locations network discussed earlier.

If UseAtomic is true, then the versions of locations designed for atomic execution are used, and in addition each thread process is put in parallel with a process At_Reg(i) whose job it is to prevent the thread from performing any signal actions during another thread's atomic section.

svacomp.csp provides a number of different functions for structuring and compressing these networks. The most basic is one that simply puts all the processes in parallel without any attempt at compression.

```
Compile(C) =  ListPar(CompileList(C))
 \({|iveval,bveval,bvwrite,ivwrite,start_at,end_at|})
```

This is provided mainly as a point of comparison so that the user can judge how effective compression is. The simplest (and often best) compression strategy is to apply Leaf Compression (see Sect. 8.8.1). It simply compresses the combinations of threads and associated locations, hiding the same internal actions as above:

```
CompressedCompile(C)(AS) =
LeafCompress(compress)(CompileList(C))(diff(Events,AS))
```

---

[4]A perhaps superior approach would be to transform each thread so that every read of the "non-variable" becomes a constant equal to its initial value. This would work for simple variables, but not for array components: an array of constants is, in effect, a look-up table.

The set AS is the alphabet of the specification: the events that need to be left visible to determine whether or not the process satisfies its specification. This will almost always be a set consisting of error events and signal events. In this context Errors means the set of all run-time errors {|error, verror|}, so that one way of checking to see if any such error can occur is

```
assert STOP [T= CompressedCompile(System)(Errors)
```

The best way of allowing more ambitious compression strategies is via networks presented hierarchically as trees. A basic network is a single thread, and we can compose any number of networks into a single one. The datatype that describes this is

```
datatype CmdStruct = CSLeaf.Thread
                   | CSNode.List(CmdStruct)
```

This is designed to support the following strategy:

- Each thread process is compiled and grouped with its associated locations exactly as above.
- These are individually compressed as in LeafCompress above.
- Except at the root of the tree, the sub-networks below each CSNode are composed in parallel, all internal communications hidden, and compressed.
- The list of sub-networks at the root of the tree are put in parallel and have internal communications hidden, but not compressed because (see Sect. 8.8) it is not productive to compress at the top level of a strategy.

Thus the following CmdStruct will give a compression strategy that is identical to LeafCompress: CSNode.<CSLeaf.C | C <- ThreadList> for a list, ThreadList of Threads.

The function that svacomp.csp provides to perform this hierarchically compressed compilation is

```
HierarchCompressedCompile(ct)(AS) =
PSStructCompile(compress) (CompiledStructure(ct))
                        (diff(Events,AS))
```

Here, CompiledStructure is a function that behaves like CompileList except that instead of turning a list of Cmds into a list of processes, it turns a CmdStruct into a SCTree, the type of trees of processes described on p. 177, naturally preserving the tree structure. We can therefore use the function PSStructCompile (from compression09.csp and described in the same place) to perform the compression. AS is again the set of events (almost always consisting of error and signal events) that we wish to be visible for checking against some specification.

The implementation of CompiledStructure in svacomp.csp is straightforward: it flattens out the CmdStruct into a list, applies CompileList, and structures the result into a SCTree using the original argument as a model. One can imagine more sophisticated versions in which the allocation of locations to threads takes account of the tree structure: if there is a choice, then allocate a location with multiple writers to one of these in a sub-network where as many other threads use the location as possible.

One can also imagine a function that takes a list of threads and arranges these into a CmdStruct in such a way that as many interactions as possible will be hidden early.

Exercise 18.3 In Exercise 18.1 we discussed the possibility of reading in the values required by an expression nondeterministically. What effect does compression have on the extra cost of this?

18.3 The Front End of SVA

When the author wrote the first version of the shared-variable compiler in 2000, writing programs as literal members of Cmd was the only way of using it. It became much easier to use when David Hopkins created a front end and GUI for it in 2007, together with a parser that converts an ASCII form of the language into Cmd etc. David has been kind enough to update this front end to encompass the much-extended functionality of the version of the compiler described in this chapter.

18.3.1 SVL

We have devised an ASCII syntax for the shared-variable language the tool uses, tentatively called SVL. This is deliberately simple: we intend that it is used to describe simple algorithms rather than large systems. The following text describes the language as it is at the time of writing: future versions may include further features, and of course similar technology could be used to model shared-variable versions of real programming languages.

A *script* consists of the definitions of one or more programs, and also contains direct definitions of CSP_M constants and processes used for setting defaults for the compiler and defining specification processes, amongst other things. Any line of the script that begins %% is CSP_M and is included directly in the CSP scripts that the parser generates. At the time of writing, constants such as MaxI and MinI, and default array indexing and initialisation data are included this way: see the example files for details.

The script also contains the declaration of shared variables, arrays and constants. We can globally declare integer and boolean variables by name. Integer variables are assumed to range over {MinI..MaxI} unless an upper bound is given, in which case the given variable ranges from 0 to that bound. Thus

```
int i,j=3;
bool b;
int %4 k=2;
```

declares two integer variables over the full type of integers admitted by the program, the second of which is initialised to 3, one boolean variable and one integer variable limited to the range {0..4} and initialised to 2. Any variable that is not explicitly initialised is initialised to a default value. We may similarly declare integer constants as in const c=5.

Integer and boolean arrays can be declared, as in

```
int [] ia;
bool [5] ba;
```

The first array takes a default index type, and the second {0..4}.

Threads are defined via names with zero or more integer parameters. Thus

```
PP(n) = {ia[n] := 2;
         ib[n] := true}
```

defines, for each integer n, program code that will translate into a Cmd, in which the name n represents an integer constant whose value is determined when the name is used in a program. The name for a thread with no parameters takes the form PQ(), not PQ.

If, as discussed on p. 432, you wish to override the automatic allocation of locations to threads for the purpose of compression, then you can use the syntax

```
PP(...) = C with S
```

where C is the program text of a thread, and S is a set of variables and array components that the compiler is directed to group with it.

If, for example, you do not want some components of the array number to be grouped with any of the proper threads, you can define a thread

```
Dummy(i) = skip with {number[i]}
```

Including some threads of this form in the final program will not change its overall semantics, but will affect the way the compression strategies used in Sect. 18.2 work. Specifically this tactic will reduce the size of the thread-plus-variable processes compressed as the system is composed. This can be useful if these processes get too large, but will typically reduce overall effectiveness of the compression. See below for some more ideas of this type.

The syntax of the SVL terms named as threads directly reflects the structures of the types Cmd, IExpr and BExpr introduced in Sect. 18.1.1. It is illustrated by the examples quoted in this chapter and the next: all subsequent shared-variable programs other than the versions of the bakery algorithm in Figs. 18.2 and 18.3 are in SVL, as of course are all our SVL example files. A full description of SVL syntax can be found in the documentation accompanying SVA.

A program is then formed as a list structure whose leaves are the thread names discussed above with their parameters instantiated. Thus

```
<PP(1),PP(2),<PP(3),PP(4)>,PQ()>
```

is one way of describing the program in which the five threads mentioned run in parallel. The reason for having a structured tree rather than a simple list is because the most usual way of running such a program is by using the hierarchical compression strategy discussed on p. 433, for example

```
MyProg = hierarchCompress <PP(1),PP(2),
                            <PP(3),PP(4)>,PQ()>
```

Typically you will use this ability to group threads together when two threads happen to use each other's locations to a significant extent, so there is extra mileage to be gained from compression. One interesting possibility is in connection with the Dummy(i) idea described above. If the thread T uses the locations seconded to Dummy(i) for i=1,2,3, then instead of enumerating the full state space of T and its variables and compressing in one go, you could try, for example

```
<T,Dummy(1),Dummy(2),Dummy(3)> or
<<<T,Dummy(1)>,Dummy(2)>,Dummy(3)>
```

as a part of a larger structure. These have the effect of first compressing T with the rest of its locations, and then either in combination with all three of the extra ones, or with them added one at a time, mimicking the behaviour of InductiveCompress (see p. 179).

Which works best in a particular case will depend on the peculiarities of the given example.

The core of SVA is an extended parser that not only parses SVL in the conventional sense but also generates a full CSP model of it by translation to the CSP_M input format used by the compiler svacomp.csp that we have described in this chapter. The compiler, naturally, is included in the resulting CSP files.

18.3.2 The GUI

The GUI of SVA is much less complex than that of FDR: it simply allows you to load an SVL script and run either individual or all assertions from that script using the translation described above.

By far the most interesting feature of the GUI is the debugger, which translates any counter-example found by FDR into the language of shared variables and displays it analysed process by process as illustrated in Fig. 18.1.

18.3.3 Possible Extensions

In the next chapter we will introduce several significant additions to SVL. We will, for example, discover a way of implementing richer data-types. There are many other ordinary programming constructs that we could have added. In this section we briefly discuss a possible additional change to the program execution model.

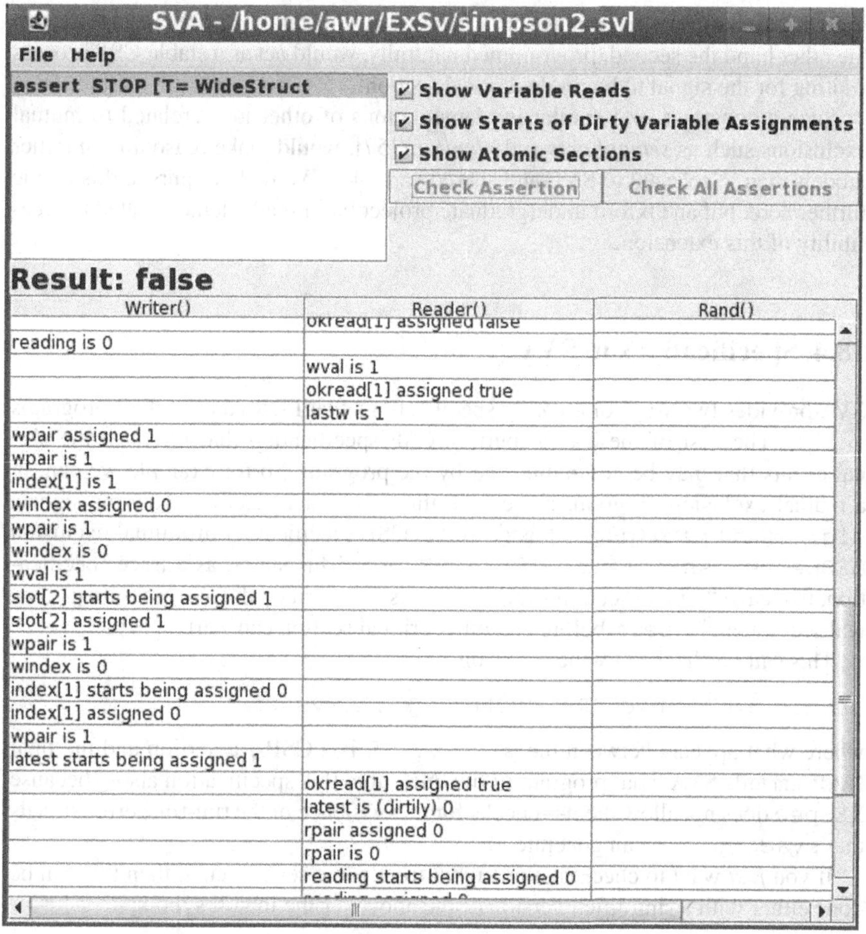

```
┌─────────────────────────────────────────────────────────────┐
│  ⬛        SVA - /home/awr/ExSv/simpson2.svl         _  ◆  ✕  │
├─────────────────────────────────────────────────────────────┤
│  File   Help                                                  │
├─────────────────────────────────────────────────────────────┤
```

assert STOP [T= WideStruct   ☑ Show Variable Reads

                                    ☑ Show Starts of Dirty Variable Assignments

                                    ☑ Show Atomic Sections

                                    ┌──────────────────┬────────────────────────┐
                                    │ Check Assertion │ Check All Assertions   │
                                    └──────────────────┴────────────────────────┘

Result: false

Writer()	Reader()	Rand()
	okread[1] assigned false	
reading is 0		
	wval is 1	
	okread[1] assigned true	
	lastw is 1	
wpair assigned 1		
wpair is 1		
index[1] is 1		
windex assigned 0		
wpair is 1		
windex is 0		
wval is 1		
slot[2] starts being assigned 1		
slot[2] assigned 1		
wpair is 1		
windex is 0		
index[1] starts being assigned 0		
index[1] assigned 0		
wpair is 1		
latest starts being assigned 1		
	okread[1] assigned true	
	latest is (dirtily) 0	
	rpair assigned 0	
	rpair is 0	
	reading starts being assigned 0	

Fig. 18.1 The SVA window analysing a counter-example

As we said in the introduction to this chapter, we are deliberately concentrating on the model of interaction at the opposite end of the spectrum from CSP—all variables and no synchronisation rather than all synchronisation and no variables.

There is something to be said, however, for allowing some constructs which work by synchronisation into the language. For example rather than having to build each mutual exclusion used in a program out of shared variables, we could create a language construct as an abstraction of this. So, for example, getmutex(a) and releasemutex(a) might respectively claim and release the mutex token a.

svacomp.csp might implement these either using shared variables or using direct synchronisation between the relevant threads and a mutex process that looks exactly like the CSP specification of mutual exclusion MESPec defined below. There would be an interesting difference between these two, in that a process waiting for a critical section in the first would, as in our implementation of Peterson's and other shared-variable mutexes, engage in a *busy wait*, constantly testing identifiers. On the other hand the second, programmed naturally, would act as a stable CSP process waiting for the signal to begin the critical section.

Such a construct, and similar implementations of other ideas related to mutual exclusions such as *semaphores* and *monitors* [57], would make reasoning in richer models than $\mathcal{T}$ relevant to SVL and shared variables. We will not pursue this theme further here, but an Oxford undergraduate project has already demonstrated the feasibility of this extension.

18.4 Specifications in SVA

SVA provides two ways of creating specifications that FDR can check of programs in SVL. The first of these is to build a CSP specification that refers to the signal events that may be communicated by the program. So for example we can, in a mutual exclusion program, make each thread's critical section show the signals `sig(css.i);sig(cse.i)` and use the CSP specification of mutual exclusion `MESpec = css?i -> cse!i -> MESpec`. This states, as a trace specification, that each "critical section start" `css.i` is followed by the corresponding "critical section end" `cse.i` before any other critical section can start.

This can be checked by the assertion

```
assert %- MESpec [T= System -% in System
```

where what appears between the `%-` .... `-%` is a CSP_M assertion and the final `System` tells SVA what program to run. Note that this specification also—because `MESpec` does not allow them—checks for the existence of the run-time error signals that `svacomp.csp` can generate.

If you *just* want to check that no signal from some set S occurs, then this can be done either with a simplified version of the above, or the inbuilt syntax:

```
assert nosignal S in P
```

Similarly you can check that a given boolean b is always/never true during P's execution by running one of the checks

```
assert always b in P
assert never b in P
```

In these checks, b is always run atomically.

One can, naturally, envisage more expressive logical assertions than these, for example by automating the checking of part of LTL as discussed in Sect. 16.4. The model of time that applies here is less well defined than there (where we had a never-ending series of *tock*s) so it will probably not make sense to use the next-state operator $\bigcirc$.

Exercise 18.4 Show how, given an SVL program `System = <P(),Q(),...>` and the boolean expression b, you can create a new `System'` where a check for the signal `notalways` is equivalent to `assert always b in System`.

18.5 Case Study: Lamport's Bakery Algorithm

The bakery algorithm was designed by Leslie Lamport [78] as a mutual exclusion algorithm that works between an arbitrary number of threads, all potentially needing to perform critical sections that must exclude all the others. It works roughly on the principle by which some shops have a machine dispensing tickets that allocate "turns" to customers: the tickets are marked with ever increasing numbers and there is typically a display that shows which number is being served.

There are, however, some significant differences between the shop algorithm and Lamport's version. The former clearly has a single server handing out tickets, but in the bakery algorithm each process computes its own ticket value. These return to 0 each time there is no-one waiting. The distributed and unsynchronised nature of the bakery algorithm means that tickets are not necessarily issued in sequential order and may indeed take equal values. To resolve the latter problem the nodes are given an index that is used to give priority in the case that two ticket values are equal. In the following, $(a, b) < (c, d)$ if $a < c$ or $a = c$ and $b < d$.

The description of the algorithm in Fig. 18.2 is taken from Lamport's original paper, modified only by turning the $0/1$ integer array *choosing* into a boolean array, and converting the **goto** commands into an equivalent control structure in our own language.

Thus thread i first sets the boolean $choosing[i]$ to **true** so that any other thread can see that it has started to seek to acquire the mutual exclusion "token" but has not yet selected its ticket value. Then it selects its ticket value as one greater than the maximum of the values it reads for all the $number[i]$s. Lamport emphasises that this is not intended to be an atomic calculation.

Having selected its ticket value, thread i looks at the variables of each other thread j (the loop also looks at $j = i$, but that is unnecessary since both of the sub-loops will terminate immediately). For each j it waits until thread j is not choosing and either has a greater ticket value or an equal one when $j \geq i$. When this is done for all j our node can assume it has claimed the notional token and can perform its critical section. When it is finished it simply sets $number[i]$ to 0.

```
iter
    begin integer j;
        choosing[i] := true;
        number[i] := 1 + maximum{number[1], ..., number[N]}};   (*)
        choosing[i] := false;
        for j = 1 step 1 until N do
            begin
                while choosing[j] do skip;
                while number[j] > 0 and ((number[j], j) < (number[i], i)) do skip;
            end;
        critical section;
        number[i] := 0;
    end
```

Fig. 18.2 Original bakery algorithm

```
iter
    begin integer j;
        turn[i] := 1;
        turn[i] := 1 + maximum{turn[1], ..., turn[N]}
        for j = 1 step 1 until N do
            begin
                while turn[j] > 0 and ((turn[j], j) < (turn[i], i)) do skip;
            end;
        critical section;
        turn[i] := 0;
    end
```

Fig. 18.3 Simplified bakery algorithm

This seems straightforward until one realises that the various nodes are potentially changing their variables at the same time at arbitrary rates relative to one another. For example, two threads might be calculating their maxima at essentially the same time, but need not see the same values from the other threads.

In many other presentations of this algorithm, for example [15],[5] the roles of *choosing* and *number* are combined into a single array, say *turn*, with the approximate relationship

- $turn[i] = 0$ corresponds to $number[i] = 0$ and $choosing[i] = false$;
- $turn[i] = 1$ corresponds to $number[i] = 0$ and $choosing[i] = true$;
- $turn[i] > 1$ corresponds to $number[i] = turn[i] - 1$ and $choosing[i] = false$.

as shown in Fig. 18.3.

The above programs translate naturally into SVL except for the N-way *maximum*, which therefore has to be implemented using a loop. The one we will regard as standard is the following, where temp is an additional local variable:

```
temp := 0; j:= 1;
while j<= N do
  {temp := max(temp,number[j]);
   j := j+1};
  number[i] := temp+1;
```

This (which incorporates the algorithm's increment to the maximum) seems to the author to correspond well to what we would expect of a *maximum* operation, since it accesses each of the things to be maximised once, and only writes once to number[i].

We will give a number of alternatives on p. 460 and analyse them.

Quite apart from potential variations in the implementation, there are two significant problems when we attempt to verify the bakery algorithm using SVA and FDR. The first is a common one: the algorithm is intended to work for any number of

---

[5]This is just an example of a paper where this version is used. The author is not sure where it originated.

threads, whereas a concrete implementation we give can only have a fixed number. The second is that the number [i] values range over arbitrary non-negative integers, while SVA can only handle finite sub-ranges of the integers. Indeed it is not hard to see that even with two threads it is possible that the number [i] s can grow unboundedly: imagine one always entering the queue waiting for a critical section while the other is performing its.

In this section we ignore both of these problems (though we will solve them in Sect. 19.6) and study implementations with fixed numbers of threads; and look for errors other than the number [j] s exceeding their bounds. Of course you can verify that any chosen bound for the integer type is inadequate by running a check that does look for run-time errors. The reader is encouraged to see and experiment the example files containing both versions of the bakery algorithm.

The usefulness of the compression strategies described in the previous sections, as well as the problems caused by the state exploration problem, is well illustrated by the statistics which you can find on p. 450.

18.6 Case Study: The Dining Philosophers in SVL

The reader should already be very familiar with the dining philosophers problem from the many earlier references to it in this book (see the index). All of those were programmed in CSP and relied on synchronous communication to manage the distribution of the resources that are otherwise known as *forks*. We could equally well replace each fork process by a mutual exclusion algorithm, so that each philosopher now has to obtain the right to perform the critical section of both its adjacent ones in order to eat. We can easily create versions of both the symmetric and asymmetric dining philosophers out of the following components, each of which uses a mutual exclusion algorithm called Dekker's algorithm [36]: see also Exercise 19.1. As with Peterson's and Hyman's algorithms, there are a pair of threads indexed by 1 and 2. In our new model of the dining philosophers, each fork is replaced by making every pair of adjacent philosophers run a separate mutual exclusion. Thus each philosopher engages in two of these mutexes, and must be in the critical section of both of them in order to eat. The following routines represent what a philosopher has to do to obtain and release one or other end of the jth mutex/fork. The two ends, in common with our representation of Petersons's and Hyman's algorithms, are labelled by the parameter i being 1 or 2.

```
GetCS(j,i) =
b[j,i] := true;                  RelCS(j,i) =
While b[j,3-i] do                  t := 3-i;
  {if t[j]==3-i then               b[j,i] := false;
   {b[j,i] := false;              signal(putsdown.(j-1+i)%N.j)
    While t[j]==3-i do Skip;
    b[j,i] := true};
signal(picksup.(j-1+i)%N.j)}
```

Here, Phil(j) gets the i=1 side of (virtual) fork j, with Phil((j+1)%N) getting the i=2 side. Note that we have added as signals the CSP events that the philosopher would have synchronised with the forks in previous models. The jth philosopher (for i in {0..N-1}) can then be defined

```
Phil(j) = iter{GetCS(j,1);GetCS((j+1)%N,2);
                signal(eats.j);
                RelCS((j+1)%N,2);RelCS(j,1)}
```

This is a "right-handed" philosopher because it always seeks the fork (mutex) at index j before it does the one at index (j+1)%N. A left-handed one would perform these tasks in the opposite order. We know that the parallel composition of these N processes can deadlock when implemented in CSP, and must expect some analogous behaviour here. Over CSP this was discovered because the system failed a liveness as opposed to safety property, and it is natural to expect the same here.

We have already seen that safety (traces) properties are handled in very similar ways in CSP and SVA, both using traces. This is not the case for liveness properties. SVL processes never deadlock in a straightforward sense, since any thread that has not terminated can always perform an action. What actually happens in this SVL version when each has picked up one fork is that they all enter an eternal, but *busy*, wait for the availability of the second mutex, going round and round a loop checking for this for ever. The danger is not that the system can reach a state where nothing can happen, but rather that it can reach a state where nothing *useful* can happen.

In this world without deadlock, and where our system's behaviour is unaffected by the external environment, we need to find a different way to specify that systems have liveness properties.

Given that we have labelled everything that represents definite progress with a signal event, it is natural that we might want to prove the following: *from every reachable state, a signal* **will** *occur at some future time*.

However, with the model we have established so far this is not something we can aspire to because there are no *fairness* assumptions in our model. We allow the various threads to interleave completely arbitrarily, including the possibility that one thread will perform an infinite sequence of actions while the rest do nothing. So, for example, if one of a pair of processes involved in a mutex is in its critical section, it is possible that only the other one may perform actions, taking the form of an eternal loop waiting for the conditions allowing it to proceed with its critical section.

We therefore need to weaken our goal to proving that *from every reachable state, there is* **some execution** *that leads to a signal*. This is a reasonable aspiration for SVA processes without fairness.

We have already seen each of these specifications considered in Sect. 16.4 when we considered the extent to which LTL could be decided using FDR. For these two specifications, the first can be written $\Box\Diamond X$ while the second requires a branching time temporal logic. Here, X is the set of events that we want to be (i) unavoidable and (ii) always reachable at every point in the execution. The first (i.e. the one that our system will not satisfy), proved to be reasonably straightforward while the other needs to be weakened to "every finite trace s of P has an extension of the form $s\hat{}t\hat{}\langle x\rangle$ for some $x \in X$": *AlwaysPossible*(P, X).

For any non-empty subset X of the signals used in its definition, the symmetric version of the dining philosophers fails *AlwaysPossible*(P, X) because of the classic deadlock in which each philosopher picks up their right-hand fork. Similarly the asymmetric version in which there is at least one right-handed and one left-handed philosopher passes each such check.

This is illustrated in the accompanying file `svdphils.svl` where this specification is translated into CSP. Since this check involves having the whole system on the left-hand side of a refinement check, and therefore normalising it, FDR is able to handle rather smaller numbers of philosophers than it can for more straightforward checks.

The present version of FDR does not handle the sort of fairness that is required to reason about definite progress such as $\square\Diamond S$ in shared-variable systems of the type dealt with in SVA: what we would need there would be a way to build in an assumption that in any infinite execution each thread performs an infinite number of actions unless it terminates or throws an error. Techniques for handling both this and LTL (as well as other temporal logics) are well understood (see [25], for example) and use automata-theoretic analysis frequently involving *Büchi automata* to reason about fair systems. Until this style of analysis is added to FDR at some later date, and provided it still proves possible to use some effective compressions on at least the thread/variable combinations, we have to conclude that *SVA as a front end to FDR is excellent for reasoning about the safety properties of shared-variable systems, but has considerable weaknesses for reasoning about liveness properties.*

This also teaches us that relatively sophisticated techniques for reasoning about LTSs such as those involving infinitary liveness properties and fairness, seem to be much more necessary in the context of systems that, like complete SVL programs, are simply observed by the environment rather than needing to interact fully with it regularly.

The property that all N philosophers do not simultaneously hold a fork is, of course, a safety property and the reader will find that SVA/FDR check this considerably more quickly than the liveness property discussed above.

The author's favourite way of avoiding this situation is the asymmetric ring already discussed in this section. This is not because the author is left-handed, but rather because it creates a network that does not require an external patch to make it deadlock free, into which category the other well-known resolution of the deadlock falls, namely the *butler* or *footman* who refuses to allow a philosopher to sit down at the table if all his or her companions are already there [60]: see p. 55.

We will, nevertheless, study this second solution in the rest of this case study, since it teaches us some interesting lessons about shared variable programming and atomicity. The series of attempts at this model described below appear in separate files `svdphilsb`*i*`.svl` for *i* in {1,2,3}.

The natural way to implement this restriction in SVL is to add a counter, accessible by all the philosophers, of how many are seated. Before approaching the table, they check that the counter is strictly less than N-1, add one to it as they sit down, and subtract one when leaving the table. The following is a somewhat naïve implementation of this.

```
Phil2(j) = iter{
              if count < M-1 then
                {count := count + 1;
                 GetCS(j,1);GetCS((j+1)%N,2);
                 signal(eats.j);
                 RelCS((j+1)%N,2);RelCS(j,1);
                 count := count - 1}
                }
```

The reader will find that running this system (with all philosophers initially away
from the table and *count* initialised to 0) creates "out of range" errors for count.
This is, of course, because the assignments are not implemented atomically and
so, for example, the effect of either incrementing or decrementing count can be
removed by running it in parallel with a second increment or decrement.

The immediate conclusion is that we need to make the statements assigning to
count atomic, either by using the explicit atomic construct or by using a mutual
exclusion algorithm such as the bakery algorithm. We can, of course, *implement* the
atomic construct in terms of the others by using a mutual exclusion algorithm that
extends the exclusion over *all* the threads rather than just between a subset of them.

Making these assignments atomic, producing a new version Phil2(j), does
remove the run-time errors (on the assumption that count ranges over {0..N}),
but does not achieve the objective of preventing all the philosophers from sitting
down at once. Therefore the same "deadlock" can still happen. The reason for this
is that, when N-2 philosophers are sitting at the table, the only two non-sitting
philosophers can both check count at the same time, and find it is N-2. They then
sit down at the same time and increment count twice to N.

In order to achieve the desired effect we need to transform our program so that
the test of count < N-1 and the increment that follows if this is successful come
within the same atomic section. This seems to require the use of a local variable, as
in the following version:

```
Phil3(j) = boolean waiting
           iter{
              waiting := true
              while waiting do
                {atomic{if count < N-1 then
                         {waiting := false;
                          count := count + 1}};
                 GetCS(j,1);GetCS((j+1)%N,2);
                 signal(eats.j);
                 RelCS((j+1)%N,2);RelCS(j,1);
                 atomic{count := count - 1}}
                }
```

Notice that this now performs one eats.j each time round the main loop, whereas
the original program sometimes performed none.

This program works satisfactorily. We could add signals into the two atomic sections to represent the sits.j and getsup.j events of the CSP model on p. 53.

Exercise 18.5 What is the effect on the execution of the system built from Phil3s if the whole while waiting loop is made atomic rather than just its body? Reason about this problem first, trying to spot an undesirable behaviour. Are the signals presently placed in the program sufficient to let SVA show this undesirable behaviour? [*Hint: the answer to this question depends on whether you have added the* sits.j *event, and if so exactly where you have placed it.*] If not, add as many as are needed to do this.

Exercise 18.6 Create an SVL program in which the atomic sections of Phil3(j) are implemented using the bakery algorithm. How would you expect the times taken to check that all N philosophers can never sit at once to compare?

Exercise 18.7 An alternative to having N processes implement mutual exclusion themselves (as in the previous exercise) is to use one or more extra threads to do it for them.

(a) What should the interface between a single thread process and such an *arbiter* be? Think of each process as having one or more boolean flags it writes (e.g. "I want to enter my critical section") and the arbiter as having one or more for each of its clients (e.g. "Client j can start its critical section").

In designing this interface you might like to consider whether it prevents a single client performing two critical sections when the arbiter only meant it to have one.

(b) Design an arbiter that uses your interface, and which checks its clients, when appropriate, in round-robin fashion to find the next one to allow a critical section.

(c) Implement this in conjunction with the network of Phil3(j)'s, implementing their atomic sections.

Exercise 18.8 Now design an arbiter that is composed of N threads, one coupled with each philosopher. They work by passing a "token" around the ring between them in a single direction, which is implemented by variables that are shared between consecutive threads in the arbiter ring.

How does the behaviour of this ring arbiter compare to your round-robin sequential arbiter?

Exercise 18.9 Notice that the single process arbiter of Exercise 18.7 has something in common with the Butler process we are representing with the variable count, in that each of the philosophers has to ask the arbiter's permission to do something.

Use the techniques, including signalling techniques, you developed for that exercise to remove the count variable from philosophers, and place it inside a modified arbiter that now represents the behaviour of the Butler. Naturally the philosophers will now have to ask its permission to sit down and signal it when they get up.

18.7 Notes

The author wrote the first version of the shared-variable compiler in late 2000, and reported this work in [124]. For obvious reasons it was difficult to persuade many others to use a tool whose input language was a CSP type, and so not a great deal happened until David Hopkins's undergraduate project of 2006/2007 in which he built a front end for it. A summary of this work was reported in [64]. The version of SVA presented in this chapter and the next was developed especially for this book, and greatly extends the earlier one, for example by allowing non-constant array index expressions and using compression. The back end (svacomp.csp and other .csp files) was written by the author supported by the extension of CSP_M by Phil Armstrong to encompass Proc as a first-class type, and the front end was again written by David Hopkins.

Chapter 19
Understanding Shared-Variable Concurrency

In this chapter we look at some more advanced ideas in shared-variable program-ming. First we contemplate a less kind, but arguably more accurate, model of shared variables than the rather obvious one used in the previous chapter, and show how the bakery algorithm, at least in one of the two commonly seen versions, works nev-ertheless. We then see a further case study, namely an algorithm (Simpson's 4-slot algorithm) that attempts to bridge over the difference between the more optimistic and pessimistic versions. We then look at how to derive an appropriate notion of *refinement* between partial SVL programs and use it to study alternative algorithms for computing *maximum* as used in the bakery algorithm, as well as showing how each SVL program is equivalent to one in which each assignment and expression can be evaluated atomically. Finally we return to the bakery algorithm and see how to show that suitable versions of it work for arbitrary numbers of nodes and with unbounded ticket values.

19.1 Dirty Variables

Imagine that one process is trying to read a shared variable while another is writing it. What value does it get? Our variable processes $IVAR(x,v)$ and $BVAR(x,v)$ do not model this situation since reads from and writes to it are each instantaneous CSP events, so do not overlap.

In an unsynchronised implementation without some sort of mutual exclusion to keep reads and writes apart, this is not realistic. We can give SVL an alternative semantics in which either all overlapping reads and writes give a nondeterministic value to the read, or where those of some selection of locations are *dirty* like this. (We will refer to variables of the type modelled previously as *clean*.) To do this we assume that a set of $DirtyVars$ has been defined and that for each of these we have events representing the start and end of each write—a read between these two events getting a nondeterministic value chosen from the type of the variable. The easiest way to implement this is to have a thread writing to such a variable perform

A.W. Roscoe, *Understanding Concurrent Systems*, Texts in Computer Science,
DOI 10.1007/978-1-84882-258-0_19, © Springer-Verlag London Limited 2010

each `ivwrite.i.x.v` or `bvwrite.i.x.v` twice, and to have the corresponding variable process expect writes to come in pairs. That is what SVA does at the
time of writing, and what we will assume in the rest of this section.

We assume here that two *writes* to such a variable should not overlap, and make
it an error if they do. This is not an issue in the common case where each location
is only written by a single thread. See Exercises 19.1, 19.2 and 19.3 for further
examination of this issue. The definition of an integer variable therefore becomes

```
IVAR(x,v) = let t = ctype(x)
       Dirty(i) = iveval?_!x?y:t -> Dirty(i)
            [] ivwrite?j.x?_ -> (if i==j then SKIP
                                 else verror.x -> STOP)
        within
        (iveval?_!x!v -> IVAR(x,v)
         [] ivwrite?jj!x?w ->
             if not(member(w,t)) then verror.x -> STOP
                    else
                        if member(x,DirtyVars) then
                        (Dirty(jj);IVAR(x,w))
                        else IVAR(x,w))
```

The state `Dirty(i)` is the one in which our variable is giving arbitrary results for
reads pending the completion of the write by thread i that is currently taking place,
and during which it is an error for a different thread to write to this location. This
state is ended by the second of the pair of `ivwrite.i`s that thread i now creates.

In systems with `atomic` sections, the `Dirty(i)` state has to allow for threads
other than i starting an atomic section between the beginning and end of the write.
In that case the end of the write cannot happen until after the end of the atomic section, and reads of this variable from within the atomic section get a nondeterministic
value.

Likewise, the compilation of a boolean assignment now duplicates the `bvwrite`
event for dirty locations.

```
MainProc(Bassign.(el,e),j) =
         let Q(lv) =
         let P(rv) = bvwrite.j.lv.rv ->
                     if member(lv,DirtyVars)
                         then bvwrite.j.lv.rv -> SKIP
                         else SKIP
                 within BExpEval(e,P,j)
         within BLvEval(el,Q,j)
```

We could also, of course, spread out reads of shared location into a start and an
end, and make the result nondeterministic if any write of the same location happens
in the interval between them. The reason this is not implemented as standard is that
the asynchrony already present in the execution model of SVA makes it unnecessary.
If a "long" read of this form could overlap a write to the same location (necessarily

by another thread), then SVA will find an execution in which the single-event implementation of read occurs during the dirty phase of the write, which of course will return a nondeterministic result. In other words, the single read event can happen at any point between the beginning and end of the "long" one.

It would be necessary to use such long reads if two processes *reading* one location at the same time could cause problems, but we assume that such problems do not occur. It might also be necessary if a single read action could return the value of more than one location, since such a read could overlap writes to two of these locations, that did not themselves overlap. All the reads and writes we consider are from and to single locations.

Long reads are relatively unattractive to implement from the point of view of state space since an IVAR or BVAR process would need to remember details of each read currently in progress.

We might, in some circumstances, want to treat a read/write conflict as an execution error, as we do for write/write conflicts. In this case, the occurrence of a read event during a Dirty phase would trigger verror.x, just as the definition above does for a write event. It would be easy to modify SVA and SVL to allow for this.

There is a strong argument for wanting shared-variable algorithms in which writes are not protected from other accesses to the same location by mutual exclusion to be correct even when all shared variables are dirty. We could perhaps make an exception for boolean-valued locations that are only written to by a single thread, thanks to the following argument (which implies a simple transformation of the process doing the write):

- A boolean write either leaves the current value the same or it changes 0 to 1 or 1 to 0.
- Since there is only the single process writing the location, it can know in advance of the write whether the value is to be changed or not.
- If the value is not going to be changed the write can be cancelled, so there is no dirty phase. Not doing this write is equivalent to a "clean" one from the point of view of all processes reading the location.
- If the value is going to be changed it is reasonable (though not uncontroversial) to assert that the value read changes monotonically so that, say, one never reads 0 then 1 when overwriting the value 1 by 0. The effect of such a write is therefore the same as a clean one.

We call this strategy *write-when-different* and see an interesting application of it in the next section.

One of the most interesting properties of Lamport's original version of the bakery algorithm is that it is tolerant of all its shared variables (*number* and *choosing*) being dirty, as the reader can easily check by setting these locations as dirty in the script:

- In input to svacomp.csp, the set DirtyVars contains the names of dirty variables. For example, if this set is empty then all variables are clean, and if it is ivnames or bvnames then it consists of all integer or boolean locations respectively.

- In SVL the word `dirty` is put before the declaration of a variable or array, as in `dirty int[4] slot;`.

The simplified bakery algorithm (without *choosing*) satisfies the mutual exclusion specification with clean variables, but does not work with dirty ones. It is easy to see why: a process that is assigning a *turn* value greater than 1 might create a moment when a second process will read value 0. While this can still happen in the original version, that moment is protected by `choosing[i]` being 1, which eliminates some of the risk: once `choosing[i]` is set, no other thread attempting to enter a critical section can look at thread i and believe that it is not presently requesting, or in, a critical section until it has left the critical section.

Making *local* variables (i.e. unshared ones) dirty does not make any semantic difference to a program since there is nobody who can read them in the dirty phase. On the other hand, making them dirty certainly increases the number of transitions that the variable and thread processes perform as they proceed, as well as the number of states in the state space of the combination of the thread and its variables.

If you look at the state space of running a compressed check with dirty local variables, it will, despite this, be identical to the same check with clean local variables. This helps illustrate why compression works so well in conjunction with SVA. Many of the steps that the combinations of threads and their own variables take are, like this extra step in a local write, things that do not directly affect the external view of the combination. They are just computational progress, and `diamond` compression has the effect of eliminating these steps, amongst others, after they have been hidden. The existence of "progress" steps (such as testing or incrementing loop variables) is very common in shared variable programs, to the extent that just about any non-trivial thread will have many. This helps to explain the effectiveness of compression in SVA as shown, for example, by the bakery algorithm with three threads and `MaxI=8`. With and without compression the version tried by the author has 1605 and 7.36 M states. Increasing to four, five and six threads increases the compressed version to 41 K, 2193 K and 135 M states, whereas the uncompressed version had grown beyond the author's patience for four, even with `MaxI` reduced to 6. These figures, of course, illustrate not only the effectiveness of compression but also the impact of the state explosion problem! When thinking about these figures you should remember that increasing the number of threads not only adds in extra processes but makes each one more complex because of the longer loops.

Making shared variables dirty will usually increase the compressed state space, however, and will *always* result in a system that is trace-refined by the one with clean variables.

Exercise 19.1 Dekker's algorithm, the mutual exclusion algorithm that we used in the dining philosophers in Sect. 18.6, is described below in the same style we used for Peterson's and Hyman's algorithms in the last chapter. `b[i]` are shared booleans and `t` is a shared integer variable that ranges over the thread numbers {1,2}.

```
iter {
  b[i] := true;
```

```
While b[3-i] do
  {if t==3-i then
              {b[i] := false;
               While t==3-i do Skip;
               b[i] := true}
  }
CRITICAL SECTION;
t := 3-i;
b[i] := false}
```

Notice that here, unlike in the other examples we have examined in the context of dirty variables, there is a variable (t) that is written to by both threads. Analyse it to see if it satisfies the mutual exclusion specification with and without its variables being dirty.

What happens if the two assignments following the critical section are interchanged?

Exercise 19.2 Analyse Hyman's and Peterson's algorithms to see whether they are guilty of concurrent writes (i.e. ones that might overlap and cause the error event in Dirty to occur).[1]

Exercise 19.3 Suggest some alternatives for the model of dirty variables that bans concurrent writes. You might like to consider the following cases separately:

(a) What if the concurrent writes are all of the same value?[2]
(b) What if the underlying type is boolean so that a pair of clashing writes are either the same or cover the entire type?

19.2 Case Study: Simpson's 4-Slot Algorithm

When one thinks about it, it is a great deal more surprising that the original bakery algorithm is tolerant of dirty variables than that the simplified one is not. Dirty variables seem to be a remarkably challenging obstacle to creating a correct shared-variable program, at least unless we use mutual exclusion to ensure that no thread ever attempts to read from one while it is being written to, and that no write to one

---

[1] We have already seen one mutual exclusion algorithm, namely the bakery algorithm, in which no location is written by more than one thread. A second is Knuth's algorithm [77], an implementation of which can be found with the examples accompanying this chapter.

[2] In the theory of concurrent algorithms, researchers sometimes consider a parallel machine model in which multiple processors are allowed to make simultaneous writes to the same location, but only if all the written values are the same: a Parallel Random Access Machine with *Common Concurrent Writes*, see [39].

starts while it is being read from. The device used in the original bakery algorithm
of having a `choosing` flag that protects a write can be seen as a weak version
of this: it prevents a second thread reading the protected variable while it is being
written to, provided the read starts after the write. It can be seen that either this or
full mutual exclusion can easily have the effect of holding up a thread that wants
to read a location. In one case it has to wait until it can perform its critical section
of accessing the location; in the other it has to wait until `choosing[j]` is unset
before it can rely on the corresponding `number[j]`. Waits like these have the
potential to create "deadlocks" in which each thread is prevented from getting any
of the mutual exclusions it wants for reading or writing in a way similar to the one
we saw in Sect. 18.6, the shared-variable implementation of the dining philosophers.

Simpson's 4-slot algorithm [148] is an attempt to rectify this: it assumes there are
two processes, one of which can write to a shared variable at any time and one can
always read from it. It seeks to create a clean shared variable of a given type from
four dirty ones of the same type and several boolean flags. It should be emphasised
that this algorithm was intended for hardware implementation by its inventor, Hugo
Simpson. Separate processes may write and read the variable at any time, and the
algorithm seeks to ensure that slots read from and written to simultaneously are
different, but that, where reads and writes do not overlap, the algorithm gives the
same results as a variable process with atomic reads and writes. It can be viewed as
a component of a rather different sort of asynchronous system compared to the sort
discussed in Sect. 17.4.

For reasons that will soon become apparent, the literature on this algorithm usually assumes that the boolean flag variables it uses are clean, sometimes stated in
terms of the reads from and writes to these locations being atomic. In this section
we will *not* usually make this assumption.

In the following model the `Reader` and `Writer` processes just perform their
tasks over and over. In a real application the body of each loop would be called when
an enclosing thread wanted to read or write the variable, but of course we should
bear in mind that the threads below are interleaved completely arbitrarily and so can
simulate any such real application.

```
Writer =
{iter
    {wval := inp;
     wpair := !reading;
     windex := !index[wpair];
     slot[wpair,windex] := wval;
     index[wpair] := windex;
     latest := wpair;
    }
}

Reader =
{iter
    {rpair := latest;
```

```
reading := rpair;
rindex := index[rpair];
outp := slot[rpair,rindex];
}
}
```

Here, `inp` represents the value that we want to be written (and which we assume here is a value set by another thread) and `outp` is the value returned by the read. The array of `slots` is shared between these two threads, as are the four booleans `reading`, `latest`, `index[true]` and `index[false]`. Apart from `reading`, which is written to by `Reader`, they are all written only by `Writer`. The rest of the variables are all local to one or other thread.

While it is perhaps more difficult to get a clear intuition for this algorithm than, for example, the bakery algorithm, we can nevertheless see that it should satisfy a number of useful properties such as the following:

- If a *read* is executed in the interval between two iterations of the `Writer` loop, then the most recently written value is read.
- If a *read* pauses then the value written is, thanks to `wpair := !reading;`, to a different slot from the one that is being read from.

It is not easy to understand the dance that the two threads perform in general, though, particularly if we assume that the four boolean flags are dirty.

Fortunately it is easy to adapt the above program, not only to run it on SVA, but also to analyse it. The only issues about adapting it are that, above, `slot` is a *two-dimensional* array indexed by booleans, and `index` is also indexed by booleans. We can convert this to the SVL language by firstly interpreting all the booleans in the above programs as integers 0=`false` and 1=`true` and secondly replacing `slot[a][b]` by `islot[2*a+b]`. Negation of a boolean becomes 1-x for the corresponding integer.

Consider first the claim that there is never a read and a write performed on the same slot simultaneously. This is easily verified by making all of the shared locations, both slots and flags, dirty, setting the type of data (i.e. what is stored in the `slots`) to be {0,1}, initialising `inp` to be 0 and never letting it change, and checking that `outp` never takes the value 1. The value 1 could be read just when `Reader` reads from a slot that it is in its dirty phase. It can equally be checked by making the flag variables dirty and the slots exclusive. The fact that this specification (i.e. that 1 is never read) holds seems, as with the bakery algorithm's tolerance for dirty variables, rather remarkable.

Since our program is obviously **NoEqT** data independent in the type of data (stored in `slots`, `inp`, `wval` and `outp`), either of these two checks clearly proves that the slots are preserved as exclusive in Simpson's algorithm, even when the flags are not assumed to be clean and the type of data is arbitrary.

A second property we would like to hold is that every read returns a value that, while it may not be the *most* recently written value, is one that is either *being* written or at some *recent* time was the most recently written one.

It seems reasonable to interpret the italicised *recent* in the last sentence as meaning "during the execution of the current read cycle". Therefore what we actually demand is that the read value may be any one of

- the value of the most recently completed write at the start of the current read cycle,
- the value of any write that was happening at the start of the current read cycle,
- the value of any write subsequent to the above.

Again relying on data independence, we can easily check whether this holds by arbitrarily writing 0 or 1 on each write cycle and modifying the `Reader` and `Writer` as follows

- There is a new integer variable `lastw` that remembers the value of the last completed write.
- There is a new boolean array `okread` indexed by the data values $\{0,1\}$: at the end of each read cycle `okread[i]` tells us whether a read of value i is legitimate under the above specification. At the start of each read cycle `okread[i]` is set to `true` if either `wval` or `lastw` takes value i; otherwise it is set to `false`.
- Each time a write cycle is performed, `okread[wval]` is set to `true`.

Regrettably, this specification fails when all the locations are dirty, though it succeeds if the flag variable `latest` is removed from `DirtyVars`. (See the file `Simpson2.svl`.) Interestingly, the trace that SVA discovers when `latest` is dirty involves this variable being assigned the same value that it had before the write: the error involves the opposite value being read during the dirty phase of the write.

This suggests that, for this and perhaps the three other shared boolean variables, we might employ the write-when-different trick described on p. 449, and only assign to them when they are to change. Modifying the assignment to `latest` in this way makes the above *recentness* specification true even if we still interpret the same variables as dirty. (Recall that we argued there that there was a reasonable case for asserting that a boolean variable treated in this way might be relatively easy to implement as clean: we are not relying on this here.)

There is one further specification that it is natural to demand of any reasonable model of a shared variable: it must be *sequentially consistent*, meaning that if we read a series of values from the variable and remove consecutive duplicates then we get a subsequence of the initial value of the variable followed by the values written to it in order. In other words, we cannot carry out two consecutive reads and get an older value on the second read.

The **NoEqT** data independence of the algorithm in the type of data means that we can run a rather cunning[3] check for this. We arrange that the initial value of the variable is 0 (every `slot[i]` equals this) and that the sequence of writes performed is a completely arbitrary number of 0s followed by an arbitrary number of 1s. If it

---

[3]Note that this, and the earlier checks in this section, resemble the check for a data-independent process being a buffer described on p. 406.

were possible to get an out-of-sequence read value then it would be possible to read a 0 after a 1, because there is an execution in which the newer value that gets read coincides with the very first 1 that is written. In other words, if the nth member of the input sequence can be read before the mth, where $n > m$, we consider the case where the first 1 to be input appears at place n.

We can therefore arrange a check on this basis: the input value inp is initialised to 0 and assigned (cleanly[4]) 1 at an arbitrary point in the execution by a third thread, and we check if outp is ever 0 when it has previously been 1.

This check succeeds if all the boolean flags are clean, but fails if any one of them is write-when-different but dirty (meaning, say, that on writing one of them that is 0 to 1, consecutive reads might see 1,0 before it settles to 1). To run these checks, see Simpson3.svl.

At least for the three flags set by Writer, there is an interesting explanation for this problem. It is easy to see that each one of these flags can directly affect the choice by Reader of which slot is read from next. Suppose that the Writer's execution gets suspended mid-way through such a critical write to flag f, which when complete will tell the Reader to look at a more newly-written slot. Now suppose that the Reader runs through twice in this period, the first time getting the changed value of f and the second time getting the old one. (This is possible in our model since f is in the middle of being written and can change its value arbitrarily while this is true.) Since the Reader uses no state that it has set prior to a particular read, it will inevitably get the value from the new slot on the first read and the old one on the second. This argument demonstrates that both Simpson's algorithm and any other with a similarly "memory-less" Reader cannot have the sequential consistency property in the presence of the dirty flag variables, when the dirty period can extend over two read cycles like this.

The author knows of no way of solving this problem by the addition of further (data-independent) slots or a finite number of boolean flags. Indeed, he conjectures that there is no solution of this type. We can, however, solve it by building on what we have already established about Simpson's algorithm when latest is made write-when-different, namely that access by the two processes to the slot avoids all dirty reads and that the value read by the reader is always recent. The essential idea behind our solution is to augment each slot with an integer counter that is always written to or read from along with the "real" slot value. We know that these counters and slots are read cleanly *as a pair*: the value the Reader sees for one of these augmented slots will always be the pair of values the Writer wrote to it earlier or which was there initially. We also know that each counter/data value combination that Reader gets is recent. If each write cycle then increments and writes the counter—the first write getting counter 1, the second 2 and so on—it should be easy to detect out-of-sequence reads.

We can therefore implement the following modified algorithm:

---

[4]It is legitimate to make clean writes to locations such as this and okread[i] that are shared between threads and introduced by us for specification purposes, because they are not part of the algorithm itself, merely tools to help us observe it.

```
Writer2 =
{iter
    {wval := inp;
     counter := counter+1;
     wpair := !reading;
     windex := !index[wpair];
     slotcounter[wpair,windex] := counter;
     slot[wpair,windex] := wval;
     index[wpair] := windex;
     if latest!=wpair then latest := wpair;
    }
}


Reader2 =
{iter
    {rpair := latest;
     reading := rpair;
     rindex := index[rpair];
     thiscounter := slotcounter[rpair,rindex];
     if thiscounter > lastcounter then
                    { outp := slot[rpair,rindex];
                      lastcounter := thiscounter};
            }
    }
```

Note that this Reader2 does not read a slot that was written no later than its previous one. outp is therefore left at its prior, more recently written, value. Of course the slotcounter locations should be treated as dirty, but we know this will have no effect thanks to the established properties of Simpson's algorithm. Given this, it is obvious that the revised algorithm never returns an out-of-sequence result. It is also clear that the value of any read is always at least as up to date as the one produced by the original algorithm.

It is therefore fair to argue that we have *already* verified the cleanness and recentness properties of this algorithm, and that the no-out-of-sequence property is obvious. This is fortunate since the revised algorithm is infinite state, thanks to the counters.

We can nevertheless run the revised algorithm directly for a small number of writes, whatever value we pick for MaxI. Later in this chapter we will see techniques that can prove both the similarly limited bakery algorithm and this one correct in the presence of an unbounded integer type.

In a practical implementation, in order to work in the presence of completely arbitrary interleaving, the counters need to be large enough to hold the value of the maximum number of writes that could conceivably occur during a run: presumably 64 bits would be sufficient in most cases. With care it should be possible to use smaller values when the length of time that a variable can remain dirty is bounded.

Of course if we can build boolean flag variables in which a write-when-different is effectively clean, there is no need for the elaboration with counters.

Our modified Simpson's algorithm can be thought of as a *data refinement*: we have refined the slot variable of the original algorithm with write-when-different into a pair of variables, and relied on the properties that the original algorithm guarantees to ensure that the counters are transmitted accurately to the `Reader`.

The idea behind our modified algorithm is close to using the idea of *protocol layering* discussed on p. 86. We use the write-when-different algorithm as an inner layer to guarantee recentness; the outer layer using message sequence numbers guarantees no-overtaking. This analogy cannot be taken too far, however, since the layered approach would naturally generate parallel processes for the reader and writer: we certainly do not want this here since it would mean more shared variables!

Exercise 19.4 Construct a Simpson's algorithm CSP_M script that tests the following specification: *the value of each read is one of the four most recent writes.* (Make an appropriate adjustment at the start of the run when there have been three or less writes.)

Even with all locations clean, the algorithm should not satisfy this specification. How can we be sure that any algorithm that never blocks reads or writes, which is arbitrarily interleaved, and which prevents dirty reads of values of the data-type, can never satisfy this specification even if "four" is increased?

Exercise 19.5 Notice that Simpson's algorithm is limited to a single reader and a single writer of our variable. Discuss the issues that would be involved in increasing the numbers, and see if you can solve the problem. Could a number of reading and/or writing processes share the use of a single `Reader/Writer` agent?

It could be argued that in a fully asynchronous world this latter (agent sharing) technique is less good than having the corresponding code embedded within the thread that actually creates or consumes the value, because the reading and writing agents may not get scheduled sufficiently often. Do you agree?

19.3 Observing and Refining SVL Programs

One of the most interesting properties of any translation of another language into CSP is that it automatically gives a definition of *refinement* between programs: refinement between terms in a language like CSP holds just when it does between the CSP translations.

As explained in Sect. 18.6, the only form of refinement check that usually makes sense for SVA is over finite traces, since the CSP processes it creates can frequently diverge due to unfair executions. Aside from the use of `AlwaysPossible` on p. 442, every check we have used for SVL has been of the complete system against a fixed CSP specification constructed in terms of `Errors` and signals to judge its correctness.

There is, of course, a second important role that we would like refinement to have, namely helping us to judge when one *partial* program refines another: can we replace the *maximum* algorithm we selected for the bakery algorithm by another without introducing any undesirable behaviour?

The compiler as described to date treats the program supplied to it as a closed system. In particular, its locations are neither read nor written to by any outside entity. To judge a partial program, one that will fit into a program context like the one where the maximum algorithm is placed, we need to take into account how it interacts with the rest of the program through the shared use of locations.

The refinement relations described in this section are implemented in a special file, refsva.csp, *which acts as a front end to* svacomp.csp.

There are actually three sorts of context we need to consider:

- In $C[P]$, P only appears within atomic statements[5] created by $C[\cdot]$. *In such contexts, parallel processes cannot read from or write to P's locations while they are running. So P is only influenced by the initial values in its locations and only influences other parts of the system via the values it leaves behind in locations it can write to and they can read from. Semantically speaking, such P can be viewed as functions from their initial state to the combination of their final state and the possibly empty sequence of signals produced. We will call this a sequential context.*

  When reasoning about such a P, we need to tell SVA which of its locations might be written to by preceding code or read from by subsequent code. For this purpose the user defines two sets of locations: SeqWrites, which contains all locations where writes by preceding code might leave a value other than the initialisation to be read by P, and SeqReads, which contains all locations that P might write to and subsequent code read from. It is important that these sets contain not only those locations that might be read from or written to by the rest of the thread within which P sits, but also the relevant ones in other threads, made sequential by the atomic statement surrounding P.

- In $C[P]$, P only appears at the level of the final parallel combination: in other words it plays the role of one or more complete threads. *In such contexts, the initial values of locations are all defined statically by the context or by P itself, and there is no process that runs afterwards to use the final values. However, some other threads may be able to read from and write to locations used by P. We therefore model P in much the same way as for complete programs, only allowing the environment (playing the role of these other threads) to read from the locations* ParReads *and write to* ParWrites.[6] We will call this a *parallel* context.

- If P appears as a part of a single thread but is not forced to be atomic by that thread, we need to consider both of the sorts of influences discussed above. This

---

[5]This type of context also applies to any case where there is no parallelism in the complete system.

[6]In the case of integer locations we only consider the case of writes of values within the content type of the given location, since, thanks to our error regime, no thread will attempt any other write.

is a *general* context. There is no need in this case to include locations written to by other threads in SeqWrites or ones read from by other threads in SeqReads, since the interfaces required by ParReads and ParWrites will give the environment all relevant access to these.

For the last two of these, there is a further parameter that defines how our term interacts with other threads: ext_atomic is a boolean that is true when we want to allow external threads to go into atomic sections, preventing any activity by our term during that period. We can see that this is necessary from the following example: assuming that x and y are initialised to 0, and that ParReads={x,y}, ParWrites={} and SeqWrites={}, consider the following pair of programs:

```
PP: iter {x := 1;        QQ: iter {x := 1;
          x := 0;                  y := 1;
          y := 1;                  x := 0;
          y := 0}                  y := 0}
```

If ext_atomic is false, then these two programs refine each other in a parallel or general context. Any read of x or y can get the values 0 or 1. If, on the other hand, ext_atomic is true, then PP is a proper refinement of QQ, which can give both variables the value 1 during the same atomic section, something impossible for PP. This example can be found in extatomic.svl.

For both sequential and parallel contexts, we need to allow the environment to assign to and read from some of *P*'s locations. In the sequential case, assignments are only possible before *P* runs and reads are only possible after *P* has finished, whereas in parallel contexts there is no restriction.

What we therefore do is implement a channel along which an "external thread" can write to locations in a set ExtWrites and read from those in ExtReads. This will give us exactly what we need to consider parallel contexts where ExtWrites equals ParWrites and ParReads=ExtReads, and be adaptable to handle sequential contexts and general ones. SVA allows such reads and writes as though they were performed by the "thread" with index -1. It prevents any such reads and writes when the process *P* we are considering is within an atomic section, because if the environment were to be replaced by one or more threads, they would not be allowed to read or write while *P* is in an atomic section. For this reason, provided that *P* obeys the rule that no atomic section sends more than one signal, there is no need to make visible the start_at.j and end_at.j events that the simulation of *P* performs.

When ext_atomic is true, the external thread can enter and then leave an atomic section via start_at.-1 and end_at.-1.

For example, if we were comparing two implementations of thread i in the original bakery algorithm, it would be natural to define

```
ParReads = {number[j],choosing[j] | j <- {1..N}}
ParWrites = {number[j],choosing[j] | j <- {1..N}, j!=i}
ext_atomic = false
```

Recall that when we introduced the implementation of *maximum* on p. 440, we said this was one of many alternatives. The following are four options, with the previous one being `Maximum A`

```
Maximum A:                          Maximum B:
temp := 0; j:= 1;                   j := 1;
while j<= N do                      while j<=N do
  {temp := max(temp,                  {number[i] := max(number[i],
            number[j]);                          number[j]);
   j := j+1};                         j := j+1};
  number[i] := temp+1;              number[i] := number[i]+1;


Maximum C:                          Maximum D:
j:= 1;                              j := 1;
while j<= N do                      while j<=N do
  {temp := number[j];                 {if number[j] > number[i]
   if temp > number[i]                then number[i] := number[j];
   then number[i] := temp;           j := j+1};
   j := j+1};                        number[i] := number[i]+1;
  number[i] := number[i]+1;
```

If the `number[i]` only take non-negative values, these are all equivalent as programs in a sequential language, which is the same as saying that they are equivalent in SVL if each of them is made `atomic`, or that they are equivalent in sequential contexts. To verify this, set `SeqWrites` to `{number[j] | j <- {1..N}}` and `SeqReads` to `{number[i]}` (`ParReads` and `ParWrites` not being relevant to sequential contexts). Note that the `number[j]` (`j!=i`) are included in `SeqReads` because the other threads may have assigned to these before the atomic section begins.

There are subtle differences between the algorithms, however, when parallel threads are allowed to see and alter the values of the `number[j]` locations, as is the case in the bakery algorithm. We will assume that the `temp` and `j` variables are local to the particular thread and cannot be seen outside it.

We can compare these algorithms in two ways. The first is to use versions of the complete thread `i` with the various `Maximum` algorithms substituted, and the second is to compare the algorithms themselves in the way appropriate for a general context. Example files are provided which do this both ways, for particular values of `i`, `N` and `MaxI` that can be adjusted by the reader.

Run-time errors are quite common in these systems because of the way 1 is added to a value that can easily be the largest possible for the type of the `number[j]`, and the result assigned back to a location of that type. For one system `P` to refine another one `Q`, it is entirely reasonable to demand that when `P` generates an error event then so can `Q`. There is a problem nevertheless: the counter-examples found to refinement may (and frequently do, without the constraint described below) arise from events that *follow* error events: in other words `P` and `Q` can both perform a trace of the form `s^<error.i>`, but `Q` can then perform some other event that P cannot. It seems unreasonable to differentiate processes on the basis of what happens *after* an error. It seems clear that we should not distinguish between processes if their only differences follow run-time errors, and so the framework for refinement that SVA uses prevents all events that follow members of Errors. It is reasonable to term this assumption *weak error strictness*, by analogy with divergence strictness. We will introduce the strong form in Exercise 19.7.

This and other issues related to deciding questions of refinement between SVL terms in any of the three sorts of context are addressed by refsva.csp, the refinement wrapper[7] for svacomp.csp. It is this file that uses the parameters ParReads, SeqWrites etc.

When building the general context model of P, a Cmd, we need to be able to compute its initial state from its trace. This is because when we compare the traces of P and Q, we need to know if a given behaviour of Q started in the same state or not. We should therefore allow writes to the locations SeqWrites at any time strictly *before* P starts running, with any location that is not written to in this way taking the value that the program initialises it to. These have to be left visible in the trace so that when we are testing the refinement of one program by another, we always compare them from identical starting states. To mark the end of this initialisation phase we introduce a special signal PStart that the model communicates at the point that P starts running. Similarly, to distinguish the final state of P in which SeqReads can occur, we introduce a signal PEnd that it communicates when it has terminated. The SVL program that is run is therefore signal(PStart);P;signal(PEnd). We can then put this running code in parallel with a CSP process:

```
GRefReg0 =
PStart -> GRefReg1(false)
[] ivwrite.-1?x:inter(SeqWrites,ivnames)?_ -> GRefReg0
[] bvwrite.-1?x:inter(SeqWrites,bvnames)?_ -> GRefReg0

GRefReg1(b) =
PEnd -> GRefReg2
[] ivwrite.-1?x:inter(OTWrites,ivnames)?_ -> GRefReg1(b)
[] bvwrite.-1?x:inter(OTWrites,bvnames)?_ -> GRefReg1(b)
[] iveval.-1?x:inter(OTReads,ivnames)?_ -> GRefReg1(b)
[] bveval.-1?x:inter(OTReads,bvnames)?_ -> GRefReg1(b)
[] ext_atomic and (not b)&start_at.-1 -> GRefReg1(true)
[] ext_atomic and b&end_at.-1 -> GRefReg1(false)
[] (not b)&
   (([] x:Union({Signals,ISignals}) @ x -> GRefReg1(b))
   [] ([] x:Errors @ x -> STOP))
```

---

[7]refsva.csp does not disable the other functions of svacomp.csp, and in fact the parser in SVA's front end always uses the combination of these two files, even when no refinement between SVL terms is tested.

```
GRefReg2 =
iveval.-1?x:inter(SeqReads,ivnames)?_ -> GRefReg2
[] bveval.-1?x:inter(SeqReads,bvnames)?_ -> GRefReg2
```

This notices the initialisation, running and final state phases and allows the appropriate external accesses to the locations, and also stops P when a run-time error occurs. The boolean parameter on the middle state is true if the external state has claimed a current atomic section. If it has, then the activities of the process we are modelling are prevented.

We are now in a position to test the refinement relation between the different Maximum algorithms. This is implemented in the file CompareMax.svl.

ParReads and ParWrites are both {} when modelling a sequential context. For parallel contexts we do not need the PStart and PEnd signals. Parallel contexts are used to check the effects of how a complete thread of the bakery algorithm is affected by the different Maximum algorithms: we can compare them for refinement.

So what of our Maximum algorithms? SVA and FDR can only test refinement between them for fixed values of i and N, and fixed finite type of integers stored in the number[j]s. If one tests them for N = 3 and then for i=1,2,3 separately, with MaxI=4, one finds that:

- All four are indeed equivalent when the algorithms are put in a sequential context, which forces the maximum algorithm to be executed atomically.
- When not atomic, A properly refines B, C, D; Version D is properly refined by A, B, and C. B and C are equivalent.

Refinement comparisons of terms typically take significantly longer than checking some simple property of one or other system. As with the AlwaysPossible check in Sect. 18.6, this is because a more complex process has to be normalised.

Quite aside from the three basic types of refinement that we have defined, and depending on the sort of context, we have also shown how to tune the refinement question according to the assumed abilities of the rest of the program to read from and write to shared locations and go into atomic sections. There is fortunately a simple result that links all of these ideas.

Theorem 19.1 *When* P *and* Q *are members of* Cmd, *then*

1. P *sequentially refines* Q *for given sets* SeqReads *and* SeqWrites *if and only if the same general refinements apply with both* ParWrites *and* ParReads *empty, and* ext_atomic=false.
2. P;Iter Skip *parallel refines* Q;Iter Skip *for any sets* ParReads *and* ParWrites *if and only if the same general refinements apply with both* SeqWrites *and* SeqReads *empty, and* ext_atomic *the same in both cases.*
3. *Suppose the general refinement holds for a quintuple* (SeqReads,Seq-Writes,ParReads,ParWrites,ext_atomic), *and a second quintuple* (SeqReads',...,ext_atomic') *is contained in the first, in the sense that* SeqReads'⊆SeqReads *etc. and* ext_atomic' => ext_atomic, *then the same refinement holds over the second quintuple.*

4. *Exactly analogous results hold for sequential and parallel refinement, with pairs and triples of parameters respectively.*

The first two parts of the above result follow directly from the structures of the contexts used to test the refinement. In the first they give identical behaviours. In the second they give identical behaviours except that the general one inserts PStart at the beginning of each trace. The reason for the sequential composition with a non-terminating process in this part is that parallel refinement ignores termination, whereas general refinement does not since it is detectable from the event PEnd.

The third and fourth parts are straightforward once we realise that the CSP model we get of P with the weaker set of observations (i.e. SeqReads' etc.) can be obtained from that with the stronger one by putting it in parallel with *STOP*, synchronising on all the events (reads, writes, start_at.-1 and end_at.-1) that the observer is allowed to try in the stronger environment but not in the weaker.

Exercise 19.6 What refinement relations hold between the following simple programs in a general context, where SeqReads, SeqWrites and ParReads are all {x}, and ParWrites = {}. Assume MinI=0, MaxI = 5, and x is of type {MinI..MaxI}?

A. x := 1
B. x := x; x := 1
C. x := 1; x := 1
D. x := 1; x := x
E. x := x/x
F. x := (x-x)+1
F. x := (x+1)-x

Would your answer change if ParReads became {x}?

Exercise 19.7 Recall that we made programs *weakly* error-strict on p. 461 by insisting that no event follows an error. The best analogue in standard CSP for this is the fact that no event ever follows ✓. A better analogue for the divergence strictness of some CSP models would be to insist that as soon as a process becomes able to communicate an error signal it is immediately equivalent to CHAOS (Events), the process that can perform every legitimate trace.

Define and implement (in terms of existing operators) a CSP operator *StrictTr*(A, P) such that whenever the process P performs any member of A it can also perform any trace at all. Thus, for example, *StrictTr*(a, b → a → Q) should be equivalent to b → *CHAOS* over the traces model $\mathcal{T}$. [You might find the *throw* operator Θ_A useful here, but it is not essential over $\mathcal{T}$.]

If we routinely made our refinement models of SVL terms strongly error strict by applying StrictTR (Errors, .) to them, how (if at all) would your answer to Exercise 19.6 change?

19.3.1 The Bakery Algorithm Revisited

If we replace one term with another that refines it inside some context, then the context will continue to refine any specification it satisfied before. If, on the other hand, we replace it by any other term, we cannot be so sure.

Since `Maximum A` is incomparable under the refinement relation with the others on p. 460, we simply do not know at this stage whether either the simplified or original bakery algorithm will continue to satisfy mutual exclusion when `Maximum A` is replaced by any of the others. In the author's experiments involving up to 6 threads with `MaxI` up to 12, all of the versions did satisfy mutual exclusion with the exception of the original algorithm with `Maximum D`. However, *both* the simplified and original algorithms fail the specification with these parameters when the line `number[i] < number[j]` of `Maximum D` is replaced[8] with `number[j] >= number[i]`: an apparently innocent change that would not change the outcome of the conditional statement in a sequential program.

This actually conceals two distinct alterations in the behaviour of this thread as in the context of shared variables: it reads the values of `number[i]` and `number[j]` in the opposite order, and in the event of equality carries out the assignment.

The latter of these in particular is anything but innocent since we find that after the comparison has been carried out with equal values, thread `j` might have altered, even to 0, the value that gets assigned to `number[i]`. We find that it is therefore possible to run the changed algorithm in the context where, say, `i=2` and `number[1]` stays at value 3 throughout, but thanks to `number[3]` changing from 3 to 0 at a crucial moment the value of `number[2]` is assigned 0 before the program looks at `number[4]`.

But of course exactly the same could have happened had `number[3]` changed from 4 to 0, and the original `Maximum D` would also have committed the error. On reflection, version D should not be regarded as a reasonable maximum algorithm in a shared-variable environment, since the type of behaviour discussed here means that it might return a value as the supposed maximum which is less than one of the `number[j]` that never changes while it runs: there is no way that we can therefore claim that the failure of the bakery algorithm, when it is used, represents a problem with the original descriptions of the algorithm on pp. 439 and 440.

There are, of course, two further versions of the comparison above that the reader can try, namely ones that just make one of the two changes discussed above: the results are different for these, too.

What all of this does show is how remarkably difficult it sometimes is to understand and reason about shared-variable programs. One reason for this is that one thread can be influenced by what others do at just about any time. This is different from CSP, where the only influences on a process are the events that it explicitly performs.

---

[8]Furthermore, this replacement only created a problem with at least 5 threads.

It also shows how much we need methods that are capable of proving versions of the bakery algorithm for all numbers of threads and arbitrary integers. See Sect. 19.6 for these.

19.4 Atomic Equivalent Programs

Programs would be easier to understand if we did not need to break down individual program statements (assignments etc.) into multiple events. What we will show in this section is that every SVL program can be transformed into one which is equivalent and where the only uses of shared variables occur in atomic assignments. The actions of any such program are therefore determined by how the assignments and signals performed by different threads interleave.

It is intuitively clear that where an assignment le := re uses no shared location it is equivalent to atomic{le := re} because whether or not it is punctuated by reads and writes by other threads does not matter. The location represented by le is not changed by any of the external writes, and neither is the calculation of the expression re. Finally, it does not matter when an external read of any of this thread's shared locations happens during the period when le := re is being executed, since it does not change any of them!

Now suppose that in carrying out our assignment we execute no more than a single evaluation or write of a shared location during its execution, and that if it is a write then the location is clean. That was stated carefully, because in fact, thanks to array indices (which may of course be nested), the separate evaluation of the expressions on the left and right of :=, and the fact that we may be writing to a location we have already read from, there is no bound on how many times a single assignment can access a given location.

Imagine an execution in which our single-shared-access assignment was carried out atomically at a particular point in the overall sequence of reads and writes. Then executions in which the single shared access happen non-atomically, and atomically at the instant of that access, are equivalent in the sense that the same value is assigned to the same location and the state visible to other threads is the same.

We can thus claim that any such assignment is not changed in its effect by making it atomic. This claim can be generalised. Suppose a thread reads a location x, that other threads can read from but not write to, as part of executing an assignment. Then the effect is no different whether x is read as part of the assignment itself or if the read is from local lx, where lx := x has been performed immediately before: the value read is certain to be the same in either case.

We therefore deduce that any assignment in which at most one access of a shared location occurs that can either be written to by another thread, or is written to by this assignment, is equivalent to running the same assignment atomically. We cannot prove this in general on SVA but we can prove the equivalence for any particular example, using refinement.

Note that if some components of a given array are shared and some are not (unusual but possible), it may not be possible to determine in advance whether a particular assignment actually accesses a shared location. Similarly it is not in general possible to determine, in advance of executing an assignment, which location(s) will be accessed.

If our program had assignments only of this limited shared access form, and where no shared location appears in any other place in the program (and they could occur in the booleans controlling while and conditional constructs, and in isignal expressions), we would have achieved our overall goal, modulo the cleanliness constraint. We will show later how to overcome this constraint, but for the time being we will assume that all locations are clean in our examples.

It is actually reasonably straightforward to transform any program construct so that it conforms to this pattern, and indeed to require additionally that the booleans controlling while and conditionals, and the integers output by isignals are single local variables. We will call this, when all the assignments are indeed made atomic, the original program's *atomic equivalent form*.

We will first consider how to transform a general assignment. What we do is create a program that makes exactly the same fetches and performs exactly the same evaluations in the same overall order, and then writes the same value to the same location, but which obeys the rule that each line follows the above rules. svacomp.csp first evaluates the location to be assigned to, then the value to be assigned, and then performs the write, so that is what the transformed code must do too. In order to work out which fetches it performs and in which order, one has to study the expression evaluation code, and especially the code for working out which fetch to perform followed by a substitution. In the transformed version we make all such fetches to new local variables, and when an expression has to be evaluated (to calculate either an array index or the final assigned value) to do that in a separate line, assigning the result to a further local variable. The assignment a[x+a[x+1]] := y+x*y, where all the locations mentioned are fully shared, could be transformed into

```
lv1 := x;              -- the leftmost x but also gets
                       -- substituted into a[x+1]
lv2 := lv1+1;          -- inner array index
lv3 := a[lv2];         -- value of a[x+1]
lv4 := lv1 + lv3;      -- index in a[] to which assignment
                       -- will be made, completing LHS
lv5 := y;              -- fetched because of leftmost,
                       -- but substitutes for both y's
lv6 := x;              -- x on RHS
lv7 := lv5 + lv6*lv5;  -- value to be assigned
a[14] := lv7;          -- the actual assignment
```

where the lvi are local variables. This program is equivalent because it performs the same fetches in the same order and then writes the same value to the same location. You can prove the equivalence (without any restrictions on dirty variables) of the original assignment and this program using general refinement, and find a similar expansion for any other assignment. Since we know that each line of the above program is equivalent (under the restrictions) to its own atomic version, it follows that the original assignment is similarly equivalent to the above program with atomic added separately to each line.

If x were only written to by this thread, there would be no need for the separate assignments to lv1 and lv6, with x being used in place of these local variables.

The crucial part of this transformation is that no line that we add atomic to generates more than one effect that can pass information in or out of the system, namely an external write or read, a signal or an error event. This is because, if two were generated, they could be split in a non-atomic execution but not in an atomic one, meaning that the two would in most cases not be equivalent. If we know that no run-time error will occur, there is no good reason to evaluate expressions such as assigned to lv4 and lv7 on separate lines.

There is nothing magical in the particular way in which SVA evaluates assignments that enables them to be transformed in this way. For example, if SVA was changed so that it evaluated the right-hand side of an assignment first, the above transformation could easily be changed to reflect this. See Exercise 19.9 for insight into this.

We can remove all non-local variables from an isignal or a conditional command: isignal(a,e) just becomes lv := e; isignal(a,lv) and if b then P else Q becomes lbv := b; if lbv then P else Q for new local variables lv and lbv. It is easy to see that in each of these pairs of programs, aside from accesses to local variables, the two processes perform exactly the same actions. Similarly, lbv := b;while lbv do {P;lbv := b} replaces while b do P.

If such a transformation is carried out on every one of these three constructs that uses a shared location, we can obtain an equivalent one where the only uses of shared variables are in assignments, and all conditionals, loops and signals use only local variables. We then use the above strategy to convert every assignment making more than one shared variable access, to a sequence. The result is that we have a program where every assignment and signal can be made atomic, and where all conditional decisions are in fact made atomically.

There is in fact little problem in extending this model to allow for dirty variables. We first note that the above transformation of an assignment into multiple steps is valid both for clean and dirty locations. The problem comes when we make the final line, which does the assignment itself, atomic, since other threads are then banned from reading the location during its dirty phase. The solution comes in two parts: in order to achieve the desired effect when other threads *read* this location, we replace sdl := lv (the last assignment of the result of the transformation above, necessarily to a shared dirty location from a local variable) by

```
atomic {sdl := randt};
atomic {sdl := lv}
```

where `randt` is a dirty variable with the same type as `lv` assigned by the thread
`iter {randt := randt}`, so any read from it gives a random value.[9]

If only one thread can write to `lv` (so no write conflicts can arise), the above is
sufficient. Otherwise we need to "shadow" the location `sdl` with a (local) boolean
flag `bsdl` (initially false) and replace the above by

```
atomic {if bsdl then Error
                else {bsdl :=   true;
                      sdl := randt}};
atomic {sdl := rv;
        bsdl := false}
```

where `Error` creates an error message to simulate the one that our model of a write
conflict to a dirty variable creates (p. 448). Exclusive locations would be handled
similarly.

Note that since the location `sdl` is completely determined by the time the final
assignment of the original transformation takes place, we can (i) always tell if it *is*
dirty and (ii) can be sure that the location written to will not change between the
two atomic segments implementing the dirty assignment.

It is obvious that, except in cases above where we had to simulate conflict errors,
none of our transformations can affect whether an error action can take place in a
system. With the possible exception of the very last transformation above (reproducing the error created by a write conflict), the actual error event reported is exactly
the same.

The fact that the results of our transformation *are* equivalent to the original program is illustrated in several accompanying files. Of course in defining "equivalent"
here, no local variables may be visible from the outside; but there are no other restrictions. We will see an interesting application of these results in Sect. 19.6.

One of the benefits of the style in which we have cast refinement, and therefore
the equivalence of SVL terms, is that programs using `atomic` sections may be
equivalent to ones without. This is because we have not had to make the beginnings
and ends of internal atomic sections visible to the outside world.

Indeed, given the existence of algorithms like the bakery algorithm that allow for
mutual exclusion amongst an arbitrarily large number of threads, it is not hard to
see that every SVL program is equivalent to one that has no `atomic` constructs at
all, although some realignment would be needed if such a program were to be put
in parallel with other thread(s) that did use `atomic`.

Exercise 19.8 Transform the following assignments into atomic equivalent programs.

(a) `a[a[a[0]]] := a[a[1]]`
(b) `a[y+z] := a[z+y] + a[y+z]`

---

[9]Another, seemingly more efficient, way of achieving this effect is set out on p. 472.

Exercise 19.9 Adapt the code of the functions `IExpEval`, `ffetchi` and `subsi` from `svacomp.csp` to create a program which converts `Iassign(lv,e)` (with `lv` is a local variable) into an atomic equivalent program.

Now do the same for when `lv` is replaced by an arbitrary expression representing an integer location.

Test your program on the example `a[x+a[x+1]] := y + x*y` and on the assignments in the previous exercises.

19.5 Overseers: Modelling Complex Data-Types

SVA and SVL only give direct support to very simple data-types, namely booleans, integers, and arrays of these. There is no reason why one should not wish to study programs that share access to more complex objects such as sets, relations, queues, stacks and trees. We may well expect that the operations that nodes carry out on these structures are atomic, and there might well be some internal properties of the representations (data-type invariants) that need to be maintained, in the sense that each operation has to maintain them.

For example, one might want to represent a queue or a stack as an array with operations *empty* (represented as a boolean that is true when the structure is empty), *add* and *remove* (each represented as an integer variable and a boolean flag that the thread sets when it wants the corresponding operation to happen). Note that these last two operations are partial: a *remove* is impossible from empty and *add* is impossible when already full.

SVL and SVA allow for a special sort of process, *overseers*, that can help us achieve such effects. Overseers, while respecting the atomic sections of other threads, always run with priority every time one of its variables is written. We can then implement the circular array model of a queue as the following thread, where the variables have their obvious meanings:

```
local a:array[0..N-1] of integer;
if add_flag then
 if size=N then signal(overfull)
      else {size := size+1;
            last := (last + 1)%N;
            a[last] := add_data;
            if size == 1 then remove_data := add_data;
            add_flag := false}
else if remove_flag then
  if size=0 then signal(removefromempty)
      else {size := size-1;
            first := (first+1)%N;
            if size > 0 then remove_data := a[first];
            remove_flag := false}
else skip
```

The other threads can access `size` like any other location, but must access the
others in the following ways:

```
atomic {add_data := v; add_flag := true}

atomic {v := remove_data; remove_flag := true}
```

Unless we want to add extra and probably unintended atomicity into the given
thread, the variable v should be local to the given thread (i.e. not itself shared).
So to add b*c to the stack, or record the value of a `remove` into b where b and c
are shared, we would write

```
v := b*c;
atomic{add := v; add_flag := true};

atomic {v := remove; remove_flag := true};
b := v;
```

These uses of local variables ensure that the accesses to the stack and the other
shared variables occur distinctly, rather than atomically. This is, of course, based on
the principles seen in Sect. 19.4.

Overseer processes do not themselves have atomic sections: they do not need
them since they always run with priority. In order to avoid clashes of priority, two
overseer processes may not share locations with each other. Overseer processes
give themselves priority access to their own locations as follows, as implemented
in `svacomp.csp`. An overseer process has four modes,

- `Inactive` (which they are initially). In this mode they allow any process to read
  from and write to their locations.
- `Inactive_at(j)`: ordinary thread j is in an atomic section, so only it can
  read from and write to the overseer's locations.
- `Active_at(j)`: the same except that while in the atomic section, thread j has
  written to at least one of the overseer's locations, meaning that the overseer will
  go into active mode when the atomic section ends.
- `Active`: entered when either an ordinary thread writes to an overseer variable
  from a non-atomic position, or when the `Active_at(j)` mode ends. In this
  mode the overseer runs its own code and allows no other process to read from or
  write to its locations. It goes back to `Inactive` when the code terminates.

Now that we have built a queue in this way, it can be used by a single thread,
one adding and one removing, or many threads. The processes pushing things onto
it will share add and add_flag with it, and those taking things from it will share
remove and remove_flag. All can read size. One could have many separate
queues (with separately named variables) in a network, with each individual queue
action being effectively atomic thanks to the use of overseer processes.

We will see another use of these processes, also involving data-types, in the next
section. Both there and those we have seen in this section, the interactions between
an ordinary thread processes and an overseer are always protected by the use of

atomic sections. To prevent such atomicity from changing the semantics of a program it is a good idea to use the transformations described for creating atomic equivalent programs.

Exercise 19.10 Modify the queue implementation given above into a (last in first out) stack, in which the bottom end of the stack is always placed at a [0], with the top varying depending on the number of items already there. You should create a shared variable to indicate the current size, and partial operations pop (analogous to remove) and push (analogous to add).

Exercise 19.11 Model a set of integers as a sorted list, with variable size and operations add, remove and isin, each of which have a single integer parameter, with the last returning a boolean that is true if and only if the parameter belongs to the set.

Using the sorted list representation should make remove and isin efficient.

Exercise 19.12 On p. 438 we commented that it might be an advantage to implement checks of LTL specifications in SVL. Show how an overseer can implement the specification $b' \mathcal{R} b$ for boolean expressions b and b', meaning that b is true at every moment until b' *releases* it, in the sense defined in Sect. 16.4. Do you think this is possible without using an overseer?

19.6 Abstraction in SVA

On p. 440 we highlighted two problems that mean it is not trivial to verify the whole bakery algorithm, namely the unboundedness of the number of threads on the one hand and the ticket values on the other. Each of these can be solved by adding a degree of abstraction into our model.

19.6.1 Two Threads out of Many

Reading Lamport's original justification of the algorithm in [78], we realise that he concentrates on just a pair of threads. Instead of looking at the global state, he demonstrates that an arbitrary pair of them never break mutual exclusion, without relying on what the other threads are doing. Clearly this is a great simplifying insight, since if a given implementation does break mutual exclusion the actions that do breach it come from just two processes.

Concentrating on the original algorithm, we can build an implementation in which the mutual exclusion of a particular pair of threads is examined by giving only these two the ability to perform the signals css.i and cse.i.

We can assume that the two threads we are considering are $i < j$. The only effects the other threads k now have is in the values they set for the shared variables that are read from by threads i and j.

For specific values of i and j it makes sense to try to prove that the two threads are mutually exclusive by running them in a context where the variables set by other threads (choosing[k] and number[k] for k!=i,j) are always arbitrary. For if threads i and j achieve mutual exclusion in that context, they will achieve it in parallel with any other threads at all that are subject to the same rights to read from and write to shared variables.

The author has implemented these arbitrary values in two different ways. The first was to run simple processes as the "other" threads whose only activity is to repeatedly assign random values (as for on p. 468) to the locations associated with them. The second was to run only threads i and j, and to put all of the other threads' locations in ExtWrites (see p. 459). This means that these locations can now have an arbitrary value assigned to them at any time by a write from "thread" -1. This proved enormously more efficient for all the variations on the bakery algorithm that we have considered (original and simplified, with many variations on the *maximum* algorithm, and with and without dirty variables). The results (see bakeryproof1.csp) were almost exactly as expected, but were slightly tidier in respect of the incorrect maximum algorithm Maximum D. The parameters used were MaxI=10, N=5, i=2 and j=4.

- Without dirty variables, both original and simplified algorithms satisfy mutual exclusion for versions A, B, C of Maximum, and fail for all versions of Maximum D (see p. 464).
- Exactly the same result holds for the original algorithm with dirty variables, but all versions of the simplified algorithm then fail.

This choice of the parameters other than MaxI is clearly a significant one, since it means that there is another node less than both i and j, one between them and one greater than both. A little thought reveals that this demonstrates the correctness of the algorithm for any number of threads, since the effects that an arbitrary number of threads in any one of these three gaps can have are no more general than the single randomising thread. We can, however, make this clearer by making threads 2 and 4 look at notional threads in these gaps a nondeterministic number of times, so that any behaviour possible of any such pair is contained in our abstracted system. Thus, in both the maximisation and waiting loops, we make these nodes wait for threads 1,3,5 a nondeterministic number of times (including zero). The following shows a version of Maximum B modified to have this effect. The uses of (k mod 2)=0 just exploit the fact that our two real threads have indices 2 and 4, and the notional ones have indices 1,3 and 5. Here, randb is a random boolean which may change in value between consecutive reads.

```
k := 0;
while k<=N do
  {if (k mod 2)=0 or randb then
          number[i] := max(number[k],number[i])
   if (k mod 2)=0 or randb then k := k+1};
number[i] := number[i]+1;
```

The effect of this code is that, for each of k = 1,3,5, number[i] is max-ed with an arbitrary number of of arbitrary values of its type, bearing in mind that these number[k] can also change between reads. This mimics the presence of an arbitrary number of nodes in each of the gaps that these values of k represent. When k=2,4 the assignment to number[i] happens precisely once, using the number[k]s of the two real threads.

The file bakeryproof2.sva shows this applied to maximum A and B in the original algorithm. These are, of course, correct with or without dirty variables.

We have therefore given a complete automated proof that these versions of the bakery algorithm work for any number of threads at all. The strategy of this proof was:

1. Break down the correctness condition you want to prove into many similar parts, parameterised by the threads that actually perform the signal events seen in a counter-example trace for the overall specification. Here there are two threads: the one n already in its critical section, and the one m that enters it illegally at the same time. (Note that this is the same strategy used for proving the correctness of a routing algorithm in Sect. 17.3.)
2. For each such part, identify the (hopefully) small number of threads that we rely on to make that part true. In our case these are just n and m.
3. Abstract away the other threads and their actions on the variables that threads n and m read in an appropriate way.
4. Abstract away the relevant threads' (for us n and m) interactions with the others in a way that simulates the ways these behave with any number of others present.

In some examples these steps may not all be possible, but even the factorisation of the original check into parts might give benefits thanks to the increased amount of compression possible when some signal events are hidden.

Exercise 19.13 Consider the following assertion about the original bakery algorithm: *For all i, the value assigned by the line*

$$number[i] := 1 + maximum\{number[1], \ldots, number[N]\} \quad (*)$$

is, for any j, at least $1 + min$, *where min is the least of the initial value of number[j] and all values assigned to it during the period when* $(*)$ *is being executed.*

Formulate a file that seeks to prove this for general i and j, emulating the structures in this section. [Note that the cases $i < j$ and $j < i$ are now distinct since the specification is not symmetric in i and j.]

Is this property true for the following cases?

(a) Maximum A with clean variables.
(b) Maximum D with clean variables.
(c) Maximum A with dirty variables.

19.6.2 Finitely Representing an Infinite Linear Order

Every check we have carried out to date on the bakery algorithm has been with a sub-range of the non-negative integers as ticket numbers. We have had to ignore the run-time errors that appear when the number[i] or turn[i] values exceed this limit. We cannot therefore claim to have proved that the bakery algorithm always works, only that no error can appear before these values get out of range.

As was the case with the number of threads, we can solve this problem by generalising, or abstracting, the system. In the discussion below we will concentrate on the version above in which we are examining two threads programmed to simulate an arbitrary number in the three gaps in the thread ordering; but exactly the same strategy can be used with any fixed number of threads.

Just as in the previous case, we need to find a finite way of simulating every behaviour of the algorithm when it is using unbounded integers in number. The key to discovering this is to examine what threads do to these integers:

- They compare integers, both in the maximisation process and when waiting for another thread to complete its critical section.
- They add one to an integer, where the role of this operation is clearly to find a value that is strictly larger than the one that is added to.
- They use constants with known position in the order, and assign these to array components, as are the results of additions and maximisations. (There is one, namely 0 in the original bakery algorithm. The simplified algorithm also uses 1.)

We can regard these integers and the ones that represent loop/thread indices as separate types. We will call the type of number[i] values *Ticket*. In fact the program would work with *Ticket* any linear order L (i.e. a transitive relation $<$ such that exactly one of $x < y$, $x = y$ and $y < x$ holds for all x and y) with the following properties:

- We have a fixed element 0 of L.
- For every element x of L we can find $next(L)$ which is the least element strictly greater than x.

It is clear that we can implement *max* over any linear order, and $next(x)$ takes the place of $x + 1$. What we will do in this section is to show how to build a finite model that establishes the correctness of the bakery algorithm implemented over any such order.

It is certain that we cannot use such a type *Ticket* directly in our implementation, since the model would then be anything but finite. What we will in fact do is produce a finite model using a special finite *FinTicket* type which can simulate any behaviour for an arbitrary *Ticket*. In other words, any execution of the bakery algorithm implemented over *Ticket* has an analogue—with the same css.k and cse.k actions, as the original.

We will not do this by making *FinTicket* a finite linear order—for next cannot then be universally defined—but by making it record the relative place the location it represents has amongst the *occupied* members of *Ticket*, namely the values of *Ticket* that are held by some location (whether shared or local) meaningful to at least one thread.

There are one or two special values in the type *Ticket* depending on whether we are using the original or simplified algorithm, namely 0 and perhaps $1 = next(0)$. We need to record accurately whether a specific location (a *slot*) has one of these values. We will therefore, for the original algorithm where only 0 is special, imagine a map from the *Ticket* values in the state of our system to $0 < v_1 < \cdots < v_M$ (where M is greater than the total number of such values) as follows:

- Any value which is 0 will map to itself.
- Any value which is greater than 0 will map to v_k, where that value is the kth smallest amongst all those values that are not 0.

If we do this then we can still decide every comparison between two ticket values, since this mapping is always strictly monotonic. For the system we are considering, of two real threads reading from their own locations and those of three notional ones, the transformation clearly achieves the goal of making it finite state. However, it also creates some problems:

- If a single ticket value is changed, we might have to change the index of every single slot, for example because a slot that was previously the only one having value 1 is given either 0 or becomes the maximum one.

  The solution to this problem is to maintain, using an overseer, the indices using a monitor that refreshes them completely every time one is changed.
- This in turn creates a problem when a thread is in the middle of a calculation involving the indices, since the overseer will not alter the values that our thread may have input but not yet used. So, for example, if the overseer changes the indices x and y while the thread is carrying out x := max(x,y), the value that gets assigned may be the greater of the *old* value of x and the *new* value of y.

  The solution to this is to make all of our threads' operations atomic. In general, of course, this would change their behaviour, but we have already shown how to build atomic equivalent programs where this is not an issue.
- If *next* is applied to a value that is not already the greatest, we *do not know* whether it should become equal to the next greatest value in *FinTicket* or get a new value beneath that. For the answer depends on what the actual ticket values are, not their indices, which is all that we are remembering.

  Our solution is to make a nondeterministic choice whenever this situation arises. As we will see later, this can require quite a bit of shuffling of the indices, particularly as we may be creating an extra member of the order in the middle.

  It is important to realise that by converting what is in fact a deterministic choice into a nondeterministic one, here on the grounds that we have abstracted away the data that is required, we are creating an anti-refinement or abstraction of the original behaviour, just as we did in the previous section when assuming that "other" threads could assign anything. A counter-example in an abstracted system of this sort does not guarantee that there is one in the original, but if the abstracted system refines some specification then so does the original.

We can therefore use the ideas of overseers, atomic equivalents and abstraction, all seen in previous sections, to complete our proof.

The following is a program for the original bakery algorithm with Maximum A, modified so that (i) it takes account of the proof methods for arbitrary numbers of threads seen in the last section and (ii) every use of an identifier of *Ticket* type can be made atomic.

```
iter
  {choosing[i] := true;
   temp := 0;
   j:= 1;
   while j< N do
     {if randb or (j mod 2 = 0) then
                  temp := max(temp,number[j]);
      if randb or (j mod 2 = 0) then
                  j := j+1
     };
   number[i] := temp+1;
   choosing[i]:=false;
   j := 1;
   while j< N do
     {
      if randb or (j mod 2 = 0) then
        {while choosing[j] do skip;
         lnj := number[j];
         b := lnj>0 and ((lnj,j)<(number[i],i));
         while b do
           {lnj := number[j];
            b := lnj>0 and ((lnj,j)<(number[i],i));
           };
        };
      if randb or (j mod 2 = 0) then
        j := j+1
     }
   signal(css.i);
   signal(cse.i);
   number[i] := 0
  }
```

To run, each of the abbreviations (lnj,j)<(number[i],i) is expanded into (lnj < number[i]) or ((lnj = number[i]) and (j < i)). This makes no difference in evaluation since all these variables are local or (in the case of number[i]) writable only by this thread. Note that Maximum A required no transformation to make its assignments equivalent to atomic ones, but that a significant transformation was required to the second half of the program.

Now that we have this code we can enumerate the slots whose positions need to be remembered in the order. The obvious inference is that there are N=5 slots of the form number [k] and two local ones for each of our two active threads, namely temp, lvj. In fact we can do better than this:

- We do not need to reserve a slot in the partial order for the locations number [1], number [3] and number [5]: the only role of these is to hold varying random members of the order for the threads 2 and 4 to read.[10] What we do need to ensure is that when these are read they might give values in any place in the order of the read slots.

- Examining the programs for threads 2, 4 reveals that temp and lvj are used in separate phases of the program. We can therefore share a location between them: one for each of threads 2 and 4. We will call these locations temp [2] and temp [4] below.

It follows that we need the following room in our order:

- The special value 0 that needs to be kept separate because it has a definite control effect on the program.

- Room for the four slots mentioned above, all of which may be different and different from 0.

- Both through reading the random number [i] and the incrementing step at the end of the initial maximisation, a value can be calculated that is not one of the present four or 0. We therefore include extra spaces in the order (one between each consecutive pair, and an extra one at the top) for this purpose.

We therefore use {0..9} as *FinTicket*, interpreting 0 as itself, mapping the four slots that are not 0 to as many of 2, 4, 6, 8 as are needed, with the odd numbers playing the roles of the gaps. The overseer's duty will be to arrange our four slots into this form whenever one of them is changed.

For example, if

$$0 = \text{number}[2] < \text{number}[4] = \text{temp}[4] < \text{temp}[2]$$

then the overseer will map number [2] to 0, number [4] and temp [4] to 2, and temp [2] to 4. The assignment number [4] := temp [4] +1 will certainly lead to number [4] being greater than temp [4], but from the information above we do not know whether it is still less than, or is equal to, temp [2]. This reflects the nondeterminism discussed above. The way we implement this is to modify the assignment so that it randomly adds 1 or 2 except when the result would be 10. This therefore becomes a nondeterministic operation on our abstracted type rather than a deterministic one on the integers.

The reason why we need this nondeterminism here is that we cannot tell from the above whether temp [2] is only 1, or at least 2, greater than temp [4].

What the overseer produces is a standardised representation of the ordering of 0 and the four slot values. The values used are independent, for example, of adding

---

[10]Indeed, it is practically better to have all three of these slots replaced by a single one randi representing a random value. The most efficient way to achieve a random value is to make a variable such as randi or randb writable by the external environment. See the example scripts.

any constant onto the non-0 slots. We therefore have a finite-state representation of an arbitrary mapping of the slots into a suitable linear order: so we have collapsed the infinity of tuples of slots that can arise in runs with any suitable order such as the non-negative integers, into a finite number, which is in fact 132 (1 in which all four slots are 0, 4 in which three are, 18 in which two are, 52 in which one is, and 57 in which none are 0).

One definition of an overseer process that achieves this is given below. Here hits is a boolean array initialised to False that is used to record which of the values {0..9} is present in the four slots. These are then used to construct a mapping omap from this set to {0,2,4,6,8} based on the principles discussed above, and the mapping is applied to the four slots to standardise their values.

```
hits[number[2]] := True;
hits[number[4]] := True;
hits[temp[2]] := True;
hits[temp[4]] := True;
nextw := 0;
kk := 0;
while kk<9 do
  {kk := kk+1;
   if hits[kk] then
     {nextw := nextw+2};
      omap[kk] := nextw;
   hits[kk] := False}
number[2] := omap[number[2]];
number[4] := omap[number[4]];
temp[2] := omap[temp[2]];
temp[4] := omap[temp[4]];
kk := 0;
while kk<9 do
  {kk := kk+1;
   omap[kk] := 0}
```

Notice how the loops here are structured so that the integers kk and nextw never exceed MaxI=9. The combination threads 2 and 4 and this overseer are implemented in bakeryproof3.svl. This is a good-sized check (over 250 M states after two compressions involving processes with more than 1.1 M states), in which the author experimented with different allocations of locations to these three and some "dummy" threads to produce a reasonably efficient result. See that file for further discussion.

The fact that this system passes the mutual exclusion specification *and has no run-time errors* means that we have proved that the original bakery algorithm with version A of *maximum* guarantees mutual exclusion for any number of threads provided that the *Ticket* values are chosen from a linear order of the sort described on p. 474, with the +1 interpreted as the *next* operation. For we have shown that the control behaviour of our thread models (where ticket values are drawn from the abstraction of an order) is an anti-refinement of that of the ones defined using the real order, where in each case ticket values from nodes other than 2 and 4 are treated as random. We saw in the previous section how the proof for this arbitrary pair establishes correctness for an arbitrary number of threads.

We should reflect on the use of the atomic equivalent program in this proof. It is necessary because of the particularly intrusive nature of the overseer process we have used here. The examples seen in Sect. 19.5 all maintained the internal consistency built using integer and boolean values that were interpreted as such in the world outside the overseers. The role of the overseer in the present section is to maintain a partial injective mapping from the infinite type used by the real-world threads to the finite type used in our representation. The representation of a single value can change *while a thread process is holding it*. In the example quoted above:

```
0 = number[2] < number[4] = temp[4] < temp[2]
```

If the assignment `number[2] := 0` occurs then, while the real-world values of the other three slots do not change, their representations all decrease by 2 (from 4 and 6). The overseer changes these values as they sit in the variables, so all is well provided no thread either (i) is part-way through evaluating an expression based on several values altered by the overseer or (ii) has calculated an expression based on pre-change values but not yet output this value (either by writing to a location or along an `isignal`). These bad cases are excluded by running the atomic equivalent form with all assignments made atomic.

So what the main check in `bakeryproof2.svl` actually does is prove that the atomic equivalent of the stated version of the algorithm works. We can infer that the ordinary version of this algorithm works because we know that any thread is equivalent to its atomic equivalent.

The proof presented in this section is complex, but it does go well beyond the traditional role of model checking, namely the proof of a fixed and finite-state version of a system. It was achieved through two different sorts of abstraction. The first sort comes from replacing thread behaviour that depends on some parameter (in this case the number of threads) by more nondeterministic behaviour that does not. The second sort was to discover what properties of an infinite data-type our threads appeared to be using (in our case the relative order of ticket values) and find a way of getting the same information from a finite representation.

It is straightforward to adapt the proof method set out in this section to other variants of the bakery algorithm, bearing in mind that this exercise only makes sense if the simpler transformation presented in Sect. 19.6.1 meets the mutual exclusion specification with error events hidden. The same technique also works for the final version of Simpson's 4-slot algorithm on p. 455 with the counter. Since, in that example, one process generates the values of the counter in sequence, and all the other one does is read, copy and compare them, the linear order there can be mapped to consecutive integers. There is no need to leave the odd numbers as gaps.

It seems likely that the same approach will work wherever an otherwise finite-state system depends on counter-like variables where it is the relative order of these rather than the actual values (aside from a finite set of special values like $\{0\}$) that controls the program.

This technique will also work with other infinite data structures such as partial orders and graphs, where abstractions suitable for a given application can be found.

Exercise 19.14 Adapt the proof in this section so that it works for Maximum B and Maximum C. Do these proofs require four slots, more or less?

Exercise 19.15 Adapt the proof in this section to the *simplified* bakery algorithm. How many slots are required?

Exercise 19.16 Prove the sequential consistency and recentness of the version of Simpson's algorithm from p. 455 with counters, so that the effect of an unbounded space of counters is reproduced in a finite type as discussed above.

19.7 Notes

Simpson's 4-slot algorithm [148] was brought to my attention in September 2008 by John Fitzgerald. Much of the analysis of it in Sect. 19.2 parallels that in John Rushby's paper [141], though using rather different tools, and the idea of write-when-different comes from that source. The augmentation with counters is, as far as I am aware, original.

The first implementation of overseers in SVA was by David Hopkins. They were introduced to avoid difficulties that he and I had discovered in other models of prioritised execution in SVL-style processes. In those, we had only allowed low-priority threads to perform a step when high-priority ones specifically executed an idle statement. Since typically this led to high-priority threads evaluating an expression to decide if each idle was allowed, it gave rise to some very unwieldy results. Since none of the activities of low-priority processes could be hidden when they had to synchronise with idle, this type of prioritisation would have greatly damaged the effects of compression. For these reasons the present version of SVA does not include this latter priority model, relying rather on overseer processes that do nothing until particular locations are written to.

Simpson's 4-slot algorithm is a favourite example [16, 53] for authors proposing semantic tools for understanding and developing programs (as opposed to model checking them) using ideas such as separation logic. The author believes that studying some of these treatments (which generally assume that the boolean flags are all clean) relative to ours may convince some readers of the practicality of model checking.

The bakery algorithm has long been one of the favourite examples for those interested in analysing concurrent programs. The reader will be able to find many other treatments to compare to ours.

Chapter 20
Priority and Mobility

In this chapter we show how CSP can be used to model systems that rely on the ideas of *mobility* and *priority*, both topics that have traditionally been thought of as beyond the scope of CSP and its models.[1] We begin with a case study that illustrates ways in which these things can be dealt with.

20.1 Case Study: Knight's Tour

The *knight* is a chess piece which moves two steps horizontally and one step vertically, or two steps vertically and one step horizontally, as shown in Fig. 20.1. A *knight's tour* of a $N \times M$ board is a complete list of all the squares on the board so that none appears twice and each apart from the first is reachable from the previous one by a knight's move. A *knight's circuit* is a knight's tour such that where the knight can reach the start in one further move. Figure 20.2 illustrates a knight's circuit of the standard 8×8 board discovered by FDR when applied to the script described in this section.

The fact that a knight alternates black and white squares means that no circuit is possible for an odd-sized board, and it is obvious that there is no knight's tour of square boards with side 2 or 3. In general, if there is a knight's circuit starting at one square then there is obviously one starting at any.

It is easy to code a CSP system that can communicate *done* if and only if, for a chosen size of board, there is a knight's tour, or circuit, starting at any chosen square. This takes essentially the form already seen when we solved Sudoku puzzles in Sect. 4.1.

```
Empty(p) = move.p ->
Full(p) Full(p) = done -> Full(p)

Board = [|{done}|] x:Coords @ Empty(p)
```

---

[1] There have been a number of approaches to extending CSP by priority: see Sect. 20.4.

A.W. Roscoe, *Understanding Concurrent Systems*, Texts in Computer Science, DOI 10.1007/978-1-84882-258-0_20, © Springer-Verlag London Limited 2010

Fig. 20.1 The central knight
can move to any of the
indicated squares

Fig. 20.2 Knight's tour
generated by FDR

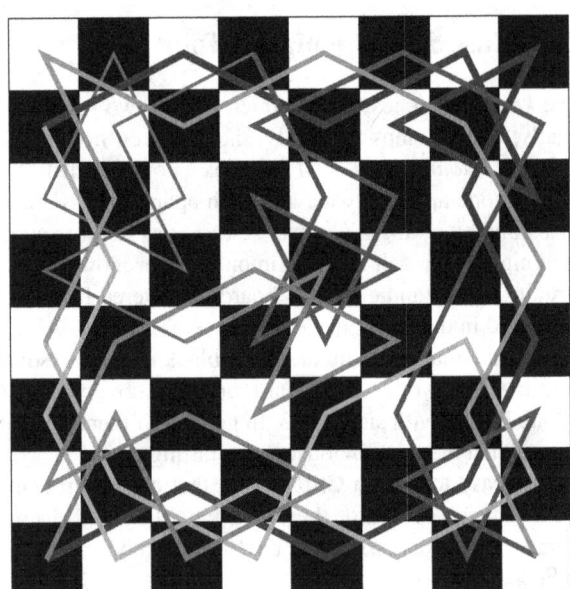

```
TKnight(p) = move?q:adj(p) -> TKnight(q)

CKnight(p) = move?q:adj(p) -> CKnight(q)
             [] p==start & done-> CKnight(p)
```

```
Circuit = Board [|{|move,done|}|] CKnight(start)
```

```
Tour = Board [|{|move|}|] move?p -> TKnight(p)
```

where Coords are the coordinates on an N x M board, and adj(p) are the Coords reachable in a single knight's move from p.

So we have one parallel process that remembers which of the squares have already been visited, and a knight process that enforces the move rules. The event done occurs just when all the squares have been visited and, in the case we are checking for a circuit (in which the knight's final position is where it started from), the knight is back at start.

There is no reason to suspect that the state space sizes of the resulting systems are hugely less than the natural bound of $2^{N \times M}$, and indeed actually running the resulting checks illustrates the state explosion problem so well that it proves impossible to perform them for anything other than a relatively small board. In particular, at the time of writing, FDR cannot solve (at least within the bounds of the author's patience!) the standard 8×8 case using either standard search or the divergence-based DFS search described on p. 167.

The knight's tour problem has been studied for hundreds of years, and a heuristic known as Warnsdorff's algorithm was discovered in the early 19th century:

- When there is a choice of which square to move to next, always choose one whose number of remaining unvisited neighbours is minimal.

It is far from obvious how to modify the above program so that FDR will only explore paths that obey this heuristic. It would be easy with a single sequential process that remembers both the square p where the knight is and which squares V have been visited, for we could easily compute the legitimate next moves under the above heuristic and allow moves to just the computed squares. There are two major drawbacks to this: firstly it would be completely impractical on FDR because of the size of this sequential process, and secondly it would offer no new insights into the nature of process interaction.

It is straightforward to modify the Empty(p) processes above so that they know how many of their neighbours are free, and to add a data field to the move channel that records how many squares are free next to the one the knight moves to:

```
CtEmpty(p,n) = move.p.n -> CtFull(p)
             [] move?q:adj(p)?_ -> CtEmpty(p,max(n-1,0))
```

```
CtFull(p) = done -> CtFull(p)
          [] move?q:adj(p)?_ -> CtFull(p)
```

```
Alpha(p) = {|move.q, done | q <- union(adj(p),{p})|}
```

These processes are composed using alphabetised parallel with the stated alphabets.

If we could declare a *priority* relation amongst the move.p.n events so that no move.p.n can happen when there is a move.q.m available with m < n, then running this revised board in parallel with our Knight process would implement the search strategy implied by Warnsdorff's algorithm when run on FDR.[2]

Unfortunately the CSP notation, at least in the form we have studied it to date, does not support priority. In this chapter we will see ways in which we extend CSP to support it.

One possibility is to have the knight, whenever it is at position p, interact with all those squares in adj(p) to discover which of the empty ones has the smallest number of free neighbours, before finally making its choice. That raises the question of how we can get a single process to interact with a variable set of processes. In essence we need the alphabet of the knight's interactions that gather information from its neighbours to change as it moves around. The knight is literally *mobile*.

The topic of mobility in process algebra means the ability for a process to move around and change which processes it interacts with. In the knight's tour example, there is a clear connection with physical movement of the process, but it is often better to think of mobility as primarily being the *channels* moving, rather than the processes. In our example this would correspond to there being some sort of manager process that holds the connections to all the squares other than the ones the knight is currently adjacent to. Every time the knight moves from p to p', this manager would swap the connections between the knight and the members of adj(p) for the ones with adj(p').

This sounds complicated and, if done like this, it would be. CSP, however, provides us with a different way of achieving the same effect. We can arrange it that the knight always communicates with *all* squares when trying to decide what the smallest free number of a member of adj(p) is, but only those empty squares that are in adj(p) participate in the negotiation. For this we need to include all {|move|} events in the alphabet of each square, so that it always knows whether it is adjacent to the square with the knight in. In the following there is an extra state of a square PriEmptyA for when the square is empty with the knight adjacent.

```
PriEmpty(p,n) =
    move?q:adj(p)?_ -> PriEmptyA(p,n-1)
[] move?q:diff(Coords,union(adj(p),{p}))?_
                                      -> PriEmpty(p,n)
[] morethan?_ -> PriEmpty(p,n)

PriEmptyA(p,n) =
    move.p.n -> PriFull(p)
[] move?q:diff(Coords,union(adj(p),{p}))?_
                                      -> PriEmpty(p,n)
[] morethan?_:{k | k <- {0..n-1}} -> PriEmpty(p,n)
```

---

[2]By "search strategy" here we mean that all allowable next squares are explored rather than just one.

```
PriFull(p) =
    done -> PriFull(p)
[] move?q:adj(p)?_ -> PriFull(p)
[] morethan?_:{k | k <- {0..7}} -> PriFull(p)

PriKnight(p,n) =
n<8 &  morethan.n -> PriKnight(p,n+1)
[] move?q!n -> PriKnight(q,0)
```

What happens here is that the processes adjacent to the knight allow morethan.k events only when k is less than the number of free neighbours they have (i.e. this process has *more than* k free neighbours). The other squares (i.e. the full and non-adjacent ones) place no restriction on these events: it is as though they are not participating in the agreement. Notice that the knight (PriKnight(p,0)) first checks that all adjacent squares have at least one (morethan.0) free neighbours, then more than 1, 2, 3, ... until this is not true. At that point, provided one of the neighbours is empty, one of them q will permit move.q.n. Note that this now gives a precise implementation of our heuristic, with appropriate morethan.n events inserted into the trace.

This coding allows knight's tours to be discovered on very much larger boards. Our reason for including it here is that it illustrates that:

- Priority between classes of event can be implemented by stepping through the classes, highest priority first, and arranging that processes agree by explicit communication when they *cannot* perform each action. These last communications, naturally, do not change the state of any process other than the one that is "implementing" the priority, here the knight.
- The effect of mobile communication can be achieved by making *all possible* processes synchronise on potentially mobile actions, in such a way that all processes that do not presently have the right to "use" a particular action (a) always accept this action and (b) never change their state when the action occurs.

We can therefore conclude that, at least to some extent, CSP's many-way synchronisation allows both priority and mobile channels to be simulated. In the rest of this chapter we will explore ways in which these simulation ideas can be extended, as well as other approaches to modelling these phenomena.

Exercise 20.1 We described Warnsdorff's "algorithm" as a *heuristic* because following it does not always lead to a solution when only a single next square is chosen at each step. Discover the (very straightforward) FDR check on the implementation described above that demonstrates this.

Exercise 20.2 Create a Sudoku script that solves the types of puzzle seen in Sect. 4.1, where the order in which the squares are filled with numbers is dynamic rather than fixed: ensure at each step that the next square is always one of those that have the least remaining options. You will need to prioritise the moves filling in

Fig. 20.3 Blank grid for "Samurai" Sudoku: see Exercise 20.3

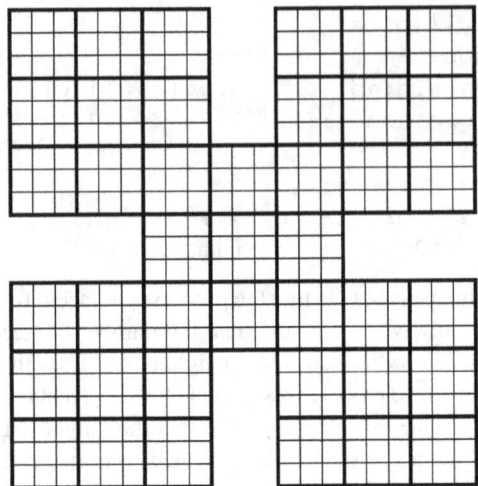

an empty square by the size of `inter(Symbol,{v(q) | q <- adj(p)})` where `v(q)` is the contents of square `q` in the current position.

There is a subtle difference between this case and Warnsdorff's algorithm: where the latter is ambiguous, we want the search to follow all highest-priority options. But in Sudoku, since we can choose which square to fill in next without eliminating possible solutions, we only need to follow a single square giving the largest size of the above set. Show how `chase` (p. 370) can achieve this effect. (So as to show the efficiency of this approach, ensure that you use the coding style in which only a single generic square process is compiled and renamed many times, as seen on p. 113.)

Make sure that you understand why it is appropriate to use `chase` in this example, but not in the knight's tour case study above.

Exercise 20.3 The author has found the coding for Sudoku implied in the previous question the best CSP/FDR approach by some way. He has found it to work well for "Samurai" Sudoku puzzles[3] in which you have to solve five 9×9 grids simultaneously since each 3×3 corner of the central 9×9 grid overlaps one corner of each of the other four 9×9 grids. Figure 20.3 shows an empty grid.

Build a script that solves such puzzles based on the previous exercise.

20.2 Priority

Priority is a natural concept in defining and running transition systems, but has never been part of "mainstream" CSP. In this section we examine some ways of imple-

---

[3] At the time of writing these puzzles appear regularly in The Times and other newspapers.

menting it in CSP and FDR, and also try to understand the obstacles to including it in the core theory.

We have already met some flavours of priority. In Sect. 14.5 we gave *all* hidden (i.e. τ) actions priority over *tock*, the event representing the regular passage of time. This used an *operational* understanding of priority, and so will be our main understanding of priority in this section.

Priority means preferring some actions that a system can perform to others. This preference can, as in the example above, be based solely on the event name. In other cases it might depend on which process is performing the event, or on some operator like a prioritised version $\boxminus$ of $\Box$ within a process.

The last of these options causes conceptual problems such as deciding what happens when the priority orders of different parallel processes cannot be resolved, as in

$$(a \to STOP \boxminus b \to STOP) \parallel_{\{a,b\}} (b \to STOP \boxminus a \to STOP)$$

This is unfortunate from the point of view of the CSP purist, since a prioritised choice operator would fit extremely well into the style of the notation. Because of these problems we will not examine this option further.

The second option requires decisions, for example how do we prioritise a synchronisation between a high- and a low-priority process relative to actions from processes with intermediate priority. Provided we do not use forms of parallel in which two processes can independently perform the same action, it is clear that this form of priority can be implemented in terms of a priority order amongst events.

There are also interesting questions about how priority should interact with hiding and the powers of the environment to choose between events. Recall that the usual CSP understanding of events is that the visibility of an event corresponds to the possibility of it being block-able by the environment:

- Should hidden events have priority over visible ones,[4] or should τ actions inherit the priority they had before hiding? In particular, should the *availability* of a high-priority visible action pre-empt a low-priority τ? If so, it would change much of our understanding of how the transition systems implementing CSP behave.
- Should the fact that one visible event has priority over another prevent the environment from choosing the second? If the answer to this is "yes", then presumably the priority order we assume between events is the order in which the environment prefers them; but it would spoil the usual symmetry between the external environment and the other processes a prioritised one interacts with. Or should priority only come into effect once hiding has occurred, as a way to choose between two τs?

These questions are not supposed to have a single correct answer. Indeed the issues they raise just help to illustrate why it is not easy to integrate priority fully into CSP.

---

[4]Recall that in Sect. 14.5 we observed that in timed modelling they should have priority over `tock`.

Therefore the following is not intended to be the *only* reasonable interpretation of priority within CSP, but the author believes it is the one that fits best into the established framework and theory of the language.

Specifically, we add a *prioritisation* operator $\mathbf{Pri}_{\leq}(P)$ to the language, for any partial order $\leq$ on a subset of Σ. It imposes priority between the members of $\mathrm{dom}(\leq)$ and τ at the specific syntactic level where it is applied: its use does not imply that these events are prioritised at higher or lower levels. The operational semantics of $\mathbf{Pri}_{\leq}(\cdot)$ do not fit into the CSP-like combinator framework discussed in Chap. 9 because they involve negation, so we present them in SOS style. The first two rules below tell us that this new operator does have a CSP-like treatment of τ and $\checkmark$.

$$\frac{P \xrightarrow{\tau} P'}{\mathbf{Pri}_{\leq}(P) \xrightarrow{\tau} \mathbf{Pri}_{\leq}(P')}, \qquad \frac{P \xrightarrow{\checkmark} P'}{\mathbf{Pri}_{\leq}(P) \xrightarrow{\tau} \Omega}$$

If a member of Σ is not in the domain of $\leq$, then its behaviour is unaffected:

$$\frac{P \xrightarrow{a} P'}{\mathbf{Pri}_{\leq}(P) \xrightarrow{a} \mathbf{Pri}_{\leq}(P')} \quad (a \notin \mathrm{dom}(\leq))$$

Events that do belong to $\mathrm{dom}(\leq)$ can only happen when neither any higher priority events nor either of τ or $\checkmark$ can occur.

$$\frac{P \xrightarrow{a} P', P \xrightarrow{\tau}\!\!\!\!\!/\;\; \cdot, P \xrightarrow{\checkmark}\!\!\!\!\!/\;\; \cdot, \forall b \neq a.a \leq b.P \xrightarrow{b}\!\!\!\!\!/\;\; \cdots}{\mathbf{Pri}_{\leq}(P) \xrightarrow{a} \mathbf{Pri}_{\leq}(P')} \quad (a \in \mathrm{dom}(\leq))$$

It is of course this last clause that actually implements priority. Without this treatment of τ and $\checkmark$ the semantics would be much more dependent on precise patterns of τs than we would like: if we want to maintain the property that τP is semantically equivalent to P, then any Q-event that P's initial events may prevent in $\mathbf{Pri}_{\leq}(P \,\Box\, Q)$ must also be prevented by the initial τ of τP in $\mathbf{Pri}_{\leq}((\tau P) \,\Box\, Q))$.

Notice that the prioritisation used in Chaps. 14 and 15 falls precisely into this format. In the basic form the only prioritised action is $\{tock\}$, but we might also envisage cases in which different "time-like" events would have different priorities, all lower than τ and all independent of ordinary visible events.

Since the operational semantics of $\mathbf{Pri}_{\leq}(P)$ is not CSP-like, we should not be surprised that it is not possible to give a semantics for it over all CSP models. For example, if $a \leq b$ and $a \neq b$, then

$$\mathbf{Pri}_{\leq}((a \to STOP) \sqcap (b \to STOP)) \quad \text{and} \quad \mathbf{Pri}_{\leq}((a \to STOP) \,\Box\, (b \to STOP))$$

have different sets of traces, even through the processes inside $\mathbf{Pri}_{\leq}(\cdot)$ have equal trace sets. This shows that we cannot calculate $traces(\mathbf{Pri}_{\leq}(P))$ from $traces(P)$. Similar problems hold for $\mathcal{F}$, $\mathcal{N}$ and some of the richer models discussed in Chaps. 11 and 12.

It is, however, possible to give a semantics to this operator in models as rich as *refusal testing* $\mathcal{RT}$ or $\mathcal{RT}^{\Downarrow}$ (see p. 262), where we can see what a process refuses before every visible event. This is because we can specify that no prioritised event ever occurs except when the set of all higher priority ones has been refused. Over $\mathcal{RT}$ we have

$$(X_0, a_1, \ldots, X_{n-1}, a_n, X_n) \in \mathbf{Pri}_{\leq}(P) \Leftrightarrow (X_0', a_1, \ldots, X_{n-1}', a_n, X_n) \in P$$

where $X_i' = X_i$ if $a_{i+1} \notin \mathrm{dom}(\leq)$, and $X' = X_i \cup \{b \mid a < b\}$ otherwise, where $\bullet \cup X = X$ and $a < b$ means $a \leq b \wedge b \nleq a$. This is related to what we discussed in Sect. 11.2.2.

A similar restriction on the divergence and termination of $\mathbf{Pri}_{\leq}(P)$ is required:
$$(X_0, a_1, \ldots, X_{n-1}, a_n, \omega) \in \mathbf{Pri}_{\leq}(P) \Leftrightarrow (X_0', a_1, \ldots, X_{n-1}', a_n, \omega) \in P \text{ where}$$
X_i' is as above, and $\omega \in \{\Uparrow, \checkmark\}$.

As this is written, this model of priority is anticipated[5] as an addition to FDR via a `prioritise(P,R)`, where R is the set $\{(a,b) \mid a \leq b\}$ representing $\leq$.

It will be implemented in a way similar to the `chase` operator seen in Sect. 16.2.5, namely as a wrapper that converts one state machine (representing the behaviour inside the operator) into another (the resultant behaviour visible outside it). This is, naturally, implemented in terms of available transitions, with the wrapper needing to work out which events in $\{\tau, \checkmark\} \cup \mathrm{dom}(\leq)$ are possible for the current "inside" state before allowing any event in $\mathrm{dom}(\leq)$ "outside".

The fact that we can define our new operator over $\mathcal{RT}$ and $\mathcal{RT}^{\Downarrow}$ is, nevertheless, practically important:

- Any compression operator such as `sbisim` which is valid over these models can be used inside the `prioritise` wrapper. Others, such as `diamond`, cannot be used safely there.
- Any refinement-based development in which components are replaced by refinements, etc., is valid provided that all the refinements used inside this wrapper are at least as strong as [R= or [RD=.

Returning to the knight's tour example, we can put an order on { |move| } by declaring that `move.p.n`≥`move.q.m` if and only if n < m or (p,n)=(q,m). Since, in `move.p.n`, n is the number of still-free neighbours of p, the network consisting of `CtEmpty(p,card(adj(p)))`s, with this priority order applied, also has the effect of making FDR follow Warnsdorff's algorithm, without the extra `morethan.n` events seen earlier.

It should be clear from our treatments of the knight's tour that we sometimes have a choice about how to implement priority: either using the `prioritise` function relative to some order, or by programming the nodes in a network so that they can

---

[5]It is often now possible to devise checks over the divergence-strict refusal testing model $\mathcal{RT}^{\Downarrow}$ which achieve the same effects as ones involving priority: implementation behaviours that do not follow priority rules are "disposed of" using the don't care properties of **div**. An example CSP$_M$ script can be found on this book's web site.

not only perform the natural communications of a system, but also perform extra, special ones representing their *inability* to perform higher priority ones. Thus in this example the event morethan.n is performed by an adjacent square p to indicate that it cannot perform move.p.n.

To perform an event of less than the highest priority we have to know that no higher priority one can occur. This might happen by prioritise checking this directly, or by special events occurring which prove this in some other way. To look at this another way: the prioritise operator can tell directly when no higher priority action can happen; without it the processes that *might* have performed a high-priority action need to *perform special actions* which are only in the model for that purpose. In the example above, the events morethan.k act as guards that prevent low-priority events happening when there is a higher priority one available. In the knight's tour, the guards happen before low-priority events, but it is sometimes useful to have them *synchronise* with low-priority events. In other words, a process with a high-priority event in its alphabet signals that this event is impossible in its present state, and that signal synchronises with a low-priority action from another process.

This latter model is particularly appropriate when the priority order on events is derived from one on the processes in the network. When a high-priority process can do no proper event it is programmed to communicate a special event, say noop, with which all events from lower-priority processes synchronise.[6] We will see this model in action in Sect. 20.2.2.

Exercise 20.4 Take the basic models of a 9×9 Sudoku puzzle PuzzleM and PuzzleB and make them more efficient using prioritise:

(a) Fill the nine 3×3 squares in turn.
(b) Fill in all missing 1s, then all 2s, etc. until all missing 9s.

20.2.1 Statecharts

A rather large example of the latter approach using noop can be found in [140], where a CSP compiler (in the spirit of SVA) is developed for Statemate statecharts [49]. There are a number of variants of *statecharts* used to design (typically embedded) systems: they are a sophisticated graphical version of state machine description which allows both concurrency and hierarchy amongst states: when a particular state is active there might be other state machines active within it. Figures 20.4–20.7 show a statechart describing a burglar alarm, which is included as a case study in [140]. Statemate statecharts have a two-level timing model as described below.

- Figure 20.4 shows that the alarm consists of a controller and a key pad. This shows that they run in parallel.[7] The timing model of Statemate statecharts is that

---

[6] A one-to-many renaming is applied to noop so that it can synchronise *separately* with each of these events, so that the latter are not forced to synchronise with each other.

[7] In the terminology of statecharts: these are *and* states as they are both active at the same time. States in a sequential state machine are *or* states: only one is active at a time.

Fig. 20.4 Overall structure
of burglar alarm

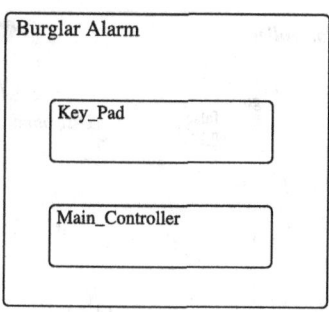

external sensors (here, the boolean *press* and integers *key* (the most recent digit to
be pressed on the key pad) and *alarm* (if non-zero, the most recent alarm sensor
to have fired)) are read each *big* time step tock, and then as many small time
steps occur with as many enabled actions as possible, until no more are possible.
Timers advance on big time steps only, and in this example refer to the length of
time that the machine has been in a particular state such as *Leaving*.

- Figure 20.5 shows the Main_Controller component moving between a number of main states, depending on interaction with the key pad, timers and sensors.
  Each time the user presses the correct 4 digit combination, the key pad will set
  the boolean *go*. Notice that each action is guarded by a boolean that determines
  whether or not it is enabled, and consists of a (possibly empty) series of assignments to variables. This example makes no use of event labels and signals (which
  act very like boolean flags).

  The black circle represents the state from which a state machine with actions
  is turned on, where the initial action is more than a null action. Here, it initialises
  three variables.

- Figure 20.6 shows the key pad. It consists of two parallel state machines, with
  the main one having a hierarchy of states. The *Pad_Active* state enables five sub-
  machines to activate. Four of them are there to check that the user enters the
  4-digit key code correctly, and the other to ensure that if either the user is inactive
  for too long or has too many unsuccessful tries the state is left: note that here
  the actions of a sub-machine are promoted to actions of the higher-level state.
  ch(press) is a boolean value meaning that the variable *press* has changed in the
  most recent big time step.

- Figure 20.7 shows the detail of the *Digit* machines and the *Key Manager*
  in Fig. 20.6. The definitions of the former are designed so that whenever
  the last four digits input during a single *Pad_Active* state are the sequence
  $\langle d[0], \ldots, d[3] \rangle$, the variable *en*[4] is set, meaning that the higher level action
  that sets *go* and returns to *Pad_Inactive* fires.

  In statecharts such as this, actions of a high-level state such as *Pad_Active* always
have priority over those of any state machines it contains such as *Digit*[2]. So, for
example, the action that *Pad_Active* performs itself (i.e. setting *go*) has priority over
those performed by sub-machines, even when these are promoted.

  Different versions of statechart have other prioritisation rules as well: for example, when a particular state can perform several actions, there is often a priority

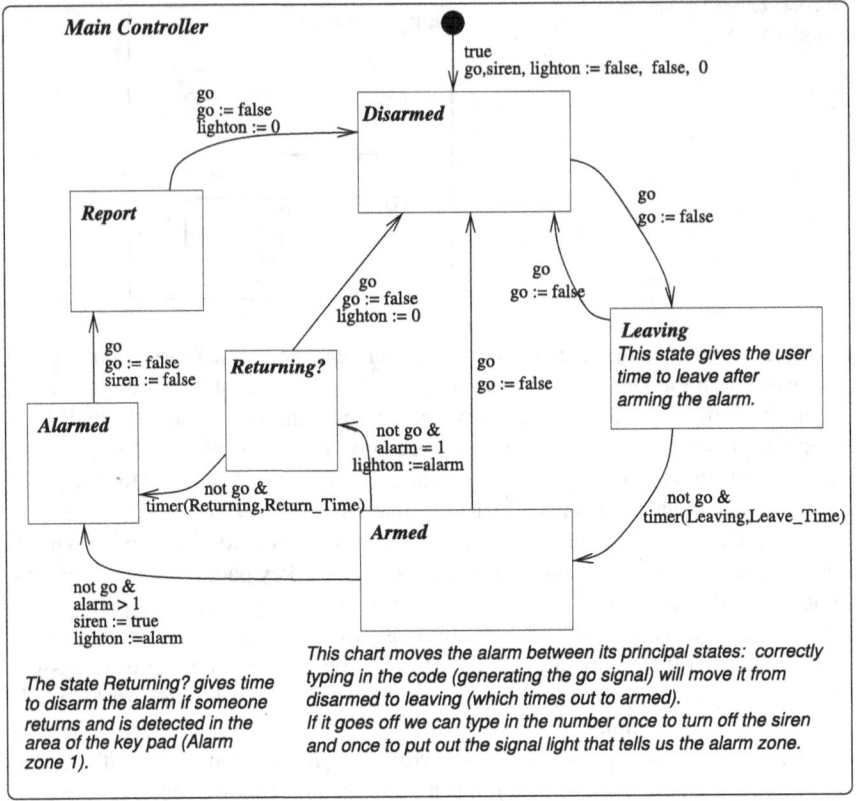

The state Returning? gives time to disarm the alarm if someone returns and is detected in the area of the key pad (Alarm zone 1).

This chart moves the alarm between its principal states: correctly typing in the code (generating the go signal) will move it from disarmed to leaving (which times out to armed).
If it goes off we can type in the number once to turn off the siren and once to put out the signal light that tells us the alarm zone.

Fig. 20.5 Burglar alarm main controller

order to select which one happens. (In the example above, except for the priorities discussed in the last paragraph, we have made sure that no state ever has more than one enabled action.) In some models, where several concurrent states can all perform actions, they all perform them simultaneously. In others there is a priority order amongst the states so that only the highest priority enabled one moves in a given time step.

Exercise 20.5 One of the main differences between our treatment of shared variables in the previous two chapters and statecharts is that, while SVA uses a completely asynchronous model, statecharts use "barrier synchronisation", where all components perform as many actions as they can, all synchronise (through the timing model) and then carry on.

(a) What modifications would you make to the SVL language to allow all processes to synchronise?
(b) How would you modify the SVA compiler to accommodate this new construct?

Burglar Alarm: number pad

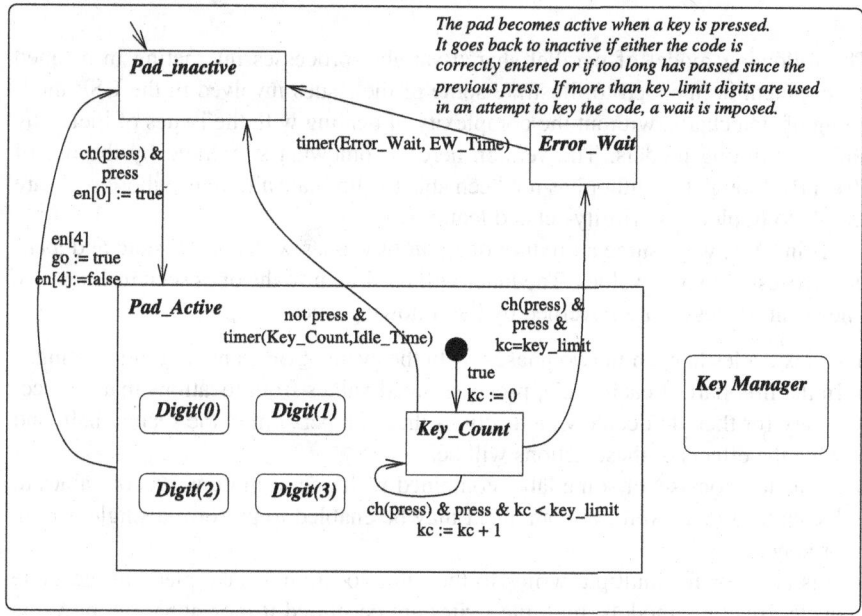

The pad becomes active when a key is pressed. It goes back to inactive if either the code is correctly entered or if too long has passed since the previous press. If more than key_limit digits are used in an attempt to key the code, a wait is imposed.

The five constituents of Pad_Active all run in parallel while that state is running. Key Manager runs in parallel with the main machine.

Fig. 20.6 Burglar alarm key pad

Burglar Alarm: number pad components

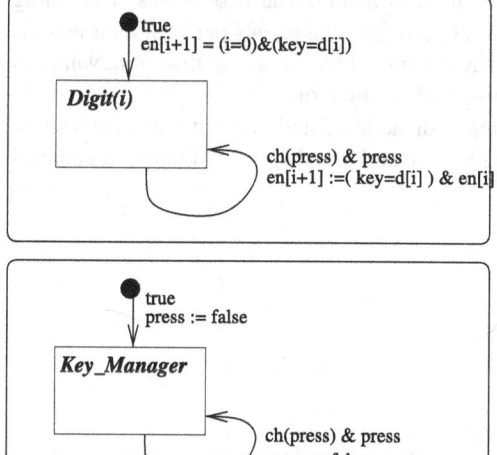

If the digit just pressed is d[i] and the most recent digits pressed are d[0]..d[i−1] then enable the next process in the chain.

press will become true each time the user enters a digit, and key takes the value pressed. The function of this process is to ensure that press is only true immediately after the user's input so a user-change is always from false to true.

Fig. 20.7 Key pad components

20.2.2 *Synchronous Two-Phase Automata*

The following model of parallel shared-variable processes interacting in a timed environment is intended to illustrate some of the issues involved in the CSP modelling of statecharts, without the complexity of dealing with the issues of hierarchy and their timing models. The version here is somewhat simplified by the use of $\mathbf{Pri}_{\leq}(P)$, though the author has not been able to eliminate all events whose roles are simply to implement priority-related features.

As in SVA, we assume a mixture of *agent* processes with control state and *location* processes to hold values. The latter will be similar to the ones seen in Chap. 18. The agent processes are governed by the following rules.

- Clock cycles happen in two phases, with the events tock and mid alternating.
- In the first half of each cycle, processes read values from locations that are necessary for them to decide which actions they can perform in the second half, and what the effects of these actions will be.
- An action consists of some label combined with one or more writes of values to locations. On a given cycle an agent may be enabled to perform a single action, or none.
- It is an error for multiple writes to the same location to take place in the same cycle. [In some models, multiple writes are permitted if they agree on the value that is written.]
- The agents are prioritised by some partial order, and no action occurs if one in a more highly prioritised agent is enabled.
- In each cycle, all the actions that are (i) enabled and (ii) not forbidden by the above rule, occur. Actions do not synchronise with each other.

The first four bullet points above describe a common mode of parallel interaction which we can call the *two-phase synchronous model*. The two phases are reading and writing. The model is synchronous because all the agents perform their actions in lock step. We will see on p. 496 that this model has some significant advantages when it comes to understanding, testing and verification.

The code for an individual time step of an action could therefore take the following form, where n is the index of the process, and c is the name of one of its control states.

```
Step(n,c) =
let Act(S) =
mid ->
  (let trueguards = <act(S) |
              (g,act)<-actions(n,c), g(S)>
   within
     if #trueguards > 0 then
        let (action,assts, next) = head(trueguards)
        within
         action -> Perform(asgts);tock -> Step(n,next)
         else
```

```
        let Allower = noop -> Allower
                      [] tock -> Allower
          within tock -> Allower
  )
  [] tock -> Step(n,next)
within
  Reads(n,c,Act)
```

Here

- S represents the local state required to compute the actions of agent n in state c. It is assembled by Reads(n,c,Act) performing reads of variable processes as necessary, as in the definition of IExpEval in SVA (see p. 426). Act is then supplied, again like the argument of IExpEval[8] with the fully assembled state within Reads.
- Act(S) is a process which performs mid and then *either* the highest priority of its enabled actions, *or* an arbitrary number of noops if there is none.
- actions(n,c) is a list of pairs, each component of which is a function of S. g is a boolean condition deciding whether an action is enabled, and act is a triple: the event labelling the action, a list of assignments that is performed if the action fires, and the state which the agent moves to. In a given state c, the action that occurs is the first in the list for which g evaluates to true.
- Perform(assgs) is a process that carries out the list of assignments assgs before terminating.

Recall that we want actions to occur from all agents that (i) have enabled actions this step and where (ii) no higher priority process has an enabled action. There does not seem to be a way of achieving this via $\mathbf{Pri}_\leq(P)$ alone: we can certainly carry out the actions in priority order, but something needs to tell the lower-priority agents whether they can do theirs or not. There are a number of solutions to this, and the one we employ here is to have each low-priority action synchronise with the noop of every higher priority process. The event noop is present in the above model just for this reason: the fact that it is there to allow lower priority events explains the name of the state Allower.

This can be achieved by the renaming:

```
Agent(n)[[noop <- noop, noop<-a |
          m <-lower(n), a <-actions(m)]]
```

where lower(n) are the agents with lower priority than n.

This solution actually ensures that rule (ii) in the previous paragraph is enforced without using $\mathbf{Pri}_\leq(P)$ at all. Notice, however, that in the second (i.e. post-mid phase), our agents can communicate tock before they have performed an action, even when one is enabled. It follows from this that our model does not enforce rule (i). We can, however, enforce this by the simple priority order in which tock

---

[8]This is the *continuation* style of programming, as described on p. 426.

has lower priority than all other events. The fact that this is essentially the same as the way discrete timed modelling is achieved by giving τ priority over *tock* is not surprising: both are examples of *maximal progress*.

Exercise 20.6 Suggest CSP$_M$ implementations for Reads and Performs used in the implementation above.

Determinism of Two-Phase Models

Two-phase models such as the one described above make the various agents run in lock-step. They retreat from the idea that concurrent systems consist of a number of separate and independent processes interacting, because an important element of that independence, namely timing, has been taken away. Of course in a given application it may or may not be natural to run a system synchronously like this, but there are a number of models of parallel execution that it fits very well.

- Register transfer level of digital circuit design, in which circuit components read values in the first part of a clock cycle and write them on the second.
- Array processors in which many calculations are done in parallel on different parts of memory, in small steps.
- Bulk Synchronous Processing (BSP) [149], in which a network of processors are handed individual locally independent jobs at the start of a long clock cycle, and synchronise when all are finished.

The main virtues of the two-phase model are that it makes the execution model a good deal more understandable than the one in which systems consist of a lot of self-timed processes, as well as far more deterministic. A consequence is that almost all circuit designs are clocked, despite the huge alleged speed and energy-efficiency advantages of asynchronous circuits.

If all the agents are deterministic processes (i.e., given that we know what control state one is in, then the assignments it performs and the next control state it moves to are functions of the present values of its variables), then it does not matter in what order the various agents in a two-phase system perform their reads and writes. This is because the reads and writes are separated, with all agents agreeing on the values of locations at the end of the read phase, and because there are never two writes to the same location. So our system will always, from a given starting state, perform the same reads and writes getting/writing the same values and move to the same result state independently of the order in which the agents happen to perform their reads and writes.

This not only makes the agents' execution a good deal easier to understand, but also means that any automated analysis of a program in this form can take advantage of its determinism: it need not consider all the different orders of performing these actions, and indeed need not even remember any intermediate states that appear while a sequence of reads and writes is being carried out.

CSP/FDR offer two different ways to exploit this: one is to *hide* all reads and writes and apply the chase operator (see p. 370), and the other is to apply a priority order to fix the order in which these events happen. Both of these can be regarded as a form of *partial order method* of exploring only part of a transition system.

It is also worth remarking that, as we have already observed in this book, a deterministic system is much more suitable for testing than a nondeterministic one.

20.3 Mobility

20.3.1 An Introduction to Mobility

A parallel network can be *static*, in the sense that the structure of the network does not change as it evolves: the number of processes and the channels connecting them are fixed, even though the states of the component processes change with time. The opposite of this is a *dynamic* network. CSP (or at least its process algebra version) has always allowed for dynamic networks in which one process can split itself, and its interface with its environment, into several parts that may communicate with each other. Historically these were often built by recursing through the piping ($\gg$) and enslavement operators, and many examples can be found in [19, 117] and TPC. Typical examples were buffer processes that expanded to accommodate more data, and binary divide-and-conquer algorithms such as Quicksort, in which a node representing the routine would enslave two copies of itself to handle smaller instances of the same problem that it would calculate from its input data. We saw various examples in Sect. 5.3.

The advent of FDR has tended to focus attention on static uses of CSP, since the tool is optimised for use with static systems, where there is a fixed parallel/hiding/renaming composition of processes, and many dynamic systems are naturally infinite state.

The concept of *mobility* as now understood in the world of concurrency theory applies to networks that can not only grow dynamically, but can also reconfigure themselves. As a network evolves, a process in it might (as in our knight's tour example) need to talk to different neighbours. While in that example the knight knows who it has to talk to based on its position, in general we might well want to communicate channels between processes. Imagine a device that is physically moving from the area covered by one mobile phone mast to another. One possible way of dealing with this would be for the first mast to communicate a connection with the second to the device, thereby handing the device over to the second mast.

By far the most prominent theory for reasoning about mobile systems is the π-calculus [92, 93, 143]. This is explicitly a calculus of passing channel names over channels, that extends the CCS model of concurrency (see the footnote on p. 220). As with CCS, connections between systems are always binary and based on connecting the output end ($\overline{x}$) of a channel to the input end (x). Neither CCS nor the π-calculus relies on process alphabets to determine connections, and so π-calculus processes do not explicitly own channels: mobility is modelled by the way processes use the channel names they pass to each other. For example, process P might create a new channel name, and pass this to processes Q and R. The latter might then use this to talk to each other, say Q for output and R for input.

The most interesting aspect of the *theory* of the π-calculus comes from the ability of processes like P to create new names and pass them to other processes for them to use. For in a clean theory it should not matter what these names are.[9] If the names were completely arbitrary then some names which processes create might be equal to others that the system uses, or not, purely nondeterministically. π-calculus makes the basic assumption that such coincidences do not happen, just as in reasoning about cryptographic protocols in CSP, as in Chap. 15 of TPC, we build in the assumption that the keys, nonces etc. created by different processes are distinct.

At the level of bisimulation-based congruences, the theory of name creation leads to there being a number of alternatives for the "right" notion of equivalence for π-calculus: see [143], for example. The author has recently shown how a full semantics of π-calculus can be given in CSP [131]. In other words, for each π-calculus process, we can create a CSP process that models it accurately.[10] Any *channel based* CSP model (see p. 241) then gives a semantics for π-calculus, complete with a theory of refinement, for example.[11]

Readers interested in discovering more about π-calculus are advised to study a book on this topic such as [92, 143], and those interested in it from a CSP perspective should study [131]. What we will do in the rest of this section is to discuss ways in which mobility can be included in the CSP language, and mobile systems verified on FDR.

20.3.2 Towards a "Mobile CSP"

In this section we discuss some options for designing a version of CSP with mobility.

The fact that π-calculus can be translated faithfully into CSP proves that there is no problem, in principle, in handling mobility in CSP. Similarly, the example in Sect. 20.1 showed a very practical way of programming systems where the set of channels that a process communicates on varies as the state changes. In this, all potentially "mobile" events are, at the level of the CSP implementation, always synchronised by all processes, but processes that are not using an event at any particular moment simply agree to it happening without changing state.

---

[9]It is at least as true to say that π-calculus is a calculus of *names* as it is to say that it is a calculus of *mobility*. It models mobility as a by-product of these names and CCS's model of parallelism.

[10]In fact, the position is a little more complex than this: depending on how one wants to treat the generation of fresh names, there are a number of alternative translations. These differences are, fortunately, only cosmetic in the sense that all the alternatives yield exactly the same equivalence for the π-calculus over every CSP model $\mathcal{M}$.

[11]The fact that all CSP models are based on *linear* observations greatly simplifies the semantic treatment of fresh names. There appears only to be one natural congruence over the π-calculus for each CSP model.

An example of this is provided by the state PriEmpty on p. 484, which is the state that an empty square has when the knight is not adjacent. It agrees to *all* morethan.n events because the knight is only interested in the numbers of empty neighbours its *adjacent* empty squares have. Since all other squares agree to any number n, the global synchronisation gives the *effect* of a synchronisation between the knight and those squares it wants the information from.

Just because it is possible to simulate π-calculus in CSP, this does not make CSP a mobile language. In the next few sections we will look at the problem of adding mobile constructs into the CSP language itself, in the same way that π-calculus does for CCS. Naturally we want to do this whilst preserving as much of the natural elegance of CSP as we can. The author does not claim to have discovered a single best way of doing this, so here we present some options and some issues that remain to be resolved.

Because there are no alphabets in π-calculus, alphabets do not have to change to accommodate mobile behaviour. If a π-calculus program "knows" a channel name c, it can choose to input, to output, do both, or neither over c. In other words, the programmer is free to write programs that achieve the effects of mobility because the CCS model of parallelism does not need to do "housekeeping" on alphabets. As we will see shortly, this is a great advantage. On the other hand, CCS's model of parallelism is in other senses much more restrictive than CSP's, for example by not allowing many-way synchronisation and always hiding synchronised communication.

So in designing a mobile CSP we have not only the opportunity to be more expressive in the possibilities for parallel interaction, but also the problem that a calculus of names is no longer enough to add a natural notion of mobility.

20.3.3 Pass the Port!

π-calculus makes the simplifying assumption that channel names are the only things communicated over channels. It would be an enormous change to CSP to make this same restriction.

We therefore add an extra type into the components that CSP channels can have, namely port. For simplicity we restrict ports to appearing solely as direct components of channel types (so we do not allow them to appear in constructed types, sets, sequences etc.) and restrict them to at most one per channel type.

Furthermore we give the option to split declarations with a * to define at what granularity things based on a given name are passed over channels. The idea is that channels that are passed over channels consist of the name plus specific values for all its type components up to exactly *, or to the end if there is no *. Process alphabets and hidden sets must respect this casting of declared events. They always consist of sets of these *ports*: the event name plus all data components up to but not past any *. For example, in our hypothetical Mobile CSP$_M$, the declarations

```
channel a:*port
channel b:A*port.Bool
channel c:A
channel d:*A
```

would all be legal, whereas

```
channel e:A*port.port
channel f:*(port,A)
```

would not, where in each case A is some finite subset of `Int`.

The difference between c and d is that d is a port and must appear by itself in alphabets etc., whereas c is not. Instead c.1 and c.2 are ports and can be in separate alphabets and be passed individually down channels. The objects passed over the port components of channels are the following.

(a) Fully specified ports that have been explicitly defined with a * such as b.n (n of type A) and d from the examples above.
(b) Any completely specified event that has no * in its declaration, such as c.n.

Note that in the above declarations all instances of the type port occur after *. This is not essential although there may be good reason to say that if a channel declaration has both a * and a port component, then the * is to the left of the port.

There are good arguments both for and against a type discipline over ports themselves. In other words, we could use a port of Int as part of a channel's type rather than just port. In the rest of this chapter we will assume that there are no subtypes enforced over port, so that, for example, a port can pass itself.

It is clear that renaming has the potential to muddle up ports. Our default position will be not to allow renaming of ports in mobile versions of CSP.

20.3.4 Closed Worlds

Things are relatively straightforward in cases, like the knight's tour, where the set of channels to be passed around is fixed from the outset and where, while the alphabets of processes in a parallel composition might change, the set of processes does not.

We will therefore specify a mode of composition in which there is a fixed number of processes, and where the union of the alphabets of the participating processes does not change, even though the individual alphabets can change.

When communicating an event that includes a port value p, we will allow the notations $p-$ and $p+$ as part of a component process description, meaning that, when this communication happens, the process loses or gains the value communicated over p as a member of its alphabet.

We will allow one further opportunity for communicating ports. When a process communicates over a port where the data passed *does not* include another port, we will allow $+$ and $-$ markings on the whole communication. The effect of communicating such an event with a $-$ is to remove the port from the process's alphabet. Communicating one with a $+$ has no effect in this case, since the port must already be in its alphabet in order for the communication to have appeared.

The fact that there is at most one port communicated per event means that we can put the $+$ or $-$ on the whole event for the first case above, not just the port component.[12]

So if we had two processes in our network that synchronised $c.p+$ and $c.p-$, then the first would gain, and the second lose, p. We place the restriction that where, in any given synchronisation, one of the processes has a $-$ marking on the port field, another must have the opposite marking. This maintains the union of the alphabet over the complete composition $\bigoplus_{i=1}^{n}(P_i, A_i)$ with $\bigoplus$ being a new operator that runs these processes in closed-world parallel. We will call this the *no loss* principle. We frequently (as in Example 20.1 below) end up adding $+$ more as an assertion of continuing membership rather than a new addition to a process's alphabet.

We allow multi-way synchronisations, including ones where there are more minuses $(-)$ than plusses $(+)$.

It is easy, though not particularly instructive, to give a combinator operational semantics for this operator. In this, the component processes events have the $+$ and $-$ markings attached so that the alphabet components of the operator can evolve with each event, and so that we can prevent combinations from breaching the no loss rule.

It is also possible to implement this operator in standard CSP using the trick described above in which processes that do not have an event in their alphabet do not block it.

The implementation is a great deal simpler if we *know* that, by construction, the network satisfies the no loss rule, for then we can let the network interact in the natural alphabet of events. We will assume this here.

We transform each alphabetised process (P, A) into one that (i) allows for changes in A and (ii) never blocks an event outside A. In the following we assume that the combined alphabet of the overall composition is Sigma, that VSigma is the same but where ports can have the $+/-$ markings, and that we have a disjoint copy of it called VSigmap. For any subset B of VSigma, prime(B) is the corresponding subset of VSigmap.

If x is in VSigma and A is a subset of Sigma, then modify(x,A) is the new alphabet that results from the communication of x from alphabet A. This is A, perhaps with the value of the port in x added or subtracted.

The process Reg(A) keeps track of A and adds in the "don't care" communications outside A. At this level the latter are in VSigma', whereas the events P performs are in VSigma.

```
Reg(A) = [] x:diff(VSigma',prime(A)) @ x -> Reg(A)
         [] x:A @ x -> Reg(modify(x,A))
```

---

[12] The author has found this convenient when devising a CSP_M version of this sort of mobility.

We can then combine this with P, applying a renaming U which forgets both the $+/-$ labels and the primes. So, for example, U would map `c'.3.p+` to `c.3.p`. The model of this closed-world parallel system can now be described:

```
MLift(P,A) = (P[|VSigma|]Reg(A))[[U]]
```

```
CWparallel = [|Sigma|] i:{1..n} @ MLift(P(i),A(i))
```

The author's CSP_M script implementing Example 20.1 below uses a slight variation on the above model. This exploits knowledge of what ports may be, and which never are, communicated over the example's channels.

It should be noted that the model below does not work without the prior knowledge that this system satisfies the no loss rule, since otherwise if a port remained in no alphabet this combination would communicate in a completely unrestricted way over it.

Example 20.1 (Mobile telephony) This example is not actually about mobile phones (see Exercise 20.9 for this), but illustrates a use of mobility in the modelling of telephony in general.

We will suppose there are two sorts of process, *phones* and *exchanges*, with each phone being connected to one or more exchanges. Phones connect to one another via the network of exchanges. We want a pair of phones in an active call to have a dedicated pair of channels connecting them. These will be channels that are permanently attached to the two phones. In this model we will assume that there is only one such channel $c(x)$ per phone x, which is permanently in its alphabet. These are the only ports that are ever communicated over channels, and the only units by which alphabets vary.

We first define the states of the process *Phone*(x), where x is its number. The first state represents the phone when inactive:

$$Phone(x) = lift.x \rightarrow LPhone(x)$$
$$\square\, called!x?e?c+ \rightarrow Ringing(x,c)$$

A phone with no active call, but with handset lifted:

$$LPhone(x) = dial.x?y \rightarrow \mu cing.(call.x?e : Exch(x)!y!ch(x)+ \rightarrow Waiting(x)$$
$$\square\, busy.x?e \rightarrow cing)$$
$$\square\, hangup.x \rightarrow Phone(x)$$
$$\square\, busy!x?e \rightarrow LPhone(x)$$

Here, *busy.x.e* tells an exchange that the phone is busy, so cannot be called right now.

In state *Ringing*, the phone has received a call, with handset down, so is ringing. If the exchange tries to open another call, it replies it is busy. The incoming call can be cancelled via *Cancel* on the imported channel:

$$Ringing(x, c) = ringing.x \rightarrow Ringing(x, c)$$
$$\square \; lift.x \rightarrow c.Pickup!ch(x)+ \rightarrow$$
$$(ch(x).Confirm+ \rightarrow Incall(x, c)$$
$$\square \; ch(x).Hungup+ \rightarrow c.Cancel- \rightarrow CallOver(x))$$
$$\square \; busy!x?e \rightarrow Ringing(x, c)$$
$$\square \; c.Cancel- \rightarrow Phone(x)$$

Caller is waiting for connection:

$$Waiting(x) = hangup.x \rightarrow GetBack(x)$$
$$\square \; ch(x).Pickup?c'+ \rightarrow c'.Confirm+ \rightarrow Incall(x, c')$$
$$\square \; ch(x).Isbusy+ \rightarrow CallOver(x)$$
$$\square \; busy!x?e \rightarrow Waiting(x)$$

If we have started a call and then hang up, we need to recover the other end of our channel:

$$GetBack(x) = ch(x).Pickup?c+ \rightarrow c.Hungup- \rightarrow ch(x).Cancel+ \rightarrow Phone(x)$$
$$\square \; ch(x).Cancel+ \rightarrow Phone(x)$$
$$\square \; busy!x?e \rightarrow GetBack(x)$$

While the call is open the following pair of states apply. There are two states to avoid deadlock when both users talk at once!

$$Incall(x, c) = say.x?m \rightarrow Incall'(x, c, m)$$
$$\square \; ch(x).Talk?m+ \rightarrow hear.x.m \rightarrow Incall(x, c)$$
$$\square \; hangup.x \rightarrow (c.EndC- \rightarrow ch(x).EndC+ \rightarrow Phone(x)$$
$$\square \; ch(x).EndC+ \rightarrow c.EndC- \rightarrow Phone(x))$$
$$\square \; ch(x).EndC+ \rightarrow c.EndC- \rightarrow CallOver(x)$$
$$\square \; busy!x?e \rightarrow Incall(x, c)$$

$$Incall'(x, c, m) = c.Talk.m+ \rightarrow Incall(x, c)$$
$$\square \; ch(x).Talk?m'+ \rightarrow hear.x.m' \rightarrow Incall'(x, c, m)$$
$$\square \; hangup.x \rightarrow (c.EndC- \rightarrow ch(x).EndC+ \rightarrow Phone(x)$$
$$\square \; ch(x).EndC+ \rightarrow c.EndC- \rightarrow Phone(x))$$
$$\square \; ch(x).EndC+ \rightarrow c.EndC- \rightarrow CallOver(x)$$
$$\square \; busy!x?e \rightarrow Incall'(x, c, m)$$

The following state applies after a call or busy reply. It is just waiting for the user to hang up.

$$CallOver(x) = hangup.x \rightarrow Phone(x)$$
$$\square \; busy.x?e \rightarrow CallOver(x)$$

In this model Bob's phone, in making a call to Alice, sends the "far end" of its channel to Alice's phone via the exchange network. If all goes to plan, hers begins to ring and when Alice *lifts* her phone she sends her own channel to Bob. They then talk (with a phone's own channel being *to* it) until one of them hangs up. This last event causes each to send the other's channel back over itself.

We don't care in this model about how the mobile channels are implemented: it might be through the same hardware as exchanges, or it might be by Internet or a radio frequency.

The exchange model we have to build is therefore just a deadlock-free routing network that sends Bob's channel forward to Alice. It has to be able to do two further things:

- Accept a *busy* signal from Alice and reply appropriately to Bob.
- Handle a *cancel* signal over the channel it is passing.

So it could be based on any of the deadlock-free routing algorithms we saw in Sect. 4.2, with the addition that the alphabet of any node includes the call channels it is currently holding. The version based on the non-blocking ring (p. 83) could be as follows:

$$NBX0(n) = ring.n?y?c+ \rightarrow NBX1(n, (y, c))$$
$$\square\, call?x!n?y?c+ \rightarrow NBX1(n, (y, c))$$
$$NBX1(n, (y, c)) =$$
$$ring.n?y'?c'+ \rightarrow NBX2(n, (y, c), (y', c'))$$
$$\square\, local(y, n)\&(called.y.n.c- \rightarrow NBX0(n)$$
$$\square\, busy.y.n \rightarrow c!Isbusy- \rightarrow NBX0(n))$$
$$\square\, nonlocal(y, n)\&ring.(n \oplus 1)M!y!c- \rightarrow NBX0(n)$$
$$\square\, c.Cancel- \rightarrow NBX0(n)$$
$$NBX2(n, (y, c), (y', c')) =$$
$$local(y, n)\&(called.y.n.c- \rightarrow NBX1(n, (y', c'))$$
$$\square\, busy.y.n \rightarrow c!Isbusy- \rightarrow NBX1(n, (y', c')))$$
$$\square\, nonlocal(y, n)\&ring.(n \oplus 1)M!y!c- \rightarrow NBX1(n, (y', c'))$$
$$\square\, c.Cancel- \rightarrow NBX1(n, (y', c'))$$
$$\square\, c'.Cancel- \rightarrow NBX1(n, (y, c))$$

Notice how the use of mobile channels enables the way in which calls are connected (namely the above exchange model) to be separated from the mechanisms for maintaining and closing down the calls.

A CSP_M script implementing the above example using the simulation discussed in Sect. 20.3.4 of ⬚ can be found on this book's web-site.

If we put the phones and exchange nodes above in parallel without any hiding, the resulting system is deterministic, as can be verified for specific values of parameters using FDR. All the component processes are deterministic, and of course ordinary (non-mobile) alphabetised parallel preserves determinism, so we should not be too surprised. Perhaps the main reason why this property is preserved for our closed-world parallel is that the individual process alphabets are (in this example) functions of the visible trace.

The only situation in which closed-world parallelism would not preserve determinism is in the possible but odd case that one of the processes could have different markings $(+,-$ or none) on the same event after the same trace.

Exercise 20.7 Modify the telephone example above so that the caller receives tones as follows:

(a) A *ready* tone when the phone is ready to dial.
(b) A *ringing* tone when the called phone is ringing.
(c) An *engaged* tone when the called phone is busy.

Exercise 20.8 Extend it further with one or more "modern" telephone features such as caller ID, call waiting, and call diversion.

   Would these, or any other feature you can think of, require phones to have more than one dedicated mobile channel each?

Exercise 20.9 We might define a *mobile* phone to be one whose nearby exchanges vary with time. Suggest some mechanisms, as additions to our existing model, which allow for this. Here phones' connections to exchanges might be mobile as well as their connections to each other.

20.3.5 *Opening Out*

We have seen above that the closed-world concept of mobility causes no real problems to CSP. There are a number of interesting problems that have to be solved before we can broaden the ideas of mobility so that we can mix mobility freely with ideas such as hiding, renaming and dynamic networks.

- What is the meaning of $(c.p+ \rightarrow P) \setminus \{|c|\}$? This process apparently increases its alphabet by c through the communication of a *hidden* event. Is it possible for a process to increase its alphabet silently like this, and if so how can such changes be implemented when the change of this process's alphabet would naturally change an enclosing context's, as in

$$((c.p+ \rightarrow P) \setminus \{|c|\} {}_A\|_B Q) {}_{A \cup B}\|_C R$$

How is Q to know that its events on p must suddenly start synchronising with P? How is the inner parallel composition to know that its alphabet changes on the hidden action of one of its components?
   One possible approach to this is to have such events hide not to τ, but to some semi-visible token $p+$ that can be seen by outer contexts.
- Should we adopt the π-calculus semantics for generating new names, namely that $vx.P$ creates a new name bound to x that is distinct from all others and cannot be communicated over until it is output? It should be noted that the synchronisation

model of CSP makes it a good deal less clear when a name has been output from a process.

Indeed there are interesting questions arising from the interplay of this question and the previous one: can a name be output over a *hidden* channel? Hopefully not, but how does this square with the fact that the process with the hidden action may be changing its alphabet?

- Or should we adopt a model where all channels exist globally and so do not have be *extruded* from scope as in π-calculus?
- How, if at all, can we allow renamings of the data components of events that are ports?

It does not seem to the author that there is a single most elegant answer to these questions, and so we do not make any concrete proposals here for how to generalise to a concept of mobility that can extend the full generality of CSP. He has no doubt, however, that it will be possible to generalise the model of the previous section in various interesting ways.

There may well be some merit, in developing a mobile CSP, in moving back to Hoare's notion of a process-with-intrinsic-alphabet (see p. 65) rather than the bald processes we have generally used in this book. Of course these alphabets would now vary with time.

There is a lot to be said for contemplating these questions alongside some case studies that can resolve these and other questions. But before one does this we might also want to use case studies to decide just what is needed. We ought to be looking for ones where the combination of general mobility and CSP could do something that none of CSP, CSP with closed-world mobility and π-calculus could do by themselves.

20.4 Notes

There have been at least three previous combinations of CSP and priority, all somewhat more ambitious than ours since they have looked at prioritised choice. On the other hand none have attempted to confine themselves (as we have) to existing CSP models. These have been Colin Fidge [40] who took an algebraic and operational approach, relating his work to the PRIALT command of OCCAM [69] and to ADA, Gavin Lowe [86] who looked at the combination of time and priority, and Adrian Lawrence [79] created complex models to express prioritisation. The connections between priority and refusal testing were noted by Phillips in [107].

People have been interested in the possibility of a mobile variant of CSP ever since the π-calculus was developed. For most of this period the author's attitude was that there was no point in simply reproducing what the latter notation could do so elegantly. However, the entreaties of people like Peter Welch and the development of the expressivity result Theorem 9.1 inspired him to look at this subject, both by developing the CSP semantics for π-calculus reported in [131] and in looking at possibilities for incorporating mobility into CSP. There are two distinct ways we could have approached the latter: developing a calculus concentrating solely on the ideas necessary for handling mobility in a *simplified* CSP (essentially the approach taken by π-calculus relative to CCS); or adding mobility into as much of the language as possible. Since the motivation for having mobility is that it is a useful modelling tool, we have taken the second approach but have certainly not solved the entire problem. Mobile calculi have recently found use in biological modelling, for example [106, 114] as well more obvious applications such as security [1].

The author's work on mobile CSP has been aided by discussions with Gavin Lowe.

Notation

This glossary sets out some of the mathematical notation in this book. Descriptions marked thus^I have a reference in the main index. For notation, such as *initials*(P) and *Chaos*, with an obvious alphabetical place in the index, you should refer directly there.

Many pieces of notation whose use is relatively localised (to a single chapter or section) are not included below. An example is the notation associated with Sect. 17.4 on buffer tolerance.

Sets and Numbers

$a \in x$	set membership (true iff a is in x)
$x \subseteq y$	subset ($\forall a . a \in x \Rightarrow a \in y$)
$\emptyset$	the empty set
$\{a_1, \ldots, a_n\}$	set containing these elements
$x \cup y, \bigcup X$	union
$x \cap y, \bigcap X \; (X \neq \emptyset)$	intersection
$x \setminus y$	difference ($= \{a \in x \mid a \notin y\}$)
$\mathbb{P}(x)$	powerset ($= \{y \mid y \subseteq x\}$)
$x \times y$	Cartesian product ($= \{(a, b) \mid a \in x \wedge b \in y\}$)
$x \to y$	the space of all functions from x to y
$\mathbb{N}$	natural numbers ($\{0, 1, 2, \ldots\}$)
$\mathbb{Z}$	integers ($\{\ldots, -2, -1, 0, 1, 2, \ldots\}$)
$\mathbb{R}$	real numbers
$\mathbb{R}^+$	non-negative real numbers
$\oplus, \ominus$	addition and subtraction *modulo* the appropriate base

Logic

$x \wedge y$	conjunction (x and y)
$x \vee y$	disjunction (x or y)

A.W. Roscoe, *Understanding Concurrent Systems*, Texts in Computer Science, DOI 10.1007/978-1-84882-258-0, © Springer-Verlag London Limited 2010

$\neg x$ negation (not x)
$x \Rightarrow y$ implication ($\equiv (\neg x \vee y)$)
$x \Leftrightarrow y$ double implication (($x \Rightarrow y) \wedge (y \Rightarrow x)$)
$\forall x.\chi$ universal quantification (χ holds for all x)
$\exists x.\chi$ existential quantification (χ holds for at least one x)

For LTL notation see p. 381.

Partial Orders

$\bigsqcup X$ least upper bound
$\bigsqcap X$ greatest lower bound
μf least fixed point of f

Communications

Σ (Sigma^I): alphabet of all communications
$\checkmark$ (tick) termination^I signal
τ (tau^I): the invisible action
$\Sigma^{\checkmark}$ $\Sigma \cup \{\checkmark\}$
$\Sigma^{\checkmark,\tau}$ $\Sigma \cup \{\checkmark, \tau\}$
$a.b.c$ compound event (see p. 14)
$c?x$ input^I
$c!e$ output^I
$\{|a,b|\}$ events associated with channels (see p. 15)

Sequence/Trace Notation (See pp. 30 and 36)

A^* set of all finite sequences over A
$A^{*\checkmark}$ $A^* \cup \{s^\frown\langle\checkmark\rangle \mid s \in A^*\}$
A^ω set of all infinite sequences over A
$\langle\rangle$ the empty sequence
$\langle a_1,\ldots,a_n\rangle$ the sequence containing $a_1,\ldots,a_n$ in that order
$s^\frown t$ concatenation of two sequences
$s \setminus X$ hiding: all members of X deleted from s
$s \upharpoonright X$ restriction: $s \setminus (\Sigma^{\checkmark} \setminus X)$
$\#s$ length of s
$s \downarrow a$ (a an event) number of a's: $\#(s \upharpoonright \{a\})$
$s \downarrow c$ (c a channel) sequence of values communicated on c in s
$s \leq t$ ($\equiv \exists u.s^\frown u = t$) prefix order

$s \parallel_X t$ $(\subseteq \Sigma^{*\checkmark})$ generalised parallel[I]

$s \parallel\mid_S t$ $(\subseteq \Sigma^{*\checkmark})$ interleaving[I]

$\overline{S}$ closure[I] of S $(= S \cup \{u \in \Sigma^{\omega} \mid \forall s < u.s \in S\})$

Note that sequence-like notation is also used to denote vectors indexed by arbitrary sets, usually with reference to mutual recursion, for example $\langle B_s^{\infty} \mid s \in T^* \rangle$.

Transition Systems (See Sect. 9.1)

$\hat{C}$ The set of nodes in transition system C

$P \xrightarrow{a} Q$ $(a \in \Sigma^{\checkmark,\tau})$ single action transition

$P \xRightarrow{s} Q$ $(s \in \Sigma^{*\checkmark})$ multiple action transition with τ's removed

$P \xmapsto{t} Q$ $(t \in (\Sigma^{\tau})^{*\checkmark})$ multiple action transition with τ's retained

$\tau^*(P)$ $(\{Q \mid P \xRightarrow{\langle\rangle} Q\})$ τ-expansion of P (see p. 358)

$P \text{ ref } B$ P refuses B

$P\Uparrow$ P diverges

Processes

The syntax of CSP_M is set out in the documentation for FDR that can be found on this book's web-site. There is a slightly out of date version in Appendix B of TPC.

$\mu p.P$ recursion[I]

$a \to P$ prefixing[I]

$?x : A \to P$ prefix choice[I]

$(a \to P \mid b \to Q)$ guarded alternative[I]

$P \Box Q$ external choice[I]

$P \sqcap Q, \sqcap S$ nondeterministic choice[I]

$P \rhd Q$ sliding choice[I]

$P \mathbin{\triangleleft b \triangleright} Q$ conditional choice[I]

$b \& P$ conditional guard (see p. 14)

$P \parallel Q$ synchronous parallel[I]

$P \,_X\!\parallel_Y Q$ alphabetised parallel[I]

$P \parallel_X Q$ generalised parallel[I]

$P \parallel\mid Q$ interleaving[I]

$P \setminus X$ hiding[I]

$f[P]$ renaming[I] (functional)

$P[\![R]\!]$ renaming[I] (relational)

$P[\![a/b]\!]$ renaming[I] (relational, by substitution)

$P; Q$ sequential composition[I]

$P[a \leftrightarrow b]Q$ link parallel[I]

$P \gg Q$	piping[I] (or chaining)
$P /\!/_X Q$	enslavement[I]
$P \bigtriangleup Q$	interrupt[I]
$P \,\Theta_A\, Q$	throw[I]
$P[x/y]$	substitution (for a free identifier x)
P/s	'after'[I] operator
$P \downarrow n$	restriction to depth n (model dependent)
$\mathcal{L}_H(P)$	lazy abstraction[I]
τP	P "prefixed by" a single τ action (equivalent to P)
$fv(P)$	P's free variables/identifiers

Semantic Models

$\mathcal{T}$	traces model[I]
$\mathcal{N}$	failures/divergences model[I]
$\mathcal{F}$	stable failures model[I]
$\mathcal{R}$	stable revivals model[I]
$\mathcal{A}$	stable acceptances (ready sets) model[I]
$\mathcal{RT}$	stable refusal testing model[I]
$\mathcal{FL}$	linear behaviours (acceptance traces) model[I]
$\mathcal{M}^{\Downarrow}$	finitary divergence-strict extension of $\mathcal{M}$
$\mathcal{M}^{\Downarrow\omega}$	infinitary divergence-strict extension of $\mathcal{M}$
$\mathcal{M}^{\sharp}$	"seeing past divergence" extension of $\mathcal{M}$
$\sqsubseteq_T$	traces refinement
$\sqsubseteq_{FD}$	failures/divergences refinement
$\sqsubseteq_F$	failures refinement (i.e., over $\mathcal{F}$)
$\sqsubseteq_{FL}$	refinement over $\mathcal{FL}$)
$\sqsubseteq$	refinement over whatever model is clear from the context
$P \leq Q$	strong order[I] (over divergence-strict models)

References

1. Abadi, M., Gordon, A.D.: A calculus for cryptographic protocols: the spi calculus. In: Proceedings of the 4th ACM Conference on Computer and Communications Security (1997)
2. Aceto, L., Hennessy, M.: Termination, deadlock and divergence. In: Proceedings of MFPS89. LNCS, vol. 442. Springer, Berlin (1989)
3. Anderson, P., Goldsmith, M.H., Scattergood, J.B., Teitelbaum, T.: An environment for integrating formal methods tools. http://www.grammatech.com/papers/uitp.html (1997)
4. Barrett, G.: The fixed-point theory of unbounded nondeterminism. Form. Asp. Comput. **3**, 110–128 (1991)
5. Barrett, G., Roscoe, A.W.: Unbounded nondeterminism in CSP. In: Proceedings of MFPS89. LNCS, vol. 442. Springer, Berlin (1991)
6. Bengtsson, J., Larsen, K., Larsson, F., Pettersson, P., Yi, W.: UPPAAL.a tool suite for automatic verification of real-time systems. In: Hybrid Systems III. Springer, Berlin (1996)
7. Bergstra, J.A., Klop, J.W.: Process algebra for synchronous communication. Inf. Control **60**, 109–137 (1984)
8. Bergstra, J.A., Klop, J.W.: Algebra for communicating processes with abstraction. Theor. Comput. Sci. **37**(1), 77–121 (1985)
9. Bird, R.S.: Introduction to Functional Programming Using Haskell, 2nd edn. Prentice Hall, New York (1998)
10. Blamey, S.R.: The soundness and completeness of axioms for CSP processes. In: Reed, G.M., Roscoe, A.W., Wachter, R.F. (eds.) Topology and category theory in computer science. Oxford University Press, London (1991)
11. Bloom, B.L.: Structural operational semantics for weak bisimulations. Theor. Comput. Sci. **146**, 26–68 (1995)
12. Bloom, B.L., Fokkink, W., van Glabbeek, R.J.: Precongruence formats for decorated trace semantics. In: ACM Transactions on Computational Logic (2004)
13. Boigelot, B., Godefroid, P., Willems, B., Wolper, P.: The power of QDDs. In: Proceedings of SAS (1997)
14. Boigelot, B., Wolper, P.: Verifying systems with infinite but regular state spaces. In: Proceedings of CAV (1998)
15. Börger, E., Gurevich, Y., Rozenweig, D.: The Bakery Algorithm: yet another specification and verification. In: Specification and Verification Methods. Oxford University Press, London (1995)
16. Bornat, R.: Separation logic and concurrency. In: Formal Methods: State of the Art and New Directions. Springer, Berlin (2010)
17. Broadfoot, P.J., Roscoe, A.W.: Embedding agents within the intruder to detect parallel attacks. J. Comput. Secur. **12**, 379–408 (2004)

A.W. Roscoe, *Understanding Concurrent Systems*, Texts in Computer Science,
DOI 10.1007/978-1-84882-258-0, © Springer-Verlag London Limited 2010

18. Brookes, S.D.: A model for communicating sequential processes. Oxford University D.Phil. thesis (1983) (published as a Carnegie-Mellon University technical report)
19. Brookes, S.D., Hoare, C.A.R., Roscoe, A.W.: A theory of communicating sequential processes. J. ACM **31**(3), 560–599 (1984)
20. Brookes, S.D., Roscoe, A.W.: An improved failures model for CSP. In: Proceedings of the Pittsburgh seminar on concurrency. LNCS, vol. 197. Springer, Berlin (1985)
21. Brookes, S.D., Roscoe, A.W., Walker, D.J.: An operational semantics for CSP. Technical report (1988)
22. Brookes, S.D., Rounds, W.C.: Possible futures, acceptances, refusals, and communicating processes. In: Foundations of Computer Science, 1981, SFCS'81 (1981)
23. Broy, M.: A theory for nondeterminism, parallelism, communication and concurrency. Theor. Comput. Sci. **45**, 1–61 (1986)
24. Buschmann, T.: Efficient checking for parallel attacks in Casper. Oxford University M.Sc. Dissertation (2006)
25. Clarke, E.M., Grumberg, O., Hamaguchi, K.: Another look at LTL model checking. Form. Methods Syst. Des. **10**, 1 (1997)
26. Clarke, E.M., Grumberg, O., Jha, S., Lu, Y., Veith, H.: Counterexample-guided abstraction refinement. In: CAV 00. LNCS, vol. 1855. Springer, Berlin (2000)
27. Colouris, G., Dollimore, J., Kindberg, T.: Distributed Systems, Concepts and Design. Addison-Wesley, Reading (1994)
28. Creese, S.J.: Data independent induction: CSP model checking of arbitrary sized networks. Oxford University D.Phil. Thesis (2001)
29. Creese, S.J., Roscoe, A.W.: TTP: a case study in combining induction and data independence. Oxford University Computing Laboratory Technical Report (1998)
30. Creese, S.J., Roscoe, A.W.: Verifying an infinite family of inductions simultaneously using data independence and FDR. In: FORTE/PSTV'99, 5–8 October 1999
31. Creese, S.J., Roscoe, A.W.: Data independent induction over structured networks. In: Proceedings of PDPTA2000
32. Davies, J.W.M.: Specification and Proof in Real-Time CSP. Cambridge University Press, Cambridge (1993)
33. Davies, J.W.M., Schneider, S.A.: A brief history of Timed CSP. Theor. Comput. Sci. **138**, 2 (1995)
34. Davies, J.W.M., Jackson, D.M., Reed, G.M., Roscoe, A.W., Schneider, S.A.: Timed CSP: theory and applications. In: de Bakker et al. (eds.) Real Time: Theory in Practice. LNCS, vol. 600. Springer, Berlin (1992)
35. de Nicola, R., Hennessy, M.: Testing equivalences for processes. Theor. Comput. Sci. **34**(1), 83–134 (1987)
36. Dijkstra, E.W.: Cooperating sequential processes. In: The Origin of Concurrent Programming: from Semaphores to Remote Procedure Calls. Springer, Berlin (2002) (paper originally published in 1965)
37. Dijkstra, E.W., Scholten, C.S.: A class of simple communication patterns. In: Selected Writings on Computing, EWD643. Springer, Berlin (1982)
38. Een, N., Sorensson, N.: An extensible SAT-solver. In: SAT (2003)
39. Fich, F.E., Ragde, P.L., Wigderson, A.: Relations between concurrent-write models of parallel computation. In: Proceedings of the Third ACM Symposium on Principles of Distributed Computing (1984)
40. Fidge, C.J.: A formal definition of priority in CSP. ACM Trans. Program. Lang. Syst. (TOPLAS) **15**, 4 (1993)
41. Fournet, C., Hoare, C.A.R., Rajamani, S.K., Rehof, J.: Stuck-free conformance. In: CAV (2004)
42. Francez, N.: Fairness. Springer, Berlin (1986)
43. Garcia-Molina, H.: Elections in a distributed computing system. IEEE Trans. Comput. **31**, 48–59 (1982)
44. Godefroid, P., Long, D.E.: Symbolic protocol verification with queue BDDs. Form. Methods Syst. Des. **14**(3), 257–271 (1999)

45. Goldsmith, M.H., Martin, J.M.R.: Parallelization of FDR, Workshop on Parallel and Distributed Model Checking (2002)
46. Goldsmith, M.H., Moffat, N., Roscoe, A.W., Whitworth, T., Zakiuddin, M.I.: Watchdog transformations for property-oriented model-checking. In: FME 2003. Springer, Berlin (2003)
47. Graf, S., Steffen, B.: Compositional minimisation of finite-state systems. In: Proceedings of CAV'90. LNCS, vol. 531. Springer, Berlin (1990)
48. Guessarian, I.: Algebraic Semantics. LNCS, vol. 99. Springer, Berlin (1981)
49. Harel, D.: Statecharts: a visual formalism for complex systems. Sci. Comput. Program. **8**, 3 (1987)
50. He Jifeng, Hoare, C.A.R.: From algebra to operational semantics. Inf. Process. Lett. **46**, 2 (1993)
51. He Jifeng, Hoare, C.A.R., Sampaio, A.: Normal form approach to compiler design. Acta Inform. **30**, 701–739 (1993)
52. Heitmeyer, C.L., Jeffords, R.D.: Formal specification and verification of real-time system requirements: a comparison study. US Naval Research Laboratory Technical Report (1993)
53. Henderson, N., Paynter, S.: The formal classification and verification of Simpsons 4-slot asynchronous communication mechanism. In: FME 2002. Springer, Berlin (2002)
54. Hennessy, M.: Algebraic Theory of Processes. MIT Press, Cambridge (1988)
55. Henzinger, T.A., Raskin, J.-F.: Robust undecidability of timed and hybrid systems. In: Proceedings of HSCC 00. LNCS, vol. 1790. Springer, Berlin (2000)
56. Hinchey, M.G., Jarvis, S.A.: Concurrent Systems: Formal Development in CSP. McGraw-Hill, New York (1995)
57. Hoare, C.A.R.: Monitors: An operating system structuring concept. Commun. ACM **17**, 10 (1974)
58. Hoare, C.A.R.: Communicating sequential processes. Commun. ACM **21**(8), 666–677 (1978)
59. Hoare, C.A.R.: A model for communicating sequential processes. In: McKeag, R.M., MacNaughten, A.M. (eds.) On the construction of programs. Cambridge University Press, Cambridge (1980)
60. Hoare, C.A.R.: Communicating Sequential Processes. Prentice Hall, New York (1985)
61. Hoare, C.A.R., Brookes, S.D., Roscoe, A.W.: A theory of communicating sequential processes. Technical Monograph PRG-16, Oxford University Computing Laboratory (1981) (draft of [63])
62. Hoare, C.A.R., He Jifeng: Unifying Theories of Programming. Prentice Hall, New York (1998)
63. Hopcroft, P.J., Broadfoot , G.H.: Combining the box structure development method and CSP. Automated Software Engineering (2004)
64. Hopkins, D., Roscoe, A.W.: SVA, a tool for analysing shared-variable programs. In: Proceedings of AVoCS (2007)
65. Huang, J.: Extending non-interference properties to the timed world. Oxford University D.Phil. Thesis (2010)
66. Hudak, P., Jones, S.L.P., Wadler, P.L., et al.: Report on the programming language Haskell, a non-strict, purely functional language. Sigplan Not. **27**, 5 (1992)
67. Hughes, J.: Graph reduction with super-combinators. Oxford University Technical Monograph PRG-28 (1982)
68. Hyman, H.: Comments on a problem in concurrent programming control. CACM **9**, 1 (1966)
69. Inmos Ltd., OCCAM2 Reference Manual. Prentice Hall, New York (1988)
70. Jackson, D.M.: Local verification of reactive software systems, Oxford University D.Phil. Thesis (1992)
71. Jones, C.B., Roscoe, A.W.: Insight, innovation and collaboration. In: Jones, C.B., Roscoe, A.W., Wood, K.R. (eds.) Reflections on the Work of C.A.R. Hoare. Springer, Berlin (2010)
72. Jones, G., Goldsmith, M.H.: Programming in OCCAM2. Prentice Hall, New York (1988)
73. Josephs, M.B.: Receptive process theory. Acta Inform. **29**, 17–31 (1992)

74. Kahn, G., MacQueen, D.B.: Coroutines and networks of parallel processes. In: Information Processing. North-Holland, Amsterdam (1977)

75. Kanellakis, P.C., Smolka, S.A.: CCS expressions, finite state processes and three problems of equivalence. Inform. Comput. **86**, 43–68 (1990)

76. Kleiner, E.: A web services security study using Casper and FDR, 2008. Oxford University D.Phil. Thesis (2008)

77. Knuth, D.E.: Additional comments on a problem in concurrent programming control. Commun. ACM **9**, 5 (1966)

78. Lamport, L.: A new solution of Dijkstra's concurrent programming problem. Commun. ACM **17**, 8 (1974)

79. Lawrence, A.E.: CSPP and event priority. In: Proceedings of CPA (2001)

80. Lazić, R.S.: A semantic study of data-independence with applications to the mechanical verification of concurrent systems. Oxford University D.Phil. Thesis (1997)

81. Lazić, R.S., Newcomb, T.C., Roscoe, A.W.: On model checking data-independent systems with arrays without reset. Theory Pract. Log. Program. **4**, 5–6 (2004)

82. Lazić, R.S., Newcomb, T., Roscoe, A.W.: Polymorphic systems with arrays, 2-counter machines and multiset rewriting. In: Proceedings of INFINITY (2004)

83. Lazić, R.S., Newcomb, T., Roscoe, A.W., Worrell, J.B.: Nets with tokens which carry data. Fundam. Inform. **20**, 251–274 (2008)

84. Leuschel, M., Currie, A., Massart, T.: How to make FDR Spin: LTL model checking of CSP by refinement. In: FME 2001. Springer, Berlin (2001)

85. Levy, P.B.: Infinite trace semantics. In: Proc. 2nd APPSEM Workshop (2004)

86. Lowe, G.: Prioritized and probabilistic models of timed CSP. Theor. Comput. Sci. **138**, 1 (1994)

87. Lowe, G.: Casper: a compiler for the analysis of security protocols. In: Proceedings of CSFW (1997)

88. Lowe, G.: Specification of communicating processes: temporal logic versus refusals-based refinement. Form. Asp. Comput. **20**, 3 (2008)

89. Lowe, G.: On CSP refinement tests that run multiple copies of a process. ENTCS **250**, 1 (2009)

90. Milner, R.: A Calculus of Communicating Systems. LNCS, vol. 92. Springer, Berlin (1980)

91. Milner, R.: Communication and Concurrency. Prentice Hall, New York (1989)

92. Milner, R.: Communicating and Mobile Systems: The π-calculus. Cambridge University Press, Cambridge (1999)

93. Milner, R., Parrow, J., Walker, D.: A calculus of mobile processes, I and II. Inf. Comput. **100**, 1 (1992)

94. Mislove, M.W., Roscoe, A.W., Schneider, S.A.: Fixed points without completeness. Theor. Comput. Sci. **138**, 2 (1995)

95. Mukkaram, A.: A refusal testing model for CSP. Oxford University D.Phil. Thesis (1993)

96. Murray, T., Lowe, G.: On refinement-closed security properties and nondeterministic compositions. ENTCS **250**, 2 (2009)

97. Olderog, E.R., Hoare, C.A.R.: Specification-oriented semantics for communicating processes. Acta Inform. **23**, 9–66 (1986)

98. Ouaknine, J.: Discrete analysis of continuous behaviour in real-time concurrent systems. Oxford University D.Phil. Thesis (2001)

99. Ouaknine, J.: Digitisation and full abstraction for dense-time model checking. In: TACAS. LNCS. Springer, Berlin (2002)

100. Ouaknine, J., Worrell, J.B.: Timed CSP = Closed Timed epsilon-automata. Nord. J. Comput. **10**, 99–133 (2003)

101. Ouaknine, J., Worrell, J.B.: On the decidability of metric temporal logic. In: LICS (2005)

102. Palikareva, H., Ouaknine, J., Roscoe, A.W.: Faster FDR counterexample generation using SAT-solving. In: Proceedings of AVOCS 09 (2009)

103. Paulson, L.C.: Isabelle: A Generic Theorem Prover. Springer, Berlin (1994)

104. Peterson, J.L., Silberschatz, A.: Operating System Concepts, 2nd edn. Addison Wesley, Reading (1985)

105. Peterson, W.W., Weldon, E.J. Jr.: Error-correcting Codes. MIT Press, Cambridge (1972)
106. Phillips, A., Cardelli, L.: A correct abstract machine for the stochastic pi-calculus. In: Transactions on Computational Systems Biology. Springer, Berlin (2005)
107. Phillips, I.: Refusal testing. Theor. Comput. Sci. **50**, 241–284 (1987)
108. Plotkin, G.D.: A structured approach to operational semantics. DAIMI FN–19, Computer Science Dept., Aarhus University (1981)
109. Puhakka, A.: Weakest congruence results concerning "any-lock". In: Theoretical Aspects of Computer Software, pp. 400–419. Springer, Berlin (2001)
110. Reed, G.M.: A uniform mathematical theory for real-time distributed computing. Oxford University D.Phil. Thesis (1988)
111. Reed, G.M., Roscoe, A.W.: A timed model for communicating sequential processes. Theor. Comput. Sci. **58**, 249–261 (1988)
112. Reed, G.M., Roscoe, A.W.: Analysing TM_{FS}: a study of nondeterminism in real-time concurrency. In: Yonezawa, A., Ito, T. (eds.) Concurrency: Theory, Language and Architecture. LNCS, vol. 491. Springer, Berlin (1991)
113. Reed, J.N., Roscoe, A.W., Sinclair, J.E.: Responsiveness and stable revivals. Form. Asp. Comput. **19**, 3 (2007)
114. Regev, A., Panina, E.M., Silverman, W., Cardelli, L., Shapiro, E.: BioAmbients: an abstraction for biological compartments. Theor. Comput. Sci. **325**, 1 (2004)
115. Roggenbach, M.: CSP-CASL: a new integration of process algebra and algebraic specification. Theor. Comput. Sci. **354**, 1 (2006)
116. Isobe, Y., Roggenbach, M.: A generic theorem prover of CSP refinement. In: TACAS 2005. Springer, Berlin (2005)
117. Roscoe, A.W.: A mathematical theory of communicating processes. Oxford University D.Phil. Thesis (1982)
118. Roscoe, A.W.: Denotational semantics for OCCAM. In: Proceedings of the Pittsburgh Seminar on Concurrency. LNCS, vol. 197. Springer, Berlin (1985)
119. Roscoe, A.W.: Routing messages through networks: an exercise in deadlock avoidance. In: Proceedings of 7th OCCAM User Group Technical Meeting. IOS Press, Amsterdam (1987)
120. Roscoe, A.W.: Topology, computer science and the mathematics of convergence. In: Reed, G.M., Roscoe, A.W., Wachter, R.F. (eds.) Topology and Category Theory in Computer Science. Oxford University Press, London (1991)
121. Roscoe, A.W.: An alternative order for the failures model. J. Log. Comput. **2**, 5 (1992)
122. Roscoe, A.W.: Unbounded nondeterminism in CSP. J. Log. Comput. **3**, 2 (1993)
123. Roscoe, A.W.: The Theory and Practice of Concurrency. Prentice Hall, New York (1997)
124. Roscoe, A.W.: Compiling Shared variable programs into CSP. In: Proceedings of PROGRESS Workshop (2001)
125. Roscoe, A.W.: Finitary refinement checks for infinitary specifications. In: Proceedings of CPA (2004)
126. Roscoe, A.W.: Seeing beyond divergence. In: Proceedings of "25 Years of CSP". LNCS, vol. 3525. Springer, Berlin (2005)
127. Roscoe, A.W.: The pursuit of buffer tolerance (2005). web.comlab.ox.ac.uk/oucl/work/bill.roscoe/publications/106.pdf
128. Roscoe, A.W.: On the expressive power of CSP refinement. Form. Asp. Comput. **17**, 2 (2005)
129. Roscoe, A.W.: The three Platonic models of divergence-strict CSP. In: Proceedings of ICTAC 2008. Springer, Berlin (2008)
130. Roscoe, A.W.: Revivals, stuckness and the hierarchy of CSP models. J. Log. Algebr. Program. **78**, 3 (2009)
131. Roscoe, A.W.: CSP is expressive enough for π. In: Jones, C.B., Roscoe, A.W., Wood, K.R. (eds.) Reflections on the Work of C.A.R. Hoare. Springer, Berlin (2010)
132. Roscoe, A.W.: On the expressive power of CSP. Available from http://www.comlab.ox.ac.uk/people/publications/personal/Bill.Roscoe.html
133. Roscoe, A.W., Armstrong, P., Pragyesh: Local search in model checking. In: Automated Technology for Verification and Analysis. Springer, Berlin (2009)

134. Roscoe, A.W., Broadfoot, P.J.: Proving security protocols with model checkers by data independence techniques. J. Comput. Secur. **7**, 147–190 (1999)

135. Roscoe, A.W., Gardiner, P.H.B., Goldsmith, M.H., Hulance, J.R., Jackson, D.M., Scattergood, J.B.: Hierarchical compression for model-checking CSP or how to check 10^{20} dining philosophers for deadlock. In: Proceedings of the 1st TACAS. LNCS, vol. 1019. Springer, Berlin (1995)

136. Roscoe, A.W., Goldsmith, M.H.: The perfect 'spy' for model-checking crypto-protocols. In: Proceedings of DIMACS Workshop on the Design and Formal Verification of Cryptographic Protocols (1997)

137. Roscoe, A.W., Hoare, C.A.R.: The laws of OCCAM programming. Theor. Comput. Sci. **60**, 177–229 (1988)

138. Roscoe, A.W., Lazić, R.S.: What can you decide about resetable arrays. In: Proc. VCL2001

139. Roscoe, A.W., Woodcock, J.C.P., Wulf, L.: Non-interference through determinism. J. Comput. Secur. **4**(1), 27–54 (1996)

140. Roscoe, A.W., Wu, Z.: Verifying Statemate statecharts using CSP and FDR. In: Formal Methods and Software Engineering. Springer, Berlin (2006)

141. Rushby, J.: Model checking Simpson's four-slot fully asynchronous communication mechanism. SRI Technical Report (2002)

142. Ryan, P.Y.A., Schneider, S.A., Goldsmith, M.H., Lowe, G., Roscoe, A.W.: The Modelling and Analysis of Security Protocols: The CSP Approach. Addison-Wesley, Reading (2001)

143. Sangiorgi, D., Walker, D.: The π-calculus: A Theory of Mobile Processes. Cambridge University Press, Cambridge (2001)

144. Scattergood, J.B.: Tools for CSP and Timed CSP. Oxford University D.Phil. Thesis (1998)

145. Schneider, S.A.: Unbounded non-determinism in timed CSP. ESPRIT SPEC project deliverable (1991)

146. Schneider, S.A.: Concurrent and Real-Time Systems: The CSP Approach. Wiley, New York (2000)

147. Schneider, S.A., Treharne, H.: Verifying controlled components. In: Integrated Formal Methods. Springer, Berlin (2004)

148. Simpson, H.R.: Four-slot fully asynchronous communication mechanism. IEE Proc. Comput. Digit. Techn. **137**, 1 (1990)

149. Valiant, L.G.: A bridging model for parallel computation. Commun. ACM **33**, 8 (1990)

150. Valmari, A.: A stubborn attack on state explosion. Form. Methods Syst. Des. **1**, 4 (1992)

151. Valmari, A., Tienari, M.: An improved failures equivalence for finite-state systems with a reduction algorithm. In: Protocol Specification, Testing and Verification XI. North-Holland, Amsterdam (1991)

152. van Glabbeek, R.J.: The linear time—branching time spectrum I. In: The Handbook of Process Algebra. Elsevier, Amsterdam (2001)

153. van Glabbeek, R.J.: The linear time—branching time spectrum II. In: CONCUR (1999)

154. Walker, D.J.: An operational semantics for CSP. Oxford University M.Sc. Dissertation (1986)

155. Walker, D.J.: Automated analysis of mutual exclusion algorithms using CCS. Form. Asp. Comput. **1**, 1 (1989)

156. Wei, K., Heather, J.: Embedding the stable failures model of CSP in PVS. In: Integrated Formal Methods. Springer, Berlin (2005)

157. Wolper, P.: Expressing interesting properties of programs in propositional temporal logic. In: Proceedings of the 13th ACM POPL (1986)

158. Yantchev, J.T., Jesshope, C.R.: Adaptive, low latency, deadlock-free packet routing for processor networks. IEE Proc. E, May 1989

Index

A

Abstraction, 104, 125, 176, 413, 414

Acceptance (ready) set, 162, 174, 199, 256, 258, 260, 262, 358, 359, 361
  minimal, 175, 314
  saturated collection of, 314

Acceptances (ready sets) model
  stable ($\mathcal{A}$), 260–262, 265, 266, 270, 271, 282, 310, 312, 358, 362

Acknowledgement messages, 87

ACP, 293

'after' operator (P/s), 40

Algebraic operational semantics (AOS), 294, **299–305**

Algebraic semantics, 23–29, 33, 189, 236, **293–317**

Alphabet, 3
  explicit *vs* implicit, 49
  of a process, 49, **65, 66**
  transformation, *see* renaming

Alphabetised parallel ($_X\|_Y$), 49–**57**, 97, 104
  as conjunction of trace specifications, **61–64**
  in terms of $\|$, 59, 61
    X
  indexed, 51
  laws of, 50, 51
  termination of, 136
  traces of, 53
  with intrinsic alphabets, 65

Alphabetised process, 177, 183

Alternating bit protocol (ABP), **87–91**, 93, 112, 127, 410
  may diverge, 99

AOS form, 294, **295–305**

Armstrong, Philip, xii, 184, 446

assert, 144

Assignment, 9, 135, 423, 426, 465, 466

Asynchronous systems, 407, 420, 452

Atomic equivalent program, 465–469, 471, 476, 479

Atomicity, 420, 425, 429, 444, 452–455, 459, 465–469

B

Bag, 58, 381, 406

Bakery algorithm, **439–441**, 445, 450–453, 458, 459, 464, 465, 468, 471–480
  simplified, 440, 450, 451
  tolerant of dirty variables, 449

Barrett, Geoff, 184, 186, 279

Barrier synchronisation, 492

Behavioural model, 23, 42, 219, 229, 255–270

Binary futures model, 268

Bird, Richard, 150

Bisimulation, **194–200**, 378, 498
  divergence respecting weak (DRW), 196–199, 257, 364, 365, 369
  maximal, 195, 197, **200**, 358, 364
  strong, 174, 195, 196, 199, 214, 217, 358, 361, 364, 369
    and divergence, 198
  weak, 196, 197

Breadth first search (BFS), 162, 166, 167, 374, 375

Brookes, Stephen, xi, 227, 267, 317

Broy, Manfred, 291

Buffer, 8, 94, 97, 102, 110, 125, 280, 381, 406–412, 415, 497
  failures specification of, **121, 122**
  failures-divergences specification of, **122**
  infinite, 8
  law 1 (BL1), 110, 122
  law 5 (BL5), 110, 122

A.W. Roscoe, *Understanding Concurrent Systems*, Texts in Computer Science, DOI 10.1007/978-1-84882-258-0, © Springer-Verlag London Limited 2010